Mainstream of America Series ★

EDITED BY LEWIS GANNETT

THE HOUSE

DIVIDES

By PAUL I. WELLMAN

THE HOUSE DIVIDES

DIVIDES

The Age of Jackson and
Lincoln, from the
War of 1812 to the Civil War

PAUL I. WELLMAN

DOUBLEDAY & COMPANY, INC., *Garden City, N.Y.*
1966

Library of Congress Catalog Card Number 66–12025
Copyright © 1966 by Paul I. Wellman
All Rights Reserved. Printed in the United States of America
First Edition

To
CHANCELLOR FRANKLIN D. MURPHY
distinguished scholar without pedantry,
superb leader by virtue of
inspiration, wisdom and strength,
wearer of his many high honors lightly,
whose humor, warmth and common touch
have won him the devotion of
his countless friends.

A house divided against itself cannot stand.
Abraham Lincoln in his Springfield
speech, June 16, 1858

Contents

List of Maps

Acknowledgments

In the preparation of this book, I owe much to Lewis Gannett, for his careful and intelligent page-by-page criticisms and suggestions. I must also acknowledge the helpful contributions of Walter I. Bradbury, and the encouragement and oversight of the book as a whole by Ken McCormick. The library of the University of California at Los Angeles has freely put its vast resources at my disposal, and thus placed me under great obligations to it. There are others, but to Mrs. Betty Vedder, for her long-continued collation of material and preparation and proofreading of the manuscript, my especial thanks.

PAUL I. WELLMAN

BOOK I

The Rise of
Andrew Jackson

Crisis at New Orleans

1

THE morning of January 8, 1815, dawned cold and dismal, with a smothering fog that caused the shivering men of the American army below New Orleans to huddle about their fires, while it obscured all vision beyond fifty yards or so, and turned to white hoarfrost on the ground.

Voices, muted by the heavy mist, could be heard up and down the miserable mud trench, grumbling, coughing, sometimes quarreling, sometimes laughing briefly; the voices of many men, just awakened, uncomfortable and weary. On the upper floor of the scattered Macarté house, just behind the trench, stood the general himself, half-shivering in the chill that seemed to penetrate his very bones, staring with almost hypnotic intensity into the clouding fog, as if by sheer will power he could pierce it with his sight.

He was Andrew Jackson, a tall, lank Tennesseean, major general in the regular army, and commander of the misfit "army" that was the last hope to prevent the British from capturing New Orleans and overrunning all Louisiana.

The United States was in the later stages of a disastrous war. Repeatedly, in this so-called War of 1812, British arms had disgraced American forces on land—though by no means on the seas—until men wondered in discouragement if soldiers of the young nation could ever face and defeat the redcoated armies from abroad.

Andrew Jackson was here to attempt that very thing, and it must have seemed to him that as a capsheaf to the multitude of discouragements he had suffered, in trying to gather a fighting force, and overcome problems of provision, arms, organization, as well as the underlying hostility of some of the people in this city, the fog that morning came as a disheartening climax.

Behind that shrouding mist he was sure the British army, containing regiments from the celebrated Wellingtonian forces that had defeated Napoleon's best in the Spanish campaigns, and led by a famous general, Sir Edward Pakenham, the Duke of Wellington's own brother-in-law, was already standing to arms. Jackson had carefully laid his plans for the impending battle, by every standard the most critical in his life, and perhaps in the life of his nation; and it was bitter knowledge that this unforeseen weather hazard might well set all those preparations at naught.

During the previous night, in which he hardly closed his eyes, he had listened to the clanging of distant hammers, which he interpreted as the emplacement of new enemy batteries. That could only mean another and greater bombardment, a barrage to prepare the way for the coming attack. By everything he could now hear—distant shouts of command, clatter of arms, a multiplicity of other sounds—he believed that the enemy was marshaling for a major assault, perhaps already sweeping toward him. And he could not even see his foe.

The fog in fact prevented his even seeing the full length of his own battle line—the crude mud trench, with its low mud rampart strengthened in places by cotton bales, extending from the Mississippi River on his right to the cypress swamps on his left, and manned by the strangest, most heterogeneous force a commander ever put together.

When he first came to defend New Orleans from the British army that threatened the city, he had in desperation mustered some showy Creole "holiday companies," organized to march in bright uniforms on gala occasions but hardly to fight; and with them a gang of red-shirted pirates from Jean Laffite's crews, some Negro freedmen, and even a company of Choctaw Indians. Except for these, and some seven hundred relatively steady regulars, the bulk of his army consisted of frontier militia.

The frontier hunters in homespun shirts and coonskin caps, carrying the long rifles peculiar to the people of the forest, he placed on the left wing of his defenses. Those long rifles, and the foresters' special skill with them, were the core of his plan of defense.

Most of his precious thirteen cannon were on his right, together with the regulars, the Creoles, the Negro freedmen, and the pirates. He had revealed the emplacements of his few pieces of artillery to the enemy during a reconnaissance in force made against him a few days before. Now, on the basis of that discovery which he had purposely revealed to them, he hoped the British would send their heaviest columns against the American *left* wing, where the cannon were few, but where waited those tobacco-chewing marksmen. In the previous days he had painstakingly trained them in what he expected of them. They were divided into three ranks. At an order the first rank was to mount the firestep, discharge its rifles with sure aim, step down to be succeeded by the second rank, and then the third rank in like order, by which time the first rank would have their pieces loaded and ready to take their places on the firestep once more.

But everything depended on clear visibility. The nimble frontier rifles were, in a measure, Jackson's "secret weapon." As one well-known authority has pointed out: at one hundred yards—the accepted battle range of the military musket such as most of the British soldiers carried—only forty percent of hits on a target four feet square were expected, and even this average suffered from misfires. In contrast, the American rifle accounted for fifty percent of hits on such a target at *three hundred yards;* while at two hundred yards—twice the musket's effective range—"the border marksman aimed with deadly certainty for the foeman's head or heart."[1]

If the major British assault came against his left, Jackson had hoped to give it a great and shocking surprise; but now the fog blanketed everything. Should the scarlet lines suddenly appear out of the mist only fifty yards away, he had little expectation that his men could do enough execution to halt or even blunt the terrible British bayonet rush.

Under such conditions disaster would result—another in the seemingly interminable succession of defeats American armies had suffered in this ill-advised war. All of Jackson's strenuous activities—his brilliant and sudden dash on the British base at Pensacola, his incessant labors in disciplining his men on the very field of battle, his audacious night attack two weeks before which temporarily confused and halted the enemy—and all his plans and hopes for the future of his country as well as himself, would be set at naught by a freak of the weather.

Then, all at once, a light breeze sprang up, grew stronger. The fog began to shred away. Suddenly he and his men, as the mists dissipated, saw the scarlet ranks before them, advancing over the frost-covered stubble of the cane fields, already almost within extreme rifle range.

From the British lines artillery and Congreve rockets began a bombardment. Preparation for the attack. The final battle for New Orleans was on.

2

Major General Sir Edward Pakenham watched his splendid regiments go forward as they always did—stern, brave soldiers in red coats and white crossbelts, getting a bad job over as soon as possible, knowing that death awaited some of them, but not shrinking from it.

The famous British discipline was evident in the perfectly dressed

[1] Lynn Montross, *War Through the Ages* (1960).

lines, the smartness with which orders were obeyed. Such discipline, such smartness were to be expected; for these were the finest soldiers in the world, most of them veterans of the Napoleonic wars, seasoned, confident, intent on their objective, which was the destruction of the enemy before them.

Almost within sight, behind the wretched muddy fieldworks where the Americans crouched, stood the rich city of New Orleans, the prize almost within the grasp of Pakenham's army. Pakenham knew from civilian inquiry and from one American deserter who came into his lines, that the enemy force was hastily assembled and mostly un-trained—in other words, "militia." The British commander had su-preme contempt for American militia, which had fled with something like unanimity before every advance of disciplined forces in battles previously fought.[2]

Yet though his officers and men were confident of victory, the com-mander himself did not share this confidence. Pakenham was a fine-looking man, thirty-seven years old, ruddy, blue-eyed, with a figure made to display a dashing uniform, and undoubted courage. He was a seasoned and distinguished soldier, the hero of the great British vic-tory over the French at Salamanca, where he personally led the de-cisive flanking attack. Furthermore, he had a large stake in the capture of New Orleans—the governorship of the city and its province, with the perquisites entailed, and the promise of an earldom.

Nevertheless, when he took over command of the army after (by some very adroit and bold amphibious maneuvers) it was brought to this position on what was called the Plain of Gentilly, he had, fol-lowing a reconnaissance in force, expressed doubts concerning the ad-visability of a frontal attack on the enemy works to Vice-Admiral Sir Alexander Cochrane, commander of the British fleet and therefore overall commander of this expedition which he had transported and landed.

Cochrane, an arrogant and self-willed man, had already laid a heavy hand on the defenseless American eastern littoral, including the cap-ture of Washington and the burning of its public buildings, while plundering Alexandria. Since these things were accomplished by land-ing parties he sent from his fleet of warships and transports, he had profound disdain for what he called the American "dirty shirts." When, therefore, Pakenham expressed his reservations, the admiral's scorn

[2] He was not alone in this contempt. An American officer, General Winfield Scott, had voiced extreme disgust with militia, and particularly militia officers, describing the latter as "sunk in either sloth, ignorance, or habits of intemperate drinking . . . Swaggerers, dependents, decayed gentlemen . . . utterly unfit for any military purpose whatever."

was so biting that the general felt it a point of honor to make the assault.

But on this Sunday morning, January 8, things had not gone well. Pakenham's plan of attack was well conceived. His total force amounted to 14,200 men, of which fifteen hundred, under Colonel Thornton, had been detached the previous night to cross the Mississippi in boats and capture some fieldworks and batteries on the opposite side of the stream, the guns of which would then be turned upon Jackson's main position. There were other regiments on various duties guarding communications and baggage. Nevertheless Pakenham could count on perhaps ten thousand veteran soldiers for his major attack, the signal for which was to be a rocket fired into the sky.

Opposed to this the American general had some 5700 men, of whom twelve hundred were in the fieldworks across the river, and others detached to watch various approaches the enemy might make in the rear. In his trenches, therefore, he had no more than four thousand men.

Yet on that morning Andrew Jackson, in contrast to his adversary, thought of nothing but victory.

Pakenham had first planned a night attack, but to his annoyance he learned that Thornton's side diversion was delayed by a shortage of boats and the Mississippi's strong current which swept units two miles downriver before they could land. Daylight came, and with it the heavy morning fog which favored his advance by its concealment. The rocket signaling the onset was sent up, but very soon the mist was dissipated by the wind, and at six o'clock his dispositions were fully revealed.

As Jackson had foreseen, the heaviest British column, under Major General John Gibbs, was directed against the American left flank. A second column under Major General John Keane moved forward along the river under the protection of the levee toward Jackson's right. Behind these a reserve of fifteen hundred men under Major General John Lambert was poised to follow with a *coup de grace* whichever blow of the two-pronged attack was most successful.

3

Forward moved the British regiments, step perfect, bayonets fixed, drummers in the rear of each company beating the time, faces of all, officers and men alike, reflecting the desperate earnestness of the superb fighting men these soldiers were.

Keane, by the river, delayed his attack just out of gunshot, his men crouching under the river levee to avoid fire from boats or ships on the stream, and prepared to close when the main column struck the foe, in what today would be called a "one-two punch."

Gibbs' men, in battle front, marched on, to within four hundred, then three hundred yards of the mud rampart. There they experienced a surprise. From the American lines burst a rifle volley—a volley fired at a range hardly credible in war of that era, but bringing men down.

Not for an instant did the British ranks break step or falter. But that first volley, which should have been succeeded by a pause while the men reloaded their pieces, was followed almost instantly by a second volley, a third, a fourth—a seemingly continuous storm of lethal lead.

Clouds of smoke, seamed and streaked by flashes of fire, shrouded the American ramparts. And every one of those flashes came from a hunter's rifle, *aimed at some particular mark*—not merely in the general direction of the enemy as was the usual musket practice in war.

The British front ranks seemed to wilt to the ground. Rearward ranks had great holes ripped and torn into them.

It was unbelievable! No troops ever faced concentrated fire so continuous and deadly before, certainly not at such ranges. Not even Wellington's veterans could go forward in the teeth of that sleet of death.

Regiments in the van wavered. Then, to the consternation of their surviving officers, they halted in disorderly little groups, fired a volley that could do no possible harm to the enemy, and began to fall back. The retreat gained momentum as it communicated itself to the rear ranks. Presently it was a rout, the men desperately seeking safety from what seemed a scythe of death mowing them down.

Unprecedented! Incredible! Disgraceful!

Officers beat at their men with flats of swords, trying to halt their flight. Poor Gibbs was weeping with shame. "The men will not follow me!" he told Pakenham brokenly. "I can't get them to come on."

To Pakenham it was a moment both of disgrace and despair. His professional reputation, all that had been promised him in the event of victory, were at stake.

Once out of rifle range the fleeing troops were rallied by mounted officers, pummeled and bullied into ranks, and ordered to turn their faces once more to the enemy.

Now, led by Keane, a fresh regiment came obliquing across the field from the river column. Red jackets, tall black headdresses, plaid kilts— it was the Ninety-third Foot, better known as the Sutherland Highlanders. Every man in that unit was six feet tall or over—a rawboned, fierce, half-savage mustering, Covenanters all, who prayed and fought with equal fury. They had never known defeat on any field.

To Pakenham, watching the wreckage of his first attack, they represented a renewal of hope. "Thank God, the Ninety-third!" he exclaimed. "Rally on the Ninety-third!"

Colonel Dale, commander of the Highlanders, had seen the decimation of the troops in the first assault. He knew that he and his men were to lead a forlorn hope. But he merely handed to a surgeon his watch and a letter.

"Give these to my wife," he said. He did not expect to return.

Into battle front swung the splendid Highlanders, their bagpipes skirling the wild, blood-stirring music of Scotland. Behind the Sutherlands other regiments followed in extended ranks, tier on tier of scarlet lines, steel-tipped with bayonets. They had thrown off their knapsacks and the mere fact that they were ready once more to face the terrible American fire showed the kind of men they were.

Pakenham, though already wounded, rode forward with his men. So did Gibbs and Keane.

The Highlanders reached the prone red figures scattered on the ground where the first assault had suffered so severely. Not a man in the grim Scottish ranks faltered.

Again, with a searing crash, the blast of fire and smoke came from the deadly parapet. Mercilessly ripped by the incessant hail of bullets from those smoke-clouded ramparts, the Highlanders were sustaining slaughter chaotic and terrible.

Still, kilts swinging, they went on. There was something majestic about their advance. Time and again the regiment—what was left of it—closed ranks. And still it marched forward.

Down went Colonel Dale, killed instantly. Other officers fell to rise no more. The Scots did not know it, but behind them Pakenham was dead. Gibbs was dying. Keane, terribly wounded, was down. The rank and file of the entire column was scourged and smitten by death.

Yet the scarlet lines stumbled on, over the bodies of their comrades, as if sheer momentum would carry them to the hostile rampart. But that rampart was wreathed with an unceasing cloud of smoke from which the rifles never stinted their deadly roar.

Fascines and ladders were to have been brought to help mount the parapet. They did not arrive. At last the Highlanders, with every officer down, came to a halt before the rampart. Major Wilkinson of the Twenty-first North Britain Fusiliers ran forward, followed by perhaps a hundred men, chiefly Scots. Only twenty reached the parapet. Of these all, including the major, died, or were wounded and captured.

The survivors of the Highlanders, unable to go forward, too proud to retreat, simply stood where they were, falling about their colors. At last, still in formation, they grudgingly fell back, since all the rest of the army had fled. The Americans wildly cheered them.

4

To all intents and purposes the battle was over. At Jackson's right, advanced squads of the British river column, led by gallant young Colonel Rennie, reached a bastion extending out in front of the line. They perished there. The rest of the column was driven back.

Across the river Thornton, so long delayed, at last reached the American works and gained an advantage of no value. The Americans fell back after spiking every cannon that might be turned against Jackson.

By then the whole British force on Jackson's immediate front was in retreat, and Thornton felt impelled to follow that example.

General Lambert, who because of the death or disablement of three superiors, Pakenham, Gibbs, and Keane, found himself senior commander of the British army, could only gather his men and prepare to take his remaining troops back to their ships.

Thus ended the Battle of New Orleans, the most crushing defeat a British army ever sustained in modern times. So humiliating was it that some British historians have found difficulty in accepting it. Others have taken refuge in criticizing Jackson's generalship.

Actually, Jackson made few mistakes in judgment and none in action. His sudden dash on Pensacola the previous November forced the British to blow up their Fort Barrancas, depriving them of a base in easy reach of both Mobile and New Orleans. He divined that the convoy sailing from Jamaica was intended for New Orleans, but he thought at first the invasion might be by the logical route of Mobile, so he kept his forces fluid, since the British controlled the seas and might strike at any point along the Mississippi Delta country. When he did discover the point of attack, he moved with lightning speed and resource to repel it. A daring and brilliant night counterattack the night of the previous December 23 had stunned the British army and fixed it in its lines for a time, giving him a sufficient breathing space to prepare his own defenses.

As to the assault itself, so heroic yet so disastrous to the British, if anyone should shoulder the blame for its failure it was not Pakenham but Admiral Cochrane, whose overconfidence and arrogance sent Pakenham into it.

Jackson's peculiar and brilliant tactical device of rapid and devastating rifle fire was made possible by deception. Pakenham believed the left flank was the weakest, when it actually was the strongest.

The American general even gave his riflemen a frontiersman's mark to shoot at. In the forests, rifle practice usually employed a V, cut in paper or bark on a tree, rather than a round target. "Cutting the V" meant hitting the exact point of the V. Jackson pointed out to his men that the white crossbelts of the British soldiers met in a V just above the belt buckle, thus furnishing a familiar sort of target for deadly marksmanship.

Of the shooting of his hunters, he later said with soldierly satisfaction that they fired "with briskness of which there have been few instances, perhaps in any country."

This was corroborated by a British officer[3], who said, "Never before had British veterans quailed. But it would be silly to deny that they did so now . . . That leaden torrent no man on earth could face. I had seen battlefields in Spain and in the East . . . but nowhere . . . such a scene."

The bloody statistics of the battle substantiated this statement. The British lost more than two thousand men, killed, wounded, or taken prisoner. The American loss was seventy-one, of whom thirteen were killed.

In the end it was Andrew Jackson's wonderful leadership that won the battle. There are three factors that make men outdo ordinary human capability in battle: blind obedience due to rigorous and severe drill and training; *esprit de corps,* which consists of pride in the unit or branch of service; and projection of the personality of the leader.

Of the first two factors, Jackson's troops had none. Of the last, the inspiration of his own personality, they had a superlative degree. Jackson made it a point to inspect each unit as it came under his command, and he did not inspect them sitting on a horse and watching them pass in review. On foot he went down the line of each company, and for an instant each man found himself looking into the piercing blue eyes of the general. That man never forgot the thrill of the experience, nor did he ever lose his belief in the leader. The Creoles Jackson mustered, thought and talked French or Spanish, and many had small liking for America and Americans. The Barataria pirates gave loyalty to no flag, except perhaps the Jolly Roger. But these fought as fiercely as the regulars and the foresters, compelled by the same cause—absolute loyalty to and emulation of their commander.

5

All war is waste. But never were valor and lives worse wasted than at the Battle of New Orleans. Though it was impossible for the commanders of either side to know it—for communication by sail across

[3] Quoted by Augustus C. Buell, in *A History of Andrew Jackson.*

the Atlantic took weeks of time—the battle actually was fought ten days after the signing of the Treaty of Ghent, which ended the war.

Yet if it did not immediately affect those negotiations, New Orleans served a mighty purpose in the glow of national pride it gave the people. Perhaps if any date could be named as the beginning of the new spirit of national consciousness among Americans, it might be January 8, 1815, when Jackson won his bloody victory.

Unhappily, the so-called United States were anything but united during and even before the War of 1812. New England and the South were at odds, and both, to a degree, were suspicious of the rising West. New England's behavior, in particular, was highly dubious. At the outset of the war, sneeringly referred to as "Mr. Madison's War," the courts of Massachusetts, Connecticut, Rhode Island, and Vermont held that their governors could decide in their own discretion whether or not they should place their militia at the disposal of the government. Newspapers in the area inveighed against the war. Ministers of the gospel preached against it, some of them drawing "strange and subversive parallels from the scriptures." Mercantile and shipping interests were partly responsible for this, and surviving Federalism played a great role, culminating in the near-treasonable Hartford Convention.

The peace treaty, announced within a few days after the news of Jackson's "miracle victory," swept the country with a wave of enthusiasm. What though the treaty left matters virtually unsettled? The American people had gained a mighty new confidence in themselves. Time had been given the young nation to grow up and expand.

And out in the West a man had appeared with qualities so remarkable that he alone of all Americans in history was to give his name to an Age.

CHAPTER TWO

Forerunners of Empire

1

THE raw, new West won the Battle of New Orleans, for in the final analysis it was the long rifles of Tennessee and Kentucky hunters that cut to pieces Pakenham's brave regiments. And the man who commanded in that battle—and won forever the fealty of the West— was himself a Westerner.

Andrew Jackson was in many respects a personification of the West. In extreme degree he embodied nearly all the excellences as well as many of the defects of the period in which he became such an over-mastering figure. His thoughts and impulses were always clear, even when mistaken; and his code undeviatingly high. Yet he was filled with contradictions.

In vehemence, obstinacy, and vindictiveness toward his enemies, he was astonishing. But he was equally superlative in chivalry, honor, valor, power of perception, and the courage of right purpose as he saw it. No understanding of his character is possible without knowledge of the raw social crucible in which it was compounded.

It must be remembered that the West, in the early decades of the nation's history, was considered to be all that region lying west of the Appalachian Mountains, and extending to the Mississippi River. The trans-Mississippi country, at that time, was hardly thought about, save as an impossibly remote and barren waste.

Before the Revolution, the West had hardly existed, for the first scattered forts and little settlements beyond the mountains could not be dignified as an entity, political or otherwise. The East, roughly divided into New England, the Middle states, and the South, was old and well established. New England, headed by Massachusetts, had been the abode of sober merchants, farmers, and seafaring men for generations. The Middle states, especially Pennsylvania and New York, were leaders in finance and commerce. The South, with Virginia as its monitor, was aristocratic, graceful in manners and ways of life, and creating by wealth and leisure a gentry of capacity and eloquence from which sprang many of the great molders of thought in colonial and post-Revolutionary days.

With the Revolution it was as if the youthful nation felt the stir of strength within it and looked out upon the world for any test. A restless pioneering spirit led to the burgeoning of American genius in many fields. It was the era of great inventions, some of them revolutionary and epoch-making; of a flowering with remarkable fecundity in realms purely intellectual, which produced a brilliant literature; of the stimulation of scientific achievements; of far-flung activities of Americans on the seas.

But the greatest and most important exemplification of the new aggressive and creative spirit of America was the sudden explosion of the population westward. With the Revolution it was as if a floodgate was opened, and a ceaseless stream of humanity began pouring into what until then was an almost unpeopled wilderness.

2

The question naturally arises as to why it took nearly two centuries from the first settlements on the Atlantic seaboard, before white populations crossed over the Appalachian Mountains in sufficient numbers to create new commonwealths. The answer to this is threefold: the great American forest; the extreme difficulty of travel; the hostile Indians.

William Pinhorne, a man of sound judgment and well acquainted with the country, wrote in 1694 to Governor Benjamin Fletcher of His Majesty's Province of New York, a report on the Champlain route where a campaign against the French was contemplated, of which this is a paragraph:

It is Impossible to marche with any party of men to Canada by Land, either in winter or summer, but they must passe a Considerable Part of ye way over ye Lake, ye Land on eache side being extream steep and Rocky, mountains or els a meer morasse cumbred with underwood, where men cannot goe upright; but must creep throu Bushes for whole days marches, and impossible for horses to goe at any time of ye yeare.

The fact that Governor Fletcher's campaign (which ignored Pinhorne's advice) was abortive, is not important for this narrative. But Pinhorne's description of the difficulty of traveling through the wilderness is; for it might have been written with equal force of almost any proposed route through the great forest which then, and for more than a century after, formed an almost impenetrable barrier against expansion of settlement from the seaboard colonies.

One who views the Midwest states today, with their populous cities, great industries, broad and rich fields, and vast networks of communications of all kinds, must find it difficult to imagine the primeval wilderness which once stretched for a thousand miles westward to, and even beyond, the Mississippi, unbroken except for occasional open spaces like islands in the great green growth.

That forest was a veritable ocean of verdure, extending almost illimitably away, climbing over mountains, striding across rivers, continuing on and over the farthest horizons. The tangle of huge trees which composed it, some of them one hundred and fifty feet high, with trunks in many cases ten or twelve feet in diameter, at times shut the sun away from sight for miles at a stretch. To make the forest more impassable, the ground was covered by trunks of fallen trees, crisscrossed in a wildly disordered abatis and in various stages of decay. Dense thickets choked the spaces between the great upright trunks, and the whole was knitted and laced together by tough, twisting vines like the webbing of monstrous spiders. Morasses, caused by interruption of outflow of rains and melting snows, added the difficulty of their treacherous and uncertain extents.

Within the dark, forbidding wilderness prowled dangerous wild beasts. Deadly reptiles slithered through the underbrush. Even more perilous were the Indians, many of them fiercely hostile. In the North tribes like the Winnebagos, Shawnees, Miamis, Ojibwas, Ottawas, and others bloodily resisted white invasion of their hunting grounds. In the South Cherokees, Creeks, Choctaws, and their congeners provided plenty of unwelcome spice for the lives of settlers.

But land hunger was inherent in the English colonists, and land was America's greatest single resource after independence was won. In spite of perils and hardships, in spite of the constant death toll exacted by the wilderness, there was a straining toward the forest country beyond the mountains even before the Revolution. At one time, in 1763, the British government, by royal proclamation, forbade settlement west of the Alleghenies; but already when this so-called "Proclamation Line" was established, many frontiersmen lived beyond the marker, a constant and fruitful cause of troubles with the Indians.

After the Revolution the migration over the mountains was almost miraculous in its unplanned and almost instinctive, yet enormous scope. By difficult trails across dangerous passes, or down wild rivers, moved such a relentless stream of people that a new transmontane area of America was created almost overnight, as it were.

It was an area that produced for a time—since it was cut off from the East by mountains and other barriers—something closely akin to

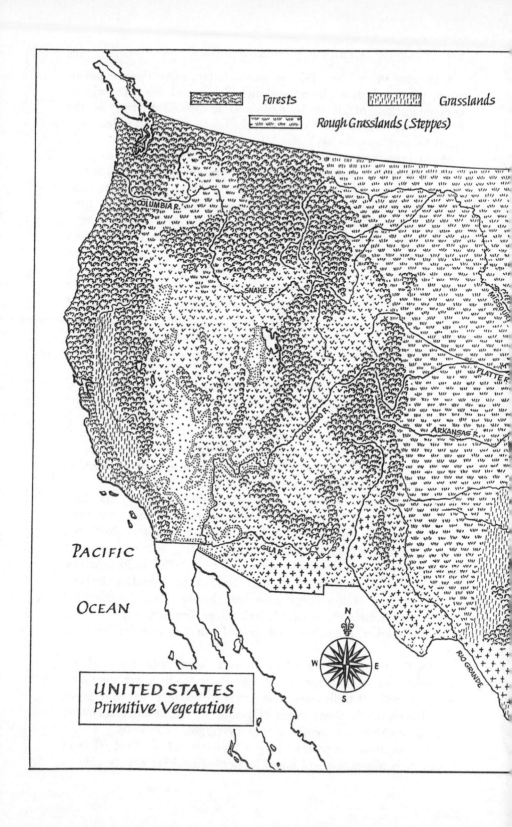

Forests   Grasslands

Rough Grasslands (Steppes)

COLUMBIA R.

SNAKE R.

MISSOURI

PLATTE R.

ARKANSAS R.

COLORADO R.

GILA R.

PACIFIC

OCEAN

RIO GRANDE

N
W   E
S

UNITED STATES
Primitive Vegetation

Deserts   Scrublands

Swamps   Semiarid Wastes

THE GREAT LAKES

OHIO R.

RED R.

MISSISSIPPI R.

ATLANTIC

OCEAN

GULF OF MEXICO

palacios

a separate people. Their modes of living, their values, even their speech became different.

The backwoods families which first penetrated the wilderness lived by necessity existences hard and crude, and of almost barbaric simplicity. Their lives were filled with danger; they never knew whether the next hour might not bring the shrill howl of the war whoop, and death would be upon them. "While about their work, in the open or the forest, a single glance had the gathering power of a fisherman's net and the analysis of a microscope . . . They walked with a soft, swinging stride, keeping themselves always well poised, for no man ever knew whether his next move would be a leap to the right or the left, a dive behind a log, a dash ahead or a rush backward over the path he came."

It was hope that brought these people into the wilderness and kept them there; hope of freedom and escape from restrictions on their lives that customs, economics, even the laws, of the older Atlantic seaboard communities imposed. Able to bring very little with them in their migration, what they had and used was chiefly fashioned from what they could get in the forest about them.

As an example: the family of Thomas Lincoln, migrating from Kentucky to southern Indiana in 1818, lived for a time in a "half camp"—a miserable hovel of poles, branches, dried grass, and mud, with two living trees as corner posts, closed on three sides only, the open side turned to the south and a log fire burning before it day and night. Later a member of the family said, "We lived the same as the Indians, 'ceptin' we took an interest in politics and religion."[1]

Later they bettered themselves somewhat. They built and moved into a log cabin, with a dirt floor, no windows, and a hole for a door. Seven-year-old Abraham Lincoln slept cold, in a tiny loft on a heap of leaves.

This was no isolated example; in fact it was rather typical of the backwoods people. Yet complaints about their hardships and dangers were few. They had chosen their environment and they made the best of it.

The backwoods people were usually unlettered, childishly curious about the affairs of others, spoke a jargon at times almost incomprehensible to strangers, bathed infrequently if at all, considered a hunting knife the best of utensils to transfer food to the mouth, drank whiskey so raw that it seared a delicate palate, often appeared indolent to the verge of inertia, and sometimes, especially when "in licker," were inclined to be quarrelsome.

They shared another American habit, almost universal among the

[1] Carl Sandburg, *The Prairie Years.*

men at least, that was offensive to fastidious observers. They chewed tobacco and spat, noisomely and incessantly. Mrs. Frances Trollope, a somewhat supercilious Englishwoman wrote in 1832:

I hardly know any annoyance so deeply repugnant to English feelings, as the incessant remorseless spitting of Americans. I feel that I owe my readers an apology for the repeated use of this, and several other odious words; but I cannot avoid them, without suffering the fidelity of description to escape me.

Fighting, among primitive peoples, is a source of relief from the sheer monotony of existence. Cut off from the outside world, having no intellectual life and no pleasures except, perhaps, eating, drinking, and procreation, they seek some means to vary the humdrum of their lives. Indian braves took the warpath, as often as not, to escape boredom. The same general truth applied to white frontiersmen, but since wars—except sudden defensive wars against Indians—were infrequent, they sometimes fought with each other.

Each settlement or neighborhood usually had its champion or "bully"—a term, incidentally, slightly differing in meaning from that most generally accepted today, and more akin to the logging camp "bull of the woods," or boss fighter. On occasion hand-to-hand combats were so ferocious that some modern writers have felt that their ferocity has been exaggerated by legend. It is not exaggerated.

"Rough and tumble" was the word for this kind of fighting, and no rules governed it. The object was always to disable, maim, even kill an opponent. Kicking in the crotch or belly, breaking of backs or limbs, throttling, biting off ears or noses, gouging out of eyes, and similar barbarities were all reckoned allowable. There are eyewitness accounts of such brutalities. Major Eluries Beatty, who was in Louisville, Kentucky, in 1781, wrote in his diary:

Saw the barbarous custom of gouging practiced between two of the lower class of people here; their unvaried way of fighting. When two men quarrel, they never have any idea of striking, but immediately seize each other, and fall and twist each other, [thrusting] thumbs or fingers into the eye and push it from the socket until it falls on the cheek, as one of those men experienced today, and was obliged to acknowledge himself beat, although he was on top of the other—but he, in turn, had bitten his adversary most abominably . . . It chilled my blood with horror to see this unmanly, cruel condition these two men were left in today from this manner of fighting, and no person, although a number stood by, ever attempted to prevent them from thus butchering each other, but all was acknowledged fair play . . . One of these . . .

gougers, was a perfect bully; all the country round stood in awe
of him, for he was so dextrous in these matters that he had, in his
time, taken out five eyes, bit off two or three noses and ears and
spit them in their faces.[2]

Further testimony to the frequency of such occurrences is a law—
similar to other statutes in Virginia, Indiana, Kentucky, and elsewhere
—promulgated in the Ohio Territory in 1798, which read in part:

> Whosoever . . . shall voluntarily, maliciously, and on purpose,
> pull out or put out an eye while fighting or otherwise . . . shall
> be sentenced to undergo confinement in jail . . . and shall also
> pay a fine of not less than fifty dollars and not exceeding one
> thousand dollars, one fourth of which shall be for the use of the
> Territory, and three fourths . . . to the use of the party grieved,
> and for want of means of payment, the offender shall be sold
> into service by the court . . . for any time not exceeding five
> years, the purchaser finding him food and raiment during that
> term.

Such laws establish the practice of "gouging" beyond the realm of
legend, and the severity of the penalty—by which a white man could
be sold into slavery—indicates the gravity with which the matter was
regarded.

Yet with all these, and perhaps other vagaries, it must not be supposed that the frontier people were all violent, or that they lacked in
generosity, kindness, and industry. The wild bullies who did the fighting described above were few in comparison with the great numbers
of men who sought no quarrel—although they would defend themselves
if a quarrel was thrust upon them. They enjoyed competition. For
example, Abraham Lincoln, reared on the frontier, never fought a
"gouge fight" in his life, so far as is known. But he was the best
wrestler, jumper, and weight lifter in his backwoods settlement and
was admired accordingly.

Hospitality was free, open, and unstinted—as far as the resources
of the house could extend them. Women, when they got a chance,
enjoyed the company of other women, and took pleasure in comparing their household arts and crafts, and praising each other's children. Men were friendly and approachable, and greeted a stranger
with simple warmth. Men, women, and children in their incorrigible
curiosity, did not hesitate to ask the most personal questions of newcomers, which usually were answered frankly and without resentment.

Any occasion for a community gathering was eagerly seized upon:
families sometimes traveled whole days to be present and participate

[2] W. E. Connelly and E. M. Coulter, *History of Kentucky* (5 vols. 1922).

in an "infare" given to a young couple just starting housekeeping together; or a log-rolling, cabin-raising, or turkey-shoot; even a funeral was an occasion for the nearer neighbors meeting—and sitting up with the corpse overnight before the burial, with maybe a gourd of whiskey now and then to restore mournful spirits, was part of the frontier protocol when it was possible.

Most of the time, however, frontier life was lonely; and the labors and adventures of the people of the forest seem almost unparalleled. The very reduction of the vast forest—by hand labor alone—is in itself a sufficient monument to their doggedness and industry.

3

American frontiersmen developed surpassing skill with two things: the rifle and the ax. Pakenham's soldiers could testify to the first. William Cobbett, an earlier English observer, said of the second, "They were the greatest wielders of the ax the world has known."

Strangely enough, the pioneers appear to have shunned at first the open areas in the forest, where it would seem tillage was easiest. This was because of beliefs they held as to the nature of soils as indicated by forest cover. Hardwood growth was considered proof of "strong" soil; pine woods indicated "weak" soil; but open stretches where no trees grew at all were thought to have "sour" soil.

Furthermore, since the backwoods families had lived all their lives in forest country, they naturally turned to the forests. Trees sheltered them, furnished wood for all manner of necessary articles from dwellings to pannikins, and in addition were the natural habitat of game birds and animals, so necessary for food and sometimes for garments, even adornment.

Deer were plentiful for hides and meat. Beaver, raccoon, wolf, fox, marten, mink, otter, and bear provided fur and in some cases—as with bear and raccoon—grease for various purposes as well as meat. Wild turkey, swans, grouse, ducks and geese teemed, and especially was this the case with the myriads of passenger pigeons, which swarmed in such incredible numbers that they at times dimmed the sun when flying overhead and broke down the limbs of great trees when they crowded together to roost. Streams furnished trout, pike, catfish, and others of the finny tribe. It is small wonder that the Indians relinquished such unparalleled hunting grounds with reluctance.

The white man, however, was not primarily a hunter. He was an agriculturalist, using game only to supplement what he could raise, and he went resolutely at the incredible labor of clearing spaces in the forest for tillage. The usual practice was first to "girdle" trees in a given "patch," by cutting away the bark in a ring around their trunks, causing them to die. Some sunlight fell through the bare branches, permitting crops to be planted and grow.

But eventually trees, even if dead, must be felled. So the axmen spat on their hands, "sized up" the probable fall of the tree they were attacking, and with wonderful skill and rapidity brought it down. Since there was no way to remove the huge trunks, and no market in that day for timber, they had to be burned where they lay before the land could finally be cleared. A constant haze of smoke in the air and a smell of burning wood characterized all new forest settlements.

Meanwhile, before the final felling took place, logs of proper size were cut and trimmed from smaller trees, invitations sent out, and by community effort—spiced by pannikins of whiskey and perhaps ending with fiddling and a dance—a cabin was erected, and with rough furniture already provided, life was ready to start for a new family.

There were degrees of axmanship. Some men so excelled that they had wide reputations. And as there were degrees in skill there also were various gradations of dwellings created by the ax. In general the cabins could be divided into two classes, each reflecting the skill of the owner who cut the logs for the structure. One, with corners crisscrossed and ends protruding at the corners, was called "hog-pen finish." A finer axman, who neatly squared and fitted his logs, had a house described as "dove-tail finish." Since a man who fell below standard thus demonstrated it, residents in the more neatly finished dwellings felt a certain superiority.

But such differences in standing were very slight, for the frontier was nothing if not independent. Mrs. Trollope, with her complacent snobbery, wrote about the "American poor," "cottagers," and the "lower classes," and even made an effort to compare the "peasants" of the United States with "those of Europe." She wound up in considerable confusion because the American Westerner simply would not fit her preconceived ideas of a peasant, such as she knew in Europe.

She found wages higher and food more plentiful and of better variety for "the poor class" in America, than in England—to say nothing of whiskey, the universal use of which she deplored. The women, she felt, aged early because of toil, and she was impatient with them for the following reason:

> The horror of domestic service, which the reality of slavery and the fable of equality have generated, excludes young women from that sure and most comfortable resource of decent English girls.[3]

[3] Mrs. Frances Trollope, *Domestic Manners of Americans.*

Without understanding it, the lady had put her finger on the great difference between the frontiersman and the Old World peasant. She did not realize that she was gazing upon perhaps the most redoubtable group in the world, the borderers who for decades, by sheer fortitude and at terrible losses, had held their ground against continual attacks of murderous Indian raiding parties until they developed self-confidence, the ability to fight singly if necessary, almost incredible courage, and with it restless eagerness to see beyond their immediate surroundings. Already, when Mrs. Trollope saw them, their vanguards were the trappers and traders up the wild Missouri, the mountain men in the hostile Rockies; and they would be the blazers of the Oregon, Santa Fe, and California trails, the spearhead of the Forty-niners, the future conquerors of the Far West.

That "fable of equality," as she sneeringly called it, was no fable to Americans. A quick stiffening of pride was what caused girls to reject "domestic service." They, and their men, would have had difficulty in assimilating the idea that they belonged to "lower classes."

Americans on the frontier, for all their awkward manners and ungainly speech, considered themselves every whit as good as the next person—including Mrs. Trollope. In short they were anything but peasants. They were forerunners of empire.

The dream fostered in America and elucidated by Thomas Jefferson —especially in those words of his in the Declaration of Independence that "all men are created equal"—had very much to do with the westering migration. In the East, debt and monopolies kept a man down. The wealthy and powerful displayed too much of an inclination to ape the snobbery of Britain, where the remnants of a feudal system still existed, where family and aristocratic birth were more important than ability and worth, and where, as one writer put it, "One must know who are one's superiors, else how can one know who are one's inferiors?"

To be "his own boss," to be independent, to truckle to no one, to rely on what he himself produced and not on wages paid by another, was the dream of every American, one of the impelling motives that sent people streaming westward.

4

"Politics and religion," the interests one of the Lincoln relatives held out as differentiating the life of the pioneers from that of the Indians, were continually absorbing. So strongly inbred was the democratic ideal that men, even on the most remote frontiers, were jealous of their right to vote, and listened eagerly to political discussions.

Sometimes their lack of learning was ludicrous. Oliver H. Smith, who ran for Congress in Indiana in 1826, related in his memoirs that when he held a joint debate with his opponent, a judge:

The whole country was there. The judge was speaking and for the first time introduced the new subject of railroads. He avowed himself in favor of them . . . and then, rising to the top of his voice: "I tell you, fellow citizens, that in England they run the cars at thirty miles an hour, and they will yet be run at a higher speed in America." This was enough. The crowd set up a loud laugh at the expense of the judge. An old fellow standing by me bawled out: "You're crazy, or do you think we are fools; a man could not live a moment at that speed." The day was mine.[4]

On another occasion, when two candidates discussed the tariff, Smith noted:

The people knew but little about it, but what they heard was decidedly against it . . . One old fellow said he had never seen one, but he believed it was hard on sheep.

Even more intense was the interest in religion. It was the period of the "Great American Revival." Camp meetings were the order of the day and whole families came from long distances to camp around the meeting places. At times there was a tent for the revivalists, but more often the eager congregations sat on wooden benches in the open and listened to the exhortations of the evangelists who preached from wooden platforms.

Unlettered and rude, the frontier cared little for a tolerant religion. What it craved was violence in the pulpit, a strong smell of brimstone and fire, furious declamation, and turgid polemics. The Methodist, Baptist, and Presbyterian persuasions all lent themselves easily to such pulpit pyrotechnics. Mrs. Trollope was shocked by the "sectarian license," as she put it. Her description of one sermon, Methodist in this case, is an illustration of the general type:

The sermon had considerable eloquence, but of a frightful kind. The preacher described with ghastly minuteness, the last feeble fainting moments of human life, and then the gradual process of decay after death, which he followed through every process up to the last loathsome stage of decomposition. Suddenly changing his tone, which had been that of sober accurate description, into the shrill voice of horror, he bent forward his head, as if to gaze

[4] Oliver H. Smith, *Early Indiana Trials and Sketches* (1852). Smith later became a United States Senator.

on some object below the pulpit. As Rebecca made known to Ivanhoe what she saw through the window, so the preacher made known to us what he saw in the pit that seemed to open before him. The device was certainly a happy one for giving effect to his description of hell. No image that fire, flame, brimstone, molten lead, or red hot pincers could supply, with flesh, nerves, and sinews quivering under them, was omitted. The perspiration ran in streams from the face of the preacher; his eyes rolled, his lips were covered with foam, and every feature had the deep expression it would have borne, had he, in truth, been gazing at the scene he described. The acting was excellent.

It was also effective. There were, of course, plenty of sinners in the West, and since the object of each revival was to bring as many converts as possible to the "mourner's bench"—thus turning each camp meeting into a sort of scoring contest for the evangelists—the field for conversions was rich. Under the lashings of tongue from the preachers, men, women, and even young children, rolled upon the earth, shrieked, shouted, went into contortions, and wept, in a perfect saturnalia of emotional excitement.

While it is to be doubted that all who were thus "struck with conviction" remained godly for long—whiskey barrels stood conveniently about the camp meetings and religion was, after all, thirsty work—it cannot be denied that many remained as godly as they knew how to be for the rest of their lives.

Emotions so stimulated required some sort of release, and hot-blooded young men and warmly receptive girls often found it with each other. There was a frequent rise in the birth rate of illegitimate babies after great camp meetings. One witness of the times wrote:

> There may be some who think that a camp meeting is no place for love-making; if so, they are much mistaken. When the mind becomes bewildered and confused, the moral restraints give way, and the passions are quickened and less controllable. For a mile or more around a camp ground the woods seemed to be alive with people; every tree or bush had its group or couple, while hundreds of others in pairs were seen prowling around in search of some cozy spot.[5]

Inevitably, criminal rascality was present. For example, the notorious outlaw, John A. Murrell, frequently attired himself in "clothes of a Methodist cut" and attended camp meetings, setting himself forth as an evangelistic preacher for the purpose of robbery on the side. "I preached some damn fine sermons," he boasted to one man. He also "scattered a lot of queer [counterfeit] money among the pious,"

---

[5] J. M. Keating, *History of the City of Memphis and Shelby County* (1888).

committed several robberies, and with the help of confederates stole some fine horses.

While it is true that the preachers were nearly always ignorant men —it required no seminary training to become a frontier preacher, a man only needed a strong voice, a "gift of gab," and some knowledge of the scriptures—it is also true that they were in the main men of powerful convictions and courage almost heroic.

Circuit riders went their lonely way through the wilderness, bringing religion to isolated settlements regardless of weather and regardless of danger. One of them, William Lambuth, youthful and quite frail, encountered the dreaded maniacal murderers, Micajah and Wiley Harpe, on a trail in Tennessee. They not only spared his life but they did not even rob him, almost the only instance of the kind when they had a man at their mercy, and it could only have been his faith-inspired resolution that saved him.

Godly men lived in almost every community. They gathered the people into churches, and their influence in maintaining not only the moral level of their communities, but respect for law and public responsibility can hardly be overstated. Those old frontier preachers, most of whom farmed for a living, and gave without financial recompense their services in their ministries, had much to do with the fact that religion and politics, both gospels of equality, united to reinforce and make permanent the democratic ideal of the West.

5

While the backwoods people existed crudely, it must not be supposed that all persons in the West lived at such a level. As towns and nascent cities grew up, fine homes even by modern standards were built, and their owners lived as near the level as they could to the Tidewater aristocracy of the seaboard, from which many of them had come, and to which all of them aspired. This was true also of many large plantations in the era of prosperity, where gracious dwellings that still please the eye in the South were evidences of wealth, luxury, and culture.

Thus, Andrew Jackson, after a youth of grinding poverty on the Carolina frontier, sought to create for himself and his wife a life as country gentlefolk, and succeeded in doing so, with slaves at his beck, a stable of blooded horses, fighting cocks in his pens, cattle and sheep in his pastures, corn and cotton in his fields, and a beautiful home, The Hermitage, still preserved today as a shrine to the man who built it and also to a way of life. In that home, incidentally, was a brace of fine, well-kept dueling pistols ready at any moment to take up the gage should his somewhat touchy sense of honor be affronted.

Many others, particularly the large cotton growers in the South, possessed greater property assets and lived on a grander scale than did Jackson. And here it is time to touch on that singular and tragic division in manners, mores, and economic outlooks, fostered by slavery, which grew up between the North and the South, and especially between the West and the Cotton states.

The invention by Eli Whitney, in 1793, of a ridiculously simple device called the cotton gin, revolutionized cotton growing by making easy and rapid the separation of the seeds from the lint, thus solving the greatest single problem in cotton culture at the very time when the British textile industry—and also that of New England—offered a tremendous demand for the fibers, for manufacture into cloth. As a result Negro slavery began its perilous upward climb.

Slavery is almost as old as the human race; and Africa was—and still is—the land of slavery. According to the figures quoted in a debate in the British House of Lords on July 14, 1960, there were then more than a million Negro slaves in Africa, almost all of them owned by other Negroes, and half a million in Arabian countries, not all Negroes by any means, with slavery existing also in some Indian provinces and in Malaysian districts.

The first African slaves were brought to America by a Dutch ship in 1619. Even before this there were *white* slaves in the Jamestown Colony in the form of "indentured servants." Though the number of African slaves increased, indentured white persons outnumbered Negroes during the seventeenth century even in the Southern colonies, and always outnumbered black slaves in the other colonies, until the indenturing was abolished.[6]

In 1776 African slaves in the United Colonies were estimated at 502,132, of whom some 15,000 were held in New England. But New England farmers and manufacturers found Negro slave labor too expensive and too difficult to train, to be economic. On the other hand, New England shipowners made a highly profitable business of importing human chattels into the South even after slavery was abolished in their home states.

It was thought at one time that slavery would die out of its own lack of efficiency. Thomas Jefferson, himself a slaveowner, in his original draft of the Declaration of Independence, condemned the slave trade, although the pertinent clause was in the end omitted.

Although importation of slaves from Africa after 1807 was prohibited by Congress, the invention of the cotton gin revived the mori-

[6] Edward Channing, A *History of the United States* (6 vols. 1905–25).

bund institution of slavery and cotton production increased tremen-
dously. Larger and larger areas were cleared, particularly in the
opening "Southwest," not only for cotton but for sugar cane and rice,
and since Negroes were adapted both to the hot climate and the simple type of work, more and more slaves were needed. By the opening
of the Civil War nearly four million were held, chiefly in the Cotton
states, but also in the so-called Border states.

Slave ownership was always uneven. Of the white population of
the slave states, totaling 6,242,418 in 1850, only 255,258 families owned
any slaves, and of these only one-third owned ten slaves or more. On
many smaller farms owners worked in the fields side by side with their
slaves, although on the large plantations Negroes worked under the
supervision of overseers.

Because of slavery the South developed a caste system, strongest
in Virginia, South Carolina, and the Mississippi Delta country. At the
top were the wealthy planters, who lived luxuriously, were educated,
and generally controlled politics. Particularly in North Carolina and
the Border states a large and important middle class of merchants,
professional men, and lesser landowners, some of whom owned a few
slaves, dominated their own sphere. Still lower were the "poor whites,"
who lived in squalor and were looked down upon even by the more
fortunately situated slaves. Lowest of all were the slaves themselves,
the "house servants" having some privileges, but the "field hands"
none.

Between the West and the slaveowners antipathy grew. The Ohio
River was a sort of boundary between free soil and slave soil, and the
rich lands north of the river began to produce crops which in time
grew to surpluses, so that the area became the granary not only of
the East, but of the South, and to a degree of Europe also. The planters, who devoted their own acres to their "money crops"—chiefly cotton—complained about the prices they had to pay for pork, beef, corn,
and wheat flour. The Westerners disliked the haughty and aristocratic pretensions of the planters.

The stage was being set for the awesome cataclysm that was to
come.

CHAPTER THREE

The Indian and the Westward Tidal Wave

1

EVER westward swept the land seekers. Affluence could be obtained through land—land speculation—or so it was believed. But where the backwoods family was content with a "patch" just large enough to be comfortably cultivated for subsistence, Eastern speculators thought in terms of thousands, sometimes hundreds of thousands, of acres, obtained through government grants, and for sale and resale.

Where was this land to come from? At the expense of the Indians, of course. One of the unhappy records of American history is the expulsion of the red men by the whites. It began with the first colonial settlements, and continued through the nineteenth century, by which time virtually all attractive and valuable lands had been occupied by the ever-encroaching white man.

Under standards of morality now current—and it should be remembered that such standards change with changing conditions and changing generations—that occupation can hardly be justified. But something stronger and more powerful than theoretical or even actual moralities was in control here. An authentic race migration was under way, one of the mightiest in the annals of man, imbued with a westering instinct that carried it eventually to the distant Pacific Ocean, and changed history as well as the map. It could no more be halted than a tidal wave.

The Indian, of course, was in the way. And the frontiersman's instinctive antipathy toward the natives was not alone due to land hunger. Racial hostility, a long history of atrocities, and radically different ways of life also played their part.

The migration westward was no organized invasion of territory. White families going into the wilderness had no governmental stimulus or backing; in fact they frequently ventured beyond the frontiers against governmental opposition, even against governmental laws.

The settlers were simple people, seeking only for room to live in. They selected what they considered likely spots in the wilderness, cleared it of trees—at enormous labor—cultivated it, fenced it, and eventually hoped to make it productive and valuable.

The Eastern Indians, on the other hand, were for the most part hunters and warriors, though they also planted cornfields in traditional areas. They had no desire for change. But change was inherent in the white frontiersmen's attitude toward the land. If they cut down the forest, they substituted for it fields of growing crops. If they drove out the wild game, they introduced more valuable domestic animals as replacements.

It is only fair to the pioneers to say that it is far easier for us, in this modern day, to be philosophical and romantic about the Indians at a safe time and distance, than it was for those who lived cheek by jowl with them when they were neither safe nor distant.

It should not be forgotten that the first white men to build tiny settlements on the Atlantic seaboard literally had to fight for their lives when, far outnumbered, they were almost swept from the continent. The ferocious bloodlust of some tribes was to blame for many white men's wars against them, just as white men's greed for land caused many Indian attacks on the settlements. When Andrew Jackson first reached the Cumberland settlements in Tennessee, many persons were still living who not only were then in the presence of a constant threat of Indian incursion, but could remember an entire lifetime of almost incessant Indian wars, lasting for decades, with all the peculiar horrors that forever accompanied them.

Nor is it to be forgotten that many tribes participated in those wars, at times when there was no threat which they, or even the white men, conceived, against their "hunting grounds," real or vaguely claimed. Or how greedily the tribes accepted bribes from the French, English, and Spanish governments to tomahawk white settlers, disembowel their wives, and dash their babies' heads against trees to kill them.

As an example of the above, the French—who employed Indian war parties against the English settlers in all the colonial wars—during the French and Indian War starting in 1756, in particular, induced Menomini, Winnebago, Potawatomi, Ottawa, and Illinois warriors, hundreds of miles from the nearest settlements, to cross the Alleghenies and wreak their bloody destruction there. Even from up in Canada the French sent Wyandot (Huron), Nipissing, Chippewa, Montagnais, and Algonquin war parties into the settlements. And all of these at that period were far from any present probability—or any considered probability of the future—that white settlement would menace them. Of course, settlement did eventually reach them, but *at that time,* it would have required prophetic vision for anyone, red or white, to envisage the peopling of the far forests by settlers. Those Indians went on their forays for loot, and scalps, and the love of bloodshed and destruction, and returned to their distant villages quite serenely confident that nobody could reach them for reprisals.

In Pontiac's War, commencing in 1763, the allied Indian tribes scourged the Pennsylvania and New York frontiers so terribly that it was deemed by some impossible to maintain them. And throughout the Revolution the British, by similar tactics, loosed upon American settlements the terrible Iroquois, the Shawnee, Miami, Delaware, Ottawas, Chippewa, Kickapoo, and other tribes in the North; while from the South British and Spanish agents prodded the Cherokee, Creek, and Chickasaw tribes into bloody incursions.

In those wars, which largely consisted of Indian attacks on settlements, there were of course white thrusts back at them, and some of these were disastrous. Braddock's and Grant's defeats in the French and Indian War, were added to by the terrible massacre at Fort George when Montcalm's Indians got out of control. In Pontiac's War an entire area was devastated, and all the Western forts captured, their defenders killed, except Detroit, Pitt, and Niagara. After the Revolution came Harmar's bloody defeat and the St. Clair disaster.

The Indian tribes were decimated, true, but by disease, notably smallpox and measles—the latter deadly to a people with no immunity built up against it. But there were no Indian battle losses to compare with the disasters cited above, and in the continual raids on the scattered cabins very few Indians ever were slain.

There is no question that there were many Indians notable for intelligence, a certain nobility, and to a degree statesmanlike qualities. Names like Pontiac, Tecumseh, and Brant among the Eastern Indians come readily to mind.

Oratory was the chief, almost the only, intellectual art of the red men. Their languages lent themselves to it, symbolism was inherent in their outlook, and their audiences of their own kind were appreciative listeners. We have speeches by such chiefs as Cornstalk, Red Jacket, Logan, Big Elk, and Joseph, which have the ring of true eloquence. All Indian leaders were orators, for it was necessary to convince their followers before any proposition was accepted, since they had no true organization, and leadership was largely a matter of personal prestige. But where there were some Indians of capacity and high qualities, the rank and file of the tribes were savages in every respect.

Most tribes were warlike. They had not lived in peace with each other before the white man came. Almost constantly they raided and fought, slaughtering women and children of rival tribes as well as men. These wars were one reason why, by best estimates, there were at most hardly a million and perhaps as few as 350,000 Indians within the present area of the United States when Europeans first arrived on the continent.

Indians went on the warpath for revenge, hereditary hatred, glory, hope of plunder, relief from boredom, or simply for love of murder. War was the chief, almost the only, way for an Indian male to win distinction. Long before the white man came into contact with them, the Iroquois were engaged in relentlessly destroying the tribes around them. That ferocious confederation of warriors *within historic times* wiped out a score or more of lesser tribes, totalling upward of 75,000 persons. Of the Iroquois Francis Parkman wrote:

> But for the presence of Europeans [they] would probably have subjugated, absorbed, or exterminated every other Indian community east of the Mississippi and north of the Ohio.

Prevalence of intertribal warfare made the first step of westward settlement easier for white men, because for safety from raids by each other the Northern Indians and the Southern Indians had drawn widely apart. The southernmost towns of the Iroquois, Miamis, Shawnees, and others, were north of the Ohio, along the Muskingum, Scioto, Miami, and Maumee rivers. The northernmost towns of the Cherokees, Creeks, and Chickasaws, were south of the Tennessee River. That intervening space, which became known as the Middle Ground or Neutral Ground, enabled a white population to move in between the two hostile aggregations of tribes whose warfare had forced them so widely apart, with comparative ease at first, so that Kentucky achieved statehood in 1792, and Tennessee in 1796. This does not mean there were no Indian troubles in that period. Hundreds of white persons died in the migration.

The Indians, who habitually butchered women and children as well as men in their wars against each other, continued this practice against the white people. Cruelty was so common among them that to show mercy was considered a weakness. Frequently—though not always—captured prisoners were tortured to death, and the records are full of examples of ingenuity in drawing out to the last quivering instant the agony of a helpless victim.

Lacking true military organization, raiding was the favorite Indian method of warfare; and loot was as large an incentive as scalps to the raiders. With the advance of white settlers into the forests, the major attention of warlike parties became concentrated on them, for various reasons: The loot was greater and more prized, including weapons, horses, various tools and implements, clothing, bed coverings, and an endless variety of trinkets which were seized almost as avidly as were useful articles. It was said that white scalps, the color of which might be brown, golden, red, or other colors, instead of the universal black of Indians' scalps, formed a variation pleasing to a savage sense of decoration when worn as fringes on leggings, or flourished on a wand in a scalp dance. Finally there was, of course, the instinctive hatred of the white man as a member of a different race, as well as because he was invading Indian hunting grounds.

Each frontier family faced its dangers alone, unless there was a communal fortification like that at Boonesborough, where several families lived together. Surprise was the major Indian tactic. Usually attacks on isolated cabins occurred early in the morning, the war party having concealed itself around it during the night. As the family came forth at dawn, a signal from the Indian leader brought a volley from the guns of his warriors, usually aimed to bring down the men. Then the whole party leaped with savage fury to cut off from the cabin any who survived the first blast, and to try to carry the cabin itself.

Adult males, old or ugly women, and young children were murdered indiscriminately. Young and comely women, and sometimes children old enough to travel, were on occasion carried away as captives. The children were frequently adopted into the tribe and trained as members of it, often becoming reconciled and fully "Indianized." The young women became camp drudges, and usually in the end were taken as "wives" of the Indians who claimed them as personal captives.

The mischief done by Spanish, French and British agents, in stirring the natives to hostility and furnishing them with arms and supplies, made the frontier conflict even more bitter.[1] It cannot be wondered that even a generation later the faces of the frontier people bore the stamp of all known distresses, and that their hatreds were deep-bitten.

This much in extenuation of the too often maligned pioneers of the American race. There was reason for their detestation of the red men, a detestation shared by so great a man as Andrew Jackson, who certainly saw enough of the Indian peril and devastation in his young manhood, and who in his maturity at the head of a frontier army conquered the Southern tribes.

---

[1] Even after independence was won, the malign work of John Graves Simcoe, governor of Upper Canada, Alexander McKee, British Indian agent, and Captain Joseph Banbury and Lieutenant Prideaux Selby of the British army, in advising Indian strategy and preventing peace conferences with the Americans, prior to the debacle of St. Clair's army has been well documented. So also are the manipulations of Colonel Edward Nicholls among the Seminoles of Florida, and those of Spanish governors of Louisiana, in stirring and arming the Creek Indians, and in keeping Alexander McGillivray, half-breed chief of that tribe on an annuity amounting to $2500 a year to insure his continued hostility to Americans, to say nothing of the Spanish payments to the ineffable General James Wilkinson to spy on his own country.

2

"Indian lands" had no documentary titles, were ill-defined, not individually owned, often disputed by several tribes among themselves. Indeed, Indian tribes often abandoned one hunting ground and moved long distances away to another, with no thought of sentiment, let alone of leaving property behind in the territory they left.

The concept of individual ownership of land came when white settlers moved into the wilderness, cleared small patches of ground, built cabins, or sometimes erected small forts, and prepared to fight off reprisal. Great bravery, or at least dogged endurance was required of those men and women who lived on the frontier, with death always near at hand.

For a time the United States came perilously close to losing the transmontane territories. Kentucky and Tennessee, receiving no help, and not even sympathy for their losses and trials from the national government, experienced a tide of dissatisfaction which made some of their leading men listen with considerable interest to offers by Spain of support and a free market for Western produce on the Gulf, and free navigation of the Mississippi, if the West would ally itself with Spain, rather than with the United States.

But with the adoption of the Constitution in 1789, the government strengthened its hold on the West. The Northern Indians were dealt with at Fallen Timbers by General Anthony Wayne, the Creeks by General Jackson at Horse Shoe Bend, and Tecumseh's allied tribes at Tippecanoe by General William Henry Harrison. It was government policy to gain title to lands claimed by various Indian tribes. Sometimes entire areas were vacated by treaty—frequently after losing wars, as was the case with the Iroquois after the Revolution, the allied tribes of Ohio after Wayne's campaign, and the Creeks after their defeat by Jackson.

Another method frequently employed was simple fraud. No better illustration of the singular blindness of even high-minded men to the moralities in dealing with Indians can be cited than the policy of Thomas Jefferson as President. Jefferson was able, evidently without qualms, to write General William Henry Harrison on February 27, 1803:

> To promote this [Indian] disposition to exchange lands which they have to spare and we want, for the necessaries which we have to spare and they want, we shall push our trading houses, and be glad to see the good and influential individuals among

them in debt; because we observe that when these debts get beyond what individuals can pay, they are willing to lop them off by a cession of lands.

"Lopping off debts" became a settled policy and an easy one. To the Indian, credit was a new and wholly delightful experience. Hitherto he had obtained what he had by the toil of hunting, or by plunder when his wars were successful, or sometimes by theft. Now white traders were telling him to take what "necessaries" he needed—even those he really did not need—and pay for them later (in the pleasantly dim future) with furs or other products of the forest he would bring in.

The Indian did not consider the fact that all goods thus sold to him were doubled, trebled, or even quadrupled in price. And of course animal life was becoming scarcer in the forests. But let the future take care of itself; especially since one of the "necessities" he was able to buy was liquor, which produced a pleasing sensation of well-being; even though often followed by most unpleasant headaches and nausea as he recovered from the debauch.

Some of the concoctions sold to the savages were brewed by methods dreadfully heartless, for the traders cared nothing for the well-being of the Indians. One recipe for "Injun whiskey" which has come down to us, and which illustrates the standards, is as follows:

Take a barrel of lake or river water, add three plugs of chewing tobacco and five bars of soap, stir half a pound of red pepper into the mixture, throw in some dead leaves, and boil until the liquid turns brown. Then add two gallons of alcohol and two ounces of strychnine, stir thoroughly, strain, and bottle.

The strychnine gave a stimulating sensation which made up for the small amount of alcohol used, and in this dilution was not fatal. The dead leaves gave "color," the soap gave "bead," and the red pepper "bite." The tobacco produced nausea—no Indian, the traders said, thought he was really drinking unless he was afterward sick as a dog.

The awful brew was cheap and easy to make, and some Indians would trade a bundle of furs—or go into debt for a like value—to get a bottle of the concoction. As one man said, "After a few drinks of the stuff, you could prop Indians up in the corners as if they were paralyzed, unable to close their eyes." Quite naturally, such "whiskey" led not only to drunkenness and sickness, but to laziness and sometimes violence among the Indians themselves.

Accounts were kept only by the traders—the Indian had no duplicate record—and could be changed at any time by a scratch of the pen.

Even when an Indian did hunt and trap, he frequently discovered that fur-bearing animals had already been killed off or driven out of his hunting grounds. His debts increased as additional credit was advanced by traders who knew they would eventually be reimbursed by the government. At last the Indian grew discouraged about ever freeing himself from his burden.

Thus, in 1836, the Potawatomi, a small and insignificant tribe, was found to owe creditors $130,974.60. This sum was paid off by the government in three years, but meantime the tribe had contracted new debts amounting to $22,761.04. At last the Potawatomi "settled" their obligations by ceding all their hunting grounds in Indiana. The example is typical of many.

East of the Mississippi, eventually, "civilized" tribes like the Iroquois, Cherokee, Choctaw, Creek, and Seminole, "semi-civilized" tribes like the Delaware, Miami, Winnebago, Wyandot, Chippewa, and Potawatomi, and "wild" tribes like the Ottawa, Sauk and Fox, Kickapoo, and their various congeners, all were removed, by war, government purchase, debt settlement, or mere pre-emption by settlers, from their hunting grounds to beyond the Mississippi, or in some cases north into Canada, save for a few scattered remnants.

In this period the government ceaselessly acquired native territories at an average cost of a few cents an acre—less than 3½ cents an acre up to 1825—and sold it to settlers at two dollars an acre, for revenue, this price gradually scaling down until the free homestead laws were enacted; or else disposed of extensive tracts to speculators who had political or financial influence.

The rapidly accelerating removal of the Indians offered almost unlimited possibilities for white expansion. After the admission of Kentucky and Tennessee, Ohio gained statehood in 1803, Louisiana in 1812, Indiana in 1816, Mississippi in 1817, Illinois in 1818, Alabama in 1819, Missouri in 1821, and Michigan, Iowa, Wisconsin, and Minnesota were to follow.

The West, unruly, hardened by suffering and hardship, obdurately brave, self-reliant and progressive, was becoming an entity. Its people had begun to identify themselves. Already it was producing men who could be accounted notable. Henry Clay was one. Andrew Jackson was even greater. There would shortly be others including the gangling lawyer from Illinois, Abraham Lincoln. Westerners were proud to call themselves by that name. They were to take charge of the nation's destiny, and in the span of a single generation carry the American idea across the entire continent to the far Pacific and there maintain it.

CHAPTER FOUR

The Tennessee Firebrand

1

BONE and marrow of the West was Andrew Jackson, the borderer who came not only to dominate his section but the entire nation. He was a man whose appearance, far from being that of the popular conception of a hero, was almost whimsical—although no man ever dared laugh at Andrew Jackson.

He was tall—six feet one inch—with narrow shoulders, excessively thin body, storklike legs; his long, homely face, pitted by smallpox and with the scar of a sword cut on one cheek, was surmounted by a stiff brush of hair, red in his younger days, snow-white in his later years. His eyes were brilliant steel blue; and his voice, rather than being a roar to inspire troops in battle, was shrill, becoming a high-pitched scream in moments of excitement or anger.

Yet for all these less than ideal physical characteristics there was about the man something that seemed to dwarf others with whom he came into contact, a kind of electric magnetism that caused his followers to love and follow him to the death, and with this a will so strong and unbreakable that its counterpart has rarely been seen in history.

He was born in a log cabin in the Waxhaw district of South Carolina; a posthumous child whose father died about a month before his birth, which took place March 15, 1767. His parents, Andrew and Elizabeth Jackson, were Scotch-Irish, having emigrated from the Protestant north of Ireland; and his mother, a titian-haired little woman, who was both brave and wise, provided her son with some of his notable characteristics—his keen mind, red hair, unflinching courage, loyalty to duty, sense of honor, and inflexible purpose.

Always a partisan, the boy instinctively sided with the patriot cause in the Revolution, and was a dispatch rider before he was fifteen. Out of that conflict he came with a sword scar on his face—inflicted by a drunken subaltern of Tarleton's British dragoons while the lad was a prisoner—and smallpox pits, souvenirs of the disease he caught while in a British prison.

Both his elder brothers, Hugh and Robert, died in the Revolutionary army, one from wounds, the other from sickness. He lost his mother also, who contracted the deadly typhus, then known as "ship fever," when she went to nurse sick American soldiers in a British prison hulk. From these several circumstances he acquired a hatred for Britain and all things British that lived through his life.

When Elizabeth Jackson bade her sole surviving son farewell—and it was for the last time, though neither of them knew it—she said:

"Andy . . . never tell a lie, nor take what is not your own, nor sue for slander . . . *settle them cases yourself.*"

That injunction was the guiding rule of Jackson's life. Above all things he prized his word, he was honest to the point of going into near-bankruptcy twice by paying off notes of others which he had endorsed; and he never permitted a slur against himself or anyone he loved to pass unnoticed, until at last he became President and felt that he must not allow the office to be involved in the quarrels of the man.

His hair-trigger temper was notorious. Formally or informally he challenged or was challenged to mortal combat by many men. Among them were: Colonel Waightstill Avery (they met, but the quarrel was composed and both fired in the air); Lewis Robards, at the time the husband of Rachel, Jackson's future wife (Robards hastily absented himself); General John Sevier, then governor of Tennessee (three times, exchanging shots with him twice though without fatalities); Judge John McNairy and the judge's brother Nathaniel McNairy, also Senator William Cocke (the quarrels in each of these instances being smoothed over by intermediaries without actual meetings); Charles Dickinson (whom he killed for slurring Rachel, and from whom he received a wound in return that wrecked his health for the remainder of his lifetime); General Winfield Scott (who declined on religious grounds); Thomas Swann (whom he caned after being challenged, but scorned to fight); and Thomas Hart Benton and his brother Jesse (in a tavern brawl during which Jesse Benton shot Jackson treacherously from behind, almost ending his life). There were other quarrels and near duels, and in every instance Jackson felt he had just cause.

This sounds as if the Tennesseean must have been an intensely quarrelsome man. That conclusion needs qualification. He lived in an era when the code of the duel was upheld by most gentlemen, and because of his strong personality and outspoken views, he made enemies, sometimes deadly foes.

In his frontier boyhood Jackson was accustomed to wearing linsey and buckskin, and living in grinding poverty; yet by his unaided efforts he became a lawyer, a judge, a senator, a great general, a substantial land owner, a gentleman as the term was understood in his

UNITED STATES
The New Nation, 1783 – 1800

LAKE OF THE WOODS
INDEFINITE
BOUNDARY

INDEFINITE
BOUNDARY

Grand Portage

L.SUPERIOR

CANADA
(ENGLISH)

MAINE
(TO MASS.)

Pointe-au-Fer

Oswegatchie

Montpelier

Portland

Ft.Michilimackinac

L.HURON

VT.
1791

N.H.

Concord

L.MICHIGAN

DIVISION LINE
1800

L.ONTARIO

Ft.Ontario

Oswego

Boston

MISSISSIPPI R.

Ft.Detroit

Ft.Niagara

Albany
NEW YORK

MASS.

L.ERIE

CONN.

Providence R.I.

NORTHWEST

Ft.Miamis

PENNSYLVANIA

N.J.

Hartford

New York

Trenton

Pittsburgh

Philadelphia

Ft.Recovery

Marietta

Baltimore

Wilmington

TERRITORY

Cincinnati

Washington

MD.

DEL.

Vincennes

VIRGINIA

Richmond

Cahokia
Kaskaskia

Norfolk

MISSOURI R.

LOUISIANA

KENTUCKY
1792

Raleigh

(SPANISH)

Nashville

NORTH CAROLINA

New Bern

TENNESSEE
1796

Ft.San Fernando
(SPANISH)

MISSISSIPPI R.

SOUTH
CAROLINA

Columbia

GEORGIA

Charleston

Ft.Nogales
(SPANISH)

Savannah

Natchez

CLAIMED BY SPAIN
UNTIL 1795

ATLANTIC OCEAN

Ft.Adams

SPANISH

FLORIDA

N

GULF OF MEXICO

BAHAMAS

(ENGLISH)

Miles

0   100   200   300

palacios

CUBA
(SPANISH)

time, and finally President of the United States. Though he had little formal schooling his mind was such that he could grasp the largest questions and bring them to solution; and he cultivated a style of speech and manner so graceful and gracious that it charmed all but his enemies.

All this he accomplished in spite of the fact that through most of his active life he was the victim of chronic ill-health that might have killed most men, or at least made of them helpless invalids. Though he suffered constantly from pain and illness, by the very power of his will he achieved gigantic feats in every sphere he entered.

His youth was wild enough. Admitted to the bar when he was twenty, he left the Carolinas and threw in his lot with the West, crossing the mountains to the Cumberland settlements in what became Tennessee. A contemporary described him at that period as a "roaring, rollicking, game-cocking, horse-racing, card-playing, mischievous fellow," who, if tradition is to be trusted, drank heavily and sowed his wild oats with mulatto mistresses as did other young blades of the time.

Yet for all his wildness and homeliness he made a not unfavorable impression on another class of contemporaries—the girls of quality who knew him. Long afterward one of them, a sprightly young lady named Nancy Jarret, wrote of him:

> His ways and manners . . . were most captivating . . . We all knew that he was wild . . . that he gambled some and was by no means a Christian young man . . . [but] either calm or animated there was something about him I cannot describe except to say that it was *a presence* . . . This I and all the other girls . . . talked about among ourselves.

A presence. Even so early in life Andrew Jackson was making felt that remarkable, magnetic personality which one day would rule armies, even the nation.

When he arrived on the frontier the Cherokees were warlike, an aftermath of the Revolution. One of his first activities in the West was fighting Indians—both Cherokees and Creeks, who frequently raided around the infant town of Nashville. "On an average of once in every ten days throughout 1789 someone was killed within a few miles of Nashville."

Wrote John Haywood of that hectic year:

> On the 20th of January the Indians killed Capt. Hunter and dangerously wounded Hugh F. Bell. A party of white men collected and pursued the Indians . . . [who] fired upon the pursuers, killed Maj. Kirkpatrick, and wounded J. Foster and Wil-

liam Brown . . . In the spring of the year, at Dunham's Station, the Indians killed a man of the name of Mills; in May they killed Dunham, and in the summer Joseph Norrington and another Dunham. They kept up hostilities during the whole summer and killed a number of persons whose names are not remembered . . . Near the mouth of Sulphur Fork of the Red River, the Indians fell upon two moving families by the name of Titsworth and killed their wives and children. Killed Evan Shelby and Abednego Lewellen as they were hunting in the woods . . . Came to Buchanan's Station and scalped John Blackburn near the spring on the bank of the creek, and left a spear sticking in his body.

To say the least, times were lively in Tennessee, and Jackson was in the midst of it, dividing his time between Indian fighting and the practice of law. In this period, at the head of nineteen men, he relieved Robertson's Station, which was besieged, then pursued the Indians and defeated them. When the Cherokees rose again in 1793, Jackson fought against them in a campaign during which the frontiersmen, under the overall command of General Sevier, broke the fighting power of the Indian nation. The Cherokees killed the father of Jackson's wife, Colonel John Donelson, one of the founders of Nashville. What he witnessed in murders and atrocities and destruction in those Indian raids and the campaigns that followed them affected Jackson's viewpoint toward Indians forever.

2

The last Cherokee campaign came after Jackson's marriage to Rachel Donelson Robards, a marriage that had a determining effect on his life. Hitherto he had been free to follow his own bents, go where he wished, and in his actions consider nobody but himself. He speculated in land, bought slaves to till his plantations—called Hunter's Hill and The Hermitage—acquired acreage near Natchez on which he built a log house, negotiated for trading rights with Don Esteban Miró, Spanish governor of Louisiana—who was at that time busily engaged in trying to wean the West away from America to Spanish dominion. He also made a good record as a lawyer and as a prosecuting attorney in the Cumberland circuit.

But where he was successful in most things, in the one most intimate part of his life he seemed doomed to misfortune, futility, and wrath.

His wife Rachel, when he first met her, was married to another man. At that time she was a beauty, very attractive to men who fairly besieged her before and after her marriage to Lewis Robards, of

Harrisburg, Kentucky. The evidence is that she did her best to live circumspectly and tread the tricky path pretty women so often must tread—by being charming and delightful, while at the same time holding at arm's length men they like and do not wish to offend. She might have been successful in this delicate feminine artistry had not her husband been of "a mean and jealous nature."

Robards saw the admiration other men displayed toward her. Presently he voiced suspicions, followed by groundless accusations, so that Rachel, a daughter of the numerous and important Donelson family of Nashville, twice left him. On the first occasion she fled to her mother's home, where she first met Jackson, then a boarder there. At that time Jackson also met Robards, who had pursued his wife to Tennessee, and according to his version "mildly remonstrated" with him about his injustice toward her. Knowing Jackson, the "mildness" of the remonstrance, leaves some room for speculation. It ended in a challenge to meet on the field of honor, which Robards discreetly and speedily avoided.

A reconciliation between Rachel and her husband was tried and failed, and once more Rachel returned from Kentucky to Tennessee, her escort on this hegira being none other than Andrew Jackson himself, who, according to his best biographer, Marquis James, acted at the request of the Donelson family to see her safely home. The girl—she was then only twenty-three, though she had been married three years—expressed fear of actual physical danger at Robards' hands, and took an opportunity to float downriver with a flatboat fleet commanded by Colonel John Stark, a friend of the Donelson family, to Natchez. Not surprisingly, Andrew Jackson, who by this time was heels over head in love with Rachel, also floated with the same fleet, ostensibly on business, but actually "to keep an eye out for her safety."

At Natchez word came that Robards had obtained a divorce through an act of the Virginia General Assembly[1]—that being the only legal way to obtain such a separation at the time. Rachel wept when Jackson broke the news to her, for divorce in that day was considered a disgrace. Her sorrow changed to joy, however, when he offered her marriage; and feeling themselves free to do so, the couple was wedded by a magistrate in Natchez. What they did not know was that Robards had asked for and received only an enabling act, whereby *if he could show cause* the marriage would be dissolved. Robards engaged to publish the terms of the act for "eight weeks consecutively in the *Kentucky Gazette*." This he did not do, but waited in scoundrelly silence for two years, when he went to court and got his

---

[1] The date of this act was July 20, 1790, just twelve days before Kentucky ceased to be a part of Virginia.

actual divorce on the grounds that during that period his wife had been "living in adultery with another man"—namely, Andrew Jackson.

Adultery? This *was* disgrace, and Rachel was crushed by it, though she was innocent of any conscious wrongdoing. Furious and bewildered, Jackson searched the law books and found that, under the terms of which he and his wife had been ignorant, the charge was technically true. He would then have sought out Robards with his pistols, had not Rachel's tears prevented. The couple went through the marriage ceremony again, but the scandal, thus unintentionally incurred, hung over them for all future time.

In her shame, poor Rachel sought obscurity and concealment—two goals impossible to achieve for the wife of a man like Andrew Jackson. Throughout their subsequent life together she became more and more recessive, unable to grow with her husband, until she actually was a social and even a political handicap to him. Yet from the time of their marriage Andrew Jackson never wavered in his loyalty to her.

3

When Tennessee became a state in 1796—and tradition says that Jackson suggested the name—he was a leading member of the constitutional convention, and he became the state's first Representative in Congress. His term in that office was chiefly distinguished by his opposition to the policies of President George Washington on three counts:

Washington was an aristocrat and a Federalist, a party which believed the government should be kept in the hands of men of family and property. Jackson was not.

Washington rebuked the frontiersmen for occupying certain Indian lands supposedly protected by treaties. Jackson had no sympathy with the Indians.

Washington, knowing America's military weakness, was willing to compromise with England, even to the point of permitting the hated impressment of men from American ships, rather than fight. Jackson would have fought.

The Representative from Tennessee was one of twelve Members of Congress who refused to vote in favor of the resolutions felicitating Washington for his services to the nation. It may be added that in no way did this appear to cloud the majestic reputation of the first President, or the feeling of the people for him.

Thereafter Jackson served a short term in the Senate, followed by six years as judge of the Supreme Court of Tennessee. As a judge Jackson was just, fearless, and incorruptible. On one occasion he upheld the dignity of the court with a pair of pistols which he leveled over the judicial desk. He believed in the rights of property, and one of his charges to a jury is preserved: "Do what is *right* between these parties. That is what *the law always means.*"

After the Louisiana Purchase of 1803, Jackson sought appointment as governor of the new territory. President Thomas Jefferson, however, appointed William C. C. Claiborne governor of the District of New Orleans (south of the present northern border of Louisiana), and Brigadier General James Wilkinson governor of the District of Louisiana (comprising the northern part of the territory).

Jackson later was to save Claiborne's territory, by then become a state, in the Battle of New Orleans. As for Wilkinson, Jackson, who knew a traitor when he saw one, had for him only complete loathing.[2]

Rejection of his application for the gubernatorial appointment came at a low point in Jackson's fortunes, for he had to sell off one of his plantations, Hunter's Hill, and go into debt on the other, The Hermitage, in order to pay off losses due to speculations and defaulting by others on notes he had done them the favor of endorsing for them.

In the midst of this depression Aaron Burr, in disgrace because of his fatal duel with Alexander Hamilton, arrived at Nashville, May 29, 1805. Jackson was grateful to Burr for his championship of the cause of Tennessee when the controversy over the admission of the state was taking place in Congress, and entertained him at The Hermitage with utmost hospitality.

It was during this visit that Burr sought to interest his host in his "colonization" scheme, but in vague terms, buttressed by assurances—probably true—that Henry Dearborn, then Secretary of War, was secretly privy to it and approved of it. At the time war with Spain seemed imminent and Burr wished to be on hand in the West, hoping to regain public favor by leading American troops should the conflict break out. He counted on the help of his "friend," General Wilkinson, not knowing that Wilkinson was at that moment in the pay of Spain,

---

[2] History has since revealed the amazing treacheries of Wilkinson. Of him, John Randolph of Roanoke said in Congress: "Human nature has never appeared in so degraded a form—the double traitor—the most finished scoundrel that ever lived—the only man I ever knew who, from bark to core, is a villain." Wilkinson was involved with Spain in the plot to detach the West from the United States, which failed. His financial venality in dealings with Spanish governors brought him large sums of money. Even when he was commanding officer of the United States army, he was carried on the Spanish government payrolls as "Spy No. 13," and received annual payments for his services in that regard. It is generally agreed that he originated the so-called Burr Conspiracy, then turned traitor on his fellow conspirator for political and monetary advantage. Yet, though he was tried three times before court-martials, he always escaped punishment. He failed disgracefully against the British in the War of 1812, and died forgotten in Mexico City in 1825. See Royal Ornan Shreve, *The Finished Scoundrel.*

and revealing every detail of the plan for colonizing a Spanish grant on the Ouichata River in Louisiana—a likely jumping-off place for a military invasion of Texas—to his employers in Mexico City.

Jackson was interested. He was now a brigadier general of Tennessee militia, and the "inevitability" of war with Spain as represented to him by Burr—whose representations were nothing if not elastic—aroused his martial ardor. He endorsed the scheme—what he knew of it, which by no means was the entire story—before Burr returned to the East.

4

Meantime the Master of The Hermitage needed money badly. "My creditors are growing clamorous," he wrote.

He chose a truly desperate expedient to repair his fortunes. A Major John Verell, embarrassed by debt, owned a horse, a magnificent stallion named Truxton, which had recently lost a match race with Greyhound, a gelding belonging to Lazarus Cotton.

Jackson, as superb a judge of horseflesh as the West knew, looked Truxton over and came to the conclusion the horse had lost the race to Greyhound through lack of condition. He bought the thoroughbred by assuming Verell's debts to the extent of eleven hundred and seventy dollars, and giving three geldings, with a bonus of two other geldings if Truxton should "win a purse in the fall ensuing."

This was unconventional financing, even by horse-trading methods, but Jackson had no cash, and he made his risks all the greater by assuming Verell's obligations in order to get Truxton. Thereafter he set about conditioning his new property, and matched him for a return match with Greyhound, for a side bet of five thousand dollars, and other considerations. How he raised such a sum at the time is a mystery since he already was "near, if not within, jail bounds for debt." Probably some of his loyal friends advanced the money to him.

In any case the betting on the race was heavy, for the general's friends backed their faith in Jackson's judgment, while their adversaries placed their money on the record—which was that Greyhound had previously defeated Truxton.

This time Truxton won, and Jackson's finances were at least temporarily eased.

But horse racing very soon brought the Tennessee firebrand into a deadly quarrel. After beating Greyhound, Jackson bought the gelding, and soon after defeated with him a horse named Tanner, owned by Captain Joseph Erwin of Nashville, for another five-thousand-dollar wager.

Erwin offered as part of his forfeit notes he held—a proper procedure, in a country where real cash was extremely scarce. Thereupon a troublemaking young lawyer named Thomas Swann carried to Erwin and his son-in-law Charles Dickinson, a story in which he misquoted Jackson about the exchange. Dickinson asked for an explanation, and Jackson replied that someone had retailed to him "a damned lye."

At this Swann, eager for the limelight, wanted to fight a duel, but Jackson contemptuously refused. Instead he went to Nashville and caned Swann for his presumption.

Now came a climactic event. Jackson's Truxton was matched against Erwin's famous stallion Ploughboy, for three thousand dollars. The meeting had to be postponed because Ploughboy went lame, and Erwin was further disgruntled by paying an eight-hundred-dollar forfeit.

On the second date it was Truxton that was ailing with an injured thigh. But Jackson refused to withdraw—to the jubilation of the Erwin crowd, who knew of the stallion's injury. Additional wagers to the amount of two thousand dollars were offered by the Erwins—and covered by Jackson. Other persons bet land, horses, slaves, and other property amounting to thousands of dollars in the intense excitement the race aroused.

The day of the race was rainy, the track slippery. But to the amazement of everyone—perhaps even of Jackson—Truxton won in straight heats.

Feelings were heated. At a convivial gathering Dickinson made a snide remark about the unconventionality of Rachel Jackson's marriage. Jackson heard of it and warned Erwin to restrain his son-in-law. But the offense was repeated.

After some newspaper exchanges Dickinson sent a "card" to a Nashville paper, the last paragraph of which stated that "the Major General [Jackson] . . . [is] a worthless scoundrel, a poltroon and coward."

Jackson at once challenged. Dickinson accepted.

At dawn, May 30, 1806, Jackson faced his antagonist with pistols at twelve paces. Dickinson was known to be an expert shot. Jackson, less skilled, was sure the other would hit him, perhaps mortally, but he concentrated his entire will on killing the detractor of his wife.

At the signal there was an instantaneous puff of smoke from Dickinson's pistol and Jackson felt a heavy shock in his side. He swayed momentarily, then straightened.

"Great God, have I missed him?" cried Dickinson in horror.

He recoiled a step, but resumed the mark at the referee's order.

Jackson raised his pistol and pulled the trigger. The hammer stopped at half-cock.

"Hold, sir—" someone cried.

But Jackson remorselessly drew back the hammer and fired. Dickinson fell, mortally wounded. He died that night.

Though Jackson could feel the blood running down from his own wound into his boot, he mounted his horse and rode forty miles back to Nashville, an amazing feat of Spartan fortitude considering the nature of his hurt. Later he made a statement, much quoted as an index of his iron will, "I would have killed him if he had hit me in the brain."

His wound was more serious than he or his doctors knew. The surgeons could not probe for the pistol ball because it was too near the heart. Actually it broke two of his ribs and embedded itself deep in the left lung. There it remained all his life, an unceasing source of pain and illness. A brilliant medical study has this to say of it:

> After this fateful affair of honor Jackson suffered from ever-recurring attacks of chills and fever, followed by coughing and hemorrhages from the lungs . . . The symptoms point to . . . diagnosis that the bullet, together with particles of clothing and bone, caused an abscess of the lung. As long as his abscess was sealed off, it would produce fever and pain in the chest. The abscess would spread gradually, the fever rise, and chills and fever would alternate with profuse sweating. Finally the pressure of the abscess and the digestive power of the pus would cause a perforation into the bronchial tube. Through this opening the pus would drain and be coughed up with blood. The severe strain of the coughing and the sudden emptying of the abscess cavity would leave the patient feeling faint and exhausted, but soon after the fever would drop and he would feel revived.[3]

That vicious cycle of septic fever and coughing hemorrhages continued throughout Jackson's life. Doctors thought he was suffering from tuberculosis, then a very common ailment. But tuberculosis in so virulent a form would soon have killed him, whereas he lived on through a life, the truly great achievements of which followed this tragic duel.

5

Hardly had Jackson recovered from his wound enough to be up and about when Burr sent him money to build five flatboats. The work was begun. Then a young man calling himself Captain Fort arrived in Nashville, professing himself to be of Burr's party, and talk-

[3] Rudolph Marx, M.D., *The Health of the Presidents.*

ing freely and importantly about Burr's plans. At last he stated that the object of those plans was "to divide the nation."

From this source Jackson learned that General Wilkinson, of whom he could believe anything, was involved in the plot. At once he was convinced that the whole scheme was rotten.

He immediately wrote warning letters to Washington, including an offer to President Jefferson tendering the services of his Tennessee soldiers "in the event of . . . aggression . . . *from any quarter.*" To Burr he sent a missive "in strong tones," stating that until his suspicions were cleared no further intimacy could exist between them.

Now Burr arrived—just ahead of a proclamation by Jefferson that a "military conspiracy" existed. He assured Jackson "upon his honor" that his project was approved by the government. At this Jackson released two of the five flatboats to Burr, but sent his nephew Stockley Hays along with secret letters of warning to Governor Claiborne at New Orleans.

Burr went on down the river. Next Jackson received a letter from Dearborn, Secretary of War, which along with instructions to "render abortive such an expedition," contained a vague hint that Jackson might be in favor of Burr's scheme.

The Tennesseean wrote a scorching reply. The first draft of this letter (later modified and amplified) shows his feeling.

> Henry Dearborn, Sir: Colo. B. [Burr] received at my house all the hospitality that a banished patriot was entitled to. But sir, when proof shews him to be a treator [*sic*] I would cut his throat with as much pleasure as I would cut yours on equal testimony.

The upshot was that Burr, betrayed by Wilkinson, was arrested and taken East to be tried at Richmond, Virginia, for treason. And Jackson, ready to testify against the perfidious general, traveled there at his own expense, and on the street publicly denounced Wilkinson as "a double traitor," crying out, "Pity the sword that dangles from his felon's belt, for it is doubtless made of honest steel!"

That was fighting talk, an open invitation to a challenge. But portly, slippery Wilkinson sized up his lean, furious opponent and swallowed the insult.

Burr was acquitted on the rulings of Chief Justice John Marshall, and Jackson returned to his home.

He wrote a friend, William Preston Anderson, while still in Richmond, "I am more convinced than ever that treason was not intended by Burr; but if it ever was, you know my wishes—that he may be hung."

Whatever else he thought or felt, Andrew Jackson's one great loyalty was to his country.

6

The War of 1812 came on—an ill-begotten, ill-conducted war, but one which Jackson enthusiastically espoused: first, because he detested England; second, because he saw prospects of territorial gain in a successful war; third, because he was a born fighting man and welcomed a chance to unsheathe his sword.

At an urgent request from the War Department he led two thousand Tennessee riflemen to reinforce the troops defending New Orleans, commanded by his old enemy, James Wilkinson. The volunteers traveled in part by flatboats, in part by the Natchez Trace, famed for its murderous robbers. Wilkinson claimed to see dire peril of a British invasion. The fact that such an invasion did develop two years later does not mitigate the fact that at this time there was no immediate danger of it. Power-loving Wilkinson schemed to get additional troops and arms under his command; nothing more.

When Jackson reached Natchez, February 13, 1813, he learned that William Eustis, who succeeded Dearborn as Secretary of War, had been dismissed for inefficiency, and was himself succeeded by John Armstrong, who was to prove equally inefficient.

But there was this great difference: Eustis was at least honest, while Armstrong was a friend of General James Wilkinson. He was, in fact, a member of the intriguing cabal, including General Horatio Gates, the treacherous General Charles Lee, Henry Dearborn, and Wilkinson himself, which plotted to displace General George Washington as commander of the American armies during the Revolution. This would have meant the loss of the war, and had not the soldiers of the Continental Army made it clear that without Washington they would not serve, the plot might have succeeded.

Now Armstrong, in behalf of his old companion in intrigue, dispatched an order to Jackson which read in part:

> The causes for embodying and marching to New Orleans the corps under your command having ceased to exist, you will . . . consider it as dismissed from the public service and take measures to have delivered to Major General Wilkinson all articles of public property . . .

How Andrew Jackson bristled at that! Knowing full well that Wilkinson had connived in this strange communication, the Tennesseean refused to obey it. He would not dismiss the young men for whom he had made himself personally responsible, nor turn them over to Wilkinson whom he already believed to be a traitor.

When Wilkinson's officers came to receive the "government property"—in other words the arms of his men—Jackson showed them a
copy of the law creating the volunteer army which specified that
every man who had served one month or more was "entitled to a
stand of arms." Then, turning an exasperatingly scornful back on
Wilkinson, he led his boys home.

On that long march he hired wagons out of his own pocket to carry
provisions. Often he lent his own horse for sick men to ride. It was
during that weary journey that his men, seeing him always striding
back and forth along the line, encouraging and directing, bestowed
on him in pure affection the name that clung to him forever—Old
Hickory—calling him after the toughest thing they knew.

It was also during that long march that he presumably drank contaminated water or otherwise acquired the chronic dysentery which
plagued and weakened him all the rest of his life.

As if to cap his misadventures, Jackson engaged in a tavern brawl
in Nashville on November 4, 1813, which did him little credit. His
adversaries in this fight, which grew out of an outburst of Jackson's
flaming temper, were Colonel Thomas Hart Benton, formerly his
friend and later in the Senate his greatest champion; and Benton's
brother Jesse.

In a confused scuffle that took place in the lobby of the City Hotel
where the Bentons were staying, Jesse Benton shot Jackson from behind, shattering his left upper arm; Colonel Benton fell backward
down some stairs; and Jesse Benton was only saved from a severe
wound, perhaps death, when Jackson's friend General John Coffee
missed a pistol shot in the smoke-filled room.

They carried Jackson over to the Nashville Inn and that night his
blood soaked through two mattresses before it could be stanched. But
in spite of the urging of his doctors who feared infection and gangrene, he stubbornly refused to have his arm amputated. A lead slug
lodged in his arm, causing an infection of the bone which became
chronic and caused periodic trouble to add to his other ailments, until
it was removed by a surgeon in 1832.

7

Thus far Andrew Jackson had shown few characteristics of greatness. A gambler, a brawler, and a duelist, his wounds seemed to have
put a period to any prospects of advancement. He was carried to The
Hermitage to be nursed by Rachel, and his mind reached the lowest
ebb of despair.

Yet while he lay in bed, trying to regain strength after his disastrous encounter, word came thundering that the Creek Indians, led by their chief, Red Eagle—usually called Weatherford by the whites, after his father, a Scottish trader named Charles Weatherford—had surprised, sacked, and burned Fort Mims, just north of Mobile, massacring all but thirty-six of five hundred fifty-three men, women, and children there. There is no question but that the Creeks in this rising were armed and incited by British and Spanish agents.

Andrew Jackson was too weak and sick to sit a horse, but he was not too weak and sick to fight. When news of the massacre reached him, along with word that war parties were spreading north, carrying fire and death to the settlements, he exclaimed, "By the Eternal! These people must be saved!"

Before the authorities at Washington could intervene with some political appointment, he called up his riflemen, placed John Coffee in command of his cavalry, and with the prospect of action acting like an elixir, Jackson joined his small army at Fayetteville, Tennessee.

He still could hardly sit in his saddle, and at times during the nights his pain was so great that he stood for hours braced up by his good arm slung over a sapling, spiked between two posts in his tent for that purpose. Yet by sheer will power he led his men.

Jackson conducted a campaign like a duel, with a remorseless aim to destroy the enemy. Though some of his men reached the end of their enlistments and went home, he kept others and was joined by a regiment of regulars. These he led in a campaign which forever crushed the warlike power of the Creeks.

Penetrating the Indian country after several indecisive battles, he reached the Creek citadel at the Horse Shoe Bend on the Tallapoosa River. There, March 27, 1814, riding a white horse in person at the head of his troops, he stormed the Indian fortification, destroyed the defending warriors, and for this victory received a promotion to major general in the Regular Army—he had previously been major general only in the Tennessee militia.

An interesting and important footnote to this battle is the fact that it was therein that young Sam Houston, then an ensign in the regulars, was twice wounded leading charges, and so distinguished himself that he won the attention and thereafter the strong friendship of Jackson, with results that affected history.

Five hundred and fifty-seven Creek warriors died at the Horse Shoe Bend. Not long after this terrible defeat the Creek chief, Weatherford, walked into Jackson's camp and calmly identified himself.

"I have come to give myself up," he said.

At Jackson's first bitter denunciation, he drew himself up. "Well may such language be addressed to me now," he said. "There was a time when I . . . could have answered you . . . I could animate my warriors to battle, but I cannot animate the dead . . . I beg you to send for the women and children . . . who have been driven into the woods without an ear of corn . . . They never did any harm. But kill me, if the white people want it done."

All his life long Jackson admired courage as much as any other quality in a man. He poured Weatherford a glass of brandy and took one himself. Then he promised to help the women and children and Weatherford promised to persuade his braves to peace. They shook hands and the chief stalked out of camp with not a hand lifted to halt him.

The Creek war was ended. After this campaign Jackson, who was now named commandant of the Seventh Military District, embracing Tennessee, Louisiana, and the Mississippi Territory, went on to his tremendous victory at New Orleans. From the depths of a barroom shooting brawl he had risen in a matter of months to become the most popular figure in the nation.

8

By no means, however, was the rimrock Westerner, Andrew Jackson, ready to rest on his laurels. Very shortly, by his grim frontier logic and incredible activity, he brought new territory into the United States. Florida was a Spanish possession, but in little more than name. It was a belief of men as disparate in views as John Quincy Adams, the Secretary of State, and Jackson himself, that whoever held Florida held a pistol at the heart of the republic—a simile given semi-graphic form by the pistol-like shape of Florida itself.

The British use of Florida during the War of 1812 made this danger manifest, and when Colonel Edward Nicholls of His Majesty's army made an "offensive and defensive alliance" with the Seminole Indians in the province *after the war was over,* and stirred those warriors to make raids against American settlements in Georgia, the situation grew tense. The fact that Nicholls' "alliance" was disavowed by Lord Castlereagh, British Foreign Secretary, seems not to have been communicated to the Seminoles who fancied themselves strong in possession of an ally who would supply them indefinitely with arms, ammunition, and perhaps even military aid.

The Seminoles were an offshoot of the Creek tribe, swelled in numbers by Creek warriors after Jackson defeated them in 1814, who carried with them their hatred of American frontiersmen. Another force in the disturbance south of the international border was a horde of escaped slaves, chiefly from Georgia, as hostile to white Americans as the Indians.

The first serious "incident" was in fact created by the Negroes. About eight hundred of them had taken possession of a fort, built and abandoned by the British during the War of 1812, on the Apalachicola River, sixty miles south of the Georgia border. It had been left stocked with arms—a dozen pieces of artillery, twenty-five hundred muskets, five hundred carbines, five hundred swords, four hundred pistols, three hundred quarter casks of rifle powder, seven hundred and sixty-three barrels of common powder, and other war matériel. The Negroes seized the abandoned fort, armed themselves, and believed themselves impregnable.

In 1816, they became so bold that they attacked an American convoy which was ascending the river with supplies for Fort Scott, an outpost just above the border in Georgia. Four sailors were shot, and one captured. The latter the Negroes bound, covered with tar, and burned alive.

But the convoy returned, this time with some gunboats, July 26, 1816. In the fort at that time were three hundred and forty-four Negroes, including some women and children. During the bombardment that followed, a red-hot shot from one of the gunboats penetrated the fort's magazine. In the shattering explosion resulting not only was the fort wrecked, but every soul in it except three miserable, stunned survivors, was killed.

Though the Seminoles were not involved in this affair, they made their presence felt elsewhere. It was their practice to raid northward into Georgia, loot, burn, and slay, then retreat back into Florida to the security of Spanish territory.

Unfortunately for them, when Andrew Jackson was ordered South to chastise them with his Tennessee riflemen, he treated the "border" for what it was to the frontier—a fiction.

To John C. Calhoun, then Secretary of War, he wrote:

> The Spanish Government is bound by treaty to keep the Indians at peace with us. They have acknowledged their incompetency to do this, and are consequently bound, by the laws of nations, to yield us the facilities to reduce them. Under this consideration, should I be able, I shall take possession of the garrison [of St. Marks] as a depot for my supplies, should it be found in the hands of the Spanish, they having supplied the Indians; but if in the hands of the Indians, I will possess it, for the benefit of the United States, as a necessary position for me to hold, to give peace and security to the frontier.

This notice that Jackson not only intended to capture a Spanish fort or forts, and if he felt the evidence justified, hold the captured posts and territory, was alarming to the timid souls among the politicians.

But communications being what they were it was too late to head
him off.

Already Jackson had become a symbol in men's minds of the kind
of nation they preferred—brilliant, aggressive, willing to fight if need
be, able to conquer if it fought, and viewing as its destiny the entire
continent. If he made a further great success he might become a serious danger to the reigning political powers. One Westerner in particular thought that Jackson might be a serious threat to him personally. Henry Clay of Kentucky, who had from the beginning been an
expansionist, found himself suddenly opposed to expansion—if Andrew
Jackson brought it about.

Jackson did bring it about. In a lightning campaign he scattered the
Seminoles, forced the surrender of the Spanish fort of St. Marks, destroyed the village of Boleck (called Bowlegs) the principal Seminole
chief, won three brief battles, executed two British subjects whom he
captured, and created a multiplicity of international incidents.

The captured Britons, a Scottish trader named Alexander Arbuthnot, and Lieutenant Robert C. Ambrister, formerly of the British Royal
Colonial Marines, were charged with inciting the Indians to attack the
American frontier. Tried before a court-martial at Fort St. Marks, they
were found guilty. Arbuthnot was hanged, Ambrister shot by a firing
squad.

Thereafter Jackson marched westward and as speedily captured
Pensacola and its forts—for the second time, since he had already, dur-
ing the War of 1812, done so to prevent the use of the facilities by the
British in their advance on New Orleans.

A truly magnificent furore ensued. Both Britain and Spain made
the strongest representations to the United States government. The
British, on consideration, realizing that their nationals probably were
quite guilty of the actions for which they were executed, and being
busy with the postwar settlement of Europe which followed the final
defeat of Napoleon, withdrew their protests.

The Spanish, however, demanded that General Jackson be disavowed and punished. But Old Hickory had a great and unexpected
supporter—at the moment—in the Cabinet. John Quincy Adams, Secretary of State, had the courage to face the other members, including
Calhoun and even President Monroe, in taking a strong line opposing
the Spanish demands. He cited the British activities in Florida both
during and after the War of 1812, and remarked bitterly that despite
those activities not "a whisper of expostulation was ever wafted from
Madrid to London."

In point of fact Jackson had confronted the world with a *fait accompli*. Taking advantage of it, Adams proceeded to negotiate a
treaty of far-reaching consequences with Spain.

In this he was supported by the manifest temper of the people. That temper was discovered by Henry Clay when he, alarmed that the fame of Jackson threatened his own great political power in the West, led an effort to censure him in Congress. Thirty days of debate was climaxed by a speech accounted one of Clay's greatest orations.

"Recall to your recollections the free nations which have gone before us!" he trumpeted. "Where are they now and how have they lost their liberties? If we could transport ourselves back to the ages when Greece and Rome flourished . . . and ask a Grecian if he did not fear some daring military chieftain, covered with glory, some Philip or Alexander, would one day overthrow his liberties? No! No! . . . [he] would exclaim, we have nothing to fear from our heroes . . . Yet Greece had fallen, Caesar passed the Rubicon . . ."

It was vain. Congress voted down the resolutions of censure. As the historian George Dangerfield has observed:

> As for Mr. Clay, his speech had been one of his greatest efforts, but its most striking result had been the enhancement of Jackson's reputation; and the Speaker was soon to learn that, in politics as in legend, it is easier to unbottle the djinn than to seal him up again.

Clay had only succeeded in erecting against himself a lifelong enemy who would remorselessly check and finally destroy his greatest ambitions.

Meantime Adams, negotiating with Don Luis de Oñis y Gonzalez, the Spanish minister, obtained the cession of all Florida—which Spain obviously was too weak to govern, let alone defend, assuming five million dollars' worth of claims against that nation. At the same time, in agreement with Oñis, he set a definite Southern boundary to the Louisiana Purchase, with the Arkansas, Rio Grande, and Sabine rivers as delineators, thus yielding Texas to Spain. This was not in agreement with Jefferson's understanding, and the French government's instructions to the intended captain-general of the province in 1802 indicated that the province, in the eyes of Napoleon who obtained it from Spain, extended to the Rio Grande.

Andrew Jackson never agreed with the border as laid out, and hotly denounced it. He always thought that Adams too easily accepted the line of the Red River and Sabine in order to facilitate his negotiations for Florida, and the dispute would be fruitful of trouble later.

But at least Florida was now United States territory, open for settlement, and the man who, rightly or wrongly, accomplished this was Andrew Jackson.

CHAPTER FIVE

"Bargain and Corruption"

1

THANKS to the jealous animosity of Henry Clay, General Jackson, already the military hero of the country, had been projected upon the national political scene as well. He had arrived in Washington during the debate over Clay's resolution to censure him, and there "the hypnotic sway of his will" made its first great impression on the nation's capital.

After the resolutions were defeated, Jackson was received with ovations in Philadelphia, New York, and Baltimore. He attended a levee at the President's Mansion, which was fresh in its first coat of white paint, and soon to become familiarly known as the White House. There "the company pressed about him" so that to the rather sour viewpoint of John Quincy Adams, it was "General Jackson rather than President Monroe who was giving the reception."

But he was ill again, from a combination of the dysentery and his chest abscess, and returned to Nashville, where he built for Rachel a new house at The Hermitage, on a site selected by her, and had the first of a long series of portraits painted by Ralph W. Earl, who was to remain a member of his household for seventeen years.

He sought rest, but he could not rest because of his financial troubles, caused by a panic due in part to the demand by the Bank of the United States that currency of private banks be redeemed in specie. Many "wildcat" banks went to the wall, Tennessee was prostrate, and Jackson had a personal experience of the power of the Bank of the United States over the lives of the people, which he did not forget.

While he still struggled with these problems he learned that Spain had been dilatory in ratifying the Adams-Oñis treaty, and he offered "with the smiles of heaven [to] endeavour to place once more the american Eagle upon the ramparts" of various Florida forts, "and then beg leave to retire if I survive."

But before any such action was necessary, the Spanish minister hastened to deliver the ratified treaty. President Monroe at once offered the governorship of the new territory to Jackson, possibly hoping by this means to shelve that too volatile personality. After at first refusing, Jackson changed his mind at the pleas of friends, and accepted.

His tenure of the post of governor of Florida was short and stormy. It included a clash with Don José Callavala, Spanish governor of West Florida, who refused to make the formal transfer of the territory. Callavala speedily found himself in jail, the documents were seized by Jackson, the United States flag unfurled on the official staff in Pensacola, and Callavala was released—to hurry to Washington with profuse complaints of his treatment, in which he received scant sympathy from the Secretary of State.

The flag raising occurred July 17, 1821. On October 5, the same year, Jackson notified the President that "having organised the Government . . . and it being in full operation," he was resigning to return to his home.

But there was no peace for him even at The Hermitage. "He is not a well man and never will be unless they allow him to rest," wrote Rachel to her niece Mary Donelson. "He has done his share for the country . . . In the thirty years of our wedded life . . . he has not spent one-fourth of his days under his own roof."

The country was not willing to allow him the rest for which Rachel prayed. There was talk that Jackson might be brought forward for the Presidency itself; in fact men already were working secretly on this project.

But Old Hickory's first intimation of this design seems to have caught him by surprise. He was felt out on the subject by a friend, George Washington Campbell.

"I really hope you don't think, George, that I'm damned fool enough to believe that!" exclaimed Old Hickory. Then, "No, sir; I may be pretty well satisfied with myself in some things, but I'm not vain enough for that."

Yet his friends went on with their work. It required a deal of doing. National tickets had always been selected by Congressional caucuses of the different parties. There was in 1824 only one real party and it was conceded that William H. Crawford would obtain the Jeffersonian Republican endorsement.

So the Tennessee legislature was offered a resolution "that the name of major-general Andrew Jackson be submitted to the consideration of the people of the United States." It was carried unanimously.

Old Hickory learned of this action with little display of interest. "I have never been an applicant for office," he wrote. "I never will . . . I have no desire, nor do I expect ever to be called to fill the Presidential chair, but should this be the case . . . it shall be without exertion on my part."

But if Jackson proposed not to exert himself, the same was not true of various others who had their eyes on the White House which would be vacated at the conclusion of President Monroe's second term.

Each section of the country had its candidate or candidates, representing different interests and all possessing great political potency. In the West—Jackson's own area—Henry Clay was an avowed candidate, and exercising all his great political powers and personal charm to attain the place he had always sought.

In one respect Clay saw eye to eye with Jackson, although they did not exchange views on the subject. Both were expansionists, both dreamed of a continental nation, far exceeding the populated areas of the time, in Clay's own words, "reaching northwestwardly to the Pacific, and more southwardly to the River Del Norte [Rio Grande]." This vision, which contemplated the Oregon Territory, did not, however, equal Jackson's greater vision, which included also California and all the regions intermediate.

The Cock of Kentucky, as he was sometimes called, had spent the years of Monroe's administration doing everything in his great power as Speaker of the House to thwart and handicap the President's program, and especially the actions of John Quincy Adams, Secretary of State. This was in large part because of his resentment over Monroe's appointment of Adams to the State Department, when he believed he should have received the honor.

Clay had been first to get himself nominated for the election of 1824, and knowing that the tariff was opposed in the South and West, while it was upheld in the North, he had attempted to gain adherents in both sections by what he called the "American System" in a speech delivered March 30 and 31, 1824. He proposed to eliminate "dependence on foreign markets" by a tariff which would "check the decline of American industry," with the result that as manufactures flourished there would be created a greater market "for the surplus of agricultural products." He expected to win the election and be the next President.

A second, and very formidable candidate, was William H. Crawford, the Secretary of the Treasury. Crawford, born in Virginia, was a plantation owner and resident of Georgia. He represented Southern thought, and particularly the thought of the more conservative elements. At the beginning of the campaign he was regarded by many as the most probable winner of the coming election, for he controlled the machinery of the "regular" Republican (Democratic) organization, which he used inexorably.

Third in the list was John Quincy Adams, the Secretary of State. Adams, a Massachusetts man, had almost the united support of New England. He was a son of John Adams, the second President, and at the outset of his career had been a Federalist like his father. But in his maturity he renounced the party of Alexander Hamilton, became a Jeffersonian Republican, and continued to uphold that political persuasion. A typical New Englander, puritanical and cold of manner, he was the most erudite of the candidates, a graduate of Harvard, a lawyer, widely traveled with much diplomatic experience, and possessing numerous intellectual interests.

Yet another Presidential hopeful was John Caldwell Calhoun, the Secretary of War. He was from South Carolina, Southern in viewpoint like Crawford, but representing the newer viewpoints of his section. He had been, for instance, one of the "War Hawks," like Clay, which plunged the United States into the War of 1812 with Great Britain. A man of great logical powers, he was yet able to argue himself out of first one stand, then another. At this period he was an ardent expansionist, supported the tariff, and was a strong nationalist. But he was an energetic and constant political manipulator, and his various changes of conviction and action form one of the interesting studies in American political history.

Against all this display of influence, activity and energy, Jackson sat almost silent. He declined a proffered appointment as Minister to Mexico, and the nearest he came to forwarding his own candidacy was an elaboration of his first statement:

> My undeviating rule of conduct through life . . . has been neither to seek or decline public invitations to office . . . As the office of Chief Magistrate of the Union . . . should not be sought . . . so it cannot, with propriety, be declined . . . My political creed prompts me to leave the affair uninfluenced by any expression on my part . . . to the free will of those who alone have the right to decide.

2

Yet by 1823 the politically sagacious could see that the silent candidate was showing astonishing strength. The luster of his name drew supporters like a magnet.

Senator John Williams of Tennessee was coming up for re-election, and Williams was a Jackson foe, who had lost few opportunities while in Washington to make statements of detraction about the general. One of his assertions was that Jackson was weak in his home state. Because no one else could beat the incumbent who had what he believed were all the votes he needed in the legislature where, in that day, the Senators were elected, Old Hickory reluctantly allowed his name to be presented for the office. He won an astonishing victory, retiring Williams to private life and a consideration of the fruits of opposition to the man who was now being referred to over the country as the Old Hero. Jackson at the time was fifty-six years old, and looked older because of his chronic illnesses and the fact that his stiff brush of hair, once red, had turned nearly snow-white.

When he went to Washington in December of 1823, he found that his seat in the Senate chamber was next to that of Thomas Hart Benton, whom he had not seen since the near-fatal day when the tavern brawl took place in Nashville. Benton, now a Senator from Missouri, was a redoubtable personage, and when he and Jackson confronted each other there were those who expected an explosion. Instead the two exchanged courtesies, cordially shook hands, and resumed a friendship, broken by their long feud, which had important bearings on the future.

In Washington the general lived at an inn operated by Major William O'Neale, where his friends, Senator Eaton and Representative Houston, also stayed. There he met another who was to play a part in his future. Major O'Neale's eldest daughter, Margaret, was a girl of more than ordinary beauty, and less than ordinary discretion. She was hardly more than twenty, though she had been married four years, her husband, Lieutenant John B. Timberlake of the U. S. Navy, being absent much of the time on cruises. Whispers concerning her circulated giddily.

Most frequently coupled with hers was the name of Senator John Henry Eaton of Tennessee, a friend of Jackson and a widower who had befriended her and her family. One Congressman wrote, "Mrs. Timberlake was considered a lady who would . . . dispense her favors wherever she took a fancy . . . Eaton's connection with . . . [her] was notorious."

But the girl, bright and amusing, pleased Old Hickory. He refused to believe anything against her; and was in consequence to suffer some serious inconveniences, not to say embarrassments, in defending her name.

Meantime the election drew inevitably closer. Complications were occurring. One of the most important was that Crawford was felled by a stroke of paralysis and lay confined in his bed.[1]

Calhoun, discovering that he had no chance in the Presidential race, took the more modest course of running for the Vice-Presidency, leaving only Jackson, Adams, Clay, and Crawford in the lists. The campaign thundered toward its close, with Old Hickory unruffled by every

---

[1] The cause of the stroke is believed to have been an overdose of lobelia, administered by a country doctor during an attack of erysipelas suffered by Crawford.

criticism that could be hurled at him. He had no formal political organization as had his rivals, but his name was sufficient to bring cheers at every militia muster, barbecue, and mass meeting. "Rowdies . . . the very dregs of society," one anti-Jackson newspaper called his supporters. They were the common people, at last bestirring themselves.

In that period there was no single Election Day. The twenty-four states could choose their own dates, between October 27 and December 1. As a result, and because of the slowness of communications, the final results were not known until the middle of December. Jackson who had gone to Tennessee to vote, returning with Rachel, learned the tidings in Washington. In the Electoral College the amateur politicians supporting Jackson had won for him ninety-nine votes—an amazing plurality considering the nature of the campaign he had waged, or rather refused to wage. Adams was second with eighty-four. Crawford, with forty-one, was in third place. And Clay was fourth and last with thirty-seven.

There was no majority, so for the second time in history, Congress, by constitutional stipulation, must choose the President.

3

Washington, the awkward and unlovely fledgling capital of the young United States, had been called "a city of magnificent distances" by a derisive foreign visitor. On the evening of February 8, 1825, it seemed to deserve all of that appellation save the adjective "magnificent." The word "dreary" might well have been substituted instead.

Here and there a few collections of buildings huddled—about the Navy Yard, the Arsenal, and the Capitol itself, which still was under reconstruction after the British arson of 1814. About halfway between the Capitol and the old town of Georgetown stood the White House. A lengthy stretch of unpaved mire known as Pennsylvania Avenue, which connected these two edifices, and both of them with Georgetown, was lined for much of its length with unpretentious inns, boardinghouses, shops, and tenements.

Elsewhere a few muddy wheel tracks crossed in erratic fashion the snow-covered and vacant fields on which thin cattle shivered, little resembling the straight, geometrical patterns laid out by L'Enfant for the street plan of the Federal City.

The week had started with cold and dismal rains, followed by a light snow, which in the roads turned to ugly slush and mud through which any who ventured forth must struggle. Cheerless and uncomfortable, the evening of February 8 was one on which it might be supposed that sensible men would remain under shelter, close to warm firesides.

Yet on this night a more than usual traffic of horsemen and equipages plied back and forth and an air of intense excitement pervaded the capital. On the morrow Congress was to choose a President of the United States.

This accounted for the travelers hurrying between various headquarters, seeking information, running errands, exerting pressures for favored candidates, or asking favors. The names of three men were on the tongues of everyone.

The three were John Quincy Adams, the cultured New Englander and a proved statesman, yet with few personal friends; Andrew Jackson, whose chief distinction at this time was a brilliant military record, with little experience or taste for politics, yet a man who made and kept steadfast friends even faster than he made steadfast enemies; and Henry Clay, the Speaker of the House of Representatives, the only real politician of the trio, and indeed the wiliest and smoothest of his era.

Since none but the top three in the Electoral College could be considered by Congress, only Adams and Jackson really were qualified for election, because it was now definite that William H. Crawford, who stood third in the number of electors chosen, would be unable to serve. Yet though Clay was thus eliminated, it was he who hoped to wield the decisive power in the election on the morrow.

At this time Henry Clay was at the height of his powers. As described by a contemporary he was "tall and thin, with a rather small head, and gray eyes, which peered forth less luminously than would have been expected in one possessing such eminent control of language. His nose was straight, his upper lip long, and his underjaw slight. His mouth, of generous width, straight when he was silent, and curving upward at the corners when he spoke or smiled, was singularly graceful, indicating more than any other feature the elastic play of his mind. When he enchained large audiences, his features were lighted up by a winning smile, the gestures of his long arms were graceful, and the gentle accents of his mellow voice were persuasive and winning. Yet there has never been a more imperious despot in political affairs than Mr. Clay. He regarded himself as the head-centre of his party—L'état, c'est moi—and he wanted everything used for his advancement."[2]

Born April 12, 1777, in Virginia, he was educated as well as the times permitted, studied for law, and entered the Kentucky bar at the age of twenty-one. From the law he turned swiftly to politics.

[2] Ben: Perley Poore, *Perley's Reminiscences*.

From the beginning he had a passion for oratory, because he considered it the surest way to gain command and power over men's minds, and he improved on his native ability until at this period he was considered America's foremost orator—a distinction in which he would later be supplanted by Daniel Webster.

Clay married into one of the wealthiest families in Lexington, Kentucky, and in addition to his undoubted gifts as a trial lawyer, inherited a large legal business from this association, which made him a rich man for the times, able to live in luxury.

Early in life he preached gradual emancipation of the slaves; yet in a few years he was buying and selling Negroes and upholding the Fugitive Slave law. A self-proclaimed defender of the poor and down-trodden, he at the same time served the money interests, defending the right of factory owners to employ women and children at mere pittances, with the sophistry that "Constant occupation is the best security for innocence and virtue, and idleness is the parent of vice and crime."

As a campaign issue he opposed the charter for the Bank of the United States in 1811, yet later became an attorney for that institution and made its recharter the chief issue of his second campaign for the Presidency. He fought against a strong army and navy, then became one of the leading "War Hawks," helping to drive the United States into the War of 1812, for which it was ill-prepared.

Appointed to the peace commission which wrought the inconclusive Treaty of Ghent ending that war, he quarreled constantly and violenty with John Quincy Adams, who was the real, though not the titular, head of the commission. As one historian has noted, "Neither Clay nor Adams was a man who took pleasure in silence if it was possible to speak . . . these two articulate persons discharged their batteries upon each other. There were scenes of towering rage . . ."[3] Yet, to their credit, they swallowed for a time their differences when they met the British commissioners, and "trembling with rage— their best arguments unanswered and their worst epithets still undischarged"—they managed to present a united front so that in the end the treaty at least did not contain the humiliating concessions demanded by Britain.

As a Member of the House of Representatives, Clay quickly rose to the top and became Speaker, consolidating his powers as no previous holder of that office had ever done, until he became a virtual dictator. Now this man, so winning, so warm when he wished to be; shallow yet dextrously giving an impression of depth; this man proposed to decide in the balloting next day who should be President.

[3] George Dangerfield, *The Era of Good Feelings.*

4

Clay disliked both Jackson and Adams; the first because, a Westerner, Jackson had ventured into the political field and thus deprived Clay of votes that he believed might have elected him; the second because of old enmities, and because Adams had been chosen over himself as Secretary of State by President James Monroe.

Andrew Jackson at this time was almost of two minds as to whether or not he wished to be President. He was almost fifty-eight, and in poor health. Furthermore, his wife dreaded the thought of the limelight that so public a life would focus upon her.

A more oddly assorted couple than General and Mrs. Jackson would be hard to find. He was tall and thin; she short, over-heavy, dowdy, and given to the frontier custom of smoking a corncob pipe. Eastern snobs looked down upon her, and she knew it. A pro-Adams newspaper had made open reference to this feeling:

How can the voters justify themselves and posterity to place such a woman as Mrs. Jackson at the head of the female society of the United States?

This was only the beginning of a campaign of detraction which would drive her to her grave. The irregularity in their marriage—through no fault of their own—would feed the malice of her husband's enemies in the years ahead.

On Jackson's side there was protective affection for her; on Rachel's absolute adoration of him. Her feelings had much to do with his attitude toward the voting on the morrow.

Quite different was the feeling of John Quincy Adams. With all sincerity he believed that he was not only better qualified for the Presidency, but more deserving than Jackson. He was in his fifty-eighth year, a few months younger than the general, and he had performed great services for his country.

A son of the second President, John Adams, he was reared in an atmosphere of culture and trained for public life. He had been a Senator and Minister to both the Netherlands and Russia, perhaps influencing the intervention of Czar Alexander I which led to the treaty conference at Ghent. It was Adams who was the real spearhead of the American commission that negotiated the Treaty of Ghent; which ended the war, if not with gains for his country, at least without losses.

As Secretary of State it was he who negotiated the purchase of

Florida from Spain—after Jackson demonstrated Spain's inability to police much less hold that province—and set the Spanish-United States boundaries of the Louisiana Purchase. He was, moreover, the chief author—this was no secret—of the Monroe Doctrine, which was the greatest claim to fame of President James Monroe.

Yet Adams had not the gift of making and keeping friends. A portly man, of no great physical stature, he had a huge bald head, a mouth wide and grim which indicated determination or perhaps stubbornness, and cold gray-blue eyes under heavy gray brows. He laughed almost never, his manner was aloof and chill, and he was often brusque as if almost contemptuous, in his discourses with other men.

He resented Henry Clay and had described the Kentuckian as "a gamester in politics as well as cards."

Yet though it was true that Clay "liked the ladies, gambling and wine perhaps too much," he was a man of enormous capabilities, and on this evening of February 8, in spite of their mutual dislike for each other, he was preparing to throw all of his potent influence into the scales in behalf of John Quincy Adams.

5

To Henry Clay it was a case of the lesser of two evils—to himself. While Adams disliked him, Jackson had been his open enemy ever since Clay attempted to get Congress to condemn the general's actions in the Florida campaign against the Seminoles. Jackson was never notable for forgetting unfriendly acts.

But beyond this, Clay had a deeper interest in the coming vote. To him the succession to the Presidency seemed to lie through the office of Secretary of State. Had not Thomas Jefferson held that post under Washington, James Madison under Jefferson, and James Monroe under Madison? Now John Quincy Adams, Secretary of State under Monroe, seemed to Clay the best bet for President in this election.

Whoever was elected, Clay desired to be Secretary of State. Jackson had been felt out in this matter. When, early in January, a smooth young intermediary named James Buchanan—who would one day himself be President—suggested that Clay might help Jackson if Jackson would agree to the arrangement, the general snorted, "Before I would reach the Presidential chair by such means . . . I would see the earth open up and swallow both Mr. Clay and his friends, and myself with them!"

The rebuff was abrupt. But on January 9, a Sunday, Mr. Clay and Mr. Adams dined together and conferred until late in the evening. That they discussed matters of "great public importance," Adams confided to his diary. He was inexplicit as to what those matters were, but wrote that Clay remarked that certain friends of Adams had urged "considerations personal to himself [Clay]." As a revealing little item, Adams added that Mr. Clay had "no hesitation in saying that his preference would be for me."

That evening Adams and Clay reached an "understanding," if not a "bargain." The first word was later used by Adams apologists, the second by his foes. "Understanding" has as one definition, "a mutual agreement, not formally entered into, but having definite engagements." "Bargain" in its harshest sense signifies a formal contract. Actually, with a man like Adams, an understanding was sufficient. He would not go back on his spoken word. In return for Henry Clay's support, John Quincy Adams, if elected, would name the Kentuckian Secretary of State.

Shortly afterward Clay formally announced that he would support Adams, and at the same time Daniel Webster, fresh from a visit with Thomas Jefferson, was circulating a statement of the Sage of Monticello, as to Jackson: "He is one of the most unfit men I know of for such a place."[4]

Yet in spite of these portents, Jackson's supporters continued to believe their candidate would be elected. Had he not received the plurality of the popular vote? It was, said the Jacksonians, a mandate from the people.

6

The morning of February 9 dawned clear and cold. Long before Congress convened, crowds of people splashed through the mud to the Capitol on horseback, in carriages, even on foot, to gain better seats for the coming spectacle.

The House of Representatives in that day numbered among its members some men destined to loom gigantic in the history of the nation. Besides Clay there were such personages as Daniel Webster, John Randolph of Roanoke, Martin Van Buren, Edward Everett, George McDuffie, Sam Houston, and others of equal caliber. The voting would be by states; in other words populous states, such as New

---

[4] Jackson who was to be the great perpetuator of Jefferson's teachings, never liked the man himself, nor did Jefferson feel any more cordial toward the Tennesseean. They met only twice in person, and both those occasions were formal ones, so they could hardly have discussed theories of government with each other. Jackson considered Jefferson weak, while Jefferson when asked by Monroe if it would be a good idea to appoint Jackson to the Russian mission, exclaimed, "Why, good God! He would breed you a quarrel before he had been there a month!"

York and Pennsylvania, with large delegations in Congress, could cast only one vote each, putting them on a par with scantily populated states like Missouri and Illinois, each of which had only one Representative. Since there were twenty-four states, thirteen were required for a majority.

In the general election Jackson had carried eleven states, and his supporters hoped the states carried by Crawford might, since their man could not serve, swing over to the Jackson column. They also hoped he might obtain the votes of Missouri and perhaps even Kentucky, the legislature of which had memorialized its Congressional delegation to vote for Jackson.

They did not, however, reckon on Henry Clay and his power as Speaker of the House. Though his manner was charming, gracious, even gay as usual, Clay knew his dangerous position. He knew that Adams had nine firm states, Daniel Webster lately had won over Federalist Maryland to the same cause, and Louisiana was safe—for the moment. That made eleven. Clay must have both the borderline states—Missouri and New York—to gain his vital majority for Adams.

Above everything he wished to avoid a deadlock, feeling that if one occurred the trend would overwhelmingly swing over to Jackson. All that morning he had used every bit of his tact, charm, promises of preferment, even hints of reprisal, trying to whip members into line. Just before noon Missouri's one Representative, John Scott, in the face of a blistering denunciation by Thomas Hart Benton, announced he would vote for Adams.

New York was now the crucial state—and New York was split exactly down the middle, seventeen votes for Adams, and seventeen in the hands of Van Buren, to vote for Crawford. Should New York fail to reach a decision on the first ballot the deadlock which Clay dreaded would occur.

As the hands of the clock in the hall approached two o'clock, Clay took his place on the Speaker's dais. The Members went to their seats. The galleries were jammed to capacity. At the stroke of two the Senators, forty-seven in number, filed in. Senator Jackson, the forty-eighth, was absent, since he felt it would be improper for him to appear, because he was a candidate.

The Speaker announced that the Electoral College having been counted, John C. Calhoun of South Carolina was elected Vice-President. There was, however, no majority for President and it therefore became the duty of the House to select the Chief Magistrate from among the three highest candidates in point of Electoral College ballots, the votes to be by states.

John Randolph of Roanoke, a Jackson man, and Daniel Webster, an Adams man, were appointed tellers. Each state upon deciding its candidate, should write that name on two pieces of paper, one of which would be dropped in a box before Randolph, the other in a box before Webster.

Intense excitement gripped the assemblage as one after another the heads of the state delegations advanced to the front and dropped their ballots in the boxes. At last only New York had not cast its ballot.

In this furiously disputing delegation sat an old man with white hair and a worn face. He was General Stephen Van Rensselaer, an honorable man, with a record of war service for his country, but torn by indecision. As both sides stormed at him, he at last dropped his head on his desk as if in prayer. On the floor he saw a piece of paper— a discarded Adams ballot. Taking it as a sign the old man dropped it into the box as his vote. It broke the tie in favor of Adams.

A few minutes later when Webster and Randolph both announced that thirteen states were for Adams, seven for Jackson, and four (complimentary) for Crawford, a roar of triumph from the Adams supporters almost shook the domed ceiling. The galleries had to be cleared before Clay could announce that John Quincy Adams was duly elected the President of the United States.

The mighty business was finished. The House adjourned. "It was impossible to win the game, gentlemen," said John Randolph of Roanoke bitterly. "The cards were stacked."

Randolph's rancor toward Clay never ceased. Later he was to excoriate the Kentuckian as follows: "So brilliant, yet so corrupt, which, like a rotten mackerel by moonlight, shines and stinks."

7

Of all the persons most interested Andrew Jackson seemed the least perturbed. In fact he appeared almost relieved. He said, according to Hezekiah Niles, editor of *Niles Register*, that "he had no doubt but that a great proportion of the citizens would be satisfied by the choice . . . he observed that many . . . were unpleasantly situated, seeing they were compelled to act either against Mr. Adams or himself . . . And he further remarked that it was a matter of small moment to the people who was their President, provided he administered the government rightfully."

Graciously he refused a proposal that he be given a testimonial dinner because "it might be viewed as conveying . . . a feeling of complaint which I sincerely hope belongs not to any of my friends." Later, as a gesture of gratitude, he did give a champagne supper to twenty-two of those friends who had stood by him.

One man, however, had an uneasy conscience, and that man was

John Quincy Adams. He showed it the evening after the election when he attended a reception at the White House. Jackson who also attended the reception met Adams in the East Room. As related by a witness:

> General Jackson, who was escorting a lady, promptly extended his hand, saying pleasantly: "How do you do, Mr. Adams? I give you my left hand, for the right, as you see, is devoted to the fair. I hope you are very well, sir." All this was gallantly and heartily said and done. Mr. Adams took the General's hand and said, with chilling coldness: "Very well, sir; I hope General Jackson is well." The military hero was genial and gracious, while the unamiable diplomat was cold as an iceberg.

Very shortly afterward, Jackson learned that the reports of Henry Clay's appointment as Secretary of State were true. Then, for the first time, the old warrior's rage flamed high. To Major William B. Lewis, a neighbor and friend near Nashville, he wrote a furious letter:

> So you see the *Judas* of the West has closed the contract and will receive the thirty pieces of silver. his end will be the same. Was there ever witnessed such bare faced corruption?

Bargain and corruption! Fighting words. Those words became a slogan, a rallying cry.

Actually, no corruption was involved, in the sense that money or other valuable property changed hands. But to Jackson, and to thousands of others, the bartering of support in exchange for an office of such high importance, was corruption in a deeper sense.

The rigging of the Congressional vote by Clay had a vital influence on history. Because of it Andrew Jackson became what he had not been before—an active, driving, furious candidate for the Presidency at the next election.

In retrospect it is perhaps fortunate for Jackson and even for the nation that he did not win his first campaign. He was not at that time ready for the Presidency. Having been in the truest sense "drafted," he had made little preparation for statesmanship. His ideas for governing the nation were few. He accepted the nomination and would have served if elected, like the soldier he was, expecting only to do his duty as best he could and try to govern justly and with such wisdom as was given him.

But now he had four years for contemplation, for forming a political philosophy, and for rallying many disparate groups to his standard of democracy. If the chance came to him again he would be ready for it.

CHAPTER SIX

The Bitter Taste of Victory

1

THERE can be no question as to the patriotism or dedication of John Quincy Adams. As a Senator, a diplomatic envoy in the courts of Europe, a leading member of the commission which fought so doggedly in negotiating the Treaty of Ghent, and as Secretary of State he had more than proved himself.

Nevertheless, as a President, he lacked certain qualities which make for a successful political administrator. He had no gift for winning people, which is essential in one who would lead. Of himself he wrote, quite frankly, "I am a man of reserved, cold, austere, and forbidding manners; my political adversaries say, a gloomy misanthropist, and my personal enemies, an unsocial savage." To this self-appraisal an Englishman, W. H. Littleton, who encountered him in 1812 when he was United States Minister to Russia, added this bitter sketch of him:

> Of all the men whom it was ever my lot to accost and waste civilities upon, [he] was the most doggedly and systematically repulsive. With a vinegar aspect, cotton in his leathern ears, and hatred for England in his heart, he sat in the frivolous assemblies of [St.] Petersburg like a bulldog among spaniels; and many were the times that I drew monosyllables and grim smiles from him and tried in vain to mitigate his venom.

Granted that Littleton was prejudiced, not only against Adams but against any American, he nevertheless touched upon some salient traits of the man he described. Adams was a puritan in the least pleasant sense, and among the qualities of that type of puritan is self-righteousness. In spite of his integrity and intellectual powers, he had no friends of the intimate variety, and repelled rather than inspired those with whom he worked.

In naming Henry Clay Secretary of State—whether by "bargain" or no—he attached to his administration a man almost his antithesis in character and personality. Clay was eloquent and polished. He had a personality so pleasing that it was said of him "he could charm the devil out of hell." Where Adams was abstemious, Clay was fond—almost too fond—of the pleasures.

"His great fault," commented Albert Gallatin, "is that he is devoured with ambition." That supreme ambition was the Presidency. Though he could be beautifully courteous to anyone who might help him, he at times gave way to terrible rages, and his quarrels with Adams during the long ordeal at Ghent were notorious. As Speaker of the House he had done all he could to hamper the policies of President Monroe and Secretary Adams; but once he became Secretary of State, he gave complete support to that same Adams, who now was President. All this was in furtherance of his ambitions, yet the years would show that in his way he was devotedly loyal to the United States. "America loved him," as one historian put it, "but never quite trusted him."

Against these two now in power, was to be arrayed politically a man whom the common people were to trust more fully perhaps than they have trusted any other in the history of the nation—Andrew Jackson.

When Clay dragooned Congress into giving the Presidency to Adams, Old Hickory had been an inactive, almost unwilling candidate, yet he came within an ace of winning the nation's highest office. Now he was fiercely determined to beat both Adams and Clay. The "corrupt bargain" cry fired his battle spirit, while at the same time it convinced him that the voters of America had been cheated of their rightful wishes.

In this, had he known it, Adams with his puritan conscience secretly agreed with him. His diary contained the sentiment that his election to the Presidency had not taken place in "a manner satisfactory to pride or just desire; with perhaps two-thirds of the whole people adverse to the actual result." This sentiment, however, did not prevent him from accepting the office and doing his best with it.

That best was hardly good enough. Between them, Adams and Clay made blunder after blunder. The President's first Message to Congress provided examples both of Adams' idealism and his political inexpertness. He recommended a national university, government financing of scientific explorations, establishment of a uniform standard of weights and measures, building of an astronomical observatory, creation of a Department of the Interior, reform of the patent laws, and internal improvements on a huge scale.

Today that program sounds sensible; indeed, a great portion of it has been accomplished in the intervening years. Yet the method of its presentation in 1825, scolding Congress, as it were, for "refraining from exercising its powers for the benefit of the people," as constituting "treachery to the most sacred of trusts," angered many members of that body. The bold embarkation on schemes and plans not yet even discussed with the legislative branch, and a most unfavorable comparison of the United States with "foreign nations . . . advancing with gigantic strides," brought upon his undoubtedly surprised head a storm of heated abuse.

Jefferson's postulate that the best government was the one that governed least was still concurred in by many important men, and the unfavorable comparison with monarchical powers of Europe produced cries of "Tyranny," and the accusation that "All Adamses are monarchists."

Jefferson himself saw the Message as "a new chapter" in Federalist doctrine, in which interpretation he was mistaken. Adams had, at one time, it is true, been a Federalist, but he long had been a Republican, though with a typical scientific viewpoint toward governmental policies.

Clay, the thorough politician, disagreed with the planned economics of the Message, as did most of the other members of the Cabinet. But Adams, with his usual bullheaded stubbornness, presented it. He was far ahead of his times and the fact did much to destroy him.

As a climax, the annual report of Richard Rush, the Secretary of the Treasury, contained a forceful and outright recommendation for a strong protective tariff to create "a flourishing state of manufactures."

Against this, which was now considered an Administration tenet, both the South and the West strenuously protested. The tariff, spokesmen of those sections held, was no more than a scheme to strengthen the industrial North at the expense of the agricultural South and West.

It remained for the most eccentric as well as one of the most brilliant of the Southern spokesmen to provide the words that linked Adams and Clay in a manner so devastating that it was never forgotten by the American people.

Randolph, called "the Lord of Roanoke," was assuredly one of the most aberrant figures ever to hold a seat in Congress. As described by a contemporary:

He was at least six feet in height, with long limbs, an ill-proportioned body, and a small, round head. Claiming descent from Pocahontas, he wore his coarse, black hair long, parted in the middle and combed down on either side of his sallow face. His small, black eyes were expressive in their rapid glances, especially when he was engaged in debate, and his high-toned and thin voice would ring through the Senate Chamber like the shrill scream of an angry vixen. He generally wore a full suit of heavy, drab-colored English broadcloth, the high, rolling collar of his surtout coat almost concealing his head, while the skirts hung in voluminous folds about his knee-breeches and the white leather tops of his boots. He used to enter the Senate Chamber wearing a pair of silver spurs, carrying a heavy riding whip, and followed by a favorite hound, which crouched beneath his desk . . . Every ten or fifteen minutes, while he occupied the floor, he would exclaim in a low tone, "Tims, more porter!" and the assistant door keeper would hand him a foaming tumbler of potent malt liquor, which he would hurriedly drink, and then proceed with his remarks, often thus drinking three or four quarts in an afternoon.[1]

His shrill voice and strange, almost beardless countenance, covered with fine lines, were perhaps due to an illness in boyhood which prevented him from ever having normal sexual intercourse with a woman. But an unwise remark on his virility uttered by an opponent brought a scathing retort from Randolph: "Sir, you pride yourself upon an animal faculty, in respect to which the Negro is your equal and the jackass infinitely your superior."

His enemies, driven almost beside themselves by his withering invective, used to say that he was mad, or at least half-mad. Perhaps this was not so at this time, but he certainly died in 1833 suffering from what probably would now be described as *dementia praecox*.

In 1825, as a member of the Senate, he was at the height of his powers as a fierce, almost demoniacal advocate of the South, and enemy of everything Adams stood for. Invariably the galleries would be crowded when he spoke, because although his discourse sometimes was rambling, at other times he might discharge some of the most quotable denunciations ever heard in those august halls.

He had a dislike for Calhoun, who as Vice-President presided over the Senate, and one day, opening one of his tirades he began in this fashion: "Mr. Speaker! I mean Mr. President of the Senate and would-be President of the United States, which God in his infinite mercy avert!" And with that he continued his diatribe.

Calhoun took the ground that he did not have the right to call a Senator to order, and Randolph roamed free. At various times he called President Adams "a traitor," Daniel Webster "a vile slanderer," John Holmes "a dangerous fool," and Edward Livingston "the most contemptible and degraded of beings, whom no man ought to touch, unless with a pair of tongs."

But it was for Clay that he reserved his choicest vitriol. An opportunity to pour out his vials came when President Adams accepted an invitation to send representatives to a Congress of American Republics which was to meet at Panama. Knowing that Clay strongly advocated this step, when the debate on the conference began in the Senate, Randolph charged that the invitations from Colombia and Mexico ac-

[1] Ben: Perley Poore, *Perley's Reminiscences.*

tually did not exist but were "forged, with the connivance of the President, in the State Department," and that "they have the footprints and flesh-marks of the style of that office as I shall show on a future occasion." Going on and rising to his climax, he shrilled that this was the work of "the coalition of Blifil and Black George—the combination, unheard of till now, of the puritan and the black-leg!"

Henry Fielding's novel *Tom Jones* was widely read at the time, and the allusion was well understood. In the book Blifil is a canting hypocrite, Black George a rascally gamekeeper. It was the word "black-leg" that infuriated Clay, since it was obvious that it was applied to him since nobody could ever accuse him of being a puritan. He sent a challenge to Randolph and the latter, waiving all rights of immunity for statements made on the floor of the Senate, accepted.

Before the duel Randolph confided to his second, General James Hamilton, that he did not intend to fire at Clay. When the meeting took place, the Lord of Roanoke, who was one of the best pistol shots in the South, forgot that his weapon was set on hair-trigger and accidentally discharged it before the word, harmlessly of course, for the muzzle was pointed at the ground. An effort was made to stop the duel, but Clay, insisting the shot was accidental, demanded that it go on. Randolph's pistol was reloaded. This time he waited until his adversary fired, then discharged his own weapon into the air.

Clay's pistol ball punctured a hole through Randolph's coat near the hip but drew no blood. "I might as well have fired at a pair of tongs," Clay later remarked, referring to Randolph's excessive gauntness.

On the occasion, however, as soon as the shots were fired, Randolph threw his pistol on the ground and advanced toward the Secretary of State with an outstretched hand. Clay met him with equal warmth.

"You owe me a coat, Mr. Clay," said Randolph with a smile.

"I thank God the debt is no greater," said the Kentuckian with sincerity.

The duel, though bloodless, served to focus the attention of the public on the speech that occasioned it. The words "Blifil and Black George—the puritan and the black-leg," remained a part of the American common language for years thereafter.

2

Meantime Andrew Jackson, who had resigned from the Senate to devote himself to his plantation—and his new ambition to defeat the two men who combined against him—was answering correspondence he received from all parts of the country, and entertaining guests, among whom was the Marquis de Lafayette, then making a triumphal tour of the country for which he had fought as a young man.

And doing a great deal of thinking.

His thinking began with the very cause for his undertaking his campaign. He believed in his heart that the Adams-Clay combination had defeated the wishes of the common people of America. The common people, therefore, became the base for his theories of government.

In his career thus far, he had passed through all the stages from buckskin frontier to broadcloth gentry. By his mode of living and his interests at this period he seemed naturally allied with the aristocracy which ruled the land. But Jackson knew what it was to labor and bear privation, and he did not forget his beginnings.

There was Alexander Hamilton's cynical theory: "All communities divide themselves into the few and the many. The first are rich and well-born, the other the mass of the people . . . The people are turbulent and changing; they seldom judge or determine rightly . . . Give, therefore, to the first class a distinct, permanent share in the government. They will check the unsteadiness of the second, and, as they cannot receive any advantage by a change, they therefore will ever maintain good government."

Hamilton was dead, killed by Aaron Burr's pistol in the Weehawken duel; and the Federalist Party hardly existed except among a few bitter-enders. The new Republican Party of Jefferson had gained such ground that it created in America virtually a one-party system. But into the fabric of this party, conceived originally as the party of equality, had crept as always the industrial, commercial, and financial interests, masking their Hamiltonianism with new words and mottos, but working for the same end.

The new and hidden Federalism had among its spokesmen the two foremost orators of their day: Henry Clay and Daniel Webster. It was Webster who asserted to the Massachusetts constitutional convention in 1820: "Power *naturally* and *necessarily* follows property . . . A republican form of government rests not more on political constitutions than on those laws which regulate the descent and transmission of property."

This was pure Hamilton doctrine. But Clay made it sound more palatable with his "American System" argument in which he advocated a "protective" tariff, to encourage industries on the high-sounding ground that it would increase the "home market" for products of American farms.

It was no mere accident that both of those gentlemen were on the payroll as attorneys of Hamilton's creation, the Bank of the United States. That great financial house, designed by Hamilton as a privately owned profit-making institution to enjoy special access to the public

funds, for the purpose of stabilizing American finances, regularly subsidized the *American Quarterly Review* in its propaganda fight
against universal manhood suffrage, in which it published such statements as the following:

> The lowest orders of society ordinarily mean the poorest—and
> the highest, the richest. Sensual excess, want of intelligence, and
> moral debasement, distinguish the former, intellectual superiority,
> and refined social and domestic affections, the latter.

Jackson was aware of such utterances, also that a formidable proportion of the men of wealth and power subscribed to them; but already he had taken a leading part in writing universal manhood suffrage into the constitution of Tennessee. The Bank of the United
States became to him a symbol of the vested interests. It was destined
to become one of the greatest bones of contention between Clay and
himself.

In those years at The Hermitage, he identified himself with the people. As he grappled with the problems confronting them, he came to
understand the common Americans as few have ever understood them.
Ever afterward he sincerely fought for what he considered their rights
and best interests. As Martin Van Buren later said, "They were his
blood relations—the only blood relations he had."[2]

3

Slowly developing his political philosophies at The Hermitage, and
in so doing arriving at conclusions at variance not only with the arch-
conservative Federalism, but with the loosely liberal Jeffersonianism,
Jackson began to gather his forces for the political battle ahead as a
general mobilizes an army.

Many factors worked for him. He was the popular hero of the nation, with a military reputation unblemished by a single defeat, and
garnished by brilliant victories. His integrity was unquestioned, even
by his enemies. While he was a gentleman planter, he also was a back-
woodsman by upbringing and early life, thus being agreeable to both
classes, and talking the language of each when called upon to do so.
Above all his extraordinary personality impressed almost everyone
with whom he came into contact. He had never entered publicly into
discussions on the chief political questions of the day, yet, while

---

[2] Jackson's father died before his birth. His mother and both his brothers lost
their lives during the Revolution. His marriage to Rachel was without issue. Andrew Jackson, Jr., his adopted son, was one of Rachel's nephews.

he was not on record, men knew him to be one of positive actions, no fence-straddler or temporizer, whom it would be interesting to watch when he did take hold of an issue. Finally, the "bargain and corruption" cry had turned thousands of voters against Adams and Clay.

His opponents rang all the changes on his reputation for gambling, intemperance (in his early years), arbitrariness, and irascibility. But these things did not greatly prejudice him, at least in the minds of Southerners and Westerners, where he was known to be just and forthright if rigid and impetuous.

Over the country important political figures began to draw to him, men like Martin Van Buren of New York who had once campaigned for Crawford, Amos Kendall the Kentucky journalist who formerly was publicist for Clay, Duff Green of the *United States Telegraph*, Thomas Hart Benton of Missouri whose former enmity had turned to powerful friendship, even—at this time—John C. Calhoun of South Carolina, when that lean Southerner saw his present chance for the supreme honor was gone, and decided for a time at least to ride the tail of Old Hickory's kite.

In Tennessee he had the beginnings of a well-drilled organization of friendly supporters, including Senator John Henry Eaton, John Overton, Major William B. Lewis, and General Sam Houston as the inner circle.

A word here about Sam Houston. After he caught the eye of Jackson by his spectacular gallantry at the Horse Shoe Bend and recovered from his severe wounds sustained in that action, he was chosen by the general for his personal staff. When he resigned from the army, over an affront he considered he had received from John Calhoun, then Secretary of War, he studied law in Tennessee under Jackson's personal sponsorship, became attorney general of Tennessee, a general of militia, and a Representative in Congress. "Houston," said Old Hickory, "is a truly noble minded fellow." He was grooming him for governor of the state when William Carroll's term was finished, and to that office Houston was elected in 1827. Throughout the younger man's extraordinary and romantic career, Andrew Jackson kept a fatherly eye on him. It was as if, having no children of his body, Jackson regarded Houston as a son of his spirit, with results destined to be epic and historic.

By now Henry Clay, who believed he had maneuvered himself into the succession for the Presidency, and John Quincy Adams, who hoped for a second term, were thoroughly alarmed by the rising tide of enthusiasm for Jackson. And it was at this time that one of the vilest campaigns of detraction in the history of American politics began.

Failing to shake the growing popularity of the Tennesseean, his foes stooped to making capital of the unfortunate but wholly innocent cir-

cumstances of his marriage to Rachel. Reports of the manufactured
scandal concerning his wife reached Jackson's ears when it was still
only word-of-mouth gossip set afloat here and there. To Sam Houston
he wrote in smoldering vein:

> I have lately got an intimation of some of his [Clay's] secrete
> movements which if I can reach with possitive and responsible
> proof I will wield to his political and perhaps to his actual de-
> struction. he is certainly the bases [t], meanest scoundrel that
> ever disgraced the image of his god . . . Even the aged and
> virtuous female is not free from his . . . slander—but *enough,
> you know me.*

Houston knew Old Hickory very well. He had, indeed, trained for a
duel of his own—in which he critically wounded General William A.
White, with pistols at five paces[3]—under the eye of Jackson himself.

He was alarmed that the next step might be a challenge sent to
Clay, which could only hurt the general, because it would tend to con-
firm the charges of his enemies as to his impetuous irascibility. Perhaps
Houston alone, of the general's circle of friends at that time, could
have succeeded in accomplishing it, but when the younger man
pleaded with Jackson to contain his fury, Old Hickory with an effort
did so.

Meantime Eaton went directly to Clay and demanded an explanation. The Secretary of State denied that he knew anything about the
canard. Eaton, however, doubted Clay's sincerity, and so informed
Jackson.

Now slander descended still further, from word-of-mouth gossip to
print. First came a handbill published by an East Tennessee enemy
of Jackson, which said that the general had "spent the prime of his life
in gambling, in cock-fighting, in horse-racing . . . and to cap all tore
from a husband the wife of his bosom." The handbill went on to add
that a vote for Andrew Jackson would be a vote to sanction a code
whereby if a man should fancy his neighbor's "pretty wife . . . he
had nothing to do but take a pistol in one hand and a horse whip in
the other and . . . possess . . . her."

Next the administration newspapers took it up and gave it wider
circulation. First the Cincinnati *Gazette*, a pro-Clay journal, published
a biased account of the divorce and its charges of adultery, omitting to

---

[3] The distance between the antagonists, extremely short, was a sportsmanlike
concession by Houston to the poor marksmanship of White. The duel grew out
of a quarrel stemming from Houston's loyal support of Jackson, and fortunately
White, although shot in the groin, recovered, for which nobody was more thankful
than Houston himself.

mention the innocent misunderstanding which caused the technical transgression. This reached crescendo when the *National Journal,* official mouthpiece of the Adams administration, took up the foul story.

Knowing what was being said about her, poor Rachel was in an agony of shame and misery. She tried to keep away from people, and wept much, a woman suffering torments she did not deserve, and which she was helpless to escape. It began to tell severely on her, mentally and physically, so that Jackson was alarmed for her.

A committee of the most prominent men in the Nashville district— not all of them by any means Jackson supporters, but all honest men who wished to bring the truth to light—wrote a calm and accurate statement of the true facts of the case, telling of Rachel's misery with Robards (who was since deceased), the supposed divorce, her marriage in good faith with Jackson, the actual divorce by *ex parte* proceedings, the remarriage to comply with the letter of the law, the virtuous lives of the couple before and after that event. This was published by Duff Green in his *Telegraph,* running to ten full columns of type.

But it did nothing to stop the attacks of Clay's spokesmen. The details of that long campaign of vilification need not be gone into in this narrative; they were all different notes played on the same string. But one typically vicious statement should be quoted. It appeared in a pamphlet, published by Charles Hammond, editor of the Cincinnati *Gazette,* and said to be distributed under the franks of administration congressmen. It posed the bald question:

"Ought a convicted adultress and her paramour husband be placed in the highest offices of this free and christian land?"

But by this time Andrew Jackson had himself under iron control. "How hard it is to keep the cowhide from these villains," he wrote his old friend John Coffee. And though he once framed what was evidently the preamble to a formal challenge to Clay, he discarded it.

Meantime, in Washington, Duff Green published a report that John Quincy Adams had pre-marital relations with his wife—a pure fabrication of course, since the puritanical Adams would never have been guilty of such misconduct. Green sent a copy of his paper to Jackson with a note, "Let Mrs. Jackson rejoice, her vindication is complete."

How he reasoned that a false report of misconduct by Adams and his wife "vindicated" a false report of misconduct by Jackson and Rachel is obscure. Jackson's reply was an immediate and sharp rebuke. "I *never war against females* and it is only the base and cowardly that do." That ended that.

Without much question a word from Adams or Clay to the overzealous administration publicists would have halted them just as Jackson stopped Green. They did nothing to that end.

There were other assaults on Jackson. His record was raked over and he was charged with everything from murder to conspiracy against his own country.

The celebrated "Coffin Handbill," containing crude representations of eighteen coffins, symbolizing that many persons supposedly brought to their deaths by Jackson, included Dickinson, John Woods who was executed for refusing to obey orders in the face of the enemy during the Creek campaign, six militiamen executed for desertion or mutiny during the New Orleans campaign, and Arbuthnot and Ambrister, executed for inciting the Seminoles in Florida to war against Americans. This does not total eighteen, but the formulators of the broadside were not stingy about numbers. Nor did the fact that all of these, except the duel with Dickinson, were military executions carrying out court-martial sentences, seem to bother them.

The old story that he had "conspired" with Aaron Burr was revived —but it was as speedily dropped when it was discovered that Henry Clay had been Burr's attorney in his trial for treason.

Toward the end of the campaign, in sheer desperation, Charles Hammond wrote in his *Gazette* that "Jackson's mother was a prostitute and his father a mulatto who sold an older offspring of that union into slavery."

By this time the press had overreached itself. The people became weary of the vilification, many turned to Jackson in sheer sympathy, and what had started as sensation turned to disbelief.

Throughout this Jackson remained outwardly calm. As Election Day neared in the fall of 1828, even Adams and Clay knew they were in for a crushing defeat at the hands of the voters.

They did not dream it would be so devastating. When the returns were all in—and in that day of slow communications it required weeks to gather them—Andrew Jackson had one hundred and seventy-eight votes in the Electoral College to Adams' eighty-three.

4

The real tragedy was Rachel Jackson's. For years, since the day she discovered that her first marriage to Jackson had been technically illegal, even though it was remedied at once by going through a second ceremony, she shrank from public gaze. Divorce was in itself disgrace in that day, and imputations of immoral conduct a shame almost impossible for her to bear.

As the campaign went on efforts were made to keep the worst of the filthy stories from her, but she knew what was going on. Day by day she seemed to fade.

The Hermitage was constantly filled with guests, among whom Jackson walked and talked with gravity and courtesy, but Rachel seldom appeared. She confined herself to an upstairs bedroom where only her closest friends were admitted.

"The enemies of the General have dipt their arrows in wormwood and gall and sped them at me," she wrote a friend. "They have Disquieted one that thaey had no rite to do."

When the results of the election were announced to her, she told Major Lewis, "For Mr. Jackson's sake I am glad. For my own part I never wished it."

Her appearance changed alarmingly, showing the effects of her long ordeal. Wrote Henry R. Wise, a Virginian who came to Nashville to practice law, and visited the family:

> Mrs. Jackson was once a form of rotund and rubiscund beauty, but now very plethoric and obese . . . [She] talked low but quick with a short and wheezing breath.

She was sincerely grateful for Wise's visit, and talked with him of her old home in Virginia, with which he was familiar, and the church she attended as a young girl.

Two doctors, old Dr. Samuel Hogg, and young Dr. Henry Lee Heiskell, frequently called upon her, with faces of growing gravity as they observed her symptoms. They bled her repeatedly, but she continued to droop. Andrew Jackson was overwhelmingly worried about her. When he learned the outcome of the election he said, "I am filled with gratitude. Still, my heart is depressed."

Senator Eaton wrote her from Washington, assuring her that "the storm has abated," and urging her to look forward to receiving full honor and attentions in Washington. But it did not comfort her. To Henry Wise she said:

"I assure you I had rather be a doorkeeper in the house of God than live in that palace at Washington."[4]

She had to make numerous wardrobe additions, and submitted to being measured and fitted, but in mid-December, whether because she overheard spiteful feminine comment concerning her on a visit to Nashville, or learned the true depth to which her name had been dragged in the newspapers and ordinary gossip, she sustained a shock which made her hysterical. Jackson did his utmost to comfort her, but

[4] Alben W. Barkley of Kentucky, Vice-President in the Truman administration, made a similar remark, paraphrasing Psalms 84:10 just prior to his death.

shortly after, December 17, she suffered an attack, described by her doctors as "spasmodic affection of the muscles of the chest and left shoulder, attended with irregular action of the heart." The symptoms were those of what is now called a coronary thrombosis.

She was put to bed, bled, and seemed better. On December 22 she begged to be allowed to sit up, which she was permitted to do. But while her husband and the doctors were consulting in the next room, she cried out, "I am fainting!" and collapsed in the arms of Hannah, her Negro serving maid.

Efforts to revived her failed. Almost crazed by grief, Jackson at first refused to believe her dead, and ordered four blankets spread on the table on which she was laid out, so, "If she does come to she will [not] lay hard on that table."

All that night he sat beside his dead, his long fingers clutching his whitened hair, eyes dry, speechless.

She was buried the afternoon of December 24, and ten thousand persons forgot their Christmas Eve celebrations to crowd the garden, lawn, and surrounding grounds of The Hermitage to do honor to her and her bereaved husband. At the end, after the ceremony of interment, for the first time tears coursed down the old general's ravaged cheeks. He lifted his voice, and it seemed to come from the tomb itself:

"I know it is unmanly, but these tears are due to her virtues . . . she has shed so many for me."

He paused, shaken by grief, then mastered the choking in his voice:

"In the presence of this dear saint I can, and do, forgive all my enemies. *But those vile wretches who have slandered her must look to God for mercy!*"

He waited for the grave to be filled, then turned back to the house, leaning on the arms of friends.

It was the end of a period, the beginning of another, in the life of Andrew Jackson and in the history of his nation.

BOOK **II**

*The Defender of
the Union*

CHAPTER SEVEN

The Problem, and the Dream

1

Old and lonely, physically feeble and sick, Jackson began his journey to Washington early in January, by steamboat from Nashville to Pittsburgh, and thence to the capital by stagecoach. The general's health by now had become a topic of national discussion and there were those who freely stated that interest was as great in his successor as in himself.

Mrs. Trollope, the peripatetic English authoress, witnessed his arrival at Cincinnati. She recorded:

> He wore his grey hair carelessly, but not ungracefully arranged, and, in spite of his harsh gaunt features, he looks like a gentleman, and a soldier. He was in deep mourning, having very recently lost his wife; they were said to have been very happy together . . . [A] greasy fellow accosted him thus:
> "General Jackson, I guess?" The General bowed assent.
> "Why, they told me you was dead."
> "No, Providence has hitherto preserved my life."
> "And is your wife alive, too?"
> The General, apparently much hurt, signified the contrary, upon which the courtier concluded his harangue by saying, "Ay, I thought it was the one or the t'other of ye."

The incident shocked Mrs. Trollope's sense of the proprieties. What she did not understand, and perhaps was incapable of understanding, was that Andrew Jackson would not have dreamed of avoiding, or resenting, such questioning. He now considered that he belonged to the public.

When Pittsburgh was reached and the overland journey began, he refused a private equipage and took the public stagecoach. To avoid the labor of climbing in and out of the coach each time a halt was made and the people clamored to see him, he rode on the high front seat with the driver. There he would rise and stand patiently, hat off, in sun or rain, to acknowledge the cheers of the village crowds.

The strain was great, but when he neared Washington, February 12, 1829, his friend John Henry Eaton spirited him into the city by a carriage to Gadsby's Hotel, thus avoiding a strenuous public entry. Eaton was now married—to Peggy O'Neale Timberlake, she of the spicy reputation. Her husband, the naval lieutenant, had committed suicide while on a cruise, apparently because his records as purser of his ship were so involved that he saw nothing but disgrace ahead of him. Eaton's marriage to her was with Jackson's approval, almost at his command, when he wrote:

If you love Margaret Timberlake go and marry her at once and shut their [the gossips'] mouths.

Old Hickory's arrival was quickly known in the capital, and during the days intervening before his inauguration, March 4, Washington was jammed with a new and startling array of visitors. Backwoodsmen, farmers, immigrants, old soldiers, shopkeepers, editors, and adventurers of every kind swarmed, drawn by the mere presence of the Old Hero. Washington society and the pompous gentry of politics were horrified. Said Daniel Webster, "Strange faces filled every public place, and every face seemed to bear defiance on its brow." They were the common people, come to see one of their own assume the nation's highest office.

Jackson seemed at first unsure of himself, feeling his way. His cabinet as announced was composed of less than top-grade men: Martin Van Buren of New York, Secretary of State; John Henry Eaton of Tennessee, Secretary of War; Samuel D. Ingham of Pennsylvania, Secretary of the Treasury; John McP. Berrien of Georgia, Attorney General; John Branch of North Carolina, Secretary of the Navy; and John McLean of Ohio, Postmaster General—the last a holdover from the Adams administration.

Upon these nominations Jackson's enemies leaped. "The millennium of minnows!" exclaimed William Wirt, formerly Attorney General.

The chief criticism centered on Eaton—not because of himself, but because of his wife, whose romantic adventures had titillated Washington. Undoubtedly she had the power of attracting men, and she knew it, and exercised it in ways sometimes audacious. Inevitably she earned the hatred of the other women, which she returned in full measure. Her marriage to Eaton after her first husband's death had not lifted the obloquy from her.

Congressman C. C. Cambreleng of New York, at the time of her wedding, had written Van Buren:

Poor Eaton is to be married tonight to Mrs. T——! There is a vulgar saying of some vulgar man, I believe Swift, on such unions —about using a certain household . . . and then putting it on one's head.

The deletion was Cambreleng's, and the man he meant to quote was Montaigne. But his point was not obscure.

"She will never be admitted to society!" exclaimed Margaret Bayard Smith, a doyenne of that society.

But when a delegation of Tennessee Congressmen called on Jackson to protest the appointment, he stormed at it with one of his famous rages, and the delegation retreated.[1] Yet the Eaton affair was to be one of the touchiest problems of his first administration.

On March 4, Old Hickory, who had vetoed any kind of a parade, walked with a few friends to the Capitol. It was noticed that John Quincy Adams absented himself from the ceremonial. He had left Washington the night before.

Andrew Jackson, "tall and thin, his white hair pushed straight back from his forehead, his long face reamed with wrinkles, his eyes sharp and commanding . . . was a noble figure," as he took the oath of office before Chief Justice John Marshall, who was his very antithesis in political thought. When he stooped to kiss the Bible, he was greeted by "such a shout as never before arose in Washington," followed by the thunder of cannon firing a salute.

So great was the enthusiasm of the thousands who massed about the east front of the Capitol to see the new President and hear his brief address, that it was with difficulty that they were kept back from almost crushing their beloved hero.

"Persons have come five hundred miles to see General Jackson," wrote Daniel Webster sourly, "and they really seem to think that the country is rescued from some dreadful danger."

Perhaps they were right, comments a modern historian.[2] A sharp change in American history had been marked: the final death of the theory of aristocratic government, the beginning of the era of democracy. A strong hand had been placed upon the rudder of the

[1] Jackson's rages were often calculated. Wrote Henry A. Wise: "He knew that the world counted him of a temperament . . . impassioned, impulsive, and inconsiderate in action; and he often turned this mistake as to character into a large capital of advantage. He was a consummate actor, never stepped without knowing and marking his ground, but knew that most men thought he was not a man of calculations. This enabled him to blind them by his affectation of passion and impulse." George Bancroft said that Jackson was "mild by nature and putting himself into a rage only when it would serve his purpose." See *The Age of Jackson*, by Arthur Schlesinger, Jr.

[2] George Dangerfield.

nation, and in face of the various critical questions which were to
rise in the next few years a lesser hand might well have faltered disas-
trously.

None who could crowd in were barred from the reception held in
the White House after the inauguration. Wrote Ben: Perley Poore who
was present:

> On their arrival at the White House, the motley crowd clam-
> ored for refreshments and soon drained the barrels of punch
> which had been prepared, in drinking the health of the new Chief
> Magistrate. A great deal of china and glassware was broken, and
> the East Room was filled with a noisy mob. At one time General
> Jackson, who had retreated until he stood with his back against
> the wall, was protected by a number of his friends, who formed
> a living barrier around him. Such a scene had never before been
> witnessed at the White House, and the aristocratic old Federalists
> saw, to their disgust, men whose boots were covered with the
> red mud of the unpaved streets, standing on the damask satin-
> covered chairs to get a sight of the President of their choice.

Patiently and good-humoredly, Jackson underwent this rather trying
ordeal, since, as he considered, the White House and all within it belonged to the people.[3] The opening of some additional barrels of
punch out on the lawn, lured away enough of the crowd to permit
the President to escape to his rooms at Gadsby's Hotel, from which
he later made a more private return to the White House.

2

How can one describe the transcendent, almost mystical effect that
the assumption of the office of President of the United States has upon
those who assume its majestic dignity and vast responsibilities? Hardly
any of those who have donned the mantle of Chief Magistrate, have
failed to become greater in so doing. Andrew Jackson did not achieve

---

[3] An interesting story connected with the site of the White House was recorded by Poore: The land on which it stands belonged originally to a crusty old
Scot named David Burns. Burns donated some land for public edifices, and pros-
pered by selling other land for building lots. But when President George Washington called upon him to ask for a little more land, the old curmudgeon rebuffed
him. Washington, whose temper was always short, departed saying, "Had not
the Federal City been laid out here, you would have died a poor tobacco planter."
"Aye, mon!" responded Burns, in his broad Scottish burr, "An' had ye nae married
the widow Custis wi' a' her nagurs, ye would hae been a land surveyor yet, an'
a mighty poor one at that." In the end, however, Burns was persuaded to donate
the land which comprises the site of the White House and Lafayette Square.

true greatness until he entered the White House. Nor did Abraham Lincoln, before he attained that same place of high honor and mighty decisions.

The new President had none of the training in statesmanship that his predecessor had brought to the office. But he possessed something John Quincy Adams lacked—a deep and genuine relationship with the people, a feeling for them and an understanding of them, which Adams never had or could have. Van Buren said of him, that he thought "to labor for the good of the masses was a special mission assigned to him by his Creator."

Once in the White House he began to learn at first hand the difficulties of the President's duties, the intransigence of politicians, the glacial slowness of Congress, the ceaseless jealousies and treacheries of intrigues beneath the surface. He dealt with his problems in the only way he knew how—directly, sometimes harshly, even relentlessly. But he was guided always by his feeling for the American people.

"With every year, every month of his Presidency," wrote Dangerfield, "he grew in stature, because his education as President was founded upon a simple idealism—one might almost say a simple faith —that 'a plain system, void of pomp, protecting all and granting favor to none' was the system that 'the genius of our people requires.'"

Since his wife's death his health had deteriorated. The old abscess in his lung caused violent coughing and the spitting at times of blood, his shoulder often ached from the leaden ball lodged in it, and dysentery returned to give him pain and sap his strength. Yet from his almost limitless resources of will power he summoned strength to accomplish his tasks.

At the very outset he was beset by job-seekers, for a large share of the government patronage was in his hands. Some of his strongest supporters, notably Martin Van Buren, presented him with long lists of "worthy" persons, with whom he was expected to replace those he would turn out of office. He did make many appointments, but when he was enjoined to sweep the offices clean, he showed great reluctance to do so in many cases.

Jackson has been criticized as instituting the "Spoils System" into government. This is not true. The second President, John Adams, made appointments on a purely political basis. Thomas Jefferson did not hesitate to remove Federalists to make room for Democrat-Republicans. Madison, Monroe, and John Quincy Adams, inheriting from Jefferson, had little reason to make wholesale changes. But Jackson brought in a new theory of government, and so long had some of the office-holders been at the public trough that corruption had crept in.

Yet Jackson was no wholehearted spoilsman. In the period of a year when he was supposed to have made a wholesale sweep of government offices, he actually replaced only 919, or about one-eleventh of the entire number. Though he replaced McLean who refused to obey instructions for dismissals in the Post Office Department, by appointing him to the Supreme Court, and appointed in his stead William T. Barry of Kentucky, and later made a policy of taking advantage of the four-year tenure act, it remains a fact that in the entire eight years of his two administrations, he replaced not more than one-fifth of those he found in office when he assumed the Presidency.[4] The coining of the phrase "To the victors belong the spoils," by Senator William L. Marcy of New York, in 1832, helped give Jackson the reputation of a ruthless spoilsman, but actually he replaced about the same proportion that Jefferson had done before him. It remained for the Whigs, who came to power in 1841, to make the clean sweep that Jackson did not. Thereafter, with each change of administration, wholesale dismissals and appointments of political favorites became the rule until long after the Civil War.

This sort of housekeeping annoyed Old Hickory. When he had done all he proposed to do, and a host of would-be office holders retreated from Washington, some with disappointed threats of rebellion, he smiled. Those discontented ones only wanted "a tit . . . to suck the Treasury pap," he said, somewhat inelegantly, but mordantly. By this time he knew what he was doing.

Yet when he turned to more important problems, he almost at once found himself involved in something as ridiculous as an unreasonable woman's cat-fight against other unreasonable women. It created a domestic difficulty in Jackson's own household, swiftly blew itself up into a matter of important political interest, and came to a climax through the rivalry of John Calhoun, the Vice-President, and Martin Van Buren, the Secretary of State, for the premier position—under Jackson—in the government.

---

[4] Sometimes he absolutely refused the importunities of subordinates. General Solomon Van Rensselaer, a Federalist, who had been appointed Postmaster of Albany, New York, by Adams. Van Buren scheduled him for removal, but the old man went to Washington to call upon the President. Alone in the study with Old Hickory, he brought up the subject of his office, and that the politicians wanted to take it from him. When the President did not reply, the aged postmaster began to take off his coat "in the most excited manner." Jackson stared at him. "What in heaven's name are you doing? Why do you take off your coat here?" he asked. Replied the old petitioner, "I am going to show you my wounds, which I received fighting for my country against the English!" "Put it on at once, sir!" exclaimed Jackson. "I am surprised that a man of your age should make such an exhibition of himself!" Then he dismissed his ancient foe with a promise that his job was safe. When later Van Buren and Silas Wright, of New York, urged Van Rensselaer's removal, Old Hickory sprang to his feet. "I take the consequences; I take the consequences!" he said. "By the Eternal! I will not remove that old man—I cannot remove him! Why, Mr. Wright, do you know that he carries more than a pound of British lead in his body?"

Peggy O'Neale Timberlake, the girl who had amused the old general at her father's inn, with her wit and lively charm, in the days when he lost his first election at the hands of Congress, had since that time been widowed, by the suicide while on a cruise at sea of Lieutenant Timberlake. She had married again. Her second husband was Senator Eaton, Jackson's close friend, and his Secretary of War.

Mrs. Peggy Eaton was now in her middle twenties, beautiful, vain, vindictive, and utterly self-willed. When she found that, because of gossip about her romantic adventures, she was being snubbed by other Cabinet ladies, she was eager, with feminine fury, to humble all of them.

She knew that her position was strong, not only as the wife of one of the President's oldest friends, and by her own acquaintance with the general, but in Old Hickory's known instinct to defend "slandered womanhood," an outgrowth of the sufferings he had seen his late wife, Rachel, undergo. Of this situation Peggy Eaton proceeded to take advantage.

By frequent calls at the White House, she cultivated anew the friendship of the old warrior, who had always smiled at her pert ways in the old days. Thus far she succeeded, but another obstacle presented itself.

In the Executive Mansion, Mrs. Emily Donelson, wife of Major Jack Donelson, Jackson's nephew and secretary, was the official hostess for the old widower, her uncle. Emily, a pleasant, pretty young woman, instinctively disliked and distrusted Peggy Eaton, and from the first there was a *sub rosa* feminine war between them.

To cap this, Jackson one day received a letter from Dr. Ezra Styles Ely, a Presbyterian minister of Philadelphia, which contained a series of charges against Peggy Eaton. In part it read:

> From girlhood, sir, this woman has borne a bad reputation. You must be aware that the ladies of Washington will not speak to her, and have not for some time past. I must tell you that a gentleman, the morning after the British Minister's ball, said at his tavern breakfast table that "Mrs. Eaton brushed by him last night pretending not to know him; she had forgotten the time when she slept with him." I am informed that her servants are told to call her children Eaton, not Timberlake, for Eaton was their real name. Furthermore, a clergyman of Washington has lately told me that Mrs. Timberlake had a miscarriage when her husband had been absent for a year. As to Mr. Eaton, his own friends, seeking to save him from this woman, persuaded him to board elsewhere than at the tavern she frequented. I should also remind you, sir, that your late and lamented wife, Mrs. Jackson, had a bad opinion of this woman. And it is stated by numerous

witnesses that Mrs. Timberlake and Eaton took trips together, and traveled as man and wife, recording it in hotel registers, in New York and elsewhere. For your own sake, for your dead wife's sake, for your administration, for the credit of the Government and the Country, you should not countenance a woman like this.

Jackson called Eaton to him and showed him the letter. Eaton declared it a "tissue of lies." Jackson set to work to unravel the accusations. O'Neale's former boarders to the number of a dozen gave affidavits that they knew of no "bad name" Peggy bore. The gentleman alleged to have spoken of "sleeping" with her—a Mr. Hyde—denied ever making such a statement. Landladies at lodgings where Eaton had stopped with Peggy (and her husband), said their conduct was correct.

Peggy, with John Eaton, visited the White House, where she wept hysterically over the "injustices" done her. Jackson, always agitated by a woman's tears, and with his strong instinct to defend "traduced females," believed her. He called a cabinet meeting, to which he summoned both Dr. Ely and Dr. Campbell, naively expecting the two reverend gentlemen to "set the calumny straight." To his astonishment and wrath both clergymen refused to exonerate Mrs. Eaton.

In this manner Peggy Eaton's sexual innocence or guilt became a public, almost a national issue—the last thing that Old Hickory, in the kindness of his heart, had even dreamed. So far as is known, Andrew Jackson continued to believe in Peggy's innocence all his life.

3

For the time being the personal affairs of Mrs. Eaton were placed in the background, for the President must grapple with the tasks of preparing his first message to Congress. That document, when it appeared, was vigorous, forthright, and controversial, like its author, and it contained a number of thought-provoking sections.

In foreign affairs, the new President called attention to France's twenty years of delay in settling American claims agreed upon for damages sustained in the Napoleonic wars; the fact that Britain still kept closed to Americans her ports in the West Indies; the continued dispute over the American-Canadian boundary of Maine; and the movement by some Southern states to annex Texas, at that time unquestionably a Mexican province. In all these issues he proposed "to ask for nothing that is not clearly right and to submit to nothing that is wrong."

The message next turned to domestic issues. There was the tariff, a thorny problem Jackson had inherited, bitterly opposed by South Carolina as the "Tariff of Abominations," for which he suggested a compromise; the question of removal of Indians to permit white settlement, which he favored; internal improvements, toward which he was manifestly lukewarm until the national debt was paid; and finally, the Bank of the United States. The President pointed out that the Bank's charter would expire in 1836, and suggested the advisability of considering another agency, more in the public interest, which might replace it, since, "it has failed in the great end of establishing a uniform and sound currency."

The last item was explosive. The Bank of the United States, a brain child of Alexander Hamilton, was originally established in 1791, its charter expiring in 1811. A twenty-year charter was given to the "second bank" in 1816.

Under this charter the Bank's capital and note limits were set at $35,000,000, of which the government subscribed one-fifth. It was the official repository for public funds, which it could use for its own banking purposes without payment of interest. It was not taxable by the states, and no rival institution could be chartered by Congress while it existed. Of its twenty-five directors only five were named by the government. For all these privileges it paid a bonus of one and a half million dollars per year and performed the services of transferring public funds and making public payments from government funds, without charge.

To Jackson, so great a private monopoly, upheld by the government, yet independent of the government, was a danger to the people. For one thing it too closely allied the government with the commercial and financial interests, to their advantage. For another, its power over the currency was such that it could even create artificial panics, if it chose, for political or other purposes.

The Bank's president was Nicholas Biddle, a brilliant, capable, and altogether extraordinary person, handsome, suave, always fashionably attired, and with considerable literary talents. He had the tastes of the aesthete, but with it a reckless daring, some said a lack of scruples.

Power had badly warped his perspective. In his view the Bank was on a level with the government; so much so that he instructed his subordinates that no officer of the government, from the President downward, had the least authority or right to interfere in the concerns of his institution. The Bank's interests were paramount, even over the interests of the nation.

Biddle read Jackson's unveiled reference to his Bank with astonishment, mingled with anger. But on consideration he bided his time. After all, the old general's term would expire in 1833, and the Bank's charter ran to 1836. His confidential reports told him that Jackson's health was so precarious that he might not even be able to serve out his full four-year term. For the present the banker said nothing and did nothing.

Other points in the message to Congress created violent controversy. There was a roar of protest from the South because the tariff was not condemned outright. Western land speculators who had dreamed of appropriations for roads, canals, and other public improvements to enhance values in their districts were outraged; the more so, because the cunning juxtaposition of the policy of paying off the national debt had appeal for many voters.

As if testing him, Congress passed a bill for a turnpike in Kentucky. The President sternly vetoed it, with a veto message so worded that though Henry Clay, still in retirement in Kentucky, blasted it with a speech, Clay's own supporters saw that Old Hickory, appealing to the people over the heads of the politicians and contractors, had won their approval.

"The document relied on Old Hickory's power over the imagination of the masses, and his uncanny ability to make his measures their measures—a phenomenon of statesmanship the country was to see more of in the seven tumultuous years to come."[5]

4

One subject on which the first message to Congress was silent, but which was deeply implicit in the state of the whole nation, was sectionalism, which had grown to such serious magnitude that even an optimist—and Andrew Jackson was a hard realist on such questions— would have considered it bordering on the perilous.

John C. Calhoun had once spoken gloomily of the "North and the South and the West," and wondered if they could ever be kept together. The North, to which he referred, was the portion of the original states of the Union lying, roughly, north of the Potomac River. His West was the area lying west of Pennsylvania and New York, and north of the Ohio River. The South, to Calhoun, was the rest of the country, south of the Potomac and Ohio watercourses. Lack of good communications as well as differences in backgrounds accounted for part of the provincialism which at this time loomed threateningly. But chiefly the sectional biases could be traced to economic situations.

It was in the North, and particularly in New England, where the

[5] Marquis James, *The Life of Andrew Jackson.*

stony soil and adverse climate handicapped farming, that the extraordinary ingenuity and energy of the Yankee mind had within one generation converted handicraft industries, in important measure, into power manufacturing. Textile machinery, designed so that relatively inexperienced operatives could make cheaply and efficiently various fabrics; interchangeable mechanisms for mass production; inventions in wood working and metal; and the use of steam to operate machinery, combined, with a growing demand for manufactured products, to bring factories by the hundreds into being, making everything from firearms and clothing to agricultural implements, tools, household appliances, even hats and clocks.

Sooty chimneys appeared in the picturesque New England country, each representing a constantly rising demand for labor. Farmers and immigrants by the thousands became factory workers, their women and even children drawn into the same system. About the plants rose towns, then cities, and the trend toward urbanization which would continually accelerate had its beginning.

At first, lacking individual capital, men adopted corporate organizations to assemble funds and pool abilities. The shipping industry, long a dominant factor in the North, was called upon to provide money for manufacturing. Before long protective tariffs and rapidly expanding demands for goods, made the corporations profitable, self-sustaining, and powerful. And since money gravitated to the cities, important municipalities like Boston, New York, and Philadelphia, became financial centers, their control of credits a factor of ever-growing force in the nation at large.

In the South, on the other hand, though there was some shipping, and relatively few manufacturing plants, the country as a whole remained agricultural, and the trend was more and more toward large plantations and a one-crop economy—chiefly cotton, although in districts adapted to them, sugar and rice also were "money crops."

In the days of high cotton prices increasingly large areas of virgin land were broken and devoted to the growth of the fiber. With increasing acreages came, of course, the increasing growth of slavery, for the plantations based their economy on slave labor.

The one-crop tendency had the effect of making the area further dependent, on the North for manufactured articles, and on the West for food. While it is true that many planters became wealthy, and lived in great houses, amid luxurious surroundings, it is also true that pursuit of money for its own sake, was not a Southern trait to the extent that it was in the North.

The West, by the time Jackson became President, had accomplished part of the great task of clearing the immense forests, and soon became as devoted to agriculture as was the South. But the

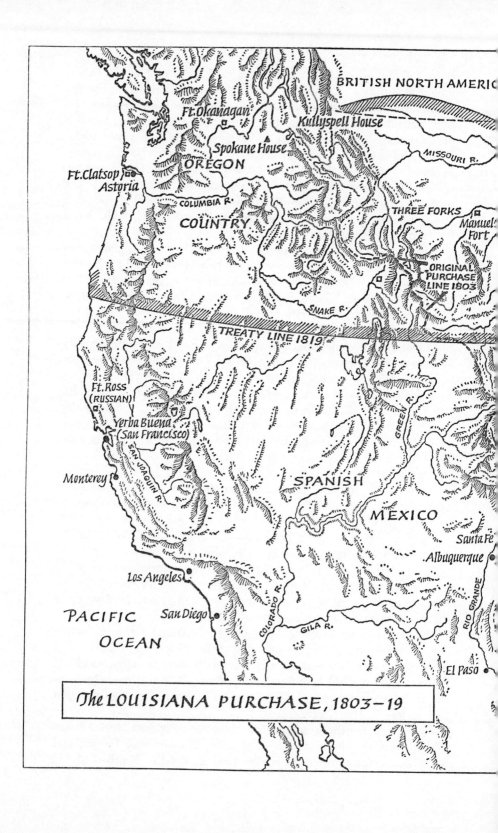

The LOUISIANA PURCHASE, 1803–19

West's rich soil permitted the growth of varied crops, such as grains, meats, and fruits, so that it increasingly produced surpluses and became a source of supply for both the North and the South. At the same time the absence of slave labor, together with the individual industry of the inhabitants, made for smaller but better cultivated farms.

The North was developing a growing antipathy toward slavery, and had come to dislike the aristocratic bearing of Southern planters and their families. In a measure the North also resented the West, because the latter siphoned off labor which the factories needed and urgently wished to retain.

The South scorned the "grasping" Yankees, and resented their attitude toward slavery; while at the same time it complained about prices it had to pay for pork, flour, and other products from the West.

The West distrusted the slaveowners of the South and the financiers of the North almost equally, especially since, being a new country, it had a large debtor class.

With sectionalism growing more and more rancorous, the nation was pulling in three different directions.

But there was a fourth element to the national picture—the frontier. Jackson was fully aware of its yeasty stirrings, and its constant movement; and also of international complications that might ensue. He informed himself to as great a degree as possible on the far-flung activities westward. But he kept to himself his great dream of a transcontinental nation, and the way in which it might be affected by events taking place far beyond the horizon toward the setting sun.

5

It was sufficiently difficult to keep track of the restless adventurers out beyond the Mississippi. The fur trade and the desire, apparently inborn in some Americans, merely to have "elbow room" had caused the frontier to overleap the Mississippi, and the seemingly arid plains beyond, even the great mountain chains in the virtually unknown Far West.

Fur there was in great variety, but the main object of the trade was beaver fur—for the making of beaver hats. Fine hats in the early part of the century often were called "beavers," and the manufacture of this headgear had offered a constant demand for beaver pelts almost since the first settlements in the continent.

Even before the young army captains, Meriwether Lewis and William Clark, began their epic exploration across the continent in 1804,

trappers were fanning out across the great country beyond the Mississippi. "Mountain men" they soon were called, and they were a class
by themselves. George Frederick Ruxton, British army officer and
sportsman, who hunted in the Western mountains—and, some say, did
a little spying on the side for his government—left a description of a
typical mountain man:

> His body [was] bent over his saddle horn, across which rested
> a long and heavy rifle, his keen gray eyes peering from under
> the slouched brim of a flexible felt hat, black and shining with
> grease. His buckskin hunting shirt, bedaubed until it had the
> appearance of polished leather, hung in folds over his bony car-
> cass . . . he *appeared* to look neither to the right or left, but in
> fact his little twinkling eye was everywhere . . . Acquainted with
> every inch of the Far West, and with all the Indian tribes who
> inhabited it, he never failed to outwit his red enemies, and
> generally made his appearance at the rendezvous with galore of
> beaver . . . When attacked by Indians [he] invariably fought
> manfully, and with all the coolness that perfect indifference to
> death or danger would give . . . His rifle cracked away merrily,
> and never spoke in vain; and in a charge—if it came to that—
> his keen-edged butcher knife tickled the fleece of many a Black-
> foot . . . His iron frame defied fatigue . . . and, when game was
> scarce and they suffered hunger . . . [he] never grumbled . . .
> [but] chewed away at his shoes with relish even, and as long as
> he had a pipeful of tobacco to his pouch was a happy man.

Of laws the mountain men knew little and cared less. What they
wanted they took, and as a result their constant clashes with the wild
tribes made their chances of long life slim indeed. They recognized
no artificial boundaries, and American parties not only explored most
of the Louisiana Purchase, but had not hesitated to cross over into
Canada, and to trap in Mexican territory to the south. Their activities
were stimulated by rivalry which grew intense not only between
American fur companies, like those of Astor, Ashley, Sublette, and the
Choteaus, but the Hudson's Bay and North West companies, the great
British firms which were the forerunners of empire for England.

National loyalties here played their role. On one occasion, May 23,
1825, while a "brigade" of Hudson's Bay trappers led by Peter Skene
Ogden was trapping near the Great Salt Lake in what is now Utah,
twenty-five American trappers rode up to his camp, with the flag of
the United States "ostentatiously displayed." An armed clash was
averted, but the Americans planted their camp within a hundred
yards of the Hudson's Bay headquarters, and began to outbid Ogden
for the furs his own men brought in. When Ogden protested, the

Americans cocked their rifles and told him that this was United States land on which he was trespassing. Ogden retreated northward with his trappers. The oddest quirk about the whole proceeding was that the land over which they disputed belonged neither to the United States nor Great Britain. Both parties were on Mexican soil at the time.

Perhaps no class of men ever lived lives of greater or more continuous adventure than the mountain men. They worked their lonely trap lines in the countries of wild and spectacular horseback tribes, like the Sioux, Cheyennes, Blackfeet, Crows, and Comanches, among fierce desert tribes like the Apaches, among other tribes like the earth lodge Pawnees and Arikaras, and the plank house, totem pole tribes like the Haidas and Nootkas of the far Pacific Coast. Almost all those tribes at one time or another were warlike.

The mountain men were contemptuous of cold, hunger, thirst, and privations of every kind. Death was always close at hand, even anticipated, and the average career of a free trapper was no more than three or four years. Only the more fortunate survived Indian ambushes, encounters with the ferocious grizzly bears, floods and avalanches, drunken brawls among themselves at their annual rendezvous, or any of the countless other perils of the wilderness.

The beaver era ended, roughly, about 1835, not because all the beaver had been trapped out, as has been mistakenly supposed. The virtual extermination of beaver did not come until the settlement of the West. The end of the era came because men of fashion stopped wearing beaver hats, as the style turned to silk hats.

Yet in the years between about 1804 and 1835, the trappers became familiar with every great geographical feature in the Far West. Among them some became famous, like Kit Carson and Jedediah Smith—men with genuine nobility of character—and also Jim Bridger, Broken Hand Fitzpatrick, Old Bill Williams, and others. But there were also among them scoundrels of the worst type.

One and all, however, they traversed with indescribable endurance the deserts, scaled the lofty mountain chains, discovered passes across the ranges, traced out the rivers to their sources, and all this with the utmost recklessness and daring.

A mountain man might start in the spring from an Indian village where he had wintered in the Wind River Valley, trap the Wasatch Mountains by June, cross the desert to the Sierra Nevadas by July, hunt in the central valley of California in August, climb the barbarous Siskiyous into the Oregon country in September, and be back with his Indian friends by October. He would have journeyed in that time on foot or horseback—depending on his fortunes—many hundreds of miles, over the wildest and most rugged country, would have starved at times, suffered thirst at others, and never for one day, even one minute, been free from danger. And all this merely from his inborn desire to see "what was on the other side of the hill."

American ships had early visited the Pacific Coast to trade, and in 1792 Captain Robert Gray in the *Columbia* discovered the mouth of the great river he named after his vessel, thus establishing a United States claim to the Oregon country.

But the Pacific was reached overland by stark adventurers soon after. Lewis and Clark built their wintering post, Fort Clatsop, at the mouth of the Columbia in 1805, before starting back on their exploration. John Jacob Astor's men erected the short-lived post Astoria, near the site of Fort Clatsop in 1811, and though they had to cease operations, they provided another claim to the watershed.

By 1826 the remarkable pathfinder and far-rover Jedediah Strong Smith reached California by way of the old Spanish Trail and across the Mojave Desert. This same Jedediah Smith discovered, among other things, South Pass, which later was to be the key for the Oregon Trail.

Other trappers like Smith entered California, and some of them stayed there, with interesting later results. When the government explorations went West, their leaders had little to do but follow the guides who knew the country already.

Of these matters Jackson kept himself informed as far as possible. His interest in the Far West is shown by the episode of an army captain with a flamboyant name, Benjamin Louis Eulalie de Bonneville. He was born in France, but his father brought him to America and he graduated from West Point. Fired by stories of wealth gained by the fur trade, he applied in 1831 for a leave of absence, to take a company of trappers into the Far West and explore, while trapping.

Major General Alexander Macomb, commanding general of the U. S. Army, referred the request to Lewis Cass, then Jackson's Secretary of War, and Cass conferred with Jackson. Permission was granted, and the conditions defined give a good idea of what was in the mind of the President and, presumably, his advisers:

> [Explore] the country to the Rocky Mountains and beyond, with a view of ascertaining the nature and character of the several tribes of Indians inhabiting those regions . . . the quality of the soil, the productions, the minerals, the natural history, the climate, the geography and topography, as well as the geology, of the various parts of the country within the limits of the territories belonging to the United States [and] between our frontier and the Pacific . . . in short, every information which you may conceive would be useful to the government.

It will be perceived that something far more important than trapping was here involved. "To the Rocky Mountains and *beyond*," and "between our frontier and the Pacific," are to say the least remarkable phrases, inasmuch as the territories of the United States then stopped short at the continental divide of the Rocky Mountains. The interest in the "quality of the soil," and the "productions" (i.e. natural resources), as well as minerals, climate, geography, and even geology of the areas to be surveyed could only mean interest in their capabilities for supporting settlement of populations.

Jackson knew that the day had long passed when some explorer could wave his sword at the mouth of a river and proclaim that all the lands drained by that stream belonged to his king or his nation. *Occupation* was the only way to establish possession of a territory. The Far West to him was an empty land—a vacuum of wasted lands and resources. Nature abhors a vacuum, and it was inevitable that the tide of population would presently flow over the West.

There were a few Spanish-Mexicans in California and New Mexico, and Indian tribes roamed over much of the wilderness. But to the American mind, these did not use the land, which fairly cried for the plow, the seed, and the harvest; or else offered resources for profit like minerals and timber.

Bonneville followed orders. Though his expedition was far from successful as a trapping venture, he was the first to prove that wagons could be taken over South Pass—a great step toward the Oregon Trail —he explored the rich interior basins, he even sent a side expedition under Joseph Reddeford Walker, which crossed the Sierras, discovered Walker Pass (and incidentally the wonderland of Yosemite), and laid out one more trail for later emigrants to follow into California.

His mapping and general observations of not only the western Louisiana Territory, but also portions of the Oregon country and the Mexican unoccupied areas of the mountains, were so excellent that his report was the first true geographical knowledge of the Far West—all, without question, eagerly studied by the President when it was made available to him after Bonneville's return in 1835. Though Bonneville considerably overstayed his leave he was commended and reinstated at once in command.

Later Jackson personally dispatched a secret service operative, William Slacum, who crossed Mexico, took ship up the Pacific Coast, sized up the Oregon situation including agricultural productivity and lumbering wealth, observed how the British interests were encroaching on the area, and incidentally took a look at California, including San Francisco Bay, all of which he duly reported. This report and that of Bonneville had considerable bearing on the events of the future in the Far West.

Commerce was making history too. As soon as Mexico won independence from Spain in 1821, William Becknell of Arrow Rock, Missouri, resolved to test the new political situation. Previously American trade had been barred in Spanish territories, and traders had their goods confiscated and sometimes spent considerable periods in prison.

But Bill Becknell, an old Indian fighter and veteran of the War of 1812, was daring and venturesome. With twenty-one men and a pack train of goods, he struck west, passed the site at the bend of the Missouri where Westport (and present-day Kansas City) would rise, and followed the Arkansas River to just past its juncture with the Purgatoire. Thence he turned south, with difficulty crossed the Raton Pass, and reached Taos and Sante Fe.

"My father saw them unload when they [Becknell's Party] returned," H. H. Harris later recorded. "When their rawhide packages of silver dollars were dumped on the sidewalk [at Arrow Rock] one of the men cut the thongs and the money spilled out and clinking on the stone pavement rolled into the gutter. Everyone was excited . . ."

And well might they be. The profits from this trade were to be enormous. Hitherto the New Mexican settlements had been supplied by a long, slow, and expensive mule-pack trail, through dangerous Indian country, all the way from Veracruz. American goods could be transported far more cheaply, and were purchased eagerly.

Next year Bill Becknell led a new expedition—this time with *wagons,* three of them. On this occasion he crossed the Arkansas River near where the present town of Cimarron, Kansas, now stands, and angled toward the Cimarron River. Not knowing the country, his men did not know that they were embarking on a waterless desert until they were too far to turn back. For two days, with only a pocket compass to guide them, they marched, seeing mirages, in the last extremity of thirst. A buffalo blundered into their path and was killed. The beast had recently drunk its fill and on the water filling its stomach the travelers eased their parched throats. One of them, years later, said "nothing ever passed his lips which gave him such exquisite delight as his first draught of that filthy beverage."[6]

But they knew now they were close to a river, and soon discovered it. Revived they pushed on, took their wagons up some high and rocky cliffs at one place, but reached Santa Fe in good time. For the first time wheeled vehicles had crossed the plains. As Hiram Martin Chittenden noted, this was five years before Ashley's men took wheeled cannon to the Salt Lake Valley, eight years before Smith, Jackson, and

[6] Josiah Gregg, *Commerce of the Prairies.*

Sublette took wagons to Wind River, and ten years before Bonneville took them to Green River.

The "covered wagon" of frontier story had made its appearance. When later a route was discovered to the Oregon country, by Jesse Applegate's Oregon Trail, with a branch which led to California, the epic of the wagon people and their great migration to the Far West could not long be delayed.

These matters were of deep interest to Andrew Jackson, but his most immediate concern on the frontier was with a Mexican province called Texas, where American settlers already had gone in numbers and were beginning to be restive over the treatment accorded them. Texas was to be the springboard for the vast Western expansion which not only Andrew Jackson, but his friend Thomas Hart Benton, and his enemy Henry Clay, clearly foresaw.

CHAPTER EIGHT

The Challenge

1

T HAT December found Andrew Jackson again weak and ailing. His legs swelled, so that his physicians feared dropsy, and his agonizing cough returned. Two men, both intensely ambitious, watched these symptoms with varying emotions.

In direct line to the succession by statutory definition, was John Caldwell Calhoun, the Vice-President. Tall and dark, without an ounce of superfluous flesh, his steel-trap mouth rarely smiling, and his long black hair thrown back from his forehead, he looked, as a contemporary described him, "like an arch-conspirator, waiting for the time when he could strike the first blow."[1] Twice he had been a pre-campaign candidate for the Presidency, and twice he had been forced to accept the Vice-President's role—a role that irked him, since he could not even participate in the Senatorial debates over which he presided.

Though Calhoun had no real loyalty to Jackson, and once had expressed feelings of bitter opposition to the general—which were to be revealed later to his embarrassment—as Vice-President, he would become Chief Magistrate should the Presidency become vacant. On one or two occasions, when Jackson suffered recurrences of his severe illnesses, Calhoun perhaps had moments of hope that he might step into the White House through the President's death or incapacity. But Old Hickory's rawhide constitution brought him back each time, and Calhoun took to brooding. Men marked his intense preoccupation. When he presided in the Senate he was an impressive, almost forbidding figure, with his hollow cheeks, and eyes so black and piercing that "they seemed almost to reflect light in the darkness." But he kept his thoughts to himself and waged his secret political war with skill and caution.

In the hidden duel of ambitions his rival was Martin Van Buren, the Secretary of State. Van Buren was short, plump, and pompous, with gray hair curling about his head, and a rubicund complexion. He

---

[1] Ben: Perley Poore.

dressed with extreme care, though always soberly, and it was whispered that he spent so much time before the big mirror in his apartment that there was a large worn spot on the carpet. Yet the man was not a fop. He merely believed that he should dress well to make a good impression.

When first he went to Congress it was predicted of him by Rufus King, of his own state, New York, that "Within two weeks Van Buren will become perfectly acquainted with the views and feelings of every member, yet no man will know his." The prophecy was sound. So complicated and skillful were his political maneuvers, that he won the sobriquet of "The Little Magician." Yet Van Buren had this redeeming quality: he was a sincere and faithful friend and supporter of his chief, Andrew Jackson.

In affairs of state the personal lives of beautiful women, down through history, often have had consequences more far-reaching than their intrinsic importance justified. It is curious and ironic that the boudoir adventures of a woman as shallow and indiscreet, but also as attractive, as Peggy Eaton, seem to have played an unexpectedly important role not only in the political but even in the historic events of her time.

Peggy, though shunned by all the cabinet wives—indeed by all the leading women of Washington society—nevertheless possessed the firm friendship, toward both her husband and herself, of the old general. Van Buren observed how obviously neglected she was by others of her kind. He was a widower, so could make himself agreeable to her, and out of loyalty to the President, he made special efforts to entertain her.

Calhoun, whose wife was one of those who refused to receive Peggy, noted the cordiality of the Secretary of State toward her. Appraising the situation, he arrived at the conclusion that the combined hostility of all the leading women of Washington was a force that sooner or later must discredit Peggy, even in the eyes of her champion, Andrew Jackson. With this may have come the corollary thought that if Van Buren continued to uphold her, when she fell she might take him with her.

Thereupon the Vice-President became the major figure in the anti-Peggy Eaton forces.

Peggy fought back. Taking her somewhat subservient husband with her, she once more visited the White House, where she again employed the feminine weapon of tears as she complained to the President of the manner in which she had been isolated by the cabinet members and their wives. Little understanding the complexities of women, the old soldier called a cabinet meeting and read a paper charging some of the members and their families, though not by name, with "avoiding Mrs. Eaton and thereby excluding her from society and degrading her." He ended by saying that he would not part with John Henry Eaton, and if members of the cabinet could not harmonize with him they should withdraw, "for harmony I must and will have."

It was an extraordinary thing for a President to do. Washington gasped to see the fine, white-haired old general put through paces that threatened to make not only himself but his administration ridiculous, by a vain, selfish, perhaps even guilty woman; for Jackson believed in his simplicity that he was defending a creature innocent and unjustly maligned.

Calhoun soon realized that instead of strengthening himself with the President, he had badly weakened his position. Jackson showed visibly greater friendship toward Van Buren; and Jackson, provided he lived, might well be able to name his successor in the White House.

Calhoun's political theories, like those of Henry Clay, changed remarkably during his career. Born in the South Carolina uplands in 1782, he married a cousin who brought him a large plantation. At once his interests became those of the planters, rather than those of the upland frontiersmen and small farmers from whom he sprang, and in 1811 he went to Congress.

At first he was a nationalist and a supporter of the tariff. But South Carolina had opposed the tariff as far back as 1820, when her legislature protested against all such Congressional measures. With the passage of the Tariff of 1828, Calhoun wrote an *Exposition*, which declared the tariff "unconstitutional, unequal, and oppressive; and calculated to corrupt public virtue and destroy the liberty of the country." At the time it was perhaps no more than a political thesis—such as Jefferson sometimes wrote, with no intention of implementing—since he still very much wanted to be President.

The Vice-President's dream obviously went at least far enough to project an eventual division of the nation, and it is not too great a supposition that he hoped to become the head of the seceded section, once it became apparent that he could not be head of the whole Union. His enemies, indeed, compared him to Milton's lost archangel, who believed it "better to reign in hell than serve in heaven."

How much Peggy Eaton and her feminine spites and ambitions had to do with Calhoun's changes of views may be argued; but some have called her an indirect and distant trigger to the Civil War.

As the coolness between Calhoun and the President grew, Calhoun's position became more and more separatist and sectional. Some leaders of the South believed that their section stood in danger of extinction at the hands of the fast-growing North, and that the institution of slavery on which they depended, was threatened. But the slavery question was too inflammable to be raised, at this time, as an issue. In opposition to the tariff, however, Calhoun saw a weapon for establishing the principle of state sovereignty, which in turn might lead to nullification of federal laws, and perhaps secession.

The question of state sovereignty depended on an interpretation of the Constitution. The so-called "strict constructionists" leaned upon the Tenth Amendment, which stated: "The powers not delegated to the United States by the Constitution, nor prohibited by it to the States, are reserved to the States respectively, or to the people." This, it was held, meant that the individual states were sovereign in their own right, as against the central government, and the theory had already been expressed in various ways. Jefferson and Madison formulated the conception in the Kentucky and Virginia Resolutions of 1798–99, protesting against the Alien and Sedition laws. New England later invoked the concept in opposing the embargo and the War of 1812. It now was adopted and developed by Calhoun and his coterie of politicians in South Carolina, for the purpose of nullifying the tariff laws.

The opposite interpretation, that the nation was paramount, was based on the very opening words of the Constitution, "We the people of the United States." *The people* created a National Government, and "delegated to it certain sovereign powers." Therefore individual states were not sovereign powers, but were subject to the sovereignty of the people of the entire nation as a whole. Daniel Webster phrased it thus:

"[The national government] is established by the people of the United States. It does not say by the people of the several states. It is as *all* the people of the United States that they established the Constitution."

A wide divergence of opinion existed here. It was to brew the direst consequences for the nation in future years.

2

In taking his next steps, Calhoun moved carefully. Before he acted, he felt, it was important to discover how the President stood in the matter.

There were reasons to think that Jackson might not be unsympathetic toward the underlying theme of Calhoun's thinking. Old Hickory was a slaveowner, a planter, a native of South Carolina, and he had received his strongest political support from the South and West. But Jackson proved sphinxlike on the subject.

It was noted that one of the President's favorite friends in the Senate was Robert Y. Hayne, of South Carolina, whose views on the tariff and state sovereignty were well known. For this reason, perhaps as much as any other, Hayne was chosen as the instrument for a salvo in behalf of state sovereignty, which it was hoped would find support in all the Southern and many of the Western states.

The occasion was well arranged. Using as a springboard a resolution concerned with the sale of public lands, not particularly germane to his subject, Hayne, an orator hardly matched in the South, which in that day was notable for its orators, launched forth suddenly and unexpectedly, on a speech that brilliantly set forth the theory of state sovereignty with all the concomitant principles involved. So effective was his effort that it created consternation among the strong Union advocates in the Senate, who hardly saw how anyone could reply to it on short notice.

But sitting in the Senate, listening closely, was a short, stalwart man, very dark in complexion, with a massive head, "a vast triangular breadth of jaw," and thick black eyebrows overhanging cavernous eyes of extraordinary brilliance—Daniel Webster. He devoted intense concentration to every word of Hayne's address. When the session closed he announced he would answer it on the morrow.

Next day, January 26, 1830, the Senate was packed, and even the lobbies and halls of the Capitol were crowded almost to suffocation. When Webster took the floor his face was grave, even portentous. With a brief exordium, he called for a reading of the resolution on which Hayne had launched his speech, thus calling attention to the artifice employed.

Then, gathering his mighty powers he began one of the greatest orations in American history, his famous "Reply to Hayne." For three hours his magnificent organ tones, and his matchless eloquence with its mighty Miltonian phrases, held every hearer as in a hypnotic trance. And when he concluded with the solemn yet inspiring words, "Liberty *and* Union, now and forever, one and inseparable!" he brought his auditors to their feet in an ovation such as the Senate has rarely if ever heard before or since.

Webster had spoken, with awesome thunder—but for the North. It remained to hear what the man whose opinion the rest of the nation most eagerly awaited would have to say on the subject.

Thomas Jefferson, now dead these four years, had set forth the conclusion that the Union was "a federation by the consent of the states," upon which Calhoun placed his interpretation that consent, if given, can be withdrawn as an inherent right. He and his followers now planned a banquet, ostensibly to celebrate the birthday of Jefferson, but really to "smoke out" Andrew Jackson on the issue, under circumstances where it was believed he would hardly dare openly oppose the manifest feelings of his strongest political supporters.

All Jeffersonians of any prominence would wish to attend such a banquet. It was skillfully managed. The occasion would be brilliant; there would be a series of toasts by eloquent speakers, building toward a toast to the Virginia and Kentucky resolutions of Jefferson, to be followed by the final set toast given by Hayne himself, which would draw an analogy between the time of Jefferson's pronouncement and the present moment when the government was, to his viewpoint, again assuming tyrannical powers over the states.

By courtesy the first volunteer toast would be that of the President, and Calhoun and his group confidently expected that after the eloquent build-up Andrew Jackson would hardly consider it politic to go against his own party spokesmen, his own people, and the "principles of democractic justice" as presented. With Old Hickory on record as an ally, or even neutral, Calhoun would have what is now called a great "breakthrough" toward his next daring maneuver.

Jackson accepted the invitation to the dinner which honored the great father of democracy. In the months since he arrived in Washington, old, grief-stricken, weary, and hardly knowing to whom he could turn for friendship, the general had proved to enemies and friends alike that he had a volcanic inner force that made light of difficulties. Now, though he seemed cordial to everyone, his strange, stern, white-faced personality immediately dominated the room as he entered it.

Calhoun himself escorted him to the place of honor at the head of the first table—of which there were two. Thomas Hart Benton—who had excoriated Webster after the latter's speech—sat beside him. At the other end of the table was Calhoun, with Hayne at his right. Up and down the tables could be seen most of the important political leaders of both the South and West, a very notable assembly. One delegation, from Pennsylvania, pointedly had withdrawn, after looking over the printed list of toasts, and seeing their trend. But when Jackson picked up and glanced over the program, he set it down serenely, without a change of expression. From this Calhoun's coterie surmised that he at least did not disagree with its tenor. Though Old Hickory hardly spoke, everyone was conscious of his every movement.

Dinner completed, the toasts began. Calhoun rose and eulogized Thomas Jefferson, paying a flattering little tribute also to "our distinguished and beloved President, here present, a true exponent of the principles which he so splendidly shares with the late Sage of Monticello."

Applause. The President remained unmoved.

Twenty-four toasts followed—half of them, it was said, written by

Calhoun himself—together forming a superb edifice of forensic archi-
tecture, culminating in a brilliant oratorical flourish by Hayne, making
the final argument for state sovereignty.

The climactic moment had now come. The President of the United
States was introduced.

As Jackson rose, the whole assemblage rose spontaneously with him,
cheering and applauding. The old soldier stood silent, with raised
glass, until quiet was resumed and the gentlemen took their seats.
Every ear strained to hear him; the atmosphere fairly crackled with
excitement.

The old general fixed his intense blue eyes on Calhoun. In the utter
stillness that fell his voice was clearly heard:

"Our Union: *It must be preserved!*"

A gasp, then silence as if everyone held his breath. Calhoun could
not have looked more staggered if someone had struck him a blow.

But Andrew Jackson still stood grimly, his glass raised, a sign that
the toast should be drunk standing. There were men at the tables who
perhaps would almost have preferred drinking poison, but under the
sheer compelling power of Jackson's will, they began to get to their
feet, some promptly, others unwillingly. Calhoun rose, but his hand
trembled so that he spilled a trickle of wine upon the white tablecloth.

The old soldier raised his glass to his lips; and every man present
obeyed the unspoken command and did likewise.[2] When the toast
was drunk, the President excused himself to return to the White
House. Two men rushed to intercept him. One was Hayne, his face
pale, who asked anxiously if, before his toast was given to the newspapers for publication, the general would permit the insertion of one
word.

"What word?" asked Jackson.

"The word 'Federal,' making it 'Our Federal Union—'"

Hayne thought this might give the statement a less uncompromising
flavor. But Jackson, realizing it only strengthened his position, gave
permission, and so his toast appeared in print next day.

The second who reached him before he left the room was Thomas
Hart Benton, the great bull of a Missourian, who once had been Jackson's deadly enemy. Now, extending his hand, he exclaimed, "Sir, in
one sentence you have done more than Daniel Webster did in three
hours of oratory. You have convinced Tom Benton."

Old Hickory grasped his hand, well pleased. "If I only did that, it
would be worth everything," he said. He meant it. Benton was speak-

---

[2] They did not know that originally Jackson had framed his single sentence:
"Our Union: It must *and shall* be preserved!" Van Buren induced him to leave
out the two words as perhaps unduly antagonistic.

ing not only for himself, but for the West, which had been waiting to hear Andrew Jackson's pronouncement.

Calhoun attempted a reply to the President's toast which was the essence of anticlimax: "The Union, next to our liberties most dear . . ." But when Jackson departed the banquet "fell to pieces," and Calhoun was left to the melancholy contemplation of how that which began as a brilliant fanfare for state sovereignty had been punctured by one brief, stern sentence.

Benton was not wrong in his estimate of the importance of Jackson's trenchant phrase. Webster had aroused tumultuous applause, and his speech (carefully amended and polished) was published and widely distributed. But Webster spoke as a Northerner, and particularly as a New Englander. A large part of his speech in fact was devoted to defending the record of Massachusetts, whose behavior in the War of 1812 had drawn Hayne's fire.

But Jackson spoke for all the country—even for those in South Carolina herself, like stanch Joel Poinsett, who believed in the Union. His six words—increased to seven at Hayne's request—carried more weight at that time than did Webster's hours of thunderings.

It was his first clash with Calhoun, and he came off with all the honors. Furthermore, as one writer stated it, "From that hour, thereafter, the vigilant old President watched the South Carolina conspirator . . . with the searching eyes of unslumbering suspicion."

Uncompromisingly Jackson had laid down the principle that the United States was sovereign over any individual state, or any individual person, however ambitious. It was a principle, now first enunciated by a President, which later would be terribly enforced in a war under the leadership of another President, like Jackson a Westerner and a dedicated champion of the Union—Abraham Lincoln.

3

Ambition is not a defect in any man, if it is properly pursued. Nor, for that matter, is a change of position on a political issue, when that change is a matter of conviction.

And it should be remarked that the whole theory of state sovereignty did become a matter of intense personal conviction to John Calhoun in his later years.

But if he might be upheld on that score, he did have one failing hard to condone: he was not always entirely candid.

One matter on which he was equivocal was his behavior during the period when Andrew Jackson was under fire for his actions in Florida during the Seminole campaign. In the heated three-day cabinet argument that followed on that occasion the representations of British envoy, and the demands by the Spanish minister for restitution of all losses and "punishment of the general [Jackson]," President Monroe and every member of his cabinet, except John Quincy Adams, were for disavowing Jackson. Calhoun, then Secretary of War, whose order sent Jackson on the campaign, was particularly censorious, and would have sacrificed the general to smooth over the international crisis.

All this, as the atmosphere cleared, and particularly as Jackson grew in national stature, the South Carolinian was anxious to cover up and have forgotten. He had in fact personally assured Jackson that in those troublous days he was one who upheld his cause in the cabinet.

This avoidance of the strict truth now returned suddenly to confront him.

To go back in history for a brief look: While Calhoun was Secretary of War, in 1818, a delegation of Cherokee Indians, in Washington for negotiation over some of their lands, was brought to visit him in his office. They were shepherded by a young army lieutenant, who had taken them East under Jackson's orders, and who was especially qualified for the mission because he had lived among the Indians, knew their language and customs, and was the adopted son of one of their chiefs. To make himself more agreeable to them, the lieutenant even attired himself in Cherokee costume; which was perfectly good diplomacy if one knew Indian ways.

Calhoun received the Cherokees courteously, but he called the lieutenant before him later and harshly reprimanded him for appearing "dressed as a savage." The fact that the young officer was still suffering from wounds received in the Creek War did not excuse him in Calhoun's mind for his lack of punctilio. To make matters worse, Calhoun next accused the lieutenant of complicity with slave smugglers —a charge the officer quickly and definitely proved false. Even then the Secretary of War expressed no regret for his hasty accusation; nor did he investigate the crooked politicians who really were guilty of the offense charged.

The young officer was Lieutenant Sam Houston. All his life Houston was notable for two traits: unswerving loyalty to his friends; unending resentment toward his enemies. He now considered Calhoun an enemy, and forthwith resigned his commission, to study law and enter politics. Years later, in Jackson's second Presidential campaign, Houston obtained possession of a letter which he used to seek retribution. It had been written by former President Monroe, and it indicated that Calhous had *not* supported Jackson in the Florida argument—quite the contrary.

Old Hickory said, when he saw the letter, "My hair stood on end for an hour." But Martin Van Buren was at hand, striving to keep the

path of the campaign smooth, and since the letter was not entirely
specific, Jackson allowed himself to be soothed so that no open break
with Calhoun occurred at the time. Calhoun, of course, was unaware
that the general had seen such a letter.

Ever since he assumed office Jackson had found Calhoun a vexing
problem. Now Calhoun was advocating nullification, which would
inevitably lead to disunion. To anyone who fully appraised Andrew
Jackson, his pronouncement at the Jefferson Day banquet should have
been no great surprise. He was close-mouthed, and with unerring instinct he reserved expression of his sentiments until Calhoun's strata-
gem gave him the perfect opportunity and rostrum publicly to state
them. The President's single greatest loyalty was to his nation. The
mere threat of disunion aroused his iron opposition. Calhoun failed to
read the signs.

It happened that very soon after the banquet episode Jackson received from William H. Crawford, who had been Secretary of the
Treasury during the Florida cabinet arguments, a letter which recalled the one Houston had shown him previously, concerning Calhoun. Houston was now out of the picture, having resigned his governorship of Tennessee for reasons sufficiently bizarre, and after that
plunged into the wilderness, to live once more among the Indians. But
Crawford's letter revived all the former implications.

The writer, who had never fully recovered from his paralysis, was
at this time a judge in Georgia. He sought to cover up his own actions
during the cabinet debate over Jackson, but stated positively that Calhoun had been ready and willing to have the general arrested and
disgraced to mollify Spain and Britain.

Jackson read the letter—the vindictiveness of which did little credit
to Crawford—and sent a copy of it to Calhoun with a curt covering
note:

> Sir . . . The Enclosed copy of a letter from William Crawford,
> Esq . . . was placed in my hands yesterday . . . My object in
> making this communication is to announce to you the great sur-
> prise which is felt, and to learn whether it is possible that the
> information given is correct . . . I am, sir, very respectfully,
>   Your humble servant, Andrew Jackson.

Calhoun was stunned. He wrote a letter of explanation, labored and
partly directed to show Crawford's kindred responsibility. But he
could not explain away his position in 1818, nor, what was more damn-
ing, the deception in both his letters and personal statements, whereby
he had concealed that position from Jackson in all the intervening
years.

It was final and decisive parting of the ways. Thence onward Calhoun could only devote himself to the constantly increasing effort to erect state sovereignty as a national issue. In the following years he was to turn his very considerable talents of logic and expression to his "great and almost interminable rationale": his interpretation that the Constitution was in reality a protection "against the tyranny of a political majority"; the presentation of the tenet that powers delegated by the states could be withdrawn by them at will; and the bolstering of the position that if any "sovereign" state felt its will ignored by the federal government, it could threaten nullification, or secession, and if need be carry them out.

CHAPTER NINE

The Bank and Henry Clay

1

MEANTIME the exasperating Peggy Eaton affair was coming to a head. Wrote John Campbell, a friend of Jackson's and a close observer:

> How Old Hickory (who always becomes greater by difficulties) is to get out of the Scrape [of the Eaton affair] I cannot say . . . The President . . . *believes* Eaton & his wife are innocent & would no longer be Andrew Jackson if any earthly consideration of popularity could induce him to give way and surrender them up.

All true, but Peggy herself was making the "difficulties" even more difficult for the old general. Her effrontery caused rebellion in his own household. Emily Donelson, a kind and unselfish young woman, at last had too much. In a tearful scene she announced that she was leaving the White House with her family, and returning to Tennessee. Her husband, Jack Donelson, persuaded by a moving letter from Jackson, agreed to remain on to the close of the Congressional session before he followed her.

When she learned that Emily Donelson was to leave, Peggy Eaton sensed a great triumph for herself. Washington gossips already were calling her the "Unofficial First Lady." Perhaps her ambitions went even higher—it would be in keeping with her character. But in reality the departure of Emily Donelson was the beginning of Peggy's downfall.

Quite unexpectedly the President decided to return to the West with his niece and her children. His reasons were not entirely personal. A curious and rather knotty problem had presented itself in the disputes over Indian lands in the Southern states.

Georgia, in 1802, had ceded to the United States western territories she claimed (now included in the states of Alabama and Mississippi) in consideration of a payment of $1,250,000, and the stipulation that Indian title to lands within the state should be extinguished "as early as the same can be peaceably obtained on reasonable terms." But the Cherokees, who held considerable lands in Georgia, had been guaranteed possession in the Holston Treaty of 1791. They made several treaties giving up part of their country and permitted roads across the rest of it in succeeding years, but they insisted on clinging to much of it.

The "extinguishing" process was going far too slowly to satisfy the citizens of Georgia. At length the state by legislative enactment extended its authority over Indian lands within its borders. Settlers already had been drifting into Cherokee country, particularly after gold was discovered there in 1828–29.

The Cherokees, recognized as a sovereign nation in a succession of treaties, went to the courts, and litigation reached as high as the Supreme Court, the final ruling of which, in favor of the Indians, Georgia openly flouted. Now two other states, Alabama and Mississippi, also became interested in having the Indians removed, for the red men occupied great areas of prime cotton land, rapidly increasing in value. They joined Georgia in her demands. Not only Cherokees, but also Choctaws, Chickasaws, and Creeks were affected by the brewing problem.

To Andrew Jackson, the old borderer and Indian fighter, there could be only one side to this controversy—that of the settlers. But refusal to obey the dictates of the Supreme Court was a form of nullification. He knew he would have to deal with nullification in South Carolina, and he wished if possible to avert nullification in other states, which would dangerously complicate matters.

Therefore he did what no other President did before or after: he attended in person a great Indian council, to persuade the tribes to accept the inevitable and move to new lands across the Mississippi which he was providing for them. The Choctaws had given him a formal invitation, and he set the meeting place for all the four tribes to gather at Franklin, Tennessee, south of Nashville.

The Chickasaws from Mississippi were first at the appointed place, but the Choctaws were late in arriving. The Cherokees and Creeks do not seem to have sent any representatives, though undoubtedly some of their warriors may have been present as observers.

Jackson went to the council at no little security risk. There were Indians present who probably had personal hatreds against him because of his border activities, and feeling was heated among even the least violently inclined because of the wrongs they felt. Here, now, was the supreme chief of the white men, within reach, even in their power, temporarily at least. A shot fired or a blow struck might eliminate him forever.

But the tall, erect white-haired soldier walked among them with not one evidence of fear. Older Indians who knew him called him Sharp Knife, and there were Choctaws present who had fought under him at New Orleans. Sharp Knife gravely greeted the chiefs who came to shake his hand, and the Indians were given a feast. When the usual lengthy preliminaries of all Indian councils were completed, including the smoking of the ceremonial pipe handed from one to another, the President of the United States addressed the assemblage through an interpreter:

"Friends and brothers: . . . You have long dwelt on the soil you occupy, and in early times before the white man kindled his fires too near to yours . . . you were a happy people. Now your white brothers are around you . . . Your great father . . . asks if you are prepared and ready to submit to the laws of Mississippi, and make a surrender of your ancient laws and customs and live peaceably . . .

"Brothers, listen—To these laws [of Mississippi], where you are, you must submit—there is no alternative. Your great father cannot, nor can Congress, prevent it . . . Do you believe that you can live under those laws? That you can surrender all your ancient habits, and the forms by which you have been so long controlled? If so, your great father has nothing to say or advise . . . Where you are, it is not possible that you could ever live contented and happy . . .

"Old men! Lead your children [instead] to a land of promise and of peace before the Great Spirit shall call you to die. Young chiefs! Preserve your people and nation . . .

"Brothers listen— . . . Reject the opportunity which is now offered you to obtain comfortable homes, and it may not be offered again . . . If you are disposed to remove, do so, and state the terms you may consider just and equitable . . ."[1]

His speech concluded, he returned to Nashville, leaving to John Henry Eaton, the Secretary of War, and his old friend General John Coffee the actual discussion of terms. Four days later he learned that the Chickasaws had agreed. His words had made such an impression that the Choctaws, Cherokees, and Creeks also capitulated later.

He had succeeded so well that all the Southern tribes, except the Seminoles, moved without armed resistance—though as it turned out, with much unwillingness, loss and suffering—to the trans-Mississippi. The Northern tribes also moved eventually. Two tribes went to war rather than move. In Florida, the Seminoles took to the warpath in 1835 and killed many soldiers and citizens before they finally were

[1] Excerpts from his speech as published in the *Western Sun*, September 25, 1830, which in turn had republished it from the Nashville *Republican* of a previous date.

conquered in 1842. Most of them were transported to what is now Oklahoma, but a remnant still lives in the Everglades of Florida. In Illinois and Wisconsin a faction of the Sauk and Fox Indians waged the so-called Black Hawk War, in 1832. There were numerous killings on both sides, but the Sauks and Foxes were defeated and forced to comply. Serving as a captain of a militia company in this war, was a young man named Abraham Lincoln.

By 1840 all of the Indians east of the Mississippi—about 60,000 persons—had been removed except for a few here and there who were allowed to remain.

When he returned to Washington, Jackson was at least hopeful that if he had to face nullification it would be one crisis at a time. He settled down to attack this and other problems of his administration.

From his cabinet he received little help or even loyalty. In the Peggy Eaton troubles only Van Buren, and of course Eaton himself, had been of any assistance. The others—perhaps coerced by their wives—followed Calhoun's lead in that travesty of social behavior. Furthermore, Postmaster General Barry, Attorney General Berrien, Secretary of the Navy Branch, and Secretary of the Treasury Ingham could not be counted upon to back him in the coming battle with the Bank of the United States for which the President already was preparing.

In their place he accepted the advice and assistance of a group of friends who often met informally at the White House to discuss problems. Among these were Amos Kendall, who helped draft many of Jackson's official communications and formed a sort of news bureau for the Presidential acts and statements; Francis Preston Blair, the diminutive editor of the Washington *Globe*, which now—since Duff Green and his *United States Telegraph* had swung over to the support of Calhoun—was the official administration newspaper; Jack Donelson, the President's nephew and secretary; Martin Van Buren, John Henry Eaton, and sometimes Thomas Hart Benton. Old Hickory's enemies derisively dubbed this group the "Kitchen Cabinet"—a name that stuck and in later years became in some sort an honor.

Uncomplainingly the old general shouldered the extra work necessitated by the dissension in his official family. Plagued as he was and laboring beyond his strength, matters were made no easier for him by Peggy Eaton, who continued to flaunt her entree into the White House, to the intense irritation of her feminine rivals.

Calhoun, bitterly jealous of Van Buren, at this time published a pamphlet attacking the Secretary of State as a political troublemaker. He only succeeded in causing Old Hickory's hackles to rise once more. Thus the South Carolinian cut the last bridge behind him.

At this juncture a curious little sequence of events relieved the

President of at least one—and not the least annoying—of his problems. It was Van Buren who one day startled Jackson by tendering his resignation, carefully making it clear that he did so to "smooth" matters for his friend and chief. Jackson received the resignation reluctantly, but with gratitude for Van Buren's ostensible unselfishness.

When it was announced to the cabinet, John Henry Eaton at last was brought face to face with himself. With unmistakable clarity he saw the schemings of his wife in a new light. Suddenly he spoke up:

"Gentlemen, this is all wrong. I am the one who ought to resign."

"Will your wife agree?" asked Van Buren slyly.

"She will agree," grimly said the harried husband, his mind at last made up. His resignation was duly presented and accepted.

The "reign" of Peggy Eaton was ended.

She had ruined her husband politically. Though, after his resignation, he was appointed governor of Florida and later minister to Spain, he never again could win an election in his own state, Tennessee.

Other cabinet resignations—in some cases asked for by the President—followed, creating a sensation in Washington and over the country. Jackson replaced the departed gentlemen with others of greater capacity, for by this time he had been given time to observe and study men. General Lewis Cass of Ohio replaced Eaton as Secretary of War. Edward Livingston of Louisiana, an old friend of the New Orleans days, succeeded Van Buren as Secretary of State while the latter was appointed minister to England. Others were Levi Woodbury of New Hampshire, Navy; Louis McLane of Delaware, Treasury; and Roger B. Taney of Maryland, Attorney General. Taney, little known at the time, carelessly attired, tall and lean, with squinting eyes due to bad sight, and tobacco-stained teeth, was to prove one of the nation's finest legal minds, and one day would succeed John Marshall as Chief Justice of the Supreme Court.

With the unwilling exit from the Washington scene of Peggy Eaton, Emily Donelson and her children returned to the White House, and for the first time since he occupied it, the Executive Mansion became a pleasant place for Andrew Jackson to live in, as pretty Emily invited young people of her own age to come as guests and brighten the great house. The general seemed visibly younger and stronger.

2

In the midst of this, in December 1831, a figure right out of the pages of romance stepped upon the stage. Sam Houston, who was governor of Tennessee when Jackson left for Washington, had sustained an almost incredible reverse of fortune. He was married, January

22, 1829, to Miss Eliza Allen, accounted beautiful, a daughter of a prominent family living near Gallatin, Tennessee. The bride was eighteen, the groom had just turned thirty-four.

Houston was already campaigning for re-election, and was considered quite sure of defeating William Carroll, his opponent, when, on April 16, 1829, he stunned the state by resigning his office and withdrawing from the race, in a letter to William Hall, Speaker of the Tennessee Senate, in which his only reason was given as "private afflictions . . . deep and incurable."

What he was referring to was the fact that his bride of less than three months had left him and returned to her father's home. Who was to blame? It is evident that Eliza was immature and unprepared for marriage. They had not gotten along well from the very first day after their wedding, when the girl, for no apparent reason, told Mrs. Robert Martin, when they stopped overnight at the Martin plantation, that she hated her husband.

Speculations were endless, but Houston never in all his life revealed his story to anyone, except a hint in a heartbroken letter to Colonel John Allen, Eliza's father.

In that desperate missive he wrote:

> Whatever had been my feelings in relation to Eliza at one period, I have been satisfied and believe her virtuous . . . That she is the only earthly object dear to me God will bear me witness. Eliza stands acquitted by me. She was cold to me, and I thought she did not love me; but she knows that such was one cause of my unhappiness . . .

This letter indicates that he had at one time accused or at least suspected her of unfaithfulness, but later believed her innocent; also that she was unresponsive to his lovemaking.

Publicly, Houston only said, "Remember that whatever may be said by the lady or her friends, it is no part of the conduct of a gallant or generous man to take up arms against a woman. If my character cannot stand the shock, let me lose it."

That was all, concerning a mystery that left generations of historians speculating as to just what happened.

Houston was gone and the speculations wildly circulated. His enemies freely stated that he had "wronged" his wife: in what manner they did not specify. Comparatively recently (in 1962) some documents were disclosed which purport to give Eliza's version of the story, or at least explain her behavior. She seems to have talked to Balie Peyton, later a Congressman, shortly after her separation from Houston and his astounding resignation followed by his leaving the world of civilization. Peyton, fifty years later, in 1878, dictated to his daughter his recollection of what Eliza said. In substance it was as follows:

"I left General Houston because I found he was a demented man. I believed him to be crazy. He is insanely jealous and suspicious. He required me to promise not to speak to anyone, and to lock myself in my room if he was absent . . . On one occasion . . . after he was gone, I found he had locked the door and carried off the key, leaving me a prisoner until late at night . . . He gave additional evidence of an unsound mind by his belief in ghosts. He was timid and averse to being alone at night, on account of these imaginary and supernatural influences . . ."[2]

Allowing for possible inaccuracies on the part of Balie Peyton, in reciting a memory half a century old, this statement has the unhappily familiar sound of divorce court charges made by women who assert "extreme cruelty" in asking for separation from their mates. Houston was splendidly sane. If he was "suspicious," perhaps Eliza gave him cause to be—there is a hint of this in his letter to her father. As to his fear of being alone at night, on account of "ghosts," this is too ridiculous to give a second thought. If anything, the statement merely shows evidence that poor Eliza felt in need of self-justification when she realized the catastrophe she had caused.

3

After he left Nashville, Houston for a time lived with his old friends the Cherokees, in what is now eastern Oklahoma. Jackson learned of his tragedy with regret, for he had important plans for the younger man. Some have speculated that had it not been for Eliza Allen, Sam Houston might one day have occupied the White House.

In the Indian country the self-exile drank heavily, and for a time took Tiana Rogers, an Indian woman, as wife under Cherokee custom. Twice before his 1831 appearance the spectacular Houston had visited Washington clad in the garments of a Cherokee. The first time was in 1818, when as an army lieutenant he brought a group of Indians to Washington, and encountered the displeasure of John Calhoun, then Secretary of War. The second instance was in January 1830 when, after being made a "citizen of the Cherokee Nation," he went to Washington as ambassador for that tribe to protest against certain corrupt

[2] Published in the *Nashville Tennesseean*, August 19, 1962.

Indian agents—five of whom were dismissed—and to bid on supplying rations at a rate cheaper, for superior quality, than the rations then being supplied.

Largely through the efforts of Duff Green, of the *United States Telegraph*, a friend of John F. Hamtramck, one of the agents dismissed, Houston's bid was rejected. On this third visit, in December 1831, he arrived in Washington accompanying, but not a member of, another Cherokee delegation; and with certain interesting plans in his head.

After his visit of the previous year Houston had been accused by Dr. Robert Mayo, in a statement written to Andrew Jackson, December 2, 1830, as follows:

> Houston is organizing an expedition against Texas; to afford a cloak for which he has assumed the Indian costume, habits and associations, by settling among them in the neighborhood of Texas . . . and by the co-operation of the Indians in the Arkansas Territory and recruits among citizens of the United States . . . form a separate and independent government.

There was some truth to this, although Houston's "intentions" toward Texas seem to have been more alcohol-inspired than thought out. He had received letters from various speculative persons, urging such a project and offering services and even funds for it.

But Jackson was attempting with indifferent success to purchase Texas from Mexico, and wanted nobody to muddy the diplomatic waters. When Houston returned to the Indian country, he was kept under surveillance lest he do something rash, and the general wrote him a letter of fatherly admonishment, asking his "pledge of honor" never to "engage in any enterprise injurious to your country, that will tarnish your honor."

Houston gave the pledge.

And now he was back in Washington for the third time, frankly trying to raise funds for a personal visit to Texas—for exactly what purpose he did not disclose. The raising of such funds was difficult, perhaps because of his reputation for drunkenness, acquired during his years among the Cherokees.

At this time Houston was a mature man, who "stood six feet six inches in his socks,[3] was of fine contour, a remarkably well propor-

[3] His Army record gave his height as six feet two inches. It presumably was based on his measurement when he enlisted at the age of eighteen during the War of 1812. Not only are Army records notoriously inexact, but Houston could have grown considerably after that age. Six feet, six inches, seems to be the accepted height for his maturity.

tioned man, and of commanding and gallant bearing; had a large, long head and face and his fine features were lit up by large eagle-looking eyes; possessed of a wonderful recollection of persons and names, a fine address and courtly manners and a magnetism approaching that of General Andrew Jackson. He enjoyed unbounded popularity among men and was a great favorite with the ladies."[4]

He appeared in Washington clad in the habiliments of a Cherokee chief, complete with buckskin coat, moccasins, blanket, and a bowie knife at his belt. Jackson received him at the White House as before, buckskin and all. Texas undoubtedly was on his mind when he invited the visitor to dinner, and studied him carefully. Old Hickory believed that the province legitimately belonged to the United States under the terms of the Louisiana Purchase from Napoleon, whose records show that he regarded the Rio Grande as the southward limit of the territory Spain yielded to him. The President, moreover, was concerned about the thousands of American colonists in Texas, living and working there, acting as a sort of buffer against the wild Comanches and Kiowas of the plains, and growing rebellious as one after another of their constitutional rights were taken from them by a series of Mexican dictators. He had tried to buy Texas for $5,000,000, but the offer was rejected.

During the third Washington visit Houston enlivened things by trouncing an Ohio Representative named William Stanbery, for a baseless attack on Jackson during which he inquired oratorically on the floor of Congress, "Was not the late Secretary of War [Eaton] removed because of his attempt fraudulently to give Governor Houston the contract for the Indian rations?"

No fraud was involved, and after the infuriated Houston was through with him—though Stanbery attempted to shoot his assailant with a pistol that misfired—the Congressman took to his bed for a few days to nurse his contusions, and Houston was summoned before the House of Representatives to answer a charge of assaulting a Representative for words spoken in a debate.

Once more Jackson called Houston to the White House. The President knew that his enemies were trying to create a grave incident out of the street fight, to get at him indirectly. Looking over Houston's bizarre buckskin attire, he tossed a silk purse across the table.

"Dress like a gentleman and buck up your defense," he said.

Houston did as directed, going to a tailor for "a coat of finest material, reaching to my knees, trousers in harmony of color and the latest style and cut, with a white satin vest to match." He always looked most impressive in fine garments.

[4] Judge Jo Conn Guild, *Old Times in Tennessee.*

The trial lasted a full month and aroused national interest. He largely conducted his own case, although his attorney was Francis Scott Key, author of *The Star-Spangled Banner*. At the end he made a speech so appealing and eloquent that the galleries gave him an ovation. The House—to uphold Congressional immunity—voted that he be punished, but with the mildest punishment possible, a reprimand. When, on May 14, Andrew Stevenson, Speaker of the House, gave the reprimand he so surrounded it with encomiums for Houston's services to the country that it amounted to an accolade rather than a condemnation.

Once more Sam Houston had become a public figure to be reckoned with. Thereafter he and Jackson had another long conference. There can be little question that they came to an understanding of some kind on the Texas matter. Jackson advanced him five hundred dollars for expenses, and Houston departed—as a confidential representative of the President.

4

In his months in office Old Hickory had impressed the capital more and more with his qualities of mind and person and with the power of his will. He came to Washington advertised as a "savage" with backwoods manners and rude speech. Instead he proved to be courteous, even urbane, well spoken, with a courtly manner that won ladies and gentlemen alike. Daniel Webster somewhat ruefully confessed, "My wife is for him, decidedly."

He possessed, according to Benton, a power of "judgment, with a rapid and almost intuitive perception, followed by an instant and decisive action." And he had, moreover, developed a remarkable flair for political strategy, together with an almost unprecedented hold on the imaginations of the people.

He had need for these things for he now faced an adversary whose tactics were more subtle than those of any opponent he had ever faced.

Quietly Nicholas Biddle had been working to neutralize the President's opposition to the Bank of the United States. His first efforts were directed at influencing Old Hickory himself. Using the great resources of his Bank, he established a branch in Nashville, and appointed some of Jackson's friends on the board of directors. He went further, and placed Jackson men on boards of others of his twenty-five branches, from one end of the country to the other, on the theory that their self-interest would induce them to intervene with the Chief Magistrate.

Meantime he continually subsidized newspapers to win their support, and extended financial "courtesies" to important political figures of all persuasions, including loans which, in one instance, permitted repayment at fifty cents on the dollar.

When the President showed no signs of relenting, Biddle played his ace card, nothing less than a bid to Jackson in person. He knew that the old soldier's darling ambition was to pay off the national debt. Making a visit to the White House, the banker coupled a plan whereby the public debt would be extinguished—by the help of his institution—with a proposal to recharter the Bank ahead of time. The public debt then was $48,522,000, and Biddle's suggestion included a flattering hint—that the last installment of the debt might well be paid on January 8, 1833, the anniversary of the Battle of New Orleans.

Jackson thanked the banker but did not take the bait. In his next message to Congress he stated that the Bank of the United States was of doubtful constitutionality, and urged a substitute for it, "Founded upon the credit of the Government and its revenue." The showdown had become inevitable.

5

The issues of the tariff and the Bank were matters of absorbing interest to Henry Clay, as the election year of 1832 approached. The brilliant Kentuckian, disappointed and bitter, had retired to his plantation after Jackson smashed his political plans in 1828. But it was impossible for him to remain idle long. Still pursuing his dream of the Presidency, he induced the Kentucky legislature to elect him to the Senate in 1831, and quietly and smoothly began to gather together the opponents of Jackson—and they were not few—to weld them into a party of his own.

John Quincy Adams' wing of the Jeffersonian Republican party had called itself National Republican, while the Jacksonian wing was known as Democratic Republican. These terms were quickly shortened to Nationals and Democrats, and when Clay took over the former its popular name became Whigs.

That fall of 1831, Clay was nominated for the Presidency by the Whigs, and from the beginning he mustered powerful support among the industrialists, the great merchants, the financial interests, the diehard Federalists, in fact conservatives of all kinds. Watching Jackson's rift with Calhoun, Clay believed he also could receive the backing of the state sovereignty faction.

Although the President at times expressed the desire to retire from public life, he realized that he could not now surrender the wheel of the ship of state in the face of the crises impending. He announced that he would seek re-election, and since Van Buren had not been confirmed as minister to England,[5] he insisted over considerable opposition that his former Secretary of State should be his running mate.

Clay took the initiative in the coming battle. On the Senate floor Thomas Hart Benton thunderously attacked the Bank of the United States as "too great and powerful to be tolerated in a government of free and equal people." But Clay, the master politician, quietly assayed the Members of Congress. Then he proposed to Biddle that the Bank's recharter be brought up *at once,* with the assurance that he could command the necessary votes to carry it in both Houses. His reasoning for this political strategy was that if the recharter was carried Jackson, with the bill before him, would be weakened whether he signed it or vetoed it. In either event he would alienate large and important elements of the nation.

Clay had the Presidency very much in view. Previously he had advised against this very move; and now Biddle at first hesitated. But the banker had grown arrogant with power, until he actually considered his institution on a level with the government itself, "beyond political good or evil," and at the same time regarded himself as the most powerful man in the nation, except perhaps the President—and perhaps not even excepting the President.

He allowed himself to be persuaded by Clay that he and his Bank could override any opposition, especially when that opposition was headed by a backwoods statesman like Jackson. On January 9, 1832, petitions for the recharter—*four years ahead of time*—were presented to both Houses of Congress.

The first great head-on collision of principles had come. Hamiltonian Federalism faced Jacksonian Democracy; property control of government faced control by the populace; the aristocrat faced the commoner.

Jackson sensed Biddle's imperial attitude, and he knew the struggle would be fierce if he undertook it. But he considered the Bank "a hydra of corruption," gaining its great wealth and power through government patronage. And he had witnessed the spectacle of flush times in the West, followed by panics and distress, which he blamed on the Bank's manipulations of currency and credits. He was ready to do battle against it.

[5] By a contrived tie vote Calhoun had the satisfaction of casting the deciding ballot against Van Buren's confirmation. Over this act he was gleeful. "It will kill him, sir, kill him dead," he exulted. "He will never stir, never kick."

Quoth Thomas Hart Benton, "You have broken a minister, sir, and elected a Vice-President." He might well have said, "and elected a President," for from that day Van Buren was Jackson's choice as his successor.

When he called a council of war, however, both Benton, leader of the administration forces in the Senate, and James Knox Polk, who led those forces in the House, warned him that Clay and Biddle had the votes to carry the recharter proposition in this session. They, and others of his advisers, urged him not to imperil his own prestige as well as that of the administration, by fighting a losing battle. Old Hickory listened to them grimly, then gave his orders: Fight the recharter, fight it to the finish, fight it to the last ditch.

Knowing he would lose, what he demanded was in essence a lengthy rear-guard action to delay the final vote as long as possible. Why? The old soldier had learned a great deal about politics. He saw that a quick decision would be a triumph for Clay and the Bank; while the longer final action was delayed, the more opportunity there would be to air the issue fully, so that the people would know the Bank and what it stood for; and, equally important, so that they would know the men who advocated this recharter four years ahead of time, and their real reasons for such precipitate action.

Like good lieutenants Benton and Polk took their orders, and at once began one of the lengthiest, most spectacular battles of Congressional history. Beneath all his bull-roaring, Benton was well conversed in parliamentary tricks; and Polk, comparatively new in the House of Representatives (he had succeeded Sam Houston when the latter became governor of Tennessee), though young and of unassuming appearance, was a shrewd political tactician.

Between them they devised and employed every kind of parliamentary expedient to postpone the final conclusive vote. Investigating committees held hearings; amendments were offered, and amendments to amendments; efforts were made to table, efforts to refer the recharter resolution to some committee which might not find it expedient to report it out; and each of these moves must be debated with incessant oratory, which occupied the legislative halls for weeks, turning into months.

In the meantime, the old soldier in the White House, employing the talents of Kendall and Blair, saw that all the debates, all the evidence amassed by the Jackson spokesmen, reached every newspaper that would publish them. These were, confessedly, chiefly country papers and small papers, for the more important journals in most cases had other ideas, for one reason or another.

In those days there seemed to be a special bond between Jackson and Kendall, a bond based on physical pain and illness. Kendall was bent nearly double by torturing arthritis. The President, with his lung abscess and his other ailments, sometimes had to lie on a couch to work. Often the two labored late at night, Kendall, with his bent back, crouching over sheets of paper on which he scribbled, while the President on a sofa, suggested or discussed questions with him. Between them the general public was made acquainted with instances of violations of the Bank's charter, abuses of the same, and other questionable points in the Bank's conduct, brought out in the battle raging then in Congress.

In spite of all his great skill in parliamentary proceedings, Clay found himself unable to gain the quick decision he desired; even though he was aided by all the power Biddle and the Bank could put at his disposal. Smooth lobbyists converged on Washington, using every art to win Congressmen to the side of the recharter. Loans continued to be made on almost ridiculously easy terms, and the Bank continued to subsidize newspapers on an increasing scale. An estimated two-thirds of the journals sided with the Bank. Many of these received direct loans from the Bank, although most of them perhaps yielded to advertising appropriations.[6]

6

Exciting scenes sometimes took place in Congress. Daniel Webster, like Clay on the payroll of the Bank as an attorney, thundered his denunciations at the anti-charter forces. Clay, lean, canny, at times charming, at other times bitterly sardonic, recognized Benton as his major opponent.

Thomas Hart Benton was at this time a large, powerfully built man, with black curly hair and sidewhiskers, strong Roman features, and a stentorian voice that compelled attention. In debate he had been compared to a wild buffalo which would "rush forward with blind fury upon every obstacle." Frequently he and Clay clashed.

On one occasion Clay sarcastically made reference to Benton's brawl with Jackson in 1813, adding that the Missourian had remarked that should the general be elected President, "Congress would have to guard itself with pistols and dirks."

Instantly Benton bounded to his feet. "That is an atrocious calumny!"

"What!" said Clay. "Can you look me in the face, sir, and say that you never used such language?"

"I look," retorted Benton, "and I repeat that it is an atrocious calumny, and I will pin it to him who repeats it here!"

---

[6] One of the glaring examples of subsidization was the *New York Trade Advocate*, a Jackson newspaper until, just after it received loans totaling nearly $135,000, it completely reversed its policy and supported the Bank with bitter editorials against the President.

Clay's face flushed with anger. "Then I declare before the Senate that you said to me the very words!"

"False! False! False!" roared Benton, moving wrathfully toward Clay.

The chamber was in an uproar. Other Senators hastened to intervene before blows were struck, for both men were known to be duelists.[7] Senator Littleton W. Tazewell, who was occupying the chair, hammered with his gavel and called the belligerents to order.

After some moments Benton cooled off and said, "I apologize to the Senate for the manner in which I have spoken—but not to the Senator from Kentucky." Immediately Clay responded, "To the Senate I also offer an apology, to the Senator from Missouri, none."

Later, however, the two men were induced to shake hands and the quarrel was not pursued—at least on the field of honor.

Contrary to Clay's implication, Benton stoutly supported Jackson, both in his first and second campaigns. The men, once foes, had developed warm mutual respect and friendship.[8]

At last, under Clay's remorseless pressure, the delaying actions one by one were surmounted. The final vote no longer could be delayed.

Nicholas Biddle in person came from Philadelphia to witness his triumph. On June 11 the bill for recharter passed the Senate 28 to 20, and the House 107 to 95. That night Biddle gave a victory party at a Washington hotel, with such a flow of champagne that several

---

[7] Clay had exchanged shots with Humphrey Marshall in Kentucky, in 1808, both men being wounded; and, as previously related, had called out John Randolph of Roanoke in 1826, puncturing that gentleman's coat tail with a pistol ball, although Randolph fired into the air. In addition to his near-deadly affray with Jackson, Benton met Charles Lucas, a lawyer, in a formal duel on "Bloody Island" near St. Louis, in 1827, and mortally wounded his antagonist while receiving a slight wound on one of his knees in return.

[8] On January 12, 1832, three days after the resolution to recharter was presented to Congress, the ball fired by Jesse Benton, the Senator's brother, was removed from Jackson's shoulder, without anesthetics, the old Spartan standing erect, with a firm grip on his walking stick, and showing no expressions of pain as the surgeon cut into the arm and removed the ball.

During the debate over the Bank—and perhaps at this very time when Clay and Benton clashed in the fiery manner described—Jackson sent the "memento" to the Missouri Senator, by the hand of Francis Preston Blair, with a note to the effect that he was "returning an article that he believed was rightfully the property of the Benton family," and concluding with assurances of friendship.

Benton received the pistol ball and its twinkling little note with a chuckle. "No," he said, "I can't accept it. Please take it back to the President and say to him for me that he has acquired clear title to it in common law by twenty years' peaceable possession."

"Only nineteen years," Blair reminded him.

Benton roared with laughter. "Well," he said, "in consideration of the extra care he's taken of it—keeping it constantly about his person, and so on—I'll waive the extra year."

august members of Congress had to be assisted to their carriages afterward.

"What if the President vetoes the bill?" Clay was asked.

"If Jackson vetoes that bill," he retorted, "I'll veto *him!*"

When the bill reached the White House July 3, the President was in bed, suffering from another of his recurring illnesses due to the old lung abscess. Van Buren, back from England, visited him and found him "pale and haggard, propped up by pillows."

"The Bank, Mr. Van Buren," said the old warrior, "is trying to kill me, *but I will kill it!*"

He did not change his purpose, though most of his cabinet advised against a veto. With the help of Donelson, Kendall, and finally Taney, he drafted a veto message. One paragraph contained the core of the whole:

It is to be regretted that the rich and powerful too often bend the acts of Government to their selfish purposes. Distinctions in society will always exist under every just Government. Equality of talents, of education, or of wealth cannot be produced by human institutions. In the full enjoyment of the gifts of Heaven and the fruits of industry, economy, and virtue, every man is equally entitled to protection by law; but when the laws undertake to add to these natural and just advantages artificial distinctions . . . to make the rich richer and the potent more powerful, the humble members of society—the farmers, mechanics, and laborers—who have neither the time nor the means of securing like favors to themselves, have a right to complain of the injustice of their Government.

Demagogic? It is true that the remarkable document was a political weapon. But it is also true that it stated the sincere beliefs of the President of the United States, and thus in fact escapes the charge of demagoguery made against it by the enemies of the administration.

Aghast when he read the veto message, Nicholas Biddle fairly shouted at Henry Clay, "It has all the fury of a chained panther, biting at the bars of his cage!" Daniel Webster gloomed, "It manifestly seeks to influence the poor against the rich. It wantonly attacks whole classes of the people, for the purpose of turning against them the prejudices and resentments of the other classes."

But over the nation the message was read with sober agreement. Working men, small farmers, the old Jeffersonians, the common folk everywhere, felt that the President had championed them.

Belatedly, Clay realized the desperate impasse into which he had maneuvered himself, and made every effort to override the veto.

Daniel Webster, now indisputably the greatest orator in America, made the chief speech attacking it, and Biddle distributed 140,000 copies of the address. But these and all other efforts of Clay's forces failed. On July 13 the veto was sustained.

7

The Bank issue was squarely in the Presidential campaign and on it Henry Clay must rise or fall. In vain he and Biddle threw all their resources into the battle. The social status of Mrs. Peggy Eaton was dug up. "King Andrew I" was the sobriquet applied to Jackson. The "spoils system" was paraded. Newspapers beholden to the Bank savagely assailed the President. A campaign of fear was launched with predictions of financial catastrophe if Jackson was re-elected. Many stores and factories notified their workers to "vote their bread and butter"—in other words cast their ballots for Clay and the Whigs. A meat wholesaler in Cincinnati announced that the prices he would pay farmers for pork would be cut in half if Old Hickory was not defeated.

But everywhere "Jackson Clubs" sprang up, with a hickory tree, trimmed of all foliage except a tuft on top, placed before the door of the headquarters of each club. Torchlight parades—then organized for the first time—marched through village streets, "halting in front of the houses of prominent Jackson men to cheer, while before the residences of leading Whigs they would often tarry long enough to give six or nine groans."

In this wild excitement Andrew Jackson remained calm. "It will be a walk," he said, out of his almost uncanny knowledge of the people.

It was. In the electoral college, when the returns were all in, the count stood: Jackson, 217; Clay, 49; William Wirt, candidate for a curious little splinter party, the anti-Mason party, 7; and John Floyd, of Virginia, 11 votes, all being from South Carolina which deliberately threw its votes to him rather than vote for Jackson, perhaps as a declaration of nullificationism growing ominously in the state. The popular vote was 687,502 for Jackson to 530,189 for Clay.

"Third term!" chanted some of the President's partisans.

But he resolutely shook his head. He had certain things to accomplish. After that he wanted only to return to private life.

On the way back to the capital after going to Nashville to vote, he had another severe coughing spell, raising much blood. Those around him were alarmed, but not Old Hickory. Lying in bed he showed them a clipping from the *Boston Courier*, which expressed the final bitterness of the men and powers he had defeated:

There is one comfort left: God has promised us that the days of the wicked shall be short; the wicked is old and feeble. It is the duty of every good Christian to pray to our Maker to have pity on us.

Jackson grinned. "I have no intention of dying for the gratification of my enemies," he said.

Next day he was up, and shortly after proceeded to Washington.

CHAPTER TEN

The Old Soldier Strikes

1

EVEN before Jackson's return to Washington, South Carolina was in a frenzy, and a great national crisis faced him.

His administration from the first had been complicated by a tariff law which was a subject of bitter contention. Though it became a law before he went into office, he found himself saddled with it, and ironically his own supporters needed to stand guilty of its enactment.

In 1827, led by Martin Van Buren, who sometimes was too cunning for his own good, a group of Jacksonian Congressmen framed a new tariff, for purely political purposes. It provided higher duties not only on manufactured goods, but on raw materials especially needed by New England—the latter included to induce the New England Congressmen to vote against it and defeat it. This, the Van Buren planners believed, would make it a convenient campaign issue on which to unite the West and the Middle States, and thus elect their candidate. Unexpectedly, enough New Englanders voted for the bill to make it a law, and it was signed unwillingly by John Quincy Adams, who was then President.

It was an unwise tariff, a drastic tariff, a tariff soon to be called the "Tariff of Abominations." Agriculture benefited to no important degree; and the planters of the South felt that it was a means of allowing tribute to be levied on them by the bankers and industrialists.

In particular the Tariff of Abominations aroused a rising storm of rage in South Carolina. Jackson himself recommended that it be modified in his first message to Congress. But though a new tariff, more equitable than the old, was passed in 1832, South Carolina's blood was up and the compromise did not appease the tariff opponents. The compromise in fact pleased nobody in particular.

Jackson's position was crystal-clear. Though he did not agree with all provisions of the tariff, while it still remained a law he considered it his duty to enforce it.

Even before he began his second administration the crisis was upon the nation. His handling of that crisis was memorable.

During the recess of Congress, Calhoun and Hayne had returned to

South Carolina, where they at once organized a convention. Within a fortnight after the results of the election were known, the convention, presided over by Hayne and dominated by Calhoun, on November 24, 1832, brought forth a resolution declaring that after February 1, 1833, the tariff acts were void and "not binding upon this State or its citizens." Furthermore, the use of force in an attempt to collect duties in South Carolina would be met by secession.

The cloven hoof of the institution of slavery was here involved. It had been an issue of ever-increasing bitterness since the debates that led to the Missouri Compromise of 1820; and it is a mistake to suppose that all its proponents were men of evil will. Slavery, as Allan Nevins has pointed out, was a heritage of the South, like the English language and the system of laws. Southerners believed that cheap labor was essential to the production of their great staple crops. Slaves did for them then what power machines do now.

The fact that they themselves were victims of slavery—which required large capital so that most proprietors were in debt, was by its very nature inefficient, and reduced much of the population to a state of near poverty—was recognized by a few. But most blamed the impoverishment on Northern "manipulations of government policy to the disadvantage of the South."

With relation to the Negroes, the South had another problem. The North, which in general opposed slavery—and yet had a settled prejudice against the Negro[1]—had no real race problem. There were a few tens of thousands of Negroes in the free states, while in the South there were some 3,000,000, and in many districts the black population exceeded the white. There is no question but that the South reared itself a bogey in the general fear of what would happen if that large population of Negroes was freed from the discipline of slavery. Abortive slave revolts, such as the Nat Turner uprising in Virginia, in 1831, with its attendant massacres, made many believe that such scenes might be repeated on a mass scale if all slaves were given liberty.

But there was a humanitarian wave abroad, strongest naturally in those states where slaves were not held, although some Southerners also advocated gradual manumission of slaves. In the North the extremists formed a group called the abolitionists. And human nature being perverse, the rise of agitation in the North created resentment in the South and there appeared a group equally extreme there, the so-called Fire-Eaters.

First and last the extremists in both the North and South did an

[1] Several states, including Indiana, Iowa, Illinois, and Oregon passed Negro-exclusion acts barring colored people from entering them or settling within their confines.

incredible amount of harm. Moderates in both sections distrusted them but gradually were whipped by them into a frenzy. The bitterness that led to the Civil War was in great degree bred by the hate propaganda of the Abolitionists and Fire-Eaters.

2

Meantime ambitious politicians found that this fear in the South, of the growing antipathy of the North to their institution,[2] was a fertile field for their manipulations. Calhoun's theory of state sovereignty, with its twin collaterals of the right to nullify and the right to secede, was quite eagerly accepted as a solution to this danger, in South Carolina, at least.

But in 1832 Calhoun and his followers in the nullification movement carefully and discreetly kept slavery in the background. The "Tariff of Abominations" was the stalking horse, though the issue of slavery seethed beneath the whole state sovereignty agitation.

Thus, before his second term even began, Andrew Jackson faced the greatest test of his administration, a test he had foreseen.

The South Carolina ordinance was announced while Congress was still in recess. But the old general did not need Congress. General Winfield Scott was hurried to the threatening area, with instructions to strengthen forts, make sure of the loyalty of federal troops, and cooperate with the seven revenue cutters and a ship-of-war sent to Charleston harbor to command the rebellious city with their guns.

To loyal Joel Poinsett, who still upheld the Union in South Carolina, Jackson dispatched by courier—the mails were no longer trustworthy —a message:

> No state or states has a right to secede . . . Nullification therefore means insurrection and war . . . I will meet it at the threshold and have the leaders arrested and arraigned for treason . . . In forty days I can have within the limits of So. Carolina fifty thousand men, and in forty days more another fifty thousand.

[2] Slave property, at least on paper, was important to its possessors. A few large owners had great numbers of slaves. For example, an item in the Richmond *Whig*, in 1854, said of the Hairston family of Virginia, that they were "rich in Negroes" as follows: "Sam Hairston owns 1700—Mrs. R. Hairston owns 1300—Marshall Hairston owns 700—Robert Hairston owns 950—Harden Hairston owns 600—and George Hairston owns 200 after giving off to his children some 700. Here is an aggregate of nearly 6000 slaves in the possession of one family. Their land property is said to be valued in proportion. Their government of slaves is said to be at once humane and successful. The annual increase in the whole family is thought to be three or four hundred. The united wealth of the Hairstons cannot fall short of $15,000,000."

But when, amid scenes of tense excitement, Congress hurriedly met to hear the President's message, the calm tone of that document disappointed some. No mention was made of resisting nullification. Instead, there was a recommendation for a further reduction in tariff, which the President long had wished.

John Quincy Adams, who had overset tradition by returning to the Lower House of Congress after being defeated for the Presidency—and where, incidentally, he was one of the strongest advocates of the Bank of the United States—voiced bitterly the opinion of tariff-minded New England: "The message goes to dissolve the Union . . . and is a complete surrender to the nullifiers."

Not yet, after all these years, did he know Andrew Jackson. On the very day his message was read to Congress, the President, with his Secretary of State, Edward Livingston, was laboring on a proclamation against nullification, which was given to the world December 9, 1832. One of the greatest state papers of the Jackson era, indeed, one of the greatest in the entire history of the nation, it set down certain principles so clearly that it was a foundation upon which later leaders in the cause of the Union were to base their stands.

The power of one state to annul a law of the United States, the proclamation declared, was "incompatible with the existence of the Union." The right of secession was denied. "The Constitution forms a *Government*, not a league . . . To say that any state may at pleasure secede from the Union is to say that the United States is not a Nation."

Other cogent points were made, in a manner firm and uncompromising, and the document ended with a solemn warning:

> Fellow-citizens of my native State, let me admonish you . . . I have no discretionary power on the subject . . . Those who told you that you might peaceably prevent . . . [the execution of the laws] deceived you . . . Their object is disunion . . . Disunion by armed force is treason. Are you ready to incur its guilt? If you are, on the heads of the instigators of the act be dreadful consequences . . . [Your] first magistrate cannot, if he would, avoid the performance of his duty . . .   Andrew Jackson.

Through the loyal states swept a wave of enthusiasm. Parades were held, bonfires flamed, militia companies offered their services; state legislatures passed resolutions denouncing nullification; newspapers condemned it and its leaders; John Quincy Adams and Daniel Webster for once sided with the President, and even Henry Clay fell silent and did not criticize.

Not the least important of the results of the proclamation was that it was read, thoroughly, completely, and studiously, in the frontier village of New Salem, Illinois, by a tall young man whose father said of him that he "always looked as if he had been chopped out with an axe." Abraham Lincoln was then twenty-four years old. He had just failed in a business venture, and though he had a hankering for politics his humble ambitions did not then dream of any office much higher than a seat in the state legislature. He was not a Jackson man; in fact at this time he was a Clay admirer. But the proclamation took hold of his wonderful and retentive mind. As one of his greatest biographers, Albert J. Beveridge, wrote:

> [The Proclamation] was to be the model used by Lincoln twenty-eight years later, when composing his First Inaugural. All arguments that ever had or have since been advanced for national supremacy against secession, were presented in Jackson's Proclamation, and stated, too, with a moderation and kindly appeal that added to their compelling power. Thus in his twenty-fourth year Lincoln was given a sublime example of the force of calm but strong method in public discussion, even on the gravest of subjects and in the most perilous of crises.

In South Carolina, however, the document was received quite differently. Hayne, now governor, issued a counterproclamation to the effect that he would maintain the sovereignty of South Carolina or "perish beneath its ruins." Young men formed companies of "Mounted Minute Men," with due regard for showy uniforms, and proper social standings.

Jackson grimly waited for the first overt act. Virginia offered to mediate, and was rejected. Georgia, Mississippi, and Alabama, upon whom South Carolina had counted as backers, remembered Old Hickory's Indian policy, so beneficial to them, and remained neutral. Van Buren, now elected though not inaugurated as Vice-President, counseled caution and was sternly rebuked by the President.

On January 4, 1833, John Caldwell Calhoun, having resigned as Vice-President although his term would have run to March 4, took his seat in the Senate and swore to uphold the Constitution. It was observed that he had "a pale, attenuated look, as if in bad health," and his hair had grown noticeably grayer. He flaunted his sectionalism by disregarding the unwritten rule whereby Senators were expected to appear in black broadcloth, and instead wore a suit of white cotton nankeen, as a symbol of the Cotton Kingdom.

While in South Carolina he had published a lengthy *Address* which went farther than his former *Exposition*, and in which he accepted full leadership of the nullification movement. The nationalist of 1824 thus made the full circuit and became the sectionalist of 1833.

"The Union *will be preserved*," Old Hickory said when he first read the *Address*. He now regarded Calhoun as the prime troublemaker.

On January 16—fifteen days before South Carolina's nullification ordinance was to take effect—Jackson asked Congress to give him authority to use military forces to collect customs. When Congress appeared slow to act, he was ready, on January 25, to use his powers as commander-in-chief of the armed forces, by issuing a proclamation warning that he was prepared to march with troops.

The proclamation was never issued. Considering the preparations being made by the wrathful old man in the White House, South Carolina decided to back away from her perilous position. A message to Washington stated that the nullification ordinance had been suspended "pending the outcome of the tariff debate."

There was much oratory in Congress, especially by Southern Senators, including John Tyler of Virginia, who would one day be President. But already Jackson had won his most important victory.

Bills for the reduction of the tariff were introduced, one in particular by Representative Gulian C. Verplanck of New York being especially well received, particularly by those who wished to conciliate the radical opponents of the tariff. But during debates over it, to the astonishment of everyone, Representative Robert P. Letcher of Kentucky, a close friend of Henry Clay's, rose and moved to strike out every word of the bill except the enacting clause, and insert in lieu of it a bill introduced in the Senate by Henry Clay, which was a formal abandonment of his so-called "American System," and has since been called the Compromise Bill, intended to heal disaffection and prevent a rupture in the Union.

The authorization of the President to use the army in the crisis— dubbed the Force Bill by its foes—was carried through Congress with both Benton and Webster cooperating for once in its support. Old Hickory was ready to face the emergency if it arose.

Meantime the tariff bill was in the throes of Congressional disputation. Calhoun and the South Carolina delegation were beginning to realize the danger in which they had placed themselves. When the Clay tariff bill was presented to them, Calhoun at once objected to parts of it "most emphatically."

It was at this point that Senator John Middleton Clayton of Delaware, a Whig, stepped into the picture as a mediator. Daniel Webster, when he was asked about a further compromise, was immediate and emphatic in his answer:

"No! It will be yielding great principles to faction. The time has come to test the strength of the Constitution and the government."

He was speaking both as a dedicated Union man and as a representative of the Northern manufacturers many of whom had hurried to Washington to oppose any lowering of tariff rates.

But Clayton knew that a tariff bill must be passed and that all the nullifiers must vote for it, thus cutting them off from the plea of "unconstitutionality." The contest of wills was squarely between Andrew Jackson and John C. Calhoun with momentous results hanging on the outcome.

Calhoun and Clay conferred, and each was unyielding. The President was fully aware of the secret meetings and the situation as it then existed. When Letcher visited him to sound him out on further compromises, the stern old man made clear his position.

"Compromise!" he exclaimed. "I will make no compromise with traitors. I will have no negotiations. I will execute the laws."

Later, during a White House reception, he dropped the remark—and he had a way of dropping apparently casual remarks that were most forcibly meant—that though he would not interfere with resolutions or manifestos, "If one drop of blood be shed in defiance of the laws of the United States, I will hang the first man of them I can get my hands on to the first tree I can find."

Word of this was quickly carried to George McDuffie, Representative from South Carolina, and Calhoun's chief coadjutor, who flew to Calhoun himself. Both gentlemen were uncomfortably aware that Jackson might choose them, since they were handy and trees plentiful, for this unhappy sort of attention.

Again Letcher visited Old Hickory, to learn if the remark had been correctly reported.

"By the Eternal!" the old general assured him, "I would hang them higher than Haman!"

When a little later one of Calhoun's friends expressed, in the hearing of Thomas Hart Benton, a doubt that Jackson would really carry matters so far as to execute a Member of Congress, the Missourian grimly replied:

"When Andrew Jackson starts talking about hanging, men begin looking for ropes."

Calhoun was understandably alarmed by this startling picture of the President's wrath. How much farther did he dare to go?

Clayton and Clay assembled the manufacturers who opposed the tariff cuts, and asked them to yield to the compromise in the interests of conciliation. The manufacturers agreed, though reluctantly, to withdraw their opposition.

Now Clayton, who had all the while been the go-between in his efforts for peace, made his last appeal to the Calhoun faction. They were unyielding. The crisis had arrived, for if the tariff was passed over their opposition, all South Carolina would be inflamed.

Clayton remonstrated with Calhoun, pointing out the danger, the folly of his course. At last Clayton said that if the nullifiers did not pledge to vote for the bill in its entirety, he would move to lay it on the table so that the old tariff would remain in force.

"The President will then," he added, "be free to execute the laws with full vigor."

It was the last chance. The proposed tariff bill would provide a gradual reduction in the tariff in the course of ten years, so that none of the interests would be severely harmed.

In the Senate the scene was tense when the bill came up for a vote. The nullifiers voted for the amendments until they came to the last. All at once Calhoun resumed his violent opposition. The session was in its last day but one, and the day itself was late.

Suddenly Clayton rose, and as suddenly executed his threat. He moved to lay the bill on the table, and declared it would remain there. Clay begged him to withdraw his motion. Others pleaded for a little more time.

Calhoun and his friends, facing a sudden terrible situation, withdrew behind the colonnade back of the presiding officer's chair, and conferred briefly and heatedly.

They showed signs of yielding and Clayton announced that he would withdraw his motion temporarily, but that unless every member of the nullification bloc voted for the tariff bill, he would renew it.

One of the South Carolina delegation went to Clayton and begged that Calhoun, at least, might be spared the mortification of appearing on the record in favor of "a measure against which, at that very time, and at his instance, troops were being raised in South Carolina, and because of which secession was determined by that state."

Not one jot would Clayton yield. "Nothing can be secured," he said, "unless his vote appears in favor of the message."

There was a brief adjournment. When the Senate met again, and the bill was taken up, the nullifiers and their friends, one after another, withdrew their objections on one pretext or another. At length, when all had voted except Calhoun, he rose, "pale and haggard, for he had a most terrible struggle."

He stated that since the bill was "a compromise to which South Carolina could accede with dignity," he would vote in the affirmative.

It was a bitter pill for him to swallow, but he had found it expedient to bow to Andrew Jackson's heroic will and unfaltering purpose.

The next day, March 4, Andrew Jackson took the oath of office in a quiet ceremony in the Hall of Representatives, as he began his second term. Eleven days after that, on March 15, which was Old Hickory's sixty-sixth birthday—although this assuredly was pure coincidence—South Carolina rescinded the ordinance of nullification.

The nation went wild with joy over news that civil war had been averted. Jackson's popularity reached a peak higher than ever before. Daniel Webster extolled him in an address.

It was the greatest single act of the President's administration. Secession and civil war had been halted—the basic tenets of the Union were firmly laid.

But the old general received the acclaim calmly. His mind had fathomed the turbid waters of nullification more deeply than others. He knew that beneath everything the fundamental issue was slavery, and that issue would grow. In gloomy prophetic vein he wrote to his friend, John Coffee, April 9, 1833:

"The nullifiers in the South intend to blow up a storm on the slave question . . . This ought to be met, for be assured these men will do any act to destroy this Union and form a southern Confederacy, bounded, north, by the Potomac River."

CHAPTER ELEVEN

Rise of a New Star

1

T HE letter was dated Natchitoches, Louisiana, February 13, 1833, and the President's eyes blazed with interest as he read it:

Gen. Jackson, Dear Sir: Having been so far as Bexar [San Antonio], in the province of Texas, I am in possession of some information that may be calculated to forward your views, if you should entertain any, touching the acquisition of Texas by the United States.

That such a measure is desireable by nineteen-twentieths of the population of the Province I cannot doubt. They are now without laws to govern or protect them. Mexico is involved in civil war. The Government is essentially despotic and must be so for years to come. The rulers have not honesty and the people have not intelligence.

The people of Texas are determined to form a State Government and separate from Coahuila, and unless Mexico is soon restored to order and the Constitution revived and re-enacted, the Province of Texas will remain separate from the confederacy of Mexico.

She [Texas] has already beaten and expelled all the troops of Mexico from her soil, nor will she permit them to return. She can defend herself against the whole power of Mexico, for really Mexico is powerless and penniless. Her [Mexico's] want of money taken in connection with the course Texas must and will adopt, will render the transfer of Texas inevitable to some power.

If Texas is desireable to the United States, it is now in the most favorable attitude perhaps that it can be to obtain it on fair terms—England is pressing her suit for it, but its citizens will resist, if any transfer should be made of them to any other power but the United States.

There was more, including a description of the country, and a warm expression of fealty to Andrew Jackson and the Union. It was signed by Sam Houston.

A suggestion . . . or a report?

The context quite clearly reveals that this was no mere observation of an interested individual. It rather indicates the careful *report*—secret, of course—of a representative sent to obtain information. Certain phrases: ". . . to forward your views, *if* you should entertain any," and "*if* Texas is desireable to the United States," have the sound of discretion, as if the writer was not acquainted with the President's leanings on the subject discussed. Yet Andrew Jackson was an open, avowed, and unashamed expansionist, and nobody knew this better than Sam Houston. The discreet phrases quite evidently were inserted so that if the President should not wish to be involved, he could disclaim any connection.

At the same time this now-famous missive contained vital on-the-ground information of importance which could not fail to arouse Old Hickory's keenest attention. Of all the outthrusts of the frontier, on which he had kept an observant eye for years, this in Texas was the most momentous at that moment. Jackson was acquainted with the internal struggles of Mexican "strong men" for supremacy—and how all of them appeared to be overfree with the firing squad and the hangman's noose. The observation that the situation "will render the transfer of Texas inevitable to *some power*," coupled with the information that "England is pressing her suit for it," was a matter for concern. Britain was in her great period of imperialism, and relations were not yet entirely cordial between her and her former colonies. With Canada on the north, the West Indies on the east, and now Texas on the south, the United States—so felt Jackson—would be like a nut between the jaws of a nutcracker. Nevertheless the President of the United States could not yet take any official part in events in Texas. He made no reply to Houston's letter; but he watched with deepening interest the events developing there.

2

Houston, whom adversity had changed into a strange and brooding giant, had found affairs in a state of profound unrest in Texas, when he entered that province in December 1832.

Spain, which until 1819 had refused to permit any foreign entry into her American provinces, had changed her policies in that year by permitting colonization in Texas, by Americans and other non-Spaniards. The Adams-Oñis "Treaty of Amity" had then just been concluded, whereby, in exchange for the cession of Florida, the United States agreed to a boundary of the Louisiana Purchase which, Spain felt, confirmed her possession of Texas. Now Spanish administrators thought it would be excellent policy to permit the *Americanos* to enter, for by so doing they would immediately become a buffer against the wild and bloodthirsty tribes like the Comanches, the Apaches, the cannibal Karankawas, the Caddos, and others, which had created such continuous danger and devastation that after two centuries of nominal occupation Texas still was almost empty of civilized people.

Save for a few strongholds such as Nacogdoches, Goliad, and San Antonio (usually called Bexar at that time), nearly all the missions and *presidios* established in Texas in those two hundred years had been destroyed and looted, with massacres of their *padres* and settlers, so that their very locations in some cases were forgotten. As it turned out the Americans did form a most effective barrier against the raiding tribes. When Indians attacked their first settlements, the colonists responded with celerity and deadliness that astounded the red men. In not too long a time the latter showed a marked preference for avoiding those straight-shooting, unterrified *Americanos,* and their raiding usually skirted the new colonies, aiming instead for less explosive Mexican settlements to the west in New Mexico, and southward across the Rio Grande.

As for the guarantee of her possession of Texas, Spain soon had no further interest in that. In 1821, after a series of revolutions had been put down, Mexico at last was successful in winning her independence, and Spain had lost her richest outpost in the New World.

The American colonists fully realized their danger in entering the new territory, menaced as it was by the Indians; but land hunger brought them into Texas by hundreds at first, and then by thousands. First to make legal application for a tract of land, under the new Spanish policy, was Moses Austin. He was a native of Connecticut, who had made a fortune mining lead in Missouri, then lost it when the Bank of St. Louis, in which he was a large stockholder, failed in 1818.

Austin looked to Texas for a new start. In 1820 he traveled to San Antonio to offer his petition, in which he undertook to establish three hundred families as colonists along the Brazos River. His journey was filled with hardship, and on his return he took sick, and died soon after reaching Missouri, June 10, 1821, probably from pneumonia contracted through exposure.

He never knew whether his petition had been granted, for his death occurred before the confirmation came. But hoping for success, on his death bed he charged his son, Stephen Austin, to complete the venture.

Before the son could carry out his father's wishes, a sudden and dramatic change occurred in Mexico. General Augustín de Iturbide, a royalist commander, went over to the revolutionaries with his whole army, forcing Spain to recognize the independence of the new nation by the Treaty of Cordova.[1] Iturbide declared himself emperor—an arrangement which did nothing for the peace and serenity of the country.

While this revolution was in process Stephen Austin brought in the "First Three Hundred" families, and began settling them along the Brazos River, where the soil was rich, though the area was exposed to Indian attacks. His father's agreement with the Spanish administrators had founded the Empresario System—the word *empresario* meaning contractor.

Under that agreement colonists were to receive 640 acres of land, with 320 acres additional for their wives, 100 acres apiece for each child, and 80 acres for each slave. A premium was thus placed on large families and slaveholding. It was specified that all colonists must be Catholics, or become Catholics before entering the territory; and that they must show credentials of good character, and swear to an oath of allegiance to the King of Spain.

Austin, however, found on his arrival with his people that the government had changed. He must obtain a new authorization from the Mexican authorities now. So he made a lonely and dangerous journey —the country was in chaos and robbery and murder frequent along the trails—to the City of Mexico. There, after twelve months of patient negotiation, he at last obtained confirmation of his grant by the Mexican congress.

The terms he gained were even more favorable than those his father had obtained from the Spanish viceroy. Land grants were as follows: one *sitio*, or square league—4338.18 acres—of grazing land, and one *labor*—174 acres—of tillage land, adding up to a little more than 4500 American acres, to each head of a family. Unmarried men received only one-fourth of a *sitio*. The new arrangement no longer placed a premium on large families and slavery. Good character, compulsory Catholicism, and an oath of allegiance to Mexico, were required.

With the success of the Austin colony, other *empresarios* flocked in, among them Robert Leftwich, Hayden Edwards, Green De Witt, Ben Milam, James Powers, and David G. Burnet, until the map of Texas was virtually covered by grants, some of which, however, were never carried into effect.

The impetus to colonization was such that by 1830 almost 20,000 Americans had taken up homes in Texas, tilling the land, building towns, and fighting off Indians. In spite of the required certificates of "good character" not all these new citizens of Texas were of the better

---

[1] In this treaty the nation was first officially named *Mexico*, from its chief city and district. Hitherto it had been known as New Spain. It is a curiosity that the province of New Mexico bore that title a couple of centuries before the nation did.

class. Some were shifty, if not shady, in their characters and past histories. It was in those days that the expression "G.T.T."—"Gone to Texas"—became a byword, when sundry persons, for various imperative reasons usually connected with transgressions of the laws, fled from the United States to the Mexican province. The vast majority of the settlers, however, were hard-working, honest, capable, self-sufficient, and—within limits—law-abiding.

They had need of leadership, for conditions in Mexico were in an almost constant state of disorder. Iturbide was forced to abdicate in March 1823, by a new revolution of which a major figure was a certain General Antonio López de Santa Anna. It was the beginning of a long succession of revolutions, counterrevolutions, massacres, and bloodshed in general, which Mexico and Texas were to endure; and at the bottom of every one of them was the figure of a small, melodramatic, cunning, cruel, vain, and treacherous man, that same Santa Anna.

Santa Anna first gained prominence by engineering the revolt by which Iturbide was deposed and Guadalupe Victoria became president in 1824. Victoria served four years amid incessant troubles between the conservatives-clergy and the liberals, fomented largely by Santa Anna. When Gómez Pedraza was elected president in 1828, his defeated rival, Vicente Guerrero, raised the standard of revolution, with Santa Anna his chief general. Santa Anna was defeated by Pedraza—and lost some face thereby—but the dogged half-Indian Guerrero fought his way into the capital and Pedraza fled into exile. Hardly was Guerrero in his seat of office when Santa Anna turned against him, this time under the banner of General Anastasio Bustamante, and forced Guerrero to vacate his office in 1829, after which the unfortunate ex-president was shot. Bustamante assumed the presidency January 1, 1830, abolished the Mexican constitution, declared himself dictator, prohibited any further entrance of Americans into Texas, suspended *empresario* contracts, stopped introduction of Negro slaves (but did not mention Mexico's parallel peon system), and showed general hostility to the colonists already in Texas.

Guerrero, it was true, was a usurper, having seized the office from Pedraza; but Bustamante was a usurper also, having wrested the presidency from Guerrero. After two troubled years a strong party of Mexicans bethought themselves that Pedraza was, after all, the lawful president. A revolt of the self-styled "legitimatists" began against Bustamante. And Santa Anna, who already had turned against Iturbide, Victoria, Pedraza, and Guerrero, now appeared in the field as one of the "legitimatist" leaders against Bustamante—whom he had helped into office—and in behalf of Pedraza, whom he had helped to oust.

The Texans did not attempt to unravel all the complicated convolutions of Mexican policy. But in the uprising against Bustamante they sided with Santa Anna, perhaps because he seemed to them—at that time—the lesser of the two evils.

They had sufficient reasons to detest Bustamante, who in addition to his other acts against them, had placed heavy duties on imported goods, closed most of the Texas seaports, and garrisoned the province with Mexican troops whose commanders were given authority to impose martial law whenever it suited them to do so.

The Mexican occupation troops were of the worst quality, composed largely of convicts taken out of prison to be "enlisted," together with "vagabonds and disorderly persons," and other recruits "obtained by entrapment and decoy." They were further brutalized by harsh and often cruel methods of "discipline," and it is hardly to be wondered that they continually committed thefts, robberies, rapes, and murders of people among whom they were garrisoned.

Without any particular leadership, the Texans in the summer of 1832, drove the Bustamante forces out of Anahuac, Velasco, Goliad, and Nacogdoches, in a series of impromptu engagements which demonstrated one thing very clearly—the superiority of the long rifle in the hands of an expert over the weapons of the Mexican soldiery. By the end of the summer not a Mexican soldier remained in Texas, except for a small garrison of about seventy in the *presidio* at San Antonio.

3

This was the situation when Houston arrived in Texas, and which he reported in his letter to Andrew Jackson. He very quickly became acquainted with the men who had come into prominence during the Bustamante troubles, among them big Jim Bowie, inventor of the famous knife and one of the deadliest duelists of his time; William Barret Travis, a fiery South Carolina opportunist; and, of course, Stephen Austin, the real leader of the Texas colonists.

Austin did not look the part of a leader. Slender and of moderate height, his face suggested a dreamer rather than a fighter. With his slightly balding forehead, almost femininely wide eyes, and a nose too long so that it weakened his mouth and chin by comparison, he nevertheless was a dedicated and courageous man, who had accepted responsibility for Texas when he was only twenty-seven years old, and carried it like a burden on his shoulders. He was abstemious, humorless, and reticent although he liked to preside at public meetings, listen to debates, and act as an expert on rules of order. He never married, but lived with his sister and her husband, James F. Perry.

Over and over Austin had proved his bravery, in the Indian wars of the early colony, as well as in journeys of hardship and danger. Yet he was not by temperament a soldier, as he showed by his irresolution and overcaution when, later, he commanded a Texas army for a time.

He did not believe in himself. "My temper," he wrote, "is naturally hasty and impetuous . . . My disposition is by nature, also, open, unsuspecting, confiding, and accommodating almost to a fault. I have been, therefore, subject in a peculiar manner to imposition. Experience has enlightened me as to this latter deficiency, I fear, almost too late, for I am apprehensive of having fallen somewhat into the opposite extreme."

Houston met Austin. In fact they both were members of the "consultation" which sat at San Felipe de Austin, and drew up a state constitution for Texas and a petition for separation from Coahuila, to which Texas then was joined, and from which it was governed.

Bustamante had been overthrown and fled from the country in 1832, so that Pedraza became president just in time to serve out the last six months of his elected term—with Santa Anna the real power in the government, waiting for the moment when he himself could assume the supreme office.

He achieved this ambition in May 1833. At that time Austin, patient, long-suffering, self-sacrificing, began the long journey to the City of Mexico, to present the petition and state constitution to the government for ratification. He did not return for two years. Santa Anna ordered his arrest. He was imprisoned for a time in the old dungeons of the Inquisition. Later he was removed to another, less noisome prison. Eventually he was released but he did not return to Texas until September 1835. In all that time he was never tried on any charge, nor was his petition answered.

Meantime Houston, in spite of the decree prohibiting entrance of Americans into Texas, began practicing law in Nacogdoches, and even became a "Muldoon Catholic"—that is, he was inducted into the faith by a singularly broad-minded priest, Padre Miguel Muldoon, who was a convenience for Americans who wished to adopt the form of Catholicism required in order to own land in Texas. Contributions to the ecclesiastical treasury were, of course, expected from such "converts," but otherwise they were permitted a wide latitude in their activities.

As for Houston, he varied his law practice—which included as his largest client the Galveston Bay and Texas Land Company—with travels, sometimes in Texas where he visited Americans who might be helpful for a *certain* project; at other times into the United States, where on one occasion he visited Andrew Jackson, just then filled with frustrated fury at the behavior of his envoy, Anthony Butler, who had made a botch of the effort to purchase Texas from the Mexican government.

An English traveler, G. W. Featherstonhaugh, had a glimpse of him in December 1834, when he was at Washington, Arkansas Territory, a hamlet hardly thirty miles north of the Texas border, and wrote:

> General Houston was here, leading a mysterious sort of life, shut up in a small tavern, seeing nobody by day and sitting up all night. The world gave him credit for passing these waking hours in the study of *trente et quarante*, and *sept' a lever;* but I had seen too much passing before my eyes, to be ignorant that this little place was the rendezvous where a much deeper game . . . was playing. There were many persons at this time in the village from States lying adjacent to the Mississippi, under the pretence of purchasing government lands, but whose real object was to encourage the settlers in Texas to throw off their allegiance to the Mexican government.

By the date of this observation Santa Anna had appeared in his true colors. In a proclamation called the "Plan of Cuernavaca," May 1834, he made public apostasy of his declared beliefs in liberalism; joined the clergy in pronouncing against religious reforms; backed the wealthy property owners; discarded the slogan of equality between races; repealed the constitution of 1824; and substituted a new constitution written by himself, under which he assumed absolute power as president-dictator.

He knew of the unrest in Texas, but he delayed in dealing with it for a few months while he put down, amid unprecedented scenes of massacre and rape, opposition to his regime in Zacatecas. That done, he sent forces, under General Martin Perfecto de Cos, his brother-in-law, to crush any rebellion in Texas.

The Texans had some warning of this when dispatches from General Cos to Tenorio were seized, but the first personally to see physical evidences of this design was Jim Bowie. Restless and always on the move, Bowie sent a letter, written June 22, 1835, to Dr. J. B. Miller, *jefe político* at Brazoria:

> I left Matamoros on the 12th of the present month. All vessels in the port were embargoed for the purpose of transporting troops to the coast of Texas. The commandant, General Cos, forbid all foreigners from leaving the city under any circumstances. I run away and succeeded in getting this far safe. Three thousand troops had reached Saltillo on their way to Texas. All this may or may not be news to you.

A thrill of alarm, followed by indignation, went through the province. Committees of Safety were formed, and men began to drill as militia companies. There were several minor clashes with Mexican detachments, but General Cos occupied San Antonio without any real opposition.

Then, early in September, Stephen Austin arrived back in Texas, gaunt and pale from illness and mistreatment. He had at last been released by Santa Anna, who thought he would continue to counsel for peace in Texas. But Austin had seen enough of the dictator and his methods.

"War is our only recourse," he declared in a public statement. "There is no other remedy. We must defend our rights, ourselves, and our country, by force of arms."

Texans rallied around their great *empresario*. Wearied of broken promises, injustices, and repudiation of their constitutional rights, twenty thousand Americans—including the women and children—defied a nation of seven million people, ruled by a vengeful and pitiless despot, with that nation's armies, weapons, and resources at his command.

4

Desperately unprepared though they were, the Texans did not behave as if they considered such odds too great. In frontier homes men usually had a long rifle handy, over the door or mantel, or leaning in a corner. Down came the guns from the racks, and the Texans swarmed toward the enemy, some on horse or mule, some on foot, some riding three or four together in a wagon. What they proceeded to do, not only then but throughout their war for independence, must always be classed among the miracles of military history.

The Texans brought their own arms and ammunition, and they were garbed as they came, without any pretense at uniforms. Of very different appearance were the troops they were to meet. Whatever failings Santa Anna's soldiers might have, they were invariably handsomely uniformed, the officers especially resplendent with epaulets, sabre-taches, and plumes. But the undisciplined Texans beat them as fast as they could get to them.

The first real battle was at Gonzales, September 20, where a detachment of two hundred Mexican cavalry, sent to seize a six-pounder cannon—used chiefly to fire off Fourth of July salutes—were met by 168 Texans under Colonel John H. Moore. The long rifles began to speak, gaudy cavalrymen spun out of saddles, and leaving their dead behind the Mexicans fled all the way back to San Antonio.

On October 9 another Texas posse—it could hardly be called a military force—under a Captain Collingsworth, captured Goliad, together with two pieces of artillery, three hundred muskets, and about $10,000 in money for the payment of Mexican troops.

Austin arrived at Gonzales and was promptly elected commander of the Texas "army." His men were undisciplined, without organization, commissary, or proper officers, but they were brimful of fight. At once the march began toward San Antonio, the provincial capital. Austin at first had only 350 men, but he was considerably reinforced by more men who came up and "fell in" without any formality in his straggling column.

Sam Houston and others had been busy appealing for aid to the United States. New Orleans sent two companies of cavalry, called "the New Orleans Grays," who contrasted with the rest of the army in their natty gray uniforms. Others arrived—all at their own expense—from Arkansas, Missouri, Tennessee, Kentucky, and Louisiana, as well as other states, eager for adventure and willing to fight for Texas.

As they neared San Antonio, Jim Bowie, now bearing the rank of colonel, with an advance force of ninety-two men, routed an enemy detachment of more than three hundred infantry and cavalry. The Texas rifles again were the difference. Though much better uniformed than the *Americanos*, the Mexican soldiers had a regrettable habit of shutting their eyes just as they pulled the trigger. Sixty-seven of them were killed, and at least as many wounded. The Texans, who fought from cover until the order came to charge, lost just one man killed; none were wounded.

By this time the army before San Antonio had increased to about eleven hundred men. Austin, however, could not be induced to attack the city, or even lay close siege to it.

Meantime the consultation had taken another decisive step. Because of his obviously superior knowledge of military affairs, General Sam Houston was appointed commander-in-chief—over Austin's head. At the same time Austin was notified that he was to go as a commissioner to the United States to gain aid if possible. When the *empresario* departed for his new duties, Colonel Edward Burleson, an old Indian fighter, succeeded to command of the forces before San Antonio.

There was a little skirmishing, but the army in the main remained idle, and grumbling grew. Many of the men, tired of indecision, simply walked out of camp and headed home, until not more than eight hundred remained.

On December 3, Burleson announced that he would attack San Antonio, and was cheered by his men. Next day, however, he changed his mind. The enemy outnumbered him and were fortified in the city.

It seemed too grave a risk to take, with a horde so undisciplined and disorganized as he had to command.

Then Colonel Ben Milam, rifle on shoulder, walked out in front of the ranks, his hat cocked over one eye, and drolly called, "Who'll go with old Ben Milam into San Antonio?" There was a roar of enthusiasm.

Virtually ignoring Burleson, the Texans attacked before dawn next day. Cos had carefully placed his cannon to sweep the streets of the city, and by every rule should have blown his enemies off the face of the earth. But the attackers did not know the rules, and did not follow them. Instead of advancing up the streets, they burrowed their way from house to house, breaking through the soft adobe walls with crowbars, as they fought their way toward the *presidio* in the center of San Antonio.

It was disconcerting to Cos, especially when the Texans approached near enough in their odd, unorthodox way, to pick off the gunners at his cannon. In the four days that the fighting continued he lost between three and four hundred men, including dead, wounded, and desertions. Incredibly, the Texans lost only two killed—one of them was old Ben Milam—and twenty-six wounded.

The battle ended when Cos surrendered his army of 1105 men, twenty-one pieces of artillery, five hundred muskets, and much ammunition and other war matériel. Colonel Francis Johnson, who succeeded Milam in command of the attackers, paroled the Mexican general and his men, and sent them marching south to the Rio Grande, without arms, but with sufficient provisions for the journey.

Not one Mexican soldier remained in Texas.

5

Despite the general rejoicing over this astonishing victory, Houston was not one of those who had rosy hopes that the war was won. He knew that Santa Anna would bring up heavy forces soon, not only to suppress the rebellion, but to exact revenge for his personal loss of face—the humiliation of his brother-in-law, General Cos.

He recognized, moreover, the great weakness of Texas—its extreme individualism which made it difficult to weld it into a unit of any kind. His forebodings were justified. Almost immediately the Texan habit of pulling in many different directions made itself apparent. There was jealousy among the numerous self-styled commanders of the army. Colonel Johnson, and Dr. James Grant, a Scottish adventurer who had managed to get himself slightly wounded in the attack on San Antonio, proposed a quixotic invasion of Mexico, including the capture of Matamoras, and held forth promises of rich loot to win men over to their project. In this move they were joined, at first, by Colonel James W. Fannin.

With most of the army they started on their march. Houston, riding hard, overtook the errant forces, which were proceeding without orders either from himself or the provisional government. But the easy victory of San Antonio had made the army "cocky," to use Houston's phrase, especially the newly arrived volunteers from the States. When he denounced the project as "piratical war," and lectured the men on the dangers of such a movement as they were embarking on, they scornfully rejected his pleas.

A general in the humiliating position of having had his army literally stolen from him, Houston rode northward, writing ahead to Governor Smith:

> No language can express the anguish of my soul. Oh, save our poor country! . . . What will the world think of the authorities of Texas? . . . I do not fear,—I will do my duty!

On his way back to San Felipe, Houston received word that on February 5, 1836, Santa Anna had crossed the Rio Grande, heading for San Antonio. His force was estimated at eight thousand men, accompanied by a huge train of artillery and baggage with several thousand horses and mules for its transport; and also by hundreds of women camp followers—a quite usual adjunct of a Mexican army of the period, it being held that women were as necessary as food for the soldiers.

At this news he dispatched Colonel Bowie with twenty men to San Antonio where Colonel Joseph C. Neill was guarding an abandoned mission, somewhat fortified, called the Alamo. Bowie's orders were to blow up the place and transport its available cannon northward for the new army Houston intended to form. Again Texas councils were divided. Neill did leave the Alamo, to serve bravely later at San Jacinto, but James Bowie and William Barret Travis remained to hold the fort.

Fannin, a former slave trader with dubious antecedents but large military ambitions, believed that he, not Houston, should have supreme command. Though he parted company with Johnson and Grant, he remained sullenly at Goliad with about four hundred men.

Houston, now acting as a delegate from Refugio, rode to Washington-on-the-Brazos, where a constitutional convention was being formed, largely through his efforts. What Texas desperately needed was a real government, a declaration of independence, a constitution, and a reorganization of the available fighting forces. The convention, which he dominated, duly adopted the constitution; passed a resolution of independence from Mexico; elected a president, David G. Burnet; and "confirmed" Houston as commander-in-chief of the army.

News was bad and growing progressively worse. Santa Anna was determined to subjugate Texas in a manner that would never be forgotten. Eastward, toward Matamoros, he sent his best commander, General José Urrea, with a thousand men to intercept the rash Johnson-Grant forces. His agents were busy in the north stirring up the Comanche Indians. With the main body of his army he himself struck across the country for San Antonio.

On February 28 a hard-riding courier brought to the convention a message from the Alamo, dated February 24, and signed "W. Barret Travis, Lt. Col. Cmdt." It contained a fervent appeal for reinforcements, and ended, "If this is neglected, I am determined to sustain myself as long as possible . . . *victory or death.*"

Bowie no longer was able to command. Injured in a fall while helping mount a cannon on the walls, he lay suffering from pneumonia, probably caused by a broken rib that punctured a lung. The Alamo contained just 183 men—not enough fully to man its walls. Before it Santa Anna had brought his whole army and his massed artillery.

The day before Travis' message was received, though the convention did not then know it, Urrea had surprised Colonel Johnson and about seventy men at San Patricio. Johnson and two or three others escaped, but all the others were butchered.

Still the convention toiled on. It could send no help to Travis, although Houston wrote Fannin, then at Goliad, to relieve the Alamo. Fannin started to move, found the going slow, returned to his former camp and left the besieged garrison to its fate. The convention, meantime, was kept at its necessary work of organization by the driving energy of Houston.

On March 6 another courier arrived from Travis, bearing his last message on earth: "I hope your honorable body will hasten on reinforcements . . . Our supply of ammunition is limited."

One of the convention fire-eaters, Robert Potter, moved to adjourn, and in a body, "march to the relief of the Alamo." Houston pointed out how foolish and futile such an action would be. He told the convention to remain at its task until it created a government. Meantime he would go to the front and try to organize troops to defend the convention from the Mexican invaders.

Clad in a buckskin coat, high-heeled boots with spurs carrying three-inch rowels, a broad-brimmed hat, and wearing a sword at his side, the general started south accompanied by four other men—five Texans to face Santa Anna and his well-equipped army of seven thousand men.

One of the men was dispatched as a courier to Goliad, where Fannin sat with his four hundred men, commanding that reluctant officer to join Houston at Gonzales. Toward Gonzales the commander with his three remaining companions rode.

He did not then know it, but March 6 marked the fall of the Alamo. The heroic defense of the mission had been crushed before he reached Gonzales.

The story of the siege of the Alamo has been told and retold. On February 23 the first shot was fired as the head of the Mexican army appeared, by Travis himself. The Mexicans ran up a blood-red flag, signalizing "No Quarter," and the same afternoon made their first assault. It was driven back with heavy loss by the rifles and cannon of the defenders.

Next day, February 24, Travis sent his first message to the convention. Though Fannin did not relieve him, thirty-two brave men from Gonzales succeeded in reaching the mission, and these raised the defending forces to the number of 183.

For eleven days the siege continued. Each time the Mexicans came within range of those Texas rifles they lost men. One battalion of engineers that tried to bridge an aqueduct which ran close to the walls, lost thirty men in a few minutes of hot shooting and had to retreat.

With all of his army up by March 5, Santa Anna prepared for his climactic effort. There is a story, told by one Moses Rose, who escaped just before the final assault, that Travis paraded his men in the mission patio, made a heroic speech, and then offered them the choice between attempting to escape and remaining to die in the Alamo. Drawing a line across the front of the rank of men with his sword, he asked all those who would stay with him to step across that mark. The entire file crossed—even Bowie, who though lying helpless on a cot asked his friends to carry him across—save one man, Moses Rose. He alone was unwilling to die. Climbing the wall, he leaped down on the other side and managed to make his way through the Mexican lines safely. His story, told to Mrs. Mary Ann Zuber and her son, W. P. Zuber, who sheltered him, was written down by them, and it was published in the *Texas Almanac* for 1873.

Whether this account is absolutely true or not is a matter for speculation, especially since Rose dropped out of sight and was not seen again. It has, however, become part of the folklore of America.

What took place thereafter is history. At four o'clock on the morning of Sunday, March 6, the Mexican bugles sounded the assassin notes of the *Deguello*—the "Cutthroat Song."

From all sides at once, heavy columns of Mexican soldiers attacked. The first assault was repelled by the bitter fire of the Texas rifles, leaving the ground strewn with dead and wounded. A second charge immediately followed. Once again the handful of defenders drove back the assault in which more than two thousand men took part.

Santa Anna was furious. He galloped forward to direct the attack in person. There were too few defenders to man the walls, and he sent fresh troops against the west wall, which was almost denuded of riflemen.

This time the overwhelming weight of numbers told. Mexican troops surmounted the wall, broke through the gates. The Texans were butchered, fighting desperately. Bowie, lying on his cot in the baptistry of the old mission, was said to be the last fighting man to die. He had his famous knife at his side and his bed was covered with pistols. Before they reached him with their bayonets several Mexicans gave their lives to those pistols and that deadly knife.

Three women, a child, and a young Negro slave boy were the only survivors. One line has commemorated the magnificent fight the Texans made: *Thermopylae had its messenger of defeat; the Alamo had none.*

6

On March 7, the day after the Alamo fell, Urrea struck the rash Dr. Grant, with some seventy men, at Agua Dulce. Only two of the small force escaped. Grant himself was lanced to death by Mexican cavalrymen.

Houston learned of this soon after he reached Gonzales, March 11. There he also learned definitely of the fate of the Alamo and the extermination of its defenders.

At Gonzales he found what he called 374 "effective men"—although some had no ammunition and all were lacking in supplies. He could not face Santa Anna where he was. The only possible strategy was to retreat. Houston was never one to confide his plans or the reasons for them to others. The retreat from the first was not popular. Texans had an instinct to fight, and they did not comprehend the niceties of their leader's strategy. Instead they complained bitterly, even threatened mutiny. Houston hardly had the authority to keep them on the march, but his personality compelled them, and they unwillingly obeyed.

His maneuvers were in fact cunningly planned. He was like a hare pursued by hounds, and he adopted the tactics of the hare. Instead of retreating in a straight line, he continually changed the direction of his march. The baffling zigzag course he adopted forced Santa Anna, who did not know exactly where to find him, to break up his army into four divisions, each seeking to bring the Texans to a stand. Mean-

time the pursuing Mexican forces were continually being weakened
by the necessity of guarding their extending lines of communication,
the difficulty of transport in a rain-soaked country—the weather was
continually bad and the rivers were high—and the necessity of forag-
ing. Meantime Houston picked up a few more men for his army each
day that he marched.

Northeast from Gonzales, Houston led the way to Burnham's Crossing of the Colorado. There he camped for nearly a week, hoping for
the arrival of Fannin's troops. But Fannin did not come. He, too, had
met disaster at the hands of Urrea.

First, Fannin delayed too long in obeying Houston's summons. Then
he divided his forces. A detachment of twenty men under Captain
King was sent to remove some families at Refugio. When King did
not return in due time, Fannin sent Colonel Ward with a hundred
men to help him.

Urrea gobbled up these two detached parties, then turned on Fannin himself. That officer at last had begun his long-delayed march.
Urrea overtook him March 18, as he reached Coleto Creek. There was
a brisk fight, Urrea's cavalry twice being driven back, but Fannin was
wounded. When artillery was brought up to shell them, the Texans
surrendered on a promise that their lives would be spared.

But Santa Anna countermanded the terms of surrender and ordered
all "foreigners" shot as pirates. When Urrea protested, he received an
angry reprimand.

At dawn, March 27—Palm Sunday—the prisoners were marched out
and brutally shot down. Even the wounded were dragged from their
beds and butchered. Some few escaped but 330 men died that day.

Because his direct orders had been disobeyed by men who thought
they knew better than he, Houston had lost 183 men at the Alamo,
70 under Johnson, 70 more under Grant, and, all together, about 400
under Fannin—more fighting men than he had with him when he
crossed the Colorado.

To his friend, Major George Hockley, he said gloomily as he rode
past his handful, "There, Hockley, goes the last hope of Texas."

From the Colorado—where a Mexican force under General Sesma
caught up with him but preferred not to cross in the teeth of those
rifles—he changed his course to almost due east, reaching the Brazos
at San Felipe.

He did not cross the river. Instead he turned north up the Brazos,
and when two of his company commanders angrily refused to march
"away" from the settlements they were "supposed to protect," he made
a virtue of necessity and "commanded" them to guard the crossings.

All this time his army was hampered, delayed, and handicapped
by the hundreds of fleeing families he was shepherding along. Re-

ports of the massacres by Santa Anna added to the terror of the help-less, and the episode still called by Texans the "Runaway Scrape" was under way.

At Groce's plantation Houston crossed the Brazos, seeing that the refugees were over the river before he took his army across the swol-len stream. From there, after a brief rest, he started east again, toward Galveston Bay. The zigzag course he had taken was paying returns. The enemy by this time was thoroughly scattered. Houston had led the Mexican forces over more rain-drenched country, across more swollen rivers, through more canyons, mesquite, cactus, and mud, than they had ever dreamed could exist. The difficulties of transpor-tation were such that Santa Anna had to send his current mistress back to San Antonio, and was able to bring this far only one piece of artillery out of the massed batteries with which he had assailed the Alamo.

North of Houston's army was General Ganoa's pursuing force; to the west were Sesma and Santa Anna himself; farther south General Filisola led a force; while General Urrea was coming up the coast around Matagorda Bay to cut him off.

The Texans reached Buffalo Bayou, and there their enigmatic gen-eral had his first stroke of good fortune. His scouts captured two Mexican dispatch riders. From the papers they carried Houston learned that Santa Anna himself was at New Washington, on Galves-ton Bay—*within one day's march of his army.*

From the hunted, Houston suddenly became the hunter. Thus far he had compelled his men to march by sheer force of personality; but now when they learned that they might at last come to grips with their enemies, his men became eager to follow him.

Leaving his sick and otherwise unfit men at the Harrisburg Crossing of Buffalo Bayou, Houston marched rapidly east toward Lynch's Ferry, where the bayou ran into the San Jacinto River. On the night of April 20 he camped his little army in a thick growth of trees beside Buffalo Bayou, and there, the following morning he at last collided with Santa Anna.

The Mexican dictator had learned of the presence of the Texas army. With more than a thousand men he appeared before it, and made a brief reconnaissance, in which the long rifles took a sharp toll from his advance parties. Santa Anna was content to withdraw them, and he camped three quarters of a mile away at the top of a low rise looking down on the Texas position. His army was arranged in a sort of arc to cut off all possible retreat, for he believed he had the Texans now and he was only awaiting reinforcements which he knew were coming.

Next morning at about 8:30 o'clock General Cos—who had violated his parole—arrived with 540 men, swelling Santa Anna's force to more than 1500. Against these Houston could muster exactly 783 men.

Later Houston said that he allowed Cos to come up because he "did not want to take two bites of one cherry." Actually, he seems to have made an error in planning. He might have attacked Santa Anna when the forces were more nearly equal. Instead he would now have to fight at odds of nearly two to one.

But if that was an error, he made none subsequently. Deaf Smith and some other scouts were dispatched to cut Vince's bridge over Vince's Bayou in the rear. This may have been one of Houston's most important moves in the events of that day.

All morning of April 21 he gave no order to prepare for battle. Instead, to keep his officers busy, he called a council of war and proposed a question: Should they attack or await the enemy's attack?

All except two of his field officers voted to await the enemy's attack.

Without announcing his decision Houston walked away from the council. At 3:30 in the afternoon he suddenly ordered his men to form in battle line. His reasoning was simple: knowing that Cos's men would be resting somewhere in the rear of Santa Anna's army after their forced march, and counting on the Mexican national habit of the *siesta*, he reckoned on a surprise.

At four o'clock he gave the order to advance, with the watchword, "Remember the Alamo!"

Marquis James, Houston's greatest biographer, has eloquently summed up the mighty issues hanging on that command:

"The mastery of a continent was in contention between the champions of two civilizations—racial rivals and hereditary enemies, so divergent in idea and method that suggestion of compromise was an affront. On an obscure meadow of bright grass, nursed by a watercourse named on hardly any map, wet steel would decide which civilization should prevail on these shores and which submit in the clash of men and symbols impending—the conquistador and the frontiersman, the Inquisition and the Magna Charta, the rosary and the rifle."[2]

Up the hill, in a thin line, went "the Last Hope of Texas," Sam Houston riding at the head.

His calculations were remarkably correct, and his men were well upon the Mexicans before an alarm was given. Santa Anna's position had been barricaded with baggage wagons, pack saddles, and other impedimenta. In this barricade Houston's two small cannon—a gift to Texas from the people of Cincinnati—blasted a hole. Then over the defense went the Texans like a wave, their rifles spurting death.

Houston's horse was killed under him. He mounted another and

[2] Marquis James, *The Raven.*

felt it also die beneath him while a bullet struck his ankle. He was assisted onto a third horse, and still he continued to lead his men.

The execution of the rifles was merciless. The Mexican army fell to pieces in frantic rout. But the Texans were "remembering the Alamo." Santa Anna had butchered their comrades, and they were in no mood for mercy. Over that field the maddened avengers raged. When the craze for slaughter was appeased, the tally as officially given was 632 Mexicans killed, 208 wounded, 730 prisoners. The 730 prisoners no doubt included the 208 wounded, and the figure of dead added to it makes the Mexican loss 1362. Fewer than two hundred of Santa Anna's men escaped. Among the dead were one general, four colonels, two lieutenant colonels, and seven captains.

The Texans lost six killed and twenty-five wounded, of whom two died later. One of the wounded was General Houston himself. After the battle was won, he collapsed from loss of blood and lay on a blanket under a tree, giving orders, while a doctor cared for his wound.

Above everything he wanted Santa Anna—alive. But where was Santa Anna? His silken marquee was found empty, with evidences of a very hasty departure by its owner.[3]

On the day after the battle, toward evening, a patrol of Houston's men found a "bedraggled little figure" wearing a blue cotton smock, a filthy leather cap, and red felt slippers. It was Santa Anna. The smock and cap were slave garments he had taken from a deserted cabin to disguise himself. The red slippers, and a linen shirt with diamond studs which he now wore beneath the smock, were what he had on when he fled. He had removed his silk drawers, which he soaked and muddied while trying to ford Vince's Bayou.

[3] One student of the Battle of San Jacinto has produced evidence of a piquant nature to account for the Mexican dictator's lack of alertness when the battle began. Two days before, when he was at Morgan's Point (New Washington) from which President Burnet and his fleeing cabinet had just escaped to Galveston Island, Santa Anna's attention was attracted by one of James Morgan's female slaves. She was "a decorative, long-haired, mulatto girl" about twenty years old. Santa Anna, who was noted for his "voluptuous habits," usually had a mistress in his entourage, but he had been without one for several days since he sent his last of the line back to San Antonio. Now he took the pretty slave girl along to serve that purpose. According to William Bollaert, an English ethnologist, who interviewed the girl, Emily, and her owner two years later, she freely stated that she was with Santa Anna in the presidential marquee at the time of the attack by Houston. Colonel Morgan, her master, said that she was "closeted" with Santa Anna when they heard the cry, "The enemy! They come! They come!" Santa Anna left Emily and ran out of the tent, where he mounted a horse and fled. She said that he was in such haste that he was clad only in silk drawers, a linen shirt with diamond studs, and a pair of morocco slippers. After the battle the girl was returned to her master, Colonel James Morgan, to whom she first related these circumstances. See Frank X. Tolbert, *The Day of San Jacinto* (1959).

This was where Houston's order to destroy Vince's bridge paid off its most handsome dividend. Santa Anna could not swim, and after one attempt to wade the bayou, which was too deep to ford, he hid in the long sedge grass. There was a story that he bogged down his horse trying to force it across the bayou, but evidently he did not do so, for the horse, a black stallion confiscated from Allen Vince, who built the bridge named for him, was found grazing on dry land afterward.

His captors did not know who he was; but at the sight of him some of the prisoners held in a corral near the Texas camp, took off their hats, and murmured *"El Presidente! El Presidente!"*

At once Santa Anna was taken before Houston who lay, with his foot bandaged, under the tree. Houston invited his "guest" to take a seat on an ammunition box and summoned an interpreter. The Mexican, fond of orotund phrases, produced one now:

"That man may consider himself born to no common destiny who had conquered the Napoleon of the West; it now remains for him to be generous to the vanquished."

"You should have remembered that at the Alamo!" growled Houston.

Visibly shaken, the prisoner, who was addicted to eating opium, asked for some. His own case, captured in his marquee and containing the drug, was brought. He ate some of it and seemed to recover his poise.

It was generally and enthusiastically agreed among Houston's men that lynching was not only merited but demanded in a case like the prisoner's. He had pitilessly ordered hundreds to death; it was only right and fair that he should taste some of those pangs to which he had condemned others. There were many present who had lost relatives or friends in Santa Anna's massacres, and the sight of him kicking at a rope's end would have been balm to their spirits.

But Houston had suddenly changed from a soldier to a statesman, and a far-seeing statesman at that. He knew that Santa Anna alive was of much greater value to him and Texas than would be Santa Anna dead. He restrained his men sternly, and Santa Anna, who could not but have felt increasingly nervous as he saw those fierce Texas eyes wistfully appraising his neck for "noose size," became very willing to do anything to mollify his captors.

Obediently, therefore, he agreed to everything as Houston dictated terms of an armistice, and under the stern eye of the wounded giant Santa Anna wrote orders to each of his army commanders in Texas, directing them at once to retreat from Texas soil.

President Burnet, in his retreat on Galveston Island, quickly learned of the destruction of the Mexican army and the detention of the Mexican dictator. He visited Houston's camp, and received from the general a letter, containing certain propositions as a basis for a treaty arrangement with Santa Anna.

By this agreement, sometimes called the Treaty of Velasco—since it was signed at Velasco, Brazoria County, where the prisoners were taken from San Jacinto—Santa Anna, identifying himself as the *de facto* ruler of Mexico, pledged immediate cessation of hostilities, indemnification of persons whose property had been taken or destroyed by his forces, and that all Mexican troops should evacuate all territory, "*passing to the other side of the Rio Grande del Norte.*"

That last provision is worth noting, in view of later disputes. Thus early Texas set her border on the Rio Grande, and received agreement from the head of the Mexican government.

In a later, secret treaty between Burnet and Santa Anna, the definition of this boundary was repeated. Santa Anna stipulated that upon his return to Mexico—where Burnet agreed to send him—he would "arrange for the favourable reception by the Mexican cabinet of a mission from Texas—that a treaty of amity and commerce should be established between the two republics—and that the Texan territory was not to extend *beyond* the Rio Grande."

The later repudiation of this boundary by Mexican authorities did not alter its validity in the eyes of Texas, or those of the United States when Texas joined the Union.

By the splendor of one man's leadership the war was won and Texas had gained her independence. One of Sam Houston's first dispatches announcing his victory went speeding by fast couriers to his old friend and patron through all those years, Andrew Jackson.

CHAPTER TWELVE

"Right or Wrong, My Country"

1

PRESIDENT Andrew Jackson viewed the Texas adventure as a key step in his grand vision for his nation. Nor was Texas the only focal area in the old general's plans.

He was openly and sincerely an expansionist. Expansionism was the theme of the period. Britain, France, Spain, Portugal, Russia, had all shown the way. The first two mentioned were in great periods of imperialism at that very time.

Jackson's friend, Commodore Stephen Decatur, now unfortunately dead as the result of a duel, had proposed a toast at a dinner in 1816:

"Our country! In her intercourse with foreign nations may she always be in the right; but our country, right or wrong!"

The naval hero's words almost exactly expressed Andrew Jackson's life creed. To him there was no higher morality than the prosperity, safety, and advancement of the United States of America.

It was in the year of the Texas revolution, 1836, that he dispatched his secret service agent, William Slacum, to bring in a full report of conditions in the Oregon country. Slacum told him that the Hudson's Bay Company, Britain's great forerunner of empire, had an important post, Fort Vancouver, on the Columbia River, in the middle of the territory to which, by Gray's discovery of the river mouth and the exploration of Lewis and Clark, the United States felt it had the rightful claim. That same company had another trading post at the village of Yerba Buena (now San Francisco) in the great San Francisco Bay, which Slacum had visited in behalf of his chief. This indicated a southward reach into California which might be alarming.

On the credit side, Slacum reported that a considerable farming community had grown up in the rich Willamette Valley, south of Fort Vancouver, and though most of these people were French Canadians—who felt little loyalty toward the British government—there was a leavening of Americans, including a group of missionaries led by Jason Lee, and some mountain men, chief of whom was a violent individual named Ewing Young. Slacum further noted that farther up the Columbia River other Americans were in the country, including *women*—two of them at least, wives of missionaries named Marcus Whitman and Henry Spaulding.

Women! Andrew Jackson's eyes must have gleamed at that. Women —white women—meant permanent settlements, and Jackson clung to his belief in the old Roman rule of *occupatio*, as the only true means of possession of any country. More families, with women and children, must be encouraged to seek this new frontier.

It was not as if the Far West was occupied by a large, settled population, with laws, governments, customs, and property. The Far West was empty land, or virtually so. Its population was thin and primitive, chiefly Indian, although there were a few Mexican-Spanish settlements of no great size. Spain's claim to that great empire of mountains, forests, plains, and deserts, had been weak enough, based on explorations centuries past and never followed up by efficient settlement and development. Mexico's claim, based on the Spanish claim, was still weaker, and Mexico could not even keep her organized provinces— like California, and Zacatecas, and now Texas—from continually revolting. There was a sort of a race for those empty lands, and to Jackson, and others who thought as he did, the nation which could first occupy and make fruitful those lands deserved to hold them.

His blue gaze was not only on Oregon and Texas, but on California. In 1835 he tried to negotiate for the purchase of San Francisco Bay and its surrounding area, at that time considered the section of chief value to the United States. He authorized an offer of money for the bay area. The offer met no response, but Andrew Jackson by no means gave up his hope for a successful outcome of future negotiations.

2

The old general's second administration had not been without incident.

He made a triumphal tour of the North, where he received unprecedented ovations in Baltimore, Philadelphia, New York, Boston, and wherever else he appeared. Harvard College conferred upon him the honorary degree of Doctor of Laws, which horrified the most distinguished alumnus of that institution, John Quincy Adams.

"Is there no way to prevent this outrage?" he asked.

"None," answered his kinsman, Josiah Quincy, who was president of the college. "As the people have twice decided that this man knows

enough law to be their ruler, it is not for Harvard College to maintain
that they were mistaken."[1]

On this Northern tour he again suffered severe illness—his old lung
abscess plus the dysentery, but he was strong enough on his return
to grapple once more with Nicholas Biddle and his Bank of the United
States. Biddle was creating an "artificial" panic by discontinuing dis-
counts and demanding the return of his Bank's balances in state
banks, as a measure to show his power and bring about through public
demand the new charter he desired when his present one expired in
1836.

Jackson's move was characteristically decisive. He proposed to remove the government deposits from the big Bank, and place them in
the smaller state banks for their relief and to deprive Biddle of the
kind of power he was exercising. The first results were not encouraging. Kendall, sent to sound out certain key state banks on the matter
of receiving these funds, discovered a curious reluctance on the part
of some of them. Fear of reprisals by Biddle had much to do with
this, but there were also the strict guarantees which Jackson demanded,
and which some of the smaller banks were unprepared to give.

Yet Jackson decided finally that there were enough banks for his
purpose, and asked his Secretary of the Treasury, Louis McLane, to
order the deposits removed from the Bank of the United States. At
that time they were about $10,000,000. McLane refused. Already he
had disagreed with the proposal in a report to the President in which
he urged his fear of chaotic financial conditions should such a step be
taken.

Jackson simply removed McLane from his office by the expedient
of appointing him Secretary of State, *vice* Edward Livingston, who
went as minister to France a post which he had long desired. Mc-
Lane's successor was William J. Duane, a Philadelphia lawyer. Actually this change had been contemplated before the Bank question
arose in its present state, and Duane was McLane's own nominee for
the position he vacated.

But Duane proved equally recalcitrant. After seeking in every way
to gain the new secretary's acquiescence, Jackson appealed to Van
Buren, now Vice-President. From that gentleman he received cautious
counsel which chimed in with that of McLane; urging that while

---

[1] A comic newspaper columnist gave a version of the presentation, which was
preceded by an address in Latin. The President, the writer said, was enjoined
to reply in Latin. "*E pluribus unum*," says he. "My friends, *sine qua non*." The
item was so widely read and quoted that many persons believed Jackson used
those actual words. In reality his reply was in English, brief, gracious, and well
phrased; and afterward he set out to shake hands with every member of the
Harvard student body.

plans might well be prepared for transferring the deposits, the act itself should be delayed at least until the first of the coming year.

"Is it possible," Old Hickory asked Van Buren, "that your friends are overawed by the power of the Bank? . . . It cannot overawe me!"

He had collected still stronger evidence of Biddle's secret loans to Congressmen, and editors,[2] and money spent by him for propaganda purposes.

After exhausting every dignified effort to change the attitude of Duane—who as Secretary of the Treasury alone had the legal right to remove the deposits—the old President dismissed him September 23. Attorney General Roger B. Taney was named to the post in his stead. From the outset Taney had been with Jackson in the war against the Bank, and he gave immediate notice that government deposits would not be made in the Bank of the United States after the last day of that month.

Biddle had not thought Jackson would dare take such an action. Nevertheless he had prepared for the eventuality by getting his own Bank in condition and drawing many state banks into its debt. As Taney went about the work of preparing the chosen state banks—now known as "pet banks"—for their new responsibilities, commerce through the nation slackened, industry flagged, prices went down, workers were laid off. In every way the banker sought to make suffer the very people who were Jackson's most numerous supporters.

In the face of this and the rising cry of protest occasioned by it the deposits were removed, beginning October 1.

Biddle and Clay struck back. After a tremendous three-day speech of denunciation, Clay moved in the Senate a resolution of censure against Andrew Jackson for violating the Constitution and the law. It was passed and duly inscribed on the record. (Two years later, under the leadership of Thomas Hart Benton, the resolution was expunged.)

But censure of any kind did not halt the old general as he slugged it out with the Bank. He was clearly out of his element in the deep financial waters where Biddle was perfectly at home. His system, thrown together, could not equal the precise efficiency of the big Bank and its branches. Some of the state banks did not live up to their agreements, and one almost went to the wall.

Tighter and tighter Nicholas Biddle pulled the strings of credit, creating vast distress over the country. Delegation after delegation

---

[2] Among the editors Biddle favored in this manner was James Gordon Bennett, at this time executive head of the New York *Courier and Enquirer*, but soon to launch his celebrated *Herald*.

called upon the President, begging him to make peace with the Bank, "for the sake of the nation."

"Come not to me!" Andrew Jackson told them. "Go to the monster!"

In the midst of this excitement an effort was made to assassinate him: the first assassination attempt against a President of the United States. Ironically, it had nothing to do with the financial furore or any of the other issues of the general's opponents.

On January 30, 1835, Jackson attended the funeral of a South Carolina Congressman, Warren R. Davis, which was held in the Hall of Representatives. As he was leaving through the east entrance of the Capitol, a bearded stranger stepped from behind one of the columns of the portico, aimed a pistol at him, and pulled the trigger.

A sharp report echoed through the stone chamber and was heard by everyone in it. First to realize that an attempt was being made on his life, Old Hickory seized his walking cane like a club and lunged forward at the assailant.

Calmly the man drew a second pistol, and again a report rang out.

Men looked with horror, expecting to see the President fall. But Jackson did not step back or stagger. Instead he tried to reach the stranger who had fired.

But a young naval attaché, Lieutenant Gedney, reached the assailant first, and with a tremendous tackle hurled him to the stone steps. Others helped secure the assassin, while some sought to assist the President.

"Let me go, gentlemen!" Old Hickory cried to those who took hold of him, expecting to support him, believing he was wounded. "I am not afraid—they can't kill me—I can protect myself!"

It was found that by something very closely approaching a miracle he was uninjured. The reports heard had been made by the explosion of the percussion caps of the pistols, which for some reason failed to detonate the charges in the weapons. A contemporary report gives the unusual circumstances:

> His pistols . . . were found to be a very elegant pair, in most excellent order, and loaded with powder and ball almost to the muzzle, the barrels being about six inches long. On examining the load in one of the pistols a ball was drawn out by means of a screw . . . it was well packed, and forced down tight on a full charge of excellent glazed powder. The [other] pistol still loaded [was] tried, by putting on another cap . . . The discharge took immediate effect.

After various other trials, in which neither of the pistols missed fire in a single instance, an expert on firearms said that the chances that both pistols would misfire under such circumstances were less than one in one hundred thousand.

Intense excitement was created by the incident, and many believed that the assassination attempt was inspired. John Calhoun found it necessary to rise on the floor of the Senate and deny any complicity, and John Quincy Adams in the House proclaimed his allegiance to the President.

Jackson himself believed at first that the effort to kill him had his enemies behind it.

"I want to get to the bottom of this," he said. But he insisted that the assailant be given a fair trial.

The man was Richard Lawrence, a house painter, thirty-five years old, and unmarried. Unquestionably he was insane, as the investigation proved. He made a habit of frequenting the galleries of the Senate and House of Representatives, and the violent criticism he heard there and elsewhere against the President, turned his crazed mind on Jackson. One of his delusions was that he was the rightful king of England, and he came to the belief that in some manner Jackson stood between him and the throne. Thus the distempered criticism of the head of the government brought about the lunatic's intended act. He was confined in a madhouse.

Meantime Jackson struggled with inflation and speculation and toward the latter days of his administration ordered that only specie be accepted in payment of lands bought from the government. But gold and silver were scarce, and the demand for them increased. Some took to hiding hard money. The full effects of the financial situation were not, however, felt until his successors came into office.

But the people had by this time seized upon Jackson's slogan, "Go to Biddle!" Public censure turned upon the banker. Too late he realized that his self-created panic was his Bank's death blow. He had only succeeded in demonstrating, what Jackson had always claimed, that his Bank, as constituted, possessed too much power over the public welfare. At the close of its charter, in 1836, he sold off the branches and his Bank eventually failed.

There were to be financial vicissitudes of various kinds, and numerous fiscal experiments, before a workable national financial system finally was devised; but no private corporation would again control the money and the credit of the whole nation.

3

Compared to his internal problems, international affairs were almost a relaxation to Old Hickory. He induced Britain to open her West Indies ports to American trade, made a strong point of the American claim to the Columbia basin, and concluded several commercial treaties with a "most-favored nation" clause for the United States.

Collecting foreign indemnities was an activity he conducted with zest. Those of Spain and Denmark were easily arranged. His method of settling the claims against the Kingdom of Naples was almost mischievous. Jackson sent a commissioner to call on the king of Naples for the sums due, and the delegate rode as a passenger on one of a small fleet of five warships commanded by Commandant David T. Patterson. Into the Bay of Naples sailed the little flotilla with cannon roaring. There was a panic in the streets. Then Naples discovered that this was no bombardment, but a salute—most correct, courteous, and respectful. The king of Naples, however, took the hint. When the commissioner returned to America—on his ship of war—he carried the full amount of the debt owed.

France, however, was more difficult. For twenty years the French had delayed, offered excuses, failed to make payments promised on their agreed debt of 25,000,000 francs (about $5,000,000). At last Jackson sent a message to Congress, recommending that if the delays continued, reprisals should be taken against French property.

The French chose to regard this as an affront to the honor of France. Old Hickory replied by ordering the Navy to make ready for sea duty.

There was Gallic oratory in the Chamber of Deputies and Gallic furore on the boulevards of Paris. But the French government, headed by King Louis Philippe, knew that the matter might be too serious for forensics. The French minister, Louis Sérurier, called upon the American Secretary of State, at that time John Forsyth of Georgia.

"What do you wish, Monsieur, a collision between us?" he asked.

"We desire the execution of the treaty to which you have agreed," replied Forsyth coolly, and added that the President considered that the people of the United States were "entitled to an explanation" of the proceedings thus far.

Jackson had expressed the position that the time had come for the United States to "take redress into our own hands."

M. Sérurier hastily communicated these portents to his government.

There was a phrase then current in the West. When a man made loud boasts of what he might do to another man, that man as acceptance of the challenge would say contemptuously, "Go on—turn loose your wolf."

Jackson had, in effect, invited France to "turn loose her wolf." The American people cheered him. Marine insurance went up. Stocks flurried. But the nation was with him. What had been a stumbling block for his predecessors he had converted by just the right touch into a national issue with popular support.

France, after a little consideration, decided against "turning loose

her wolf." She tried to save face by asking Old Hickory to apologize
for the abrupt language used in his message.

"The honor of my country," said the old general in a message to Congress, "shall never be stained by an apology from me for the statement
of truth or the performance of duty." He added that he had said nothing intended to "menace or insult the Government of France," but
in view of the "peremptory refusal [of France] to execute the treaty"
the Executive requested "large and speedy appropriations for the increase of the Navy and completion of our coast defenses."

The French made a new study of the previous Jacksonian statement,
and focused upon the word *pretendu* in describing the non-accom-
plishment of the French engagements. This had been translated as
"pretended" which touched the honor of France; but a different trans-
lation might be "alleged" which was considered not offensive.

France now perceived that she might after all pay up—with honor.
Installments, with interest, began at once. Jackson had added one
more international triumph to his record.

Meantime, on January 8, 1835, he had achieved an ambition close
to his heart. On that day, the anniversary of his victory at New Orleans,
the last installment of the national debt was paid, but two years after
Biddle had proposed help to pay it.

The event was celebrated by a grand banquet, at which Thomas
Hart Benton presided. Jackson's great and stanch friend, when the
cloth was removed, made an exultant speech.

"The national debt is paid!" Benton exclaimed. "This month of
January, 1835, in the fifty-eighth year of the Republic, Andrew Jackson being President, the national debt is paid! And the apparition, so
long unseen on earth—a great nation without a national debt—stands
revealed to the astonished vision of a wondering world! Gentlemen,
my heart is in this double celebration, and I offer you a sentiment
which, coming direct from my own bosom, will find its response in
yours: 'President Jackson: May the evening of his days be as tranquil
and as happy for himself as their meridian has been resplendent,
glorious, and beneficent for his country!'"

Nothing he had succeeded in doing pleased the old warrior more
than this event for which he had worked so long and which he regarded as a sacred promise he had made to the nation.

4

But now came a new international complication, yet one which he
could not shun, and did not wish to shun.

News of the incredible victory at San Jacinto and the winning of

Texas independence went over the United States in a storm of re-joicing. Andrew Jackson's reactions were recorded by Lieutenant Hitchcock of the United States dragoons who brought the dispatches announcing the mighty consummation.

Old Hickory fairly snatched the papers from the young man's hand, and his eyes blazed as he exclaimed, "Yes, that is his writing! I know it well. That is Sam Houston's writing. There can be no doubt about what he says!"

He had the *fait accompli* of Texas in his lap. What would he do with it?

Jackson had watched the unfolding drama of the Texas war for lib-eration with the intense interest of a soldier as well as that of a states-man. Though he recognized the weakness of the colonists, he counted on his favorite subaltern, Sam Houston, somehow to bring about a victory. When, during Houston's long retreat, some of those around the President surmised that the Texas leader was fleeing for the United States border, Old Hickory indignantly repelled the idea. Houston would fight, he said. He even, according to two testimonies,[3] predicted with his finger indicating the place on the map, that the battle would be somewhere near the entrance of the San Jacinto River into Galveston Bay.

He could not intervene officially, but he did what he could for Texas.

General Edmund P. Gaines, commanding the United States troops in Louisiana, was ordered to observe "strict neutrality," but given dis-cretion to furnish aid if needed against hostile aggression by Indians, "against either Anglo-American or Mexican states." When the Co-manches, stimulated by representations and gifts from Mexican agents, began depredations in northern Texas, Gaines exercised his dis-cretionary powers and moved troops across the Sabine, occupying Nacogdoches.

It must be regarded as an act of aggression by the United States, given technical excuse by an earlier treaty with Mexico whereby both nations agreed to prevent Indian hostilities against the citizens of either. By it Gaines gave the Texans protection in their rear, and the troops in Nacogdoches later were a powerful deterrent against Mexican thoughts of a second attempt at reconquest of Texas. The Mexican minister in Washington made strong and indignant protests, but the troops remained in Nacogdoches.

---

[3] James A. Parton, *A Life of Andrew Jackson*, (2 vols. 1859–60) and the reminiscences of Nicholas P. Trist, published in the New York *Evening Post*, in July, 1856.

Texas was in critical need of finances; and when Austin arrived in the United States seeking aid for his beleaguered country, he petitioned Jackson in a letter, which read in part as follows:

It appears that Santana [*sic*] has succeeded in uniting the whole of the Mexicans against Texas by making it a national war against heretics . . . Let the President and the Cabinet and the Congress come out openly and at once, and proclaim their opinions—let Texas have some of the $37,000,000 now in the national treasury—let the war in Texas become a *National war, above board,* and thus respond to the noble feelings of the American people. Who can deny that it is a national war in reality—a war in which every free American who is not a fanatic, abolitionist, or cold-hearted recreant to the interests in honor and principles, country and countrymen, who is not an icicle in soul and practice, is deeply, warmly, ardently interested . . .

Jackson was for Texas, heart and soul; but as President he could not devote funds of the national treasury to that cause. Perhaps, however, there were unofficial ways to assist. Two weeks after this appeal to Jackson, a loan of $100,000 was made to Texas by New York financiers. Other loans from private individuals were negotiated by Austin.

All such loans, though "secured" by land in Texas, were of course highly speculative. Nicholas Biddle and his Bank of the United States flatly rejected an application for $500,000, for Biddle did not consider Texas assets as bankable securities.

How much Andrew Jackson's influence had to do with the floating of these loans is one of the secrets of history. We do know, however, that he himself "contributed to the extent of my means" to a fund for Texas, and his interest certainly did no harm to the Texas efforts to obtain financing.

5

Within a week after the news of the Texas victory, John C. Calhoun, pallid and portentous, arose in the Senate and said there were "powerful reasons" for recognizing the independence of Texas, and further than that, for admitting her into the Union.

Had any other spokesman made the proposal it would have done less harm. Calhoun by this time was the acknowledged spokesman for the slave-holding South, and his statement tended to make Texas not the national issue Jackson hoped it would be, but a sectional issue.

The President had need to tread a delicate path. He profoundly desired that Texas join the Union, but above all he wanted to keep the nation united.

Old Hickory was an expansionist, but he was no slave expansionist. He owned slaves but he believed, and had so stated, that slavery nurtured the roots of disunion. He had been one of those leaders who in the early 1830s considered proposals for gradual emancipation, not only in Tennessee, but in Virginia, Kentucky, and North Carolina; and he might have agreed with his friend Washington Irving, who observed, "In these [slave] establishments the world is turned upside down—the slave the master, the master the slave. The master has the idea of property, the latter the reality."

He had dreamed, as had Clay and Benton, of a nation extending to the far Pacific, but for the present he made no move toward even recognizing Texas, in large part because of the explosive quality of the slavery issue.

Meantime General Sam Houston, after an absence for the treatment of his wound in New Orleans, returned to Texas and was elected president of the new republic. One of his first acts was to send two men to President Jackson—Santa Anna, still a prisoner, and now expressing eagerness to "guarantee the acquiescence of Mexico to the annexation of Texas by the United States"; and a personal envoy, William H. Wharton, in whom Houston placed more faith than he did in the Mexican. The state of public feeling was quickly discovered by the arrival of the two men. Santa Anna was almost lionized by the anti-Texas element in the East, and a strangely unrealistic view of him was taken in the North, as was illustrated by a comment in the Woonsocket, Rhode Island, *Patriot:*

How can we style him tyrant who opposed the efforts of rebels and used them with deserved severity, and fought and bled to contravene the efforts of those who wished to substantiate the horrible system of slavery?

Deserved severity . . . did the writer consider Santa Anna's massacres in Zacatecas and Texas? *Fought and bled* . . . when the dictator fled like a craven and left his army to its fate?

The other side was recorded by Wharton in a report written to Houston when he reached Kentucky:

The Southern papers . . . are acting most imprudently . . . Language such as the following is uttered by the most respectable journals . . . "The North must choose between the Union with Texas added—or no Union."

Santa Anna reached Jackson first—under the wardenship of Colonel Bernard E. Bee. Old Hickory conferred with him, explored the possibility of buying the California area including San Francisco Bay— suggesting $3,500,000 as a purchase price—and another sum, not named, for the assent by Mexico to the Texas annexation. The latter idea was rejected by Wharton, who had now arrived, on the ground that "Texas would submit to no such indignity." Jackson wearied of fruitless talk, shipped Santa Anna to Veracruz and his not highly appreciative countrymen.

Jackson's second term was nearing an end and Martin Van Buren had been elected his successor. In his final days he wrote a message to Congress, in which he said, "Recognition [of Texas] at this time . . . would scarcely be regarded as consistent with that prudent reserve with which we have heretofore held ourselves bound to treat all such similar questions."

Wharton could not believe it when he read it. "Prudent reserve" hardly seemed "consistent" with the Andrew Jackson who had for years tried to obtain Texas, by purchase, advice to Houston, and contributions to the war chest of the Lone Star republic.

The old general was packing, preparing to leave the White House for his successor. But he had not, as Wharton thought, given up hope of Texas; nor had he stopped thinking.

The tenor of his thoughts was revealed in almost his last conversation with Wharton. What, he asked, were the boundaries of Texas? They had not been definitely established.

"Texas," the old warrior said, *"must claim the Californias."* This would paralyze the opposition of the North and East to annexation. "The fishing interests of the North and East wish a harbor on the Pacific," he went on. Should it be offered, they would be reconciled to the annexation of Texas.

This conversation was reported by Wharton in a letter dated February 16, 1837. "He is very earnest and anxious on this point of claiming the Californias, and says we must not consent to less," wrote Wharton. "This is in strict confidence. Glory to God in the highest."

Though no immediate action was taken on this insistent advice, it was to bear important fruit later.

And then, as his last act in office, Jackson appointed Alcée La Branche of Louisiana, "to be Chargé d'Affaires to the Republic of Texas." At midnight, March 3, the Senate confirmed the appointment.

It was the recognition for which Texas had pleaded. No longer was she a province of Mexico, but an independent nation.

The next day Andrew Jackson saw his successor, Martin Van Buren, sworn in, and became himself a private citizen.

What had he done for his country?

He gave a new concept to democracy. When the framers of the first government set up the machinery for the election of Presidents, they intended that the people at large should have little or nothing to do with the election of the Chief Magistrate. State legislatures originally were expected to choose electors, and these, by exercising wisdom and experience and a knowledge of public men which the common people presumably did not possess, would then choose a suitable President. Jackson was elected by the pressure of the people. He broke down the old system whereby Presidential candidates were nominated by Congressional caucuses. The first party conventions were a result of his beliefs and acts.

He ended, at least for a time, the Hamiltonian creed of rule by privilege; and through his foreign policy he raised the prestige of the young American nation to a height it had never before attained among world powers.

He lived by valor in both his private and public lives, provided an example of selfless patriotism, and though he wielded power like a sword, it was for the benefit, as he saw it, of the people, never for himself. As one historian has said, "He brought to the Presidency fewer personal ambitions than any man except Washington." Continuously he sacrificed himself, suffered almost all the time from pains and illnesses during his terms of office, and died poor and in debt. He was more popular with the people when he went out of office, than when he entered it.

Among his achievements not the least was the spurring of America on that avalanche-like rush across the continent which would make the far Pacific its western boundary. He knew—none better—the stupendous consequences which would follow should Texas become independent and then be annexed by the United States. To the day of his death his mind grappled with the problems inherent in such a departure for his country, and his power with the people was felt to the end.

Above all, he enunciated for all to understand, and enforced for the first time as Chief Executive, the principle of the sovereignty of the Union, a principle Abraham Lincoln was to make forever permanent.

He had deserved well of the Republic.

BOOK **III**

Manifest Destiny

CHAPTER THIRTEEN

Panic and Lands of Promise

1

GEORGE TEMPLETON STRONG was an ordinary enough man in most respects. Somewhat snobbish, a music lover, quite good looking, public spirited to a degree, with money in reasonable amounts, he was an average person, in all but one thing: he kept a diary, a journal which ran for almost forty years, and his diary is a mirror of events as he saw them. Edited and annotated by Allan Nevins it has recently (1952) been published.

As early as 1837, at the end of his sixteenth and beginning of his seventeenth years, when he was attending Columbia College in New York, the following entries appear in his diary:

April 12. Terrible lot of failures today, Mr. Hull and Abraham Ogden among them. Awful bad times. The merchants are going to the devil *en masse*. Hope they'll carry nobody else after them. . . .

April 27. Matters very bad . . . Confidence annihilated . . . Fears entertained for the banks, and if they go, God only knows what the consequences will be. Ruin here, and on the other side of the Atlantic, and not only private ruin but political convulsion and revolution, I think . . . As for the banks, they are losing from five to fifty thousand dollars daily in the way of specie . . . Where in the name of wonder is this all to end?

May 2. Matters worse and worse in Wall Street . . . prospect of universal ruin and general insolvency of the banks . . . Business at a stand; the coal in Pennsylvania mines stopped and no fuel in prospect for next winter . . .

May 3 . . . Fresh failures . . . So they go—smash, crash . . . Near two hundred and fifty failures thus far!

May 4 . . . Terrible news in Wall Street. [John] Fleming, late president of the Mechanics Bank, found dead in his bed this morning. Some say prussic acid . . . a run on the bank—street crowded—more feeling of alarm and despondency in Wall Street than has appeared yet . . . Fears entertained that tomorrow the attack will be general on all the banks; if so they'll go down and then all the banks from Maine to Louisiana must follow—universal ruin.

May 6 . . . There's a run on the Dry Dock Bank and the other banks have refused to sustain it!

May 9 . . . As I expected, there's a run on all banks, the depositors drawing out specie as fast as the tellers can count it.

May 10. Extensive news in this morning's paper. The banks (except three) have concluded to stop specie payment ! ! ! Glory to the old General! Glory to little Marty [Martin Van Buren], second fiddler to the great Magician—ay, and double patent glory—to the experiment, the specie currency, and all the glorious humbugs who have inflicted them on us.

Commerce and speculation here have been spreading of late like a card house, story after story and ramification after ramification till the building towered up to the sky and people rolled up their eyes in amazement, but at last one corner gave way and every card that dropped brought down a dozen with it, and *sic transit gloria mundi!* How people have grown rich of late! I often wondered when I heard how Messrs. A.B.C. and D. were worth a million apiece and how people were now worth half a million at least before they could be called more than paupers. I often wondered where all the money had come from and how such a quantity of wealth had found its way into the country. But there's the result of it.

This description, the more vivid since it came from the pen of a boy who knew as yet comparatively little of the workings of finance, is the opening of one of the greatest financial disasters in this nation's history.

It began with a wave of wild speculation which swept Europe and communicated itself to the United States. Eighty-nine state banks had been selected to receive government deposits after Jackson took the national funds from the Bank of the United States, and these and other financial institutions were overwilling to lend money to speculators, causing a spiraling inflation. Then Congress voted to distribute the national surplus of $28,000,000 among the several states—which took money from the banks when they needed it most. Jackson's so-called "Specie Circular" of July 1836, an effort to halt speculation by requiring gold or silver coin as payment for public lands, added to this embarrassment.

When Martin Van Buren took office the country was in a speculating debauch. Much of this was in lands. The sale of public lands leaped from 4,500,000 acres in 1834 to 20,000,000 acres in 1836. New York real estate soared to nearly double values. Farm lands on Long Island brought fantastic prices. Even waste tracts of timber in Maine and elsewhere sold "in some cases at 1000 per cent of their ordinary value."

Inevitably the reckoning came. A financial crisis first appeared in

England, causing British bankers to call in their American loans and reducing the price of American cotton. A season of poor crops further lowered farmers' purchasing power. In May 1837 a large cotton firm in New Orleans failed, involving others. Efforts of banks in New York and Philadelphia to halt the disastrous trend were futile. Merchandise prices went down everywhere, and with them the prices of real estate. Stocks fell even faster. When, on May 10, as young Strong recorded, the banks in New York suspended specie payments, others all over the country followed their example.

Everywhere business was prostrate, building operations ceased, mercantile houses failed, more than one man, seeing his fortune evaporate in the panic, took his own life. The final crash of the Bank of the United States put the cap to the disaster.

Distress was felt by every class, but in particular by the poorer people. Workers were laid off until the cities were filled with unemployed. In spite of overcrowded poorhouses and private charities, some even starved to death in the slums, or else froze to death when coal supplies failed in the unusually severe winter of 1838.[1]

2

In this national emergency President Van Buren had little to offer in the way of relief measures. It would be difficult to find a greater contrast than that between him and his predecessor. Andrew Jackson was tall, lean, stern, sometimes fiery, and frank-minded. Van Buren was short, plump, dapper, and politically sly. A contemporary describes him:

> He endeavored to establish a personal intimacy with everyone presented to him, and he ostensibly opened his heart for inspec-

[1] Mortgages on farms and homes were foreclosed to such an extent that the people and even officials sometimes took matters in their own hands to halt them. General James Findlay, a stalwart Jacksonian, and receiver of the land office at Cincinnati, provided an example of this. Bluff, hearty, and corpulent, he attended a sale where a large number of farms in the region north of Cincinnati were forfeited. He soon learned that a number of speculators were in the crowd, hoping to get property for little or nothing in the distress auction. General Findlay mounted a stump and made a little speech. He was there, he said, to offer the designated lands to the highest bidder. All the owners, he added, were honest men who because of hard times had been unable to meet their obligations, and it was hard to be forced from homes by such circumstances. Nevertheless, he went on, the law ordered that the lands be offered. "And now," he concluded, his voice rising, "I trust there is no gentleman—no, I will not say that, I hope there is no *rascal*—here, so mean as to buy his neighbor's home over his head. Gentlemen, I offer this lot for sale. Who bids?" There was no forfeited land sold that day.

tion. The tone of his voice was that of thorough frankness,
but a fixed expression at the corners of his mouth and the searching look of his keen eyes showed that he believed, with Talley-
rand, that language was given to conceal thought.[2]

Jackson, who sponsored Van Buren, made him President in spite
of opposition from some Democratic leaders. Van Buren's running
mate also was selected by Jackson. He was Colonel Richard Mentor
Johnson, who commonly was called "Tecumseh" Johnson, because it
was at first believed (though later disproved) that he killed the famous Indian chief, Tecumseh, at the Battle of the Thames, in the War
of 1812. It may not have been Tecumseh he killed, but in any case,
he was a stout fighter, and received five wounds in that battle.
Throughout he was a strong supporter of Old Hickory, had been a
Representative in Congress from Kentucky from 1807 to 1819, and a
Senator from 1819 to 1829, and he was considerable of an individualist.
One of his eccentricities—in that day particularly—was that he lived
openly with a mulatto mistress, Julia Chinn, by whom he had two
daughters, Adeline and Imogene. Both the daughters were very light-
skinned, and were given private tutoring at his home in Kentucky.
Both girls married white men and lived on land he provided for them.
It is interesting that with this relationship known, he was steadily
elected to public office in Kentucky, and was solidly backed by Andrew Jackson, a Tennesseean. Julia, his mistress, died in 1833. In the
election of 1836, while Van Buren obtained a majority of the electors, Johnson did not, but by a vote of the Senate he was elected Vice-
President. Decidedly there must have been some qualities in this
man's character that won for him—and maintained—strong friendships.

Where Andrew Jackson was a statesman, Martin Van Buren was
merely a politician. He shrank from the Texas annexation issue, and
managed to let it "simmer" during his administration. But he could
not escape the reality of the great panic, which, to do him justice, was
really not his fault.

While people starved, he temporized. At last, alarmed by failures of
banks holding government deposits, he made the first and almost the
only constructive proposal of his administration: that an Independent
Treasury be set up, isolated from all private banks, as a repository for
national funds, from which national expenses should be paid.

At once the proposal was bitterly attacked by the Whigs, led by
Henry Clay. It was Clay's plan to establish a new central bank, somewhat on the lines of the now defunct Bank of the United States. Here
was an opportunity to embarrass, perhaps wreck the Democratic administration.

[2] Ben: Perley Poore.

In this emergency John C. Calhoun, who had hitherto allied himself with Clay, unexpectedly rose as a champion of the President's proposal. Calhoun saw in the Independent Treasury at least the beginnings of workable government control of money, and he submerged his personal dislike for Van Buren, even his personal ambitions, for what he considered the common good.

Clay and he at once clashed, the Kentuckian furious at what he regarded as his ally's defection. As the debate over the Independent Treasury continued session after session—it was not finally made a law until 1841—"Clay and Calhoun passed from their discussion of national finances into an acrimonious reciprocal review of the acts, votes, and motions of each other during the preceding thirty years." That review was revealing, for each knew much of the almost secret thoughts of the other in the three decades they had sometimes battled each other, sometimes fought side by side in Congress and the government.

Meantime the depression slowly dragged its course. It reached its depths in 1841, and after that conditions gradually grew better. Yet though the nation recovered from the panic, a darker question remained: slavery. It came to the fore in a particularly ugly manner during the administration of the astute but unfortunate Mr. Van Buren.

3

The great Victorian reform movement was abroad in the land. Not only the abolition movement, but the temperance (later prohibition) movement, a campaign against the use of tobacco, feminism in general, various food faddisms, reform of some jails and hospitals, and numerous cults of religious or theoretical types, including one or two that practiced free love in the name of religion or philosophy, were products of this period.

Abolition, however, was the most explosive. William Lloyd Garrison, the leading abolition agitator, surpassed himself by denouncing the Constitution, exclaiming that "the compact which exists between the North and the South is a covenant with death and an agreement with hell—involving both parties in atrocious criminality, and should be immediately annulled."

Wrote the historian James Truslow Adams:

> The abolitionists were ready to place their cause above all others. Slavery was a great evil, which civilized mankind was gradually growing away from, but unless the abolitionists could end it immediately, they were willing to sacrifice the nation.

The abolitionists, of course, were right in their desire to extirpate slavery, but they might have been more effective had they behaved with more moderation. Many in the North and even the South wished to see the institution put at an end, and conceivably, had it not been for the furious agitators a peaceful solution, in time might have been found. But this did not suit Garrison and his following. They shouted their fiery condemnations of the South, from a safe distance in the North, stirring the most violent feelings.

The South, thrown on the defensive and resenting these gasconades, threatened abolitionists with personal violence if they entered Southern states, and demanded that Congress enact laws barring anti-slavery literature from the mails.

In the North, feeling against abolitionist radicals was almost as violent. Mobs threatened and sometimes attacked abolition speakers. Garrison himself was assailed in Boston, where he published his paper, the *Liberator,* and had to be rescued by the police who lodged him in the jail for his own safety. The *Liberator* was of such radical nature that after the Nat Turner slave uprising in Virginia, Garrison published a diatribe, apparently directed against his critics in the North, of which the following is a paragraph:

> Ye patriotic hypocrites! ye panegyrists of Frenchmen, Greeks and Poles! . . . Cast no reproach upon the conduct of slaves, but let your lips and cheeks wear the blisters of condemnation! Ye accuse the pacific friends of emancipation of instigating the slaves to revolt. Take back the charge as a foul slander. The slaves need no incentives at our hands. They will find them in their stripes . . . in your speeches, your conversations, your celebrations!

Garrison proclaimed himself a pacifist, a "non-resistant" who would not fight even to uphold his voiced principles and kept himself quite safe from slave territories. But the Reverend Elijah P. Lovejoy, a Presbyterian minister, was of sterner fiber. He published a religious magazine, the *Observer,* in St. Louis, where, although there was much sentiment for freedom of the slaves the state laws permitted slaveholding, and many persons detested the very name of abolitionist.

Lovejoy was a zealot, who attacked everyone with whom he disagreed. At first (in 1833) he advocated a gradual freeing of the slaves, such as was then in process of being carried out by the British in their West Indian possessions.[3]

---

[3] He did not suggest the exact form emancipation took in Britain. Parliament voted 20,000,000 pounds sterling to recompense the planters, and established an apprentice system for slaves, of seven years at first, later reduced to five years, as a transitional preparation for liberty. Planters in the West Indies received,

But feeling was so strong that Lovejoy's suggestions excited opposition in St. Louis. Perhaps this feeling was accentuated by the fact that he attacked not only slaveholders but also the Catholic Church—not because it had any connection with slavery, but because Lovejoy was a bigot and hated Catholics. His journal, the *Observer*, made unsavory suggestions about conduct in Catholic nunneries, and later Lovejoy published a statement: "I never said there was 'not a chaste female in the [Catholic] church'; I said as a *general truth* there was not, and I repeat it."

When threats were made, Lovejoy insisted on his right of "free speech and a free press," but finding resentment growing, he decided to move his press into Illinois, across and up the Mississippi River from St. Louis, to Alton. This, presumably, was free-soil territory.

But when his press reached the dock, a mob smashed it. Sympathizers bought him a new press. By this time Lovejoy's blood was up. He came out for immediate abolition and a state anti-slavery society, and renewed his attacks on the Catholics. A mob destroyed this second press in August 1837 and wrecked a third in September of the same year.

The men who wrecked the presses appear not to have been all Catholics, or slaveholders, so much as citizens who believed that so incendiary a journal as the *Observer* in their city, would injure Alton and prevent its growth.

On November 1, after a fourth press had been installed and no change occurred in Lovejoy's policies, a mob formed before the building where the *Observer* was published. Lovejoy had gathered some of his supporters, who were armed with guns. As the crowd began throwing stones at the building, the defenders opened fire. A young man named Bishop was killed. First blood for the abolitionists.

The mob retired and came back with firearms. In the battle that followed, during which attempts were made to set fire to the building, Lovejoy, who had twice appeared at windows and fired on the crowd outside, was shot to death on his third appearance at a door, gun in hand. After that his men surrendered, the press was thrown into the Mississippi, and Lovejoy became the first martyr for the cause of abolition. His younger brother Owen, who was with him when the

---

according to one estimate, about $400 for each slave regardless of age or sex. To have paid at that rate for as many as 3,000,000 slaves in the United States would have cost $1,200,000,000. But the slave-holders, of course, would not have agreed to a figure so low, nor the Northern taxpayers to a payment that in that day appeared so colossal. Instead they drifted into the Civil War which cost more than half a million lives, over $6,000,000,000 in treasure to the Union and Confederate governments, enormous destruction of property, loss of all slaves, and complete prostration of the South.

was killed, took to the platform and his fiery speeches were among the most effective in the abolitionist campaigns, as he recited the story of Elijah's struggles and death. If Owen Lovejoy made any mention of Bishop, the young man who was killed by the abolitionists, available records do not show it.

4

By 1840 it was apparent that Van Buren could not be re-elected even if nominated. The Whigs were in the ascendancy, and now Henry Clay, who had bowed out in the previous election when he foresaw defeat, expressed his willingness to make the race for the Presidency. Several legislatures endorsed him, and he appears to have been quite sure of his nomination by the Whig convention. To his son he wrote:

> If I am to judge from information which daily, almost hourly reaches me, there is everywhere an irresistible current setting towards me.

But the Whig convention made up its own mind, and showed considerable perspicacity in so doing. The two greatest Whig figures, of course, were Clay and Webster. But those two gentlemen had long records in politics, parts of which might not do them much good when exposed to the pitiless glare of election limelight. The Whigs instead fell upon the expedient of choosing as a standard bearer a man who was known, to be sure, but who had such a minimum of political accomplishment that he also had a minimum of enemies.

General William Henry Harrison was a military hero. He had defeated Tecumseh's confederated Indian tribes—in the absence of Tecumseh—at Tippecanoe before the War of 1812, and beat Proctor's British, reinforced by Tecumseh's warriors, at the Thames in 1813. Besides this he had served as governor of the Ohio Territory.

Furthermore, he had been willing to sacrifice himself four years before by standing as the Whig candidate when Clay refused in the face of sure defeat. The Whigs nominated Harrison.

Clay's anguish when he received this stunning news was almost pathetic. "My friends are not worth the powder and shot it would take to kill them!" he exclaimed. Then, sorrowfully, "I am the most unfortunate man in the history of parties, always run by my friends when sure to be defeated, and now betrayed for a nomination when I, or anyone, would be sure of election. If there were two Henry Clays, one of them would make the other President of the United States."

When the convention offered him the Vice-Presidency, he rejected it with disdain. That may have been his worst mistake. Had he accepted, he would have reached his life's goal, for Harrison died within a month after his inauguration.

As it was, John Tyler, the fiery Virginian who had frequently opposed Jackson's policies in the Senate, was nominated for the second spot, and thereby ascended to the White House.

The campaign that followed made no appeal to the intellects of the electorate. The Democrats, though they nominated Van Buren, could not even agree on a candidate for Vice-President, Tecumseh Johnson being rejected. Meantime the Baltimore *American* had published a sneering remark about Harrison:

> Give him a barrel of hard cider and settle a pension of two thousand a year on him and, my word for it, he will sit the remainder of his days in a log cabin.

As a matter of fact, General Harrison was moderately well-to-do, and lived a comfortable and hospitable life in his large house in Ohio. But the Whigs caught it up, pictured him as carrying an ax and wearing a coonskin cap, and the "log cabin and hard cider" campaign was on. It swept Harrison into office. The electoral college vote was 234 to 60, but the popular vote was 1,275,000 to 1,128,000.

A footnote on this election: A new party, the Liberty party, for the first time entered the Presidential field. It was frankly abolitionist and its candidate was James G. Birney, a public-spirited man of handsome face and oratorical ability, who had once been a slaveholder in Alabama, later freed his slaves and worked for gradual emancipation, and finally decided to throw his energies into immediate abolition. The new party polled scarcely 7000 votes, but it was a portent. It would be succeeded by the Free-Soil party of considerably more strength, and that in turn by a great historic party not then even dreamed of, the Republican party (not to be confused in any respect with the Republican party of Thomas Jefferson).

5

Those troublous times which saw the great panic and the beginning of a more violent abolitionist controversy, also witnessed the beginning of the most spectacular of all American population movements. The country was full of discontented men. Many had lost their homesteads in the depression; others never had succeeded in amassing property. There was, of course, still unclaimed land, particularly in the Wisconsin and Minnesota areas. But that had to be paid for; and besides a restless migratory instinct was brewing.

Oregon—that unknown country of adventure and perhaps great opportunity—was the subject of much discussion. The journals of Lewis and Clark had been published and read, telling of their exploration. Other literature was available on the topic. A visionary named Hall J. Kelley, who visited Oregon, had written about it both before and after he saw the territory. That great roving trapper and trader, Jedediah Smith, killed by Comanche Indians in 1831, had made reports to the government, including the location of South Pass across the continental divide and an account of Willamette Valley in Oregon itself. Furthermore, one of America's most popular authors, Washington Irving, had published exciting books, *Astoria* in 1836, and *The Adventures of Captain Bonneville* in 1837, which bore on the country and the territory intervening. In addition there were accounts by missionaries, such as Jason Lee of the Methodist mission on the Willamette, and Marcus Whitman of the American Board mission near what is now Walla Walla, Washington.

None of these writers seem fully to have understood the actual status of the "Oregon" country. At that time the territory included the present states of Oregon, Washington, Idaho, and those portions of Montana and Wyoming west of the continental divide, together with the southern portion of present British Columbia; and it was in the curiously anomalous situation of "Joint Occupancy" by Britain and the United States. The reason for this was that while the two nations had determined on the 49th Parallel as the general boundary between Canada and the United States as far as the continental divide, they had not agreed on a border west of that to the Pacific.

That jointly occupied territory was huge and largely unexplored. At one time or another it had been claimed by four nations—Spain, Russia, Britain, and the United States. But Spain had ceded all claims north of her Mexican territories when the Adams-Oñis treaty defined the Louisiana Purchase. Russia later withdrew her claims to anything south of the extension from Alaska down the coast to 54°40′ latitude—the present Alaska "panhandle."

Britain and the United States made a temporary agreement in 1818, renewed in 1827, under which nationals of either nation could trade or settle in the territory, until one party or the other gave a year's notice of termination. On the surface it appeared that the British had the advantage here, for the great Hudson's Bay Company, superbly organized and equipped, had the nearest established posts, and water routes by which much of the distance could be traveled; while Americans could only reach it after lengthy journeys from the Missouri settlements.

By 1841 the Hudson's Bay Company had trading posts and forts on the upper Columbia River, and in what is now Idaho, and at the mouth of the Columbia, where Fort Vancouver was commanded with imperial sway by John McLoughlin, the Hudson's Bay director of affairs west of the Rocky Mountains. Several hundred persons of at least nominal British allegiance were already in the country; and against this strength in trading posts and numbers there were only a few roving American trappers and traders, and a handful of people about the missions. Yet the British were destined to lose, for the Hudson's Bay Company interests were chiefly in the fur trade, while the Americans, once they started in that direction, went to settle on the land and stay.

6

Oregon's unorganized territory was not the only area that interested would-be migrants. By 1840 there was quite a sprinkling of Americans in California, although that was a Mexican province—by law, at least. Some of these came by sea, but others found their way across the terrifying deserts and still more terrifying steeps of the Sierra Nevada, that towering mountain range which faced the east with a wall of sheer soaring cliffs and snow-crested peaks, like a mighty protecting barrier to discourage any invasion from that direction of the soft and pleasant land it guarded.

In 1840—the beginning of the decade in which the great change was to take place—California was beautiful, peaceful, and sleepily indolent. Along its Pacific coast ranged the long chain of Franciscan missions, each with its pueblo about it; but most of the land between the mountains and the sea, from San Diego Bay north to San Francisco Bay, was occupied by immense *ranchos* operated by proud, aristocratic families of Spanish blood, who called themselves *Californios* —a distinction from *Mexicanos*, for they were in the process of winning independence from the Mexican nation.

Life on the great *ranchos* and in the villages was drowsy and contented. The land produced livestock and crops plentifully, the climate was mild, and the vistas forever beautiful. The *ranchero* class never toiled—all work was done by the Indians who had been subjugated by Spanish soldiers and Spanish *padres* into virtual slavery. Their masters wore showy attire and rode fine horses. The women of the upper class were noted for their beauty, coquetry, and their grace in the charming traditional dances. Elaborate courtesy and elegant manners were culitivated.

Understandably, the *Californios* had no desire to change their life;

nor did they expect to have to do so. In the shelter of the great saw-toothed Sierra Nevadas, they felt secure. They could not dream that the Sierra Nevadas themselves, the range of mountains which seemed their surest protection, would in the future be their actual undoing, by bringing in such a typhoon of alien populations, seeking the minerals and particularly gold in those rocky fastnesses, that in two or three years dreamy, pleasant California would be changed into a far different place indeed.

The first Americans who crossed the mountains were so fierce and desperate that they were frightening to the gentle *Californios*. They were the mountain men, Jedediah Smith and his companions leading the advance, but followed by others in increasing numbers.

Some of the Americans settled in the pleasant valleys—like stark Ike Graham, who operated a still, and Ewing Young, who dealt in horses and mules, and became one of the first colonists in Oregon. They were a rough, hard-drinking, hard-living lot, never a negligible factor in the population, even when they were comparatively few in numbers.

In 1836 there were about two hundred "foreigners" living in California. Two of these deserve special mention. One was Thomas O. Larkin, a merchant who settled in Monterey in 1832 and served there as United States consul, in the crucial years 1844–1848. The other was John Sutter, a native of Switzerland, who crossed the American continent with a band of free trappers, dwelt for a time in the disputed Oregon territory, voyaged and traded from Sitka, Alaska, then a Russian possession, to the Sandwich Islands (Hawaii), and finally reached California, where he became a citizen, wheedled a magnificent land grant of 50,000 acres from the governor, built the strongest fort in the province, and was destined to play an unwilling but decisive role in the events that altered the history of his adopted country.

Indolent and leisurely though they were, the *Californios* could not deny themselves the luxury of periodic excitement of "revolting" against Mexican authority; a natural tendency which was stimulated by the incompetence and arrogance of the officials sent from Mexico to rule over them. In one period of thirteen months, so dizzily did the whirligig of California politics revolve, four separate governors ruled: José Figueroa, who died in 1835, and Mariano Chico, Nicolas Gutiérrez, and Juan B. Alvarado, each of whom was supplanted.

So unsettled were conditions that some of the Americans discussed the idea—but in a vague and indecisive manner—of doing what Sam Houston did in Texas, by setting up a separate nation in California.

They were saved the trouble by Alvarado, who made the declaration for them. He proclaimed that California was a "free and sovereign state"; announced that duties on all foreign goods would be lowered;

called for a constitutional convention; proposed that the province be divided into two states, one from Santa Barbara south to San Diego, with Los Angeles as its capital, the other north from that dividing point, with Monterey as the capital; and began planning a body of militia to be formed and equipped.

The Mexican government had appointed Don Carlos Antonio Carrillo governor, replacing Alvarado, and the new ruler at once announced that the capital of the whole province would be at Los Angeles, then the largest pueblo in California.[4]

Alvarado refused to relinquish his office and remained at Monterey. For a time the two leaders exchanged wordy proclamations and fiery letters. But at last time for action came.

Alvarado marched down the coast and defeated Captain Juan Casteñada, a Carrillo supporter, at Ventura, in an engagement in which one man was accidentally killed. This loss of (one) life constituted something like a record in California revolutionary battles. At the later decisive engagement at La Mesa, described as "for the most part one of tongue and pen rather than of artillery and guns," Alvarado became supreme. He placed Carrillo and his brother under arrest, but soon freed them when they "accepted the change of fortune with equanimity," and settled peacefully on the island of Santa Rosa.

The victor, however, made the mistake of rounding up about a hundred American and British residents, including the noted Ike Graham. Alvarado sent them to Mexico City, but on the way Eustace Barron, a British vice-consul, obtained their release. Most of them returned to California, where many filed suit against the government for damages. A statement made by Graham to the vice-consul, which was forwarded through diplomatic channels to Washington, caused the American government to strengthen its Pacific squadron for the protection of its nationals.

The last revolt, which really separated California from Mexico and ended Mexican rule, occurred when, on the expiration of his term in 1842, Alvarado was succeeded by General Manuel Micheltorena. The new governor came from Mexico, arriving by ship at Monterey with an army of some three hundred "soldiers," of the same rascally type as those who caused the Texas uprising. In two years the thieving vagabonds had plunged California into another revolution.

It began in the south. Micheltorena determined to put it down and marched toward Los Angeles, with his three hundred men, supplemented by a force furnished by Sutter, which raised his numbers to about four hundred. The Sutter increment gave the governor a sort of

---

[4] The city of San Francisco had not yet risen on the site of the little village of Yerba Buena, nor would it do so for some years.

"secret weapon"—several score of deadly, hard-shooting mountain men, under the fierce, bearded Ike Graham. These were expected to do the actual fighting, and Micheltorena anticipated heavy carnage and a quick victory when their lethal rifles began to play upon his rebellious subjects.

But at Los Angeles General José Castro and two influential brothers, Pío and Andrés Pico, had also availed themselves of a "secret weapon"—a similar force of mountain men, enlisted in Southern California and led by a redoubtable Indian fighter named Bill Fallon. Neither of the opposing commanders knew that his adversary possessed such formidable auxiliaries. When the two armies met in Cahuenga Pass, north of Los Angeles, however, there was a hitch in the proceedings. The mountain men decided not to fight.[5]

Deprived of their deadly allies on both sides, the *Californios* were forced to conduct their battle in their usual manner. It was noisy, with much gunpowder burned and gesticulating horsemen careering about, and it lasted for two days. But what had been planned as a gory conflict became *opera bouffe*. The only blood spilled was that of one, or perhaps two, horses on Castro's side, and a mule on the governor's side. Thomas O. Larkin wrote of this engagement, if it could be called that:

> ". . . 6,000 ball cartridges were fired and high mass said the next day, giving thanks that there was no bloodshed."

Nothing was accomplished by the farcical "Battle of Cahuenga Pass," except that Micheltorena decided to resign and return to Mexico, taking his unpopular *soldados* with him. The mountain men re-

---

[5] An entertaining account of what followed was given by Major Horace Bell, one of the early chroniclers, in his *Reminiscenses of a Ranger* (1927). Forward, according to Bell, went the mountain men on each side, rifles ready, to begin the battle. But as the skirmish lines came in view of each other, advancing through the mesquite and chaparral, one of Graham's men recognized an acquaintance in the opposing force.

"Hello, Read, is that you?" he cried.

"Why, yes, McKinley," came the surprised reply. "Is that you?"

Other voices began to exclaim: "Well, by Jupiter, there's Laughlin!" "And there's Graham!" "What, Bell, are you here, too?"

Both sides now realized they were facing fellow Americans, and friends at that. Instead of shooting, the mountain men guffawed and shook hands all around.

"What in the name of the great grizzly are we fighting for?" asked someone.

"We don't give two hoots for Castro, or the governor, either," agreed others. "Let 'em fight their own war," was the final decision.

With that, both contingents withdrew to a convenient spot in the shade of some live oaks, took a drink all around, and prepared to watch the descendants of the *conquistadores* fight it out. The "battle" that followed furnished them only with amusement.

turned to their previous pursuits. Pío Pico became governor of California.

As the historian Charles Edward Chapman has noted:

"The last real vestige of Mexican rule was gone, though a shadowy allegiance was retained a few months longer."

Toward these two lands of promise—Oregon and California—the thoughts of men in the United States were turning more and more in that year of the great depression, 1841.

CHAPTER FOURTEEN

The West—and Texas

1

IN MAY 1843 the frontier settlement of Independence, Missouri, situated where the Missouri River begins its great elbow-like bend almost directly east from its north-and-south course, was crowded with strangers. Each year, at about the same time, there was bustle and ado in the muddy streets, because as soon as the grass of the plains grew green the freighter wagons of the Santa Fe traders began to leave for New Mexico. But this year a different atmosphere was in the air.

These strangers were not traders. With them were their women and children. They were *families;* and they had in their wagons household goods and supplies, even plows and scythes. These people meant to *settle,* strike down roots, develop the country in—of all places—incredibly remote Oregon.

A square-shouldered, whiskered man, Dr. Marcus Whitman, walked among the wagon people. Of them all he alone knew the way west, for Whitman, at first a country doctor in western New York, had with his wife Narcissa adventured all the way to Fort Vancouver at the mouth of the Columbia, seven years before, and then had gone up-river to establish a mission for the Indians somewhere in the wilderness. Furthermore he had taken wagons with him—at least in a technical sense, although only the running gears of one vehicle actually reached as far as the Snake River Valley beyond Fort Hall.

Marcus Whitman, one of the most dedicated men in America, had left his wife at a mission with an unpronounceable name (it was Waiilatpu), where there were one or two other white missionary women and their men, to travel east for the purpose of stirring up renewed interest in his project of converting the Indians.[1] Now he was ready to begin his return to his mission with the Oregon caravan, not only as a guide, but as a physician. Others in the westering crowd were destined to be notable. One, a self-taught Missouri lawyer, Peter Bur-

---

[1] He and his wife were murdered later by those same Indians, but that is no part of the present chronicle.

nett, would one day be the first governor of the newly created state of California. Another was Jesse Applegate, tall and raw-boned, "so homely he avoided mirrors all his life," a lawyer, surveyor, and farmer, but above all a leader, who would be one of the famous figures not only in Oregon, but in the history of all the West.

There had been previous trickles of settlers toward the Oregon country. Missionaries were first, but others were frankly "movers," intent on settlement. One handful of men with their wives and children was led over the long trail in 1840 by Joel Walker, brother of Joseph Reddeford Walker, the great mountain man and explorer. Another group, guided by a mountain man named Doc Newell, followed next year, and this caravan took the first wagons to Oregon—although the vehicles had to be floated down the Columbia, being taken apart and carried over the hard portages of that wild river. Still a third train, containing—according to some accounts—a hundred persons of both sexes and all ages, followed Dr. Elijah White, a small, self-assertive man, formerly a member of the Methodist mission on the Willamette, who quarreled with Jason Lee and was sent home. White obtained an appointment as Indian agent for Oregon, and he had the good sense to secure the services of a famous mountain man, Thomas (Broken Hand) Fitzpatrick. It was Fitzpatrick who managed to get his charges away when a party of Sioux warriors would have attacked them near Independence Rock, a landmark on the route.

All of these parties had severe difficulties, and all of them abandoned any attempt to go all the way with their wagons, although, as stated above, the Newell party floated two or three running gears down the Columbia. Dr. Whitman, however, believed that wagons could make it all the way to the Willamette Valley. He advised everyone to take "sound" vehicles, and spare parts for repairs.

May 22 the "Great Emigration"—so called because of its events, as well as the events following, rather than its size—got under way. The number of persons in this caravan have never been officially determined. Estimates run as low as five hundred and as high as "more than a thousand." Applegate and his brothers, Charles and Lindsey, believed the country to which they were headed would be good for livestock. They put the money they obtained from selling their farms into a herd of several hundred cattle, chiefly cows. Others brought cattle, too, and counting the draft oxen and mules, and the riding horses, the total of animals, by various accounts, ranges all the way from 1700 to 5000.

It was decided to move the expedition in two sections—the wagons with the families first, the cattle herd after it. Burnett captained the wagon train in the beginning, until disputes caused him to resign and allow another man to be elected in his place. Jesse Applegate bossed the "cow column" throughout. Not long after the train was on its road it was joined by John Charles Frémont, son-in-law of Senator Benton, on the first of his government financed expeditions which were designed to supplement information obtained by Lieutenant Charles Wilkes of the Navy (who during the Civil War would seize the *Trent* and precipitate an ugly international incident). Wilkes had explored the South Seas, for the benefit of the whaling industry, and discovered the Antarctic Continent. After that he sailed along the Pacific Coast, anchored in Puget Sound, and sent exploring parties to look over the interior. His report spoke enthusiastically of the Northwest, and it was Benton's lifetime dream, as it was Jackson's, to extend the domain of the United States to the Pacific.

Already Frémont had been to the Rocky Mountains. This time, in 1843, guided by Kit Carson, he was to go to Oregon—although he took a different route later from that followed by the emigrants—and thence to California. His report, published by Congress in 1845, became a guidebook for thousands of emigrants to both Oregon and California in the succeeding years.

Following the Platte River to the Sweetwater River, the caravan and its bawling "cow column" crossed the continental divide at South Pass. Applegate left a spirited account of that long migration. The wagons numbered sixty, and formed a line on the march three-quarters of a mile long. Ahead rode the "pilot"—a former army man, turned trapper and trader, named Captain John Gantt. With him a score of young men also rode, as escort and to hunt. The pilot was to select the next night's camping ground. At night the wagons would be "corraled" in a circle, families cooked the suppers, children played about, and sometimes private disputes and grievances were settled by an impromptu court which dealt out justice. The great herd of cattle was allowed to graze its fill, and then watched through the night by successive shifts of horsemen, to see that animals did not wander away. A similar sentinel system guarded the wagon corral, until morning came and the signal to begin the next day's travel was given.

Things went well enough—Dr. Whitman even delivered a baby on the road—until the caravan reached Fort Hall, a post originally built by the American fur trader Nathaniel Wyeth in what is now southeastern Idaho, but sold to the Hudson's Bay Company in 1834. There the resident factor, Richard Grant, told the wagon people that their wagons could not reach the coast.

It was a crushing blow; but that night at a meeting held by the men, Marcus Whitman assured them that the wagons could go through. He knew of the previous efforts—he himself had made one of them. Now he insisted that the present train had what the others lacked—enough manpower to build roads where they were needed.

He was wrong, as it proved. But they had to go on. There were not enough pack animals to carry the necessary articles and all the women and children, and their supplies were too short to permit any turning back.

Forty axmen chopped trees, and others "graded" a way across the Blue Mountains, hitherto impassable. But the Cascade Mountains were different. The wagons were forced to the Columbia Valley again, and had to make the same perilous journey down that river previous parties had made. Several lives and most of the property of the emigrants were lost. That route, in fact, was practicable only for the fur trade, which traveled by horse and canoe, until much later times.

Help was sent upriver by the Willamette settlers, and also by McLoughlin, the towering, white-bearded factor at Fort Vancouver, and eventually most of the weary wayfarers and some of their livestock reached the Willamette.

Difficulties did not daunt future parties. A second, larger, caravan made the trek the following year and was snowed in and spent the winter amid great suffering in the Walla Walla Valley. Most of them reached the Willamette in destitution. The emigration of 1845 was three thousand strong. It also followed the difficult trail of its predecessors, with further loss of life and property.

But at that point Jesse Applegate, the great leader in Oregon, undertook to find a better road, and instead of trying to follow previous trails, took a brand-new direction. With fifteen companions he made his way down the Umpqua River Valley, as far as present Grants Pass, then turned east along the Applegate River (named for him), and actually found the long-sought pass over the Cascade Mountains which took him to Klamath Lake. Thence they worked their way southwest over the Nevada desert, and struck the California Trail at the Humboldt River. It was still a difficult, at times dangerous road, but it was practicable all the way to Oregon, and yearly greater numbers of caravans took it to the country being opened up.[2]

The avalanche had begun. Though the Hudson's Bay Company organized land projects on Puget Sound and around Fort Vancouver, hoping to offset American migration with a flood of settlers from Canada and England, no great interest could be stimulated in schemes so far distant among those people. With the Americans it was quite the opposite. The Great Emigration of 1843 started a continuous stream of wagon people who not only took over available lands south of the Columbia, but soon lapped over into the territories north of it. The United States government, at first content to insist on the 49th

[2] A fuller account of the Great Emigration is given in *Land of Giants*, by David Lavender, another of the Mainstream of America series.

Parallel as the boundary with Canada, began to talk of a different
latitude—"fifty-four forty"—the 54°40′ at the very tip of the Russian
extension down the coast from Alaska.

2

A growing stream of wagon people took the southward branch of
the Overland Trail just beyond Fort Hall, which became known as the
California Trail. Following the Humboldt River to the great marshy
sink where that stream disappears into the ground, it cut across to the
Sierra Nevada Mountains at the Truckee Pass.

It was a hard, grim trail, but in 1846 about five hundred Americans
found their way over the mountains to the haven of Sutter's Fort at the
confluence of the Sacramento and American rivers, where they scattered to seek land or find other occupations.

The hardships of those who made it were sufficiently terrible, but
one party, led by Jacob Donner and containing eighty-seven persons
was especially unfortunate. Too late in the year the Donner party attempted the Sierras. It was engulfed by the tremendous snows char-
acteristic of that area, and the experiences of its people make one of
the most horrifying stories in the annals of America. Caught in their
miserable temporary cabins and tents by the huge drifts, they began
to die. The survivors lived on by devouring the bodies. Two children
were found by rescuers, eating the partly roasted liver and heart of
their dead father. Others had kept life in themselves by equally revolting fare. But for rescue crews sent from Sutter's Fort after a man
named Reed fought his way there through the snow, every soul in
the Donner party must have perished. As it was, thirty-nine failed to
survive. Donner Pass is still a place of ghastly curiosity on the Emigrant Trail in California.

By 1848 there were some eight hundred Americans in that province, but it would require the discovery of gold to make the stream of
emigrants become a roaring flood.

Meantime another migration took place that established white
men's habitations in a nearer, though still remote, part of the Far
West. The Mormons were a religious sect formed by a strange New
York State man named Joseph Smith, who claimed to have "direct
communication" with the Supreme Being, said he had discovered
golden tablets with further illumination on Biblical history, the Book
of Mormon, and developed a whole new theology. He attracted followers. At first small, the sect grew; and as it grew its peculiar clan-
nishness, and the policies of its leaders, caused trouble.

It was persecuted. From settlement to settlement it moved, driven from New York to Ohio, from Ohio to Missouri, and from Missouri to Illinois, where the Mormons built a thriving city called Nauvoo. Even there they could not rest. The state gave Joseph Smith an unprecedented charter for his city, which made it self-governing beyond the powers ever conferred on any other municipality in the United States, with its own courts, its own laws, even its own army.

Because of this peculiar situation, robbers and outlaws gathered within its limits, became "Mormons" in name only, and used the city as a base from which to make forays and commit crimes, after which they took refuge in Nauvoo, secure in the knowledge that the sheriff could not follow them there. The Mormon residents, largely ignorant and unlettered, with the hand of every non-Mormon turned against them, defended anyone who called himself one of them.

Knowledge that Nauvoo sheltered robbers and murderers, the fanatical attitude of the true Mormons who called all other forms of religion "works of the devil," and the arrogance of Joseph Smith in his dealings with the Gentiles (non-Mormons) caused public feeling to grow bitter against them. A "revelation" that Smith received, not only sanctioning but enjoining polygamy, and internal difficulties among the Mormons themselves, caused even graver troubles.

Joseph Smith, his brother Hyrum, and two other dignitaries of the church were arrested, and the two Smiths were murdered by a mob. The leader who succeeded Smith, Brigham Young, at last ordered his people to leave their homes and move westward.

Young, a man of great capacity as a leader and planner, conducted the best-planned migration in the history of the West. By the spring of 1846 he established winter quarters across the Mississippi from Council Bluffs, Iowa. His people followed, not in a body but strung out, some reaching the winter quarters before the others left Nauvoo.

In April 1847 Young continued the great advance. His people did not know where he was taking them, nor, perhaps, did he. All he desired was to get beyond reach of the laws of the United States, which interfered with some of the Mormon tenets, including polygamy which he and many others already practiced according to "divine revelation."

Along the way he established stations, where those who followed could rest, repair wagons, and recoup their livestock. Discipline was maintained and the wagons were kept from straggling, because only large caravans were safe from Indian raiders. The men drilled frequently as militia companies. Prayers were said morning and night, at the call of a bugle.

Not one, but many separate caravans were in the Mormon march, and all told an estimated 12,000 persons made the journey that year or the next. Many died but others pressed on. Brigham Young had told them he would lead them to a promised land. On July 20, 1847, the advance party reached the Great Basin and saw the mirror surface of Great Salt Lake, stretching for miles.

"This is the place," said Brigham Young.

As the Mormons reached the valley below through Emigrant Canyon, Young already was planning. Trees were scarce, but bricks could be made of adobe. He envisaged and carried into effect a great irrigation system—the first major irrigation project ever carried on by American whites. Farming would prosper.

But another consideration was perhaps more important to him than all the rest. This, he believed, was not territory of the United States. It was Mexican territory. He did not ask the Mexican government for permission to settle his people there. It was enough for him that there the hated laws of the United States did not run.

Before the end of 1847 more people of American background were living in the valley of Great Salt Lake than there were then residing in either California or Oregon.

3

President John Tyler, who succeeded to office when General Harrison died April 4, 1841, just one month after he was inaugurated, had been nominated for the Vice-Presidency by the Whigs for the sole reason that his presence on the ticket ensured Virginia's vote. He was not a convinced Whig. Though he had bitterly opposed Jackson on the nullification question, and resigned from the Senate in protest against the "Force Bill," he was in reality a Democrat.

Long-faced, spare framed, with a beak-like nose, keen eyes, and the perfect courtliness of a Virginia aristocrat, he was said to lack any sense of humor,[3] and was to prove to be a man who acted according to conviction, refusing to take dictates from anyone, including the party that elected him.

Though he retained the entire cabinet which his predecessor had chosen, including Daniel Webster as Secretary of State, he soon dis-

---

[3] In a tilt with Senator John Holmes of Massachusetts, in the course of the nullification debates in the Senate during the Jackson administration, he bitterly asked Holmes, "What has become, sir, of the firm once mentioned in debate by John Randolph as 'James Madison, Felix Grundy, John Holmes, and the Devil?'" Holmes rose. "I will tell the gentleman," he said, "what has become of that firm. The first member is dead, the second has gone into retirement, the third now addresses you, and the last one has gone over to the nullifiers, and is now electioneering among the gentleman's constituents. So the partnership is legally dissolved."

agreed so completely with his entire official family that every member of it resigned, save Webster alone, who was then engaged in settling the Maine boundary question with Britain, and continued to serve his country in his position regardless of his disagreements with his chief.

Internal war disrupted the Whigs, and Tyler faced the Texas annexation issue, the slavery issue, the Oregon territory issue, and the party issue. To this was added a curious brief crisis early in his administration, known as the Dorr rebellion. Strictly confined to Rhode Island, the issue nevertheless was national in scope.

Rhode Island had been backward in establishing universal manhood suffrage. It was in fact still being governed under the provisions of its original charter, given by Charles II in 1663. No person could vote unless he owned a freehold worth $150, or was the eldest son of such a freeholder. This excluded about two-thirds of the citizens from the franchise.

A strong movement grew, led by Thomas W. Dorr, a Harvard graduate, a property holder and a former Federalist who turned Jacksonian, to extend the suffrage in the state. It was opposed by the conservatives, frequently referred to as the "Landowners," who charged that Dorr would bring "undesireables" into the electorate—referring to "foreigners," and particularly Irish Catholics.

In the intense feeling that rose, the "People's Party," organized an election which, though it had no legal validity, elected Dorr governor and announced that any government interference would be met by force of arms. A small civil war thus confronted Rhode Island. Business was suspended, alarm was general. Governor Sam W. King declared martial law and asked for federal troops, which Tyler wisely refused.

In the end Dorr's "army" fled without resistance when the state militia approached, and Dorr surrendered and was tried and sentenced to life imprisonment in solitary confinement at hard labor. He was pardoned after three years, but the three years of rigorous prison treatment ruined his health for the rest of his life.

Before the end of 1842 a new state constitution was adopted—and curiously this was before Dorr was even tried—by which the franchise was given to all male citizens over twenty-one provided they paid a tax of not less than one dollar a year.

The Dorr difficulties were but one manifestation of singular unrest, tending to violence, in many places. A mob mania developed, by no means confined to the dispute over abolition and slavery. Immigrants were pouring into the United States from Europe, and as they came they created religious, economic, political, and social problems, which often provoked mob action. Irish Catholics were a special target for violence, although Germans were sometimes involved. In some places

Catholic churches were burned and priests beaten. For a time it seemed that the forces of law and order could not cope with these adjustments.

4

Slavery agitation furnished the most ominous undertone to the nation's life. In Congress almost every question became tinged with it. So many petitions asking for emancipation of slaves were presented that on the instance of some Southern members a rule was adopted providing that all petitions, propositions, or papers of any kind, which related to the subject of slavery, should if brought before Congress, be laid upon the table without liberty of debate, and receive no further action. Soon labeled the "Gag Rule," it was bitterly opposed, in particular by John Quincy Adams.

"I hold the resolution to be a direct violation of the Constitution of the United States, of the rules of this House, and of the rights of my constituents," the old man declared. He saw danger in the rule to every form of request from the nation to Congress, and with typical courage and clear-sightedness undertook a single-handed battle against it which was without parallel.

Petitions against slavery continued to come in, in increasing numbers, and since he had declared himself on the matter, most and finally all of those petitions were addressed to Adams. With unwavering firmness—and against exasperated and bitter opposition—he continued to present those petitions, one by one, sometimes as many as two hundred in a single day, demanding the attention of the House to each separate petition. Sometimes the scenes became dramatic, even dangerous. Amidst scorn and derision, against threats of expulsion and even assassination, Adams defended the right of even the poorest and humblest in the land to petition Congress.

The climax came one day early in 1837 when, after offering a new mass of petitions, none of which he was permitted even to read, he paused to arrange the papers on his desk, and suddenly glancing at one of them, took it up and in his hoarse voice exclaimed:

"Mr. Speaker, I have in my possession a petition of somewhat extraordinary character; and I wish to inquire of the chair if it be in order to present it."

Asked the character of the petition, Adams replied, "Sir, the petition is signed by eleven slaves of the town of Fredericksburg, in the county of Culpeper, in the State of Virginia . . . It is signed partly by persons who cannot write, by making their marks, and partly by persons whose handwriting would manifest that they have received the education of slaves, and I am requested to present it. I will send it to the chair."

The Speaker was James Knox Polk, later to be President. He had throughout the bitter controversy extended to Adams every possible courtesy. Now he said that a petition from slaves was a novelty, and he would like time to consider it.

A violent interruption came from Dixon H. Lewis of Alabama. "By God, sir, this is not to be endured any longer!" he exclaimed, turning toward Adams.

"Treason! Treason! Expel the old scoundrel! Do not let him disgrace the House any longer!" came cries from other members.

Quickly a resolution was drawn up by George C. Dromgoole of Virginia, followed by other resolutions of the same tenor, to the effect that inasmuch as Mr. Adams had presented to the House a petition signed by slaves, whereas bondmen had no right of petition, he should be "taken to the bar of the House and censured by the Speaker thereof."

Throughout this furore Adams remained silent. The very idea of bringing the venerable former President, now in his seventies, to the bar like a common culprit, to be reprimanded by a comparatively youthful Speaker, was disgraceful and absurd, and Polk was against it. He insisted that Adams be given a chance to speak. The old man turned upon his assailants, with a brief statement defending his right to bring up petitions. Then he went on to say:

"Now, as to the fact of what the petition was for, I simply state to the gentleman . . . who has sent to the table a resolution assuming that this petition was for the abolition of slavery—I state to him that he was mistaken. He must amend his resolution . . . he must amend his resolution in a very important particular; for he may probably put into it that my 'crime' was for attempting to introduce the petition of slaves that slavery should *not* be abolished."

A roar of mirth from the House greeted this startling reversal, and the resolutions were actually laughed out of existence.

Still the "Gag Rule" remained, and still Adams fought it. Still he maintained that it was his duty to present any petition; for the right of petition belonged to all, whether he concurred with it or was utterly opposed to it.

Five years later, in 1842, he presented a petition signed by forty-five citizens of Haverhill, Massachuetts, praying that Congress immediately take measures peacefully to dissolve the Union of States, because it was not agreeable, did not present prospects of reciprocal ideas, and would in its present form bring destruction in the end.

Adams most fervently disagreed with the aim of the petition; yet he proposed that it be referred to a special committee to outline reasons why the prayer should not be granted.

It was a petition for secession. Yet so heated was the feeling against Adams and everything he did, that its most furious assailants were Southerners from the very states that continually talked of secession. One moved to burn it in the presence of the House. Another offered a resolution to censure the member who presented such a petition. There were shoutings and scenes of tense excitement as the House adjourned for the day.

Adams' opponents believed at last they had him where they could crush him. That night a motion was framed, which charged that the petition Adams had offered involved high treason. The following day, April 25, with Thomas F. Marshall of Kentucky as spokesman, it was offered with the provision that Mr. Adams, for presenting the offensive petition, should receive the severest censure of the House.

While Marshall delivered his speech denouncing Adams, the galleries were crowded and the membership of the House was fully represented. When the Kentuckian finished he was applauded by his supporters. But Speaker John White, also of Kentucky, called for order and announced that Mr. Adams was entitled to the floor.

The old, bald, gray man, "his hands trembling with constitutional infirmity and age," rose, and after a few short remarks, said, in reply to the "audacious charge of high treason":

"I call for the reading of the first paragraph of the Declaration of Independence."

When the passage was read, which solemnly proclaims the right of reform, revolution, and resistance to oppression, the old man thundered, "Read that again!"

The reading was in fact a vindication of him, in the sentences of the nation's own Magna Charta; and the sympathetic revulsion of feeling in the House and galleries was instantly evident.

Though the debate lasted a little longer, the feeling of the members had changed. Adams was showered with compliments by his colleagues not only from the North, but from the South as well. The brave old statesman had the satisfaction of seeing the "Gag Rule" rescinded the following year; and when the next session of Congress began, he was, on the motion of Richard Barnwell Rhett of South Carolina, chosen to occupy the chair until the House was organized. He was escorted to that seat of honor by two of his foremost foes of the "Gag Rule" debates—Rhett himself, and Lewis Williams of North Carolina.

To his last day on earth John Quincy Adams upheld the right as he saw it, and "died in harness," being stricken while in his seat during a session of Congress, February 21, 1848. He was in his eighty-first year, and his death came shortly after, his final words being, "This is the last of earth. I am content."

5

The Texas question would not down. The nation was divided not only on political grounds, but on grounds of doubt concerning the advisability of further expansion. Thomas Jefferson at one time had favored *two* American nations—divided by the Rocky Mountains—feeling that a larger area would be too difficult to govern. Thomas Hart Benton himself at first thought the continental divide should be the natural limit of the nation, though he early changed his vision and in speaking for expansion made the celebrated statement, pointing toward the West: "There lies the East—there lies India!"

George McDuffie opposed acquisition of the Oregon Territory, probably on the ground that it would not be slaveholding, and said in the Senate in 1843, "If there was an embankment of five feet to be removed, I would not consent to expend five dollars to remove that embankment to enable our population to go there. I thank God for his mercy in placing the Rocky Mountains there."

New England was almost a unit in opposing expansion—anywhere. And when a resolution was introduced in the Senate for the establishment of a mail route from Independence, Missouri, to the mouth of the Columbia River, in 1844, Daniel Webster blasted it with words which sound strange today:

"What do we want with this vast, worthless area? This region of savages and wild beasts, of deserts, of shifting sands and whirlpools of dust, of cactus and prairie dogs? To what use could we ever hope to put these great deserts, or those endless mountain ranges, impenetrable, and covered to their very base with eternal snow? What can we ever hope to do with the western coast, a coast of three thousand miles, rock-bound, cheerless, uninviting, and not a harbor on it? What use have we for such a country? Mr. President, I will never vote one cent from the public treasury to place the Pacific coast one inch nearer to Boston than it now is."

The lack of knowledge of the country to which Webster referred, as shown by these remarks, extended at that date to a great many people. Even Texas, much closer than Oregon or California, was a *terra incognita* to thousands, and therefore an area of mystery and fear.

But the people as a whole were less timorous than their leaders. Sentiment grew for the annexation of Texas. When an offer for annexation to the United States came from that republic—authorized by a nearly unanimous vote of its citizens—and arrived on Van Buren's desk in August 1837, he feared the possibility of international complications; and even more so the violent opposition of the free states to any extension of slave territory. He was looking to his political fences, which would be not a little damaged if his supporters in the North and those in the South divided on this issue.

Old Andrew Jackson, retired to The Hermitage, did not share this sort of timidity, and was disappointed at the indecision of the man he personally had picked to succeed him. He remained Van Buren's friend, offered him encouragement and advice on the economic depression that scourged the administration, and backed him in his long fight for the Independent Treasury. But Old Hickory never lost sight of Texas, or of his friend Sam Houston, who had become the dominant figure and the first president of the new republic, and who was conducting its affairs with statesmanlike abilities.[4]

At the sudden and tragic death of General Harrison, who had succeeded Van Buren, Old Hickory who saw no value in the Whig President wrote:

> A kind and overruling providence has interfered to prolong our glorious Union . . . for surely Tyler . . . [will] stay the corruptions of this clique who has got into power by deluding the people by the grossest of slanders . . .

He was thinking of Texas, and placing his faith in Tyler, a Virginian who, if an opponent of Jackson's during the nullification fight, at least would not be unfriendly to the acquisition of Texas, as Harrison obviously was.

Daniel Webster, as Secretary of State, had at last completed negotiation of the Maine boundary line. It was a prickly situation, with inhabitants of the disputed territory sometimes clashing and even shooting one another. The Senate was in no mood to compromise with the British, nor was Parliament eager to give up territory to America. But one of the most curious coincidences in diplomatic history aided a happy final settlement.

Two maps came to light, one in England and one in America, in which, though differing from each other, a boundary of Maine was drawn in red. In both the British Foreign Office and the United States

---

[4] After the death of his Indian "wife," Tiana, Houston obtained a divorce from Eliza Allen Houston, on the grounds of abandonment. Eliza was represented by counsel but did not fight the case. On May 9, 1840, Houston married Miss Margaret Lea of Alabama. This marriage was very happy. They had a fine family of brilliant children. Margaret considered herself the instrument "of Houston's regeneration." She induced him to give up drinking and chewing tobacco, in fact all his bad habits—except swearing. She was never able entirely to curb the sulphurous life habit of his tongue, though she did eventually get him to join the Baptist church of which she was a member.

State Department it was believed these maps were the original maps used by the treaty makers in 1783.

But the map found in America appeared to give so much more territory to the British than they were claiming that the Senate was silenced by it; while the one found in the British Museum, on the other hand, so supported the original claims of the United States that Parliament similarly was glad to get off with a compromise. The result was the Webster-Ashburton agreement by which the present boundary of Maine was established, each country compromising by a slight cession to the other, so that the tension between the two nations was not only eased but forgotten in that matter at least. The strange part of this affair is that nobody really knows to this day, whether either of the maps was authentically what it was believed to be at the time.[5]

Webster, feeling that his chief aim was accomplished and being unable to agree with President Tyler, resigned his office. The President appointed Abel P. Upshur of Virginia, Secretary of State, and through Upshur proposed to Sam Houston, president of the Texas republic, renewed discussions of annexation.

But Houston, who at first had been eager to bring his nation into the Union, became cool to the proposal, especially after Upshur was accidently killed,[6] and John C. Calhoun was appointed in his stead. The old feud between Houston and Calhoun remained, but eventually both men rose above it, and a treaty was signed, in April 1844, whereby the United States agreed to accept Texas into the Union, and assume her public debt up to $10,000,000, all public lands of the annexed territory to be owned by the government. In this treaty Texas once again asserted that her boundary was the Rio Grande, and was accepted by the United States *on that basis*.

But when the treaty was submitted to the Senate, the fury which Van Buren had shunned arose. Northern Senators shouted that the South was seeking to extend slavery. The South bitterly returned that the North, from sheer prejudice, was attempting to prevent the nat-

---

[5] James Truslow Adams and Charles Garrett Vannest, *The Record of America* (1935).

[6] February 28, 1844, Upshur was inspecting a new type of heavy gun just installed on the ship *Princeton*, together with President Tyler, and other notables. The gun—ironically named "the Peacemaker"—was loaded and given a trial to demonstrate to the President and his party the power and efficiency of the great weapon. When it was fired the cannon burst, blowing off its lower part from the trunnions to the breech. In the terrific explosion Upshur was killed, as were Governor Thomas Walker Gilmer of Virginia and six others, while nine seamen also were injured. Senator Benton was knocked flat by the blast but uninjured. President Tyler escaped by merest chance. He had been called back from where he stood, for a conference, just a moment before the tragic accident took place.

ural expansion of the nation. A two-thirds vote was required to ratify
the treaty. It failed of passage to the bitter disappointment of two
men in particular: Andrew Jackson and Sam Houston.

6

Already the election of 1844 was occupying the minds of the American people. This time Henry Clay had clear sailing for the Whig
nomination. He had managed to destroy Tyler, by forcing through
Congress a new bill for a Bank of the United States, so worded that
Tyler was forced to veto it on constitutional grounds. Again Clay
forced the bill through Congress. Again Tyler vetoed it, and thus forever ended any hope of Whig support. He must be credited with
strong and unselfish convictions in thus signing away his political future. One of Andrew Jackson's friends wrote, "Egad, he [Tyler] has
found one of Jackson's old pens!"

Clay, now sixty-seven, was unanimously nominated on the first ballot by the Whig convention, and prepared to make the fight of his life.
He believed that Van Buren would be his Democratic opponent, and
one of his important acts even before his nomination, was to reach an
understanding with that gentleman on the Texas question. They were
both to ignore it in the campaign, thus avoiding sectional issues, and
debate relatively innocuous domestic questions only.

Neither of them, however, counted on Old Hickory. Houston, as
wily as one of the Indian chiefs among whom he once dwelt, was once
more president of Texas, after an unprofitable interim during which
one of Houston's old subordinates, with a flamboyant name, Mirabeau
Buonaparte Lamar, held the highest office. Mexico had begun to
threaten again, Lamar had incurred the overwhelming hostility of the
wild Indians, and the treasury was empty. Houston, who was forced
to watch from the sidelines because he could not succeed himself under the Texas constitution, was overwhelmingly re-elected when
Lamar's term ended. When the annexation treaty was rejected, he
engaged in quite open conversations with British envoys—which, at
this distance, appear to have been window dressing for the benefit of
the United States. But they alarmed Tyler, and seriously concerned
Jackson who wrote Houston:

> My dear Genl I tell you in all sincerity and friendship, if you
> will achieve this annexation your name & fame will become en-
> rolled amongst the greatest chieftains . . . Now is the time to act
> & that with promptness & secrecy & have a treaty of annexation
> laid before the United States Senate where I am assured it will

be ratified . . . It will be an unfailing laurel to your ploom . . .
I am scarcely able to write—the Theme alone inspires me with
the strength . . . Let me hear from you if only three lines . . .
your friend,

                                        Andrew Jackson

Deeply as he was devoted to the failing old man who had been his
mentor and sponsor almost all his life, Houston in this critical period
could not put to paper anything that would reassure him that all was
well. He wrote Jackson a long letter, saying he was willing to offer
once more to unite, but containing some arresting lines:

> Texas with peace could exist without the U. States; but the U.
> States cannot, without great hazard, exist without Texas . . . An
> effort to postpone [discussion] may be tried in the U. States,
> to subserve party purposes and make a President; Let them be-
> ware! . . . [Texas] has been sought by the United States, and
> this is the third time she has consented. Were she now to be
> spurned, it would forever terminate expectation on her part; and
> . . . she would seek some other friend [among the nations of
> the world].

Old Jackson, slowly dying, perceived the danger. He had based his
prediction that this time the Senate would ratify the treaty on the
great gains in Congress made by the Democrats in the election of
1842. Now he was sure that both Clay and Van Buren, the ostensible
candidates, would delay any action at least until after the election.
He wrote to Houston assuring him that confidential polls showed
that thirty-nine Senators would vote for annexation—four more than
the two-thirds required. Yet already it was becoming apparent that
the thirty-nine could not safely be counted upon. Both Van Buren and
Clay opposed bringing up the question at this time.
Old Hickory was seventy-seven years old, blind in one eye, seeing
only dimly from the other, confined for most of the time in his bed.
Yet now he put forth an incredible burst of energy. He had given up
on Van Buren, whose agreement with Clay was now obvious. Fever-
ishly he looked around for a man who would stand on his feet and
not act merely for political expediency. There was Lewis Cass. There
was Silas Wright. There was even John Calhoun. None filled the bill.
Someone—tradition says George Bancroft—suggested another name.
James Knox Polk. Now, Jimmie Polk . . . the old warrior was interested. Polk had been a power in Congress, and always loyal to the
tenets of his chief. Polk, to be sure, did not have much of a personality
. . . but maybe an old man might be of some help to him. At least
Polk would *act*, where others merely talked.

Polk was summoned to The Hermitage. He had never aspired to an office higher than Vice-President, but the unquenchable fire in Andrew Jackson ignited him. Jack Donelson, the general's nephew and close adviser, was sent speeding to Baltimore, where the Democratic convention was being held, with Van Buren and Cass in a deadlock for which, under the two-thirds rule then in effect, there seemed no escaping.

To the delegates Donelson submitted the name of Old Hickory's choice. An all-night session followed. At dawn an agreement was reached. By acclamation the convention nominated James Knox Polk of Tennessee, and bestowed on him the campaign appellation of "Young Hickory."

As if he were twenty years younger, Jackson swung into action. Though many of his letters were dictated to his adopted son's wife, Sarah Yorke Jackson, because of the unsteadiness of his own eye and hand, it was as if he stretched out his long gaunt arm across the nation to summon the men who still idolized him.

Without him Polk could hardly have made much of a contest against Clay. He had been greeted at the outset, with the cry, "Who is James K. Polk?" and Clay sneeringly had said he could defeat him, "with my left hand."

Compared to the inspiring appearance of the magnetic Kentuckian, Polk was unpretentious in appearance, with a figure slight and spare, a rather small head on which he wore his already graying hair (soon to be white) long and brushed back behind his ears, rather wide, gray eyes and a recessive temperament that may have been due to shyness rather than coldness. As a speaker he was almost inarticulate in comparison with the soaring eloquence of Clay's oratory.

But he was inflexible in purpose, completely imbued with the expansionist dreams of Jackson, his old friend and sponsor; he straddled no issues, and spoke from the convictions of his heart.

"Lash Clay on Texas," Jackson instructed his protégé. Polk obeyed and his forthright statements and speeches contrasted strongly with the weasel words of his adversary. He adopted another campaign cry. Sufficient Americans had settled in Oregon by this time—one estimate was 10,000—so that they were demanding organization of a territory, and the most impulsive of them wanted the still undefined northern limits set at the Russian southern extension from Alaska. "Fifty-four forty or fight," became a slogan of the Democrats. Texas and Oregon were Polk's major issues, and they caught the imagination of the people.

Old Hickory, though in an invalid's chair and often too weak even to rise from his bed, continued to use his wonderful influence. When President Tyler, rejected by the Whigs, was running on an independent ticket, Jackson induced him to withdraw, so as not to siphon votes away from Polk. From The Hermitage letters were broadcast all over the country, to arouse the old general's supporters, not only to the support of Polk, but also to the peril of losing Texas.

Slowly the tide began to rise. Clay could sense it, but he still would not believe he could possibly lose. When, in November, the voters went to the polls, suspense was so great that in many parts of the country people stayed up all night waiting for the mails.

It happened that Clay was attending a wedding party when the final results came in. He was handed a paper with the fatal figures: Out of 2,600,000 votes cast, he had lost by barely 38,000. In the Electoral College Polk led 171 to 105.[7]

When Clay read the election report he "stood for a moment as if frozen" while pallor went over his face. Then he laid down the paper, poured himself a glass of wine, and raising it to his lips with a smile said, "I drink to the health and happiness of everyone here."

Later, however, he was bitter. "The late blow that has fallen upon our country is very heavy," he said. "I hope that she may recover from it, but I confess that the prospect ahead is dark and discouraging."

7

After Polk's election, but before he was inaugurated, the outgoing Senate once more rejected the treaty Houston had offered for annexation of Texas. It was a severe setback, and Houston was gloomy. Another letter from Jackson, pleading with him not to give up hope of joining the Union, or yield to England who "wants Texas, next Cuba, and then Oregon," brought from him only an acknowledgment of thanks.

Houston's second term as president of Texas came to an end, and in his farewell address, he said somberly, "The attitude of Texas is now one of peculiar interest. The United States have spurned her. Let her, therefore, work out her own political salvation."

At this period came a strange manifestation. Houston must have been pondering the words of the message sent to him long ago by Jackson, through Wharton: "Texas must claim the Californias."

To William S. Murphy, United States chargé d'affaires in Texas, he wrote a long letter, outlining carefully what would happen should an-

---

[7] The Liberty party, which received only 17,000 votes four years before, polled 62,300 votes this time for its candidate—Birney, for the second time. This may well have been the decisive factor in the election, for a shifting of a mere 7,918 votes in the right states would have elected Clay.

nexation finally fail. It could only mean, he said, that "the Glory of the United States has already culminated. A rival power will be built up." He then proceeded to describe the new "power" as he conceived it. "The Pacific as well as the Atlantic will be component parts of Texas." This was a dark prediction that the South would secede. He even furnished a map showing the prospective extent of the Republic of Texas. It contained all of the South, including Virginia, but excluding the border states of Kentucky and Missouri, and projected occupation of all territories of Mexico to the boundary of the Louisiana Purchase, thus including the present states of Oklahoma, New Mexico, Arizona, California, Nevada, Utah, and parts of Kansas and Colorado. He proposed further to extend that domain north on the Pacific side of the continental divide to the Columbia River, taking in the present Oregon and parts of Wyoming and Idaho. Southward, he forecast that Lower California, Sonora, and Chihuahua, would also become parts of the greater Texas.

As a prediction that map was remarkable. Eventually the Southern states did secede, and in the wake of the War with Mexico soon to come, all the territories he described, except the Mexican states of Lower California, Sonora, and Chihuahua, became parts of the territory of the United States.

Meantime, Polk's victory, though it brought from the Senate a rebuff to the advocates of the annexation of Texas, in reality decided the issue after all—at least as regarded the people of the United States. His defeat of Van Buren, as a candidate for nomination, and of Clay, as a candidate for election—in spite of his own comparative obscurity in comparison with those two national figures—showed how strongly the people were attached to the principle of annexing Texas and gaining Oregon. He had an unquestionable mandate, and in his term that was to follow he sought patiently, incessantly, and laboriously to carry out that mandate. In so doing he acted rightly, decisively, and even wisely, if those actions are considered as he considered them—the obedient performance of a servant of the people to their express commands.

In view of this evident decision by the citizens of the nation, John Tyler decided to try once more, in the brief period remaining in his administration. This time he recommended to Congress immediate annexation by a *joint resolution* of the two Houses, rather than by a formal treaty. The latter method required a two-thirds vote of the Senate, the former only a majority in both Houses.

The resolution as presented provided that Texas should come into the Union as a *state*, not a territory. At once the Mexican minister in Washington presented an ultimatum that his government would consider such annexation as equivalent to a declaration of war—the first step in a series of tragic consequences which were to befall his nation, due largely to the bombastic military spirit of the Mexican governing officials.

This threat failed to deter the legislators, who passed the resolution, though by a narrow margin of twenty-seven to twenty-five in the Senate. An interesting footnote to this act of Congress is furnished by Edward S. Ellis, in *The History of Our Country:*

> The power of one vote was never shown more strikingly than in Indiana in 1844. A sick man in Switzerland County, was carried two miles in a carriage to vote for David Kelso, who was running for the state senate. The sick man was a client whose life had been saved by Kelso. The act of gratitude caused the client's death, but elected Kelso, who received one more vote than his opponent. The state senate had to elect a United States Senator. Kelso bolted the Democratic caucus and took with him a friend. This tied the votes for weeks. Then Kelso selected Edward A. Hannigan [*sic*] as a new candidate and declared that he would vote with the Whigs unless he was supported. This threat brought about the election of Hannigan [*sic*] who took his seat in the United States Senate. Then came the wrangle over the admission of Texas to the Union. The most prominent candidate before Hannigan [*sic*] entered the field had pledged himself to vote against the measure. The bill for the admission of the State passed by a single vote and that vote was cast by Hannigan [*sic.*] Thus it may be said that the vote of a dying man in the wooded hills of Switzerland County, Indiana, made Texas a state and brought on the war with Mexico.

> As a comment on the above, Edward Hannegan (the correct spelling of his name), had he voted against the resolution would have tied not defeated it, and the issue would have had to be decided by the vote of the president pro tem, a Whig and presumably against annexation. Hannegan was one of the strongest advocates of the "Fifty-four forty or fight" extremists and turned against Polk when the President finally settled for the forty-ninth parallel as the boundary of the Oregon Territory.

News of the resolution of admission was sped to Texas. Houston no longer was president there, having been succeeded by Anson Jones, but he still held the strings of power. For a time he hesitated—perhaps he was still thinking of that dream of empire extending to the Pacific. A query from The Hermitage brought him to his decision. On May 26 Andrew Jackson received news that Texas had accepted. To Polk, who by this time had been inaugurated, he wrote a note, "I knew British gold could not buy Sam Houston."

Jackson's end was very near. Houston made a desperate effort to reach The Hermitage in time to see his old friend before he died. It was a thousand-mile journey, in a coach, and his wife and infant son rode with him. Three hours before they arrived on June 8 Andrew Jackson expired.

"All is safe at last!" the old soldier had said just before his death. What was he thinking of? Texas? Yes, Texas was safe. Oregon? He believed that Polk would take care of Oregon. Did the annexation of Texas suggest to the old mind the succession of events that followed almost inevitably? In the presence of death men have sometimes been gifted with prophetic vision.

CHAPTER FIFTEEN

War with Mexico

1

IN THE July 1845 number of the *Democratic Review*, John L. O'Sullivan wrote an article which spoke of "our manifest destiny to overspread the continent allotted by Providence for the free development of our yearly multiplying millions."

Manifest Destiny. It had a ring to it. Americans caught it up and made it a watchword.

Some historians have stigmatized it as a synonym for aggression; yet it was a phrase not without idealism. Manifest Destiny expressed the unvoiced dreams and aspirations of the American people. It was a day when Americans sincerely believed they were almost the sole upholders of what they considered the sacred principle of democracy; and that it was for them not only to preserve democracy, but also to disseminate it in the world. The irresistible urge, inarticulate but almost instinctive, to occupy, develop, and make fruitful the empty lands beyond the frontier also found expression in the dynamic phrase.

The continent to the west *was* empty. Some figures are of interest in this connection. After two hundred years of Spanish, followed by Mexican, overlordship, California in 1845 had a population of no more than 12,000 "civilized" persons, and half of these were the so-called "neophyte Indians," really slaves of the *ranchos* and missions, as distinguished from about twice that number of "gentile Indians" who were still wild and unconverted to the Catholic faith.

Arizona, in that year, was peopled, apart from Indians, by no more than a thousand Mexicans of all classes, concentrated at Tubac and Tucson, the rest of the country devastated by the Apaches; and in that same year even Tubac was abandoned, what was left of its population of 249 taking refuge in Tucson, or fleeing southward.

New Mexico, as now constituted, was somewhat more "populous," containing in 1845-46 about 60,000, including a small proportion of Hispano-Mexicans, a much larger proportion of Spanish-Indian peons, and the Pueblo Indians who were included in the enumeration. That enumeration excluded the wandering bands of Navajo, Apache, and

Comanche Indians which constantly preyed on the settlements and pueblos.

Nevada was without white people; and so was Utah—the advance parties of the Mormons would not arrive there until 1847. Save for a sprinkling of settlers, and Hudson's Bay employees, the Northwest also was empty, always excluding from this count the wild hunting or fishing Indians.

In a Senate speech, March 23, 1848, Daniel Webster, who was opposing the territorial expansion following the War with Mexico, proved himself a bad prophet by predicting that Texas could hardly be expected to exceed 150,000 in population at any future time, New Mexico (then including Arizona, Nevada, and Utah) 60,000, and California "we may suppose" might "amount to sixty or seventy thousand. We will put them down at seventy thousand." He surmised that the whole territory, "in this estimate, which is as high as any man puts it, will contain two hundred and ninety thousand persons . . . a population less than that of the State of Vermont, and not the eighth part of New York."

Webster did not envision what American energy, enterprise, and foresight would accomplish, for in 1964 the estimated populations of the states mentioned were as follows:

Arizona, 1,581,000; California, 18,084,000; Nevada, 408,000; New Mexico, 1,008,000; and Utah, 992,000. These figures do not include the parts of Colorado and Wyoming included in the territory acquired.

All of that great portion of the present United States was gained as a result of the War with Mexico, in 1846–48, which became inevitable as a result of the annexation of Texas.

That war is the one of all American wars most frequently called dishonorable. Notes Lynn Montross, in his *War Through the Ages:*

> This tradition may be traced back to the rabid politics of the day, for the Whigs and Abolitionists came dangerously near to treason in their opposition. Such leaders as Clay and Webster denounced the struggle as a conspiracy to bring more slave-holding states into the Union; and a Whig newspaper declared that it would be a "joy to hear that the hordes under Scott and Taylor were every man of them swept into the next world."

Nor were Clay and Webster alone. Joshua Reed Giddings, a Whig and abolitionist of Pennsylvania, in December 1847, bitterly declared that the American army had "planted itself in the midst of Mexican cornfields" and "unarmed peasants had been murdered" including "women, children, and helpless age . . . virgins outraged." Senator Thomas Corwin of Ohio, a Whig, roared that "this desolating war" was caused by American invasion. Gathering himself, he rose to the height of invective: "Sir, . . . if I were a Mexican I would tell you, 'Have you not room in your own country to bury your dead men? If you come into mine, we will greet you with bloody hands, and welcome you to hospitable graves.'" There were other speeches of like tenor, and there may be significance in the fact that such remarks were delivered after the war was well under way and with good prospect of being won.

Sectionalism, abolitionism, and politics all were involved in the denunciations. Anything the Southern states advocated was anathema to the abolitionists and the Whigs were eager to discredit anything a Democratic administration did.

Later, the bitterness of the Civil War and the issue of slavery added to the attitude of Northern writers in particular, who went to extreme lengths in their contentions that the war was "deliberately provoked for the sole purpose of crushing a weak and unprepared neighbor, by overwhelming might."

As regards the last, far from sending "overwhelming forces" to conduct the war, the odds actually were heavily against the Americans. "The northern army," says Montross, "faced four times its own numbers in the principal battle [Buena Vista]; and as a triumph of skill over obstacles, Scott's campaign had no equal in the world during the half-century after Waterloo."

The Mexican soldiers were hardy and courageous. They were particularly strong in artillery and engineering—"two arms which are not the resources of a military rabble." It was Mexican leadership, rather than Mexican fighters, that lost the war for Mexico.

The purely political nature of the Whig opposition is made to look especially glaring by the fact that the two chief generals in the war, Zachary Taylor and Winfield Scott, both were later nominated by the Whigs for the Presidency, and Taylor was elected to that office, *primarily on his military record in the Mexican War.*

President Polk was bewildered by the Whig opposition to the war, and more so by defections in his own party. In his diary he expressed this surprise and pain, and he could not understand the injection of the slavery issue into it. On January 4, 1847, he wrote:

> The slavery question is assuming a fearful . . . aspect . . . It has, and can have no legitimate connection with the War with Mexico, or the terms of peace which may be concluded with that country. It . . . must divide the country by a sectional line and lead to the worst consequences . . . Such agitation is not only unwise, but wicked . . . I will do my duty and leave the rest to God and my country.

He had not anticipated that his desire for expansion would lead to war, and he had not wanted war. When it came he believed he was doing his plain duty in sending troops to protect Texas, and when attacked carry on the war to victory.

It is unfair to judge people of a past day by standards of today. Expansion was the morality of Polk's times. Britain, France, Holland, Russia, and Spain had shown, and were showing, the way. At the very time of the annexation of Texas, England was bidding to gain that raw young republic as a colony, or perhaps as a commonwealth—at least as a protectorate. And the United States was engaged in a heated controversy with the same power over the possession of the Oregon territory.

The world of the 1840s did not particularly blame nations for occupying undeveloped lands. There were, of course, bitter jealousies among some of the competing countries. France and England, for example, fought bloody wars over colonies. But those wars were not waged on moral grounds; they were fought for possession.

Manifest Destiny, to the Americans of 1845, seemed a prophetic term, as well as a justification. Their will, ambitions, and westward momentum, as well perhaps as their prejudices, their adventuresomeness, and their eagerness to acquire new lands, all were expressed in the phrase.

It must be remembered that the War with Mexico was by no means exclusively a Southern war. Illinois, Indiana, Ohio, and Pennsylvania regiments fought bravely by the side of regiments from South Carolina, Mississippi, and Texas. Though Henry Clay was busy denouncing the war, his son, Henry Clay, Jr., helped raise a regiment of volunteers in Kentucky, and went to the front where he was killed at Buena Vista. Daniel Webster also lost a son in the war, and many Whig leaders fought in that conflict. In truth, despite politics, the War with Mexico while it was in progress came close to uniting the nation as it had not been united in many years.

2

Let us look at the causes of the War with Mexico, which are interesting for the reason that by no means were they entirely the fault of the United States.

To begin with, Mexico gave an ultimatum that if Texas were annexed it would create a situation of war between the nations. Mexico clung to the fiction that Texas was still a Mexican province—and this in face of the fact that Mexico could not re-establish her authority there, while on the other hand the independence of Texas had been officially recognized by the United States, France, Holland, Belgium and England, before the annexation. Under international law, therefore, Texas was a *de facto* nation, with the right to dispose of herself as she pleased.

To be sure the Mexican government repudiated Santa Anna's terms of peace with Texas; which, incidentally, Santa Anna did also as soon as he was safely back on Mexican soil. But the fact of Texas independence existed, in spite of considerable saber-rattling south of the border. President Herrera, indeed, actually received a Texas agent named Treat and permitted him to submit the basis of a treaty.

Of course no treaty, or indeed understanding of any kind, was possible under conditions so unsettled as those in Mexico. Bustamante took over the reins of dictatorship again after Santa Anna lost his power through the Texas revolution; Santa Anna in turn succeeded Bustamante, to be forced into exile because of his corrupt administration. José Joaquín Herrera, next to assume power, was a moderate, fairly sensible man, and it was he who received the Texas envoy with the treaty plan. Herrera was ousted by General Mariano Paredes, a fire-eater and leader of the Mexican militarists.

Quite apart from the Texas annexation question, tensions existed in both countries. A strong anti-Mexican feeling existed among many Americans, arising out of the atrocities committed by Mexican dictators, particularly those of Santa Anna in Texas. This hostility was reciprocated by many Mexicans, especially the noisy and demagogic military and political leaders.

United States citizens had suffered damages in the periodic sacks of the City of Mexico, which took place each time the regime changed; and Mexico promised to pay reparations, which were fully adjudicated. But a sudden and peremptory refusal to make further payments created resentment in the United States.

As to the assertion that the war was "deliberately provoked," for the purpose of gaining additional territory, the facts are that the United States got into the war by degrees, the Mexicans took the first offensive actions, and the final plan for conducting the war was not formed by Polk, his Secretary of War, William Learned Marcy, and General Scott until July 1846, three months *after* actual hostilities were begun.

Conceding that Polk was an expansionist—as were Thomas Jefferson, John Quincy Adams, Henry Clay, John C. Calhoun, Andrew Jackson, and many others before him—the fact remains that he sought to settle affairs with Mexico by conciliatory methods.

In 1846 he sent John Slidell as envoy to negotiate an agreement on the Texas border, and to offer Mexico $30,000,000 cash, plus assumption by the United States of all claims of its citizens, for the peaceful cession of the New Mexico and California provinces.

The sum in this day seems small; but in that day it was very large. The entire national surplus at the end of Jackson's administration was only $36,000,000. Nobody then suspected the presence of gold in California (or, for that matter, oil in Texas), and all the country intervening between the frontier of Texas settlement and the Sierra Nevada Mountains, was regarded as a savagely inhospitable and barren desert, completely useless for human habitation, except for a few of what Webster called narrow "garters" of arable land along the sides of some streams. Polk believed he was making a fair, even a generous offer, especially since it was evident that Mexico could not keep California any more than she had been able to keep Texas.

Such an offer was not regarded as an "insult" to Mexico. Purchase of territorial areas was well recognized on a basis of international agreement. Thus, Jefferson had purchased Louisiana from Napoleon; Adams had purchased Florida from Spain; Seward later was to purchase Alaska from Russia.

But when Slidell appeared in Mexico City, Herrera, under pressure of the war party, abruptly refused to see him—which was regarded as an affront in itself to the United States. Shortly after Herrera was deposed by a military *junta*, which inaugurated in his place Paredes, leader of the war party. At this period it appears that a considerable part of the Mexican militarists actually harbored the belief that the Americans would not fight; and that if they did fight they could easily be defeated.

The sorest point between the nations was the dispute over the Texas border. Texas, in winning independence, asserted from the first that her natural boundary was the Rio Grande; and upon this Santa Anna had agreed with Houston as a stipulation for peace. In regard to this matter Mexico took an oddly inconsistent position. Though she refused to acknowledge the independence of Texas, she insisted that the border of Texas—the very existence of which as a separate political entity was not even acknowledged—was on the Nueces River, not the Rio Grande.

The Nueces, which runs into Corpus Christi Bay, at one time was the vague limit between the provinces of Coahuila and Texas, although nobody paid any attention to it, since Coahuila and Texas were considered twin provinces by the Mexican government, both being ruled from Monclova—one of the reasons for the Texas discontent and revolution.

But the United States, *by statute*, in accepting Texas into the Union, also accepted its boundaries as outlined, which meant the Rio Grande. America was therefore dutybound to defend this Texas claim, or at least adjudicate it, and Mexico had refused to meet Slidell.

3

As the tension between the countries grew, General Zachary Taylor (actually at that time a colonel holding the rank of brigadier general by brevet only, though later brevetted major general), was ordered to the disputed area. Taylor was a courageous but far from brilliant frontier soldier, and he was sent merely as a precaution.

He chose for his headquarters Corpus Christi, which is on the bay of that name, and though within the territory in dispute, about as distant as possible from the Rio Grande where trouble might brew. There he gathered a small military force, not exceeding 3500 men, all regulars, and he improved his time by drilling and disciplining them, so that "when he took the field, in organization and efficiency [it] was probably the best ever seen [up to that time] in the United States."

Mexico began concentrating troops south of the Rio Grande. When Washington was informed of this, Secretary Marcy ordered Taylor to march to that river to forestall a possible invasion by a show of strength. He took with him only about two thousand men, and met no Mexican opposition on the way south.[1]

Hindsight is better than foresight. Ulysses S. Grant, in his *Personal Memoirs*, denounced the Mexican War as "a conspiracy to acquire territory out of which slave states might be formed," although the facts are that none of the territory later acquired was in the least degree suitable for slave labor, nor did any of it become slave territory. This was written forty years after the war was fought.

---

[1] The single instance of physical opposition, however, created one of the hilarious episodes of the war. The country was full of wild cattle, which sometimes were fierce toward dismounted men. A soldier, marching on the flank of Taylor's column tried to shoo a large black bull out of the way, and finally fired at him, but missed his shot. Instantly the bull charged, horns down, tail up, snorting with rage. The soldier fled in most unsoldierly fashion into the column for safety, but right after him thundered the beast. Full into the column of marching men he rushed, "scattering regiments like chaff," with soldiers falling over one another, files breaking in undignified rout, officers swearing and unable to halt the debacle. So tangled were the men, weapons and the animal, that nobody dared fire for fear of wounding a comrade, and the bull at last galloped away unharmed. Fortunately nobody was injured, but that bull possessed the distinction of having alone thrown Zachary Taylor's army into confusion, which the whole Mexican array was not able to do in later battles. See Colonel Richard I. Dodge, *Our Wild Indians*.

At the actual time of the War with Mexico, Grant was not particularly anti-slavery. In fact he himself owned a slave *after* that war, his wife had several, and his wife's family many. During the war Grant seems to have been as eager for military glory as any other young officer.

Another statement by Grant in the *Memoirs* is "We [of Taylor's command] were sent to provoke a fight." This is simply not true.

Taylor was too unsubtle a man to send on a mission of such deep and dark subterfuges. The United States felt obliged to uphold the Rio Grande border, and Taylor was sent to occupy the disputed territory, no more. When he arrived at the river opposite Matamoros, the first thing he did was to send General William Jenkins Worth across the stream with a communication to General T. Mejía, the Mexican commander, expressing "a desire to maintain amicable relations, and . . . willingness to leave the port of Brazos Santiago open to citizens of Matamoros until the boundary question should be settled."[2]

Mejía rejected any such proposal. Besides refusing to permit Worth to have an interview with the American consul at Matamoros, he notified Taylor that the movement of the American army was "regarded as an act of war."

Thereafter events moved rapidly. General Pedro Ampudia, who arrived to take over chief command from Mejía, politely invited Taylor to retire. General Taylor, equally polite, declined on the ground that he was on United States territory, and began to build a fort opposite Matamoros.

Ampudia displayed some hesitation about what to do next. He was therefore replaced by General Mariano Arista, who had the kind of fiery war spirit President Paredes desired. Taylor learned that two ships intended to ascend the Rio Grande with supplies for the Mexican army and ordered the river blockaded. At that Arista began crossing his army over the river, with the intention of cutting Taylor off from his base of supplies, which he had established at Port Isabel.

On April 24, 1846, Captain S. B. Thornton, reconnoitering with a company of dragoons, was ambushed by a detachment of Arista's men. Sixteen Americans were killed or wounded, and others captured.

First blood had been shed—and on soil which Texas and the United States maintained belonged to them. The war had begun, the initial hostile move by Mexico.

President Polk sent a message to Congress announcing the invasion and armed clash, and stating that the patience of the United States

---

[2] Brazos Santiago was on the American side a few miles north of the mouth of the Rio Grande, and this offer sufficiently indicates Taylor's pacific intentions.

was exhausted. Congress declared that a state of war existed, and voted $10,000,000 for expenses.[3]

Polk called for 50,000 volunteers (he got about 30,000, some of whom never saw action), and asked Congress for an additional sum to "negotiate peace," it being understood this would apply should territory be acquired in the conflict now begun. The appropriation was not voted at the time, and is chiefly interesting because of a motion called the Wilmot Proviso, introduced as an amendment to the appropriation bill by David Wilmot, a portly young Pennsylvania Democrat, providing that slavery should be debarred from any lands acquired by the war.

Wilmot was a strong Unionist, a fighter for the rights of labor, a hard money man, and a leading advocate of the abolishment of imprisonment for debt. He showed courage in his Proviso, but his tenminute speech in its behalf, and the amendment itself, had the immediate effect of whetting to a new and keener edge the sectional bitterness over slavery. Southern speakers assailed the Proviso with unexampled fury, while it was as furiously upheld by Northern orators. The Proviso was voted down, but it was destined to be a constant source of friction, ever widening the rift in the nation, for years afterward.

4

Meantime the war was in progress. Zachary Taylor knew he was heavily outnumbered and in a perilous position, but he also knew how to fight. As Bernard De Voto later wrote: "What did he [Taylor] have? A sound principle: attack. A less valuable one which was to serve him as well in this war: never retreat. Total ignorance of the art of war. And an instinct, if not for command, at least for leadership."

Taylor, heavy featured, with a huge nose, wrinkled forehead, bushy

[3] The War with Mexico was to be the cheapest in United States history. Excluding the obviously gigantic expenditures of the two World Wars and the Korean War, and bearing in mind the changing dollar values over the period of time, here are, according to George Frederick Ashworth, in *Dictionary of American History*, the estimated costs of major American conflicts:

Revolutionary War		$370,000,000
War of 1812		112,912,543
Mexican War		97,705,860
Civil War		
Union	$4,486,198,881	
Confederate	1,520,033,632	$6,006,232,513
Spanish-American War		444,599,343

brows and wide-set mouth, was one of the least spectacular commanding officers in the history of the United States army. He had a
farmerish aversion to military display, so that his usual attire was ill-
fitting civilian's garb, his only mark of rank being a cap with his
general's insignia upon it. This peculiarity won for him the name Old
Rough and Ready. He rode a white horse more notable for solid if
indolent virtue than for fiery speed and action, and he liked to sit
this horse side-wise—with both legs hanging over one side, while he
read dispatches or gave orders. His men, with considerable lack of
imagination, called this horse Old Whitey.

Having learned of Arista's movements, Taylor left the partly finished fort, which he named Fort Texas, under the command of Major
Jacob Brown, with a regiment of infantry and two batteries of artillery as a garrison, and with the rest of his force marched to secure
his base at Port Isabel. This done, he turned to meet his enemy.

The Mexicans had begun a siege of the new fort which Brown defended with gallantry, and Taylor's first object was to relieve this
beleaguered outpost.

Arista had been under the impression that Taylor was retreating,
and therefore pursued. It was something of a surprise to him when he
encountered the Americans on their way back toward their fort. At
Port Isabel Taylor had received reinforcements of some marines and
some Texas volunteers, and he now headed 2228 men.

The Mexican army, numbering about five thousand, took up a position at a place called Palo Alto, and there on the afternoon of May 7,
the first pitched battle was fought.

Arista at first advanced his lines, but the American batteries played
so fiercely on the Mexican columns, that they fell back in retreat. A
charge by Arista's lancers—the favorite form of Mexican cavalry—was
likewise repulsed with loss. To add to the confusion of the battle,
wadding from some of the American cannon set fire to the high dry
grass, flames spread along the entire line, and the breeze carried the
smoke into the faces of the Mexicans. Another confused charge just
before nightfall was thrown into disorder by grape and canister from
Taylor's guns, and that night Arista withdrew his army.

In this battle, Taylor had no more than 1700 men, part of his army
not yet having come up from Port Isabel. He was much outnumbered
by the enemy's five thousand. Yet his loss was only four killed and
forty-two wounded, while the Mexicans admitted a loss of 102 killed
and 127 wounded. That great disproportion of casualties was due to
the work of Taylor's artillery.

The following day Taylor resumed his march and encountered the
enemy once more, this time at Resaca de la Palma where Arista had

formed his army in the dense chaparral and mesquite that choked a defile. Fighting here was of a desperate nature, almost at hide and seek, the underbrush so thick that units on each side frequently lost track of each other.

Once a Mexican charge nearly captured an American battery, which annoyed Taylor. One of his more spectacular officers was Captain Charles A. May, six feet four inches tall, wearing a full beard and long hair falling down his back, reckless, inclined to the bottle, and a superb horseman. He and his company of eighty dragoons were typical daredevil cavalrymen.

To May, Taylor indicated that he would like to see a certain Mexican battery captured. Away went May, his long hair flying, his dragoons behind him, leaping their horses over rocks and bushes at the dead run. They cleared the Mexican parapet and began sabering the Mexican gunners. The battery was captured. At about the same time a new American charge turned Arista's flank, and his army crumbled.

The pursuit continued all the way to the Rio Grande, where the fleeing Mexicans crossed, some of them drowning in the passage. In that battle and rout the Mexicans admitted loss was 262 killed, 355 wounded, and 159 missing, against Taylor's relatively small casualties of 39 killed and 125 wounded. Again the American batteries had dominated the day.

The beleaguered fort was relieved. Major Brown had been mortally wounded in its defense, and Taylor renamed it Fort Brown. It was the beginning of the present city of Brownsville, Texas.

All Mexicans had now been cleared out of Texas, but Taylor was not the man to let matters rest there. Without waiting for orders, he moved his army across the Rio Grande into Matamoros, which he occupied without resistance.

But there he remained for a time, expecting reinforcements, and employing his time in writing letters to Congressmen and newspaper editors, extolling his own deeds and constantly criticizing his rivals and opponents of every kind.[4]

His two small victories had aroused enormous excitement and enthusiasm in the United States, and already he was being spoken of as Presidential timber—a reference which he did nothing to discourage.

[4] "He [Taylor] established the friendliest relations with newspaper correspondents, who knew copy when they saw it. Brave, benignant, stupid, as common as your Uncle Bill, he dealt gently with the excesses of volunteers . . . While the political brigadiers kept a stream of letters going where they would do the most good, Taylor also enlarged his correspondence. Bliss, his chief of staff, corrected the spelling (he had spelled his two battles "Palialito" and "Resacka"), Taylor being of the opinion that in our perfected system, a President did not need spelling or much else."—Bernard De Voto, The Year of Decision.

5

As late as this President Polk still hoped that he might obtain the settlement of the boundary question, and also acquire the territories to the west, on which he now had his eyes, by peaceful purchase rather than by further bloodshed.

In an effort to accomplish this, Polk engaged in one of the most fantastic intrigues in the history of the nation. Still in exile in Cuba was Santa Anna, the master of treachery. There appeared presently in Washington an impressively uniformed individual named Colonel Atoche, who, it seems, was an adherent of Santa Anna.

Colonel Atoche had an interesting proposition. To Polk he suggested that certain sums of money—$30,000,000 to the Mexican nation, and, say, $500,000, to meet "present purposes" for a certain personage for whom he could speak—would permit the arrangement by that personage, when he returned to power, of a conclusion with the United States "at a show of force," whereby Texas and certain lands to the west of Texas would be ceded by the Mexican government.

With incredible naïveté Polk took all this at face value, although Santa Anna's previous long record of rascality should have been sufficient warning to him. There was, indeed, a sort of logic to it, since any Mexican regime with $30,000,000 could make itself permanent. But dealing with Santa Anna precluded any logic.

Yet it was not all loss. As an important corollary of these negotiations, the dispute with Britain over the Oregon boundary was settled. Polk, contemplating the asking of a "secret fund" from Congress to meet Atoche's proposal, sought the advice of his cabinet. The cabinet members agreed, although some had misgivings. Next the President sounded out party leaders. Thomas Hart Benton would be in favor of the sum involved. Sam Houston, now a Senator from Texas, agreed to it. There was John C. Calhoun: and Polk foresaw trouble with him. But when the South Carolinian was invited to a conference he said, yes, he would agree to pay up to $25,000,000 for the western lands.

He pointed out, however, that the existence of the fund would soon be public knowledge, and this would embarrass negotiations for Oregon. Therefore, he suggested, that instead of demanding the 54°40′ boundary on which Mr. Polk had campaigned, the President would do well to compromise immediately on the 49th Parallel—which extended the already existing line across the top of the nation. This had been Calhoun's stand from the first, and it was logical. Also it shows him as thinking of the nation as a whole and not of his own section, for Oregon could never be slave territory.

As for Britain, that nation was anxious to have the matter adjusted and in a receptive frame of mind. After some hesitation, Polk agreed and the settlement was accordingly made, clearing the atmosphere in that direction at least, although bringing upon his head much criticism, especially from the Whigs, who seemed willing enough to acquire additional territory in the Northwest, while they were against acquiring it in the Southwest.

To return to Santa Anna: He was not as naïve as the American President. The agent selected to negotiate with him, Captain A. Slidell MacKenzie, of the United States Navy, was indiscreet enough to arrive in Havana in full uniform, with the consequent publicity which could not be avoided. This exactly played into Santa Anna's hands.

Still promising that he would live up to his agreements, the archplotter was permitted to pass through the American blockade and land at Veracruz. There he instantly reversed himself, as he had done so many times before, and repudiated everything in tones of such righteous indignation that once more he was the hero of the Mexican people.[5]

Vice-President Bravo, one of Santa Anna's men, ousted Paredes from the supreme office of the land, and in December 1846, Santa Anna once more was proclaimed *El Presidente*, and made a speech of acceptance in which he promised to "punish the barbarians." Now at last Polk learned that he who sups with the devil needs a long spoon. There could be no negotiated peace.

[5] Santa Anna was in and out of power four times, and he knew perfectly how to play on the emotional nature of his countrymen. When he was in eclipse after the Texas revolution, he brought himself back in the following manner: Late in 1838 a French squadron anchored off Veracruz to collect reparations owed by Mexico. Veracruz was bombarded and occupied. At this point Santa Anna came out of retirement to "command the army opposing the French invaders."

The reparations being paid, the French squadron withdrew. But Santa Anna, wishing to make it appear that he was "driving" the enemy from the sacred soil of Mexico, advanced with a small force and opened fire on the last of the French as they embarked. He approached closer to the firing line than he intended, and was struck by a bullet below the knee, necessitating the amputation of the leg.

Of this he made full dramatic use, said he was at death's door, composed a touching and patriotic "dying request"—and thereupon rapidly recovered.

The amputated leg, however, did not recover. Santa Anna considered it a part of his sacred person, and that it had died for his country. When he was restored to power—which was quite soon—the martyred extremity was tenderly exhumed from where the surgeons who removed it had inconsiderately buried it, carried to the City of Mexico, and there interred with impressive ceremonies of both church and state, including a monument. Santa Anna, as chief mourner at this farce, dropped a pensive tear over the "grave."

Meantime the loss of his leg, his own oratorical pronouncements, and a *junta* headed by two of his generals, deposed Bustamante and once more Santa Anna reigned. This was before his exile in 1844 for corruption.

CHAPTER SIXTEEN

Buena Vista

1

LATE in June, Taylor was interrupted in his letterwriting and political interviews, by orders to proceed with the war. He was not ready for such an order and spent time frantically buying mules for his transport wagons. Volunteers had arrived at Matamoros in numbers which swelled his force to about 12,000 men, and increased the problem of feeding them, but when Taylor at last set forth he left all of them behind except some 6600 officers and men, with requisite artillery.

He reached Camargo, close to the head of navigation on the Rio Grande, July 31, and since steamboats could, at high water, reach that point, he made it his advanced base of supplies. Taylor, by this time, seems to have begun taking his candidacy for the Presidency very seriously. "He had acquired an unshakable conviction that the administration was trying to kill his candidacy by procuring his defeat in the field." Of this he complained loudly and long to his friends back in the States.

But move he must. On August 19 he set out once more, heading for Monterrey.[1] Ahead of his main army rode a body of Texas Rangers, commanded by Ben McCulloch and Jack Hays, "in outlandish dress with huge beards, looking almost like savages." The Rangers, with the episodes of the Texas revolution in their recent recollections, had a great distaste for Mexicans. When a body of enemy lancers tried conclusions with them, they simply sat in their saddles and after one blast from their rifles drew their Colt five-shooters—the first really practical repeating weapons—and cut down so many of their spear-carrying foes that the others lost their enthusiasm and with precipitation sought the safety of distance.

Moving with lumbering slowness, Taylor's army approached Monterrey. His advance division, commanded by General William J.

[1] The capital of the Mexican state of Nuevo Leon, and not to be confused with Monterey, California, which also enters into this narrative.

Worth, one of the best soldiers of the war, reached that heavily fortified town September 19.

Old Rough and Ready saw no reason to delay matters, and ordered an attack the following morning. Within the excellently engi-
neered defensive works was General Ampudia, Taylor's old adversary
of the Rio Grande, with 7000 regular soldiers and between 2000 and
3000 irregulars.

To oppose this formidably placed enemy army, Taylor had three
divisions, two of them consisting of regulars. The first was commanded
by General David E. Twiggs, who had won distinction in the War of
1812, had served in the Seminole and Black Hawk Indian wars, and
later was to be a general in the army of the Confederacy. The second
division was headed by General Worth, also a veteran of the War of
1812, and recently superintendent of the United States Military Academy at West Point, a very excellent officer whose career was cut
short by cholera, and for whom Fort Worth, Texas, was named. The
third division—made up of volunteers—had as its leader General William O. Butler, a third soldier of the War of 1812, who had served
under Andrew Jackson, was to supersede Winfield Scott in command
of the army in Mexico City, and eventually would run for Vice-President on the Democratic ticket headed by Lewis Cass in 1848, against
Taylor himself.

Subordinate to these, but contributing largely to the success of the
American arms was a brilliant group of younger officers, including
Lieutenant Ulysses S. Grant, Captain Braxton Bragg, Lieutenant James
Longstreet, Lieutenant George Gordon Meade, Lieutenant John F.
Reynolds, and Lieutenant George H. Thomas, all of whom later won
renown in the Civil War.

The artillery arm was represented by four batteries, four guns each,
of light field artillery, and three guns of siege proportions. On the
other side, Ampudia had forty-two cannon to oppose Taylor's nineteen.

Monterrey was ready for the attack. To the north it was protected
by the Citadel, a huge bastioned work built about the unfinished walls
of a new cathedral, with twelve pieces of artillery. The western end
was guarded by two strong fortifications, Cerro del Obispado and La
Federación, built on rugged heights. A line of barricades along the
San Juan River provided defenses on the south. On the east three
frowning forts overlooked a northward bend of the river—Tenería,
El Diablo, and La Libertad.

From the first Taylor's action was badly planned. He began by
ordering Worth to march to the west side of the town, thus dividing
and weakening his forces. The artillery he carried was not adequate

for breaching fortifications such as the Mexicans possessed, except for two howitzers and one mortar of his siege train.

Nevertheless, deprived of Worth's division, he sent his men in. Forward went the blue lines, charging the enemy's strong defenses with desperate courage. The Citadel and the barricades hung out heavy clouds of smoke and the shocking roar of big guns and small arms smote the ears, as the attacking party was raked from two sides.

In spite of heavy losses, the first assault reached the streets of the city. There, however, it became confused, lost momentum, and when four of its ranking officers were struck down, Taylor at last was forced to recall it. A second attack, led by Brigadier General John Anthony Quitman also was driven back after losing a third of its numbers.

Thus far the action was a failure, and Taylor and his staff fully believed they had lost the battle. But at this juncture Old Rough and Ready's subordinates took charge, as they did frequently during his campaign. The first turn in favor of the Americans came through a fortunate circumstance and the decisive action of one young officer.

In the immense confusion of the first assault, a company of the 1st Infantry under Captain Backus had reached a tannery which stood about 130 yards to the rear of Fort Tenería. The captain led his men to the roof of the building, which was flat and surrounded by a thick wall, two feet high, furnishing excellent protection for prone marksmen.

When the American force began to withdraw, Backus was on the point of retreating also, when he saw that his position commanded the "gorge" (open rear) of the enemy's battery in the fort.

Backus did not retreat. Placing his men behind the low parapet he directed them to pick off the gunners, and the guns of the company on the roof were soon banging merrily.

Just as the major attack was withdrawing, the crackling fire of Backus' men began. In the fort, stricken Mexican artillerymen slumped to the ground, or spun about and fell headlong. The murderous fusillade cleared the bastion, and the survivors fled from it for Fort Diablo, farther to the south.

Now the Americans returned to the attack. General Butler, with the 1st Ohio Volunteers, swarmed into Fort Tenería, and the first of the Monterrey outposts was captured—with five pieces of artillery, considerable ammunition, and thirty prisoners.

Yet Fort Diablo, even stronger than Tenería, defied the Americans, and drove them back with losses when they attacked it. Darkness fell, and firing ceased, except for sporadic sputters of musketry now and then through the night hours.

That first day's fighting was far from encouraging. Three times Taylor's men had been repulsed, and though an enemy fort had been captured, it was by no means the key to Monterrey. Losses had been heavy—a total of 394 officers and men killed or wounded. At this rate it appeared as if the city could not be taken without sacrificing half the army.

But meantime Worth, after a hard march which took all day because of the difficulty of getting his artillery over the roadless terrain, had reached a position from which he could fall on the western end of the city defenses. He communicated this to Taylor, and at dawn began his advance.

It was punctuated by a sharp cavalry action between the mounted Texas Rangers and a battalion of Mexican lancers. Though it lasted only a few minutes, being ended by the supporting fire of Worth's field guns, the enemy lost a hundred men on the field, and as they fled up the hill the Texans, with remorseless marksmanship, emptied many another saddle. Their own casualties were insignificant.

Flushed by the little victory, Worth's men at once assaulted the height of La Federación. Up the hill they went, led by the now dismounted Texans. A roar of musketry came from billowing clouds of powder smoke as the defenders on top opened fire. But the plunging fire of the Mexicans had the effect of overshooting its targets, and few Americans were hit as they reached the top and captured the important redoubt with surprising ease.

The fortification had been deemed inaccessible because of the almost perpendicular ascent. But that very factor favored the attackers, and soon after it fell, its sister redoubt, Cerro del Obispado, gave way also. Worth had completed his investment of the west side of Monterrey.

Now heavy and incessant firing was heard in the opposite part of the city. Taylor had resumed his attack which the previous night had halted, and his men were fighting their way into the streets. Without hesitation Worth immediately began an attack of his own, converging toward that of Taylor.

Street fighting is always ugly and costly. Ampudia had placed artillery to sweep the main avenues, but the Americans used the plan followed by the Texans in the capture of San Antonio years before. Using crowbars and axes found in one of the forts, they literally tunneled their way through the soft adobe walls, from one house to the next, occupying the housetops as they took them, driving the Mexicans back.

Square after square was thus gained, and the deadly racket of battle continued without intermission as the streets were filled with powder smoke and the Texas sharpshooters kept up a lethal decimation of the enemy forces. By nightfall Worth was within a square of the great plaza of the city, to which Ampudia had been driven by the attacks on both sides. There he halted when the darkness made operations difficult, and though the outposts continued a bickering exchange of shots, there was no real fighting.

With dawn a flag of truce came from Ampudia. The Mexican general, stunned by the remorseless advance of the Americans under circumstances so unusual, offered surrender. To save further lives, Taylor allowed Ampudia to evacuate his garrison and agreed to an armistice of eight weeks.

Monterrey was in his hands. The loss was severe—142 men and officers killed, and 340 wounded. But Taylor's army had been "blooded," and morale was high. Ampudia's army, on the other hand —with losses never determined—was correspondingly depressed.

So easy were Taylor's terms to the enemy, permitting them to retire without even surrendering their arms, that he was severely criticized. Shortly he received a dispatch from the War Department, disapproving the armistice and ordering him to give notice to the Mexicans at once that it was suspended.

2

By this time the high command at Washington at last had drawn up plans for a complete, rather than a partial, war. The capture of Monterrey had little material advantage as far as the ultimate defeat of the enemy was concerned. It had, to be sure, proved the mettle of the American soldiers. But it also indicated the impracticability of conducting a lengthy campaign through the sterile regions southward.

Scott's new plan included penetration of the west by General Stephen W. Kearny's "Army of the West," and a campaign directly against the City of Mexico by an "Army of the Centre" commanded by himself. It was decided that Taylor, whose force now was designated the "Army of Occupation," should make no further advances, but remain on the defensive and hold the northern provinces of Mexico.

General John Ellis Wool, a first-class regular officer, had marched south from San Antonio, Texas, ostensibly to occupy Chihuahua. Finding the route impracticable for baggage trains and artillery, he went instead to Monclova, and afterward, on orders from Taylor, to Parras. From there he joined Taylor's army at Saltillo.

With Wool's army and other reinforcements including the troops at Matamoros, Taylor now had 17,000 men. But the plan for the war included the occupation of Tamaulipas, and Taylor was instructed to send 5000 men, under Generals Robert Patterson, Worth, and Quitman, overland to that state, and to occupy the port of Tampico. That march was accomplished without serious resistance, and later the force at Tampico was picked up and accompanied Scott by sea to Vera-cruz.

Taylor now had only about 12,000 men, but worse was to come. Scott, about to undertake his campaign against the City of Mexico, requisitioned from him some of his best troops.

Taylor obeyed the orders of his superior, but he wrote a bitter dissent, in which he expressed the feeling that he had "lost the confidence of the government," and was being "sacrificed." One paragraph read:

> But, however much I may feel personally mortified and outraged by the course pursued, unprecedented at least in our history, I will carry out in good faith, while I remain in Mexico, the views of the government, though I may be sacrificed in the effort.

It is true that political considerations entered into these orders. Polk was aware of the growing boom for Taylor as President. While he had no intention of succeeding himself—his health in fact would have precluded this—he disliked Whigs, and Taylor was, technically at least, a Whig. Polk may have wished to curtail Taylor's press clippings by curtailing his activities. The President had made an effort to appoint a Democrat—like Thomas Hart Benton, or General Robert Patterson (who was by this time at Tampico)—head of all the armies, by creating a rank of lieutenant general for either of them. Congress, however, refused to accede to this.

It should be added that the feeling was quite prevalent, and shared by Scott, that Taylor did not have the ability to conduct any extended campaign of invasion. He was steady, but not brilliant, and on one occasion had proved inadequate to outgeneral a few hundred Seminoles in Florida. But Taylor also was thinking politics. He did not intend to allow Scott, or anybody else, to eclipse him.

In complete disobedience of orders, he took the offensive. He decided on his own authority—which presupposes complete ignorance of the country to be traversed—to take his reduced army south across the rugged mountains and waterless deserts to San Luis Potosí—and from there perhaps to Mexico City itself!

Blunderingly as usual he set out, and by February 5, 1847, he was camped at Agua Nueva, eighteen miles from Saltillo, on the road to San Luis Potosí.

Meantime Santa Anna, back in control in Mexico, had worked with almost maniacal energy raising, equipping, and training an army. The

self-styled "Napoleon of the West" made no secret of his military ambitions, and when a captured dispatch informed him that Taylor had
fewer than five thousand troops in his immediate army, Santa Anna
marched rapidly to crush him. His army contained more than 20,000
men, with twenty pieces of artillery. The soldiers were well armed
with imported weapons, so that the two-day battle that ensued was
"the first in history to be fought with percussion arms" on both sides.

Agua Nueva was situated in open fields, which offered little chance
for defensive action against superior numbers, and Taylor's selection
of it for his camp illustrates his less than brilliant military skill.

But General Wool, the regular, pointed out that the choice of
ground was a mistake. He succeeded with some difficulty in con-
vincing his superior, and Taylor unwillingly drew back his army about
eleven miles to a narrow pass called La Angostura, near a large hacienda named Buena Vista. The valley was about three miles wide, but
narrowed just beyond the hacienda, where a spur extended from the
mountains almost to the river which ran down to Saltillo seven miles
north.

Santa Anna, well served by his scouts, had hoped to surprise Taylor
at Agua Nueva. An expert reconnaissance by Texas Rangers under
McCullough and dragoons under May discovered his advance. He
found the abandoned American camp February 22 and pressed on.

In a small pass called Carnero, Santa Anna encountered an advanced party of about nine hundred Americans and attacked at once,
meantime sending flanking parties to cut off the detachment if possible. It was fortunate that Wool was in command there, instead of one
of the political brigadiers. His expert handling of his men resulted in
a fighting retreat instead of disorder. In extricating the men from the
trap in which they were almost caught by the encircling Mexicans,
Colonel Arch Yell, who had resigned as governor of Arkansas to head
a regiment from his state, showed superb gallantry.

Wool's little force fell back to where the main army was deployed
—if that word can be used in describing Taylor's somewhat haphazard
dispositions—in the gullies and across the ridges of the extremely
rough and cut-up battlefield he had chosen. Darkness was coming
down and the Mexicans did not pursue farther just then.

That night was bitter cold, with rain squalls beating the shivering
troops, often quenching their smoking fires. Cavalry videttes were out
to watch the enemy, but the Mexicans appeared to be as chilled as
the Americans, and there was no skirmishing in those cheerless hours.

Late in the evening the men, most of them volunteers and some
as yet hardly understanding what war was, since they had only recently joined Taylor, heard cheering in the distance. It was later
learned that Santa Anna was making a spread-eagle address to his

men, calling upon them to fight as heroes for their country. Their yells of "*Libertad o Muerte!*" were carried to the ears of the men in the American lines.

3

The Battle of Buena Vista is often pictured as a victory of American precision and discipline over raw and uncourageous though numerous Mexican foes. Too often that victory has been regarded as a foregone conclusion, with Taylor calmly giving orders, which his soldiers as calmly executed, unflurried by any thought of possible defeat.

No such thing occurred. The battle of February 23, 1847, on the muddy field which again and again was soaked by new rains, was one of the most fiercely contested engagements in the military history of the nation, its results often in extreme doubt, the tough Mexican soldiers fighting with sustained fury and the outmanned Americans at times driven before them, then rallying again, until by the narrowest of margins the decision finally was won.

In the first place, Taylor was not even on the scene when the action began. The previous night he had ridden to Saltillo, accompanied by a company of dragoons and the Mississippi Rifles, commanded by Colonel Jefferson Davis, who one day was to be President of the Confederate States of America, to look over the defenses there.

At dawn Mexican troops, which had reached positions in the higher mountains at the American left, began to fire at a skirmish line, thrown out by Wool, who was temporarily in command.

Then the main force of Santa Anna's army, in three columns, colorfully uniformed as always, marched out and halted in full sight of the American lines. Hurriedly Wool placed his units on the highest of the mountain spurs, taking advantage of the nature of the ground before him. That terrain was much cut by barrancas and ridges, with a network of arroyos coming down from the hills about the northern side of the hacienda Buena Vista.

The rains had ceased temporarily. On their ridge, the American force, reduced to little more than four thousand men, since the troops taken with him by Taylor were as yet absent, waited in grim silence. Their officers viewed and estimated the distant enemy, their sergeants made last minute inspections to see that guns and ammunition were in order after the wet night.

Worth had placed a battery commanded by Captain J. M. Washington, on the road below the ridge, on his right, at a point where the river cut closely to the escarpment, making the pass called Angostura (the Narrows) which the guns were to defend. In support, he placed

the 1st Illinois Volunteers on the tongue of land projecting down to
the road from the ridge, and then in his line, extending to the mountains, the 2nd Illinois, Colonel Yell's Arkansas regiment, the 2nd Kentucky under Colonel Henry Clay, Jr., and on the left the Indiana
Volunteers. Interspersed with these were light batteries commanded
by Captain Bragg, and Captain T. W. Sherman (not to be confused
with William Tecumseh Sherman of Civil War fame). In the rear
were two squadrons of dragoons and a company of Kentucky mounted
volunteers. Just at this juncture Taylor, who had heard the opening
gunfire of the battle, came hurrying back, bringing another company
of dragoons and the Mississippi Rifles, which were placed in reserve.

Santa Anna had been quick to observe that the Americans had not
occupied the heights of the mountains on their left, and he ordered
Ampudia with a column of troops to sweep over those heights and
turn the American flank. From his own left he sent General Mora y
Villamil, with another column, to move down the road and carry the
Angostura pass, which was held by Captain Washington's battery and
its supporting troops. A third column, under General M. M. Lombardini, was directed to move up a ravine and form junction with
Mora's force in the attack on the pass. Still a fourth division, under
General Ortega, constituted the reserve—and each one of these four
divisions was approximately equal to the entire American force.

Taylor arrived just when Ampudia's movement up the mountains
was first discovered, and when Wool was busy changing front of the
Indiana regiment on his left, to face this threat, meanwhile hurrying
a battery to aid in the defense.

The Battle of Monterrey had been won by his subordinates, and
to give Old Rough and Ready credit he did not now attempt to tell his
younger officers what to do. They fought the battle as conditions arose.
But Taylor did make two contributions. The first was when, just before the major onset, a flag of truce brought a curiously grandiloquent
ultimatum from Santa Anna:

> General Taylor: You are surrounded by twenty thousand men,
> and cannot, in any human probability, avoid suffering a rout and
> being cut to pieces with your troops; but, as you deserve consid-
> eration and particular esteem, I wish to save you from such a
> catastrophe, and for that purpose give you notice, in order that
> you may surrender at discretion, under the assurance that you
> will be treated with the consideration belonging to the Mexican
> character; to which end you will be granted an hour's time to
> make up your mind, to commence from the moment my flag of
> truce reaches your camp. With this in view, I assure you of my
> particular consideration. God and liberty!
>
> Antonio López de Santa Anna.

Taylor did not need the hour "granted" him to make up his mind. By the same messenger who brought the ultimatum, he returned his reply:

> General Santa Anna: I beg leave to say that I decline acceding to your request. With high respect, I am, Sir, your obedient servant.
>
> Z. Taylor

After that rebuff, Santa Anna, taking full advantage of his numerical superiority, loosed his forces.

Ampudia had more difficulty than he anticipated getting his column up the mountain and across its rugged heights, so the first heavy contact came from Mora, on the American right. Forward came the Mexican regulars, bayonets gleaming. The Washington battery began to slam grapeshot into it, and the Illinois regiments delivered such a blistering fire that the assailants recoiled.

Throughout this battle American batteries repeatedly were limbered up and sent bounding behind their galloping horses to hotly threatened points. By this remarkable mobility the field artillery exerted a tremendous effect on the outcome of the battle.

While the attack on the Angostura position was being beaten back, the ridge immediately in front of the American line suddenly burst into a cloud of smoke, through which the flashes of gunfire made vivid sparkles. Lombardini had led his column up the designated ravine, and deployed upon the ridge where he engaged Taylor's whole line, while Mexican batteries posted on the high ground overlooking the American left began blasting shells into the Indiana regiment.

Raw and inexperienced, the Hoosiers did not enjoy having those great holes torn in their ranks. Their disturbance was completed when Ampudia's men, who at last had achieved their climb of the mountains on the left, came pouring down upon them. That was too much for the recruits. They fled.

It was a moment of extreme danger. Ampudia's men rushed down in pursuit, and Mexican lancers who had been massed in cover galloped forward to complete the rout. Below the ridge, masses of enemy horse and foot pressed forward. Some of Ampudia's soldiers actually gained the rear of the American left. Taylor's position was completely turned and black disaster loomed for the whole army.

But the 2nd Illinois, supported by two pieces of artillery, refused to break, though it had to make a complete change of front. Bragg's battery, with two of Sherman's guns, galloped along the ridge, unlimbered, and began to shell the head of the Mexican column.

All this would have been insufficient had not at this moment a regiment in striking uniforms—palmetto hats, red flannel shirts, and white cotton trousers—thrown itself before the enemy. These were the Mississippi Rifles. Colonel Davis was wounded, but continued to direct his men. The Indiana regiment was rallied by its officers and returned to the battle line.

It was at this juncture that Taylor made his second contribution to the struggle. With a droll disregard of danger, he sat his horse, Old Whitey, and watched the battle surging around him. But now seeing what he thought were signs of wavering in the enemy force, he caused his horse to amble over to where Braxton Bragg was sweating with his guns, and said quaintly, "Give them a little more of the grape, Captain."

Bragg complied, the 2nd Kentucky came up, and before the murderous fire from the American front Ampudia's advance was rolled back.

For the moment the situation was restored, but matters still looked dark. Withdrawal of troops and guns from the Angostura pass to meet the flank attack left it almost undefended, and this was the key to Taylor's position.

Mora's column, not too greatly depleted by his first repulse, was formed behind a ridge, ready to attack again, and powerful reserves were at hand. Had Santa Anna thrown these forces against Angostura, he would have crushed the American right as he had almost crushed the American left, and overwhelmed the American rear. A debacle could hardly have been avoided.

But he did not recognize his opportunity, or he was too much involved in watching Ampudia's action to see it. The moment of danger passed, and the weak point was strengthened.

Even so there was a moment of excitement near the hacienda. A body of cavalry, under General Torrejón, had succeeded in getting clear around the defense position of the Americans, having broken through at the time the left was fighting for its life. Now Torrejón launched a charge from the rear on the hacienda.

He was met by the mounted Kentuckians, the Arkansas regiment, and May's dragoons, while from the roof tops of the hacienda buildings American riflemen blazed at the lancers. Torrejón was severely wounded, and his men were glad to get away from that sharp melee, with heavy loss, as they continued on their course to rejoin the rest of the Mexican army.

Now Taylor's men, gaining confidence, began to press the Mexicans on the mountain side. Massed guns intercepted the retreat when Ampudia sought to withdraw, while a terrible barrage decimated the Mexicans who were crowded in the ravines. For a time it appeared that Santa Anna's right wing was cut off and must surrender.

Just at this moment another flag of truce came fluttering forward. The messenger brought a request from Santa Anna that Taylor state his demands. Thinking the Mexican right wing might give up, Taylor gave the order to cease fire, and growled to the messenger, "I am only waiting for Santa Anna to surrender."

The white flag, the temporary cease-fire order, and the moment's truce were what the Mexican general wanted. His endangered right wing was able to extricate itself.

Almost immediately another hideous danger presented itself to Taylor's beset forces. At this time there were only three guns on the plateau, pieces which had been advanced to scourge the retreating Mexicans. With them were the 1st and 2nd Illinois, and the 2nd Kentucky.

All at once a dense column of enemy infantry came pouring up the slope, to the crest, cutting the American army literally in two. Masses of the Mexican infantry closed in on the volunteers, who retreated down into a gorge. Instantly the sides of the gorge were occupied by Mexicans who poured such a fire down upon the helpless men below that the ravine was choked with smoke. At the same time a body of Mexican cavalry swept across a salient spur and blocked the mouth of the gorge, cutting off retreat.

Destruction of the Illinois and Kentucky regiments seemed certain. But the Washington battery turned its full fury on the enemy horsemen, driving them back, and the shattered remnants of the volunteers made their escape and gained the shelter of the battery.

Then, down the ridge itself advanced the now triumphant Mexicans. Two batteries, commanded by O'Brien and Thomas, fought until the discharges from their guns literally scorched the flesh of the files of the enemy nearest them. Though these tore great gaps in the advancing column, the soldiers of Mexico came on with magnificent courage. O'Brien's battery was overwhelmed. Defeat again seemed certain.

But at the critical moment Bragg's battery galloped up, the guns were swung on the enemy and fired as rapidly as they could be worked. Sherman's battery joined them. Once more the Mississippi Rifles and the Indiana regiment appeared, coming up from the barranca at the north of the ridge and taking the Mexicans in the flank.

It was decisive. The enemy recoiled and retreated.

All day the skies had threatened, with intermittent showers of rain. Now the clouds gathered in earnest and a violent storm, with almost hurricane winds accompanied by fierce lightning and thunder, swept the contending armies. Operations on both sides nearly ceased. By the time the storm had blown itself out night was falling.

In the darkness the Americans cared for their wounded as well as they could, and prepared to renew the battle next day. It was with forebodings that they awaited the morrow's conflict, for their ranks were heavily depleted by casualties, and the men were worn out.

But when morning came, to their amazement, they could not see a Mexican, save for the dead. During the night Santa Anna had retreated from the field.

Buena Vista was history. Taylor's losses were 267 killed, 456 wounded, and 23 missing, a total of 746 out of 4769 officers and men engaged. Santa Anna lost 591 killed, 1049 wounded, and 1854 prisoners or missing. In his retreat southward across the desert he lost so many more by thirst, fatigue, or desertion that he reached San Luis Potosí with no more than 10,000 of the 20,000 with whom he had set forth.

Zachary Taylor had won the greatest single battle of the war—or rather his men had won it for him. It was the fighting ability of the individual soldiers and the initiative of his subordinates that gained the victory.

Nevertheless it went down on the books as Taylor's triumph. It was his last battle. Before long he turned over his command to a subordinate and went back to the United States to begin running for President in earnest.

"A little more of the grape, Captain," became one of the campaign sayings that carried him to the White House.

CHAPTER SEVENTEEN

War in the Amateur Manner

1

PRESIDENT Polk, now that hostilities had begun, "wanted the whole hog, not just the trotters." In particular he wanted California, which to him and most others then meant no more than the two great bays of San Francisco and San Diego. The magnificent anchorages were as yet little used, but whaling and shipping industries knew of their great possibilities and desired them.

California, since the bloodless "battle" of Cahuenga Pass, was no longer a part of Mexico except by the most shadowy of pretenses. In April 1846, Thomas O. Larkin, the American consul at Monterey, wrote Abel Stearns of Los Angeles:

> Only better government by Mexico in California can keep the people here loyal to Mexico. They already begin to look abroad for help. Some look to England, some to the United States, and a few to France. The last is a *dernier* resort . . .

Two weeks later Larkin noted:

> Overtures have been made by British agents to the Government of California to declare its independence, and at the same time requesting to declare itself under the protection of that Government and offering guaranties . . .

Polk had attempted to purchase the Mexican claim to California, as had Andrew Jackson before him, and had failed. He was aware of the condition of the province and perhaps also of the overtures of the British to take it over as a protectorate. He now proposed to obtain California by conquest.

Just prior to the beginning of the war, Thomas Hart Benton's flamboyant son-in-law, Captain John C. Frémont, on one of his several exploring tours, was in Oregon.

Polk wanted California, and Benton wanted California, but Frémont had no orders to invade California. Nevertheless, invade it he did. A copy of a dispatch sent from Washington to Larkin at Monterey, was forwarded by that official, and the bearer, Lieutenant Archibald Gillespie of the Marines, reached Frémont with it, where he was camped on the shores of Klamath Lake, May 9, 1846. That dispatch did not, as Frémont later claimed, announce that a state of war existed with Mexico. It was dated near the end of October 1845. Not until May 12, 1846—three days *after* this message reached Frémont clear across the continent—did the declaration of war take place. Its instructions to Larkin, and hence to Frémont, were merely to conciliate the Californians and make them as friendly as possible to the United States.

But the vain and self-dramatizing Frémont had larger ambitions than conciliation. He wanted to be a hero.

So he took his small exploring party down into California, to a ranch operated by Peter Lassen, a mountain man (for whom the volcano was named) on Deer Creek, north of Sutter's Fort, which was on the Sacramento River. There he mustered some Americans, chiefly mountain men, and with these succeeded in stealing some horses, "capturing" the hamlet of Sonoma and an abandoned fort, raised a flag with the crude painting of a bear on it—whence the name "Bear Flag Revolt"—proclaimed the "Republic of California," and bitterly embroiled himself with Larkin, Commodore John D. Sloat, and everyone else in authority. Three American settlers were killed, and the same number of harmless Californians murdered in the brief disorder. In thirty days it was over.[1]

2

Back on the Missouri frontier, however, something far more important was happening. Colonel (soon to be Brigadier General) Stephen W. Kearny, pursuant to orders, had organized the "Army of the West"— assuredly one of the most heterogeneous forces in history. He had three hundred regulars of his own regiment, the 1st Dragoons; two companies of light artillery; two battalions of volunteers; and the 1st Missouri Mounted Volunteers, a somewhat more than individualistic unit, commanded by Colonel Alexander W. Doniphan.

Six feet four inches tall, rawboned and strong featured, Doniphan was a lawyer whose sole military experience had been in the so-called "Mormon War" during which members of that sect were expelled from Jackson County, Missouri. Nevertheless he was to prove himself a fine leader, without fear, and something of a humorist.

---

[1] Perhaps the single permanent result of Frémont's "revolt" was the later adoption by California of the Bear Flag as its official ensign, which now flies over all state buildings.

To supplement these, Kearny was busy organizing the 2nd Missouri Mounted Volunteers, to follow his first army under Colonel Sterling Price (later a Confederate general). Even more remarkable than any of the above was the "Mormon Battalion," enlisted among members of that whiskery sect, and accompanied in some instances by their wives and families—540 persons of all ages and both sexes—who were shepherded, rather than commanded, by a much harried but excellent officer, Colonel Philip St. George Cooke. The Mormon Battalion eventually made its way to California and added to the population of that territory with offspring produced both on the way and after arriving there. To add the final incongruity to the "Army of the West," it was accompanied by four hundred wagons of the annual Santa Fe trading expedition from the Missouri River towns.

Taking the first division of his army, totaling 1658 men and sixteen pieces of artillery—and trailed by the traders' wagons—Kearny set forth on the Santa Fe Trail in June 1846. With no particular adventures he marched the 650 miles to Fort Bent, where he camped while he sent an escort to conduct James Magoffin, a trader well liked in the New Mexican capital, who had been in a secret conference with President Polk before setting out with this expedition.

In Santa Fe dwelt General Manuel Armijo, governor of the province, a man addicted to the showiest of uniforms, described as "a mountain of fat," greedy, cruel, and venal. Magoffin called upon this functionary, and they held a considerable conference. Just what transpired between them is not known to this day, but later Congress was to appropriate $25,000 to Mr. Magoffin for "expenses and money expended by him" in an enterprise undefined but having to do with this visit.

Perhaps a key to the trend of the conversation (which may very well have included the suggestion of, say $25,000, as a bribe) may be found in Armijo's later actions. First, he proclaimed loudly that he was going to "exterminate the invader." Then, with an army of four thousand men and a couple of cannon, he marched northward toward where Kearny was bringing his expedition southward. The New Mexican "soldiers" were largely Indian or peon levies, poorly armed and with understandably little stomach for a fight. Nevertheless Armijo took them to Apache Canyon, a strong position which he might have defended even with his two cannon and ill-assorted forces.

Meantime Kearny reached Las Vegas, New Mexico, and there issued a proclamation "absolving" the people of the province from all allegiance to Mexico. This proclamation was received with relief by many New Mexicans, for Armijo was a scourge to the poor and helpless under his dominion. But the American general still had to reach Apache Canyon and presumably fight his way through it.

Whether or not Magoffin's "diplomacy" had anything to do with it, as soon as he heard that Kearny had reached the other end of the canyon Armijo suddenly declared that all was lost, and ordered a retreat. Some of his officers protested at abandoning the most defensible position in New Mexico, and he was forced to threaten them with punishment for insubordination before they obeyed him. But most of his army, nothing loth, followed him precipitately all the way back to Santa Fe.

The portly governor, however, did not even stop there. Pausing only long enough to gather up several wagon loads of valuables—which he later sold at a considerable profit in Durango, Mexico—he continued his flight southward. In his hurry he neglected to take along his wife, mistresses being plentiful and easy to obtain in Mexico. The lady thus deserted was described by Lieutenant Ruxton, the British army officer who saw her later, as "Once the belle of New Orleans [but] now a fat, comely dame of forty, with the remains of a considerable beauty, but quite *passé.*"

Prior to seeing Señora Armijo, Ruxton, who was on his way north from Chihuahua, encountered Armijo himself. That worthy asked what people were saying about his actions in New Mexico. Said the bluff Britisher, "Everyone says you and the New Mexicans are a pack of arrant cowards."

With a gesture of theatrical despair, Armijo replied, "*Adios!* They do not know that I had but seventy-five men to fight three thousand. What could I do?" And with that he continued his retreat to safety.

Without firing a shot Kearny marched through the canyon thus abandoned, and reached Santa Fe. There he raised the United States flag over the governor's palace; proclaimed New Mexico (then including the present states of Arizona, Nevada, and Utah) a part of the territory of his government; appointed as governor Charles Bent, of the fur trading firm of Bent & St. Vrain; and began construction of Fort Marcy, named after the Secretary of War.

3

But Kearny's real objective was California. As soon as all these things were accomplished, or under way, he ordered Doniphan to draw up a code of laws, pacify the Indians in the surrounding wilds, and then march southward to join General Wool at Chihuahua. Thereupon he hurried westward with his dragoons and part of his artillery.

He encountered Kit Carson riding east with dispatches telling of the "conquest" of California by Frémont, and knowing no good could come of this, he persuaded Carson to turn around and guide him back on the trail west.

That difficult journey was successfully accomplished. Incidentally, Kearny's cannon were the first wheeled vehicles to cross the continent along the line of the Gila River.

The wagons of the Mormon Battalion later followed, but by a slightly different route, and a better one, for the commander, Colonel Cooke, was laying out a practicable route for a possible railroad—a route which was first to be used by the gold rush stampede.[2]

As for Kearny's expedition, it suffered one casualty, a Mexican hostler, presumably killed by Apache Indians. Kearny gave the man decent burial, including a pine slab for a headstone, on which was burned with a hot iron the following epitaph:

HERE LIE THE BONES OF SANCHO PEDRO, THE ONLY
DAMN DECENT GREASER I EVER KNEW.

KILLED BY APACHE INDIANS, 1846.

GEN. S.W.K. U.S.A.

Of equal interest was a meeting with the famous Apache chief, Mangas Coloradas (Red Sleeves), who with twenty of his warriors visited Kearny's camp October 18. Because of the treachery of Mexican and American scalp hunters, who lured a crowd of Indians to a feast and then massacred them, using a concealed howitzer loaded with slugs for the purpose, the Apaches had conducted a war of extermination against Mexicans in New Mexico and Arizona.

It developed that Mangas held no grudge against Americans, blaming the Mexicans for the troubles of his people. In fact he welcomed the Americans as allies. To Kearny he said: "You have taken Santa Fe; let us go on and take Chihuahua and Sonora; we will go with you. You fight for honor; we fight for plunder and vengeance. Their people are truce-breakers. Let us punish them as they deserve."

[2] The Mormon Battalion fought one "battle," this with wild bulls similar to the beast that assailed Taylor's column. The "engagement" took place December 11. A whole herd of bulls charged the column, and Cooke, seeing the animals coming, ordered his men to load their muskets and repel the enemy. On came the bulls in spite of the volley which seems to have been badly aimed and hastily fired. One brute reached the "battle line," hooked a horn through a soldier's thigh, and threw him over his back. Another attacked a team of mules and killed them both. One huge, coal-black bull was killed when he almost had reached Colonel Cooke himself. In this combat a number of bulls were killed, and the others finally withdrew, but it would be hard to claim a victory for the battalion in view of the confusion and destruction left. Several men were injured, perhaps one fatally, in this most curious of all battles fought under the American flag. Later Cooke named a nearby creek Bull Run, little thinking that only a few years later another Bull Run, located in far-away Virginia, would be the scene of two of the bloodiest battles in the Civil War.

When this was translated to Kearny he of course rejected the proposal, and the Apaches went away, much puzzled by such scruples.

On marched Kearny to California. Commodore Sloat, who with five vessels had been off the Pacific coast of Mexico when he learned from "reliable sources" that hostilities between that country and the United States had broken out, at once sailed north. He was in a quandary. He had no formal notice of a declaration of war, nor did he have official orders governing his actions.

But he observed that a flotilla of British warships was in the vicinity, under the command of Admiral Sir George Seymour. Sloat feared that if news of the fighting reached the English commander, the latter might intervene in California. To avert this he sailed into Monterey harbor July 2, without waiting for official dispatches, landed some blue jackets, and occupied the government buildings and town. Two days later one of his subordinates, Captain John Montgomery, took possession of the Bay of San Francisco.

On July 15 Commodore Robert F. Stockton arrived with orders to assume command of the Pacific fleet, together with official word of the state of war existing. He at once occupied the remaining ports of California, commissioned Frémont (without authority to do so) a major, and mustered in that officer's brigands as Mounted Navy Riflemen—in other words, "horse marines."

Now the Californians, angered by Frémont's and Stockton's arbitrary actions, broke out into a real revolt. A body of *rancheros* captured some unarmed Americans at the Rancho del Chino (south of present day Pomona) and would have massacred them but for the intervention of their leader, Serbulo Valera. They then marched on Los Angeles, taking their prisoners with them, and forced the Americans to withdraw from that pueblo to San Pedro, where the guns of the U.S.S. *Savannah* protected them.

4

It was at this juncture, with the Californians in a state of great excitement, that Kearny, with his advance guard numbering about a hundred men, arrived near San Diego. His dragoons and their horses were much worn and wearied by the long march, and Kearny ordered a halt to rest them.

Very quickly a contingent of *rancheros*, under General Andrés Pico, the brother of Governor Pío Pico, gathered to oppose the Americans. The natives were all superbly mounted and they were magnificent horsemen. For weapons they relied chiefly on long lances with steel blades.

Close to a little Indian village, San Pasqual, the two small forces met. A clever feint was made by the Californians, drawing the dragoons into a disorganized attack and pursuit. But the worn horses of the Americans were no match for the speedy and well-trained mounts of their adversaries. When the pursuit became strung out for a mile or more, with the American horses showing the strain of the race, Pico's men suddenly reversed direction and came charging back.

The maneuver was a complete surprise. Having fired their carbines, without much effect, the dragoons were forced to depend on sabers against lances. The longer weapons prevailed. Before Kearny could get his men together, he lost seventeen killed, and fourteen wounded, including himself. The Californians' loss was never learned, but six of their dead were left on the field.

Not until a messenger from Kearny reached Stockton at San Diego, and two hundred reinforcements came marching to relieve him, could the American general proceed to San Diego.

After the rest of Kearny's dragoons came up, with men from the fleet and volunteers among the Americans, the advance to Los Angeles was begun. Though the Californians attempted to dispute passage of the San Gabriel River, and again showed fight near Los Angeles, they were easily beaten off and Kearny entered Los Angeles on January 11, 1847. By a capitulation signed January 13 at Los Angeles, in which the Californians gave up their arms and promised to return peaceably to their homes, being guaranteed in return protection of their lives and property, the little "war" in California was over.

There were difficulties to follow, headlined by a clash between Frémont (now calling himself Lieutenant Colonel) and Kearny, when the former disobeyed orders. Later, when they returned east, Kearny caused the arrest of Frémont at Fort Leavenworth, and preferred against him charges of mutiny, disobedience of orders, and conduct prejudicial to military discipline. The flamboyant son-in-law of Thomas Hart Benton was convicted on all charges, and sentenced to be dismissed from the service. But the President remitted the punishment. Frémont, unwilling to accept clemency, resigned from the army.

By that time California was peacefully—on the surface at least—under the administration of the United States.

5

Colonel Alexander Doniphan, left at Santa Fe by Kearny, had a sufficiently difficult series of orders with which to comply. To draw up a code of laws, to pacify wild and warlike Indians in an unmapped wilderness larger than all of New England with Pennsylvania and New York included, and to march into enemy country several hundred miles with his raw and inexperienced command, would have been enough to baffle if not discourage a lesser man.

But not Doniphan. He solved the necessities of the first order by declaring the statutes of the State of Missouri legal and binding in New Mexico, with a few exceptions governing land grants, *acequias,* and similar matters peculiar to the country.

His "law making" accomplished, Doniphan next set out to "pacify" the Indians. Pueblos were visited, and promised to behave—although after Doniphan departed southward the Taos Pueblo erupted in a bloody revolt that was put down equally bloodily by Colonel Sterling Price, who with the 2nd Missouri Mounted Volunteers took Doniphan's place as military commander of New Mexico. A more difficult problem was that of reaching, and impressing, the nomadic tribes, of which the Navajos were the most numerous and at that time the most annoying.

These Indians occupied a desert area cut by deep chasms, of which Canyon de Chelly, known to many modern tourists, is an example; and intersected by rugged mountains. It was and is a country of high peaks, sterile valleys, timbered table-lands, and fields of lava, with occasional oases.

Doniphan attacked this problem in the only way he knew. With four separate columns he boldly entered the Navajo country. His loose-riding, unintimidated Missouri detachments so impressed the Navajos that they gathered at Ojo del Oso. There they listened to Doniphan's words, and promised not to do any more raiding against the Mexicans—a promise they actually kept, for a few months.

Doniphan now had accomplished the first two of his injunctions, and since Price and the 2nd Missouri had arrived to take over the garrison work, he was free to carry out the last command—to invade Mexico and make junction with Wool.

He had arrived in Santa Fe with a regiment that numbered 856 men when he set out from Missouri. But they were mostly backwoods or farm boys, and they quickly perceived that there were many ways that a young man could enjoy himself in the New Mexican capital. In fact they perhaps enjoyed themselves too well.

The New Mexicans who had dreaded treatment they expected at the hands of a "lewd and licentious soldiery," discovered to their pleasant surprise that the Missouri boys were polite, even diffident; and that their property not only was free from confiscation, but on the other hand the Americans were willing to pay for what they required at a good round price.

Cantinas remained open twenty-four hours a day, and country lads sampled strange beverages like *aguardiente,* a fiery Mexican brandy, and a still more evil potation called Taos Lightning—a whiskey distilled from wheat with powerful intoxicating effects.

They attended *fandangos* and discovered that the pretty women of Santa Fe smiled at them; and in their awkward way they pursued those smiles, not only by attempting the native dances as best their clumsy feet could manage, but by even more intimate advances. To their delight they found that the women not only were amiable, but quite willing.

It followed that some interesting amours ensued, and considerable overindulgence. When the 2nd Missouri presently arrived, its boys also plunged into these pleasures with more zest than discretion. As a result there was much sickness, including venereal diseases, and some three hundred Missourians are said to have been buried in Santa Fe, from Doniphan's and Price's regiments.[3]

As a result of all this, Doniphan left Santa Fe, in November 1846, with a force somewhat depleted by the "dissipations of the New Mexico metropolis." His march toward El Paso was unmilitary in most ways. Distinctions in rank meant little to the individualists in his little army, and the boys liked to see what was up ahead, so that there were always some unauthorized persons with the advance.

Down the Rio Grande straggled *Los Goddammies.* No other word describes it, for to call it a march signifies some sort of military progression. Doniphan rode along, cracking jokes with his men, but keeping an eye out for possible enemies. The boys out on the flanks of the so-called column could not be restrained from shooting at jackrabbits which sometimes sprang up, or at larger game when it appeared, or even at prairie owls and prairie dogs. Everything was informal, jovial, and carefree.

Lieutenant Ruxton, on his way north to Santa Fe after encountering Armijo, left the shocked impressions of a British professional soldier:

> From appearances no one would have imagined this to be a military encampment. The tents were in line but there all uniformity ceased . . . The camp was strewed with the bones of the cattle slaughtered for its supply, and not the slightest attention was paid to keeping it clear from other accumulations of filth. The men, unwashed and unshaven, were ragged and dirty, without uniforms, and dressed as, and how, they pleased . . . The most total lack of discipline was apparent in everything. These very men, however, were as full of fight as gamecocks and shortly

[3] From their favorite words, uttered whether happy or angry, at work or at play, fighting or frolicking, the Missourians gained for themselves—and hence for all Americans—the name *Los Goddammies.*

after defeated four times their number of Mexicans, at Sacramento, near Chihuahua . . . Of drill and maneuvering the volunteers have little or no idea. "Every man on his own hook" is their system in action; and trusting to, and confident in, their undeniable bravery, they "go ahead" and overcome all obstacles.—
George Frederick Ruxton, *Life in the Far West.*

It was winter, the weather was extremely cold, and with considerable suffering they dragged themselves through the dread *Jornada del Muerto*, a ninety-mile waterless stretch extending southward from Valverde to Las Cruces. But they managed to make it, and when they emerged from the desert they were in good humor and ready for anything.

On Christmas Day they reached the Brazito (Little Arm), a branch of the Rio Grande, not far north of El Paso. There they prepared to celebrate in Yuletide spirit, with a barbecue for which beeves were slaughtered, although the supply of alcoholic cheer was lamentably short. Nevertheless, making the best of things, the boys sang *Hail Columbia and Yankee Doodle,* to show their patriotism, and fired their rifles skyward in honor of the occasion.

Others did a little gambling, including Doniphan, who was engaged with some of his officers and buck privates—no distinctions of rank existed here—in a game of "three trick loo" to decide who should own a fine horse, captured that morning, when someone brought word that a Mexican army was almost upon them. Doniphan threw down his cards. "Boys," he said, "I have an invincible hand, but I'll be damned if I don't have to play it in steel now."

6

The commander of the approaching Mexican army was General Ponce de León, and he had four hundred dragoons, eight hundred infantry, and four pieces of artillery with their crews, in all more than 1400 men, besides his baggage train. Doniphan at the moment could muster only about five hundred ragged frontiersmen, the rest of his command not yet having come up because of the chronic habit of straggling for which the 1st Missouri was notorious.

Even those at hand were much scattered, some bringing wood or water, others attending to their animals. But at the appearance of the Mexicans they hurried into some kind of a battle line, every man loading and looking to his gun, and rallying to the nearest flag in sight without regard to company classification. The whole thing was most primitive and unmilitary, but within an incredibly short time the Missourians were ready for their first battle—which not a man among them doubted they would win.

Ponce de León was equally confident. He sent a messenger with a black flag, on which was painted a skull and crossbones in white, and demanded immediate surrender. The Missouri answer was negative—in an insulting sort of way. The flag bearer returned to his commander.

Mexican bugles sang out and the Veracruz Dragoons charged the American left. The Missouri boys waited until they were in easy range, then loosed on them a rifle fire so withering that the dragoons fell back quickly, harried as they fled by Captain John W. Reid and sixteen mounted men—the rest of Doniphan's boys were fighting on foot, horses to the rear.

One company of enemy dragoons outflanked the line, and managed to get in among the American baggage wagons. But the mule skinners and packers carried shooting irons too, and the dragoons were glad to get out of that hot spot—with losses.

Now de León advanced the full force of his infantry. On command, the Mexicans fired a volley, which did little damage, most of the bullets going high. But following frontier custom the Missourians flattened themselves on the ground, to present targets as small as possible.

When the smoke of the volley cleared the Mexicans, seeing their prostrate foes, jumped to the erroneous conclusion that they had wiped them out and advanced exultingly. Then *Los Goddammies* rose, and the rippling crash of their rifle volley rang out. Down went scores of the enemy, and the rest retreated in confusion.

Ponce de León had been able to bring only one of his four cannon into action—a six-pound howitzer, which fired two or three times, the cannon balls sailing calmly overhead.

James Peacock, standing in the center where a group of boys from Missouri's Howard County had gathered, saw one of them crane his neck.

"What the hell do you reckon that is?" asked the neck-craner.

"A cannon, I believe," said another.

"Let's go get it!" cried several.

Without waiting for orders a squad of the Howard County boys ran into the Mexican lines, drove off the gun crew, killing several of its members, and took possession of the howitzer.

Doniphan's center advanced, apparently on impulse—certainly without definite orders—and Lieutenant Christian Kribben, with a hastily assembled gun crew, loaded the piece and discharged it into the Mexican ranks.

By this time de León's array was in disorder, and very shortly his whole army fled from the field. They had lost 43 killed and about

150 wounded. The Missourians had none dead, and seven wounded, all of whom recovered.

As it turned out, General Ponce de León had arrived at a most timely hour. In their haste to depart the Mexican commissary left behind "sacks and wallets of provisions, and gourds of the delicious wines of El Paso . . . profusely scattered over miles of surface."

The "delicious wines" supplied an aching want. It was only three o'clock in the afternoon when the last of the living Mexicans was gone, and the Missouri boys had "a regular Christmas banquet." That night they "reposed on their arms"—the account does not say how much the captured wines contributed to their "repose"—but there were enough men who were sober to provide a "strong guard."

The Missouri boys fought at the Brazito as if for the fun of it, picking and calling their targets as they shot. Doniphan had commanded with coolness and fine military judgment, but he refused to be made a hero. Later at a welcoming banquet given him and his men when they returned to Missouri, he said humorously: "At the Battle of Brazito, I remained behind, on the hill overlooking the battle, as any prudent commander would do. I soon found the Mexicans were overshooting the boys who were below me. Their shot were falling thick all around me. I put spurs to my horse, charged to the front, hollered, 'Come on boys' . . . The boys thought I was brave as hell but they did not know what drove me there."

After Brazito Doniphan occupied El Paso, where he was reinforced with men and artillery led by Major Meriwether Clark, son of one of the famous exploring partnership of Lewis and Clark, and named after the other.[4]

For more than a month Doniphan rested his men at El Paso; but he still had his objective to reach—the City of Chihuahua. February 8, his force now strengthened by reinforcements to 824, he marched for that city.

Word about General Wool was vague. Doniphan's orders were to report to that officer at Chihuahua, 235 miles to the south. Yet he was not even sure Wool was there. In fact rumors had reached him that the army he was seeking had turned off east—as indeed it had, to

---

[4] When Clark's men marched into El Paso some of the boys thought a salute should be fired in their honor. The gun captured at Brazito was wheeled out, loaded with powder, but no wad was found to make a blank shot. In the emergency a young Missourian pulled off his socks and rammed them down on the powder. When the "salute" was fired, the socks sailed in a high arc toward the advancing column and hit one of the men in the face. He set up a loud howl, and continued caterwauling even after he found he was not injured. Asked why he so bemoaned himself, he replied, "I'd rather be shot with a solid ball than with a pair of socks worn from Fort Leavenworth to El Paso, without a change for eight months."

join Taylor. He knew that Chihuahua was a large and strong city, and that he must penetrate inhospitable sandy wastes, facing a population aroused against him, with a force of less than a thousand men. Yet his orders were to go to Chihuahua. Before he set out he paraded his troops and put to a vote whether they were willing to march with him on the hazardous adventure. The Missouri boys were all for it, except for three dissenting votes.

One dissenter was a blacksmith who later was found to be insane. The other two, in the stay at El Paso, had fallen in love with two pretty Mexican girls. Two days out on the road to Chihuahua the lovelorn youths decided that they "did not choose to march any farther with the army." They departed at night, returned to El Paso, and married the girls. Nothing was ever done to punish them.

7

At El Paso Doniphan was joined by Jim Kirker, a famous scalp hunter, who made a career of securing Apache scalps and selling them to the government of Chihuahua for the bounty of $100 for a brave's scalp, $50 for a squaw's, and $25 for a papoose's. There appears to have been some suspicion that not all the scalps were from legitimate Apaches: a Mexican's hair was similar in appearance to that of an Apache. When he came to Doniphan he said that Chihuahua owed him $30,000 for scalps, and he wanted to collect part of it if he could.

Kirker was Doniphan's scout and guide. He informed the commander that very strong fortifications guarded Chihuahua, where General José A. Heredia had prepared redoubts and entrenchments commanding the strategic crossing of the Sacramento River, sixteen miles from Chihuahua itself.[5]

Within these fortifications Heredia had 4220 men, according to a written report of the Mexican adjutant general which came into Doniphan's possession after the battle. Major Clark reconnoitered the position. His report caused Doniphan to swing his whole force off the road to the right, across a rocky arroyo, and thus gain the top of the fortified plateau.

The move surprised the Mexicans completely. They did not believe it possible to get an army over that arroyo, but the clever Mis-

[5] General de León, after his defeat at Brazito, retreated all the way to Chihuahua, where he was arrested for cowardice. When he was shown the fortifications there, he said, "Yes, those are all right; but those *Americanos* will roll over them like hogs; they do not fight as we do." An uncomplimentary simile, but a correct prediction.

sourian had bypassed much of their elaborate defenses and forced them to change front.

Heredia, taken in the flank, had to come out and face his foe in the open plateau—a situation faintly analogous to that of Montcalm when Wolfe suddenly surprised him by turning his defenses and reaching the Plains of Abraham outside of Quebec.

Doniphan even managed to manhandle his artillery down the arroyo and up to the plain above. Major Meriwether Clark had six fieldpieces, Captain Richard H. Weightman two howitzers, and there was the Brazito cannon, probably still worked by Lieutenant Christian Kribben and his amateur gun crew.

There were fourteen Mexican guns, and for a brief time these engaged Doniphan's batteries in an artillery duel. But according to an eyewitness account their aim was so bad that the balls struck the ground forty or fifty yards in front of the American line, and rebounded completely over, wounding only two men but killing several horses and mules in the rear.

Suddenly a body of 1200 cavalry, under General García Conde (former Mexican minister of war), charged. The American artillery opened on them, and the Missouri rifles clattered. Conde fell back.

At this Doniphan ordered his own cannon to advance. With his two heavy howitzers Weightman slugged the enemy's nearest battery so hard that it was silenced, whereupon a brisk charge by Captain Reid captured the redoubt in which it was placed.

Clark's lighter fieldpieces turned on the Mexicans where they had rallied in their works about their main battery. But the Missouri boys had grown impatient. The artillery was having all the fun.

In a wave they suddenly went forward. The enemy big guns, "firing ragged balls and heavy copper ore" tore gaps in their ranks but could not halt them.

Lieutenant Colonel Congreve Jackson rode at their head with a shotgun in one hand and a saber in the other. "Now, boys, every man for his turkey!" was his frontier yell. And one of the men who followed him in that charge recorded that "Almost every man singled out his [target] . . . and brought the bead to bear upon him with as much certainty as if he were shooting at wild game in the forests of Missouri."

The Americans clambered over the parapets and bastions like ants, but before they could get at the garrison the Mexicans fled in wildest disorder. Rarely has a battle been more brief. It lasted hardly more than thirty minutes; but in that short time Heredia's army was destroyed, scattering in all directions, never completely to be gathered together again. His dead numbered 304, his wounded were estimated at not less than five hundred, while seventy prisoners, including General Cuilta, were captured. The booty consisted of vast quantities of ammunition, $6000 in specie, sixteen pieces of artillery,[6] and many horses and mules for transport as well as cattle and sheep to feed the troops. Considering everything it was one of the most astonishing victories of the entire war.

Typical of their strictly amateur approach to things military, the Missouri boys crowded around Doniphan after the battle, to shake hands with him and congratulate him on what they considered a "bang up job." The colonel received these compliments with the kind of pleasure any good Missourian would show at hearing praise from friends and neighbors.

Doniphan, of course, discovered that Wool had not arrived when he reached Chihuahua and occupied that city. Nevertheless he remained there for some weeks, perplexed as to what to do next. The command had received reports on the march which were at times disquieting. Before Brazito they heard of Taylor's victory at Monterrey. But after leaving El Paso for Chihuahua they learned that New Mexico was in revolt behind them. A later report indicated that Colonel Price had put down the uprising in three battles, after Charles Bent, the newly appointed governor had been murdered at Taos by Indians and Mexicans.

In spite of this disturbing information—though it turned out the second report was nearly correct—Doniphan continued his march, and fought the Battle of Sacramento.

Even more alarming was the first rumor of the Battle of Buena Vista, which indicated that the Mexican General Urrea had defeated Taylor. The next report was that Taylor had fought a drawn battle with Santa Anna, and held his ground, but with no further particulars.

8

Doniphan had been ordered to "report" to General Wool, who quite evidently was with Taylor. He was separated by hundreds of miles from the nearest American military force, and it was up to him to decide on the next move. Before he made his decision he called his officers together for a council of war. Some were for returning to Santa Fe, others for remaining in Chihuahua, but Doniphan, bringing his heavy fist down on the table, said, "I'm for going home to Sarah and the children!" He thought that he should report to Wool—wher-

[6] One Missouri boy, William H. Richardson, wrote home with awe: "One of these cannon is a very valuable thing, being composed of silver and brass, melted together."

ever Wool was—and after having been in possession of Chihuahua for
nearly two months, ordered the next leg of the march—clear across
northern Mexico to Saltillo where Taylor and Wool were waiting after
the victory of Buena Vista.

It meant another march of several hundred miles, but the Missourians started out cheerfully. Doniphan had no maps, but he had
with him some men that were rather good at "smelling out a trail."
Ignoring the Rio Grande route, he struck boldly south, then east,
following the Rio Conchos and Rio Nasas valleys, and stopped at one
point long enough to chastise a marauding band of Comanches who
had massacred a settlement and were bearing off some Mexican
women and children. Nineteen of the Indians were killed in the brief
battle, and the women and children restored to their families.

On May 8, when they reached the Hacienda Cadenas, his men received certain news of Scott's victory at Cerro Gordo. The frontier
boys cheered, and learned later that a force of Mexicans heard the
yelling and retreated entirely out of the state of Durango where they
were then marching. At Parras they at last received a communication
from Wool. He was at Saltillo, and he directed them to join him there.
Five days later Doniphan's "lost" regiment arrived at the battle field
of Buena Vista, and saw American troops and American flags
once more.

But when the Missourians were paraded before Wool, that officer
was scandalized by their appearance. He was in his handsome trappings of war, while they were attired, as he said, "some like Mexicans,
some like Comanches." As he walked down the line in inspection,
the boys craned their necks to keep him in view, and one, reproved
for getting out of ranks, explained to Colonel Doniphan that he
"couldn't see good enough where he was so he stood out and looked
at the show."

Appearances or not, Wool knew fighters when he saw them. He
wrote an order of commendation, in which among other things he
said:

> No troops can point to a more brilliant career than those com-
> manded by Colonel Doniphan, and no one will ever hear of the
> battles of Brazito, or Sacramento, without a feeling of admiration
> for the men who gained them.

Wool was anxious to have the Missourians re-enlist. But they politely demurred. They had been gone a year, almost, and they wanted
to return home, and see their folks, and spark their girls again. So
they were ordered to be sent back to Missouri.

It must not be supposed that they departed from Mexico without some other evidences of their backwoods ways to leave the regulars laughing. The Missourians had marched hundreds of miles through country where there was not enough water to bathe. Perhaps they stank. If so they were blithely tolerant of it. After all, you do not mind a little body odor in a comrade, if he uses a rifle well and stands up to a fight beside you.

For the first time they received pay and full rations. But when they went off with every skillet, kettle, and bag filled with food, the soap they had been issued remained behind. A commissary officer called their attention to this. "Soap, hell!" said the soldiers. "What do we want with soap? We have no clothes to wash!"

They were nearly right. The clothes with which they had started their campaign had suffered the attrition of hard usage, and they had picked up almost any kind of covering to replace the garments lost. George L. Boone, one of them, recorded that "Many of the soldiers were almost naked when they arrived at New Orleans. One man marched off the ship with only a pair of thin drawers on—and they were *quite* ragged."

General Taylor visited their camp, wearing, as usual, no part of a uniform, only a short brown country coat and a straw hat. Lem White, one of the Missourians, was feeling the delightful jingle of coins in his pocket, having been paid for the first time since leaving home, and he supposed Old Rough and Ready was some hanger-on or camp follower. Going to the general, he tapped him on the shoulder and asked where he could get some good whiskey.

Taylor pointed out the sutler's quarters. "You can get it there," he told the soldier, "but you'd better not let General Taylor know you got it, for he might make trouble for you."

White got the whiskey and sought his beloved Colonel Doniphan to give him a drink. He was told that Doniphan was at Taylor's tent. Going there he peered in, saw the colonel talking to the man he had asked about the whiskey. "Who is that fat old fellow sitting in there?" he asked the guard before the tent.

"That is General Taylor," said the guard.

"The hell you say!" exclaimed White, beating a retreat in alarm. "Why, that's the very old rascal that told me where to get this whiskey!"

The 1st Missouri was sent down the Rio Grande, embarked for New Orleans, and thence up the Mississippi to their home state, where a round of barn dances and barbecues awaited them. They had traveled 3600 miles by land and 2000 by water, fought and won two battles against superior enemy forces, captured two provinces, and all in all enjoyed an exuberant good time.

CHAPTER EIGHTEEN

Scott's Great Campaign

1

Bu t these events were side-shows compared to the really decisive campaign to subdue the enemy which was being conducted by General Winfield Scott in the south of Mexico.

Scott, General-in-Chief of the Army of the United States, was an impressive personage, six feet four inches tall and weighing more than 250 pounds. He had a broad, deeply lined face, with heavy brows and gray side whiskers. Unlike Taylor, he was fond of military trappings, and insisted that his staff members should be attired in all the glitter that the regulations allowed. For this reason his soldiers called him, somewhat derisively, "Old Fuss and Feathers."

A contemporary, George Templeton Strong, thus described Scott in his diary:

> The General [Scott] is . . . strong in great things and . . . weak in little things. Any man who should listen for half an hour to the general's bad French and flat jokes, his tedious egotisms, his agonizing pedantries of connoisseurship in wine and cookery, his insipid, inflated gallantries, and his painful exhibitions of suspicious sensitive conceit would pronounce him the smallest and feeblest of created men. A silly giant, a euphuistic Goliath, if we did not know that he had proved himself a brave, prudent, skillful, brilliant, and humane commander, and a warm-hearted and excellent man. His faults, I suppose, are chiefly vanity, arbitrary disposition, and an uncertain temper . . .

Yes, those were his faults. He was almost ridiculously touchy, his temper always flying off. He quarreled with his best general, Worth, so that the latter went home to resign his commission, until news that war had been declared caused him to recall it and go to Mexico where he served brilliantly. He quarreled, in fact, with all his subordinates, and he quarreled with his superiors. Not even the President was safe from his spleen, and he did not participate in the opening actions of the war because of his differences with Polk.

Yet he had been the head of the U. S. Army for fifteen years, its real intellectual leader. His talents were all military. He proved to be a bad politician, but he was the great soldier of his day. Perhaps the news of Taylor's thrilling early victories brought him to action, for he was intensely jealous. At any rate, on October 7, 1846, he laid before Marcy, the Secretary of War, his plan for a campaign against the capital itself of the enemy country.

Under this plan he proposed to gather all available troops—including all he could siphon off from Taylor—and capture Veracruz, the American Navy meantime blockading Mexican seaports or capturing them, and rendering him aid with the transportation of his army. Once Veracruz was taken, he would then march upon the City of Mexico. Taylor disagreed strongly with the proposal that he remain on the defensive, and confronted both Polk and Scott with an act of near insubordination.

Scott had his way, as was proper, since he was the supreme military commander, and preparations for his invasion were hurried forward. Good maps of Mexico were lacking, and he had little accurate knowledge of the obstacles he would encounter. But once launched, he carried on his campaign with soldierly courage and skill, so that his advance against the City of Mexico has been pronounced by experts a triumph of resolution and expertness not equaled between the Napoleonic wars and the great campaigns of the Civil War.

With accessions from Taylor's force, including the regiments sent to Tampico, and troops he conveyed directly from the United States, Scott had about 10,000 men at the beginning of his operations. Included in that number were some very promising young officers, among them Robert E. Lee, Ulysses S. Grant, T. J. Jackson (later famous as "Stonewall"), P. G. T. Beauregard, George B. McClellan, James Longstreet, Joseph E. Johnston, George Gordon Meade, Phil Kearny, and others, whose names would resound in history as a result of their military deeds in the Civil War.[1] Some of these, like Grant, Longstreet, and Meade, had fought previously under Taylor. Braxton Bragg, Albert Sidney Johnston, Jefferson Davis, and George Thomas were still with Taylor, and another who would win fame, William Tecumseh Sherman, was acting as aide to General Stephen

[1] To show the quality of the young officers of the junior group serving in the War with Mexico, a total of eighty-three of them later held general rank in the Civil War, forty on the Confederate side, forty-three on the Union side. Of these all but eight of the Confederates, and nine of the Union officers, were West Point men. Oddly, Congress was interrupted in a debate as to whether or not to abolish the Military Academy as an unnecessary expense, by the necessity of formally declaring war against Mexico. So brilliantly did the graduates of the great war college on the Hudson perform that the question of maintaining West Point was never raised again.

W. Kearny in the campaign against California. All of these officers were on the company level, ranking as captains or lieutenants, but their contributions to the operations in which they took part, were only matched by the knowledge they gained in so doing.

Supported by the fleet, Scott had little difficulty landing his troops south of Veracruz, a walled city, heavily gunned, with a bristling fort, San Juan de Ulúa, in the harbor. Scott's brisk siege forced its surrender May 29, 1847, after which its harbor facilities and stores were available to him. Some five thousand prisoners were captured and paroled, and four hundred pieces of artillery were taken, most of which, however, were so antiquated or so fixed in the fortifications, that they were of little use to him. His losses in the siege were light—sixty-seven killed or wounded—but that in the city, including civilians, was much heavier due to the bombardment to which he subjected it.

2

Santa Anna was back in the capital after his defeat at Buena Vista. A revolt had broken out against him and he spent a little time restoring order, jailing the rebellious leaders or executing them. News of the fall of Veracruz reached him May 30, and the City of Mexico was filled with excitement and fury.

Santa Anna knew he must strike. To a huge crowd that gathered in the central plaza before the presidential palace, he made one of his inflammatory speeches, and followed that by having congress pass a decree, April 1, making him General-Dictator for the "emergency."

Immediately he issued a proclamation that he would "triumph over the invaders or die in the cause," and started for the coast, mobilizing all available troops as he did so. Among the soldiers he marshaled were many who had given their paroles after Veracruz, whom he forced into service in spite of their protests that they had promised to refrain from all hostilities.

Having ascertained the direction of his enemy's advance, Santa Anna chose the difficult pass of Cerro Gordo as the ideal place to repulse the American army. At once, with great energy, he set about fortifying it, while he gathered in his works between nine and ten thousand men and forty pieces of artillery. Only the rapid movements of Scott prevented him from rendering the position, as he thought, impregnable.

But Scott had to move. He was anxious to get his army away from Veracruz, which was subject to periodic epidemics of yellow fever. Four days after that city surrendered, on April 2, he began his march for higher and less unhealthy climes, leaving only enough men to garrison the place and form escorts for supplies that would be forwarded to him.

There were but two roads to the City of Mexico, one by Jalapa and Perote, the other by Córdoba and Orizaba. Scott chose the former because the valley of Jalapa produced crops and livestock upon which he might subsist his army, while it was—he hoped—sufficiently remote from the *vómito,* as Mexicans called yellow fever, to escape its inroads.

On April 12 his advance brigades, under General Twiggs, reached the small village of Plan del Río, and on the heights above they beheld the Mexican army ready for battle. Scott arrived at that point two days later, and the main body of his army was up by April 16.

The gigantic general faced a very severe test. Before him, towering over the village, with a stream rushing through the bottom of a deep gorge at its feet, was the eminence of Cerro Gordo. Behind it rose other mountains, "like a Titanic staircase, in successive heights."

Cerro Gordo itself had a plateau on its top, and there stood a fort of considerable strength, while commanding its precipitous sides batteries and entrenchments had been placed. Beneath the guns of this frowning fortification ran the national road from Veracruz to the City of Mexico. It could not be negotiated while Cerro Gordo was defended.

At first glance the position seemed almost impossible to assail with success. Certainly a frontal attack, which must attempt to cross the gorge—between four and five hundred feet deep—and scale the steep wall to the plateau, was a task which could only be attended by frightful loss and probable failure. The southern side was equally uninviting, for the river with its gorge curved closely about that side.

On the north side of the plateau, overlooking the road that wound through the pass, Santa Anna had placed his heaviest batteries. As an extra precaution the Mexican general had also stationed, across the narrow valley, a strong battery on a hill called Telegrafo. His camp was to his rear on level ground well protected by additional batteries.

Scott had about 8500 men, his force having been shrunk by necessities of guarding his base and communications. Nevertheless the stout-hearted old general determined to carry that pass, for if he did not do so his whole campaign was thwarted.

With him was young Captain Robert E. Lee of the engineers, one of the most brilliant of the junior officers. That very night of April 16 Lee made a daring and difficult reconnaissance, in which he discovered a way around the north side of the enemy position, beyond a ridge of mountains which screened the projected pathway from the road and hence from Cerro Gordo itself. The route he had found needed some improvements, and Lee proceeded to make them. With his company of engineers he cut a route through the underbrush, and

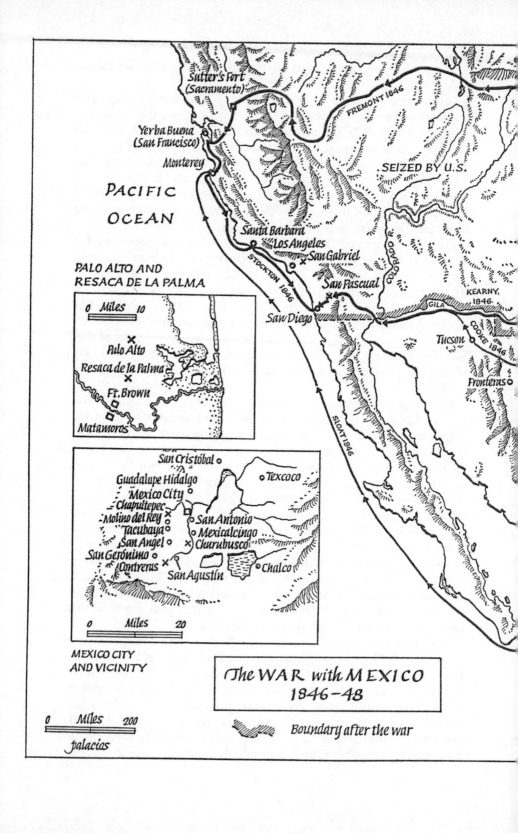

Sutter's Fort
(Sacramento)

FREMONT 1846

Yerba Buena
(San Francisco)

Monterey

SEIZED BY U.S.

PACIFIC

OCEAN

Santa Barbara

Los Angeles

San Gabriel

PALO ALTO AND
RESACA DE LA PALMA

San Pascual

COLORADO R.

KEARNY,
1846.

STOCKTON 1846

0   Miles   10

San Diego

GILA

TUCSON

COOKE 1846

Palo Alto

Resaca de la Palma

Ft. Brown

Fronteras

Matamoros

SLOAT 1846

San Cristóbal

Texcoco

Guadalupe Hidalgo

Mexico City

Chapultepec

Molino del Rey

San Antonio

Tacubaya

Mexicalcingo

San Angel

Churubusco

San Gerónimo

Contreras

Chalco

San Agustín

0   Miles   20

MEXICO CITY
AND VICINITY

The WAR with MEXICO
1846–48

0   Miles   200

palacios

Boundary after the war

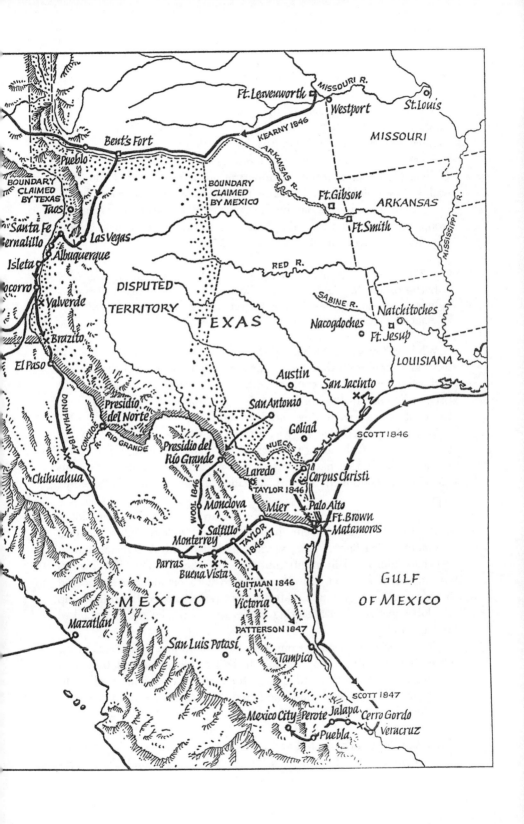

at places notched the road into the mountain sides to make it practicable for wheeled transportation, particularly for artillery.

To cover this engineering operation Scott kept the Mexicans occupied with a bombardment in front, and apparently Santa Anna remained ignorant of Lee's preparations until too late.

Scott launched his attack the morning of April 17. While General Gideon Pillow made a noisy demonstration before Cerro Gordo, General James Shields and General Twiggs followed the road—hardly more than a trail—laid out by Lee. Never was the value of regular troops and West Point training better demonstrated than in the fighting that followed. Grant wrote in his *Memoirs:*

> The attack was made as ordered, and perhaps there was no battle of the Mexican war, or of any other, where orders issued before an engagement were nearer being a correct report of what afterward took place.

While Pillow's cannon blasted the fortifications on Cerro Gordo, and were answered with thunders of artillery from above until the plateau and valley were alike choked with powder smoke, Shields led his brigade far out to the north, with Twiggs following right behind. In front, of course, went Lee and his engineers.

When he judged that he was abreast of the Cerro Gordo, Twiggs turned to his left, heading southward, his objective being a hill called Atalaya, which Lee had reported was not fortified. Shields and his detachment continued onward, seeking to cut around the enemy's rear.

Very soon, as Twiggs and his men began to climb the steep slopes of Atalaya, they found themselves exchanging volleys with a Mexican regiment which Santa Anna, warned at last of the American maneuver, had interposed in an attempt to check the advance. But Twiggs was not to be stopped. Hurrying forward with his men, he reinforced his advance unit, and as the Mexicans retreated he led the brigade up the lofty acclivity in a blistering battle. At last the height was reached and carried.

The Americans, gasping from their hard climb and fight, were given little time to catch their breath. Realizing the advantage they had gained, Santa Anna three times sent forward his troops in an effort to recapture Atalaya. Each time the fierce and deadly fire from the crest repelled the Mexican onsets.

Once a regiment of Americans actually made a brief countercharge down the slopes of their hill and attempted to cross the valley toward Cerro Gordo itself. The enemy's fire grew too heavy and Twiggs recalled the men. Thereafter Santa Anna subjected the hill to a terrific pounding of grapeshot from his batteries. Hurtling across the valley, missiles from the Mexican batteries seemed to blast the top off the hill, hurling stones and fountains of dirt, mingled with bits of shrubbery and even dead bodies, high into the sky.

The Americans grimly endured the bombardment. "Sheltering themselves in the shelving sides of the crest," they managed to get through the long, deafening afternoon with comparatively few losses.

Night fell, but the bombardment did not cease. During the dark hours, which were illuminated fitfully by the glaring flashes of the big guns across the canyon, the Americans on the crest clung to their hill while others struggled to bring up artillery to return the enemy fire.

There was no way to the top of Atalaya which animals could possibly negotiate. Even men had to scramble up and down those stony slopes. But the sweating troops, by incredible labor, letting the ponderous guns down into ravines by ropes attached to the axles, and later hauling them to higher ground by hand, succeeded before dawn in getting on the crest two 24-pound howitzers, and a 24-pound cannon. During that night also Shields made his way by the most difficult of routes, over and through a labyrinth of deep ravines and steep hills covered with prickly desert brush, to a position roughly approximating the camp at the rear of Santa Anna's fortifications, though still hidden by the intervening heights.

On the crest of Atalaya was General William S. Harney, with three regiments of regular infantry.[2] At dawn the big guns on the hill top began to thunder, and the Mexicans on Cerro Gordo had a taste of their own medicine. As the bombardment opened, Harney began a carefully planned, but not the less dashing, assault on Santa Anna's main position from the north.

Down into the ravine went his three regiments, across the national road, and then up the other side. The face of Cerro Gordo was covered by masses of thorny brushwood, through which the sweltering storming parties must force their way. Meantime the entire brow of the Mexican position was hidden by belching clouds of smoke as a plunging fire of artillery echoed through the mountains, accompanied by heavy volleys of musketry. Such was the angle of the declivity, however, that most of the Mexican missiles passed over the heads of the scrambling Americans, whose eyes were fixed on the heights above.

---

[2] Because of General Scott's personal animosity against him, Harney had been removed from command at one time, but was replaced when he appealed to Washington. His brilliant leadership in the action that followed justified his reinstatement.

At the lip of the precipice was a parapet of stone. Here bayonets clashed across the rampart as Harney's men reached it. For a few minutes the battle swayed back and forth, indecisively. But Harney was in the thick, and presently a company broke through and surmounted the wall. At that the Mexicans recoiled from it.

Pillow's demonstration in front had been repulsed with heavy loss, but it served to draw some of the Mexican army's attention from the attack on the north side. And at about the same time that Harney reached the ramparts on top of Cerro Gordo, Shields arrived at a point from which he could assail the enemy rear.

Mexican batteries went into action. Forward went Shields' men, badly cut up by the enemy artillery, but not halting. Shields fell, wounded. But Colonel Edward D. Baker, his cap held aloft on the tip of his sword, led the men on in a charge that swept over the batteries and Santa Anna's camp, cutting off the retreat of a large portion of his army.

Meantime Twiggs and the bulk of his command hurried to reinforce Harney. The three Harney regiments, though almost spent after carrying the stone bastion, rushed on as their adversaries tried to rally about the main fortification. Nothing could stop the Americans. In a wild charge upward they burst through an abatis and forced their way into the fort.

Up went a white flag, fluttering in the smoke of the battle. Santa Anna had fled, but such of his troops as were left on the plateau surrendered.

The American loss in this spectacular action was 431 killed and wounded. Mexican casualties were never known, but Scott captured three thousand prisoners, forty-three pieces of artillery, and five thousand stands of arms. Because of the impossibility of guarding so many prisoners, they were paroled. The small arms were broken up, being of no use to the American army.

3

The victory of Cerro Gordo was so complete that Scott did not encounter any further serious resistance in penetrating the high mountains that guarded the Mexican capital.

He moved his army to Jalapa, sending General Worth ahead to Puebla, so as to secure the road across the intervening heights. In so doing Worth encountered the strong fortress of Perote, which until lately had been occupied by General Gaona—one of Sam Houston's old foes of the Texas revolution. But Gaona had been ordered to retire, and Worth took possession of the strong point on April 22, clearing the road all the way to Puebla.

At Jalapa Scott found himself encumbered with sick and wounded. Though he had lately received reinforcements which brought his total force up to 10,276 men, only 8061 were effective, because 2215 were on the disabled list. The *vómito* had followed him after all, and of the sick nearly seven hundred were to die.

A halt was necessary, not only to rest the army, but because President Polk once more wished to try to negotiate a peace. To this end he sent Nicholas P. Trist, chief clerk of the State Department, as confidential agent with full instructions. Knowing Scott's sensitiveness, the President told Trist to communicate the project of the treaty to the general, and even set forth the demands of the United States. The suspicious Scott took umbrage, and a quarrel flared between the two which drew upon both of them a rebuke from Washington. Trist, thereafter, had the good sense to address a soothing letter to the irascible old warrior, and their relations became more cordial.

Though Trist succeeded in getting the British legation to convey his offer of negotiations to the Mexican government, that government gave it a flat rejection. But not so did Santa Anna. That slippery rascal sent secret agents to Jalapa who conferred with Scott. Privately, they intimated that if $1,000,000 were placed at Santa Anna's disposal, to be paid at the conclusion of peace—with $10,000 furnished at once for "present expenses"—he would appoint commissioners to confer on the terms of peace, and would recommend acceptance of the terms offered.

Sundry rogues of history have left trails hard to follow, but none were more clouded than the track of Santa Anna. His real motives in this curious piece of "diplomacy" have never been fathomed. Did he actually believe the war lost, and think that he could gain the fortune he asked, by leading his country to peace at the expense of her northern provinces? He was quite capable of that. Or was he merely working to gain time? He was quite capable of that, also.

Scott called in his generals for a conference. The question of the bribe of $1,000,000 and whether the United States government would be willing to pay it, was embarrassing. Pillow objected to it strongly as an affront to the honor of America. But Scott was in favor of trying it, and Pillow unwillingly assented. Santa Anna was informed in cipher that his proposal was accepted, and $10,000, disbursed from Scott's secret service fund, was sent to him.

With that negotiations abruptly ceased. Santa Anna was $10,000 richer, and had gained valuable time.

In the three months' delay, Scott did his best to administer the country well. Desertion, rape, and murder were punished by execution, and all supplies were purchased at fair prices—a contrast to Santa Anna's confiscations.[3]

Further depletions threatened Scott's force. Enlistment periods expired for many volunteers, who had to be sent to Veracruz, to be shipped back to the United States and discharged. Providentially, General Franklin Pierce (later to be President of the United States) arrived with fresh reinforcements of 2429 men. Thus strengthened, Scott was able to leave a garrison and his sick at Puebla, and with 10,738 rank and file, forty pieces of artillery, seven hundred supply wagons, and five hundred laden mules, he set forth between August 7 and 10, his army marching in four divisions, under Worth, Twiggs, Pillow, and Quitman, about a day's march separating them from each other on the road to the capital.

The remarkable boldness of Scott's later operations is highlighted by the fact that at Puebla he cut himself off from all communications. From this time on the army had to be self-sufficient—*and victorious*. If it met defeat it could only suffer extinction.

With Cerro Gordo he had won the key to the mountains, and he found that the mountain passes through which his road lay were undefended. Some guerrilla attacks were made on his baggage trains, which were beaten off, but no formidable army confronted him.

The route he followed was almost the same as had been followed by Cortez three centuries before. It led through the mountains north of the great snowcapped volcanic cones of Iztaccihuatl and Popocatepetl, and early in August Harney's cavalry brigade, preceding Worth's division, gazed down with awe upon the magnificent valley of Mexico, its bright verdure, its fields ripe with crops, its meadows beautiful with blossoms, its lakes like great polished mirrors, its villages sheltered among shady groves. In the distance the great capital lifted its domes and displayed its vast assemblage of buildings almost universally roofed with red tiles.

To the soldiers, the sight was entrancing; but to the Mexicans, who saw the invading army make its way downward along the tortuous road leading across the slopes of the volcanoes, the spectacle was the

[3] Scott was not entirely successful. In every army there are always scoundrels. Sile Doty, a notorious criminal, with some other choice rascals had first followed Taylor. They committed murders and robberies undetected, including thefts from American soldiers. Later Doty "joined" Scott's army, and claimed that the fine horse the general rode in the campaign and at the surrender of the City of Mexico was a gift from him—an animal Doty stole from an officer in Taylor's army, which fact, of course, was unknown to Scott. Later, in Veracruz and Puebla, the gang continued its depredations. When the army reached the City of Mexico, Doty and his accomplices returned to Veracruz—on three fine horses stolen from officers of Scott's command—and from that point sailed for the United States, their crimes undetected. See *The Life of Sile Doty.*

reverse of delightful. Fear and anger reigned in the valley. Yet Santa
Anna made no move to attack Scott as the latter's cavalry, followed
by the marching troops with a broken gleam of bayonets, and the long
trains of white covered wagons, reached the floor of the plain itself.

4

It is probable that the Mexican leader expected to defeat the Americans by force of numbers and the well-planned fortifications with
which his engineers had defended his capital, for Scott's first survey
of the terrain revealed that the approaches to the city were most difficult.

The valley in which it stood was surrounded by lofty mountains,
and the city itself at an altitude of more than seven thousand feet
above sea level; it was the wet season, and the prevailing rains had
turned the lands close to the city—which were formerly covered by
Lake Texcoco but partially reclaimed from that half-drained sheet of
water—into a heavy marsh with numerous bog-holes so deep as to
seem bottomless.

The only way to cross this morass was by several causeways, built
of stone upon raised earth embankments, all covered by fortifications.
Any movements of the army were further handicapped by several
lakes of which Texcoco, Xochimilco, and Chalco were the largest, so
that approach from the south was limited to only three of the causeways. A further impediment, acting almost as a continuation of the
barriers furnished by Lakes Xochimilco and Chalco, was a wide field
of jagged lava, called the Pedregal.

Although Santa Anna had fortified the northern approaches to the
city, particularly at the village of Guadalupe Hidalgo, and the northern boundaries of the metropolis itself, he had foreseen that Scott's
army must debouch into the southern end of the valley. With this in
mind he had prepared a series of traps into which he hoped his adversary would blunder.

The best approach, and the one he deemed most likely to be taken
by the Americans, was that between Lake Texcoco, due east of the
city, and the two smaller but still extensive lakes south of it. A causeway ran across an arm of Lake Texcoco, and Santa Anna must have
hoped Scott would attempt that obvious route, for it was guarded by
the fortress of El Peñón, situated on a great rock pinnacle completely
surrounded by marshes in which troops could not have been maneuvered. Upon this had been placed batteries of artillery that could cut
to pieces any army attempting to bypass it either by day or night. A
fortified village, Mexicalcingo, prevented any skirting of El Peñón at

a distance, even if the morass permitted troops to make such a detour.

But Scott was too canny a general to attempt the obvious. To carry El Peñón would not be worth the expenditure in men, even if possible. Yet he must go ahead, for retreat was now out of the question. Nor could he undertake any prolonged siege, for he did not have sufficient troops or supplies to conduct such an operation, while Santa Anna's force was being strengthened daily by newly arriving contingents from the provinces.

The time he had gained by his "diplomatic" exchanges with the American general had enabled Santa Anna to build up his forces so that, by his own account, he now had 22,939 officers and men, with more than a hundred pieces of artillery, to which he could add as auxiliaries hundreds of guerrillas who swarmed in the mountains behind the Americans and continually harried the outposts. It was perhaps Santa Anna's strategy to hold Scott thus at bay, until sickness, lack of supplies, and guerrilla and cavalry attacks decimated his army and made him an easy prey.

The dictator had raised morale in the city itself until it was in an ecstasy of enthusiasm. "It was like a gala day . . . as these forces were reviewed and sent to their posts. Flowers in festoons covered the muzzles of the frowning guns . . . breasts heaving in response to cheers . . . and to blossom showers and fluttering handkerchiefs of señoritas, smiling midst their tears."[4]

Fortunately for Scott, Captain Lee at this point again distinguished himself by a fateful reconnaissance. He discovered a little used road running south of Lakes Chalco and Xochimilco, which Santa Anna had not troubled to fortify because so much of it lay under water at this season of the year. Lee waded his horse in the submerged areas, and believed that with a little corduroying—logs laid side by side to form a roadway over the worst places—troops and even guns and transport wagons could be moved across it.

He reported his discovery to General Worth, who in turn reported it to Scott. The coolness between the two men remained, yet Scott saw at once that the suggested new route might be of immense advantage. Moreover it was actually a case of dire necessity with him.

Once again he resorted to a feint. While one brigade skirmished in front of El Peñón, the hard-working engineers cut the trees and laid the logs at the miriest places and the bulk of the American army, wading for long stretches on the sunken road, and dragging artillery and wagons through the heavy swales sometimes with a hundred men hauling on ropes to help the laboring horses, by August 15 had reached the drier ground beyond. Scott had succeeded in accomplish-

[4] Hubert Howe Bancroft, *History of Mexico.*

ing the "impossible" by outflanking the main Mexican defenses. The elaborate works at El Peñón, Guadalupe Hidalgo, Mexicalcingo, and the northern and eastern perimeter of the city had been neatly by-passed.

Not yet, however, were all the problems by any means solved. It has been pointed out that, facing similar difficulties in his Arcola campaign, Napoleon failed. Scott did not fail.

As soon as he recovered from his surprise at his enemy's maneuver, Santa Anna, took advantage of his internal lines and rushed troops to meet the new menace. Several strong points bristled at the Americans. Between Lake Xochimilco and the Pedregal was the hacienda of San Antonio, which had been converted into an elaborate fortification. On the opposite side of the Pedregal, centering on the village of Contreras, was another powerful defense line with one flank on the Pedregal it-self and the other against the feet of the steep mountains. Behind these two forward defenses was a still greater fortification called Churu-busco, guarding the bridge over the river of that name. Farther to the left—but threatening the rear of any army that succeeded in passing beyond them—were the fortresses of Molino del Rey, and Chapulte-pec.

5

There was some dissension among Santa Anna's generals, and one who had quarreled with the dictator over his Fabian tactics of delay, was General Valencia, who may have had ambitions to obtain for himself the supreme command. Independently, it appears, of orders from his superior, Valencia set out on a daring flank movement, which if successful might have rolled up the American army, and established Valencia's military reputation for all time.

With four thousand men and twenty-two guns he moved up to Con-treras to prepare his assault. There he paused, feeling reasonably safe. The Pedregal, at his left was as if lashed into billows of lava, tortured into weird whorls and gullies by long-dead fires from the bowels of the earth, and presenting razor edges of volcanic glass which would cut to shreds the shoes of men attempting to cross it. Valencia believed this area impossible to maneuver upon, but he did not count on the undaunted tenacity of the American engineers.

Lee—once more pioneering—discovered a faint mule track across the lava bed, and the engineers prepared to convert it into a road over which artillery and men could pass. Within forty-eight hours, by breaking away jagged points of lava and moving aside great vol-canic rocks they hacked a usable road to within striking distance of

Contreras—one of the most remarkable feats of the entire campaign.

Along this road Pillow and Twiggs moved, to be greeted by heavy fire from Valencia. They accepted the challenge, but though a way could be made across the Pedregal, the nature of the twisted, convoluted lava made it almost impossible to deploy troops. Under the merciless fire from the Mexican lines, the Americans fell back.

During this engagement, however, a brigade under Colonel Bennet Riley had picked its way, unaccompanied by any artillery, over the northern end of the Pedregal, where they took up a position between Valencia and Santa Anna's lines, by hastily throwing up entrenchments in the small village of San Gerónimo. Shortly after they were joined by another regiment under Colonel Cadwalader, which scrambled over the rough lava as Riley's men had done.

Just at this time Santa Anna suddenly appeared, with a strong force estimated at six thousand men, to relieve Valencia. The two American regiments badly outnumbered, made ready to fight for their lives, expecting attacks from both sides, when all at once a drenching rainstorm began, cutting off visibility, making any movement of troops almost impossible. Santa Anna retired to San Angel, leaving his soldiers to face the torrential downpour. The feebleness of his effort to relieve Valencia was attributed by later Mexican historians to his resentment of Valencia's insubordination, and suspicion of Valencia's designs.

Night fell again, cold and rainy. General Persifer F. Smith, who reached San Gerónimo with Shields' brigade,[5] took over the command and promptly decided, in spite of the rain, upon a night movement against Valencia.

Leaving only a few men to watch movements of Santa Anna's force —which, in the absence of their commander, remained stationary all night—Smith set out shortly after midnight to make his way to Valencia's rear, along the sides of the mountains.

Long afterward his men remembered that march. They groped their way through the forest on the slopes, sometimes slipping and falling as the rain made footing undependable, trying to keep quiet but finding it difficult to do so, and still pressing forward. Though they were favored by the steady downpour which masked sounds, they were delayed by trying to find a way along the slopes. It was not until dawn that Smith found himself in a position behind Valencia's camp, hidden from that unwary officer and his men by the brow of a low summit.

At dawn Pillow and Twiggs, out on the Pedregal, once more en-

---

[5] Shields was temporarily incapacitated by the serious wound he received at Cerro Gordo.

gaged Valencia and in the din of battle Smith's men were able to re-
load their wet pieces and arrange themselves for the attack.

Now Valencia discovered the Americans in his rear, and had two
fieldpieces swung around to check them. He was too late. Over the
top of the hill swept the Americans, fired one blinding volley, and then
charged down the slope, yelling, with bayonets fixed.

Valencia's hastily mustered cavalry was driven back upon the disordered infantry, and the scene was one of vast confusion, increased
by the stampede of the train mules, and by a new sound heard in battle
—the shrieks of terrified women, for here as elsewhere the Mexican
soldiers had brought their *mujeres de guerra.*

The American bayonets created havoc. In front Pillow closed in, his
first brigade led by General Pierce. Quickly the fight became a retreat,
a rout, a slaughter. Valencia succeeded in making his escape on a fast
horse, but the bodies of his men strewed the wet ground for a mile.

During this fighting Worth's division was stationed before the San
Antonio hacienda on the opposite side of the Pedregal, and young
Lieutenant Grant, with that unit, later described how he watched the
progress at Contreras, including the final victory and rout, adding,
"The Mexicans all the way back to the city could see the same thing,
and their conduct showed plainly that they did not enjoy the sight."

Loss of Contreras caused the defenders of San Antonio to fall back
also. Hardly pausing for breath the Americans pursued the enemy
down the two causeways to their next strong point, Churubusco.

For once, the Americans attacked that fortification immediately,
without reconnaissance or artillery preparation. Scott evidently hoped
to take advantage of the demoralization of the enemy, but Churubusco was a scientifically constructed work of great strength. It was
built about the massive stone convent of San Pablo, with embrasures
and platforms for cannon, and a bastion protecting the bridge across
the river. It was heavily gunned, also, and manned by 1400 men commanded by General M. Rincón, one of the bravest of Santa Anna's
officers.

Stalled baggage trains along the causeway gave the Americans some
screening from the fortress at first. But additional Mexican troops hurried up to support Churubusco until several thousands were in position
behind a levee that followed the course of the bank-full river.

As the American regiments came up, fire from these flanking troops
as well as that from the fortress caused heavy losses in the American ranks. Nevertheless the brigades of Smith and Riley held their
ground, some of the men within seventy yards of the bastion itself.

The convent-fortress seemed to one of the soldiers, "a very volcano,
enfolded in a dense cloud, and rumbling with the roar of artillery and
the rattle of musketry . . . [with] flashes of fire that lighted the scene

as lightning-rays the storm." From the surrounding mountains came the pealing echoes of the heavy cannonading, adding to the ear-splitting din.

Once—twice—three times, the Americans bravely charged the bastion which guarded the bridge, in the teeth of a murderous fire. Each time they were repulsed, one regiment from South Carolina leaving half its number on the field.

But now came help. After nearly two hours, one of Worth's regiments managed to cross the river some distance east of the fort. Others followed. The Mexican left was driven back, and now Churubusco was attacked in the rear.

In front there was another heroic dash by the Americans, who at last cleared the bastion. The Mexicans who had come up to support the beleaguered fortress streamed back toward the city. Rincón's ammunition began to fail, Worth pressed hard against the rear, and at last the white flag of surrender went up.

So great was the panic of the Mexicans outside the fort that American cavalry harried them to the very gates of the city, one company of dragoons, under Captain Phil Kearny, almost entering the walls. But they were recalled. In this action Kearny, later to be killed fighting for the Union in the Civil War, lost an arm.

In the two days of fighting at Contreras and Churubusco, the American loss was 139 dead and 876 wounded, a total of 1015. The Mexicans lost nearly four thousand dead and wounded, plus three thousand captured, and thirty-seven guns.

6

The way was open to the capital by the central route, but on the American left still remained two threatening strong points, a collection of stone buildings called Molino del Rey where cannon were manufactured, and the frowning eminence called Chapultepec, where once the Montezumas and later the viceroys of Spain had their palace, the buildings now converted into a military school for cadets.

Scott, who did not propose to leave fortifications in his rear, prepared to take those redoubts. But again Santa Anna cajoled him into a truce, saying again that he might discuss terms of peace with Trist.[6]

[6] Scott later said that he was governed by humane instincts, and by the consideration that if he wantonly drove away the members of the government, he might "scatter the elements of peace." He added that he shrank from immediate assault on the city because "the carnage among the citizens, their women and children, would have been frightful, as well as pillage, for the soldiers could not be controlled."

The truce gave Santa Anna time to recover somewhat from his defeats. He strengthened the outer works of the city, and received reinforcements, in spite of the conditions of the armistice, signed August 22, which expressly prohibited either side from such activities.

Trist's negotiations for peace on the terms he was authorized to offer failed. Those terms were sufficiently rigorous: cession of all territory included in the Province of New Mexico (the present United States Southwest), plus both California proper and Lower California, recognition of the Rio Grande boundary for Texas, and the right of free transit across the Isthmus of Tehuantepec, across which it was proposed to build a canal eventually.

In return he offered a sum of money to be agreed upon, abandonment of all claims against Mexico for war expenses, and assumption by the United States of claims of its citizens. Within three days it was known that these terms were not acceptable to the Mexican government.

War spirit meantime rose higher. The State of Mexico even threatened to separate from the rest of the nation if such a peace was concluded. By September Scott knew that Santa Anna was not abiding by the armistice terms, and on September 6 notified him that at noon the following day the truce would end.

The new operations began September 8, when Worth's artillery began a bombardment of Molino del Rey. His field pieces made little impression on the massive stone walls, and he sent a storming party forward. It was driven back. A second assault was more successful. General León, the commander, was killed, and the defenders retreated from the buildings into a dense cypress forest which covered the base of Chapultepec, only a short distance away.

Some old cannon molds and a quantity of powder were the only booty, and though his losses had been quite heavy, Worth did not even attempt to retain the mill, but withdrew that evening to the main American lines. The withdrawal was perhaps justified by the fact that the Molino was commanded by the guns of Chapultepec, looming near; but it encouraged the Mexicans to believe they had defeated the Americans.

Chapultepec was to be next; and the assault upon it was in some respects the most spectacular battle of the war. The Mexicans failed to reoccupy Molino del Rey and American batteries were established within it. Other big guns were stationed at different points to bombard the hill.

Chapultepec was a picturesque upthrust from the plain. Its north side was inaccessibly steep, its east and southeast nearly so. Only on the west was there a practicable slope, although a narrow road climbed it diagonally on the south, covered by a bastion. About 160 feet high, its top was a level plateau six hundred feet long, with a heavy stone castle—once a palace but now a cadet school—at the northern verge of the cliff, as a citadel. Parapets and "bomb-proofs" had been erected along the sides of the level plateau, with bastions, especially one on the west, which was guarded by a "priest cap"—a sort of redan, with three salients permitting crossfire at any attacking enemy.

The base of the hill was further fortified by a long barricade, a redan, and ditch, facing Molino del Rey. On the top were eight hundred regular troops, commanded by General Nicolas Bravo, with about a thousand in the defenses at the base. There were also present the young cadets who were taking military training at the school. The place was well supplied with artillery, some of the heaviest type.

Altogether it presented a formidable obstacle, but Scott ordered it taken. Repeated victories had raised high the elan of his soldiers, and they were ready to obey.

At dawn, September 12, Scott's guns began the bombardment of Chapultepec. His big guns, most of them captured from the enemy, wrought destruction in the castle, smashing holes through the walls and scattering dust and debris on the defenders. So well aimed was the American barrage that by noon the artillery reply from above was considerably diminished because so many guns had been put out of action. Nevertheless all that day the ceaseless roar of cannon continued. Scott was not making a second mistake like the too-precipitate assault on Churubusco, and ordered careful preparation this time. As night came on great damage had been done to Bravo's defenses, but Chapultepec still defiantly flew the banner of Mexico.

During the night firing ceased, but the defenders on the crest and below could hear the sounds of troops being marched to positions for the real assault of the morrow.

Dawn, September 13. Again the batteries roared in a final preparation. Suddenly, at eight o'clock in the morning, the big guns ceased speaking. From the Molino one of Worth's regiments issued and charged toward the hill.

It was greeted by a burst of fire which shrouded the hill with powder smoke. But the American soldiers ran forward through the hail of bullets "as if it were a light snow." Many crumpled up, through with battle forever, but their comrades dashed on, bayonets glittering and ready.

The parapet at the foot of the hill was reached. Over it leaped the storming party, driving the defenders up the slope among the huge gnarled cypress trees that covered it.

Other American regiments followed the first. In spite of canister and grapeshot, and the whizzing musket balls of the Mexicans, they drove forward, led by Pillow. The redan at the foot of the hill was carried. Pillow was wounded, but his men charged on.

Mexican engineers had mined the approach to the slope, and an officer was detailed to fire the *saucissons*—a form of fuses—but so rapid was the leaping rush of the Americans that he was disabled before he could carry out his orders, and the *saucissons* were destroyed, making the mines useless.

By this time the foot of the hill was in the possession of the attacking forces, but through the thick haze of powder smoke the castle above still could be seen emitting garish flashes of gunfire as it maintained its defense, and the deafening roar of the battle never ceased.

Ladders and fascines were brought up by the Americans. While sharpshooters below tried to keep down enemy heads above, the ladders were planted and daring men began to mount. Down came the first climbers, dead or wounded. But with great courage others took their places, and more ladders were raised against the steep rock face.

While Chapultepec continued to hang out curtains of smoke and its guns made an overwhelming racket, by sheer dogged bravery a foothold finally was gained on the lower parapet of the hill. No hesitating now. Fighting hand to hand, the Americans widened the foothold, and more and more of the attackers gained it.

A desperate charge carried the "priest cap," and at once its ten pieces of artillery—heavy guns among them—were turned on the castle. Once the flag of Mexico was seen to fall, and it was thought the defenders had surrendered. But a shell had severed its staff, and a brave soldier lifted it and lashed it again in place. The battle continued with unabated fury.

With the strength of the defense concentrated on Pillow's attack, a second storming party began to make its way up the south face. The work defending the road was carried, and the top was gained.

Now the plateau was filled with Americans, and the Mexicans were driven into the castle where a furious struggle took place. Great bravery was displayed by the beleaguered defenders. Even the cadets— lads fourteen to sixteen years old—fought heroically, and gave their young lives freely. "The blood of stripling and graybeard mingle in their flow, and bear the mournful tidings in the red-tinged waters of the aqueduct."[7]

Some of Pillow's men at last reached the roof of the castle and struck the flag. The defenders yielded. The slaughter ceased.

Many of the Mexican soldiers had bounded or slid down the east face of the hill to escape, but the total loss of the defenders in killed,

[7] H. H. Bancroft, *History of Mexico.*

wounded, and prisoners, was about nine hundred, including General Bravo, who was among those who surrendered. The American loss was 138 killed and 673 wounded in their determined assault, a total of 811 men, much greater than the Mexican loss, if the prisoners be excluded from the count.

After the fall of Chapultepec, Worth's and Quitman's men pursued the fleeing enemy all the way to the gates of the city. Now the assault on the capital itself could begin.

7

What followed was a confused period of bitter street fighting. The *garitas* (gates) of San Cosmé and Belén were the first to be carried. At San Cosmé, Lieutenant Grant distinguished himself by causing a cannon to be manhandled to the tower of San Cosmé church, from which he directed a series of discharges downward, making the abandonment of the *garita* necessary.

With his artillery playing upon the city, and his men moving forward from square to square, Scott grimly continued his advance during the dark hours. The enemy was now thoroughly demoralized. So was Santa Anna. That night he abandoned the capital, taking with him four thousand cavalry and five thousand infantry, the best of the defensive troops.

Next day, September 14, a deputation from the city government sued for a cessation of hostilities. A white flag was raised over the government building on the main plaza, and Scott made his entry in the forenoon "at the head of a brilliant suite and imposing force, midst a dense gathering of spectators who lined the streets and *azoteas* (roof tops)."

But not all Mexicans were as pusillanimous as Santa Anna. Hatred and resentment and a will to resist remained. Shots were fired at a party of officers around General Worth, bringing several down.

Scott knew the danger of allowing such a movement to grow, and took prompt and severe measures to quell it. Artillery swept the streets with grape, troops charged the crowds and stormed dwellings.

As one of his last acts before leaving the city, Santa Anna had released two thousand criminals from the prison to "fight the enemy." But the convicts proved so intent on plunder that, though they did little if any fighting, they created more havoc by looting than did the soldiers. Some of them were shot in the act of plundering their own people.

By the next day the brief uprising was completely subdued.

8

The City of Mexico had surrendered, ending the fighting in the valley which cost the victors more than 2700 killed and wounded, besides the sick, out of a force of 11,000. Scott's entire campaign, starting with the capture of Veracruz, the march from the coast, the severe Battle of Cerro Gordo, the crossing of the high mountains, and the operations in the valley itself, was almost unparalleled.

The Mexicans fully proved their bravery. It was not the Mexican common soldier who lost the war. It was the incompetence, in some cases jealousy, even cowardice and venality of his commanders that caused the shame of Mexico.

It takes nothing from Mexican bravery to say that the American soldiers had equal courage. Time and time again when repulsed they came back with desperate assaults, regardless of their own losses, which eventually won their objectives. Individually they were better fighters than their adversaries, perhaps not from a standpoint of courage, but from a standpoint of sheer formidability. They shot better, were more ferocious in hand to hand combat, showed more initiative at times. And they were far better led. The Mexican campaigns gave a foretaste of the kind of fighting men who would later, in the Union or Confederate army, astonish the world with their exploits in battle.

Trist, who had ignored an order to return to Washington, once again resumed his peace overtures. This time the Mexican officials representing their country—for Santa Anna had fled—agreed to meet with him for the discussions. General Scott had the good taste to order the negotiations conducted at Guadalupe Hidalgo, north of the city, so that the proud capital should not have its name attached to a treaty of surrender.

The treaty was signed February 2, 1848. It provided for the establishment of the American-Mexican boundary at the middle of the Rio Grande from the Gulf of Mexico to the point where that river met the southern border of New Mexico, thence west along the present line of the state, north to the first branch of the Gila River, down the middle of the Gila to the Colorado River, and from there direct west to the Pacific Ocean at a point one marine league south of the southernmost point of the port of San Diego. Trist did not press the claim for Lower California, or for the transit line across the Isthmus of Tehuantepec.

Though Mexico was prostrate and could make no demands, the United States agreed to pay that government $15,000,000, to which later was added another $10,000,000 for the Gadsden Purchase, a roughly triangular area south of the Gila—$25,000,000 in all—and also to assume all claims of American citizens against Mexico. It constituted exactly what Polk had offered before the war began. The treaty was speedily ratified by the United States Senate.

For better or for worse the United States had gained an immense new domain, and the dream of some of her greatest leaders—a two-ocean nation—had been fulfilled. With the later Gadsden Purchase, all the territory of the present states of Texas, New Mexico, Arizona, California, Utah, and Nevada, together with portions of Oklahoma, Kansas, Colorado, and southern Wyoming were acquired. It was a territory for the most part completely wild and in many parts even unexplored, but it was destined to exert enormous influence on the later course of American history.[8]

---

[8] And what of Santa Anna, whose personal vanity, greed, and treachery both to his own country and others, lost Mexico more than half of her territory? (The present territory of Mexico comprises 793,944 square miles. That of Texas, New Mexico, Arizona, California, Utah, and Nevada, exclusive of the Gadsden Purchase, comprised 810,928 square miles, and this does not include those portions of Oklahoma, Kansas, Colorado and Wyoming obtained as a result of the war.) Most of the Mexican "strong men" during the period of violence and repeated dictatorships died either by execution or assassination. Hidalgo, Morelos, Iturbide, Guerrero, Leonardo Bravo, his son Nicolas Bravo, Victoria, Mexia, Pedraza, Santmanet, Herrera, Paredes, Maximilian, Madero, Suarez, Carranza, and Villa, all were killed officially or by assassination. But Santa Anna, the man who was willing to sell out his country not once but many times, and with the blood of thousands on his hands, lived out his life and died in Mexico, poor and discredited but peacefully in bed, in 1876.

BOOK IV

*The Rift Becomes
a Chasm*

CHAPTER NINETEEN

"The Most Humble Walks of Life"

1

THE War with Mexico so occupied the attention of leaders in Congress that the first appearance in that body of a tall, homely man from Illinois was hardly noticed at first, except for a rather unfortunate episode in which he figured. Abraham Lincoln had been elected to the House of Representatives in August 1846, when the war was in full progress, Taylor was moving on Monterrey, and Kearny soon was to reach Santa Fe. Lincoln took his seat in that body in December 1847, after Scott had captured the City of Mexico, but before peace was declared.

America has been strangely the child of destiny, in that at each of its supreme crises men of surpassing ability, courage, and worth have risen to lead the nation through its periods of stress. One of these— perhaps greatest of any of them, for he faced America's direst peril —was the lanky man from the West who thus without fanfare first set foot upon the national rostrum.

Not at first did Abraham Lincoln show evidences of greatness. His character was like that of an oak tree, the product of slow, even painful building, with seasons of storm and adversity as well as seasons favorable to development. His advances at first were minute, succeeded by retrogressions; his errors were numerous. But from these he fought his way back, and errors and retrogressions alike compounded in him the toughness and depth of mental and moral fiber, the humanity, the foresight, and the inspiration which the world now recognizes in him.

Like Andrew Jackson, Lincoln was a product of the log-cabin frontier. But unlike Jackson it took him far longer to find himself and achieve his full stature as a man and as a historical figure.

A comparison between the two is not without interest. Both were tall—Jackson six feet one inch, Lincoln six feet four inches—both were lean, and both were homely, each in his own way. Both, in public speaking had, instead of the thunder tones of a Webster, high, almost shrill voices. Both were intensely human. Both had small formal schooling. Both were adept, sometimes ruthless politicans; but to both politics was a means to serve the people. Both were without any fear of consequences to their lives or to their ambitions, where matters of principle were involved. Both liked the power and prestige connected with the office of President of the United States; but both thought of themselves as instruments for right government, and both were devoted first and foremost to the preservation of the Union. Both were Westerners in the sense that the word "West" was understood in their day.

But there similarities end. Jackson was a soldier, one of the great generals of his time. Lincoln saw a few months of service in backwoods militia companies, but never was in action and belittled even the small military experience he had. Jackson, starting with nothing, built himself up a comfortable estate. Lincoln, extremely poverty-stricken in his young manhood, never achieved any considerable financial worth. Jackson acquired the speech and bearing of a man of some cultivation. To the end Lincoln remained a provincial, and even in his White House days his speech was frequently marked by the solecisms of the backwoods. Jackson was almost without a sense of humor. The rich humor of Lincoln, and his inimitable storytelling are part of his tradition. Jackson was a headlong gambler. Lincoln never gambled. Jackson, at least in his early days, was a hard drinker, and given on occasion to vivid profanity. Lincoln did little drinking in his early days, almost none at all after his maturity, and never swore except for an occasional word by way of emphasis; although it must be conceded that he told stories that were sometimes very broad, even crude. Jackson was gifted with intuitive swiftness in action. Lincoln's mind was slower, but more profound. Jackson was hot tempered, almost irascible. Lincoln possessed endless patience. While Jackson spoke well, he was a pedestrian writer, and had to call upon others more gifted in composition when he presented his great papers. Lincoln was a supreme genius when he took his pen in hand; his Gettysburg Address, for example, is pure poetry, and his important speeches and documents are studded with memorable sayings and eloquent passages.

The early life of Abraham Lincoln has been too often written to require lengthy recapitulation here. He was born February 12, 1809, in a log cabin on a backwoods farm in Kentucky, the son of Thomas Lincoln and his wife Nancy Hanks Lincoln.

The Lincoln family migrated from Kentucky to Indiana in 1816, and after Abraham reached his majority, to Illinois in 1830. The boy's early years were spent in hardship and squalor. According to the Reverend J. Edward Murr, a minister who interviewed members of his congregation who knew the Lincoln family in Indiana, the future President "lived quite on the level, if not below that of thousands of slaves whom he afterward liberated."

Lincoln's mother died October 5, 1818, when he was nine years old. His father remarried, December 2, 1819, taking as wife Sarah Bush Johnston, a widow with three children, he being forty-one years old, and she ten years younger. Sarah was a capable, kindly woman, better educated than her predecessor Nancy, who was completely illiterate. Not until she came to the Indiana cabin was it given a board floor, the pounded earth previously having been deemed sufficient by Thomas Lincoln. She also saw that the roof was fixed so that snow did not blow into the loft and cover the bed in which Abraham Lincoln now slept with her own son John Johnston. Other improvements were made including a thorough cleansing and furbishing not only of the house but of its occupants. Sarah won the undying affection of the boy Abraham, with her kindness. It was she, rather than his real mother Nancy, that he, later in life, spoke of as "my angel mother."[1]

On the forest frontier the ax was almost the most important of tools, and Lincoln in a short autobiography written in 1860, speaking of himself in the third person, said, "Abraham, though very young, was large of his age, and had an ax put into his hands at once; and from that till within his twenty-third year, he was almost constantly handling that most useful instrument—less, of course, in plowing and harvesting seasons." In his first year in Illinois, he put this skill to use by taking, and filling, a contract to split three thousand fence rails, a considerable job by any standard.

He also learned other farm work. A friend, James I. Short, said, "I used to consider myself very good [as a corn husker] but he would gather two loads to my one." Once, campaigning for the state legislature, he came upon some men harvesting wheat. It was before the day of the machine harvester and wheat was cut by means of a "cradle"—a heavy scythe with an attachment of fingerlike rods, so that with each sweep of the scythe the grain was caught and could be uniformly laid making it easier to gather for sheaving. The work required both skill and strength, but Lincoln took a cradle and led all the others around the field—and thus gained their votes.

Yet general testimony shows that he was not fond of hard labor. He was gregarious and would rather be with a group of friends, amusing them. Because he grew so rapidly and was so poor, he could never afford proper garments and neighbors later recalled his droll appearance in a homespun shirt, an old straw hat without a band, and six inches of shin bone showing between his thick-soled brogans and the bottoms of his pantaloons, which, beside being too short for him, hung from a single suspender.

In spite of his appearance, the awkward, gangling lad was a uni-

[1] Albert J. Beveridge, *Abraham Lincoln*.

versal favorite, partly because of his gift for mimicry—he frequently convulsed his listeners with "impersonations" of local evangelists, politicians, and other notables—and his inimitable stories, but also because of his obliging kindness.

All told he attended school less than a year, some of it in Kentucky, the rest in Indiana. As he himself said, "There was absolutely nothing to excite ambition for education." Yet he had a consuming hunger for knowledge, and read and reread every book he could get his hands on—*Pilgrim's Progress*, Weems' *Life of Washington*, *Aesop's Fables*, *Robinson Crusoe*, and Franklin's *Autobiography* were among his earliest readings. The Bible must have been pored over, also, although he never subscribed to formal religion. From these books, and particularly from the organ tones of the King James version of the Bible, came that sense of style which later was so notable in him.

Twice he floated all the way down to New Orleans by flatboat, bearing merchandise to that market. The first time he and his companion, Allen Gentry, had to fight for their lives when they were attacked by a gang of seven Negro robbers. The two frontier boys routed their assailants after a furious battle in the dark, but Lincoln bore as a result of that fight a scar on the right side of his head for the rest of his life. On that trip he received ten dollars a month, which he duly turned over to his father, as he did all his other earnings, which were his father's right until he was twenty-one. The second trip, however, came after he reached his majority, and he kept his wages. It was on that second visit to New Orleans that he was alleged to have said, on seeing a slave auction, "If I ever get a chance to hit that thing, I'll hit it hard." But John Hanks, author of the story, was not within a thousand miles of New Orleans at the time, and modern historians doubt the statement.

The Lincoln family did not, as has been suggested, leave Kentucky to get away from slavery. Thomas Lincoln, indeed, had been a member of the "patrollers" whose duty it was to see that slaves stayed out of mischief and were in their cabins at night. Albert J. Beveridge wrote: "Not the faintest evidence has been found indicating that slavery was so much as a contributing cause for their departure; indeed it is doubtful whether that institution made any impression, one way or another, on Thomas Lincoln's pallid mind."

2

Abraham Lincoln's young manhood was a story of disappointments. He grew astonishingly tall, with wide shoulders, powerful arms and hands, and huge feet. His deeds of strength were amazing. J. Rowan

Herndon later wrote that Lincoln was "by fare the stoutest man that i ever took hold of i was a mear child in his hands and i Considered myself as good a man as there was in the Cuntry untill he come about i saw him Lift Between 1000 and 1300 lbs of Rock waid in a box."

He could outjump, outrun, and outwrestle anybody in the vicinity. Once he pinned the leader of a gang of young hoodlums known as the Clary's Grove Boys. His prowess so aroused the admiration of his opponent, Jack Armstrong, that he latter became his great friend, and the other Clary's Grove Boys were from that time on Lincoln's devoted followers.

But above and beyond this physical power there was something far more important in him. He was not handsome, but his head was impressive. Wide cheekbones, gaunt cheeks, a mole on his face, mouth of generous width with a projecting lower lip and lines both of strength and humor, eyes dark gray and speculative under shaggy projecting brows, and a lofty forehead surmounted by a shock of coarse black hair—he was an elemental force, with no place to expend itself.

Having at his majority cut loose from his father—with whom he was not then or after on good terms—he tried several means of earning a living, until he met a man named Denton Offutt, who hired him to make the second journey to New Orleans already referred to, and later gave him a job in a store he was opening in New Salem, Illinois, north of Springfield, in present Menard County, then part of Sangamon County.

The village was forlorn, with less than a hundred inhabitants when Lincoln first made it his home, consisting of a few log cabins and crude shacks, one of those accidental frontier settlements with no real reason for existence. After Lincoln left it, it gradually disappeared until only a few crumbling ruins of log cabins remained. It has since been restored in part and made a state park.

Offutt was a wordy, visionary man, who soon decided that storekeeping was too slow, and closed his store to devote himself to speculating in wheat and corn. Lincoln was jobless. He was then twenty-three years old, and popular among his fellows. Perhaps at a friend's suggestion he announced himself a candidate for the state legislature. His humbleness, perhaps due to his vicissitudes and poverty, is rather pathetically shown in the concluding words of his written "address" to the people, asking for their support, which was published in the *Sangamo Journal*, the chief Whig organ in Springfield:

I was born, and have ever remained, in the most humble walks of life. I have no wealthy or popular relations or friends to recommend me . . . My case is thrown exclusively upon the independent voters of this county . . . But, if the good people in their wisdom, shall see fit to keep me in the background, I have been too familiar with disappointments to be very much chagrined.

To be kept in the background—that was what he was struggling against. The future was to him undefined and mysterious. He did not yet even think of entering the national arena. America was immense, unfathomable, stirring restlessly, filled with men of superlative talents and great prestige, against whom he did not dream of measuring himself. If only he could win a little place in his own small world, that would be enough for the time being at least.

3

Before the election, Lincoln had his brief taste of war. Black Hawk, chief of the Sauks and Foxes, who with his people had been much abused by white men, repented of having agreed to vacate his hunting grounds east of the Mississippi, and with some of his warriors returned to northern Illinois. Troops were rushed to meet him, and there was a call for volunteers in the state. Lincoln was one of the first to enlist. With him enlisted Jack Armstrong and the Clary's Grove Boys. Largely through their solid vote he was elected captain of their company.

Neither he nor his men knew anything of military procedure, and amusing stories have come down of their drill. Once Lincoln, marching his men across a field, was confronted by a gate. As he later said, he could not remember the command "to turn the company endwise," so he solved the impasse by calling out, "Halt. This company will break ranks and reform immediately on the other side of that gate."

The volunteers marched to the mouth of the Rock River, where there was a detachment of Regulars under Colonel Zachary Taylor. Lincoln and his men were mustered into the service by a young captain named Jefferson Davis, who later became Taylor's son-in-law.[2] It was the lanky frontiersman's first sight of two men who were to be most important in his later life.

Lincoln saw no fighting, though he did save an old friendly Indian from being lynched by his company, and helped bury five white men who had been killed and scalped in a skirmish at Kellogg's Grove. The Sauks and Foxes were crushed at the Battle of Bad Axe, and the militia went home.

[2] His bride died three months after the wedding. Davis later married Miss Varina Howell, who was the "First Lady" of the Confederacy.

Of his military experience Lincoln always made light. When he was in Congress, in the course of a speech against General Lewis Cass, a veteran of the War of 1812 and a commander against Black Hawk, who had become the Democratic candidate for President, Lincoln said, according to his written version:

> In the days of the Black Hawk War, I fought, bled, and came away. I was not at Stillman's defeat, but I was about as near it, as Cass was to Hull's surrender [in the War of 1812]; and, like him, I saw the place very soon afterwards. . . . If Gen. Cass went in advance of me in picking huckleberries, I guess I surpassed him in charges upon the wild onions. If he saw any live, fighting Indians, it was more than I did; but I had a good many bloody struggles with musquitoes [*sic*]: and, although I never fainted from loss of blood, I can truly say that I was often very hungry.

In the election which took place soon after he was discharged, he lost in the county as a whole, running eighth among thirteen candidates. But there was one significant thing in the vote: out of 208 ballots cast in the New Salem precinct, he got 205. Where Lincoln was known people were strongly for him. He needed to widen his acquaintance.

Disappointed in the election, he tried operating a store. Of the three general stores in New Salem, the least successful was one belonging to Rowan Herndon and William F. Berry. When Herndon offered Lincoln his share of the partnership, the young man accepted, giving Herndon his note for the interest he purchased.

One of the "staples" the store sold was liquor. Berry proved a more consistent tippler than he was a salesman. Lincoln, on the other hand, by this time had virtually ceased drinking. The store failed, Berry died, and Lincoln was left with a burden of $1100 in debts, which he slowly, painfully paid off in later years, with his almost fanatical honesty.

The episode was another of his setbacks. The fates seemed against him. One after another his efforts thus far had been frustrated. Other disappointments were to come, and all played a part in giving him a heavy heart. His face came to assume a look of sadness when in repose; and in his later life he suffered periods of extreme depression, from which only his natural sanity and humor rescued him.

Friends obtained for him appointment as postmaster—an appointment he received from Andrew Jackson, then President. But Lincoln was no Jackson man. His hero was Henry Clay, so much so that he became a Whig. In this he departed from the traditions of his family.

His father, his stepbrother, and his cousins all were Democrats.[3] But his admiration for Clay did not keep him from reading, with thrills, Daniel Webster's magnificent *Reply to Hayne,* and also Jackson's proclamation against nullification. He read the arguments of the other side, too, for all addresses and proclamations of the nullifiers were published along with those opposed to nullification, in the papers to which he had access. Though he said little at the time, the formation of his lifelong devotion to the cause of the Union must have dated from that year.

As postmaster—for which he received a pittance—and later as a surveyor's helper, he "made out," and continually widened his acquaintance, and won the friendship of people for whom he did favors, such as on one occasion walking several miles to deliver a letter which he knew was anxiously being awaited.

The man who hired him to help survey the county was John Calhoun, a Democrat, but no relation to the famous South Carolinian. This Calhoun, who had studied law, took a liking to the gawky young man with his strange clothes and unfailing sense of humor, and urged Lincoln to study law and try to obtain entrance to the bar. The same advice had already come to him from John T. Stuart of Springfield.

Lincoln took the suggestion, and plunged seriously into the task of educating himself. It was his way—one thing at a time, and his whole being devoted to that.

A schoolteacher named Mentor Graham helped him. For a time Lincoln boarded at Graham's cabin, and under his tutelage mastered grammar, learned some history, and gained a smattering of literature. The remarkable native qualities of Lincoln's mind so struck Graham that he later wrote that his pupil was the "most studious, diligent strait [*sic*] forward young man in the pursuit of knowledge and literature than any among the five thousand I have taught in schools."

Wherever Lincoln went in those days he had his nose in a book or carried one under his arm. He "was a very miser of time, never wasting a minute." During the day, in short rests from work, he read. He read until late at night and rose at daylight to read. While he ate, a book was propped up before him, and he hardly seemed to know or taste what he put into his mouth so great was his concentration.

At first his associates perhaps considered this devotion to books a little on the peculiar side, but his widely expanding knowledge soon won their respect and admiration. When in 1834 he again ran for the legislature, he was elected.

While he waited for the assembly to convene he continued his crash

[3] It is significant that none of his family voted for him in 1860, except for one cousin, John Hanks, who not only voted for Lincoln that year but later served in the Union Army.

program of studying. He borrowed books from Stuart, prominent as a Whig and lawyer in Springfield, who saw in the young man some extraordinary promise and befriended him. At an auction he bought a copy of Blackstone's *Commentaries,* and treasured it as a prize, studying it fiercely. With the same passionate determination he also read the *Revised Laws of Illinois.*

At that time the capital of Illinois was Vandalia. Before going to attend the legislative sessions Lincoln borrowed $200 from a friend, Coleman Smoot, of which he spent $60 for the first decent suit of clothes he had ever had—tailored to make allowances for those long legs—and used the rest for expenses. When he returned from the session he had $285 in state pay, from which his first expenditure was meeting his obligation to Smoot.

The Capitol building at Vandalia was in bad repair, but Lincoln entered it as one at last finding his chosen field. Under the leadership of Stuart, who led the Sangamon County delegation, he learned the fundamentals of parliamentary practice. He roomed with Stuart and their room became a sort of headquarters for the Whigs. Night after night Lincoln sat up until the late hours listening to interminable political discussions, sometimes adding a little sparkle to those lengthy rounds of talk, with his apt stories.

Lincoln never subscribed to the dictum of Dr. Samuel Johnson: "To succeed in politics you must be a pompous ass." Throughout his political career he was often humorous, never pompous.

His achievements as a freshman legislator were not spectacular; but he made friends on a statewide level, and he heard public issues discussed both privately and on the floor, by men of more than local fame, and whether he agreed with them or not, he learned something of the way to present ideas.

4

When early in 1835 he returned to New Salem—riding home in subzero weather—he found his standing much increased. He returned to work as postmaster and surveyor, continued the study of law, and amused his friends by yarns about the legislature and its chief figures.

He had now reached his twenty-fifth year, an age at which most young men think of the other sex. But his romantic career was as unfortunate as most of his other projects. A pretty girl, Ann Rutledge, daughter of a tavernkeeper with whom he had lodged, captured his fancy. She was engaged to another man, but later broke off the engagement. Whether Lincoln ever spoke to her in terms of courtship no one knows; but when she died suddenly, probably of typhoid, he was plunged into grief so deep, and so long continued, that some of his neighbors thought him "off his balance." It was one of the first of his periods of intense morbid melancholia, which he sometimes called "hypochondria."

Politics rallied his spirits. He stood once more for the legislature and was elected. From this time he continued in the state assembly until what he called the "fatal day" of 1841.

Meantime—as an indication perhaps of a rebound from his grief over the death of Ann Rutledge—he drifted into an engagement with a girl named Mary Owens, a cousin of Mentor Graham. He had met her before he became interested in Ann. Apparently she was inclined to plumpness—one description calls her "portly"—but she was well educated for her day, and pleasant company. The engagement, however, was a mistake. The two had little in common and Mary herself dissolved the alliance, because "Mr. Lincoln was deficient in those little links which make up the chain of a woman's happiness—at least in my case." To Lincoln getting out of the "scrape" as he called it was an overwhelming relief. He had never been in love with her; and as he put it, had been "trapped" by Mrs. Bennett Abell, Miss Owens' sister.

He attended a special session of the legislature at Vandalia, and then the regular session which began December 5, 1836. Prior to this he had taken his law examination, passed it easily, and obtained his license to practice. This session was notable for the fact that in it Lincoln and a young man who was to be the greatest political rival of his lifetime first sat in a law-making body together. Stephen A. Douglas and Lincoln had met before, but probably only perfunctorily. Now, however, they were direct adversaries; Douglas was a Democrat and Lincoln a Whig.

A contemporary, Ben: Perley Poore, described Douglas as follows:

He was industrious and sagacious, clothing his brilliant ideas in energetic and emphatic language, and standing like a lion at bay when opposed. He had a herculean frame, with the exception of his lower limbs, which were short and small, dwarfing what otherwise would have been a conspicuous figure, and he was popularly known as the "Little Giant." His large, round head surmounted a massive neck, and his features were symmetrical, although his small nose deprived them of dignity. His dark eyes, peering from beneath projecting brows, gleamed with energy, mixed with an expression of slyness and sagacity, and his full lips were generally stained at the corners of his mouth with tobacco juice. His voice was neither musical nor soft, and his gestures were not graceful. But he would speak for hours in clear, well enunciated tones, and the sharp Illinois attorney . . . developed into a statesman at Washington.

The contrasts between Douglas and Lincoln were notable: Douglas short, Lincoln long; Douglas a roaring, fiery speaker, Lincoln deliberate, often humorous; Douglas filled with robustious self-confidence, Lincoln often humble and uncertain.

From the beginning they were on opposite sides of almost every question. It was as if they were measuring each other. A gulf separated them which ever widened, a natural antagonism of personalities perhaps, a fierce and unrelenting competition that lasted almost to the end. And yet both became great men. Each would one day be the foremost figure in his party. They would vie even for the highest office in the nation, and when Douglas lost he would extend the hand of his loyalty and support to Lincoln, the victor.

That session, the tenth, of the Illinois legislature was most notable for the battle, spearheaded by Lincoln, in which eventually Springfield was made the state capital, rather than Vandalia. It was also notable for an enthusiastic but not very wise provision for the expenditure by Illinois of $10,000,000 for "internal improvements"—subsidizing railroads and canals, chiefly—and this for a state whose income that year was reported as $57,891.15, with expenditures of $55,151.91, leaving a balance of just $2,739.24! Lincoln was instrumental in that, too, and it helped him in his Springfield project. Quite shamelessly he resorted to "log-rolling" tactics. To one county he and his associates promised support for a canal, to another for roads, to still another for a bridge, yet others for railroad right-of-ways—all in exchange for their votes for Springfield as capital.

On February 28, 1837, Springfield was chosen; Lincoln became a popular hero in Sangamon County.

He was resolved to enter legal practice, and after the close of the session, April 15, 1837, he packed up his few belongings and left New Salem to take up residence in Springfield. In spite of his legislative laurels he was so poor that he hardly knew how to get through the winter. An intimate friend, Joshua Fry Speed, offered to share with Lincoln his room and bed. William Butler asked Lincoln to take meals at his home. Neither made any mention of charges. Under these conditions—almost if not quite charity—Lincoln continued to live for many months thereafter.

His friend John T. Stuart took him into partnership, his first step up in his chosen profession of law. It was an important advance. Lincoln was twenty-eight years old. From an awkward and seedy man-of-all-work, he had within a space of five years become his party's floor leader in the legislature, winner of the fight for Springfield as state capital, partner of one of the foremost lawyers in Illinois, and was generally considered the most personally popular Whig in Sangamon County. Yet he was still poor, still a failure in society, still humble in his own feeling that he lacked knowledge, perhaps lacked any great merits or deserts.

His legislative experience had revealed to him that he had a gift for words. There is a heady sensation in being able to rise and hold an audience with words and ideas formed and spoken while one is on his feet. There is pride in winning applause by means of well-turned phrases and in worsting adversaries in the rough and tumble of forensic debate.

Lincoln's most brilliant efforts hitherto, however, had been in invective; and he must have possessed a corrosive tongue, to judge by a furious outburst from W. Lee D. Ewing, after an exchange with Lincoln during the debate over the Vandalia-Springfield question.

"Have you no other champion than this coarse and vulgar fellow to bring into the lists against me?" Ewing cried out. "Do you suppose that I will condescend to break a lance with your low and obscure colleague?" Lincoln merely smiled at the tirade.

He turned this gift into a hardly admirable course: anonymous or pseudonymous newspaper lampoons. Once in his earlier days in Indiana, when two young men of his neighborhood married sisters in a joint wedding, Lincoln in a spirit of horseplay helped maneuver the brides into the wrong bedrooms on their wedding night. Presumably the mistake was discovered and set straight before too late, but the embarrassment of the couples involved was in no way diminished by an account of it, written by Lincoln and entitled *The Chronicles of Reuben*. Its Rabelaisian humor delighted the countryside, but not the victims.

Now Lincoln turned this "talent" against General James Adams, a Democrat seeking the office of probate judge against Dr. Anson G. Henry, a Whig and a friend of Lincoln. Previously Lincoln had been in a lawsuit against Adams over a disputed piece of property, and he used the occasion for a series of letters in the *Sangamo Journal*, signed "Samson's Ghost" and charging Adams with fraud in the land transactions.

It reacted against his friend Henry, however, for the people thought Adams was being unfairly persecuted and elected him by a large majority.

These lampoons were only evidences of a surface froth above a deeper current running strong and true in Lincoln's character. In the legislature he had caught a glimpse of something greater than Springfield, or even Illinois. He had seen, though afar off, the nation; even the world. He had been confronted by issues of importance to all America—slavery, abolitionism, the growing bitterness and tension between the North and South, and other problems great and complex, including the significance to the West and the entire country of means of communication, particularly the railroads, which at this period, 1837, were beginning to extend feelers from population centers. In 1830 there had been only twenty-three miles of railroad line in America. By 1840 there were 2808 miles of track in nineteen states. Henceforth the standards of Lincoln's judgment were not to be merely those of a neighborhood, a town, or even a state. He began to think in terms of the nation as a whole.

Even this early a curious fatalism seems to have possessed Lincoln. To his friend Joshua Fry Speed, whom he had helped over a period of indecision concerning marriage, he wrote that it was "fate . . . I always was superstitious; I believe God made me one of the instruments of bringing Fanny and you together, which union I have no doubt he had foreordained. Whatever he designs he will do for me next."

Later another friend, William H. Herndon, his law partner for many years, became convinced from Lincoln's talk and actions that he believed in a fixed destiny, and that he was foreordained to some mysterious and as yet unrevealed role. His moods of gloom were interwoven with a vein of something like a prophetic streak. He did not know, but some strange seer's instinct seemed to warn him of a fate, still shadowy but mighty and perhaps terrible, that awaited him.

He plunged into law practice. But his partner, Stuart, was busy running for Congress, and the law cases at first were relatively few and unimportant.

Meanwhile, November 7, 1837, at Alton, Illinois, not far from Springfield, the slaying of Elijah Lovejoy, the abolitionist editor, occurred. Lincoln held no brief for abolitionists and their methods, but this and other instances that had occurred over the country,[4] seemed to him dangerous evidences of a growing mob violence in the country. On January 27, 1838, he delivered to the Young Men's Lyceum in Springfield a speech that lacked any light-hearted humor but was spoken with earnest eloquence, on the danger and wickedness of mobs and the vital necessity of maintaining law and order.

"There is," he said, in a manner that caught his listeners, "no grievance that is a fit object of redress by mob law. In any case that may arise, as, for instance, the promulgation of abolitionism, one of two propositions is necessarily true: that is, the thing is right within itself, and therefore deserves the protection of all law and all good citizens, or it is wrong, and therefore proper to be prohibited by legal enactments; and in neither case is the interposition of mob law either necessary, justifiable, or excusable."

[4] Including the hanging of four gamblers in Memphis, Tennessee, the lynching of several Negroes and white men in Mississippi who were involved in a plot, fomented by the outlaw John A. Murrell, for a slave uprising, and the burning to death of a mulatto murderer in Missouri.

The speech gave a new dimension to Lincoln. In the confused state of feelings at the time, his logical and forceful denunciation of mob violence and his declaration for the laws and institutions created to make and preserve America, made a deep impression. His auditors began to realize that the speaker was a thinker, not merely a politician.

In the first legislative session that convened at Springfield Lincoln was defeated for Speaker by the majority Democratic vote; but as Whig floor leader, "suave and merciless," he beat down an attempt by Vandalia to recover the capital. By the end of the session national politics was the chief topic of discussion. Lincoln worked for the Whig ticket, engaged in a debate, in which he and two other Whigs met on the platform three Democrats led by Stephen A. Douglas, by that time Register of the Land Office in Springfield.

That fall of 1840 the result of the Presidential election pleased Lincoln, in that a Whig, General Harrison, was elected; but he was not pleased that his favorite, Henry Clay, had been put aside by the party convention in favor of the military hero.

5

Now occurred a strange episode in Lincoln's life. The legislature met and Lincoln, the Whig leader in the House, was always in attendance, working, cajoling, arguing, manipulating to carry through his legislative program.

But on January 1, 1841, he was present only once, for a few minutes. Next day he was there only twice, and the third day he did not appear at all.

For three weeks, until January 21, he made only brief visits to the assembly, on just four days. His absences were made more mysterious by the fact that at the beginning of the fourth week he returned to regular attendance and took up once more his work of legislation. But when the legislature adjourned, March 1, 1841, Abraham Lincoln was through with it. He never again returned to the body, and he went to his law office with "gloom fairly dripping from him."

What had happened?

Lincoln had suffered a siege of depressions and melancholia which came near to being a nervous breakdown. At one time he contemplated suicide and even wrote a poem on that subject.

The cause was a woman. Her name was Mary Todd, a daughter of Robert Smith Todd, of Lexington, Kentucky. She was one of six sisters and brothers who reached maturity, and of these, four, including Mary, had psychotic tendencies.

When she first met Lincoln, Mary Todd was twenty-one. She was not beautiful, being inclined to dumpiness, but she had the appeal of youth and vitality, being "spirited, vivacious, witty, entertaining, and fluent in conversations," though with "a tendency to sarcasm and quick, sharp repartee."

She had attended a fashionable girl's academy, and was trained for wifehood in the manner of the planter society of Kentucky, of which her father was a prominent member. She quarreled with her stepmother in Lexington, and went to Springfield to live with her sister Elizabeth, wife of Ninian W. Edwards, one of the important men of the city, and a member of whatever aristocracy it boasted.

Among those who called on Miss Todd was Joshua Speed. It was he who first introduced Lincoln to her. Another caller was Stephen A. Douglas.

According to Mrs. Edwards, her sister "loved glitter, show and pomp and power . . . the most ambitious woman I ever knew. She often and often contended that she was destined to be the wife of some future President." Lincoln was early enthralled with her, and she knew it. She therefore "flirted boldly and conspicuously" with Douglas, while Lincoln sat by miserably, listening and hardly saying a word.

Both Edwards, who had been in the legislature with Lincoln and liked him, and Elizabeth Edwards, remonstrated with Mary for her cruel treatment of the tall young man. When they asked her which suitor she intended to marry, she tossed her head and replied, "Him who has the best prospects of being President."

As it turned out she did not have a choice, for Douglas never asked her. Though she knew Lincoln was highly regarded, both in politics and law, she was at first unfavorably disposed toward him, not only because his discourse was awkward, but because of his family. Wrote Beveridge:

> The Todd and Edwards families scorned and detested the Hanks and Lincoln family; and Mary, especially, held the Hanks tribe in contempt and the Lincoln family generally—the old folks in particular—a feeling which she never overcame.

In the end, however, Mary Todd accepted Lincoln's proposal and they were engaged. He was, after all, despite his crude antecedents, something of a catch. It is doubtful that she ever really loved Lincoln; or that Lincoln ever was wholly in love with her. Herndon contended long after that the tall young lawyer buried his heart with Ann Rutledge. In any case he soon wished to get out of the engagement, and even wrote Mary "informing her of the doubtful nature of his affections and asking to be released." But before he mailed the letter his friend, Speed, induced him to throw it into the fire, and told him "If you have the courage of manhood" he must see Mary and tell her face-to-face.

It was difficult advice to follow, but Lincoln attempted to do so. The girl, quite naturally, burst into tears; and Lincoln melted, took her in his arms, and told her he would never break their engagement. When Mary told her sister of the episode, Mrs. Edwards advised her to drop Lincoln "because of their obvious unfitness for each other." But she went ahead with her plans, and the wedding was set for January 1, 1841.

It did not take place. That was the day that Lincoln displayed an almost hallucinatory frame of mind, began absenting himself from the legislature; and in that period he wrote to his partner, John T. Stuart, then in Washington, in despairing vein:

I am now the most miserable man living . . . Whether I shall ever be better, I cannot tell; I awfully forebode that I shall not.

It was perhaps also in this period that he memorized the poem of despair, written by the gloomy Scotchman, William Knox, which begins:

Oh why should the spirit of mortal be proud?
Like a fast-flitting meteor, a fast-flying cloud,
A flash of the lightning, a break of the wave,
He passes from life to his rest in the grave.

In later life Lincoln quoted that poem frequently, and there is a copy of it in his handwriting. In 1846 he told a friend that he did not then know the author of it, but had seen it fifteen years before, and later in a newspaper. Its verses on death, decay, and doleful contemplation of mortality, seemed to give him some special satisfaction in his periods of depression.

Matchmakers will ever busy themselves. One such was Mrs. Simeon Francis, wife of the editor of the *Sangamo Journal*. It was she who invited Lincoln and Mary to her house, letting neither of them know the other would be there. After a few such secret meetings they were reconciled, although there was no immediate renewal of the betrothal.

When the two became engaged again, it was an aftermath of one of the most unhappy events in Lincoln's life.

6

Among the men Lincoln met in the legislature was James Shields, an attractive, brave, and honorable gentleman, who was born in Ireland, fought in the Seminole war where he was wounded, would be twice wounded in the Mexican War, and was eventually to be elected Senator from three different states. He also served as a general in the Civil War, where he had the misfortune to encounter a certain Confederate general named Thomas J. Jackson—already called Stonewall —in the Shenandoah Valley of Virginia, suffered a severe defeat at his hands, and was wounded so seriously that he had to be invalided out of the army.

Shields was a Democrat, which was enough to condemn him in Lincoln's eyes. In the panic following the financial collapse of 1837, the State Bank of Springfield, for which Lincoln had worked to obtain a charter in the legislature, found itself unable to redeem in specie, so that the value of its notes depreciated to forty-four cents on the dollar. After a conference with the governor and the treasurer, in August 1842, Shields, who had become state auditor, acting under a statutory provision, prohibited tax collectors from receiving the paper of the Springfield State Bank.

It was the day of Jackson's "Specie Circular," but the bank was Lincoln's particular pet. Shortly, there appeared in the *Sangamo Journal*, a "letter" purportedly written by a farmer's wife, signing herself "Rebecca," though it actually was written by Lincoln. With a humorous approach and couching his words in the language of the farm and cabin, Lincoln restated his arguments for the bank, and included some galling gibes at Shields. So cleverly written was it that it "came near to being a work of art."

Two other letters followed this, both evidently by Lincoln, and both signed fictitiously. It was his old trick of anonymous correspondence. The letters impugned Shields' motives and misrepresented his words and purposes, in a not very admirable manner, since the writer was hiding under a pseudonym.

Shields "felt the lash," but said nothing. Then a fourth "Rebecca" letter appeared, badly written and lacking all the humor of the first three, and this time holding Shields up to scorn as lacking courage. It was not written by Lincoln. Instead it was the work of Mary Todd and a close friend of hers, Julia Jayne; and it was an impertinence, especially since it attributed, by implication, to the writer of the first three missives sentiments which he did not hold. Lincoln would never have dreamed of questioning the courage of James Shields.

At the time this latest screed appeared, Shields was out of town, attending another tax meeting which resulted in a reversal of his previous proclamation so that he directed tax collectors to accept the paper of the Springfield bank "at its specie value." This should have been enough, but on the day Shields returned to Springfield, the *Sangamo Journal* published a piece of atrocious doggerel, signed "Cathleen" and written by the Misses Todd and Jayne, in which they sportively announced that he had "won" Rebecca (who had now become a widow) and would soon marry her.

The letters now had been reduced to the sort of petty personal basis that young women might think important, though few others would. Still, to Shields the "Cathleen" doggerel was the last straw. He demanded from Francis, the editor of the paper, the name of the author of the "Rebecca" letters. After some hesitation, Francis named Lincoln.

It developed that Lincoln was in Tremont, a day's ride north, attending court. The angry Shields started after him on horseback. Warned by friends that Shields would challenge him, Lincoln gravely said that he was opposed to dueling, but would fight before submitting to "such degradation" as being called a coward. He might have disclaimed the authorship of the last and worst of the letters, but with Shields demanding satisfaction he refused to name the two young ladies.

The challenge came. Lincoln, as the challenged party, had the choice of weapons, and the terms he set give an unavoidable impression of burlesque even in so tense a situation:

1st, Weapons Cavalry broadswords of the largest size.

2d, Position A plank ten feet long, and from nine to twelve inches broad, to be firmly fixed on edge, on the ground, as the line between us which neither is to pass his foot over upon forfeit of his life. Next a line drawn on the ground on either side of said plank and parallel with it, each at the distance of the whole length of the sword and three feet additional from the plank; and the passing of his own such line by either party during the fight, shall be deemed a surrender of the contest.

3d, Time On Thursday evening [September 22] at 5 o'clock . . . but in no case to be at a greater distance of time than Friday evening at 5 o'clock.

4th, Place Within three miles of Alton, on the opposite side of the river, the particular spot to be agreed.

Shields was a slender man, five feet nine inches tall, so that Lincoln had seven inches advantage in height and a corresponding advantage in reach with the long and heavy broadsword. Years afterward James Lane Allen made an amusing comment on the situation, in his *Aftermath:*

> There is only one duel I ever heard of that gave me any pleasure, and that one never came off. A few years ago a Kentuckian [Lincoln] wrote a political satire on an Irishman [Shields] in Illinois—wrote it as a widow. The Irishman wished to fight. The widow offered to marry the Irishman, if such a sacrifice would be accepted as satisfactory damages. The Irishman sent a challenge and the Kentuckian chose cavalry broadswords of the largest size. He was a giant; he had the longest arms of any man in Illinois; he could have mowed Erin down at a stroke like a green milk-weed; he had been trained in duelling with oak-trees.

Lincoln had been practicing with broadswords, under expert tutelage. To his friend, Usher F. Linder, he afterward said, "I did not want to kill Shields and felt sure I could disarm him . . . Furthermore, I did not want the damned fellow to kill me, which I rather think he would have done if we had selected pistols."

Because dueling was illegal in Illinois, the Lincoln and Shields parties—principals and seconds—crossed the Mississippi into Missouri. But at the last moment reconciliations took place, the duel was called off, and everybody went home.

Though the incident was ended, Lincoln had received a lesson in good taste. It was the last time he ever ridiculed another person anonymously. He realized that he had been wrong in thus assailing a brave and honorable man, and though he sometimes used his gift of irony and even sarcasm in later speeches, he never afterward spoke an insulting word about another man.

7

One important result of the Shields episode was a new relationship between Lincoln and Mary Todd. The girl had, in her way, espoused his cause in the "Rebecca" letters, and he no doubt felt grateful to her for this evidence of loyalty. On the other hand Mary perhaps was frightened when she saw that she had been instrumental in almost causing a deadly duel, and was relieved when the affair ended peaceably.

Whatever their inner motives, the two were soon engaged again, and before Lincoln's "faltering resolution once more broke down they were hastily married"—on November 4, 1842. An Episcopal minister performed the ceremony, and according to Lincoln's best man, James H. Matheny, the groom "looked and acted as if he were going to the slaughter."

Though he would never be entirely happy in his marriage, Lincoln gained by it socially and perhaps financially. His bride was of a Kentucky family with considerable property. Mary's father was a slaveowner, and at his death in 1849, she received her share of his considerable estate, a part of her inheritance being from the sale of slaves. She was not opposed to slavery; but that did not affect Lincoln's position on the issue, in which he was taking an increasingly deep interest.

More and more his ponderings turned toward the national arena. He had not yet crystallized his thoughts and policies and it would take discipline and suffering before they became refined into the form they took. In 1843 he determined to run for Congress. There is a strong probability that Mary had a part in making his mind up, for she was, as her sister said, intensely ambitious.

But the Whigs did not nominate him in his first race. John J. Hardin was nominated and elected, and Lincoln appears to have taken it hard. In the next campaign, in 1844, Lincoln was again disappointed. Edward D. Baker was nominated by the Whigs and elected.

A son, the first of four, was born to the Lincolns, named after Robert Todd, Mary's father, and they bought a house to live in, where before they had stayed in rooms in the Globe Hotel. Lincoln's income was now around $1200 or $1500 a year—the governor of the state only received $1200 and district judges $750, so his income was for the time good. He had dissolved his partnership with Stuart, who was in Washington, and for a time shared offices with Stephen H. Logan. At length this partnership was also severed, and Lincoln invited young William H. Herndon to be his partner.

It was a historic partnership. Herndon had studied law in Lincoln's office; he would stick to him through thick and thin in all his political activities. The partnership remained in force to the time of Lincoln's death and years later Herndon, in collaboration with J. W. Weik, wrote a biography which gave the world many of the details of Lincoln's early life.

Lincoln was a Whig candidate for Presidential elector in 1844, and spoke all over the state in behalf of his hero, Clay, the Whig Presidential candidate. Polk, however, carried Illinois.

Another Congressional election was coming up and Lincoln doggedly once more announced his candidacy. "You know that my own argument is that 'Turn about is fair play,'" he wrote a supporter. That was his slogan, his theme. Hardin and Baker had each served a term in Congress, and he felt they should step aside for him. Beveridge later wrote:

> In the multitude of letters which he showered upon the Seventh Congressional District when pushing his candidacy, the practical politics of rotation was the dominant note. Grave issues were before the country, great events impending; but to these he gave no heed. In fact, he appears not to have been interested in them. So "turn about is fair play," said Lincoln and he said little else.

But Hardin announced that he also would be a candidate. In great anxiety Lincoln rallied all his friends, including those who edited newspapers. In the end, though Hardin formally denied that he ever had agreed to rotation in office, he withdrew. Since the Seventh District was predominately Whig, Lincoln's chances of election were very bright.

War clouds were mounting in the sky when Lincoln was nominated by the Whigs at their district convention, May 1, 1846. In fact the opening clashes of the Mexican conflict had taken place and the declaration of war was voted by Congress May 12. As Lincoln began his campaign war spirit was high in Illinois. None of the criticism of the war, of its motives, and of President Polk, such as later colored Whig and abolition utterances, had yet appeared.

Indeed the *Sangamo Journal,* one of the most stalwart Whig papers, was demanding that President Polk adopt a "sterner course" in dealing with Mexico. It denounced the President's attempts to conciliate Mexico on the ground that "Mexican authorities have insulted our government, and robbed our people sufficiently, to call for some other policy . . . Nothing but pusillanimity on our part will continue our present policy with Mexico."

In his campaign Lincoln supported the war. He could hardly have done otherwise. Illinois, at the call for volunteers, had a quota of three regiments, which were filled almost overnight. James Shields, Lincoln's former challenger, resigned his office as General Land Commissioner in Washington, and received a commission as brigadier general of Illinois troops. Baker became a colonel, left his seat in Congress, and raised another regiment in Illinois. Thousands of eager young men were pleading to be taken in. Eventually the state furnished seven regiments, and Illinois troops did doughty service in the war.

Lincoln's Democratic opponent was the Reverend Peter Cartwright, the notable and somewhat cantankerous Methodist circuit rider and revivalist. Neither candidate discussed slavery in their speeches, because their viewpoints were identical: "both thought it was an evil, but neither considered it a sin."

Lincoln was criticized by some because he was not a churchgoer. He was "suspected of being a deist." Among the many books he had read were Thomas Paine's *Age of Reason*, and the Count de Volney's *Ruins of Time*, both of which popularized skepticism concerning religion and were consequently anathema to church people, particularly those of the frontier. It is to be doubted that these books had any serious effect on Lincoln's thinking. Though he never united with any church, his basic feeling was fundamentally religious.

If Lincoln was criticized for his lack of churchly affiliations, however, his opponent was criticized as severely for exactly the opposite reason—as a minister of the gospel, some held, it was unseemly for him to run for public office, particularly for Congress.

In the end, Lincoln's personal popularity was unbeatable. When the votes were counted on Election Day, August 3, he polled 6340 votes to Cartwright's 4829.

There ensued a long wait, for the new Congressman could not assume his seat until December 1847. He occupied the intervening time by attending a River and Harbors Convention in Chicago, called to protest the veto by President Polk of appropriations for work on rivers and harbors—referred to by Bernard De Voto as "the annual pork." He also became involved in a case where he acted as attorney for a slaveholder named Robert Matson, in a tangled lawsuit over the status of four slaves Matson, a Kentuckian, had brought to Illinois. Apparently Lincoln had "consulted" with Matson before he understood the full implications, and felt bound by the ethics of his profession to go on with the case. Previously, in another suit, Lincoln had obtained the freedom of a young Negro girl similarly claimed; his heart was not in the Matson case, which he lost. The Negroes were declared free, and Matson left the state, evading his creditors and omitting to pay Lincoln his fee.

One flaw in his happiness was the election by the state legislature of Stephen A. Douglas to the United States Senate, December 14, 1846. Such eminence for his rival! But Lincoln had to rest content.

Meantime the war was being victoriously waged in Mexico; and Whig sentiment against it began to appear. The mortality, caused as much by sickness as by battle, brought sorrow to many homes. And politicians were now seeking some way to discredit the Polk administration by closely scrutinizing every phase of the war, its causes, and its results.

CHAPTER TWENTY

Gold in California

1

JAMES KNOX POLK was nearing the end of his term, and nearing it unhappily. Weary and ailing, he had long ago notified his party that he would not again be a candidate for the Presidency. He was suffering from dysentery, and probably malaria, and certainly from overwork. The Potomac flats with their fever-breeding mosquitoes, and the pollution of drinking water by sewage, made Washington one of the unhealthiest places in the whole country during the first half of the nineteenth century.

The President's weakened physical condition was made more intolerable by the unjust aspersions and criticisms cast upon him by his political opponents, the abolitionists and the Whigs, and even by some members of his own party. Polk was a man who felt no enjoyment of power or thrills in accomplishment. He was driven by a sense of duty, and he worked so far beyond his strength that within four months after he left office he was dead.

Polk was treated with almost uniform unkindness in our historical literature, Allan Nevins points out, until his *Diary* edited by Milo M. Quaife was published in 1910, revealing his inner thoughts and hopes for his country. Of Polk's character and achievements Nevins, who in 1929 edited a popular condensation of Quaife's four-volume work, wrote in his *Ordeal of the Union*, Vol. 1:

> A little known Tennessee politician when he entered the White House, [Polk] left an impressive record behind him. He had given the fiscal system a solid foundation; he had disposed of critical boundary issues with Great Britain in a manner honorable to both nations; carrying on a war of unexpected magnitude in a land of great distances and difficult terrain, and using generals politically hostile to him, he had raised the American flag over the enemy capital; and he had made precisely the right peace, claiming neither too little nor too much. In the difficult issues growing out of the war, he had trodden a just and moderate path

between the two sections, and favored a measure of compromise
which it was probably unfortunate that Congress did not adopt.
Endlessly abused, in the most vital fields of public activity he had
brought Congress and national sentiment to approve his measures.

His last days in the White House were darkened by the furore and
clamor of his political foes. There was opposition even to the acceptance of the territory he had won. Daniel Webster, for example, speaking March 23, 1848, during the debate over ratification of the peace
treaty stormed against the idea that the territories of California and
New Mexico would join the already admitted Texas, thus adding to
the Senate two members each from those states.

"We shall have six Senators then," he exclaimed, "for less than three
hundred thousand people! We shall have as many Senators for three
hundred thousand people in that region as we have for New York,
Pennsylvania, and Ohio, with four or five millions of people; and that
is what we call equal representation! . . . I say, Sir, that according to
my conscientious conviction, we are now fixing on the Constitution of
The United States and its frame of government, a monstrosity, a disfig-
uration, an enormity!"

Webster was assuming that the new territories would be Southern
in their feelings and attitudes. He might have been less acrimonious
had he been able to foresee that California within a year would be
seeking statehood *without* slavery—and then be opposed fiercely by
the Southerners themselves. Or that New Mexico's enormous territory
would eventually be carved into the separate states of New Mexico,
Arizona, Nevada, and Utah, none of which would achieve statehood
for many years—Nevada in 1864, Utah in 1896, and New Mexico and
Arizona not until 1912.

The dark question of slavery remained the center of the debate.
During that debate Lewis Cass, a devoted follower of Andrew Jackson
in whose cabinet he had served, and also a pillar of the Polk administration, gave voice to a fateful sentiment. When John C. Calhoun proclaimed that the new territories were the "common property" of all
the states, and that therefore slavery was legal in all those territories,
old Thomas Hart Benton, the sturdy Jacksonian, who saw in this the
seeds of disunion, denounced the theory furiously. But it remained for
Cass, a Michigan man who detested slavery, to enunciate the viewpoint which was dramatically opposite to that of Calhoun: that self-
government was inherent in the American way of life, and that the
people of the territories, therefore, ought to have the right to express
their own opinions on the question. This theory, which became known
as "Popular Sovereignty," had early and powerful adherents in Sena-

tors Benton, Douglas, and others. But it created a split in the Democratic party which had important repercussions.

Then, just at the time when the status of the territories was furnishing fulminating fuel for national dissension, something occurred in the distant West; something so unexpected, so important, so almost miraculous, that the whole course of history was changed by it, including the acts of the government and the future career of the nation.

2

Before the War with Mexico the most prosperous and influential man in California was John Augustus Sutter, a stocky, blue-eyed Swiss, with a pleasant face, a neat mustache and goatee, and an ability to get along with people. Still in his forties, he had seen much of the world. After failing in business in Switzerland, he left his family, crossed the American continent with a band of mountain men, lived for a time in the disputed Oregon country, and then went into coastwise trading, visiting Hawaii, Alaska (then Russian America), and in 1839 reaching San Francisco Bay.

Wherever he went, Sutter made friends. So well did the Russians like him that when they abandoned their Fort Rossya (present Fort Ross, California), they sold him, *on credit*, everything he wanted— their land claims, livestock, equipment, a schooner, even an arsenal of cannon and muskets.[1]

Equally well he got along with the *Californios*. Governor Juan Bautista Alvarado gave him a magnificent land grant of eleven Spanish leagues—almost 50,000 acres—and with other lands he occupied by squatter possession, Sutter controlled perhaps 100,000 acres of the best soil in California. At the confluence of the Sacramento and American rivers (the present site of Sacramento), he established a fort, which he called New Helvetia, but which was universally known as Sutter's Fort. In and about it were granaries, warehouses, mills, tanneries, dwellings, and stores; and between 700 and 800 persons, mostly his employees and their families, lived in the settlement, while his stock ranges supported 12,000 cattle, 2000 horses and mules, 1000 hogs, 15,000 sheep, and his wide fields grew wheat and other crops.

At all times Sutter's little empire offered hospitality to those who came to it. From it went the rescue parties that saved what was left of the tragic snow-trapped Donner party, and other emigrants were

---

[1] The muskets were of French make, picked up by the Russians along the snowy trail of Napoleon's disastrous retreat from Moscow in 1813.

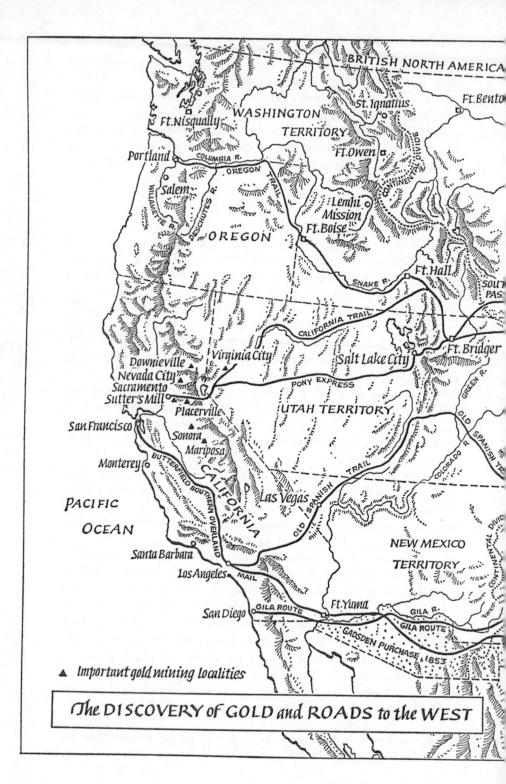

The DISCOVERY of GOLD and ROADS to the WEST

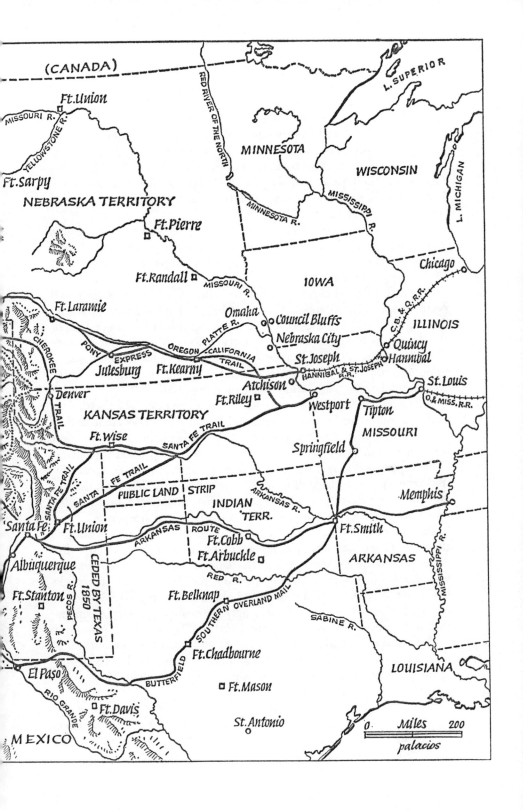

helped in like manner. A happy man, a powerful man, a genial man, a man to be reckoned with was John A. Sutter. Yet by a strange quirk of fate he became the cause of a great change which upset everything, not only in his own life, but in all of California.

When American troops occupied California in 1847, some members of the Mormon Battalion, on receiving their discharges, were employed by Sutter. In that summer while Scott was fighting his Valley Campaign, California went its peaceful way, remote from hostilities. But Sutter foresaw an increase in American population and decided on an improvement.

Americans preferred lumber for building, whereas adobe bricks were usual in California at the time. Sutter made an agreement with James W. Marshall, a mechanic, to build and operate a sawmill for him in upper country.

Marshall, a broad-chested, powerful man, dark of complexion, with features somewhat coarse, and a short beard about his chin and grim mouth, did some scouting before he chose a site on the south fork of the American River. It was about forty miles upstream from Sutter's Fort, near a fine stand of timber, with water power for the mill. Something else also was there, which he did not then suspect, but which was fraught with world-wide consequences—gold.

A flaw in Marshall's planning made the revelation. He decided to build his mill over an old dry channel of the river, deepen it with a narrow ditch, then divert water into it by a weir dam of logs to form a millrace to drive the water wheel on which he depended for power.

By September 1847, he had a crew working on the project, and by mid-January, 1848, the mill neared completion. Now Marshall discovered his miscalculation. The ditch was too shallow to bring water down with enough power for the wheel. He must deepen it.

To save time and labor, he decided to let the river itself wash out the channel. For several days he employed his men in loosening dirt and stones in the channel, while each night the full force of the current was allowed to run through and wash out the debris. Each day when the water was shut off he inspected the channel to see whether it needed further deepening. (Unwittingly he was using a miner's operation that became known as "ground sluicing.")

The afternoon of Monday, January 24, during his inspection, Marshall saw something that sparkled in the mud and sand washed out of the channel. He picked it up—a shining yellow particle. There were several others in the detritus of the tailrace.

Here was something worth investigating. He sent a boy for a tin pan and clumsily began to wash the sand. Some of his men watched him curiously, wondering what he was doing. Marshall was not excited. Nobody was excited. Yet history hung on that moment.

When he finished washing he had a small quantity of yellow particles in the bottom of the pan. Next day he panned again and found additional pieces of the yellow substance in the channel. He suggested to his crew that it was gold. The men were skeptical.

But Marshall knew something about gold. The metal is malleable— it can be beaten into very thin leaves without breaking. It resists most acids and even high temperatures without changing its nature.

His small particles matched a five-dollar gold piece in color. He hammered one of them on an anvil. It did not shatter. His foreman's wife had a kettle of lye boiling for soap-making. One of the bits of metal was dropped in this caustic and left all day. It showed no signs of tarnish.

Marshall waited only to collect a little more, then rode hard for Sutter's Fort. He arrived in a heavy rain, at once closeted himself with his employer, and brought out a pouch.

"It contained," Sutter later recalled, "what might have been an ounce and a half of gold dust, flaky and in grains, the largest piece not quite as large as a pea, and from that down to less than a pinhead in size."

Together the two men tested the substance. Nitric acid did not affect it. Weighed against silver coins, its specific gravity proved greater than silver. Sutter studied an encyclopedia.

"It's gold!" he declared at last. "Of the finest quality—at least twenty-three carats!"

He was not elated. Instead he regarded it as a misfortune, feeling that gold, if found in quantity would wreck his life and everything dear to him.[2] At first he and Marshall tried to keep the discovery from the world. But such a secret could no more be bottled up than a volcano.

One of the young Mormons at the mill, Henry Bigler, kept a diary and thus provided the only exact and certain date of the discovery in existence. His notation, in his rather uncertain spelling, reads:

> Monday, 24th, this day some kind of mettle was found in the tail race that looks like goald, first discovered by James Martial, the Boss of the Mill.

Bigler, an enterprising fellow, went prospecting on his own and found gold down the river in a gravel bed. He invited some of his Mormon friends to share his discovery. They located "Mormon Island," the first really big placer deposit.

[2] His foreboding was justified. Elbowed out, threatened, pushed aside by the furious gold seekers who later came, Sutter died a ruined man in 1880. Marshall also died in abject poverty in 1885.

News, of course, soon reached San Francisco, then a mere hamlet. At first people discounted it, but one day Sam Brannan, off and on a Mormon leader—he twice quarreled with Brigham Young and was twice excommunicated—came running up the street with his hat in one hand, and a glass bottle filled with gold dust in the other, shouting at the top of his lungs: "Gold! Gold! Gold from the American River!"

The volcano had erupted. The rush to the gold fields almost depopulated the coast towns for a time. By every available means of communication the news sped all over the world. Ships with every sail set carried the word to Hawaii, Chile, China, Australia, the Atlantic seaboard of America, and every nation in Europe. Mormon messengers hurried it across the Sierra to Salt Lake City. Hudson's Bay Company officials sped it across Canada, and to England.

Thomas O. Larkin, American consul at Monterey, reported it to Washington by way of the Isthmus of Panama, the report reaching its destination in the middle of September. Later a tea caddy filled with gold dust and nuggets was dispatched to the capital and President Polk caused it to be exhibited in the War Office. In his message to Congress, December 5, 1848, in which he urged immediate organization of the new territories, he referred to the discovery as follows:

> The accounts of the abundance of gold in that territory [California] are of such extraordinary character as would scarcely command belief were they not corroborated by the authentic reports of officers in the public service who have visited the mineral district and derived the facts which they detail from personal observation.

In California the original gold strikes[3] were followed with bewildering rapidity by others. Because of the distances and slow transportation of the times, it took months for the full effect of the world-wide excitement to be felt in California, but by the end of 1848 the first great influx of outsiders had arrived. Many came northward out of Mexico. Almost half of the male population of Oregon went to California. Before 1849 dawned between eight and ten thousand men were working in the gold fields.

[3] Oddly the discovery of gold at Sutter's mill was antedated by a little-known gold strike near the San Fernando Mission, which today is surrounded by the city of Los Angeles, in 1842. Natives worked it but water was scarce and the gold never very plentiful. It created little excitement and was almost completely abandoned when the Mexican War broke out in 1846.

3

It was 1849, however, that saw the really great, wild, almost insane stampede begin. In that year—the year of the "Forty-niners"—California received the tremendous impact of 81,000 immigrants from all parts of the world, but chiefly from the United States.

Some 30,000 went by sea, of whom 23,000 were Americans, the rest from Europe, Chile, Peru, Australia, Hawaii, China, and other far lands. Part of these took ship to the Isthmus of Panama, crossed it overland, and boarded ship again on the other side for the gold country. Disorganization of transport, bad food, and tropical diseases killed hundreds of them.

Others took the hard and stormy voyage around Cape Horn—three or four months at sea, facing the perils of storms and the extremely rough and dangerous "rounding the Horn." Every available ship was put into service, and unscrupulous men even outfitted rotting hulks so unseaworthy that some sank with all aboard. But nothing could stop or discourage the gold-seekers. On one single January day in 1849, as an example, sixty-one vessels, all crowded, left eastern ports for the long voyage to California.

Most of the gold-seekers, however—42,000, of whom 33,000 were Americans—went overland, by wagon. One route to California ran through the Apache country, along the Gila River. Another took the Old Spanish Trail, through Utah. The greatest, however, was the Overland Trail.

Few of the young adventurers—and they were almost all young, a man of forty being considered quite elderly—understood the gravity of the journey across the continent. They could not start until the grass grew green enough to support their teams of mules and oxen, and their riding horses; which meant in early May, that year of 1849.

By thousands they gathered at the Missouri River ports, Westport (now a part of Kansas City, Missouri), St. Joseph, Missouri, and Kanesville (now Council Bluffs, Iowa). Wagon trains were organized, with elected officers to command them. Then the Argonauts, as they liked to call themselves, set forth, full of optimism and almost pathetically green.

Every man went heavily armed—usually with a rifle or shotgun and a brace of pistols—against the supposed peril of the wild Indians; but it turned out that they were more dangerous to each other than were the red warriors. Many hardly knew which end of a gun to point. They pulled loaded weapons out of wagons, muzzle first, and shot themselves. They dropped guns and set them off, wounding themselves or

others. They fired wild fusillades at rabbits or antelope; and sometimes a companion was in the way. At least one man was killed "fool-
ishly holding a trunk cover for another man to shoot at." From one
end of the trail to the other, gunshot accidents caused almost daily
casualties, and more men were killed or wounded in this manner than
might have fallen in a first-class Indian battle.

As for the Indians, astonished by the appearance of such hordes of
white men—it is estimated that seven thousand wagons were on the
trail at a time, with others waiting to follow—they withdrew from the
noise and confusion, and except for stealing a few cattle and mules,
did little harm. In later years the Indians came to resent the intrusion
and wagons were attacked and travelers killed, but 1849 was almost
free from serious depredations.

The early stages of a typical journey, with the wagon train snaking
its way along the Platte River bottom, the grass green and wild flowers
blooming, was like a picnic, a gay procession. But after Fort Child
(later Kearney, Nebraska) was passed, the fun rapidly ceased.

Heavy storms drenched and chilled the travelers and made going
difficult. Flooded rivers had to be crossed and men and animals
drowned. To these dangers was added another, unforeseen and terrible. Starting at New Orleans and working its way up the Mississippi the dread Asiatic cholera appeared. Great cities in the East were
stricken, and among the victims of the disease was James Knox Polk,
who had finished his term as President only a few months previously.
Panic gripped the land because the mortality rate was so terrible, and
the plague so rapid in its course, that a man stricken in the morning
might be dead by night.

In that year of 1849 deaths from cholera on the California Trail
have been estimated as high as five thousand. Dysentery and Rocky
Mountain fever later added to the toll. The whole long route from the
Missouri River to the Sierra Nevada was lined with graves, some
marked with crude headboards or stones, but many not marked at
all.

Yet on rushed the Argonauts in their wild migration. Teams began
to give out. By the time landmarks like Chimney Rock and Scott's
Bluff were reached, broken wagons, scattered trunks, even piles of
bacon, coffee and other foods were beginning to be abandoned. The
tenderfeet gaped at buffalo, elk, and antelope, and at great villages
of prairie dogs, and each night the coyotes gave voice to their wild
mockery around the camps.

Past Fort Laramie went the wagons, and entered the mountains as
they headed for Fort Bridger. More animals died, more vehicles were
abandoned, more brief funerals held. But the Argonauts pressed on,
passed Independence Rock where many carved their names, went
through the grim cleft of Devil's Gate, surmounted South Pass, crossed

a sagebrush desert to Fort Bridger—where perhaps they obtained some supplies and refreshment—and then up the Bear River valley to Soda Springs.

Now they were bone-weary, and many had been left behind in those shallow graves. Yet the worst of the journey remained before them. Down the Humboldt River—an ugly, sluggish stream with barren banks so cut by ravines that travel difficulties multiplied—went the trail. Heat, dust, and alkali poisoning killed more animals and the river itself disappeared at last in a desolate morass called the Humboldt Sink.

Between the Humboldt Sink and the Carson River was forty-five miles of trail with no water at all. Still the wagons fought on. Joshua Breyfogle, in his diary recorded his impressions:

> Emigrants passing in crowds, nearly perishing for water . . . leaving mules, horses and oxen to starve on the plains for they can't drive them on. I don't know what will become of the back trains . . . This is the most horrid night I ever passed. The road was strewed with the carcasses of dead mules, horses, and cattle . . . The forty-five mile stretch is now almost impassable because of the stench of the dead animals along the road which is literally lined with them and there is scarcely a single train or wagon but leaves one or more dead animal, so it must be getting worse every day.[4]

By the time the Carson River was reached so many animals had died that more wagons and articles must be discarded. Because of the debris, including clothing, featherbeds, furniture, canvas covers, and other articles, all worn and beaten by the weather, this place became known as Ragtown. And after that the Sierra Nevada passes must be faced before the gold country was reached.

How many "pilgrims" died in those journeys by ship, on the Isthmus, or over the various transcontinental trails, can never be known. According to an estimate by Ralph K. Andrist, it reached "tens of thousands before the gold rush ended, late in the 1850s." Yet about as many stampeded to California each year for the next three or four years, as crossed in that historic year of 1849.

4

New and incredibly rich strikes continued to be made, and there were remarkable fortunes taken from the ground. As random examples: three men, Patrick McChristian, Jacob F. Lease, and Jasper

4 *American Heritage Magazine*, December 1962.

O'Farrell, took $75,000 in dust and nuggets from a single bar on the Yuba River. Iowa Hill yielded $20,000,000 in thirty years; American Bar and Mud Canyon, $3,000,000 each in much shorter time; Boston Ravine, $4,000,000; and Coyote Hill, $8,000,000 to name only a few.

The miner's great prize, for which he was always looking, was a big nugget. Some of fantastic size were found. The greatest California nugget, named the "Monumental," was a solid mass of gold weighing 148 pounds 8 ounces; it sold for $40,000. Another found near Carson- ville weighed 112 pounds and was worth more than $30,000. Many other large nuggets were discovered,[5] but the vast proportion of the gold was in the form of "grain and flour," which indicates the size of the particles gathered, and thousands of seekers found no gold at all.

In those months and years the mountains were strung with devices to separate the gold from the sand and earth, such as cradles, rockers, long toms, and sluices. Considerable engineering feats were performed in building flumes sometimes miles in length and made of timber, to carry water to dry mining sites; and at times rivers were diverted from their channels to permit their sands to be worked.

A Mrs. Elizabeth Farnham, who visited the mining areas, was so impressed by this aspect of the work that she wrote:

> Some of the largest mountain streams of California are now lifted from their beds for miles . . . and the earth is being searched and re-searched, washed and re-washed.

Mining towns with picturesque names sprang up—Hangtown, An- gel's Camp, Poverty Hill, You Bet, and Helltown, for example. When at last the "Mother Lode" was found in 1850—by which was meant the principal series of gold-bearing quartz veins of the Sierra Nevada, from which all "drift" and placers descended to the lower levels, it seemed that the entire Sierras were included in the great gold-bearing field.

Population grew almost unbelievably. San Francisco at first nearly deserted, with its bay so full of abandoned ships that their masts looked like a forest, soon had close to 40,000 inhabitants. Sacramento had about 7000. Hangtown (later Placerville) boasted 5600. Remote

[5] A stranger one day brought into the San Francisco assay office a nugget which weighed more than 132 pounds. It was of such symmetrical shape that he asked to have it assayed from one place only not wishing to mar its appearance. The assay showed it was of finest gold, and that weight of gold was worth in excess of $35,000. The stranger borrowed $6000 against it, and leaving it as collateral, dis- appeared. When, after a sufficient lapse of time the "nugget" was more closely examined, it proved to be nothing but a lump of lead, plated over with gold, and with gold beaten into a pocket—at the spot where the stranger insisted that the assay be made "so as not to mar its appearance."

mountain counties like Eldorado, Calaveras, Yuba, and Nevada had 20,000 to 40,000 each. (By contrast Los Angeles, today's largest California city, at that time had only 1600 inhabitants.)

The skills men acquired in the California gold fields, including the ways of discovering the metal, and of mining it, led to other great discoveries in many parts of the world—Australia, British Columbia, New Zealand, South Africa, the Yukon and Klondike regions, and in the United States Nevada, Colorado, Oregon, Idaho, Montana, and South Dakota, covering a period of almost fifty years after the California strike.

In California during the first nine years, 1848 to 1856 inclusive, the gold production was $456,000,000. All told, to the present, California has produced in excess of $1,500,000,000 in gold.

5

The effects of the California gold discovery are almost incalculable. It gave an enormous impulse to industry not only in the United States but in Europe. It created vast changes in monetary values and revolutionized commerce and finance. And it caused a shift in population as dramatic as it was important.

President Polk's policies were more than justified. By the Treaty of Guadalupe Hidalgo, and the later Gadsden Purchase, the United States paid to Mexico $25,000,000 for California and the Southwest. The cost of the Mexican War to the United States has been figured at $97,705,860. Those figures add up to $122,705,860—the total monetary cost to the United States government of all of Western America south of the Louisiana Purchase and the Oregon Territory. That cost was more than offset in the *first four years* of gold mining in California, during which $160,000,000 worth of the precious metal was taken from the mountains.

Transcending all else in importance was a "by-product" of the stampede westward—full-fledged occupation of the Pacific Coast.

California, indeed, sprang with dizzying suddenness into the population classification warranting statehood. A federal census in 1850—making little pretense to accuracy—gave the population as 93,000. Two years later a fuller census set the figure at approximately 260,000.

The question of statehood soon became a new and very hot potato tossed into the laps of Congress and the government.

CHAPTER TWENTY-ONE

The Old Giants Take Their Stand

1

NOT until mid-September of 1848 was the discovery of gold in California known in the East, and its important effects were not fully understood until much later than that. The great immediate interest of the nation in 1848 was focused on the Presidential election.

The Democratic party that year was badly divided, especially in New York, where a reform element was nicknamed "Barnburners," from the story of the stupid farmer who burned down his barn to get rid of the rats. The conservatives of the party were called "Hunkers," either from their "hunger for office," or because they were willing to "sit on their hunkers," and oppose any changes in the laws, particularly those governing slavery.

To the Whigs it was a magnificent opportunity. Four names were uppermost in their discussions about who should be their standard bearer: their two great statesmen, Henry Clay and Daniel Webster; and their two great generals, Zachary Taylor and Winfield Scott.

Both Clay and Webster thought they deserved the nomination. Clay even believed himself the man most likely to receive it. But a different leaven was working in the country. A group of young politicians had risen who were determined to control events. Among the Whigs were such men as Thurlow Weed, shrewd and ambitious editor of the Albany, New York, *Evening Journal* and boss of his party in New York; his political partner, Senator William H. Seward, who had been governor of New York, a hard-bitten anti-slavery leader and remorseless politician; Thaddeus Stevens of Pennsylvania, embittered because he limped with a club foot, but a brilliant speaker and uncompromising fighter; Truman Smith of Connecticut; and Alexander Stephens and Robert Toombs of Georgia. There was also young Abraham Lincoln of Illinois, not yet recognized as a leader.

Soon after he took his seat in the House of Representatives, Lincoln created a minor ripple by making a speech attacking President Polk and the war in general. Prior to that time he had never made a public statement in opposition to the war, and had in fact written a friend, Williamson Durley, about two years before:

I never could very clearly see how the annexation [of Texas] would augment the evil of slavery. It always seemed to me that slaves would be taken there in about equal numbers with or without annexation . . . I hold it to be a paramount duty of us in the free States, due to the Union of the States, and perhaps to liberty itself (paradox though it may seem), to let the slavery of other States alone; while, on the other hand, I hold it equally clear that we should never knowingly lend ourselves, directly or indirectly, to prevent slavery from dying a natural death.

But in Congress Lincoln followed the party line. The Whig party line was to assail the President, so Lincoln rose, December 22, 1847, and introduced a set of resolutions, known as the "spot resolutions," because they demanded that Polk admit that the "spot" where the first blood was shed in the War with Mexico was on Mexican, not United States, soil and questioned the whole basis of the war.

The resolutions were largely ignored, but Lincoln arose again January 12, 1848, and made a speech against the war which contained some vitriolic and intemperate statements. The *Illinois State Register*, back in Springfield, repeated some of them in a scathing denunciation:

I think Lincoln will find that he had better remained quiet. He will . . . regret that he voted that Illinois officers [naming them] fell while leading brave Illinoisans to "robbery and dishonor . . . in aid of a war of rapine and murder . . ."; that he has thrown upon the escutcheon of Illinois the stain of having sent six thousand men to Mexico "to record their infamy and shame in the blood of poor, innocent, unoffending people, whose only crime is weakness" . . . ; that he has declared . . . that the "God of Heaven has forgotten to defend the weak and innocent and permitted the strong hand of murderers and demons from hell to kill men, women, and children, and lay waste and pillage to the land of the just."

Apparently the Representative from Illinois realized that he had spoken intemperately, for the speech—as a reporter on the spot recorded it—was much toned down in the written version which Lincoln later offered for publication in the *Congressional Globe*.[1] In the

---

[1] The *Congressional Globe* (1834–73), succeeded the *Annals of Congress* (1789–1824) and the *Register of Debates* (1824–37). These were all privately published with consequent questionable accuracy, and members of Congress were permitted to revise their speeches before publication in them. The present *Congressional Record*, published by the government since 1873, is the official record of proceedings, and publishes not only a checked stenographic record of all remarks and formal debates, but the daily actions of both chambers of Congress.

course of his remarks, Lincoln asked when the war would cease—and two weeks later he had his answer, when the treaty of peace was laid before the Senate.

That speech was ill-timed. While it was barely noticed in Washington, Illinois did not like it. Lincoln learned this at once from reactions at home and particularly from the pleading letters of his friend and partner Herndon.

After that bitterly criticized speech Lincoln voted for a war loan of $18,500,000, and against tabling an army appropriations bill. But his anti-war speech was not forgiven. It was the greatest political mistake he ever made.

His term in Congress was undistinguished and when he returned home, he felt that his political career was ruined. He already had agreed to the "turn about" system and was not to run for the next term in Congress. His Congressional district went Democratic, and part of the blame for that was laid at Lincoln's door; and his assertion that he voiced and voted his convictions did not alter that situation.

Politics being what it is, the Whigs—including Lincoln—did a remarkable about face in the Presidential campaign of 1848. Turning their backs on men of stature like Clay and Webster, they nominated General Zachary Taylor. He was almost everything the Whigs had so bitterly denounced: a slaveowner, a Southerner, a believer in the military spirit the Whigs had decried, absolutely in favor of the annexation of the territory taken from Mexico and more.

On top of this he was one of the most unfit men ever proposed for the office of Chief Executive. He "was a man of prejudices rather than opinions," had himself never voted for President, and until the last year or two hardly knew to what party he belonged. He was almost unread, and so nearsighted that at close range he had to close one eye to focus his vision. He knew nothing of national or international affairs, and while almost mulishly stubborn when he had set his mind on any matter, was notably susceptible to influence by others.

But he had the wonderful vote-getting appeal of a military hero.

During the campaign, in which Lincoln, who helped nominate him, played an active part, Taylor had the good sense to remain on his plantation in Louisiana, and say little. Lewis Cass had been nominated by the Democrats, and Van Buren took his Barnburners into the Free-Soil party. The division in the party enabled Taylor, who received in the election 1,360,000 votes to his combined opponents' 1,512,000, to win by 163 to 127 in the Electoral College.

He was the last President ever to be elected by the Whigs.

2

Speedily it was demonstrated that Taylor's election had increased the rancor of sectional feeling. The South felt that he had been recreant in choosing a largely anti-slavery cabinet. The North suspected him of slavery tendencies.

So alarming became the situation that Douglas expressed the foreboding that never had the country stood in such peril. America needed leadership, but the new President, while honest and upright, had so little knowledge of the essential skills of politics, and so little actual intelligence, that he could not furnish it.

As Allan Nevins wrote long afterward: "What was needed was some bold appeal to the imagination of men, or some iron enunciation of principles . . . A Jefferson could have furnished the first, and a Jackson the second." But Zachary Taylor could provide neither.

It was the Senate that took the leadership relinquished by the Chief Executive; and from this time, until the ultimate emergence of Lincoln, the Senate in effect would rule the nation.

That body contained some mighty names, names of men who were nearing the ends of their careers but still were giants: Henry Clay who returned to the Senate in December, 1849, Daniel Webster, John Calhoun, and Thomas Hart Benton were still present. There were also younger men of mark: Lewis Cass, William H. Seward, Stephen A. Douglas, Salmon P. Chase, and Jefferson Davis, among them, soon to be joined by Charles Sumner.

It was an explosive admixture of minds, beliefs, abilities, and personalities. In the coming session old rivals would cross swords for the last time—Calhoun opposed to Clay and Webster—for all three of those men would be taken by death within two years. The session also would provide a spectacle of courageous and unselfish sacrifices in behalf of principle.

The new President had taken at least one decisive action. He sent a representative to urge California to form a constitution and apply immediately for statehood, leaving the slavery question up to the decision of the people of that territory. The Californians reacted at once, electing representatives to a convention which drew up a constitution in a little more than six weeks, ending October 13, 1849, and ratifying that constitution at the polls a month later. A distinctive feature of that constitution was that it *prohibited slavery*. The South was dismayed and Taylor was furiously criticized.

Bills poured into the Senatorial hopper. One, by Joseph M. Root of Ohio, a radical anti-slavery man, proposed the organization of the territories of New Mexico and Utah under the Wilmot Proviso. To counter this, Senator Henry Stuart Foote, of Mississippi, who long had opposed the states' rights school of thought, came forward with a bill to organize three territories, California, New Mexico, and Utah without any prohibition of slavery. Foote also suggested a formation of two states from Texas, divided by the Brazos River, the western division to be named Jacinto and permit slavery—which would add two more Senators to the Southern bloc. This aroused the ire of the North, of course.

To counteract the Foote suggestion Senator Thomas Hart Benton introduced a bill to reduce the boundaries of Texas to approximately its present proportions, and pay the state $15,000,000 for ceding peacefully the other land claimed, which included everything to the upper reaches of the Rio Grande, which flowed south through what is now the middle of New Mexico. Senator Stephen A. Douglas offered a constitution drawn up by Deseret (the Mormon name for Utah) with a petition for statehood with slavery excluded. Senator James A. Mason of Virginia brought forward a measure to put teeth into the Fugitive Slave law, which not only was intended to aid the recapture of escaped slaves, but contemplated a fine of $1000 for any obstruction of such recaptures.

With these tangled issues already before Congress, matters were still further complicated when President Taylor was asked to explain his actions in detail with regard to California and the other territories, especially his dispatching of a personal agent there, and what steps had been taken by that agent for bringing about the California convention and application for statehood so unpalatable to the slave-holding faction.

Poor old Taylor replied as best he could. He urged admission of California, asked that the other territories be allowed to remain in *status quo,* and refused to endorse either the Wilmot Proviso or the South's demand for the right to take slaves into the territories. In sum, he bumbled and hesitated, very much on the defensive and showing it. He faced a hostile Senate and House, and had not the slightest notion of how to maneuver, to bring about desired objectives.

Now a strange and unnatural alignment appeared. Extremists of both the free soil and pro-slavery elements seemed willing to cooperate—in secret of course—to prevent any smoothing over of the quarrels, hoping that an open rupture would occur. For both Northern radicals and Southern fire-eaters, this sort of agreement was treasonable.

The actual challenge was uttered in Congress by Thomas L. Clingman of North Carolina. He had just been in the North, he said, and felt the strong animosity of the anti-slavery movement. Under the circumstances he asserted that the passage either of the Wilmot Proviso, or abolition of slavery in the District of Columbia, were valid grounds for secession of the South. He went on to declaim that Britain's injuries which drove the colonies into revolt were less than those by the North against the South. And he wound up his tirade by saying that to break away from the North would benefit the South in many ways—lowering tariffs, gaining capital from abroad for railroad building and other improvements—and should war come, he predicted that the South, with its military tradition studded by such names as George Washington, Andrew Jackson, Zachary Taylor, and Winfield Scott, could repel any Northern coercion.

At the same time, in the North itself, feeling had grown so bitter that radical abolitionists were calling for secession from the South. Such a course was advocated by even so reasonable a man as Edward Everett, a former governor of Massachusetts and United States Minister to Great Britain, at that time president of Harvard College, though he pleaded that the separation should be brought about in a friendly spirit, "like reasonable men."

3

To face and attempt to ameliorate this bristling situation, Henry Clay turned his undoubted powers. He was now in his seventy-third year, and showing his age. His head was quite bald on top, fringed with long gray hair, his cheeks were sunken, his nose had a pinched look, but his smile retained its charm. Always he attired himself in black, with a high white shirt collar and black stock, and he no longer took the active part he once had taken in Washington social life, contenting himself usually with a little game of cards with friends, and a glass of toddy made from Kentucky bourbon whiskey.

In the early days of the session he devoted his thought to the problems before the country, and the antagonisms that threatened it. On January 29, 1850, he rose in the Senate, and in his most winning manner, with only a short introductory speech, proposed as a solution, a set of resolutions: 1. Admission of California as a free state; 2. Territorial governments to be set up in the other territories without any condition or restriction as to slavery, based on the unlikelihood that slavery could successfully be introduced into those areas in any case; 3. The boundary of Texas fixed to exclude all of New Mexico; 4. In return, the national government should assume all the Texas debt contracted before the annexation; 5. Prohibition of bringing slaves into the District of Columbia to sell and deliver elsewhere; 6. Slavery itself should not be abolished in the District of Columbia, without

the consent both of Maryland (which had given the District to the
nation), and of the people of the District, and then not without just
compensation to owners; 7. Passage of a more effective Fugitive Slave
law; 8. A formal declaration by Congress that it had no power to interfere with the interstate slave trade.

Having thus offered the basis of his compromise proposal, Clay
waited a week, then rose again to speak in its behalf. On that day
the Senate chamber was so crowded that the doors had to be closed
to prevent more seeking to enter than could be accommodated. Clay
received a tremendous ovation.

He was old and tired, but clearly and logically, in a speech which
continued that day and the next, the great Kentuckian outlined his
arguments. California, whose delegates had voted unanimously to exclude slavery, could not be accepted on any other basis, and should
be welcomed into the sisterhood of states. Texas claims to New Mexico he thought invalid, and the state if bounded as he suggested
would be large enough in any case, while the government in reality
was responsible for the Texas debts at the time of annexation. He
quoted long-dead John Randolph of Roanoke, who had referred to
the slave pens of the District of Columbia as "an abomination," and
asked why traders should drive coffles of slaves past the Capitol
building, an offense to all visitors. As for the declaration of Congress
that it had no power to interfere with interstate trade, it simply
affirmed a verdict of the Supreme Court. He pleaded for both North
and South to be magnanimous, and said that in the failure of the
North to enforce the Fugitive Slave law the South had "just cause
for complaint." Finally he solemnly warned the South that secession
would be ruinous for it. The seceding slave states would lose all their
main objectives: admission of slaves to the territories, continuance of
slavery in the District of Columbia, and any possible return of fugitive
slaves. Furthermore, secession would mean war—"furious, bloody, im-
placable, exterminating war," and it would bring sure disaster to the
South.

Henry Clay's speech was received with strong approval in some
quarters—Toombs of Georgia, for example, was filled with enthusiasm
for its courageous stand. Others agreed to it with some reservations,
and it seemed probable that Clay's proposals might find acceptance,
when a surprising turn took place.

Zachary Taylor was not in favor of it.

The old man had been convinced by Seward and some members
of his cabinet that his own, far more limited, plan should be adopted.
He was by nature stubborn, and he had a feeling against Clay who
had refused to help him in his election campaign, and also against
Webster, who was supporting Clay. Furthermore, "a morbid jealousy

rose in his breast as he found all the public applause and attention directed toward Clay."

Deprived of any administration support, Clay suddenly faced a recrudescent drumfire of opposition from the extremists of both the North and South.

Jefferson Davis, walking with a cane because of his Buena Vista wound, voiced the position of the Southern radicals. He charged the North with trying to establish "perpetual domination" over the rest of the nation, with slandering the character of the Southern people, and with denying the South equality under the Constitution.

Northern spokesmen argued that Clay's resolutions gave all the concessions to the South. Abolitionists inveighed against him as an advocate of slavery and all manner of other charges.

A week later Clay rose again, and stood like a man defending himself and his cause from multiple enemies. He was, he said, glad to find himself assailed from the two quarters, and he thought better of his poor scheme because the fanatics on both sides attacked it with equal fury.

He appealed not to the fanatics, but to the thinking men of the nation. Though he represented a slave state and sympathized with the problems of slaveowners, he considered slavery "a social and political evil; that it is wrong, as it respects those who are subject to the institution of slavery." He went on to say that he had, a year before, drawn up a plan for gradual emancipation, though he knew his own people of Kentucky would never support it.

"Mr. President," he said, addressing the chair in his ringing tones, "I am directly opposed to any purpose of secession . . . The Constitution . . . was made, not merely for the generation which then existed, but for posterity, undefined, unlimited, permanent, and perpetual . . . and for every subsequent state which might come into the Union, binding themselves by that indissoluble bond."

It was a stirring speech and had the effect of dividing opinion even in the South, where his proposals were accepted by many of the moderate, thinking men, as a hope of averting the conflict which everyone dreaded except the wild and reckless extremists of both sections.

Shortly the resolutions were referred to a select committee of thirteen—six Democrats and six Whigs, with Clay himself making the thirteenth, as chairman. The committee on May 8 made its report, presenting an "Omnibus Bill" which contained all of Clay's resolutions, in compact and unified form.

It was the sole great hope for a compromise that would avert rebellion and war. To its support Clay rallied all the outstanding Union men.

But a formidable foe, not a friend of the Union, now entered the lists. John C. Calhoun had been failing in health. Three times in the previous session of Congress, when he worked beyond his strength, he had fainted in the Senate lobby. On one of those occasions he said to Robert Barnwell Rhett, who was attending him, "Ah, Mr. Rhett, my career is nearly done. The great battle must be fought by you younger men."

He was past any thought of personal ambition. "The South—the poor South," he said, his eyes filling with tears.

It was announced, even before the Committee of Thirteen completed its deliberations, that Calhoun would appear in the Senate on Monday, March 4. Everyone knew it might be his last appearance, and that only the importance of the occasion could have brought him to expend the energy and strength necessary for such an appearance.

Again the Senate and halls of the Capitol were crowded as the gaunt figure of the "Sentinel of the South" entered, supported by Senator Mason and another friend, James Hamilton. He was thinner than ever before, his long mane of hair, now almost white, falling on each side of his sunken cheeks. A dark cloak was draped from his thin shoulders, and he gave every impression of being a man not long for this world.

When he reached his seat he sat up to receive the greetings of friends, and a member of the Senate moved that as the senior Senator from South Carolina could remain only briefly, the order of the day be waived. It was carried. Calhoun rose with some effort, then stood straight, with countenance unsmiling and stern. In a clear voice, heard distinctly all over the chamber, he thanked the Senate for its courtesy, and begged it to permit that his speech be read by his friend Senator Mason.

Then he sat down again, and as Mason read Calhoun's final statement, he remained motionless, wrapped in his cloak, "his eyes glowing with meteor-like brilliancy as he glanced at Senators upon whom he desired to have certain passages make an impression."

Flatly, the speech declared that abolitionist agitation had brought the nation near to disunion. Calhoun vainly had tried to have steps taken to prevent the disaster, but now the crisis was at hand, and the Senate was confronted with the gravest question that could ever demand its decision.

He recited the wrongs as seen by the South: violation of states' rights, exclusion from common territory, tariff laws that halted the South's progress, attacks on the character and motives of Southerners, concentration of authority of which the North was taking advantage for its own purposes.

Coming from the source it did, even though Calhoun could not personally speak it, the speech was a telling blow at the whole framework of the compromise. Southerners surrounded the old man at the conclusion of the reading, to congratulate him. To one group he said, "At any rate, be men!"

Then he was assisted from the chamber where for so many years he had been a compelling, sometimes a dominating figure, and taken home to his lodgings at Hill's boardinghouse.

The appearance of the dying old statesman, the tenor of his address, his very way of coming and going, had produced a profound feeling of sympathy, while the logic of his statements made some reconsider their previous acceptance of the compromise. It was necessary, absolutely necessary, that he be answered by one of equal caliber.

4

That man could only be Daniel Webster. Eight days before he introduced his resolutions, Henry Clay had gone to the great orator's lodgings early in the evening, and spent some time with him, explaining his purposes, and soliciting his help.

At the time Webster made no promises. He was sixty-nine years old and he, too, was in bad health. For some time he had taken regularly as a stimulant, minute doses of oxide of arsenic, as well as other medicines which his doctor prescribed. But more important than this, he had perhaps more to lose if he made the address requested of him than did Clay or any other. He was from Massachusetts, the very hotbed of radical anti-slavery conviction. He knew that he would be assailed violently by abolitionists and fanatical free-soil advocates, that he would be accused of being a traitor, and that in all probability he would be hounded from any future hope of political advancement.

Yet Daniel Webster's patriotism was as sincere as Henry Clay's. Day after day as the debate continued with growing fierceness, and especially after Calhoun's dramatic appearance, his feeling grew that it was his duty to his country to take the floor. To his son Fletcher he wrote, "I know not . . . with what weapons to beat down the Northern and Southern follies, now raging in equal extremes."

As he began work on his speech he learned that the Massachusetts Anti-Slavery Society had adopted resolutions favoring breaking up of the Union because of the slavery situation; and he was pelted continuously with letters of the most uncompromising nature, urging him to take bolder ground against slavery and the South.

He announced that he would speak on March 7—three days after

Calhoun's address. His far-seeing mind already envisaged the prospects of the cataclysm of civil war. He must avert it if possible, and he
had come fully to support Clay's compromise plan. That day an enormous crowd, surpassing any the Capitol had ever seen, struggled to
hear him.

When Daniel Webster rose, as soon as the Senate was called to
order, a breathless silence fell. His brilliant dark eyes in their cavernous sockets, his mighty forehead, his powerful jaw and wide eloquent mouth, seemed to command them. His opening words were
memorable.

"Mr. President," he began, "I wish to speak today not as a Massachusetts man, nor as a Northern man, but as an American . . . The
imprisoned winds are let loose, the East, the North, and the stormy
South, combine to throw the whole sea into commotion, to toss its
billows to the skies, and disclose its profoundest depths . . . I speak
today for the preservation of the Union. Hear me for my cause!"

Caught in the invariable spell he cast upon them, his listeners
leaned forward to catch every word. There was a momentary interruption. A tall, almost cadaverously thin man, with lank gray hair,
and wrapped in a long cloak, made his way feebly into the chamber,
and was assisted to a chair. It was John Calhoun. He had risen from
his deathbed to hear once more the voice of his old friend and colleague, so often also his antagonist and rival. There was a touching
friendship between Webster and Calhoun, a mingling of admiration,
respect, and affection, which divergence of ideas and policies never
impaired.

Webster at first did not see Calhoun, then he paused to allow the
South Carolinian to be seated, before returning into his address. Once
more the great voice, the great presence, the great mounting phrases
and sentences, building the lofty edifice of eloquence, held them. For
three hours it continued and hardly a listener stirred in his seat in
that time.

Like a master builder erecting an imperishable structure of truth
and appealing to the best in men, he first traced the history of slavery,
its existence through the ages, to the present. Willingly he conceded,
"There are thousands of religious men, with consciences as tender as
any of their brethren at the North, who do not see the unlawfulness of
slavery," and were "just as conscientious" in their support of the institution as were their Northern opponents against it.

But the world was changing, he said, and with it the feeling of the
people. Two sections of the American people held divergent views.
With irony he spoke of those who believed everything was "absolutely
wrong, or absolutely right." "They deal," he went on, "with morals
as with mathematics, and they think what is right may be distin-

guished from what is wrong with the precision of an algebraic equation."

Next he touched on the growth of the nation, the addition of new territories from which slave states were carved, and agreed that the South's devotion to slavery, the desire to extend the cotton territory, was based on the natural desire to prosper.

But what of these most lately acquired territories? Turning full to the seats occupied by the most radical anti-slavery members, he said to them, "The law of nature, or physical geography, the law of the formation of the earth," forever excluded slavery from all territory acquired from Mexico. So, "Why re-enact the will of God?" Why needlessly taunt the South by an act of Congress? He would never support any assertion of "superior power, exercised for no purpose but to wound the pride . . . of the citizens of the Southern states."

That the South had reason for feeling aggrieved at the North's failure to return fugitive slaves, he conceded. The Constitution and laws alike had been violated by this failure. "The South has been injured in this respect, and has a right to complain."

And what had been the result of abolition agitation? "The bonds of the slaves were bound more firmly," as Southern sentiment hardened. Extreme and untactful things were said by both sides, until feeling was acute and even dangerous.

But secession? Webster had heard of a convention called by some Southern extremists at Nashville to draw up plans on that subject. "What! Plot the overthrow of this Union over the bones of Andrew Jackson?" He decried the very thought in words of thunder.

His thoughts moved forward in prophecy. "Ere long the strength of America will be in the valley of the Mississippi." Could that river be cut in two by separate governments of slave states and free states? "I would rather hear of natural blasts and mildews, war, pestilence, and famine, than to hear gentlemen talk of secession . . . No, Sir! No, Sir! There can be no secession!"

Thus Webster, "with his peculiar and distinctive impressiveness of manner and majesty of bearing, swept on." It was a great speech, second only to his *Reply to Hayne*, and it so affected his hearers that next day the editor of the *Washington Republic* wrote:

> Fears . . . for the Union melted . . . and with them dwindled
> the consequence . . . of those who disturb the repose of society
> by brandishing firebrands near the altar of the temple.

At the end John Calhoun got to his feet and spoke a few words, dwelling on "broken faith" in that the Missouri Compromise, carried largely by Northern votes, was now being disavowed by the North in the question of the status of the territories.

Having spoken thus briefly, he turned and slowly made his way out of the Senate chamber, to go to his lodgings and there die. Death came soon, March 31, and among his pallbearers were both Webster and Clay, neither of whom long outlived him.

5

Webster's great speech may have quieted fears, but the wrath of the radicals in the North which broke upon his head was even more furious than he had anticipated. William Cullen Bryant, Horace Greeley, and other editors attacked him with slashing editorials in their newspapers. He was described as having "the ineffable meanness of the lion turned spaniel in his fawnings on the masters whose hands he was licking for the sake of the dirty puddings they might choose to toss to him."

Yet it was Webster's finest hour. Knowing full well the penalties, he had thrown every thought of self aside for his beloved country.

President Taylor and his chief adviser, Seward, sought to destroy the effect of his speech. Rising in the Senate, Seward decried any stronger law for recovery of escaping slaves, on the ground that it could never be enforced. What if the Constitution recognized slavery, he declaimed, his voice rising with emotion, "There is a *higher law* than the Constitution!"

He had created a phrase that was taken up by the emotionalists of the North, even though it was assailed as wrong and untenable by lawyers and conservatives on both sides. It was an appeal to individual conscience above law that was to be echoed by other speakers in the years to come.

Day after day the debate continued, and in spite of growing sentiment for Clay's compromise plan, it became ever more apparent that the stubborn old man in the White House would never agree to it.

In the course of the debate Douglas, now the acknowledged leader of the Northern Democrats, rose to disclaim any wish of the Northern Democrats to increase slavery. When Webster interrupted with a playful remark about "Northwestern Democracy," Douglas smiled and thanked him.

"There is a power in this nation greater than either the North or the South—a growing, increasing, swelling power, that will be able to speak the law to this nation, and execute the law as spoken," he thundered. "That power is the country known as the great West—the valley of the Mississippi, one and indivisible from the Gulf to the Great Lakes . . . There, sir, is the hope of this nation—the resting place of the power that is not only to control, but to save, the Union!"

In this, too, there was an element of prophecy.

As the Senate debate raged, the House also engaged in almost continuous oratory. Now the whole fate of the compromise was in balance. Webster continued to receive bitter abuse such as few statesmen have ever been called upon to face, from his own New England as well as other parts of the North.

To that he made answer: "Sir, I shall stand by the Union, and by all who stand by it . . . I mean to stand upon the Constitution . . . I shall know but one country . . . I was born an American; I will live as an American; I shall die an American . . . What are the personal consequences? . . . No man can suffer too much, and no man can fall too soon, if he suffer or if he fall in defence of the liberties and Constitution of his country."

Those were the last words spoken by Daniel Webster in the Senate. Soon he was to become, for the second time, Secretary of State, and he would die in that office.

6

As the weeks passed, the temper of Congress and the country at large grew notably quieter.

A highly advertised convention of slave states at Nashville, which had seemed a threat of secession, took place in June—and was a fiasco. Only nine states sent delegates and some of these had "very dubious credentials." The national debate over the compromise evidently had created a mood of moderation. A resolution was drawn up stating that as a "concession" the South would be willing to see the new territories divided by the Missouri Compromise line[2]—36°30′—and condemned the acceptance of the whole of California as a free state. But though Rhett composed a fulminating *Address to the People*, the convention simmered quietly to an end.

Strive as he might, however, Clay could not bring Congress to a

[2] For clarification, the Missouri Compromise was passed by Congress in 1821, as a measure admitting Missouri as a slave state, "paired" with the admission of Maine as a free state, to maintain the balance of power between slave and free states. Under its stipulated terms in the remainder of the Louisiana Purchase, of which Missouri was a part, slavery was prohibited north of 36°30′. Henry Clay, then Speaker of the House, was active in promoting the compromise, the furious debate over which startled the nation, and came, as Thomas Jefferson said, "like a fire bell in the night," marking the first truly grave sectional conflict and striking the South with fear. This line of demarcation should not be confused with the Mason-Dixon line which marked the boundary between the colonies of Pennsylvania and Maryland in 1767, was at 39°43′26″.3, considerably north of the Missouri Compromise line.

final vote on his proposals. Growing more thin, more gray, more worn each day, he labored on, trying to reconcile differences, urging that the Omnibus Bill was based not on expediency but on fairness and logic.

Zachary Taylor, in the White House, remained intransigent. The old man who had pledged himself—as a campaign gesture—not to veto any measure except on grounds of constitutionality, seemed ready to veto the compromise itself, because it did not fall in with his own plan.

Now a new crisis confronted him. Texas, aggressive and self-confident, still claimed all of New Mexico up to the Rio Grande, and, in March 1848, created by legislative enactment a "County of Santa Fe," declaring all of eastern New Mexico under Texas authority.

A convention was held in Santa Fe, and a delegate sent to Washington to apply for admission of New Mexico as a state—even though the population was too scanty to permit such a status. Taylor espoused the New Mexican cause. His plan now was to admit both California and New Mexico at once as free states—in direct opposition to the compromise measures.

Revolt at this grew even among the President's supporters. Southern Whigs in Congress appointed three representatives to call upon the old general and try to convince him of his error, and to persuade him to accept the compromise measures for the sake of peace in the nation.

Meantime Texas was making motions that looked like an invasion of New Mexico. Taylor ordered Colonel John Munro, military governor of New Mexico, to resist with government troops. A small civil war seemed imminent.

It was at this point that three Whig spokesmen, Robert Toombs, Humphrey Marshall, and C. M. Conrad—all supporters of Taylor, all Southerners, and all upholders of the Union—called upon the President. The interview must have been stormy. Thurlow Weed, entering the President's office soon after the delegation had departed, found Old Rough and Ready in such a rage that for a time he did not even speak, but paced back and forth furiously.

"Did you see those traitors?" he exploded at last. "I told them that if it becomes necessary I will take command of the Army myself to enforce the laws. And I said 'If you men are taken in rebellion against the Union, I will hang you with less reluctance than I hanged spies and deserters in Mexico!'"

This threat to men who were trying their best to preserve the Union by the compromise plan! It echoed a similar statement by Andrew Jackson, but Jackson was talking to outright enemies, not friends, of the Union. It is evident that Old Rough and Ready was confused.

And then, quite simply and with absolute finality, the tension ended.

Zachary Taylor died very suddenly, of indigestion contracted from too much iced water and milk and too many cherries, after he returned hot and tired from Fourth of July ceremonies. Death occurred July 9. He was sixty-five years old.

7

When the state funeral was over, and the Vice-President, Millard Fillmore, assumed the office of President, a fortunate change had taken place. The new Chief Executive was a devoted friend and admirer of Henry Clay. Even before the death of his predecessor he had informed Taylor that in event of a tie on the compromise measure in the Senate, he, as presiding officer, would cast the deciding vote in favor of it.

Fillmore was born poor, had been taught to write by the woman he married, and was of limited mind, yet he had worked his way up in politics. One of his first acts was to ask Daniel Webster to serve as Secretary of State, to the great chagrin of William H. Seward who had been Taylor's chief adviser and now found himself shorn of influence and power.

Clay believed his greatest victory was in sight. But parliamentary maneuvers defeated the Omnibus Bill July 31—an unexpected, crushing blow. Clay was stunned and sat "melancholy as Caius Marius over the ruins of Carthage."

He soon rallied. His greatest coadjutor, Webster, was no longer in the Senate, being now in the cabinet. Nevertheless he set out to salvage the component parts of the defeated Omnibus Bill. On the day after this decision, he gained new and valiant support—that of Stephen A. Douglas, a Democrat, who hitherto had never fully committed himself to the Omnibus Bill. Douglas saw the peril ahead, and his was the driving power which, added to that of Clay, pushed through on August 1 a bill organizing the Utah Territory.

At once the Clay-Douglas forces turned to other provisions of the compromise. Worn out, Clay was forced to take a rest at Newport, Rhode Island. But Douglas, as chairman of the Committee on Territories, did not abate his efforts, persuading other Democrats to aid in the battle which hitherto had been carried on chiefly by Whigs.

A bill was framed—and approved by Secretary of State Webster—fixing the limits of Texas as they remain today, and with it a payment to Texas of $10,000,000 for peaceful cession of the New Mexico areas claimed. It passed August 9.

California's statehood was voted August 13, and New Mexico was given territorial status on August 14. In these actions the Wilmot Proviso was forever buried, and the principle of popular sovereignty seemed tacitly accepted.

The last major provision of Clay's compromise, the amended Fugitive Slave law, was enacted August 19. It had new teeth put into it, which later were to cause anger and trouble in the North. But it was passed.

Fillmore exerted his influence in favor of these measures, and the House quickly ratified the Senate actions. In substance, Henry Clay's great contribution to the preservation of the Union, known thenceforth as the Compromise of 1850, had triumphed.

In Newport, the Kentuckian was wildly acclaimed. When he returned to the Senate, August 27, to see the last of his measures, the forbidding of traffic in slaves within the District of Columbia, passed by Congress, he was given an ovation.

In Washington everyone seemed to celebrate. There were bonfires, cannon salutes, processions. Crowds visited the homes of Webster, Clay, Douglas, and others, cheering and asking for a speech. The whole nation in fact seemed to exult with relief—all except the most radical abolition faction in the North.

Daniel Webster had paid his respects to the latter during the debates in the Senate when he laid to abolitionism's door the rising hatred between North and South. "No drum-head," he declared, "in the longest day's march, was ever more incessantly beaten and smitten, than the public sentiment in the North has been, every month, and every day, and hour, by the din, and roll, and rub-a-dub of abolition writers and abolition lecturers. This is what has created the prejudice."

Upon Webster now the abolitionists turned their full furious hatred. He was likened to Benedict Arnold and Judas Iscariot. Garrison published Webster's great speech in his *Liberator* under the headline: THE LATE SATANIC SPEECH OF DANIEL WEBSTER. Wendell Phillips, at an anti-Webster meeting exclaimed: "It is not often . . . that Providence permits the eyes of twenty millions of thinking people to behold the fall of another Lucifer, from the very battlements of Heaven down to that 'lower deep of the lowest deep' of hell." John Greenleaf Whittier thus characterized Webster in his poem, *Ichabod:*

> So fallen! so lost! the light withdrawn
>   Which once he wore!
> The glory from his gray hairs gone
>   Forevermore! . . .
> Then, pay the reverence of old days
>   To his dead fame;
> Walk backward, with averted gaze,
>   And hide the shame!

The abuse deeply wounded the aging statesman, yet he sturdily stood his ground and called on all Americans to live up to the provisions of the Compromise of 1850. Thousands responded. Great Union meetings were held in New York, Boston, and other large cities, in which he was heartily applauded. Webster must have been pleased by tributes like the one in the *Washington Republic:*

> He braved the prejudice of the North; he rebuked the intemperance of the South. He bared his breast to the assaults of fanaticism and exposed his name to the malice of faction. But he may well be content to forego the plaudits of madmen and plotters of treason, to receive the homage of a continent of freemen.

Two old men, weary and well scarred from their battles, reached their noblest hours of greatness in the long-drawn fight to save the Union they loved. Henry Clay died on June 29, 1852, in his quarters in Washington. Out in Illinois Abraham Lincoln eulogized him, and like Mercutio's "A plague o' both your houses," assailed both the abolitionists of the North and the fire-eaters of the South. Of the first he said, they would "shiver into fragments the Union of these States; tear to tatters its now venerated Constitution." As to the hotheads of the slave states he charged that in their idolatry of slavery, they denied the basic premise of the Constitution, that "all men are created equal."

Daniel Webster crossed the threshold into history four months after Clay, at his home, Marshfield, Massachusetts. Both he and Clay died believing they had saved the Union they so loved, and though the hatred of some men followed them to their graves,[3] they died happy in that comforting belief. Neither of them knew that in spite of all their sacrifices and labors the structure on which they counted to save the country would topple less than ten years later; or that the direct cause of the destruction would appear within two years after they breathed their last.

---

[3] Abolitionists refused to join Free Soilers, who with Democrats and Whigs took part in the procession as Webster was buried. Wendell Phillips went so far as to excoriate those who did so, for showing him honor in death.

CHAPTER TWENTY-TWO

The Fury Rises

1

THE Compromise of 1850, for all the effort to obtain its enactment, was at most a stop-gap. It could not permanently endure because it sought to come to terms with an institution both evil and anachronistic, which civilization in the end would not tolerate. Yet at the time of its passage there was a general belief both North and South that a grave crisis was safely past, and the slavery question permanently set at rest.

With relief, men turned to their work, or professions, or businesses; and a period of exceptional prosperity which set in added to the hopeful optimism. At that very time, however, pressures were building, impalpable or ignored by most at first, but within a decade destined to erupt into a horrible disaster to the nation—the Civil War.

From the first the amended Fugitive Slave Act was a cause of discord. It made the fanatical abolitionists furious, but it was objectionable even to the moderates in the free states. Under it a Negro claimed as a fugitive was denied bail, trial by jury, or even the right to testify in his own behalf. Federal officers were required to act as slave-catchers, and private individuals who refused to aid in arrests of refugees or aided in any slave's escape, were subject to heavy fines, imprisonment, and civil damages.

Incidents occurred. The Underground Railroad which for years had smuggled slaves over the border into Canada, increased its activities. Black prisoners were delivered from jails by white mobs. A slave-owner, in the North to regain his human property, was murdered. Yet many slaves were recaptured, and to add further injustice to the situation, a few free Negroes were carried off into slavery in the South. Pulpits and newspapers denounced the law, there were meetings of protest, and many of the Northern states in effect set about to nullify the law by simply refusing to comply with it, which increased the South's feeling of injury and aggravation.

In New England poets and authors—among them world-famed figures like Whittier, Lowell, and Emerson—stirred up the people with verse and prose. And suddenly, in 1852, a little, plain-faced, dowdy woman of forty-one named Harriet Beecher Stowe, published a book, *Uncle Tom's Cabin*, that eclipsed all the efforts of her better-known contemporaries as anti-slavery propaganda.

Mrs. Stowe, a sister of the abolitionist preacher Henry Ward Beecher, had never lived in the South, although she had made short visits across the Ohio River from her early home in Cincinnati. She knew nothing of the life she described, except by hearsay, and her book was unfair to the South, in that it did not present a balanced picture of plantation life, but described sentimentally and harrowingly extreme cases of slave suffering as if they were typical.

But *Uncle Tom's Cabin* appeared "at the moment of Fate," and its success was immediate and sensational. In its first three years it sold 300,000 copies and the total of sales by 1860 was 1,000,000—besides which it was dramatized for the stage and translated into more than twenty foreign languages.

Nothing had ever aroused emotion in America as *Uncle Tom's Cabin* did. It created fury in the North not only against slavery, but against the South itself and the Southern people. So moderate a judge as Abraham Lincoln considered it a contributing cause of the Civil War. When, during that conflict, Mrs. Stowe was introduced to him in the White House, he said, "Is this the little woman who made this big war?"

2

This growing storm of bitterness both the Whig and Democratic parties tried their best to ignore, hoping, perhaps, that it would quiet down. In the Presidential election of 1852 the Democratic nominee, General Franklin Pierce, a pleasant-enough New Hampshire gentleman who had no outspoken opinions on any controversial subject, won over the Whig, General Winfield Scott, who had no strong opinions either, and was pompous and egotistical to boot.

Ignoring the growing bitterness, however, would not soothe it, and an ambitious politician, by driving a controversial law through Congress, brought matters to an even more critical stage.

Stephen A. Douglas of Illinois had gone forward while Lincoln dropped out of the political picture, and had come to be the acknowledged leader of the Northern Democrats. With his huge head on his short, stalwart body, he was a spectacular figure as he shook back his black mane and roared in the Senate or to an audience in a hall.

In 1854 Douglas, building on precedent, devised a plan for giving territorial status to all the remaining unorganized area within the bor-

ders of the United States—roughly, that portion of the continent between the Missouri River and the Continental Divide.

The day of the keelboat, the barge, and the raft had reached its
zenith and was passing. River steamboats of magnificent appointments
had become the spectacular feature of the rivers, although keelboat
cargoes still floated down the Ohio and the Mississippi with their
tough boatmen, to Homeric carousals in Natchez or New Orleans. Instead of jeans and buckskin, the new race of river men wore brass but-
tons and gold braid, and the setting pole and sweep had been replaced in the new era of steam by the mighty splash of paddle wheels
and the sound and smoke of machinery.

In what had once been the frontier east of the Mississippi the forests at last had been conquered, and the land now was covered with
tilled fields, turnpikes, telegraph lines between the larger cities—and
railroads.

The impact of the railroads is difficult to overestimate. It should be
remembered that the first engine to draw a train in the United States,
named the "Best Friend of Charleston," went into service in the fall
of 1830 on a rail "system" of about 23 miles of track—increased to 136
in two years. Ten years later, in 1840, there were 2808 miles; by 1850,
9031 miles; and in the next decade, by 1860, the total rail mileage in
the country had increased to 30,635.

The early railroad builders faced severe problems. One difficulty
was the question of the gauge, which varied according to the railroad's
ideas as to the best practical distance between rails. For example, the
Mohawk Hudson's gauge was 4 feet 9 inches, the Camden & Am-
boy's was 4 feet 10 inches, the Charleston & Hamburg 4 feet, the Baltimore & Ohio 4 feet 8½ inches. It was impossible to switch cars or
trains from one of these systems to another, and it took years before
the Baltimore & Ohio's gauge was accepted as "standard," both in this
country and Great Britain.

Locomotives, at first inefficient and weak, had to be improved. Engineering problems of grades, excavation of cuts, bridging of watercourses, and other necessary construction all had to be surmounted
without power machinery and chiefly by hand labor. The invention
of the "T-rail" to replace the old "strap-rail" was a mighty step forward.

Most of the railroad construction was north of the Ohio River, because capital and credit were available there for the work; whereas in
the South money was largely tied up in land and slaves. This was to
prove a decisive factor during the Civil War.

The railroads generally drove turnpike companies out of business,
and canals, though longer lasting, since once built they could compete
with railroads in cost though not in speed of transportation, began slip-

ping behind. But though this revolution in transportation produced an economic shock in some quarters, that was soon overcome as it was perceived that the railroads were producing growth and prosperity.

By 1850 men were looking for new territories to be tapped by the rails. It was inevitable that with the growth of population in California and Oregon Territory, the project of a transcontinental railroad began to be much discussed, in Congress, in the newspapers, and elsewhere.

Now it happened that Douglas had financial interests both in Western lands, and in railroads. He soon realized that unless some form of territorial government was established for what was then called the Nebraska country, the railroad linking the East with the West quite probably would be built along a southern route, through Texas and the New Mexico Territory, which was at that time strongly advocated by such men as Jefferson Davis of Mississippi and Sam Houston of Texas.

Yet in all fairness, Douglas was not animated by personal interests alone. The idea of giving the territory a stable government was constructive, even necessary.

Douglas, a past master at politics, knew he must gain support from the Southern Senators if his plan was to succeed. He had another thing in view: he much desired to unite the Democratic party, which had shown signs of division lately on the slavery issue, and he believed that by giving them common cause he could weld the disparate factions of his party together. In this, of course, there may have been something of personal interest, for Douglas nursed a hope for the Presidency.

As chairman of the powerful Committee on Territories, he used his position to advantage and after bargaining with the Southern members his committee concocted a bill known as the Nebraska Bill, which would confer upon that vast area territorial status, with the provision that the question of slavery should be decided by the citizens within its borders on the principle of popular sovereignty, soon to be known as "Squatter Sovereignty." By a rewriting of the bill before it went to a vote, the huge territory was carved into two portions. The southern part, approximately following the lines of Kansas today, except that it then reached to the mountains in present Colorado, was named the Kansas Territory, while all the rest of the vast area, extending north clear to the Canadian border, was named the Nebraska Territory.

Since both parts of this new territory were north of the Missouri Compromise line barring slavery north of 36°30', Douglas' proposal was an *implicit* repudiation of that agreement. But to many Southern leaders even this was not enough. They had for thirty years considered the historic compromise an affront to the South. So at the representation of Senator Archibald Dixon of Kentucky, and after some soul-searching, Douglas agreed to a provision *explicitly* repealing that law.

He later explained that he had acted in good faith in so doing. The Missouri Compromise line already had been abrogated, he held, by the admission of California as a free state and the organization of the intervening territories on a basis of popular sovereignty. He saw no reason why the Kansas-Nebraska Territory, part of which lay farther south than the northern parts of the state and territories already admitted, should not be treated in the same manner. Besides, he pointed out, slavery in the areas involved was an academic question only, since the physical and economic factors were such that he considered it impossible for slavery to exist in one single mile of that territory.

Academic question or no, when the Kansas-Nebraska Act, with the Missouri Compromise repeal, was passed by an almost solid Democratic vote over strenuous opposition (from a strange coalition that included Whigs, anti-slavery men, and Sam Houston) Douglas expected that it would create "a hell of a storm." Of the extent of that storm, its true hellishness, and its final repercussions he did not dream.

Like a thunderbolt the Kansas-Nebraska Act struck in the North. The repeal of the Missouri Compromise opened to slavery, at least in theory, the whole of the national domain—and this included the entire Northwest not yet organized into states or even territories. A typhoon of rage was unleashed in the North. Horace Greeley, in his New York *Tribune*, stated that the Kansas-Nebraska law would create more abolitionists in three months than Garrison and Phillips and the other orators could make in fifty years.

In the South, it should be pointed out, there was little excitement about it, pro or con. Most Southern Congressmen had supported the bill in principle, but few men in or out of politics believed it would be of any real value to the institution of slavery, for the very reason that Douglas had pointed out. As Webster had phrased it, "Why re-enact the will of God?" The new areas definitely were unfitted for slave labor.

A fight was to be made for at least the Kansas Territory, however; and that fight would originate in New England, to be taken up by Missouri and the South, and have effects most baleful upon the peace of the whole nation.

3

Smarting under the bitter attack upon him in the North, Douglas went to his own state, Illinois, to defend himself. He was hooted out of a meeting in Chicago, but even threats against his life could not intimidate him. He began a determined speechmaking swing through the state, and when he reached Springfield he was challenged by an old adversary, Abraham Lincoln.

The years since Lincoln returned to his home, believing his political career was ended, had been unhappy ones. His home life was not easy. His wife Mary had such a temper that Lincoln and his oldest son sometimes ate a lunch of a slice of bologna and bread in his office in preference to home. Lincoln was also deeply disappointed in the apparent end of his political hopes. He had always been subject to periods of profound despondence, but now his gloom became constant. At times he sat silent and withdrawn, with the saddest of all possible expressions on his face, lost in thought. Yet perhaps those years were responsible for the enormous patience, understanding, and endurance of Lincoln's later years.

He devoted himself to his law practice. His legal adversaries complained that he knew by his first name every man eligible for jury duty in the entire judicial district, and it was almost impossible to win a case against him. But his acquaintanceship with men was not the major reason why Lincoln was victorious in so many of his lawsuits. His knowledge of law was supported by his long periods of meditation and he had developed an unsurpassed instinct for the just and adequate word.

When Douglas appeared in Springfield, Lincoln shook off his melancholia and confronted him. Douglas knew him of old, perhaps discounted him somewhat. Now he met a different Lincoln, a Lincoln no longer a party hack, a Lincoln who had climbed slowly and with pain to mental and spiritual maturity.

At Springfield, on October 3, 1854, Douglas spoke to a packed crowd, a fine and eloquent effort that drew applause and won back many who had deserted him over the Missouri Compromise issue. At the end of the meeting, as the crowd broke up, Lincoln stood on the stairs and announced that on the following day he would speak in answer to Douglas.

When he did so the hall was jammed again, and Douglas sat in a front seat, for Lincoln had invited him to be present. The Little Giant must have wondered and been disturbed as he listened to that speech, for it was the first truly great speech Lincoln ever made.[1]

The tall, gaunt lawyer was not now speaking for himself, or for political advancement, or even for his own city or state. He was speaking for a great principle, a national principle; and in that speech, free

---

[1] Though first delivered at Springfield, it was not fully published until he delivered it again, ten days later, at Peoria. In the Lincoln *Works* it is entitled The Peoria Speech.

from the kind of vituperation common in political speeches of the period and subject, he displayed the breadth and fairness of attitude, the basic approach to the crisis of the American nation which in varied forms were to be expressed over and over by him until the very day he wrote the Emancipation Proclamation.

He refused to admit that the Kansas-Nebraska Act was a "plot of the slave power"; yet he upheld the Missouri Compromise, traced its adoption and the reasons therefor, and called for its restoration.

He did not castigate the South for slavery, and he acknowledged the consititutional right of Southerners to own slaves; furthermore he believed they should be protected by a law which enabled them to recover fugitives, provided it "should not in its stringency be more likely to carry a free man into slavery than our ordinary criminal laws are to hang an innocent one."

On the other hand he expressed his unyielding hatred of slavery "because of the monstrous injustice of slavery itself . . . because it deprives our republican example of its just influence in the world . . . causes the real friends of freedom to doubt our sincerity and especially because it forces so many really good men amongst ourselves into an open war with the very fundamental principle of civil liberty."

He acknowledged, however, the problem of dealing with the institution. "If all earthly power were given to me," he declared, "I would not know what to do . . . My first impulse would be to free all the slaves and send them to Liberia, to their native land." Yet he conceded the impracticability of that idea, and instead urged gradual emancipation as a solution.

It was in attacking the position of Douglas on the principle of popular sovereignty that he struck his shrewdest blows. He had closely analyzed that principle. It sounded fine enough, but at what point could a people decide on the momentous question of whether they would have slavery or not? When they reached a thousand in numbers? Or ten thousand? Or thirty thousand? When they became a state?

None of these stages would suffice, for not only the territory was involved, but the *whole nation* was concerned in the decision. No mere handful of settlers on a frontier should be given the power to determine a question so momentous for millions. Furthermore the Douglas contention that slavery could not exist in the territories under discussion was a fallacy. Other slave states—Delaware, Maryland, Virginia, Kentucky, and Missouri—existed north of the Missouri Compromise line. Why would not slavery flourish in the new territories?

He closed with a burst of eloquence in which he urged all lovers of liberty, North and South, to join in regarding slavery not as "a sacred right" but as a national problem, and to "join together in the great and good work . . . so that we shall not only have saved the Union, but we shall have so saved it . . . that succeeding millions of free, happy people, the world over, shall rise up and call us blessed to the latest generations."

Tumultous applause greeted the speech. Douglas rose at Lincoln's conclusion, and in answer spoke for an hour and a half; but it was generally agreed that he had been badly worsted.

There were to be other speeches by both Douglas and Lincoln in this era of preliminary combat, but the great formal debates which would be heard later and which would crystallize national thinking had on this day found their respective champions.

At the end of Douglas' tour the clash of oratory ended—for the time being—and the Senator returned to Washington, while Lincoln went back to his law practice. He had acquired a new type of business—as a railroad attorney. From the beginning he had been interested in the progress of the railroads, and like George Washington before him—that great advocate of a system of canals—he believed that the best way to unite the nation was by good transportation and communications.[2]

While he was in the legislature he worked on bills to aid the building of new lines of rails. Now he acted as a lobbyist for the Illinois Central, and handled legal cases for the Ohio & Mississippi, Rock Island, Tonica & Petersburg, and Chicago & Alton railroads.

One case of importance was over damages to a steamboat, the *Effie Afton*, which collided with a pier of a railroad bridge over the Mississippi built by the Rock Island, and sank with its cargo. The suit presented a showdown between the era of steamboats and the new age of railroads, and Lincoln's conduct of the case was so well prepared and presented that the jury disagreed, in effect a great victory

[2] Lincoln's interest in railroads, developed in this era, had much to do with the later construction of the Union Pacific-Central Pacific line across the continent. On a speaking tour in 1859 he dined in Council Bluffs, Iowa, with a young engineer named Grenville M. Dodge, who was imbued with the dream of a railroad across the nation and had made surveys along the Platte River valley. All plans for such a line were suspended when the Civil War broke out, but even during his vast labors of conducting that war, Lincoln urged a program for building the transcontinental line. Congress worked out a plan for giving public land and loans to such a railroad, and even when his armies were reeling before the Confederate forces under General Robert E. Lee, Lincoln signed the act, July 2, 1862. By that time Dodge was a brigadier general in the Union Army. Lincoln sent for him, and between them they fixed the starting point for the new railroad at the little hamlet of Omaha, in the Nebraska Territory, across the Missouri River from Council Bluffs. When the Union Pacific started construction westward July 10, 1865, General Dodge already had been chosen as its chief engineer, and as soon as he was released from service progress on the epic construction feat became rapid and so continued, to its successful conclusion.

for his client the railroad, since the steamship company failed to collect any damages. The case had an enormous influence in establishing the legal position of the railroads, and thus changing the course of commerce in the nation.

In a patent suit by Cyrus H. McCormick against John H. Manny for alleged infringement of patents, Lincoln was associated with Edwin M. Stanton, a massive, domineering lawyer from Pittsburgh, with a huge head, and sweeping locks and beard. Stanton snubbed the "country lawyer," but Lincoln, cool and unruffled, studied him and approved of his hard-driving qualities. Later he was to choose Stanton for a place in his cabinet as Secretary of War.

4

Manifest Destiny—gone wild—began to occupy national attention. There were those who believed that destiny meant occupation of both American continents from Alaska to Tierra del Fuego. And there were Southern leaders who were eager to obtain additional slaveholding territory, in order to retain a balance of power with the North.

The day of filibustering was ushered in. That word "filibuster" is derived through English corruption from the Dutch *vrijbuiter* (freebooter) and at first was applied to the buccaneers of the Caribbean. Later, however, it came to be the name for irregular adventurers, who for loot or land, or sometimes because of mistaken patriotism, or even with a romantic desire to aid a people in overthrowing tyranny, invaded Latin American countries, and sometimes set up brief governments, which never lasted long.

Cuba was wanted by the South. Rich and lush, with an enormous population of Negro slaves, Cuba was feebly held by a weak and corrupt Spanish government. Even Northern leaders, in the earlier years, looked with acquisitive eyes on the "Pearl of the Antilles." John Quincy Adams, in 1832, expressed the opinion that possession of the island—key to the Caribbean—probably was indispensable for the safety of the Union; and Daniel Webster, in 1843, warned against permitting a really strong power to occupy the island, implying that if such occurred intervention might be necessary.

James Knox Polk had once offered Spain $100,000,000 for the island —more than for all the present American Southwest, including California—and was refused. With the election of Pierce, the gaining of possession of Cuba became part of the government policy.

But by this time the temper of the people had changed. With the growing feeling against slavery in the North, Pierce and William L.

Marcy, his Secretary of State, knew there would be strong opposition to anything done officially by the government toward acquiring Cuba, because this island inevitably would become a slave state. Nevertheless the administration continued to consider the problem and seek some solution to it.

In the South excitement was stimulated by the actions of General Narciso López, a Spanish-American soldier of fortune. Born in Venezuela, López served in the Spanish army against his countrymen in their war for liberation. When Spain lost that war, and Venezuela won her freedom, he found that his presence was no longer desired in his native land, and took up residence in Cuba. Still a soldier, when the Carlist rebellion erupted in Spain, López went there and served with such distinction in putting down the Carlists that he was made a field marshal, a senator in the Cortes, and given a lucrative appointment as governor of the Trinidad district in Cuba. That position he lost at a change of colonial administration in 1843; whereupon he devoted himself to schemes for the "liberation" of Cuba.

Without question López was brave, and without question he was charming and plausible. When forced to flee from Cuba to the United States, he made an enormous impression on some Southern leaders, notably General John Anthony Quitman, a hero of the War with Mexico, and in 1850 governor of Mississippi. With money which Quitman helped to raise, López made two filibustering attempts against Cuba, in the second of which he landed a force, for a time seemed to gain adherents, but in the end was defeated, captured, and executed.

For the time being the Cuban scheme lay idle, but other filibustering escapades drew attention. California was filled with adventurers, and therefore was a breeding spot for irresponsible activities.

As early as 1850 an oddly assorted group had set out from San Francisco to take Ecuador, and actually conquered and occupied Guayaquil for a few days.

Efforts of a group of Frenchmen, also starting from San Francisco, to colonize northern Mexico, were closely watched by a slight sandy-haired man, with heavy-lidded gray eyes so arresting that they indicated some latent force within him. He was William Walker, sometime physician, sometime lawyer, sometime journalist, eternally an ascetic, and forever dominated by a longing for fame. But for those eyes—which were to win him the sobriquet "The Gray-eyed Man of Destiny"—nobody would have dreamed that the youngish-looking man, who stood only five feet, five inches tall, and weighed less than 120 pounds, would become the greatest of all filibusters.

Walker was born in Nashville in 1824, when the fame of Andrew Jackson filled the city; and he carried an image of heroism before him throughout his life. After studying medicine and law, and writing editorials for a New Orleans newspaper, he traveled to California in 1850 as a journalist.

Walker had magnetism. From rich San Franciscans who were willing to gamble he obtained money, and he enlisted forty-five adventurers with whom he slipped out of San Francisco Bay on a ship, October 8, 1853.

La Paz, at the southern tip of the peninsula of Lower California, was his first landing place. But he found the town and country singularly lacking in anything that would suitably reward a conscientious filibuster, and sailed back up the coast to Ensenada. There he won a brief little battle with a Mexican force, and proclaimed "The Republic of Lower California" with himself as president "until the country shall be firmly established."

But establishment was far from firm. Walker ran out of food, some of his followers sullenly deserted him, and he marched most of the rest as far as the mouth of the Colorado River. Obtaining no help from the Sonorans, he dejectedly took what was left of his force back to California, where he was indicted, but not convicted, of violating the neutrality laws. He would be heard from again.

Walker did not know it, much less plan it, but his abortive expedition had one important effect. News of it reached Mexico City while James Gadsden, the American minister to Mexico, was trying to buy for the United States various portions of Mexican territory including what later was known as the Gadsden Purchase. The Mexicans needed American dollars, but nevertheless bargained.

Suddenly word came that William Walker, with a force of fearsome *Americanos*, had captured Ensenada and were marching toward the very area under discussion. Bargaining was considerably hastened, and a provisional treaty was signed December 31, 1853. For $10,000,000 the United States added 45,000 square miles to its territory—including what was then regarded as the most practicable railroad route to the Pacific Coast.

5

In the midst of all this, hardly noticed because of events nearer home, something worthy of great attention took place in the far Pacific Ocean. Japan at that time was a hermit nation, closed against the rest of the world. Her rulers rejected foreign trade attempts because they did not wish the traditions and static social conditions of their people changed in their islands.

By 1844 the United States had made a commercial treaty with China, one was made with Hawaii in 1849, and one with Borneo in 1850. But Japan remained obdurate.

In 1852 Commodore Matthew C. Perry was dispatched to secure a treaty with that country. He arrived in July 1853, and declined to leave the Bay of Yeddo until a letter he bore from President Fillmore was delivered to the Shogun, then the military and civil ruler of Japan. Japanese officials came aboard the vessels of Perry's little fleet, and carefully examined the big naval guns. Then they agreed to take the letter to the Shogun.

To give the government time to reflect upon the President's friendly proposals for mutual trade between the nations, Perry sailed for China. He returned in March, by which time the Shogun was ready with an affirmative answer. On March 31 a treaty was signed by which American vessels were permitted to enter certain Japanese ports for trade.

It seemed to most Americans at the time a minor matter. Japan was an island empire with quaint people, and there was some value in trading with them, but that was all. In actuality the adventure was epoch-making. Few events have had a more important effect not only on American history but that of the world, than this forced awakening of Japan from her slumber, thrusting her, against her will, into the main currents of the Western world.

6

Thus far filibustering had conspicuously failed of success. President Pierce issued a proclamation, January 18, 1854, against illegal expeditions against Mexico, with severe penalties attached.

But now an "incident" suddenly focused attention again on Cuba. The American steamship *Black Warrior*, on a routine voyage from New York to Mobile, stopped at Havana on February 28, 1854, and was seized by Spanish authorities. They were perhaps suspicious that the ship carried arms for revolutionaries—which it did not—but the action was considered by Americans highhanded and contrary to international port usages.

Jefferson Davis, then Secretary of War, demanded that action be taken against Spain, even at the price of hostilities. President Pierce consulted with his Secretary of State, and Marcy, while cool-headedly holding back from the naked use of force, suggested that the opportunity seemed excellent for purchasing Cuba from Spain. Spain's two most potent allies, Britain and France, were at the time involved in the Crimean crisis which soon became a war, and Spain was left alone. Marcy instructed Pierre Soulé of Louisiana, the minister to Spain, to demand $300,000 indemnity for the *Black Warrior* episode.

Soulé, French-born but an American citizen, was full of medieval notions of honor. Instead of using diplomatic language, the fire-eating Southerner delivered his note as an ultimatum, giving Spain forty-eight hours to comply.[3] Spain, of course, rejected the ultimatum and sent troops to reinforce her Havana garrison.

Many American newspapers, even in the North, by this time were demanding hot action in Cuba, including suspension of the neutrality laws and invasion. Then, unexpectedly, the Spanish authorities released the *Black Warrior* and tendered a formal apology.

That knocked the oratorical wind out of the clamorers for war. But Pierce and Marcy still wanted Cuba. Soulé was instructed to consult with James Buchanan, then minister to England, and John Y. Mason, minister to France, with regard to the Cuban question.

There ensued one of the most hare-brained acts in the history of American diplomacy. The three coadjutors met at Ostend, Belgium, wherefore what followed has been called the "Ostend Manifesto," in spite of the fact that the actual deliberations took place at Aix-la-Chapelle. From that session of so-called "diplomats," on October 18, 1854, came a report, supposed to be secret but far from that. The Ostend Manifesto recommended offering to Spain $120,000,000 for Cuba; and if that nation, "actuated by stubborn pride and a false sense of honor," should refuse to sell, "by every law human and divine, we shall be justified in wresting it from Spain . . . Under such circumstances we ought neither to count the cost, nor regard the odds which Spain might enlist against us . . ."

Almost at once the general tenor of the Manifesto became known. Spain was righteously indignant. English and French newspapers denounced it. Marcy finally was forced to send the document to Congress, where it created a ferocious tumult and newspapers joined in the fury directed at it.

Marcy, who detested Soulé, regarded Mason as "a pompous windbag," and had little respect for Buchanan, refused to accept any provision of the Manifesto. Yet in actuality it was in part his and Pierce's fault that it was ever drawn up. All three envoys knew that the administration's policy was to get Cuba if possible, and the instructions

---

[3] As a diplomat Soulé was a disaster. He challenged the French ambassador to a duel and seriously wounded him, offered other challenges, and bitterly antagonized Calderón de la Barca, the Spanish foreign minister, with whom he was supposed to do business.

given them were capable of the widest interpretations. The affair had the unfortunate effect of increasing suspicions of the European powers with regard to every motive of the United States.

7

The major parties had been divided by the Kansas-Nebraska Act, but they still dominated the American political scene. Smaller parties had challenged them and failed, including the anti-Masonic party, the Liberty party, and the Free-Soil party. But now a small cloud appeared on the horizon, hardly noticed at first and belittled later, that would grow into a storm which would sweep the Whigs out of existence and for a time submerge even the Democrats.

There was, particularly in the North, a rising tide of resentment and prejudice against immigrants who came to America, gathered in slums and voted in blocs according to what their political bosses told them to do. The Irish in particular congregating in the cities showed a talent for political regimentation. Bossism inevitably leads to corruption, and though civic corruption by no means was confined to wards dominated by voters of foreign birth, a small splinter party, calling itself the American Republican party, was launched in 1843, held a national convention in 1845, and called for reforms in the naturalization laws, including a twenty-year waiting period before citizenship could be conferred.

The party disappeared during the Mexican crisis, but shortly after reappeared in a new form, when a secret society known as the Order of the Star-Spangled Banner was organized in New York in 1849. Its expansion was rapid and by 1854 it became a political party, officially called the American party, but popularly known as the "Know-Nothings." The nickname was given it because members who were sworn into it, promised never to reveal any of its mysteries, their universal answer to all inquiries being, "I know nothing about it."

The party was against foreigners, against Jews, against Catholics, and against Negroes. It was, in fact, very similar in its foundation of prejudices to the Ku Klux Klan—not that of the South immediately after the Civil War, but that of the 1920s, particularly in the Middle West. The Know-Nothings gained such strength that in 1854 they polled a fourth of the total vote in New York, two-fifths of that in Pennsylvania, and two-thirds of that in Massachusetts, electing in the last-named state the governor and the entire legislature. Racial and religious tensions created by the Know-Nothings caused riots.

Many sincere men believed that Roman Catholicism was a threat to the nation. To illustrate, as conservative and moderate a man as George Templeton Strong, who was a Whig (at that time), wrote in his diary, September 6, 1854:

> Another Catholic *vs.* Protestant row at Newark—Irish church gutted; those infatuated, pig-headed Celts seemingly the aggressors, as usual. We may well have a memorable row here before the fall elections are over, and perhaps a religious war within the next decade, if this new element of Know-Nothingism is as potent as its friends and political wooers seem to think it. I'm sick of Celtism; it's nothing but imbecility, brag, and bad rhetoric. If the Know-Nothings were only political, not politico-religious, I'd join them.

He did not join; and the Know-Nothings, like all similar extremist groups, before and after, eventually succumbed to its own inborn destructive forces.

But all this was unimportant compared to a far more modest event, which occurred at Ripon, Wisconsin, February 28, 1854. On that day a group of men, mostly abolitionists but including also others who were opposed to the Kansas-Nebraska Act, formed what they informally called the Republican party. The following July 6 the new party had grown so that it held a convention at Jackson, Michigan, at which the name was formally adopted.

The Republican party became a catch-all for every discontented segment of citizens. It drew into its ranks Free-Soilers, anti-slavery Democrats, Know-Nothings, abolitionists, and the great proportion of the leading Whigs. Its growth was phenomenal. By 1856 it would nominate a President and make a strong race with him; by 1860 it would elect a President. It would thereafter have a continuous, sometimes a dominating, voice in the history of the nation.

CHAPTER TWENTY-THREE

Vendetta

1

Tʜᴇ growing strife over the slavery problem would not die down; and in May 1856 a sensational episode occurred in the chamber of the United States Senate that aroused nation-wide excitement and further widened the breach between the North and the South.

Senator Charles Sumner of Massachusetts was a large handsome man, with a considerable store of learning, a commanding voice, and a cultivated mastery of rhetoric. A fiery anti-slavery leader, he was also a supreme egotist, intolerant of the opinions of anyone else, with a cold superior manner. Such were his qualities that conservative Senators soon treated him as "a fanatic unfit to associate with them." He was denied committee appointments and otherwise treated in a way that wounded his overweening egotism.

That May he prepared an address entitled *The Crime Against Kansas*, which was remarkable for the stinging and offensive language that filled it. This he had printed, in advance of its delivery in the Senate, so that copies might be sent to distant cities for publication. As uncompromising a critic of the proponents of the Missouri Compromise repeal as William H. Seward advised Sumner to tone down the objectionable parts of the speech when it was given to him to read.

Sumner rejected the advice and delivered the speech just as he had written it, occupying two days in the Senate, May 19 and 20. It was a speech that was pompous, a speech filled with extravagances and exaggerations, a speech that added nothing new to arguments already adduced, above all a speech lacking in good taste and reeking with emotional spite.

Of Stephen A. Douglas, for example, he said, "The noisome, squat and nameless animal, to which I now refer, is not a proper model for an American Senator. Will the Senator from Illinois take notice?"

Douglas, perhaps a little sensitive because of his short figure, replied with a mild sarcasm. At this Sumner cried, "Again the Senator has switched his tongue, and again he fills the Senate with its offensive odor!"

In particular he assailed Senator Andrew Pickens Butler of South Carolina, a courteous, white-haired gentleman, who was not even in the Senate chamber at the time, in the following language:

"He has chosen a mistress to whom he has made his vows, and who, though ugly to others, is always lovely to him; though polluted in the sight of the world, is chaste in his sight—I mean the harlot, Slavery."

To many, because of charges of miscegenation made by abolitionists[1] against Southerners, there was in this allusion an indelicate *double entendre*, the more offensive in view of Senator Butler's blameless personal life.

In particular the reference infuriated the Senator's nephew and friend, a handsome young South Carolinian, then a Representative in Congress, Preston S. Brooks. Sumner's speech had been the subject of reproofs on the Senate floor, by Lewis Cass, and by Douglas, who, while not defending himself from Sumner's aspersions, gravely condemned Sumner's attacks on Butler, "the venerable, the courteous, the distinguished Senator from South Carolina."

But the hotheaded Brooks was not content with verbal reproofs. He decided to take physical action against the contemner of his uncle.

On May 22, the day after Sumner completed his speech, the Senate adjourned early. Sumner, however, remained at his desk, writing. Suddenly he glanced up and saw a tall man standing over him. It was Brooks.

"I have read your speech twice over," said Brooks. "It is a libel on South Carolina, and on Mr. Butler, who is a friend of mine."

With those words he began to rain blows on Sumner's head with a gutta-percha cane. The Senator tried to rise, tore his desk from the floor by an effort of strength, and collapsed under the repeated blows.

Others in the chamber pulled Brooks away, though some who witnessed the assault openly approved it. The cane used was hollow and tapering, and broke after the fifth or sixth blow; but by that time Sumner's head was cut and bleeding. So seriously injured was he that he was incapacitated for two or three years. Though he did not during that time occupy his seat in the Senate, his Massachusetts constituency loyally sent him back until he could resume it. Years later Sumner suffered a nervous condition that caused such men as Hamilton Fish, Richard H. Dana, and Ulysses S. Grant to think him partly

---

[1] The charges were unhappily true in some cases. Mrs. Mary Chesnut, wife of Senator James Chesnut of South Carolina, wrote in her diary just before the Civil War: ". . . God forgive us, but ours is a monstrous system, a wrong and an iniquity! Like the patriarchs of old, our men live all in one house with their wives and their concubines; and the mulattoes one sees in every family resemble the white children. Any lady is ready to tell you who is the father of all the mulatto children in everybody's household but their own . . ." See Manly Wade Wellman, *They Took Their Stand.*

insane. Whether this was in any respect due to the beating he received can never be ascertained.

The attack on Sumner made him a hero and martyr in the North, even to persons who did not care for abolitionists. Witness another entry of George Templeton Strong of New York, in his diary that May 22:

> News tonight that Charles Sumner of the Senate has been licked by a loaded cane by a certain honorable Carolinian Brooks for his recent rather sophomorical anti-slavery speech. I hold the anti-slavery agitators wrong in principle and mischievous in policy. But the reckless, insolent brutality of our Southern aristocrats may drive me into abolitionism yet.

Had it not been for the Brooks assault Sumner probably would have been criticized the country over for his speech. As it was, the incident created general excitement. Many Southerners upheld the right of Brooks to cane the man who insulted his uncle, while in the North the act was almost universally condemned.

The mounting fever of excitement was quickly stirred to an even higher pitch by something that was taking place far to the west.

2

At almost the same time that Sumner was receiving his beating in the Senate chamber, something more grim and fearsome than oratorical debates or even canings was transpiring in the distant Kansas Territory.

On May 21—the day Sumner finished his speech and the day before Brooks assailed him—a mob calling itself a "posse" entered the town of Lawrence, burned down two structures, and did considerable other damage before it retired. The mob was made up of pro-slavery men, mostly from Missouri; and the town they attacked was the chief citadel of the anti-slavery forces in the territory. It was the first act in what has been called the Kansas-Missouri Border War.[2]

The Border War was fought over no question of nullification or secession. Frankly and bitterly it was predicated on the question of Negro slavery, and in the tense emotional atmosphere of the period

---

[2] The story of the attack upon Sumner, which occurred May 22, was published by New York newspapers the morning of May 23. The "Sack of Lawrence," which took place May 21, because of slowness of communications was first noted in bulletins in the Eastern press, May 24, with fuller details by May 26. Thus the two events had almost simultaneous impacts on the public.

it was a logical consequence of Douglas' "squatter sovereignty" doctrine.

Even before the final passage of the Kansas-Nebraska Act, Eli Thayer, an abolitionist of Worcester, Massachusetts, with others of like mind, had organized the New England Emigrant Aid Society. Significantly, perhaps, the society had a dual purpose. The first was to fill the Kansas territory with anti-slavery settlers. The second was not so idealistic: to make a neat profit for the stockholders of the society, in land taken up near good settlements, in implements and machinery rented to the settlers, and perhaps later, in arms furnished them.

The capitalization of the society was announced at $5,000,000. Though canny New England investors subscribed perhaps only as much as $50,000 to it, word of the large announced capitalization, and also of formation of similar societies elsewhere in the East, alarmed the South, and particularly Missouri. To the Southerners it appeared that the much-detested abolitionists, not content to allow settlement of the new area to take its natural course, were going to force, on any terms, free-state colonization of the territory.

In actual fact the various emigrant aid societies had comparatively little to do with the major tide of settlement in Kansas. A few thousand zealots did make their way west under auspices of the societies, singing a hymn written especially for them by Whittier, and ill-calculated to appease hostility in Southern hearts:

> We cross the prairie as of old
>   The Pilgrims crossed the sea,
> To make the West, as they the East,
>   The homestead of the Free!
>
> We go to rear a wall of men
>   On Freedom's southern line,
> And plant beside the cotton-tree
>   The rugged northern pine!

As it happened, the first settlers in Kansas had been primarily Southerners in sympathy. They entered as soon as the territory was opened, not to establish slavery, but to get land. In the end, however, the greatest proportion of migrants to Kansas came from Western states like Iowa, Illinois, and Indiana. Though they were in general opposed to slavery, the prime purpose of these people also was to gain homesteads for themselves and their families. It has been said that, left to themselves, the settlers most likely would have created a free state, with some Southern leanings and no particular animosities. But they were not to be left to themselves.

On both sides of the border turbulent men thrust themselves into

leadership. Kansas had gaunt, ferocious Jim Lane, with his half-mani-
acal lust for power, who ended his life by suicide shortly after the
Civil War rather than face charges of corrupt practices; John Brown,
cadaverous and fanatical, with a crazed streak of murder in him, who
died on the gallows for his treasonable Harper's Ferry raid in 1859 and
thereby became a "martyr" for the anti-slavery cause; and S. N. Wood,
a lawyer and a continual troublemaker to the end of his life, who was
a chief figure in the Stevens County War of 1888, during which he
himself was killed.

Missouri had fire-eating, wrong-headed David R. Atchison, a
former United States Senator and the great political foe of Thomas
Hart Benton, who had supported the Kansas-Nebraska Act and was
determined to make the territory slaveholding; Charles A. Hamelton,
a Georgia duelist, and later a colonel in the Confederate army, who
ordered the needless Marais de Cygnes massacre; and Sam J. Jones,
who had been postmaster at Westport, Missouri, managed to get
himself elected sheriff of Douglas County, Kansas—which contains
Lawrence—and was involved in most of the serious troubles that followed. There were others, of almost equal troublemaking propensities,
on both sides.

When news came of the activities of the emigrant aid societies,
Missourians held meetings and passed resolutions, one of which, in
Lafayette County, read in part:

> Societies were formed [and] money contributed . . . for the
> purpose of buying up, and sending to the territory of Kansas
> . . . a set of deluded, ignorant, and vicious tools of knavish
> abolitionists . . . Such as would be thus bought up . . . would
> be a wicked, debased and abandoned class, dragged forth from
> the dens of filth, misery and crime of the Northern cities.

Such resolutions were far off the mark. Making the trek to Kansas
were many men of education and high mental abilities, and the bulk
of the Northern settlers were farmers, hard-working and law-abiding. In like manner the term "Border Ruffians," soon applied to the
Missourians in the border difficulties, was unjust, for there were physicians, judges, legislators, even ministers and other men of culture and
intelligence among those who upheld the slavery cause on the border.

Of course there is always a shifty, indolent, and criminally inclined
element in every frontier society, and persons of this type existed on
both sides of the border. Some violence was inevitable; the rifle and
bowie knife were much in evidence in those days, while newspapers and extremists stirred up mutual animosity.

Contemporary accounts are so prejudiced that it is difficult to find the truth in them. The free-state people had the better publicity, for the great newspapers of the country were in the North; but the slavery advocates published their viewpoints also, and there is little to choose as to exaggeration and vituperation, between accounts in the North and the South.

The first overt act, however, assuredly came from Missouri when, on November 9, 1854, hundreds from that state crossed over the territorial border and voted illegally to elect a pro-slavery delegate, John W. Whitfield, as delegate to Congress. Ironically, Whitfield probably would have been elected without this invasion, for at that time pro-slavery settlers still were in the majority in Kansas.

Eastern papers proclaimed it "an act of hostility," pointing out that the Missouri "voters" left the territory at once for their true homes. Missourians countered by saying that after the election hundreds of free-state settlers also left Kansas, as evidence that they, too, had been in the territory merely to control the balloting.

Next came another election, March 30, 1855, to choose a territorial legislature. Once more Missourians crossed the border—an estimated five thousand this time—armed with guns and carrying flags, with fifes and drums playing a march to give a military aspect to the expedition. A pro-slavery legislature was elected, which chose Lecompton as the territorial capital, and declared slavery legal. This was the "Bogus Legislature" of Kansas history. It was not recognized by the free-soil voters, who elected a legislature of their own, named Topeka as the capital, declared slavery illegal, and elected Dr. Charles Robinson "governor."

Again telegraph wires hummed, presses clattered in the East, and orators spouted invectives. Lawrence, the chief stronghold of the anti-slavery people, converted the Free State hotel into a fortress, with thick walls of masonry, loopholes for guns, and embrasures for cannon. Rifles were shipped in quantity from the East, in boxes marked "Books," "Revised Statutes," "Hardware," even "Bibles."

It was at this time that Henry Ward Beecher preached his sensational and much-criticized sermon, in which he called on "friends of freedom" to supply the Kansas settlers with Sharps rifles. "One Sharps rifle will have more moral influence upon slaveholders than a hundred Bibles!" he shouted. And so was coined the term "Beecher's Bibles" for the newly perfected Sharps rifles which played a considerable role on the frontier.[3]

[3] The books of the Sharps Rifle Manufacturing Company for the years 1855 and 1856 show that 917 of its rifles, with requisite ammunition, were shipped into Kansas, chiefly on orders from the "New England Emigrant Aid Company," the "Massachusetts Kansas Committee," "Beecher and others," and "Thayer and others." Arms of other makes, of course, were also shipped West.

3

Sam J. Jones, the pro-slavery sheriff of Douglas County, now took the stage, in the first of a series of events which led to the "Sack of Lawrence." Jones, a determined if not very wise man, appeared in Lawrence, April 19, 1856, to arrest S. N. Wood on several warrants which he held. A mob of free-staters interfered, roughly handled Jones, knocked him down, and took away his prisoner.

Jones appealed for help and Colonel E. V. Sumner sent Lieutenant James McIntosh, 1st Cavalry, with ten men and a noncommissioned officer, "to aid the Sheriff in executing the laws."

Army officers during this period were having a most difficult time. They tried to preserve peace, but they only succeeded in drawing down upon their heads the wrath of both sides. Sumner, Colonel Philip St. George Cooke, and General William S. Harney were berated by free-soil sympathizers and their papers as "merciless," "harsh," and "arbitrary," as they tried to prevent disorder. All three were stanch upholders of the Union as they proved by their later service for the flag of the United States in the Civil War.

With the backing of Lieutenant McIntosh's detachment, Jones arrested six men for whom he had warrants—although Wood had by that time departed. That evening, as the sheriff stood in the tent of Lieutenant McIntosh talking to that officer, he was shot by an assassin who crept up under cover of darkness, and then escaped unidentified. The bullet passed through Jones' body just below the heart. The wound at first was thought fatal, but he made a quick and remarkable recovery.

He was in fact well enough to ride when, only a little more than a month later, a "posse" of pro-slavery men, led by J. B. Donaldson, the U.S. marshal, invaded Lawrence to carry out orders of a grand jury which had convened under Judge Samuel D. Lecompte, a furious pro-slavery advocate, but at that time chief federal judge of Kansas by legal appointment.

The grand jury had indicted Robinson, Wood, Lane, and several others for "constructive treason." "Governor" Robinson—the title was illegal because at the time Wilson Shannon was the duly authorized governor of the territory—was arrested and held in prison four months. Others were captured also, but Jim Lane and S. N. Wood managed to make their escapes.

The grand jury also decreed that two newspapers, the *Herald of Freedom* and the *Kansas Free State*, both published in Lawrence, be "abated as nuisances," and that the Free State hotel be destroyed because it had been built as a fortress.

There was no resistance when with about eight hundred men Donaldson and Jones entered Lawrence, May 21. The free-state men who possessed arms had been warned by their committee of safety to retreat from the town to give their enemies no pretext for violence.

The "posse" needed no pretext. It broke up the presses and scattered the type of the two proscribed newspapers; confiscated all weapons that could be found, including six cannon and a few small arms; destroyed the hotel, partly by artillery fire, partly by blasting with gunpowder, and finally by flames; and burned the house of Dr. Robinson to the ground.

The people in the town, largely women and children on that day, were thoroughly frightened, but not one of them was harmed. There was some looting, probably much exaggerated in newspaper accounts.[4] One member of the "posse" was killed and two injured, largely through their own carelessness, during the destruction of the hotel. The invaders thereafter retired to their homes, some in the territory and some in Missouri.

Whether or not indiscriminate looting occurred, the "Sack of Lawrence" was screamed to the high heavens by Northern newspapers and abolition orators. In the furore over Lawrence, the same papers and speakers seemed hardly to notice a far more terrible event that occurred almost immediately afterward.

4

Living in a log cabin near the nascent village of Osawatomie, was a man in his fifties, with a sunken-cheeked ravaged face, and, according to John Murray Forbes, a Yankee observer who sided with the Free-Soilers, "a little touch of insanity about his glittering gray-blue eyes." His name was John Brown. Both his mother and grandmother had died insane, and an aunt and three uncles on his maternal side also were lunatics. He himself had a sort of crazy cunning and cruelty, combined with a disordered fanaticism that sometimes became a maniacal bloodthirstiness.

John Brown's father was a wandering jack-of-all-trades, and Brown himself, disliking school, had small education. He tried his hand at many occupations without much success. He was sued in court more than once on various charges, including embezzlement. He disliked

---

[4] Dr. Albert Morrall, a South Carolinian who was present with the "posse," later denied that Lawrence was "sacked" in the sense that stores or houses were broken into and looted. He said that restaurants which contained food might have been entered by hungry Missourians, but except for the wrecking of the newspaper offices and the destruction of the hotel and the Robinson house, there was no general devastation of which he had any knowledge. Statement in Kansas Historical Collections, Vol. XIV.

any kind of work; in fact the only thing at which he was proficient was procreation—by two wives he had twenty children.

Brown had just enough schooling to read the Bible—chiefly the Old Testament's grimmer passages. One of his favorite quotations was "Without the shedding of blood there is no remission of sins." This, of course, in his interpretation, referred to the shedding of other persons' blood, not his own. He was to do more than his share in bringing on the Civil War.

Born in Connecticut he lived for years in Ohio, where he became a fanatical abolitionist. Typically, one of his early vague schemes for combating slavery was an effort to organize a Negro "League of Gideonites," with which he proposed to resist with arms the Fugitive Slave law.

He found the free Negroes of the North more interested in peace than war, however, so his scheme fell through. When five of his sons emigrated to Kansas in the summer of 1855 to take up claims, he followed them in a wagon which he loaded with arms, ammunition, and supplies. Among the arms carried were a number of artillery broadswords, such as cannoneers formerly used as protection against cavalry charges. These weapons were shorter than cavalry sabers, straight, and razor sharp on both edges of their blades. They once had been the property of a secret society called the Grand Eagles, and each blade had an eagle engraved upon it.

The night after the so-called "Sack of Lawrence," John Brown was one of a company called, too late, to its relief. His eldest son, John Brown, Jr., was captain of a band of mounted men who called themselves the Osawatomie Rifles. Such self-assumed military titles were plentiful on the border. There were dozens of "captains," "majors," and "colonels," and even some "generals," as for example "General" Jim Lane on the free-state side, and "General" David Atchison on the pro-slavery side. John Brown himself, rejoiced in the rank of "captain," conferred upon himself by himself.

The motives for Brown's next mad act are obscure. His advocates later said that he wished to wreak revenge for the Lawrence episode on the nearest pro-slavery people handy. But a more personal reason may have something to do with it.

Along Pottawatomie Creek was a handful of log cabins, near "Dutch Henry's Crossing" where a road led to a ford over the stream. "Dutch Henry," for whom the crossing was named, was a German named Henry Sherman, who had taken up his claim there as early as 1847. With him lived his brothers William and Peter, called respectively "Dutch Bill" and "Dutch Pete."

Next to Sherman's cabin, up the creek, was one belonging to Allen Wilkinson, a lawyer, who once had been prosecuting attorney *pro tem* for Franklin County. Above Wilkinson lived William P. Doyle, his wife Mahala, and their two young sons, William and Drury. All were Southern in sympathy, although not one of them owned a slave.

Some time prior to this somebody stole from Henry Sherman two horses and twenty-four cattle. He stated publicly that "Old" (John) Brown and his son Owen Brown had driven off the livestock. Later on he accused them in a sworn affidavit and tried to prosecute them for the theft, although no conviction was obtained.

It is very probable that part of John Brown's foray was to silence the tongue of his accuser, "Dutch Henry" Sherman.

Whatever his motives, on the night of May 24, three days after the "sack" of Lawrence, gaunt, half-crazed John Brown, groped his way through the woods along Pottawatomie Creek. With him crept four of his sons, Owen, Frederick, Salmon, and Oliver, and two other men, James Townsley and Theodore Wiener. All were heavily armed, not only with guns, but with the razor-sharp broadswords.

The first cabin they came upon in the darkness was Doyle's. A knock on the door, and Doyle himself appeared.

"Come out," was the order.

Doyle and his sons obeyed, leaving Mahala alone in the cabin. The man and his sons were led off into the woods and killed, the father shot through the head, the sons slashed to death by the broadswords. All three were fearfully mangled when their bodies were found next day.

On went the murderers to the cabin of Allen Wilkinson. His wife was sick in bed, but Wilkinson was summoned outside and hacked to death.

When they reached "Dutch Henry's" house, they were disappointed. "Dutch Henry" himself, against whom Brown had his bitterest grudge, was away from home with his brother Peter. But William Sherman— "Dutch Bill"—was there. The killers dragged him into the bushes. Next day he was found with his skull split open, a deep wound in his breast, and one hand cut off. Presumably he put up a fight before he died.

Next morning John Brown was back among his free-state neighbors in the Osawatomie neighborhood, all bloodstains washed away. But he was accused, together with his sons, by Mrs. Mahala Doyle and other persons. A warrant was issued for him, but he left the territory and lurked in Nebraska with Jim Lane who also was a fugitive at the time.[5]

[5] One of the strange things connected with this episode was the effort later made to exonerate Brown of any share in it. This came after he had been hanged at Harper's Ferry and was practically canonized by the Northern press as a "martyr" to the cause of freedom. It was not until James Townsley, a member of the murder gang, made a full statement giving all details of the Pottawatomie Massacre, and naming every person who participated in it, in 1878, that the old fanatic's guilt was fully established and accepted even by his apologists.

5

"WAR! WAR!" shouted the *Border Times* of Westport, Missouri, when news of the Pottawatomie Creek massacre became known. And war it was, but not war in the grand manner, with marching hosts and the thundering pageantry of great battles. Rather it was to be a sneaking, savage, merciless little war; more like feudists bushwhacking each other than any civilized conflict.

Men would be shot from ambush, or called to their doors and shot down, or hanged without benefit of trial. There would be "battles"—really small, irregular skirmishes, yet with murderous intent on both sides—at places like Osawatomie, Black Jack, Franklin, Slough Creek, and Hickory Point. There would be another massacre—this time of free-soil men—near the Marais de Cygnes River, in which five men would die before a "firing squad" directed by "Captain" Charles A. Hamelton of the pro-slavery forces.

There would be raiding by Kansas men across the border into Missouri, and by Missouri men across the border into Kansas,[6] and in this the Kansas raiders had the advantage, for over in Missouri were prosperous farms and homes, and the loot was better than in Kansas, at that time chiefly a place of shacks and log cabins.

Some precious scoundrels were developed. For example, William Clarke Quantrill, the notorious guerrilla who *really* sacked Lawrence during the Civil War, first turned up as a killer and thief on the Kansas side where he took part in freebooting raids over into Missouri. Later he changed sides and became the prize villain of Kansas history.

Charles Jennison, leader of a gang of looters and murderers, was as deeply execrated in Missouri as was Quantrill in Kansas. In the period after Governor John W. Geary brought some kind of temporary order to the border, Jennison continued to make "retaliatory" raids into Missouri "with certain of the rougher element as his retainers," and thus kept hatreds stirred up.

Other reprehensible characters sneaked, and looted, and murdered on both sides. Though the government made efforts to put a stop to the feuding, and for a time, through the courage of Governor

---

[6] It was in this period that the name Jayhawker came to be applied to Kansans. The state now accepts it with pride but at first it was no complimentary term. One Pat Devlin, a Kansas raider and horse thief hailing from Ireland, said he had been "jayhawking" after a raid into Missouri. He explained that in Ireland "we have a bird called the jayhawk, which makes its living off other birds." The best inquiries indicate that he was referring to the shrike, or butcherbird, which has some of the worst qualities of both the jay and the hawk, to which the term appears to be applied in some parts of Ireland.

Geary, achieved some sort of a truce, the Border War did not entirely cease until secession and a far greater conflict inaugurated a new and even more terrible phase in Kansas-Missouri difficulties.

It was not the scale of the Border War that was terrible. What should have sent a tremor throughout the nation was that this was the indubitable prelude to the great holocaust of the Civil War, with its vast destruction of life, property, and the sufferings it inflicted on the American people both North and South.

BOOK V

The Irrepressible Conflict

CHAPTER TWENTY-FOUR

Events Beyond Control

1

THE Whigs were finished. Only too well had they illustrated the truism that a party which merely opposes cannot long exist.

By 1855 Lincoln, who all his active life had been a Whig, was convinced of this fact. He did not accept it easily, or happily, and he continued to keep in touch with the men he had known as Whigs, but who now might be considering other alliances, hoping always for some change in the complexion of affairs that would give him an opening once more for political advancement.

In 1854 he won his last election as a Whig, for a seat in the state legislature. But this victory was due rather to his personal popularity than to his party affiliation. As it turned out, he never sat with that legislature, because he resigned before it convened. A new ambition had taken possession of him.

When he studied the composition of the new Legislature, Lincoln perceived that it contained only forty-one "regular" Democrats, as against fifty-nine "anti-Nebraska" men—the term for those who opposed the Kansas-Nebraska Act. It was, however, by no means a solid wing of the legislature, for it included Whigs, a number of Democrats who had revolted against Douglas, a sprinkling of Free-Soilers, some Know-Nothings, and even a few Republicans.

But though it had little cohesion and no central party discipline, if this anti-Nebraska element could be kept together it might elect a United States Senator; and Lincoln wanted to be that Senator. His resignation from the legislature before sitting in it was in order that he might be eligible for consideration by that body for the Senate seat then occupied by General James Shields. Mary Lincoln, ambitious as always, hungrily desired her husband to win the honor, for the social position of a "Mrs. Senator" was very high in that day.

Though Shields was a candidate to succeed himself, it was believed even by the regular Democrats that he could not win. The leaders of that party therefore proposed to use him only as an early pace-setter when the voting in the legislature began—for at that time the legislatures still elected Senators—and after a show of strength, they would bring out Governor Joel Aldrich Matteson, who had managed to keep out of controversial issues, as their real candidate.

When the legislature met in joint session February 8, 1855, for the balloting, Mary Lincoln was in the gallery. So, of course, were other women, including the former Julia Jayne, Mary's long-time friend with whom she had collaborated in the "Rebecca" writings. Julia had since married Lyman Trumbull, a friend of Lincoln's, a Democrat, and also a candidate for the Senate, though without much apparent support. Trumbull, though a Democrat, was an anti-Nebraska man and could count on no votes from the regulars of his party.

Election required a total of fifty-one votes, for the two houses of the legislature at that time totaled exactly a hundred members. On the first ballot Lincoln led with forty-four votes to Shields' forty-one. Trumbull had five, and there were a few scattering votes for others. It was noted that the regular Democrats had voted solidly for Shields, an indication of their close party discipline.

As the voting continued, it was seen that Lincoln's early strength was fading rapidly. On the seventh ballot the regular Democrats brought forward Matteson, who received Shields' entire bloc of votes, together with the votes of some other Democrats who now swung to him. By the ninth ballot Matteson had risen to forty-five votes. Meantime Trumbull's strength had increased to thirty-five, and Lincoln suffered the humiliation of seeing his own support dwindle to fifteen.

Lincoln now knew he could not win. Trumbull, whom he personally liked, was a Democrat, but at least an anti-Nebraska Democrat. In the critical situation Lincoln threw his remaining support to his friend. Trumbull, with his own thirty-five and Lincoln's fifteen, had fifty votes, and when he picked up one in addition on the next ballot he was elected Senator with exactly fifty-one votes.

The loss of the election which at one time he seemed so close to winning, was a heavy disappointment to Lincoln, though he was philosophical about it. Mary Lincoln, however, was not philosophical. So bitter was she over the defeat that she never again spoke to Julia Trumbull.

To Lincoln it was not yet plain that the Whig power was dead in Illinois and probably in the nation. One paragraph of a letter he wrote to Joshua Speed described his confused state of mind:

> I think I am a whig, but others say there are no whigs, and that I am an abolitionist . . . [yet] I now do no more than oppose the extension of slavery. I am not a Know-nothing. That is certain. How could I be? How can anyone who abhors the oppression of negroes, be in favor of degrading classes of white people? Our progress in degeneracy appears to me to be pretty

rapid. As a nation, we began by declaring that *"all men are created equal."* Now we practically read it "all men are created equal, *except negroes.*" When the Know-Nothings get control, it will read "all men are created equal, except negroes, *and foreigners and Catholics."* When it comes to this I should prefer emigrating to some country where they make no pretense of loving liberty—to Russia, for example, where despotism can be taken pure, without the base alloy of hypocracy [*sic*].

By the time 1856 dawned—and it was a Presidential election year —he was still in a state of indecision. He had been drawn to the Republicans but had distrusted some of the abolitionist extremist leaders. Though invited, he not only refused to attend a meeting of the new party at Springfield, but rejected an invitation to serve on its state central committee. Yet the Republican party, if sectional, was full of vigor, a contrast to the moribund Whigs; and if it could be broadened and given a solid scope of policies, its enthusiasm might carry it a long way.

To Lincoln, the lifelong Whig, anything seemed preferable to the rule of the nation by a one-party system—especially when that party was the Democrats against whom he had striven all his political career. His law partner, Herndon, had already joined the Republicans and was pushing Lincoln. Considering all these things, when an anti-Nebraska convention—with a strong Republican tinge—was called at Bloomington, Illinois, May 29, 1856, he attended it as a delegate from Springfield.

It was a time of great tensions. Only eight days before the "Sack of Lawrence" had taken place. Only seven days before Charles Sumner had been caned in the Senate chamber by Preston Brooks. Only six days before John Brown had led his followers to the cruel massacre of five pro-slavery men on Pottawatomie Creek.

Old-line Whigs, bolting Democrats, even Know-Nothings, all shunned the name Republican because of its association with sectionalism and radical abolitionism. Yet at that historic meeting, Abraham Lincoln was to lay down the principles on which the Republican party would establish respectability, mature its policies, and build its success.

Ranting extremist oratory opened the convention. Then Lincoln was called upon for a speech. Whether he had prepared a formal speech for the occasion is doubtful. At least there exists no full written version of it. Probably what he said, if not quite impromptu, was at least a quick gathering together of long and ripe meditation in a determination to give some sane and constructive direction to the movement he was addressing.

He rose to speak from where he had been sitting, but a cry, "The platform! The platform!" went up. The towering, lank figure responded by moving to the platform, and when Lincoln began to speak he wrought in that crowd of men with widely differing views and objectives an almost miraculous change.

His face was grave as he began by calling for calmness and moderation; and in the most solemn and impressive manner he predicted that unless the violence in Kansas was halted, "Blood will flow . . . brother's hand will be raised against brother." It was as if Lincoln in that moment saw with a prophet's eye the dreadful storm of the Civil War, and the tones of his voice and the expression of his face were so "earnest, impressive, if not, indeed, tragic . . . as to make a cold chill creep" over his hearers.

On he went, to demand a restoration of the Missouri Compromise, and referred with sarcasm to Stephen A. Douglas. But he next asserted that the South was entitled to a "reasonable and efficient" Fugitive Slave law. "No!" cried someone in the audience; and Lincoln trumpeted back, "I say yes! It was part of the bargain . . . but I will go no further!" The crowd applauded him thunderously.

With indignation he spoke of the Lawrence episode and the Sumner affair, and though he did not mention Pottawatomie Creek, he declared that retaliation in kind would win no final victory. "Let the legions of slavery use bullets; but let us wait patiently until November and fire ballots at them in return."

His most moving eloquence was devoted to the Union which he loved, its sacredness, and the necessity, whatever the sacrifice, of preserving it. No matter what issues rose, this was above all other concerns. Rising to his toes so that he "looked seven feet tall," he flung down the gauntlet to the enemies of the Union in words that men never forgot: "We will say to the Southern disunionists, we won't go out of the Union, *and you shan't!*"

In those words Abraham Lincoln expressed his supreme Credo—the Credo on which he based every later action of his life, the Credo for which he died. With it he joined Andrew Jackson's, "The Federal Union, it must be preserved!" and Daniel Webster's, "Union and liberty, now and forever, one and inseparable!"

At his finish the convention cheered him wildly, madly, standing on the seats, throwing hats in air, waving handkerchiefs, caught up in a tremendous, unanimous enthusiasm. On that day Lincoln welded many divergent elements into a party; a party with a strong, sober, and intelligent purpose; a party that would uphold the Union to the end. Very soon there would be no hesitation about using the name Republican.

2

The Bloomington convention was a state convention only, but four days after it adjourned the great national party meetings began. First the Democrats gathered in Cincinnati, and after casting aside Franklin Pierce who wanted a second term, nominated James Buchanan for President. The Know-Nothings nominated Millard Fillmore; and the Whigs, seeing at last the disintegration of their party, also nominated Fillmore, but refused to endorse the principles of the Know-Nothings.

Now the young Republican party, which had received a tremendous access of enthusiasm and achieved a focus through the Bloomington convention, and through the speeches of some important men over the nation who leaned toward it, met in Philadelphia, June 17, the anniversary of the Battle of Bunker Hill. By the very nature of the platform it adopted—opposition to repeal of the Missouri Compromise and to any extension of slave territory, while advocating the admission of Kansas as a free state—it made itself a sectional party, for the South would not participate in it. The choice of the Republican convention as its candidate for President was John Charles Frémont, the much-publicized "Pathfinder."

Of the three major candidates thus in the field, Buchanan, Fillmore, and Frémont, the last probably was the least fit for the office. Lincoln was not for him, almost instinctively, as Beveridge has pointed out, "for Frémont's strongest characteristics were those which Lincoln did not trust—impulsiveness, insubordination, overgallantry, and dash."

But when Frémont was nominated, Lincoln (who received 110 delegate votes for Vice-President, though William L. Dayton of New Jersey was eventually nominated), loyally made a series of speeches for the candidate of his new party. No longer, however, did he fan the flames over "bleeding Kansas" which was current material for other Republican orators.

In that campaign William H. Seward, the powerful Senator from New York, in a speech at Rochester, described the dispute between the North and the South as follows: "It is an *irrepressible conflict* between opposing and enduring forces, and it means that the United States must and will, sooner or later, become either an entirely slaveholding nation or entirely a free-labor nation."

Those words echoed like a voice of doom in the ears of many. They were unfortunate words, words that did nothing to heal the wounds of the nation. Seward's "Irrepressible Conflict" and "Higher

Law" dictums became catch-words in both North and South. They marked him, somewhat falsely, as a radical, and in the end they destroyed for him any hope of the Presidency.

There were other notable speakers. Salmon P. Chase was on the stump. So was Owen Lovejoy. And now Lyman Trumbull left the Democrats, became a Republican, and thereafter was one of Lincoln's stanchest supporters. Lincoln himself devoted his time, thought, and energy to rallying the old-line Whigs to the support of Frémont and the Republican ticket.

Frémont was a difficult candidate to "sell" to the nation. For one thing, he had irregular parentage,[1] which was held against him by some of the more strait-laced in that Victorian time, and was campaign ammunition for his opponents. In a speech at Richmond, Governor Henry A. Wise declared that Frémont was "born illegitimately in a neighboring state, if not ill begotten in this very city," and added, "Tell me if the hoisting of the black flag over you by a Frenchman's bastard, with the arms of civil war already clashing, is not to be deemed an overt act and a declaration of war?"

Frémont was a graduate of West Point, and married the only daughter of Senator Thomas Hart Benton. He gained considerable publicity by various exploring expeditions in the West, financed by the government through the influence of his father-in-law, whereby he was sometimes called the "Pathfinder," although the paths he found were shown to him by mountain men like Thomas Fitzpatrick and Kit Carson, to whom they had long been familiar. During the War with Mexico, he precipitated the unauthorized "Bear Flag Revolt" in California, later was court-martialed at Fort Leavenworth for insubordination, returned to California, and became wealthy when gold was found on a ranch he owned.

In person, Frémont was medium-sized, slightly pop-eyed, affecting a straggling beard, given to bombastic language and haughty in manner. Later he would be charged with graft during the Civil War, and after that conflict he became involved in a railroad scandal.

For the present, however, he was head of a crusading party, and

[1] His father, Charles Frémont, was a French adventurer with amorous inclinations. He had been dismissed from a teaching post in a Richmond academy, for living with a woman not his wife, when he met Ann Whiting Pryor, wife of John Pryor, of Norfolk, Virginia. Pryor, a veteran of the Revolutionary War, was wealthy—and old. His wife was passionate—and young. It was not difficult for Charles Frémont to seduce her. When Pryor discovered their relations, he publicly cast her off by a printed notice in the *Virginia Patriot*, June 12, 1811. There was no divorce. The couple began a wandering career, and their son, John Charles Frémont, was born of this extra-marital union, probably near Savannah, Georgia, on or about January 21, 1813. See Cardinal Goodman, *John Charles Frémont, an Explanation of his Career* (1930).

the Republicans, with only hasty organization, carried on a fighting campaign under the slogan: "Free Soil, Free Labor, Free Speech, Free Men, Frémont." To the surprise of almost everyone they carried every Northern and Western state, except California, Illinois, Pennsylvania, and Indiana.

The final popular vote was: Buchanan 1,838,169; Frémont 1,341,264; Fillmore (who carried only one state), 874,534. The issues, of course, had been more important than the candidates, but starting from nothing the Republicans gave the Democrats a scare and an impressive indication of probable future strength. The Whigs gave up the ghost; and the Know-Nothings disappeared as a party.

3

James Buchanan, as President, began an administration doomed to disaster, for from the first events were beyond his control.

He was a tall, fine-looking man, a successful lawyer, and he remained a bachelor all his life. A defect in vision—one eye was farsighted, the other near-sighted—caused him to form the habit of closing one or the other eye, depending on whether his object of interest was near or far. Ladies with whom he happened to be conversing sometimes were disconcerted, or annoyed, or perhaps even interested, when he "winked" at them. Usually he carried his head slightly tilted to one side, also because of this defect in vision.

Smooth maneuvering brought him political advancement. It was Buchanan who, in 1825, carried the celebrated proposal to Andrew Jackson that he make Henry Clay the Secretary of State—to Old Hickory's resounding fury. Always ingratiating, always calculating, he went to Congress and later the Senate, was minister to Russia and Great Britain, and served as Secretary of State under Polk. His remarkable political quick-footedness enabled him to avoid most controversial issues until his participation in the Ostend Manifesto. Even this, perhaps, was no political error from his viewpoint, for Buchanan had his eye on the White House, and he believed that the tenor of the Manifesto—much of which he personally wrote—would gain him support in the South. In this he was correct, for it was the South that gave him the winning margin in his election.

As President, however, he could no longer avoid facing knotty problems; and even had he been a man of force and decision, he could hardly have coped with the numerous threatening situations that confronted him. Talk of disunion was growing; and this was by no means confined to the South. The Republican party was embarrassed by intemperate disunionist oratory on the part of abolitionist speakers.

The abolitionist extremists were a minority movement even within the anti-slavery forces; and, unlike Southern disunionists, they did not hold offices or lead majorities in their own states. Southern orators often identified them with Republicans; but both the Republicans and the abolitionists repudiated the connection. Garrison refused to vote for Frémont in 1856 and advised his followers not to do so. Wendell Phillips declared, "I want no man for President . . . who has not got his hand half-clenched, and means to close it on the jugular vein of the slave system." He made it clear that he did not think Frémont would do so. "No Union with slave holders!" had been Garrison's cry, and Phillips, capping it, thundered, "Treason? Treason runs in the blood that flowed on Bunker Hill!"

Of even more immediate difficulty was a decision of the Supreme Court, handed down March 6, 1857, only two days after the harried Buchanan took office. It has gone down in history as the Dred Scott Decision, because it dealt with the status of a Negro named Dred Scott, and his wife, Harriet.

The story of Dred Scott is interesting as a human document and as an example of the growing dissension of the period, arising out of contradictory opinions on the slavery question. He was born in Virginia, sometime during the administration of President Thomas Jefferson. His master, Peter Blow, went from Virginia to St. Louis, Missouri, taking Scott with him. About 1834, Blow sold him, as a body servant, to Dr. John Emerson, an army surgeon. When Emerson was ordered first to Rock Island, Illinois, and later to Fort Snelling, Minnesota (then a part of the Wisconsin Territory), the slave went with him. He was then in his early thirties.

During his tour of duty at Fort Snelling, Dr. Emerson bought a Negro woman, named Harriet, probably as a maid for his wife; and in due time Dred and Harriet were married. They had two children. Not long afterward Dr. Emerson was ordered back to St. Louis, taking his wife and the Negroes with him. In fact one of the children of the Scott family, a girl, was born on the steamboat *Gypsy*, during the journey down the river, and before the Missouri state line was reached. The second child, also a girl, was born a year later in St. Louis.

Dr. Emerson kept the Scott family as his servants, even after he was forced by ill health to retire from the Army in 1842. Two years later, about 1844, Dr. Emerson died.

It was after her husband's death, that Dred Scott, in 1846, brought suit for freedom against Mrs. Emerson, for himself and his family, on the ground that since he had lived in Illinois, he was made free under the constitution of that state, and his period of living in the Wisconsin Territory also made him free inasmuch as the Missouri

Compromise forbade slavery in that part of the domain of the United States.

Mrs. Emerson, who, with her brother, John F. A. Sanford of New York, held her former husband's estate in trust in behalf of a daughter, Henrietta Emerson, resisted the suit. Scott won in the lower court, but Mrs. Emerson appealed the case to the state supreme court.

During this time Scott remained in his humble state as a slave, and Mrs. Emerson tried to hire him out to other families. But he was at this time, to quote Allan Nevins, "infirm and inefficient and became increasingly dependent on his owners and those who befriended him." Then, in 1850, Mrs. Emerson married again, her husband being Dr. Calvin Clifford Chaffee of Springfield, Massachusetts. Chaffee was a Know-Nothing and an abolitionist, and was elected to Congress for two terms. By her marriage to him, Mrs. Chaffee, under the Missouri laws, could no longer act with regard to Emerson's estate. Her brother, John F. A. Sanford, now appears to have been the sole legal administrator.

Two years later the state supreme court heard the appeal, and a majority of the justices overruled the lower court, deciding against Dred Scott, on the ground that since he had returned to Missouri voluntarily, he therefore resumed his status of a slave under the laws of that state. In this decision the chief justice, Hamilton R. Gamble, strongly dissented.[2]

Since Sanford, administrator of the Emerson estate, lived in New York, Scott brought suit against him in the federal district court. In April 1854 the first skirmish in that court took place. The ruling being against Scott, his attorney, Roswell M. Field, appealed to the Supreme Court of the United States.

Two interesting developments occurred at this time. On May 25, Field, the Negro's attorney, wrote Montgomery Blair, later to be Postmaster General under Abraham Lincoln, that it would be well to have the constitutionality of the Missouri Compromise decided once and for all, even if the decision of the highest court in the nation was adverse to the constitutionality of the Compromise.

The second matter of interest was that Dred's appeal bond was signed by Henry Taylor Blow, a son of Peter Blow, the very man who had sold him to Emerson. The younger Blow had become a

---

[2] Gamble, who was opposed to slavery, became provisional governor of Missouri in 1861, when Claiborne F. Jackson, the elected governor, with other Southern sympathizers, withdrew from the convention called to consider the question of whether or not to remain in the Union, after they saw they were in the minority. He served until his death in 1864, and during his administration, in 1863, sought to work out a plan for gradual emancipation of slaves, the owners to receive compensation. But the radical abolitionists, who by that time had gained great power, overruled him, demanding immediate and unconditional emancipation.

strong anti-slavery man. The Blow family assisted the slave in his court fight, although they did not instigate his original suit. That Dred, who thus became a pawn in a vast national question, was financed in the costs of his extensive litigation which continued for seven years before it finally was decided, is obvious. The Blow family may have borne part of these costs, but other anti-slavery forces no doubt contributed also, as did anti-slavery lawyers who served, in most cases at least, without fees.

As a footnote, within a few weeks after the case finally was decided *against* Dred, the slave and his whole family, who had been held in servitude only technical during this period, were given their freedom.

Three fundamental questions were involved in the case: Could Dred Scott, as a Negro, claim to be a citizen of the United States with a right to sue? What was his status after being taken to free territory and then returned to a slave state? Did Congress have the right to legislate on slavery, and was the Missouri Compromise a valid use of power by Congress?

The heart of the celebrated Dred Scott Decision lay in the interpretation by the court of the meaning of the word "citizen" in the minds of the framers of the Constitution. While the aged and respected Chief Justice Roger B. Taney wrote what became the ruling opinion, and while on the main point six of the justices supported him, every one of the nine justices wrote his own opinion, and two dissented throughout.

As summed up by Allan Nevins: Three Southern judges declared that no Negro of slave ancestry could be entitled to citizenship; five Southern judges and one from the North, held that Scott's status depended on the laws of Missouri; five judges with one from the North declared that any law which excluded slavery from a territory was unconstitutional; and two Northern judges held that Scott was a citizen, the Missouri law did not control his status, and that Congress had a constitutional right to debar slavery from any territory.

Chief Justice Taney was a recognized authority on constitutional law, and had freed all the slaves he once possessed, except for two very old Negroes whom he kept merely to see that they were well care for. Yet his opinion was charged with the fury of the times, which was answered by counter fury.

In particular there was his statement that Negroes "had for more than a century [before the Constitution was adopted] been regarded as beings of an inferior order, and altogether unfit to associate with the white race, either in social or political relations; and so far inferior, that they had no rights which the white man was bound to respect."

They were not, therefore, a part of "the people" who framed that Constitution, and therefore, free or slave, Negroes never legally had been citizens.

The final findings were: That Scott was not a citizen; that slaves were property and Congress had no right to deprive citizens of property without due process, wherefore Scott's travels did not affect his status as a slave; and finally that Congress had no power to legislate slavery either in or out of the territories, wherefore the Missouri Compromise was unconstitutional.

The Dred Scott Decision delivered a stunning blow to the antislavery cause. In effect it legalized slavery in all the territories, including Kansas. It upheld the Fugitive Slave Act. It singled out the Negro *on a basis of race*, as being ineligible for citizenship and the rights pertaining thereto, including the right of appeal to the laws of the land.

So vexed were the constitutional questions and so heated the arguments, pro and con, that in the storm of abuse and counterabuse the North and South were driven still farther apart. In the North the Fugitive Slave Act became even more difficult—almost impossible—of enforcement.

It required, in effect, the Civil War to reverse the Dred Scott Decision, and two amendments, the Thirteenth which abolished slavery, and the Fourteenth which gave the Negro civil rights, to establish the full status of the race as part of the American nation.

4

Sectional problems affecting the whole nation were not the only difficulties that beset Buchanan. Even before he took office that irrepressible little egomaniac, William Walker, precipitated a crisis in Latin America that grew in proportions during Buchanan's administration.

For a generation American statesmen had thought of a canal that would connect the Atlantic and Pacific Oceans, navigable for deepsea vessels. Succeeding administrations looked for a place to construct such a waterway, somewhere in the narrowing strip of land connecting the continents of North and South America.

As early as 1836 Andrew Jackson sent a special agent to survey the possibility of such a canal across Nicaragua, where the San Juan River and Lake Nicaragua offered navigation for small ships, a waterway capable of improvement for large vessels, to within a few miles of the Pacific Ocean.

Later Van Buren made another investigation, but the "unsettled and revolutionary" character of Nicaragua made investment in such a project unattractive. During the War with Mexico, interest shifted to the Mexican isthmus of Tehuantepec, and transit rights across that neck of land were at first proposed as one of the terms of peace, but later abandoned.

England, recognizing the advantage such a shipway would give to the American shipping interests in the Asiatic trade, sought to forestall it. The War with Mexico seemed an excellent opportunity, and in 1848 a British squadron seized the little port of San Juan del Norte, at the mouth of the San Juan River. The town was renamed Greytown, and for a time was governed by the British ostensibly for the "Mosquito Kingdom,"—one of the devices by which the empire of Queen Victoria acquired British Honduras and at one time claimed much of the eastern coast of Central America. The United States protested, but at the time could do nothing about it, since the War with Mexico was occupying all the national attention and all the resources available at that time.

Soon after the war the United States took an interest again—not because of statecraft, but because of a piratical-minded financier with a foghorn voice and a remarkably incandescent flow of profanity, named Cornelius Vanderbilt, and usually called "Commodore." Among his many enterprises, which were to make him the richest American of his time, Vanderbilt established the Accessory Transit Corporation, with boats plying the San Juan River and Lake Nicaragua, and mules to carry passengers across the final few miles to the Pacific, in order to capture more than his share of the gold rush traffic which took the isthmian route to California.

The project paid well, and when, in 1853, Vanderbilt sailed in his steam yacht *North Star,* for his somewhat celebrated tour of Europe, he left Accessory Transit in charge of Charles Morgan, a ship owner, and Cornelius K. Garrison, a banker, as managers. Vanderbilt departed on his yacht, apparently not dreaming that his subordinates were as piratical-minded as himself, for he left them with powers of attorney that rapidly enabled them to gain control of Accessory Transit.

Of this Vanderbilt learned while he was still in Europe. Blazing with wrath he sailed for America; and having discovered the full extent of the conspiracy against him, dictated to Morgan and Garrison a letter still remembered for its brevity and grimness:

Gentlemen: You have undertaken to cheat me. I won't sue you, for the law is too slow. I'll ruin you. (Signed) C. Vanderbilt.

Like the freebooter he was, he proceeded against the lesser free-booters, and not only regained control of Accessory Transit, but crippled and humbled both his treacherous former associates.

Into this politico-financial skein William Walker, still in San Francisco, was drawn. Garrison, then also in San Francisco, saw in him an instrument whereby Accessory Transit might be wrested permanently away from Vanderbilt. How? By seizing control of the Nicaraguan government.

Walker, a sort of modern Don Quixote, with a mixture of absurdity, grandiose notions, idealism, very real courage, and much impracticality, was induced to take a band of adventurers from California to "liberate" the Nicaraguan people. At that time the Central American nation was being torn by one of its almost incessant civil wars. Two rival factions fought each other. Granada was the capital of the Legitimists, backed by the wealthy mining and estate owners who controlled most of the money in the country. León was the capital of the Democratists, who supposedly represented the poor and down-trodden classes.

When an invitation (procured through the influence of Garrison) came to him from the Democratist leaders, inviting him to join in the "holy war for liberty," Walker was at once fired with enthusiasm. Financing for the proposed expedition was available (furnished by Garrison's go-betweens). Walker found it not difficult to enlist men for his crusade against "tyranny."

Not only was Nicaragua rich in valuable timber like mahogany and Brazilwood; in metals, including gold, silver, copper, and lead; and in products like cacao, sugar, cotton, indigo, tobacco, grains, and fruits; but it produced cattle and other livestock. Land grants which were promised to Walker and his men seemed attractive. One of Walker's biographers[3] suggests also that the "sexual possibilities of Nicaragua where because of the continual civil wars women outnumbered men three to two, had a powerful influence on the woman-starved Californians." So usually restrained an observer as Mark Twain, who crossed Nicaragua in 1866, was able to rhapsodize over Nicaraguan beauties:

> Raven-haired, splendid-eyed Nicaragua damsels standing in attitudes of careless grace . . . damsels buff-colored, like an envelope—damsels who are always dressed the same way: in a single flowing gown of fancifully figured calico, "gathered" across the breast (they are singularly full in the bust, the young ones), and ruffled all around, near the bottom of the skirt. They have

[3] Albert Z. Carr, *The World and William Walker.*

white teeth, and pleasant, smiling, winning faces. They are virtuous according to their lights, but I guess their lights are a little
dim . . . such liquid, languishing eyes! such pouting lips! such
glossy, luxuriant hair! such ravishing, incendiary expressions! such
grace! such voluptuous forms, and such precious little drapery
about them!

Whatever the attraction (and this particular one did not interest
the ascetic Walker) he took about sixty fighting men to Nicaragua,
landing on its west coast in the summer of 1855, after a voyage from
San Francisco on the brig *Vesta*. He was welcomed by the people
of León; and at once, with fifty-six of his men, dubbed by the natives
La Falange Americana, aided by about two hundred Nicaraguan
soldiers, he attempted to capture the town of Rivas.

The attempt was a failure. When a force of five hundred Legitimatists appeared before them the two hundred native allies of Walker
suddenly lost all enthusiasm for the "holy war for freedom" and
fled. With his handful of Americans Walker defended a building and
succeeded in standing off the overwhelming numbers of his enemy,
until he was able to fall back to the coast, board the *Vesta*, and
return to León. The deadly fighting ability of his Americans was shown
in this little battle by the fact they lost only ten killed and wounded,
while the enemy suffered casualties of (an estimated) one hundred
and fifty.

He had received a reverse, but Walker quickly changed the complexion of affairs. By a brilliant series of victories, which included the
daring capture of Granada itself—the capital of the Legitimatists—he
became the dominant figure in Nicaragua, "united" the nation, and
was elected its president.

William Walker was a soldier, there is no gainsaying that; but he
was hardly an administrator. One of his first acts when he came into
power was to revoke, by decree, the prohibition of slavery that had
existed for almost thirty years. Shortly afterward he began to seize
the large estates and mines of the aristocrats. The repeal of the anti-
slavery provisions caused indignation among the poor, and the seizure
of the estates angered the rich. It would seem difficult for Walker
to do worse; but he succeeded. He antagonized a man with greater
power and fewer scruples than himself—Commodore Vanderbilt.

The Accessory Transit line still operated, and though it was then
in litigation, Walker favored the usurpers Morgan and Garrison who
had advanced him cash. He now suspended the charter of Accessory Transit, and expropriated its ships, docks, buildings, horses and
mules, and other equipment, to use the facilities for transporting his
own troops and supplies.

This annoyed Vanderbilt, who was winning his fight against Morgan and Garrison, and who soon obtained full legal control again. The Commodore, however, wrote no letters to Walker. He simply sat in his office in New York, and backed by his millions, organized a Central American alliance against the filibuster, which included Costa Rica, Honduras, San Salvador, and Guatemala. Britain was pleased to cooperate by preventing any reinforcements from reaching Walker from the east.

Abandoned now by most of his Nicaraguan allies, the soldier of fortune fought a brave but losing war. His suspension of the anti-slavery laws had alienated those in the United States who opposed the extension of that institution; and now he alienated the Southern expansionists by deciding not to seek annexation to the United States, but instead to keep Nicaragua as a sort of personal empire.

The odds were too great. On May 1, 1857, Walker surrendered to Commander Charles N. Davis of the U.S. sloop-of-war *St. Mary's* and was returned to the United States.

Though he was formally charged with violating the neutrality laws, the filibuster was still popular with the unthinking crowds. Buchanan fumbled and bumbled, and twice again during his administration Walker made new invasions of Central America. He was captured at last in Honduras—surrendering to Captain Norvell Salmon of the British warship *Icarus*—who promptly turned him over to the Honduran authorities.

William Walker died before a firing squad at Trujillo, Honduras, September 12, 1860, and with him died filibustering from the United States. He was not only an episode in the isthmian canal history, but also a symbol and symptom of the generally expanding American energy of the time, one of many filibusters. Cuba, Ecuador, Yucatán, Sonora, Lower California, all had been objectives, real or planned, of filibustering efforts; and whalers were raising the American flag on atolls all over the world. The Civil War and the development of the West turned the expansionist impulse to new directions.

5

Other issues embarrassed Buchanan even more.

Out in the Utah territory, the Mormon sect, under the unquestioned dictatorship of Brigham Young, persisted in behaving as if they were independent of, and had no loyalty to, the United States. Young entitled himself governor, the Mormons controlled territorial courts and juries, sometimes preying upon and even killing emigrants passing through to California, and openly defied government officials.

One of the most remarkable personages in America was Brigham Young. He was a burly, powerful man, with chin whiskers, a cold gray eye, and a masterful personality. Born in Vermont in 1801, he had only eleven days of formal schooling, but he made up for this lack with keen native shrewdness, force of personality, and unbending will. That he was a remarkable organizer and leader was shown by the way in which he made his thousands of followers, from different parts of the world, obey his commands without question. They worked with hive-like industry and their achievements were worthy of the highest praise.

Under Young's direction they built well-planned towns and cities, including the capital, Salt Lake City, with its ornate temple, embarked with great success on the first major irrigation project by white men in North America, raised crops and herds, paid one-tenth of all they acquired into the coffers of the church by way of tithes, and developed a community that gradually grew strong and prosperous —in what had been once a bleak desert surrounding a lake as salt as the Dead Sea.

Brigham Young brooked no opposition from his followers, or anyone else. He acted in what he believed was the interest of his people. To that end he was unscrupulous; he condoned, if he did not actually order, many murders; and he warped justice in the courts. And he gained a considerable fortune; he had a fine home in Salt Lake City called the "Lion House" because of a stone lion that stood over the portico, which had to be unusually spacious, with numbers of rooms, for in it were housed his numerous wives and children.[4]

Young was the great protagonist of polygamy, which he called "the seed of the church," and made it a part of Mormon doctrine. Under the Mormon tenets plurality of wives was not only right, but holy, and the practice was general in the territory. It may seem strange to modern thinking, but the Mormon women accepted the doctrine and became plural wives without much objection, while some were even strong defenders of it. Perhaps a reason for this was that far more women than men became converted to Mormonism in its early years, and polygamy offered some sort of a solution for the problem created by this surplus.

Over the rest of the country, however, polygamy as practiced by the Mormons aroused violent opposition. Its first exposure was one of the causes of the expulsion of the sect from Nauvoo, Illinois. Eventually

---

[4] In his lifetime, Brigham Young was married to twenty-seven women, although never that many at any one time. At his death in 1877, he was survived by seventeen wives; and he was the father of fifty-six children, of whom sixteen sons and twenty-eight daughters survived him.

Congress passed laws against it, and by 1890 all Mormons ceased polygamy, except for a few outlying communities.

But however much it was disapproved, polygamy as practiced far out in the West, did not directly affect the nation as a whole. What did create a problem was the early determination of the Mormons to resist the rule of the United States government, their violence against those not of their faith, and the manner in which they, in effect, made travel to the Pacific Coast difficult and at times dangerous, since part of Brigham Young's "empire" lay right athwart the Overland Trail.

Discipline of the church was maintained by a more or less secret body of men known as Danites (and sometimes as "Destroying Angels"). Persons who disobeyed the church laws, especially "apostates," were sometimes murdered by these agents. Emigrants passing through the country were on more than one occasion robbed, and their livestock stolen. A military surveying party of eight men, headed by Captain John W. Gunnison, was massacred.

The Mormons always denied their guilt in such murders, and laid the blame on Indians. But Judge W. W. Drummond, who had been appointed to the Utah federal district court, resigned March 20, 1857, when he found it impossible to enforce justice, and his life was threatened. He made a direct and formal charge that these Indians were directed by Mormons.

It is certain that some Mormons had great influence over certain bands of Indians, particularly the Paiutes, a people linguistically allied to the Utes of Colorado, and the Snakes and Shoshones of Wyoming.[5] One of the most influential members of the sect was John D. Lee, a foster son of Brigham Young, and a leader of the Danites, who learned the Indian languages and became a leader among them. And one instance of Mormon participation in outrages is particularly well documented—the Mountain Meadows Massacre of September 1857 in which Lee was one of the directors.

A wagon train carrying a party of 137 persons, part of them from Arkansas and the rest from Missouri, was surrounded in camp not far from Cedar Valley. Testimony indicates that Paiutes opened the attack, but that a strong party of Mormons took over and slew every adult person in the party, and all children whom they thought old enough to remember. All told 120 persons died and seventeen young

[5] Walkara, often called Walker, a Ute chief, was made a Mormon and ordained as an elder in the Mormon church. But he remained a thorough savage, was the man upon whom the Mormons laid the guilt for the Gunnison massacre, and when he died was buried according to Ute custom, with two whimpering Paiute child slaves caged alive above him to starve to death on his grave. See *Walkara, Hawk of the Mountains,* by Paul Bailey.

children were taken to the Mormon settlements, from which most were later restored to their families in Arkansas and Missouri.

Years later, after a long investigation by the government, Lee was captured and convicted of his share in the massacre. He made a confession, was sentenced to die, and was executed by a firing squad, sitting on his own coffin at the scene of the massacre.

Others guilty of murders usually escaped the penalties of their crimes, and in this category, by self-confession, were men like Porter Rockwell and Bill Hickman. Judge Drummond, after returning to the East from Utah, asserted that there was "one set of courts for Mormons, another set for Gentiles." He believed (without proof) that his predecessor in the Utah office, Judge Leonidas Shaver, was poisoned by Mormons, and he declared in his official protest to Washington that Brigham Young, who controlled the courts, sometimes pardoned murderers simply because they were of the Mormon faith.

Such a condition of affairs could not be permitted to continue, and already, before the Mountain Meadows Massacre took place, Buchanan ordered troops to the trouble spot.

The President had appointed Alfred Cummins, a courageous and capable man, to be governor of the territory, naming at the same time three new federal judges, a marshal, and a secretary. These were escorted by a military force, at first to be 2500 men, but later reduced to 1400, commanded by Colonel Albert Sidney Johnston. The expedition set out from Fort Leavenworth in midsummer of 1857.

Johnston was a first-class soldier, who made a fine record in the War with Mexico, and was destined to be killed during the Civil War, leading a Confederate army at the Battle of Shiloh. His troops were regular infantry and dragoons. But the Utah expedition is one of the least brilliant "campaigns" in the history of the United States Army.

For one thing, the army was on a peaceful mission. It even sent ahead Captain Van Vliet, to assure the Mormons of this fact, and purchase supplies from them. Van Vliet found the Mormons preparing for war. Obviously they and their leaders were hysterically excited.

For another thing the soldiers were hampered by orders which forced them to take no aggressive actions, while the Mormons were hampered by nothing.

"We will send them to hell across lots!" Brigham Young had said, speaking of the "invaders"—as he called United States troops entering a United States territory. Refusing to accept the arrival of Governor Cummins as superseding his own authority, he declared Utah under "martial law."

While Johnston rigorously kept his soldiers in leash, forbidding them to enter towns or even forage in the country about, Mormon raiders looted wagon trains, ran off horses and mules, and incited Indians to hostile actions.

Three wagon trains, consisting of seventy-five wagons, were surprised on the Green River. The trains did not belong to the government but were owned by the freighting firm of Russell, Majors, and Waddell, carrying provisions and tents for the army under contract. The wagons were burned, the livestock driven away, and the wagon drivers, some eighty men, were sent eastward with an inadequate supply of food. Many of them died of cold and privation before they reached the Missouri River settlements. This episode was to be reflected in a government financial scandal, affecting John B. Floyd, Secretary of War, in the last days of the Buchanan administration.

Johnston camped near Fort Bridger when the winter storms began. Accompanying the soldiers was a disorderly mob of camp-followers, including wives of the men—and other women. Efforts to take care of these in the severe weather did not prevent great suffering. The cold was so intense that some five hundred animals belonging to the command died. Men cut their own wood, dragging it by hand through deep snow from adjacent hills. Numbers of deaths occurred.

Though Johnston named his camp after General Scott, the soldiers preferred to call it "Camp Death."

Brigham Young had stated that he could raise eight or ten thousand men to defend the passes through the mountains; and that winter his people believed jubilantly that they had "whipped the United States." Poems were written by Utah bards, a sample verse of which follows:

> Up, awake, ye defenders of Zion!
> The foe's at the door of your homes;
> Let each heart be the heart of a lion,
> Unyielding and proud as he roams.
> Remember the wrongs of Missouri,
> Remember the fate of Nauvoo:
> When the God-hating foe is before ye,
> Stand firm, and be faithful and true.

As the winter passed and spring set in, Brigham Young realistically faced the fact that he would soon be forced to confront the small army of "God-hating foes"—who by now were thoroughly angry and spoiling for a fight. The time for big talk was past, and he ordered his people to evacuate their homes, and prepare to march south, perhaps to Mexico. Food was to be cached, and houses and other buildings to be "left in smoking ashes."

The Mormons were aghast at the realization that the United States had not been whipped after all, but faithful to the commands of their "prophet," they despairingly made ready for the journey. The homes they had worked so hard to build, the lands they had made productive with great toil, all were to be abandoned. Yet some 25,000 men, women, and children prepared to obey without question.

Fortunately, before this exodus had gone very far, Thomas L. Kane, who was well-known to Mormon leaders, went as an intermediary to Governor Cummins and convinced him "that the Mormons were rather more peaceable than average lambs, if let alone." Cummins, without an escort, accompanied Kane to Salt Lake City, and reached an understanding with Brigham Young.

The Mormons halted their evacuation, and bowed to the national sovereignty. The civil governor's authority was accepted, and it was agreed that the religion of the inhabitants should not be interfered with. The "Mormon War" was over, and President Buchanan granted full pardon to the lately rebellious people. Since that troublous period no segment of the population of the United States has established a better record for industry, obedience to the laws, and sober prosperity than the Mormons. At least one of Buchanan's problems was solved.

CHAPTER TWENTY-FIVE

Devices and Discoveries

1

ONE can hardly help feeling sorry for James Buchanan—well-meaning man, who desired nothing so much as freedom from anxieties and yet was beset with ever-growing troubles—were it not for his personal ineffectuality, and the fact that as President of the United States he allowed himself so much to be a victim, rather than a mover, of events.

Early in his administration a new thorny irritant further inflamed sectional differences. It was a book, which came from the South.

A North Carolina writer, Hinton Rowan Helper, in the title of a book he published in 1857, coined a phrase, *The Impending Crisis*, that seemed rather closely to describe the situation then existing in the nation—the ugly Kansas question; the disunionist sentiments expressed by extremists not only in the South, but in the North; and economic conditions all of which contributed to the peril of the Buchanan administration.

Helper, a disillusioned Southerner who owned no slaves, bitterly attacked the institution of slavery in his book. *The Impending Crisis* was not addressed to the abolitionists or even to the North in general. It was addressed to the middle and lower classes of the South itself—the men who were not, in general, slaveowners.

Because of his central thesis, the author was unable to get his book printed in any Southern state. At last he found a publisher in New York, and in the North his volume was widely circulated, though in the South speakers and writers united in denouncing it, and some persons were even arrested for buying or owning a copy of it.

Helper's contention was that the slaveholders had for generations kept the white people of the lower social and financial classes in ignorance of the true effect that slavery had on their personal and economic lives, molding their thoughts and prejudices so that they acted "in direct opposition" to their "dearest rights and interests." Buttressing his claims with pages of statistics (some of which he misinterpreted) he asserted that the slaveholders "owed" the poorer people of the South more than $7,000,000,000, because they had by that much impoverished the status of free labor. He even advocated general hostility of the non-slaveowners toward slaveowners; and pointed out that out of a white population of 6,185,000, in all the slave states, only about 350,000 were slaveowners or slave-hirers.

Until general liberation of slaves could be obtained, Helper argued, slaveholders should be taxed $60 a head for each slave they owned. The money thus garnered should be impounded and used to transport every black to Africa or some place in South America, or perhaps to some "comfortable settlement within the bounds of the United States"—apparently meaning somewhere in the Indian country of the West.

His scheme, of course, was completely impracticable. Colonization of freed Negroes in Africa had been tried, and it had failed, partly because of the hostility of the native Africans to the newcomers of their own race, and partly because of the sheer unwillingness of the Negroes themselves to return to Africa after living in America.

Southerners heatedly denied that there was any hostility between slaveowning citizens and those who did not own slaves. This proved to be true during the Civil War when all classes fought side by side for the Confederacy. A few border state spokesmen called attention to inequalities of taxation, education, and opportunity; but few even of these argued, at least publicly, against the institution of slavery itself.

Perhaps the most important and far-reaching effect of *The Impending Crisis* was not in the South, but in the North. Coming from the pen of a Southern writer, it created a tremendous impression. Many persons who hitherto had been unconvinced by the moral aspects of slavery, now turned against it because they realized it was an economic fallacy. Helper's book, reissued in 1859 together with a *Compendium* of its contents, were widely circulated as Republican campaign documents, and this still further alienated the people of the North and the South.

2

As if all these controversial matters were not sufficient to destroy whatever peace of mind President Buchanan may have had, the nation sustained a money panic, starting in August 1857, that was as severe in many respects as that of 1837, which plagued Van Buren.

It was the familiar result of overexpansion. Partly because of the quantities of gold reaching the financial markets from California and elsewhere, the times were characterized by extravagance and wild speculations. Money by the millions of dollars which should have been used for legitimate investment, was devoted instead to financing dubious schemes for sudden wealth.

In nine years more than 21,000 miles of new railroads had been built, much of which was speculative and as yet unproductive. Populations did not move into the territories penetrated by the new rails nearly as fast as the promoters had hoped; and little account was taken of traffic which would begin paying at once to support the projects while patronage could grow. When dividends did not accrue, railroad stocks began a decline, particularly the stocks of Western lines.

At the same time land speculations drew funds far exceeding their investment values. New territories and parts of some Western states which were not as yet populated, were almost covered with "paper cities," inviting the credulous to "invest" at fabulous prices. A contemporary source noted:

> In Kansas alone, where scarcely one legal title had as yet been granted, there were more acres laid out for cities than were covered by all the cities in the northern and middle states. Nearly the whole West swarmed with speculators, who neither intended to cultivate the soil or settle there, but who expected to realize fortunes, without labor, out of the bona fide settler. Lots in "cities," where was scarcely a house, were sold to the inexperienced and unwary, at prices equaling those in large cities.[1]

Of course the dream cities did not develop, and money was lost; but they used up available capital in the wild spree of gambling. As a corollary result, prices of food and other necessary commodities increased. The decline in railroad stocks was the first omen of the disaster to come, but the real crash began when, in August 1857, the Ohio Life Insurance and Trust Company of Cincinnati suddenly failed. It had put too much of its capital into shaky railroad enterprises.

Other institutions and individuals were affected by the fall of the Ohio company, so that announcement of its failure "fell like a bomb" in financial circles. By the first or second week in September many banks and business houses began to stop payment in specie. Three financial houses failed in Philadelphia, and the panic was on.

Crowds of people thronged the streets in front of bank buildings, demanding their savings without avail. Rumors spread wildly, increasing the terror. New York and New England banks held firm into the month of October, but even these had to succumb at last. So rapid and numerous were the failures of railroads and other corporations, that all Northern banks suspended specie payments, commerce and

---

[1] R. M. Devens, *Our First Century, Great and Memorable Events* (1876).

industry were paralyzed, and property values, even in established communities, fell from 25 to 75 percent.

Factories closed their doors, steamboats on rivers and lakes stood still, canal boats ceased to ply, railroads conveyed less than half the normal traffic in passengers and freight. Unemployment grew alarmingly. In New York alone there were 30,000 to 40,000 jobless, with winter in immediate prospect.

Mobs began to march in the streets of large cities, shouting "Bread or work!" Vandalism and looting occurred here and there, and soldiers and marines were placed on guard at the sub-treasury in New York to prevent mobs from breaking in.

Like all panics, that of 1857—from which complete recovery was not made until 1860—severely injured the incumbent administration. The South was less affected than other parts of the country, because cotton still was in demand in Europe; and this fact caused the section to become overconfident of its role as "stabilizer" of national finances, and consequently less tolerant of the North. The West and the industrial East where the suffering was worst, began to turn to the growing Republican party in sheer protest against the Democratic "dynasty," which they blamed for their trouble. This economic situation was destined to be as potent, in many respects, as the slavery question, in the Presidential election of 1860.

3

Right in the middle of the depression came the second great gold rush—a rush which occurred, strangely enough, before gold was actually discovered, at least in sufficient quantities to warrant the excitement.

It was a promotion and a fraud, gotten up in an unscrupulous effort to counteract the business decline of certain Missouri River towns, due to the depression. The fact that it developed into a legitimate, indeed vast, discovery of treasure was only incidental to its conception and launching.

On the Missouri River such towns as Kansas City, Leavenworth, St. Joseph, Council Bluffs, and smaller places, had felt the pinch of the times particularly sharply. For years they had been keyed to the migrations across the continent to the Pacific Coast, but now those migrations virtually ceased. Merchants, liquor dealers, arms suppliers, sellers of wagons, mules, horses, and oxen, keepers of inns and hostelries, proprietors of gambling places, dance halls, and sporting houses—with their establishments idle and none of that welcome traffic coming from the East to be sent onward to the West—could see nothing but ruin ahead of them. Those towns were not entrepôts of grain, livestock, or other farm products; they had no mining or lumbering to maintain them; and they had been geared to a higher level of financial and business activity than that of sleepy little river hamlets.

Only something like another gold rush would save them for the present. And another gold rush they set about creating.

To the west, between the California Trail and the Santa Fe Trail, lay a great upthrust of the Rocky Mountains, contained in what is now Colorado but was then divided between the Kansas and Utah territories. Its frowning mountain crests—which included no less than fifty-one peaks soaring to an altitude of 14,000 feet or more—were too rugged to be crossed by wagon trains. Its only population consisted of some Indian bands and a few trappers.

During the California gold rush some men who had gained experience in gold mining in Georgia took the Overland Trail along with the tens of thousands who had no experience at all. Among these was a group of Cherokee Indians, originally from Georgia, but expelled from that gold-bearing region and then living in the Indian Territory. They prospected a few of the tributaries of the South Platte River, where they found a little gold but not enough to detain them, and they soon were on the trail again for California.

They did not forget it, however, and later they passed on the information to a man named William Green Russell, who was friendly to their people. Russell had mined gold in Georgia, and he was married to a Cherokee woman.

When he returned to the Missouri River frontier in the winter of 1857, Russell organized a party of about a hundred men, including his brothers Oliver and Levi, and other whites, but mostly Cherokees, to prospect what then was vaguely known as the "Pike's Peak country." Early in the spring they started panning the streams at the foothills of the Rampart Range, and found some gold—not enough to warrant mining, but enough so that Russell decided he ought to prospect a little more.

Winter caught them in the mountains, with deep snows and cold weather. Russell made a winter camp at the point where Cherry Creek flowed into the South Platte, the site of the present city of Denver. Other prospectors, hearing of his activities, wandered in, and the camp was enlarged for them, as all waited for spring. Meantime, just to give them something to do, they "staked out," on opposite sides of Cherry Creek, two rival towns, which they named Auraria (somebody's coining from the word *aurum*, Latin for gold), and Denver (named for General James W. Denver, than governor of the Kansas Territory).

A little gold had been found, but certainly not enough to justify a rush of gold seekers to the region. Nevertheless the frontier towns, suffering from the panic, set about to create a gold rush purely to help business.

Pamphlets, containing glowing (and fictitious) accounts of rich strikes made in the mountains, were printed and distributed throughout the East and Middle West. Newspaper articles in the same vein were written. The caution of Russell's own reports, and those of other prospectors, was attributed to a selfish desire to keep those riches for themselves. Agents were sent to principal cities, and others boarded steamboats and trains, to create and whip up excitement.

The result, partly due to the restlessness and despair caused by the economic depression, exceeded the fondest imaginings even of the Missouri River town promoters. The next spring a wave of people began arriving at the Missouri. Roads were lined with wagons, steamboats crowded with passengers. Once more suppliers of goods, liquor, food, livestock, and entertainment of various kinds enjoyed a period of exhilarating prosperity.

The fact that they were sending out across the plains thousands to seek a Golconda which the men who were "wise" knew did not exist, did not trouble them. Profits were splendid. They cheerfully took from some of the "pilgrims" every dollar they owned, selling them equipment and supplies for the effort which their victims hoped would redeem fortunes lost in the panic.

The tragic outcome of this unscrupulous exploitation came, of course, when men arrived at the Cherry Creek camps and found that they had been deceived. Loud were the maledictions and fierce the anger of the dupes. One of them composed a threatening rhyme:

> Here lies the body of D. C. Oakes
> Killed for aiding the Pike's Peak hoax.

And then, quite unexpectedly and suddenly, there came a *genuine gold strike!*

There were two of them in fact, almost simultaneous, on two branches of Clear Creek, between Denver and the Berthoud Pass. And both were rich.

Now the gold rush had a legitimate reason. And "D. C. Oakes," whoever he was, and his fellow promoters, no doubt were saved embarrassment if not danger from irate gold-seekers returning empty-handed.

Horace Greeley, lured by the same propaganda that sent the first wave of prospectors to the mountains, went out to "inspect the Kansas gold fields." He had plenty to write about, and from his pen shortly appeared a picturesque description in his New York *Tribune:*

As yet the entire population of the valley [Gregory Gulch]—which cannot number less than 4000, including five white women and seven squaws living with white men—sleep in tents or under booths of pine boughs, cooking and eating in the open air. I doubt that there is as yet a table or a chair in these diggings . . . The food . . . is restricted to a few staples—pork, hot bread, beans, and coffee forming the almost exclusive diet . . . but a meat shop has just been established, on whose altar are offered up the ill-fed and well-whipped oxen who are just in from a 50-day journey across the plains.

Greeley said that five hundred of the people in the diggings had arrived within the past week, and more were coming every day; and he offered his considered opinion that very rich deposits had been found.

Such an endorsement was all that was needed. The rush grew. Lusty mining towns such as Tarryall, Hamilton, Fairplay, Golden, Gold Hill, Boulder, and Colorado City sprang up, and Denver began to grow. In the first year $1,000,000 worth of gold was taken out. More and more fields were opened. Silver and other minerals were discovered, and the mountains poured a vast new wealth into the financial bloodstream of the nation, measurably helping to restore the nation to prosperity.

Miraculously, it seemed, the "trumped up" gold rush had made good.

4

In another part of the West, differing from the snowy and pine-clad mountains of Colorado, lay the bleak, treeless country of what is now Nevada (then part of the Utah Territory). Gold prospectors had drifted over into it from the Sierra Nevada Mountains of California, and gold was found in fair quantities, particularly in the area east of Lake Tahoe and along the Truckee River.

Enough was found, in fact, to name one particular valley Gold Canyon. A camp called Gold Hill sprang up at the head of the canyon, and another on the other side of the ridge, near Carson Creek, was named Virginia City.[2] By 1858 gold had begun to "peter out," and the miners were leaving the country. Those remaining grew even more discouraged when a heavy, dark material in the earth clogged

---

[2] In honor of James Finney (or Fennimore), nicknamed "Old Virginia," a prospector who, according to his contemporary, H. T. P. Comstock, one night "on a drunk, fell down and broke his whiskey bottle. On rising he said—'I baptize this ground Virginia.'"

their rockers and generally caused trouble and profanity. They washed the gold out of it, and threw the stuff away.

In the spring of 1859 Peter O'Riley and Pat McLaughlin, working high up on the side of a hill where they had but little water to run their rocker, began to dig a hole to impound more water for that purpose. Four feet down they struck that same gummy substance. It was black, but contained spangles of gold. Their first attempts to run the curious-looking stuff through their rocker surprised them by the rich gold deposit left. But the gold taken out was light in color, and they began to fear it was "bogus"—some base metal with a gold color.

What they had run into was a great bed of decomposed ore—black sulphuret of silver. They took a wordy and important-talking individual named H. T. P. Comstock (commonly called Pancake) in as a partner, because he claimed that he had posted the ground for a ranch—a claim never proved.

On July 1 that year, Augustus Harrison, a rancher on the Truckee River, out of sheer curiosity, took a piece of the "queer stuff" to an assayer. Then the astonishing truth came out. The sample assayed at a rate of several thousand dollars per ton in gold and silver!

Thus, blunderingly, the greatest single silver deposit in the land was discovered—the great Comstock lode which was to yield more than $500,000,000 in treasure, create a state out of barren, sun-smitten Nevada, and be the chief factor in the vast silver mining industry.

5

There was enormous excitement over gold and silver, as well as coal and other minerals, including rich iron deposits in the Lake Superior regions. But at this same time came another discovery of tremendous influence upon the future civilization of America and the world.

For many years the phenomenon known as "rock oil" had been known in the Allegheny River headwaters of northwest Pennsylvania and southwest New York. Some learned pedant, with the instinct of all learned pedants to make simple things more complicated, gave it a Latin name—petroleum (from the Latin *petra*, meaning rock, and *oleum*, meaning oil)—but in English or Latin it meant the same thing, an oil believed to originate in some manner in the rocks beneath the earth's surface.

Indians knew of it before the white men, and used it in mixing their warpaints, in tarring baskets to make them waterproof, and as remedies for ailments such as rheumatism. Its first use among white people in fact seems to have been as medicine known as Seneca Oil or

Genesee Oil, which was bottled and sold over the country as a sort of panacea by glib-tongued "medicine show" men.

But its value as an illuminant also was known. The learned Dr. S. P. Hildreth wrote to the American Journal of Science in 1826, that a well sunk for salt had discharged instead great quantities of petroleum "vulgarly called Seneka Oil," and since "it affords a brisk, clear light, when burnt," predicted it might be valuable for lighting "the street lamps of the future cities of Ohio."

It was a good prediction, but at the time Dr. Hildreth wrote, petroleum was generally considered a nuisance. Men had for years dug or drilled wells for salt, and a crude method of casing with hollow logs, thus bringing brine to the surface without mixing it with the "top water" above, had been devised as early as 1806. But still the object was to obtain salt, not oil, and when oil was encountered the well was abandoned, for oil-tainted salt had no market value.

Science experimented with the substance, and in 1852 Abraham Gesner, a Canadian scientist, discovered a way to obtain kerosene from oil distilled from coal (hence the name "coal oil") and a year later introduced it into the United States for use in lamps.

Oil thus had become of some commercial value, but nobody as yet imagined that it could be produced in quantities sufficient to make it important. What appeared in water springs or lay as an oleaginous scum on certain ponds and pools, was gathered by spreading woolen cloths and wringing them out into a container when saturated.

But it was not as an illuminant, so much as a lubricant and later as a fuel that oil was to play its greatest role in history. And a demand had already become acute for lubricants before it was available in any great supply.

In America the industrial era had been developing since about 1800. Machinery needed lubrication in ever-increasing quantities. At first castor and other vegetable oils were used, and in some cases animal fats such as lard. Then came the great days of whaling, largely spurred by a rapidly growing demand for whale oil as a lubricant. But vegetable oils did not suffice in quantity, and the whale ships, wandering over the seven seas, killed off the whales until they became scarce. Industry, and the spreading railroad systems, faced a crisis.

Petroleum, even in its crude state, had lubricating qualities, and some Americans began to wonder if there might be some way to find the mysterious sources from which oil appeared here and there at the surface of the earth.

It was Colonel E. L. Drake—a railroad conductor and "colonel" by courtesy only—who first had the idea of *drilling* for oil. A bewhiskered man, he had eyes set so far apart that they seemed not to focus too well, and gave him somewhat the appearance of a startled rabbit. He nevertheless possessed a large bump of curiosity. In the winter of 1857 he traveled from his New Haven, Connecticut, home to visit the small settlement of Titusville, Pennsylvania, which was situated on the banks of Oil Creek, the stream being so named because of the large amounts of oil that ruined its water for drinking purposes.

On the way to Pennsylvania he visited the salt works at Syracuse, New York, where his idea of drilling or boring for oil may have been born. After inspecting the oil country, he went on to Tarentum, the site of many salt wells, which he studied, before returning to New Haven. All this had been done while he was on sick leave from his railroad duties.

Having deeply considered the problem, Drake formed the Seneca Oil Company with some friends, and obtained a drilling lease near Titusville, to which he returned in the summer of 1858. His plan—to drill for oil—was delayed by the difficulty of finding a salt driller who would undertake the job. Though oil had been found when drilling for salt, it seemed ridiculous to the men of the time that anyone should drill at a specific place and expect to find oil. Little was known of oil geology. Nobody had any real idea whether oil lay in large deposits, or ran in veins, or seeped through porous rock in such a way that recovery by the undeveloped methods of the time would be practicable.

So wild did the project appear in fact, that the first of all oil promoters received the nickname "Crazy Drake," and his well, when he got it started was known as "Drake's Folly."

But he continued working, corresponding, and even obtained a little money in the way of loans. At length, going back to Tarentum, he found a man named William A. Smith, usually called Uncle Billy, who had made tools for drilling for salt and for artesian water, and had drilled some wells himself. Uncle Billy agreed to take the job—at $2.50 a day—and, about the middle of May, 1859, he arrived at Titusville with his equipment.

Risking everything on his hunch, and with the crudest of derricks and most primitive tools, Drake saw to it that Uncle Billy started the well, May 20, 1859. He had, of course, struck upon the secret of finding petroleum which is the key to the whole vast industry today.

There had been an improvement over the old hollow-log casings, and Uncle Billy used a six-inch iron pipe to keep out the infiltration of water and prevent the constant caving of the sides of the shaft. With a small six-horsepower steam engine he began sending the bit down.

Gravel was first encountered—42 feet of it. No oil was found. Then shale rock was struck, and still there was no oil.

The prospect seemed discouraging. Drake was running short of funds. But still he ordered the driller to continue. Foot by foot the crude bit ate its way down until the hole was 64 feet deep, and 22 feet of shale had been penetrated, still with no result.

Then, on August 29, 1859, the first oil strike of history occurred. As recorded by a contemporary chronicle:

> At the depth of about 70 feet a large opening, filled with coal oil, somewhat mixed with water [was struck]. A small pump on hand brought up from 400 to 500 gallons of oil a day. An explosion blew it [the pump] up. One of three times its size was put in its place and during the first four days threw up 5000 gallons of oil—1250 gallons per day, or one gallon per minute for twenty-hours, fifty minutes, per day.

The strike was a rare piece of luck. After that one well, oil was never found at that depth anywhere in the area, and had Drake's well been bored only a few feet in any direction from just where it went down, the crevice would have been missed. As the *Titusville Herald* later said, "like a long, friendly arm, the vein of oil seemed to reach up to meet him."

Had the well not been successfully completed, perhaps nobody else would ever have tried the experiment of drilling. As it was, however, an industry destined to grow to gigantic proportions was born that day beside Oil Creek, in Pennsylvania. Drake had proved that oil could be brought up in quantity, but even he had no notion of the prodigious amounts of petroleum the earth could be induced to yield up in the future.

At once the first "oil boom" occurred. Merchants abandoned their stores, farmers dropped their plows, lawyers deserted their offices, and preachers their pulpits, in the hysteria. A forest of derricks sprang up in the area.

With the development of the refining process, pioneered by Samuel M. Kier of Pittsburgh, and as exploration widened and refinery methods improved, the industrial age had its limitless lubrication, the way was opened to the modern age of transportation, cities were lit and heated by natural gas, and within less than a century the oil deposits of many nations would become matters of international concern.

America seemed bursting with resources. What had once been forest country now had given way to millions upon millions of acres, in patches and squares of geometrical regularity, where fat lands were farmed and grains and livestock grew. In the South great plantations and small freeholds were white with cotton. The whole land seemed to smile. It was only the people who were at odds with life.

CHAPTER TWENTY-SIX

Lincoln versus Douglas

1

KANSAS, continued to be the major danger spot in the country. The farcical elections in that territory, already described, in which the slavery men elected a legislature that sat at Lecompton and the anti-slavery men another that sat at Topeka, with each party refusing to vote in the other's "election," had resulted in two state constitutions being presented to Congress.

There is not space in this narrative to describe all the political maneuvers by which Kansas settlers made themselves rather ridiculous, and democratic processes broke down, due to the heated feelings in that strife-torn territory. It is enough to say that the "free state" constitution was clearly illegal. The Lecompton constitution, also illegal, at least had a semblance of being framed under the statutes.

It was a curious document. Slave property, under its provisions, was made inviolable. Immigrants were permitted to bring in slaves, and emancipation of a slave without compensation and the owner's consent, was forbidden.

But a clause also offered an alternative. It was provided that a referendum should be held, to determine whether the "constitution with slavery," or the "constitution without slavery" should be adopted. If the latter prevailed, the slavery provisions would be deleted, except that there should be no interference with slave property already in Kansas at that time.

To anti-slavery people even the "without slavery" alternative was unacceptable, for some two hundred slaves—and their progeny—would remain in the territory, while others might be smuggled in and held on the presumption that they were present before the adoption of the alternative constitution. So when the referendum was held Kansas voters, with the free state element now clearly in the majority, rejected the entire constitution with both its alternatives. When they saw that they were beaten before the election, the slavery men refused to vote.

Thus far the Kansas situation was a stalemate. But at this point Buchanan made his greatest blunder. Perhaps influenced by his cabinet, which was strongly Southern in complexion; perhaps hoping that the Kansas problem might be settled by the act, since he based his policy on the technical legality of the Lecompton constitution; or perhaps fearful of secession, which some parts of the South already had threatened if the Lecompton constitution was not adopted, he decided that Kansas should be admitted under that provision.

Some of his friends warned him against the policy, even pleaded with him, but like most weak men Buchanan could be stubborn.

"I intend to make my policy a test," he said.

It was a test which was destined to disrupt his own party. Nobody saw this more quickly than Stephen A. Douglas, leader of the Northern Democrats, who felt that the question at issue went to the very heart of his popular sovereignty doctrine. As he took a train from Illinois for Washington, it became known that he would fight the Lecompton constitution on the ground that it did not allow the people of Kansas the right to decide this all-important question among themselves. Crowds at railroad stations cheered him as he rode to the capital.

Arrived in Washington, he called in person at the White House on December 3. There Douglas and Buchanan faced each other in a critical and historic scene.

Buchanan at first sought to be urbane; Douglas was positive, almost pugnacious. In that conversation the short, burly Senator from the West told the tall, white-haired President that he would denounce any message to Congress urging acceptance of the Lecompton constitution, as soon as it was read.

Anger flared in the President's eye. "Mr. Douglas," he said, "I desire you to remember that no Democrat ever yet differed from an administration of his own choice without being crushed. Beware of the fate of Tallmadge and Rives."

He was referring to two men whom Andrew Jackson had disciplined, and the Senator got the implication.

"Mr. President," said Douglas, "I desire *you* to remember that General Jackson is dead."

With that defiance, he left the White House.

2

Buchanan believed that party discipline and the administration's potent influence would carry the Lecompton constitution through both houses. Congress organized itself December 7, and next day Buchanan's message was read to both houses. It recommended the proposed Pacific railroad, condemned filibustering—and called for adoption of the Lecompton constitution.

Douglas immediately accepted the challenge. Knowing that the Democrats held a clear majority in the Senate, he could only hope to win over enough of his own party to combine with the Republican strength, to defeat it. This seemed a severe problem to attack for the Democratic strength was thirty-nine against twenty Republican and five Know-Nothing votes. He would have to swing at least eight of his own party for a majority, even if the divided opposition held together, which there was no assurance it would do.

The first day after the message was received, Douglas arose to speak against the Lecompton constitution. In that speech he stated his opinion for all to hear: that the document in question was contrary to the American principle; that it violated the spirit of the Kansas-Nebraska Act under which it was intended that the people of a territory should be able to speak for themselves; that in fact the Lecompton convention itself was not legal, in spite of statements to the contrary, for it had never been recognized by Congress; and that no constitution should be endorsed by Congress under any circumstances, which did not express the popular will.

He knew that he was drawing upon his head the hostility of the President, and he was willing to accept that hostility to uphold the principle in which he believed. He hoped to protract the debate until the North fully understood the issues at stake and would be sufficiently aroused to let the Lower House know its will in the questions.

Buchanan was right in his estimate of the Senate. In spite of the dramatic efforts of Douglas, who sought to rally the Republicans, labored with his Democratic colleagues, and spoke again and again fearlessly and brilliantly during the long battle, the Senate, on March 22, 1858, voted 33 to 25 in favor of the Lecompton resolution.

But Douglas was not beaten yet. He was irrevocably opposed to the methods being used, and when asked if he had considered what might be the cost to himself, he replied, "I have taken a through ticket and checked all my baggage!"

The Lecompton resolution still must pass the House. Senators have six-year terms, while House members have two-year terms. So the complexion of the membership of the House had changed more recently than that of the Senate. It contained 131 Democrats, 92 Republicans, and 14 Know-Nothings. But many of the Democrats were from the North, and of these at least five from Illinois, six from Ohio, three from Indiana, three from Pennsylvania, and two from New York might be definitely counted as anti-Lecompton men. There were probably others, if they could be held in line.

To this group Douglas devoted all his influence and his attention. Against him the administration forces employed every device of patronage and preferment. Feelings ran high in the debates that ensued. On one occasion, when the session lasted far into the night, a veritable melee took place, of which Ben: Perley Poore wrote a spirited account:

About half-past one, Mr. Grow, of Pennsylvania, then standing on the Democratic side of the House, objected to General Quitman's making any remarks. "If you are going to object," shouted Mr. Keitt, of South Carolina, "return to your own side of the hall." Mr. Grow responded: "This is a free hall, and every man has a right to be where he pleases." Mr. Keitt then came up to Mr. Grow and said: "I want to know what you mean by such an answer as that." Mr. Grow replied: "I mean just what I say; this is a free hall, and a man has the right to be where he pleases." "Sir," said Mr. Keitt, "I will let you know that you are a Black Republican puppy." "Never mind," retorted Mr. Grow, "I shall occupy such place in this hall as I please, and no negro-driver shall crack his whip over me." The two men then rushed at each other with clinched fists. A dozen Southerners at once hastened to the affray, while as many anti-Lecompton men came to the rescue, and Keitt received—not from Grow, however—a blow that knocked him down. Mr. Potter, of Wisconsin, a very athletic, compactly built man, bounded into the centre of the excited group, striking right and left with vigor. Washburne, of Illinois, and his brother, of Wisconsin, also were prominent, and for a minute or two it seemed as though we were to have a Kilkenny fight on a magnificent scale. Barksdale had hold of Grow, when Potter struck him a severe blow, supposing that he was hurting that gentleman. Barksdale, turning around and supposing it was Elihu Washburne who struck him, dropped Grow, and struck out at the gentleman from Illinois. Cadwallader Washburne, perceiving the attack on his brother, also made a dash at Mr. Barksdale, and seized him by the hair, apparently for the purpose of drawing him "into chancery" and pummeling him to greater satisfaction. Horrible to relate, Mr. Barksdale's wig came off in Cadwallader's left hand, and his right fist expended itself with tremendous force against the unresisting air. This ludicrous incident unquestionably did much toward restoring good nature subsequently, and its effect was heightened not a little by the fact that in the excitement of the occasion Barksdale restored his wig wrong-side foremost.

The Speaker pounded his desk and shouted for order, the sergeant-at-arms paraded the official mace among the members, and the tumult subsided. Several distinguished Congressmen "were found to present an excessively tumbled and disordered appearance," and not a few "sustained slight bruises and scratches," but when the commotion was over, "gentlemen of the opposite parties crossed over to each other to explain their pacific dispositions, and that they got into a fight when their only purpose was to prevent a fight." The chronicler noted, with satisfaction, that "no weapons were openly displayed"—unless a heavy stoneware spittoon, poised for hurling (but not used) by Congressman John Covode of Pennsylvania, could be so described.[1]

It became apparent that the Lecompton resolution would fail of passage, and Douglas, more than any other man, was responsible. His speeches and delaying tactics had aroused opinion in the North, and Congressmen were getting letters from their constituents. By a coalition of Republicans, his own Democratic followers, and even a few Know-Nothings, the offensive measure was rejected, and instead an amendment was carried, really a substitute resolution, proposed by the venerable Senator John J. Crittenden of Kentucky, Henry Clay's old friend. The substitute provided for a popular vote in Kansas for a constitution.

But the administration and the Southern Democratic leaders, still unwilling to accept the verdict, asked for a conference between committees from both houses. The result was a bill which juggled with words sufficiently to save face for the President, at least in part, while in actuality permitting the Kansans to defeat the Lecompton constitution—which they soon did.

3

Buchanan had abandoned principle for expediency; and he disrupted the Democratic party in so doing. Douglas foresaw trouble, not only for the nation, but for himself. Since the days of Andrew Jackson, his party had been the chief guide and guardian of the nation's destinies; now it had in effect become two parties—North and South, split on the questions of slavery and states' rights.

That division cut deep. Even churches divided on the slavery question. Methodist, Presbyterian, and Baptist denominations separated into two independent bodies, North and South. Episcopalians and Roman Catholics managed to avoid schisms, and some denominations were sufficiently localized—like the Congregationalists of the North— to avoid the problem of sectional feeling.

Douglas had shown courage and integrity in leading the fight against the Lecompton resolution, and by so doing had lost much of his personal popularity in the South. He saw that the growing power of the Republican party was Northern and sectional, and no very great feat of prophecy was required by him to foresee that if the Republicans

---

[1] See *Perley's Reminiscences,* by Ben: Perley Poore.

won the next Presidential election, the South very probably would rebel at being governed by a party, the interests and policies of which came exclusively from the North.

It was Douglas' firm belief that the Democratic party was the only means by which this disruption of the Union could be averted. But how to save the Democratic party and with it the nation?

By this time Douglas was immeasurably the most distinguished as well as popular of the Northern Democrats, but Southern Democrats, who did not share the enthusiasm for him, based their opposition to him on the grounds that he would fight any attempt at secession; and the sentiment for secession was growing ever stronger in the South.

If Northern Democrats regarded Douglas as their chief hope for the Presidency, many in the slave states spoke of Jefferson Davis of Mississippi as a White House possibility. Like Lincoln, Davis was born in a Kentucky log cabin, only about a hundred miles separating their birthplaces; and they were nearly the same age, Davis being a little more than eight months the senior. In a curious way Davis even vaguely resembled Lincoln physically—tall, raw-boned, and lean, with hollowed cheeks. But he was finer featured, and less homely than Lincoln. The resemblance was enhanced when both men grew beards.[2]

But this resemblance was physical only. Jefferson Davis graduated from West Point in 1828, received a commission as a second lieutenant, and spent the next seven years on active army duty. During this tour of duty the Black Hawk War took place, where, as a captain, he mustered in the Illinois militia, including Abraham Lincoln.

While serving under Colonel (later General) Zachary Taylor, at Fort Crawford, Wisconsin, he fell in love with his commander's daughter Sarah Knox and eloped with her in June 1835. Three months after their marriage the girl died, probably of typhoid fever. Davis, resigned his commission from the army, mourned her for years but eventually, a decade later in 1845, married again, his second bride being Varina Howell, a charming girl seventeen years his junior.

His family had grown prosperous in cotton lands in Mississippi, and he was elected to Congress from that state, but resigned his seat at the opening of the War with Mexico to organize a regiment of Mississippi volunteers of which he was colonel. He and his regiment showed such distinguished fighting qualities at the Battle of Buena Vista, that Davis won the praise and friendship of Old Rough and Ready, who until then had never been reconciled to the loss of his daughter.

[2] T. C. DeLeon, in *Four Years in Rebel Capitals* (1892), wrote of leaving Washington immediately after Lincoln was inaugurated and the Civil War started, and going to Montgomery, Alabama, for a time the capital of the Confederacy, where he saw Davis. He was fascinated by a sense that Davis and Lincoln looked a great deal alike, and suggested that later the critical times gave strength to Davis' delicacy and refinement to Lincoln's ruggedness.

After the war Davis was elected to the Senate, served with conspicuous efficiency as Secretary of War under Franklin Pierce, and when Buchanan became President, returned to the Senate. In the debate over the Lecompton issue he had sadly and solemnly deplored the tendency toward disunion which he saw in various parts of the country.

Personally, Jefferson Davis was elegant and courteous, but reserved and sometimes cold in manner. His ambition was boundless, and to the end of his life he believed that his chief genius was along military lines. In sum, though cabin-born he was too aristocratic in his attitudes and habits to appeal to the affections of the common people, and his sectional feelings were such that he hardly thought in the broadest national terms. When the time came he would be the spearhead of secession.

By 1858 it was becoming apparent that Buchanan could hardly be re-elected. The nickname "Ten Cent Jimmy," which was hung on him by his political adversaries because of a statement attributed to him (but never verified) to the effect that ten cents a day was enough for a workingman, created an image of cheapness and pettiness which he perhaps hardly deserved, yet which clung to him.

Studying the situation then existing, Douglas sincerely believed that he was the man most likely to unite the nation. The Presidency, always an ambition, he now felt he should seek as a duty to his country.

Before he could think of that supreme honor, however, he first must think about keeping his seat in the Senate. His term was near the end, and he must stand again for office in 1858.

Illinois had given Buchanan and the Democrats a plurality of 6500 votes in 1856, but Douglas and others had noticed this: the southern part of the state, nicknamed "Egypt," because the city of Cairo was at its tip, swung the balance for the Democrats. On the other hand, the northern part of the state, with Chicago as its chief center, was fast gaining in population; and with the demise of the Know-Nothing and Whig parties, of whom the Republicans might pick up a large proportion, Douglas knew that he was facing the fight of his life in the coming election.

4

More and more the Republicans of Illinois looked toward Abraham Lincoln as their leader. He had courage, and sound reasoning power, and he had developed into a speaker of remarkable eloquence. He was no spread-eagle orator, and though he sometimes spoke wonderful and thrilling words, he aimed to inspire thought rather than emotion. His strong and original ideas placed him in a class by himself in the West.

Lincoln had failed in one effort to win a Senate seat. But he was eager to try again. He had a powerful opponent for the Republican nomination, John Wentworth, mayor of Chicago, who had been elected to the chief post of his city by a record-making majority. There were many who believed that even if the Republicans should gain a majority in the next legislature—which would elect the Senator —Wentworth could control that body, and so elect himself.

As for Lincoln, even if he won the Republican nomination, he would have to face Douglas, the greatest, most powerful, and most eloquent Democrat in Illinois and the entire North. The stand taken by Douglas on the Lecompton question, while exciting fierce enmity among many Southern Democrats, had brought him high praise in the North, including that of such prominent Republicans as Horace Greeley, William H. Seward, and Thurlow Weed.

Douglas, preparing for his race, knew that he faced the displeasure of President Buchanan. In retaliation against the man who had defied him on the Lecompton issue, Buchanan used his patronage power to dismiss almost all Douglas supporters from federal offices; and he clearly indicated that he would extend his further displeasure to all others who backed Douglas. In Illinois, therefore, Douglas faced a rupture in his own party, of which a considerable faction, called by his supporters the "Buchaneers" (a weak pun on "buccaneers"), were administration supporters who would work against him in Illinois.

Most of the state's Democrats, however, loyally rallied to Douglas, and other elements, including old-line Whigs, inclined toward him. Lincoln, in fact, had a complaint about the adulation of his rival by Republicans in the East; and his law partner, William H. Herndon, traveled to New York to plead Lincoln's cause with Greeley, whose powerful New York *Tribune* had a wide—and influential—circulation in Illinois.

Greeley stood by his guns. "Douglas is a brave man," he said. "Forget the past and sustain the righteous."

Throughout the East important Republicans gave Herndon a cold reception and in Boston they actually seemed surprised that anyone would oppose Douglas. Undiscouraged by these indications, Lincoln went to work upon the leaders of his own party in Illinois; and he so far succeeded with them that by the time the Republican state convention opened at Springfield, June 16, he had secured endorsements from most of the county organizations. Almost as soon as the state convention was called to order it officially nominated Abraham Lincoln "for the United States Senate, as the successor of Stephen A. Douglas."

Illinois was sure to be a key state in the next Presidential election. Here were two contestants almost without equals, and possible Presidential history was in the making between them. No wonder the whole country focused its attention upon Illinois, and what was to be the most famous state campaign in the annals of the nation.

When Douglas, still in Washington, read a telegram telling of his rival's nomination by the Republicans, he gave Lincoln a sincere tribute:

"I shall have my hands full! He is the strong man of his party, full of wit, facts, dates—and the best stump speaker, with his droll ways and dry jokes, in the West. He is as honest as he is shrewd and if I beat him my victory will be hardly won."

Few of Douglas' own supporters, perhaps, agreed with him at that time. Lincoln was raw, homely in appearance, awkward, perpetually ill-clad, a failure in his political career, and he represented a political power which had become national in scope only two years before. How could he successfully oppose the famous Douglas, a masterful orator, and the leader of an old established party, with a powerful backing of friends and influence?

It is interesting to consider Lincolns' own viewpoint at this time. He had been in one of his periods of melancholy. Though he believed in himself and his policies, assuredly he was facing the greatest opponent of his life.

There was his vernacular. He was inclined to say "whar" for "where," "keer" for "care," "young uns" for "children," and these and other traces of frontier dialect were to remain with him throughout his life.[3]

Yet his confidence had grown, rather than waned. He believed in ideas, and he had learned how to express them. His almost uncouth appearance made him distinctive, while he could warm people to him with his humor and straightforwardness. Lincoln, though he knew he was the underdog, did not go into his contest with Douglas in any mood of defeatism.

Very early, in fact, he showed that he would be an antagonist worthy of Douglas' steel. Rising to address the Springfield state convention, the night after he was nominated, he made an address, which became historic as the "House Divided" speech.

He began by pointing out, with profound gravity, the danger of the situation, how all attempts at compromise on the slavery question

---

[3] Later, in his famous Cooper Union speech, he began by saying, "Mr. Cheerman."

had failed, and how agitation on that question had only grown more bitter. Then came the great challenge:

"In my opinion, it will not cease until a crisis shall have been reached and passed—

"*A house divided against itself cannot stand.*[4]

"I believe this government cannot endure; permanently half slave and half free. I do not expect the Union to be dissolved—I do not expect the house to fall—but I do expect that it will cease to be divided."

It expressed his great central concern, the preservation of the Union. Those words were to echo as a battle cry throughout the Civil War.

The rest of his speech, devoted to a recital of the issues of the day, contained some questions as to Douglas' policies, and denied that his opponent was the best instrument to achieve the exclusion of slavery from the territories.

"They [the Douglas supporters] remind us that he is a very great man," said the tall speaker in his whimsical manner, "and that the largest of us are very small ones. Let this be granted. But 'a living dog is better than a dead lion.' Judge Douglas, if not a dead lion for this work, is at least a caged and toothless one."

He paid a semi-tribute to his opponent: "Now, as ever, I wish not to misrepresent Judge Douglas' position, question his motives, or do aught that can be personally offensive to him. Whenever, if ever, he and we can come together on principle so that our great cause may have assistance from his great ability, I hope to have opposed no adventitious obstacle."

But, he added, Douglas was not with the Republicans then, did not pretend to be, did not promise to be. Therefore the cause of union and liberty must be carried on by its undoubted friends, "whose hands are free, whose hearts are in the work."

He concluded with a brief review of the Republican showing in the previous election, a party then "of strange, discordant, and even hostile elements," which yet "formed and fought the battle through, under the constant fire of a disciplined, proud, and pampered enemy," and concluded with the assertion that though the victory might be delayed, sooner or later it was sure to come.

The speech made a tremendous sensation, not only in Illinois, but over the nation. Greeley printed it entire in his *Tribune*, with an editorial of cordial praise; and thereafter Greeley ceased urging the Illinois Republicans to support Douglas.

[4] This phrase, so often quoted, was from the Bible, Lincoln's version of Mark II, 25: "If a house be divided against itself, that house cannot stand."

Democratic newspapers also paid attention to the speech—but by way of criticism. Some even denounced it as "little short of treason," since, to their view, it was an incitement to civil war.

In the eyes of both his supporters and his adversaries, the "House Divided" speech was a new manifestation of the power of Abraham Lincoln, its central declaration classic. For the purposes of his own coming campaign, however, it was not altogether helpful.

His friends, indeed, had urged him to leave out the "house divided" sequence, because it might be taken to indicate that he was a radical, whereas he was in reality a conservative. But Lincoln was more interested in his cause than in himself. He replied: "The time has come when these sentiments should be uttered; and if it is decreed that I should go down linked with the truth—let me die in the advocacy of what is just and right."

5

And what of Stephen A. Douglas? He was correct in his estimate of Lincoln as a tough opponent; but he was never known to quail before any person or any odds. Now, in spite of Buchanan's reprisals, in spite of the division of his party, in spite of criticisms leveled at him by many leaders among the Democrats, he prepared to carry on the fight with everything in him.

Before he left Washington, to return to Illinois for his campaign, he charged in the Senate that there was a secret combination between Buchanan Democrats and Illinois Republicans to defeat him for office. And indeed there was some such skulduggery in progress, but knowing Lincoln's fanatical honesty, his supporters did not dare tell him of their scheming. Wrote Herndon at this time to Lyman Trumbull:

You know he [Lincoln] does not know the details of how we get along. I do, but he does not. That kind of thing does not suit his tastes, nor does it suit me, yet I am compelled to do it—do it because I cannot get rid of it.

On the arrival of Douglas in Illinois, the change of feeling toward him was notable. The streets of Chicago, where once he had been hooted from the platform, were packed with throngs that roared a welcome to him, and from the upper windows of houses a snowstorm of white handkerchiefs were waved to him by the ladies.

Douglas lost no time in restating his position: that popular sovereignty—the will of the people—should determine what laws were imposed upon them. Lincoln sat on the platform, as Douglas spoke to a cheering Chicago audience, and Douglas made a point of complimenting his rival as "a kind, amiable, and intelligent gentleman, a good citizen and an honorable opponent."

But he charged that Lincoln's "House Divided" speech invited "A war of sections, a war of the North against the South, of the free states against the slave states—a war of extermination to be continued relentlessly, until one or the other shall be subdued and the states shall either become free or become slave." And he defended the Supreme Court in the Dred Scott Decision, on the ground that it did its duty in expounding the Constitution and construing its laws; and its decision must remain final until reversed by an equally high authority.

The following night Lincoln also spoke, pointing out how ineffective was any theory of popular sovereignty in the face of the Dred Scott Decision, and insisting that Douglas drew a wrong inference from his "House Divided" speech. He had not "invited" a war between the sections. He had merely offered a prediction—and "it may have been a foolish one." Already he had said many times that the North should not meddle with slavery in the states where it already existed; but the institution must be confined where it was, so that inevitably it would become extinct in the future.

Thus was launched the great campaign. Douglas began a swing through the state, riding with his beautiful wife and his retinue in a gaily decorated private car. At the rear of the train was a flatcar, on which was mounted a cannon that would thunder when a town was approached, to give notice that the Senator was coming.

Also on that train, but occupying a seat in one of the ordinary passenger cars, with neither wife nor retinue, rode Lincoln. It had been decided that he should follow Douglas and speak wherever the Senator spoke.

Bloomington was the first stop, and Douglas spoke to two thousand people in the courthouse square. He wore a well-cut and carefully brushed suit of blue broadcloth, and upon his massive head was a big, wide-brimmed felt hat, "which, contrasting sharply with his heavy long black hair and dark complexion, added a touch of the theatrical to his appearance."

Lincoln, arriving on the same train, dusty and tired from his trip, was described by Leonard W. Volk, a sculptor who two years later made the famous life mask of Lincoln, as "carrying an old carpetbag in his hand, and wearing a weather-beaten silk hat—too large, apparently, for his head—a long, loosely fitting frock coat, of black alpaca, and vest and trousers of the same material."

Douglas made a brilliant reply to Lincoln's "House Divided" and Chicago speeches. Just as the North would resist any effort to force slavery upon it, he said, so would the South fight if an effort was made to abolish slavery there. "I will not judge them," he declared, "lest I be judged." But he saw inevitable war if such a policy as he described became the settled policy of either section. How would Lincoln go about making all states free? How would he reverse the Dred Scott Decision? A salient point he made was that slavery could not exist in any place where the people did not want it. "I tell you, my friends," he bugled, "it is impossible under our institutions to force slavery on an unwilling people." And he asserted that the Dred Scott Decision, for that very reason, was no more than an abstraction, without practical effect.

Lincoln sat on the platform, but did not speak. "This meeting was called by friends of Judge Douglas," he said, "and it would be improper for me to address it."

Leaving Bloomington, Lincoln again rode on the same train with Douglas—"the only Lincoln man on the train"—and at Springfield he did speak, in the evening after his opponent's afternoon address. Douglas had argued the point that Lincoln favored Negro equality, and in his reply that night Lincoln said that the Declaration of Independence meant only that blacks were equals of whites in their right to "life, liberty, and the pursuit of happiness. All I ask for the Negro is that if you do not like him, let him alone. If God gave him but little, that little let him enjoy."

But Lincoln's following Douglas around was drawing ridicule upon himself. Newspapers began saying that he could get a crowd no other way.

Some of his friends thought that the tactics were wrong, and advised Lincoln to challenge Douglas to a joint debate—as had already been suggested by Horace Greeley in his *Tribune*. Lincoln finally came to a decision and sent a note to Douglas, by Norman Buell Judd, his campaign manager:

> Will it be agreeable to you to make an arrangement for you and myself to divide time, and address the same audiences at the present canvass? Mr. Judd, who will hand you this, is authorized to receive your answer; and if agreeable to you, to enter into the forms of such arrangement.

Quite naturally, Douglas did not care to debate Lincoln. As he said to his advisers, "I do not feel that I want to go into this debate. The whole country knows me and has me measured. Lincoln, as regards myself, is comparatively unknown, and if he gets the best of this debate—and I want to say he is the ablest man the Republicans have got—I shall lose everything. Should I win, I shall gain but little. I do not want to go into the debate with Mr. Lincoln."

But when Republican newspapers announced that the challenge had been given, Douglas felt that he would be accused of fearing to enter the contest. Fear was no part of his nature, and after some correspondence, he agreed to meet Lincoln once in each Congressional district of the state—except Chicago and Springfield where both had spoken—and suggested Ottawa, Freeport, Jonesboro, Charleston, Galesburg, Quincy, and Alton as the meeting places. Lincoln accepted.

6

The sun beat mercilessly down, August 21, 1858, and dust rose from the trampling of the crowd massed about the platform in the Ottawa town square, so that everything was in a haze. Bands played, people shouted.

Upon the platform, with other dignitaries, were the two men: one short, swarthy, with a mane of long black hair, and both courage and energy stamped on his mastiff face; the other tall, also dark, carelessly clothed, his lean face serious, in his gray eyes beneath their shaggy brows a look at once determined and speculative. Stephen A. Douglas and Abraham Lincoln, long-time rivals, at last were matched, man to man, in the first of the great debates that attracted the attention of the nation. Ten or twelve thousand persons had been drawn to the spot to witness the drama of the contest.

Douglas, in his booming voice, began the debate by reading a Republican resolution adopted in 1854—at the time when Lincoln was avoiding that party because of its radicalism—which called for repeal of the Fugitive Slave law, admission of no more slave states into the Union, abolishment of slavery in the District of Columbia, and no further acquirement of territory by the nation unless slavery was forever excluded from it. Then he demanded that Lincoln answer whether he was pledged to those propositions.

Twinklingly Douglas recounted his long acquaintance with his opponent. "I was a school-teacher . . . and he a flourishing grocery-keeper[5]. . . He was then just as good at telling an anecdote as now . . . could beat any of the boys wrestling, or running a foot-race . . . could ruin more liquor than all the boys of the town together; and the dignity and impartiality with which he presided at a horse-race or fist-fight . . . won the praise of everybody that was present and participated. I sympathized with him because he was struggling with difficulties, and so was I."

[5] In the parlance of the day a grocery was equivalent to a saloon, which was the meaning of Douglas' gibe.

Having brought laughter from the crowd, he recited Lincoln's history: his legislative career, and how he dropped out of sight; his brief term in Congress, and how he again dropped out of sight; his failure to win a Senate seat, and how once more he dropped out of sight. And now, said Douglas, he was back helping make the platform that had just been read.

There was more, including a new dissection of the "House Divided" speech; and a charge that Lincoln and Trumbull had conspired to wreck the Whig party to form the Republican party. He was roundly cheered as he closed.

Lincoln seemed almost humble and abashed in comparison to his assured rival, as he in turn took the platform, but he received stirring applause. He began to speak, his high squeaky voice in contrast to Douglas' booming tones, but he also got a laugh when he said that Douglas was mistaken about his being a grocery-keeper.[6]

"I don't know as it would be a great sin if I had been," he went on, and added, "It is true that Lincoln did work the latter part of one winter in a little still house, up at the head of a hollow."

Thereupon he showed to the full satisfaction of everyone that he had nothing to do with the resolutions read. Parrying the abolitionist charge, he said that he was as much for his own race having a "superior position" as Douglas, whenever the necessity of choice arose.

"There is a physical difference," he said, "between the two [races] which, in my judgement, will probably forever forbid their living together on a footing of perfect equality." Yet the Negro was entitled to the natural rights stated in the Declaration of Independence. "I hold that he is as much entitled to these as the white man . . . He is not my equal in many respects . . . But in the right to eat bread, without the leave of anybody else, which his own hand earns, he is my equal and the equal of Judge Douglas, and the equal of every living man."

Foreshadowing his famous question asked later at Freeport, he returned to the charge of a conspiracy to extend slavery over the country, which Douglas said was a falsehood.

"I know the Judge is a great man, while I am a small man, but I feel that I have got him," he said, amid cheering. "If the evidence proves the existence of the conspiracy, does his broad answer denying all knowledge, information, or belief, disturb that fact? It can only show that he was used by the conspirators, and was not a leader of them . . . I do not say that I *know* such a conspiracy to exist . . . but I *believe* it."

The Ottawa debate ended in forensic fireworks when Douglas, in

6 Yet Lincoln actually did operate a store in New Salem in 1832, in which he sold liquor, both in bulk and by the drink.

rebuttal, exclaimed, "Mr. Lincoln has not character enough for integrity and truth, merely on his own *ipse dixit*, to arraign President Buchanan, President Pierce, and nine judges of the Supreme Court, not one of whom would be complimented by being put on an equality with him."

7

Lincoln had not answered the direct questions of Douglas at Ottawa, but he was prepared for them when the next debate was held, at Freeport.

When the two candidates met at Freeport, six days after the Ottawa debate, the weather had turned raw and cloudy, with occasional fine drizzles. But an even greater crowd estimated as high as 15,000 gathered about the open-air platform. Lincoln this time was the first speaker. He faced his audience "tall and ungainly, with a lean face, homely and sorrowful looking," but there was no discouragement in his heart.

First he answered Douglas' Ottawa questions in detail. The Southern states, he said, were entitled to a Fugitive Slave law, but why talk about it since repeal of the law was not now being urged? He did not think any future territories would apply for statehood with slavery, but if one should do so, he saw no alternative but to admit it into the Union. He would be glad to see slavery abolished in the District of Columbia, provided it was done gradually, there was a majority vote for it by the residents in the District, and owners were compensated. He believed it the right and duty of Congress to exclude slavery from the territories, and though he was not in general opposed to honest acquisition of territory by the nation, he would oppose or favor such acquisition as he might think it would or would not aggravate the vexed slavery question.

Having thus stated his position, he dramatically turned to Douglas with some questions of his own. It was at this point that he raised the celebrated issue, in his second question:

Can the people of a United States territory, in any lawful way, against the wish of any citizen of the United States, exclude slavery from its limits prior to the formation of a state constitution?

Here was the real crux of the campaign. Douglas' reply was forthright: "I answer emphatically . . . that in my opinion the people of a territory can, by lawful means, exclude slavery from their limits prior to the formation of a state constitution. Mr. Lincoln knew that I had answered that question over and over again . . . It matters not what way the Supreme Court may hereafter decide as to the abstract question whether slavery may or may not go into a territory under the Constitution, the people have the lawful means to introduce it or exclude it as they please, for the reason that slavery cannot exist a day or an hour anywhere, unless it is supported by local police regulations."

There has been much discussion of Lincoln's strategy in thus bringing Douglas to state what has been called the "Freeport Doctrine." Campaign biographies of Lincoln written two years later, when Lincoln was running for President, claimed that he and other party leaders held a grave discussion on the question, fearing that Douglas' reply would lose the Senate race for Lincoln. To this, according to the story, Lincoln said, "I am after bigger game. The battle of 1860 is worth a hundred of this."

It has been brought out by Beveridge and others that there is no evidence that any such thing occurred. Douglas repeatedly had said much the same things in previous addresses and in Senate speeches —as he pointed out in his reply.

In bringing his opponent to restate this position, Lincoln was probably not thinking of any Presidential race; he was thinking of the Senate race. He was not trying to hurt Douglas in the *South;* he asked the question as a shrewd and practical politician, to widen the breach between the Douglas Democrats and the Buchanan Democrats *in Illinois.*

The important thing accomplished was that the debates had attracted such nation-wide attention that a large corps of newspaper reporters from all parts of the country was present to describe them; and by this means the Freeport Doctrine was given emphasis in national publicity, where it might have escaped the attention of some in Douglas' former pronouncements. It ruined whatever Presidential chances Douglas may have had in the South.

Other questions, put and answered, were of less importance. The debates continued. At Charleston, September 18, Lincoln made a statement much criticized later: "I am not, nor ever have been, in favor of bringing about in any way the social and political equality of the white and black races; that I am not, nor ever have been, in favor of making voters or jurors of Negroes, nor of qualifying them to hold office, nor to intermarry with white people . . ." It was a politician's statement, but it also probably was his honest belief. Lincoln never had been an abolitionist, and his opinion on this question was the opinion of the times.

Yet in the last debate at Alton, Lincoln struck with resounding force the question of *morality* in the slavery question.

"The real issue in this controversy—the one pressing on every mind —is the sentiment on the part of one class that looks upon slavery *as a wrong,*" he said, "and of another class that *does not* look upon it as a wrong. The sentiment that contemplates the institution of slavery in this country as a wrong is the sentiment of the Republican party . . . They look upon it as being a moral, social and political wrong; and while they contemplate it as such, they nevertheless have due regard for its actual existence among us, and the difficulties of getting rid of it in any satisfactory way, and to all the constitutional obligations thrown about it . . .

"On the other hand, I have said there is a sentiment which treats it as *not* being wrong. That is the Democratic sentiment of this day. . . . That class will include all men who positively assert that it is right, and all who, like Judge Douglas, treat it as indifferent and do not say it is either right or wrong . . ."

Here was the important difference between Lincoln and Douglas. Neither wished to see the extension of slavery. Both wished to quiet the anti-slavery agitation. Both were patriotic men who wished above everything to preserve the Union, and therefore deplored the growth of sectionalism.

But to Lincoln slavery was a great moral wrong, while to Douglas the issue of popular sovereignty was more important. Nothing really new or original had been said in the debates; but they had the effect of riveting the attention of America on the fact that slavery had become the paramount issue before the nation.

8

Douglas had carried on an effective fight for the prize both he and Lincoln wanted. He rallied his own supporters, succeeded in winning over many Buchanan Democrats, and even some former Whigs. But Lincoln had proved to be the more appealing candidate. He had managed to weld together sentiment so strong that he actually carried Illinois, in the popular vote.

The election, of course, was for seats in the Legislature, which would elect a Senator. The final count was Republicans 125,275; Democrats 121,090; Buchanan Democrats only 5071. The popular vote did not elect Lincoln.

The state's legislative districts had been apportioned on the basis of the last census, taken in 1850. A new census was not due to be taken until 1860. Since 1850 many of the northern parts of the state had considerably increased in population; but the apportionment was such that in the joint session of the legislature, in January 1859, Douglas received 54 votes to Lincoln's 46.

Lincoln was bitterly disappointed at his failure in his second bid for the Senate. But he did not give up. Much later he told of walking home through the dark streets on the night after the election. "The path had been worn pig-backed and was slippery. My foot slipped from under me, knocking the other out of the way; but I recovered and said to myself, '*It's a slip and not a fall.*'"

Nor was the loss in this election a fall. He had received an important plus in his campaign. The nation-wide interest in the debates had elevated him to full stature among the nation's leaders. Anyone who could slug it out with Stephen A. Douglas on such terms, and actually beat him in the popular vote—if not in the legislature—must be destined for greatness.

CHAPTER TWENTY-SEVEN

Harper's Ferry

1

CHATHAM, Ontario, was a pretty Canadian town, just across the border from the United States, and not far from Detroit, Michigan. There, on May 8, 1858, a harsh-faced fanatic lectured a group of men who secretly had gathered in a house to confer.

He was John Brown of Osawatomie, self-appointed scourge of the god of abolition. Those familiar with the painting by John Steuart Curry, depicting John Brown as a giant with tawny beard and hair, flaming eyes, and mouth opened to roar some Homeric defiance (with a tornado symbolically accentuating this violence in the background) will have gained a wrong impression of the man's actual appearance.

A contemporary description of him says that he was "a small man, with white head and beard, and cold-looking gray eyes."[1] When not speaking, his mouth was compressed grimly. He was no roaring defier of his enemies; he had courage but he preferred to do his murdering by night; and after the notoriety he received following the massacre on Pottawatomie Creek and his other fomented troubles in Kansas, he felt the territory too unhealthy for him and left it. His face was leathery and deep-lined, his figure nervous and bony.

John Brown undoubtedly was afflicted with a streak of insanity. He was ignorant, murderous by principle, and none too honest, although capable of becoming engrossed with a great obsession. His father had been an abolitionist before him and the freeing of slaves was a mania with him. The "hell-hounds" who owned slaves deserved to be visited by an angry God with death and destruction, according to his belief. The Biblical dictum "Without shedding of blood there is no remission," had become a crazy shibboleth with him. Having already murdered in the cause, he conceived it his fated role to be the flail of the Lord.

In his journeyings since leaving Kansas, he had visited the East, and particularly New England where the abolition flame burned fiercest. There he found admirers who had heard of his Kansas exploits,

---

[1] In his Kansas days Brown was clean-shaven. He grew the beard later.

some of them men of national fame like William Lloyd Garrison, Wendell Phillips, Henry David Thoreau, Theodore Parker, Frederick Douglass, and Ralph Waldo Emerson. Association with such celebrities was heady wine for the uncouth farmer-turned-murderer, and increased his ideas of his own importance and the importance of his self-appointed mission. Furthermore it gave him opportunity to solicit funds, and from these and others he had collected more money than he ever before had possessed in his almost sixty years of life.

Now, at Chatham, he laid down to his handful of followers a mad scheme—a scheme which even if successful could only create bloodshed, suffering, and destruction, yet one which stood almost no chance at all of succeeding. It was a scheme that even in its failure was destined to bring about death and troubles far out of proportion to the abilities or comprehensions of the bearded fanatic who propounded it.

John Brown's plan was nothing less than a plot to foment a gigantic slave uprising in the South, with the arming of Negroes to slaughter white persons, a wide general wreaking of havoc, even the setting up of a sort of Negro government like that of Santo Domingo, to continue carrying on a victorious war against slavery.

It was no new idea with him. As early as 1847 he discussed plans of this nature with Frederick Douglass, a free Negro orator and abolition worker. Douglass was a really remarkable personage. The son of a slave mother and an unknown white father, he learned to read and write, escaped from his owners in Maryland, earned enough money as a day laborer to buy his legal freedom, displayed exceptional speaking powers and even edited a newspaper. To him Brown outlined a system of raids through the mountain districts of the South, where he could find strongholds in which he would organize the slaves who would, he confidently believed, flock to his banner, and from which he would then continue his "war of liberation."

Now at last, from his friends in the East, to whom, however, he did not fully unfold his plans, he had obtained sufficient funds to carry out at least one raid such as he contemplated.

Expounding the plan to his followers, he went so far as to draw up a "Provisional Constitution and Ordinances for the People of the United States," with which he proposed to govern the slave-controlled area he imagined he could establish and hold.

The Chatham group solemnly "adopted" the constitution, elected John Brown commander-in-chief, John H. Kagi secretary-of-war, and Aaron Stevens captain.

Harper's Ferry, on the Virginia-Maryland border was chosen as the objective of the attack, because it offered a "gateway" to the

South and particularly to Virginia, but more importantly because in that little city was located a United States arsenal at which fine rifles were manufactured, and stores of arms and ammunition were kept, with which the slaves who revolted could be armed.

After this the "Chatham Convention" adjourned, its members going to various places to await the call for action.

2

The first step in the quixotic scheme was the appearance of John Brown, under the alias of "I. Smith," at Harper's Ferry. He received mail under that name at the post office, but did not remain long in the town. He and two of his sons rented a small farm belonging to a Dr. Kennedy, a few miles from Harper's Ferry, in Maryland. This gave them a base for spying on the town, and for the later gathering of their forces.

Learning the lay of the land was not difficult. Harper's Ferry, at that time, had a population of fewer than 2000, including about 750 slaves and 40 free Negroes. Among the free Negroes the best-known and liked was Shephard Hayward, tall, strong, and courtly, who was baggage master at the Baltimore & Ohio railroad station. Ironically, Hayward was fated to be the first victim of the guns of Brown's men, who came ostensibly in behalf of his race.

Brown observed that the arsenal, which consisted of a row of buildings along the railroad, and a rifle factory some distance away, was not garrisoned by troops, although it employed civilians, including watchmen and about sixty gunsmiths who worked during the day. The town was connected to the Maryland shore, across the Potomac River, by a bridge 900 feet long. On this a watchman stood guard at night, perhaps to keep thieves or fleeing Negroes from using it as a means of gaining refuge in the North. All in all, the capture of the arsenal, and of the town, appeared not only feasible, but actually easy, to Brown.

Messages went to his supporters and by October 16 he had gathered his men and arms for his crazy adventure, the rendezvous being Kennedy's farm. That night he elected to make his descent on Harper's Ferry, with his "army." Just how many men were in the "army" is not known. Twenty-three marched into Harper's Ferry, counting Brown himself and including seventeen other white men and five Negroes, three of whom, it afterward developed, were runaway slaves. It was later reported that other men were waiting in the vicinity to cut telegraph wires and destroy railroad tracks, "at the proper time."

Before setting out from Kennedy's place, John Brown, according to his later statement, addressed his men, adjuring them "not to take the life of anyone, if you can possibly avoid it; but, if it is necessary to take life to save your own, *then make sure work of it.*"

This may have been an apocryphal anecdote. In any case it did not appear to affect the behavior of his men in the fighting that followed.

Darkness was Brown's favorite time to operate, and it was after night fell that he led his men across the bridge. They brought with them a one-horse wagon filled with pikes for the Negroes who were expected to rise. He had gained one recruit in the vicinity, a young man named John E. Cook, who was employed as a lock-tender on the Chesapeake & Ohio Canal, which at this point closely paralleled the Potomac River on the Maryland side. Cook joined the small "army."

Nobody in Harper's Ferry dreamed of such an incursion as was taking place. The raiders were able to capture William Williams, the watchman on the bridge, and Daniel Whelan, the watchman at the armory gate, without a struggle or an outcry. Quickly they took possession of the armory buildings, and began rounding up any night strollers who came near. These prisoners were held in the engine house.

Meantime parties fanned out. One took possession of the rifle works and made some shift at fortifying it. Another went out to seek hostages and Negro slaves. This party broke into the homes of Colonel Lewis Washington, grandnephew of the first President, and John H. Allstadt, both of whom were respected planters. Having made prisoners of these two men, they announced to their slaves that they were "free," which made little sense to the Negroes. Several of the slaves were brought back to Harper's Ferry with the two planters. The Negroes thus transported did not understand where they were going or what they were supposed to do, but simply obeyed orders. When they arrived at the armory, Osawatomie Brown harangued them on "freedom" and "rebellion." They appeared to comprehend little of what he was talking about and throughout the battle that followed, they took no part.

The little interest these slaves showed in what he held out to them must have been the first real inkling John Brown had of the chimerical nature of his plan, which contemplated a leaping to arms of all the Negroes in the country at his call. He placed the apathetic slaves in custody with the other prisoners.

Colonel Washington later said that when he arrived in the engine house he found eight or ten men under guard, among whom were acquaintances of his. He seated himself among them and tried to learn what was the meaning of the strange actions that were taking place. The interior was unlighted, but John Brown addressed the group, asking their names. He then said, "It is now too dark to write, but when it is sufficiently light . . . I require that you shall each write to your friends, to send a Negro man apiece, as a ransom."

Someone asked Brown what he was trying to do. "Free the slaves," he said. And when asked on what authority, he replied, "By the authority of God Almighty."

3

At about midnight the tense silent waiting was broken by the first shots fired. Patrick Higgins, on his way to relieve his fellow watchman, Williams—who by then was a prisoner in the engine house—started across the bridge.

"Halt!" came a command.

Instead of obeying, Higgins turned and ran. Rifles flashed in the gloom and a bullet plowed a slight furrow in Higgins' scalp, but though bleeding he was not seriously wounded as he dived into a nearby inn called the Wager House.

People began to stir in their homes, wondering at the sudden shots in the night. Higgins kept a sharp lookout, for he knew the eastbound Baltimore & Ohio train was due. When it came puffing into town at 1:25 A.M., October 17, Higgins ran out and yelled a warning to A. J. Phelps, the conductor. At about the same time one of Brown's men fired at the engineer, who promptly put his locomotive in reverse and backed the train out of danger.

The arrival of the train meant performance of his duties, to Shephard Hayward, the Negro baggagemaster. Though he must have heard the shots, he probably had no thought of danger to himself as he came around a corner heading for the railroad station.

One of Brown's trigger-happy guards shot him down. Hayward fell heavily to the ground, then struggled into the station office, where Higgins and others laid him on a wide plank across two chairs as an improvised bed. There he was treated by young Dr. John D. Starry, who had been awakened by the shots and hurried to the scene. But Hayward died soon after.

Looking out of the station office door, Dr. Starry saw three armed men near the armory gate. The physician walked boldly toward them and asked for the watchman. One of the men said he did not know of any watchman. "But," he added, "there are a few of *us* here."

The doctor asked what armed men were doing at this place at night.

"Never mind, you will find out in a day or two," he was told.

Dr. Starry returned to the station without being harmed, and in a good deal of perplexity. By this time the townspeople were generally awake and much alarmed. Some thought a robbery was taking place. Passengers on the stalled train thought it was a railroad strike. When Brown sent one of the captured citizens to tell the conductor that he might proceed, Phelps declined, saying he would wait until daylight.

Just before dawn Brown sent Cook with some other men to gather in more hostages. They shortly returned, unsuccessful. Had they remained away they might have avoided the fate of the rest of Brown's "army."

Sunrise came. As soon as it was light the train that had been standing for hours in the outskirts of the town got up headway and puffed across the railroad bridge into Maryland.

Shortly afterward Daniel Young, master machinist at the rifle factory, tried to enter the place to begin work. He was halted by a man with a gun who forbade him to go in, adding that the works had been seized, and freedom given "to every slave in Virginia, in the name of God."

Young (later a captain in the Union army during the Civil War) seems to have been the first who comprehended the nature of the lawless effort at Harper's Ferry.

"If you derive your authority from the Almighty, I must yield," he replied, "as I derive my right to enter from an earthly power—the United States government." And then he added, "I warn you, however, that before this day's sun sets, you and your companions will be corpses."

He went back to where he could stop gunsmiths who might be headed for the rifle works. Some, however, went there by different routes, and these were made prisoner and detained in the works.

It began to rain, adding further gloom to the situation.

Dr. Starry returned to his house, saddled his horse, and tried to organize resistance to the raiders who held the armory. With daylight, shots began to sound from the arsenal and bullets sang up the streets. A grocer named Joseph Boerly was hit and fell, mortally wounded. Another bullet carried away the hat of Alex Kelley, a young workman. Clearly the streets were unsafe.

Someone began ringing the bell in the Lutheran church, gathering the citizens there. Dr. Starry spoke to them, telling them a gang of armed men was holding the armory. He had his horse and would ride toward Charles Town, the county seat, to get help.

Only a few of the citizens had arms—old squirrel rifles and shotguns mostly; but more guns were found in a workshop. Armed men now surrounded the arsenal, holding their fire but trying to make sure that none escaped while Dr. Starry rode hard for Charles Town.

By this time Kagi, Brown's "secretary-of-war" saw that the situation was growing serious, and sent word to the "commander-in-chief" urging immediate retreat before it was too late. But Brown refused. He still held to the fanatical belief that hundreds of slaves would come hurrying to him as soon as they learned he was there to free them. No slaves came. Not one slave in fact willingly joined him. The wagonload of Negroes brought in from the Washington and Allstadt plantations remained noncombatants, frightened and wishing only to return safely to their homes.

Thus far, in addition to capturing several persons, Brown's men had killed two—Hayward and Boerly—and wounded one slightly. But Kagi's forebodings were soon justified.

4

Dr. Starry had reached Charles Town, which was about eight miles from Harper's Ferry. In midmorning a Winchester & Potomac train, from the county seat, halted at the outskirts of the threatened town.

From it quickly descended a militia company, the Jefferson Guards, under Captain John W. Rowan, and another hastily assembled body of men, without drill and without name, led by Lawson Botts. Conductor Phelps had reported the occurrences of the night by telegraph to Baltimore, but the officials of the railroad at first thought his story "exaggerated." They learned their error shortly.

By ten o'clock the militia were in the town. The pick-up company under Botts seized the heights to the west commanding the roads in that direction. Part of Rowan's Jefferson Guards crossed the Potomac upstream in rowboats, and suddenly appeared at the Maryland end of the bridge. Oliver Brown, one of John Brown's sons, was on guard at the bridge with two other men, one a Negro named Dangerfield Newby. The three fled at the arrival of the militia, but a volley from the soldiers brought down Newby, who was killed.

Now at last John Brown realized that he was in an extremely perilous situation, cut off from all retreat. Acting as if he believed himself indeed the head of a *de facto* government, he sent a "flag of truce" to ask for an "armistice." The bearer of the white flag, William Thompson, was at once taken into custody as a prisoner.

After waiting, Brown sent two more emissaries with a white flag—his son Watson, and Aaron Stevens, the elected "captain" of the raiding crew. But the citizens and militia alike refused to recognize any flag of truce from the outlaws in the arsenal. They opened fire. Stevens fell, wounded, and was captured. Watson Brown was wounded also, but struggled back to the armory. His wound was mortal and he died hours later.

Shortly after this William Leeman, one of the raiders, attempted to make his escape by wading the river. He was spotted and killed by rifle fire, his body falling into the water.

The casualties, however, were not all on the side of the raiders. George Turner, an ex-army officer was killed while shooting at the engine house, and a little later Fontaine Beckham, mayor of Harper's Ferry, likewise fell dead from a shot fired by one of Brown's men.

The death of the mayor, a man universally popular, so infuriated the citizens that they took the prisoner, William Thompson, out of the house where he was held to shoot him. He ran onto the bridge, got through the railings, and fell into the Potomac. There he was riddled by bullets and died.

Most of Brown's men were in the engine house, but at the rifle works remained Kagi, Lewis Sheridan Leary, and John Copeland, the latter a Negro. Dr. Starry had gathered a posse, and began an attack on the works defended by these three. Kagi and his men, seeing that resistance was hopeless, tried to retreat across the Shenandoah River, which at this site ran into the Potomac. But they were seen. Bullets beat up a spray about them. Kagi was killed in midstream. Leary was fatally wounded. Copeland was unhurt, but was seized and pulled ashore. He would have been lynched there and then, had not Dr. Starry faced down the crowd, and had him lodged instead in the town jail to await trial.[2]

The long day ended with its constant racket of gunfire and the yells of men. As evening approached a shout was directed at Brown, demanding his surrender. He shouted back, replying that he would leave the armory with his men if they were allowed to cross the Potomac River without being fired upon; and that he held hostages whom he would take with him across the river as a safeguard, promising to release them on the other side. No reply was made to this proposal.

Darkness fell. Now and again it was broken by the flash of a rifle followed by the report, as the citizens and militia kept a close watch on the engine house which now had become the citadel of the invaders.

By this time the news of the insurrection was believed in the East. From Washington a company of 101 Marines—said to be the sole garrison of the capital at that time—was sent by train. It was commanded by Colonel Robert E. Lee, 2nd Cavalry, who had as his aide another professional soldier, Lieutenant J. E. B. Stuart. The Marines arrived at Harper's Ferry about midnight.

---

[2] The appearance of armed Negroes among Brown's men in this effort to cause a slave revolt, seemed to have an especially infuriating effect on the people. All these Negroes had come from the North, including the three runaway slaves; but the Virginians may have believed them to be slaves who had joined the revolt from that vicinity.

The morning of October 18 dawned. Lee, whose record in the War with Mexico had been brilliant, and who would one day be the greatest commander of the Confederate army, waited until daylight, then sent Stuart, who would be the most famous cavalry officer of the Civil War, to bear a note demanding that Brown surrender unconditionally.

It was a ticklish assignment. Brown's emissaries had been shot down by the citizens, and there was no telling what the desperate men in the engine house might do to one advancing upon them. But without hesitation, in full uniform, Stuart marched up to the door of the engine house. There, speaking through the barred door, he made the formal demand and delivered Lee's note when the door was opened a crack. Brown's reply was the same as before. He would not surrender, and would come out only on condition that his whole party be permitted to escape.

Stuart returned and reported to Lee. Such a parley for escape was of course unacceptable. As soon as he heard Brown's answer, Lee ordered the engine house attacked.

Two squads of marines ran forward at once, one on each side of the door. With sledge hammers two of their number battered the door, but though it swayed, it seemed to be secured by a rope, the spring of which deadened the force of the blows.

Seeing this, the Marines seized a ladder, forty-five feet long, and holding it as a battering ram, they ran full tilt at the door. The first blow jarred it. The second caused the door to give way, one leaf slanting inward.

Headed by Lieutenant Israel Green, the Marines rushed into the building. In a flurry of firing from within, one of the attackers was shot dead on the threshold. John Brown himself was cut down by a blow from Green's sword, and lay on the floor painfully wounded. His son Oliver was mortally wounded and died soon after, with another of the raiders. The rest were prisoners.

John Brown's lunatic raid was ended. Of his followers, ten whites, including his sons Watson and Oliver, and three Negroes had been killed; three whites, two of them severely wounded, and two Negroes had been taken prisoner. Four escaped, of whom two, Cook and a man named Hazlitt, were soon captured. One who made good his escape was John Brown's son Owen, who lived until 1889, dying in Pasadena, California.

His raiders killed five men and wounded nine, of whom all but two were private citizens.

The old man was carried out of the engine house and laid on the grass.

"Are you Captain Brown, of Kansas?" he was asked.

"I am sometimes called so," he replied.

"Are you Osawatomie Brown?"

"I tried to do my duty there."

"What was your present object?"

"To free the slaves from bondage."

He refused to implicate anyone in the North, saying, "There was no one connected with the movement but those who came with me."

But having thus far in this exchange been reasonable and even admirable, he took to boasting. He had, he said, had Harper's Ferry at his mercy and could have murdered its inhabitants and burned it to the ground, but he did not. This was sheerest rant, for from the time his party was first discovered it really had no chance to do anything but defend itself. He complained that he had been "hunted down like a beast," whereas he had treated his prisoners with courtesy. This was true except that they were kept in constant fear of death and without food for more than twenty-four hours. Then he denied that he had ever intended to seize public arms, because his "army" had guns and ammunition enough, "reshipped from Kansas." Yet Harper's Ferry was chosen for his raid for the exact reason that it contained the armory, where there were guns and stores to arm the slaves Brown expected to rise at his call. He expressed disappointment that at his demonstration he did not receive rapid reinforcements "from abolitionists settled everywhere through Maryland and Virginia, enough to take possession of both states, with all of the Negroes they would capture." But he carefully avoided saying outright that he intended to start a huge servile revolt. He could only vaguely describe what his course would have been, had he succeeded in his first stroke, except that it might have gone southwest diagonally through Virginia, "varying as circumstances dictated or required." It was evident that his distempered thinking had not really planned any moves after the capture of Harper's Ferry.

Colonel Lee peremptorily put down a cry by the citizens to lynch the survivors.

5

Instead John Brown was to be tried for treason; and he was to receive a national rostrum from which to dramatize himself and his cause.

The prisoners were indicted for treason and murder, and as they demanded separate trials, it was decided to try the leader first. It was at this point that John Brown assumed the second role of the fanatical agitator—the role of martyr.

His trial was covered and its details published by all the major Northern papers, as well as many in the South. The anti-slavery and abolitionist journals lost no opportunity to glorify John Brown and his deeds. The New York *Herald* quoted him as saying after his capture:

"I claim to be here in carrying out a measure I believe perfectly justifiable, and not to act the part of an incendiary or ruffian, but to aid those suffering great wrong. I wish to say, furthermore, that you had better—all you people of the South—prepare yourselves for a settlement of that question that must come up for settlement sooner than you are prepared for it."

John Brown had become a symbol, a symbol to be surrounded with all possible dignity and sympathetic appeal. He was imprisoned and closely guarded, but there were many who conversed with him.

His trial, which began October 27 at Charles Town, drew more newspaper reporters, magazine writers, illustrators, and other representatives of the disseminating press than had any event preceding it in history. The evidence was overwhelmingly against him, and he was convicted on all charges and sentenced to be executed December 2.

On being asked why sentence should not be passed upon him, he rose from his chair, and made the following objections:

He denied everything but what he had previously admitted—the design on his part to free the slaves—and asserted that he never did intend murder, or treason, or to excite or incite slaves to rebellion, or to foment insurrection.

He felt it unjust that he should suffer such a penalty, asserting that had he "so interfered" in behalf of the rich and powerful (instead of slaves) "every man in this court would have deemed it an act worthy of reward rather than punishment."

Finally: "If it is deemed necessary that . . . I mingle my blood with the blood of my children, and with the millions in this slave country whose rights are disregarded by wicked, cruel, and unjust enactments —I submit: so let it be done."

The gallows had been erected in a field near Charles Town. It was a crude, ugly structure, with thirteen steep steps, reaching a platform of unpainted planks on which had been erected two posts with a raw horizontal wooden bar between them and a trap door in the floor. Soldiers surrounded the field to prevent any effort to rescue the condemned man, and a huge crowd milled around outside the guard lines.

On December 2 Brown rode to the place in a furniture wagon, sitting on his coffin, his arms bound at the elbows. He wore "the same seedy and dilapidated dress" he had during his trial, but his rough boots had been replaced by a pair of "parti-colored slippers." As the wagon neared the gallows, one observer noted, Brown's "face wore a

grim & greisly [*sic*] smirk which but for the solemnity of the occasion might have suggested ideas of the ludicrous."

But the man was not afraid. He was determined to make a fine
death of it, stepped down from the wagon, waved one of his pinioned
arms at the press section and firmly mounted the steps of the gallows.
His hat was removed, the rope adjusted about his neck and a white
muslin cap placed over his face. When the sheriff told him to move
over the trap, Brown answered "You will have to guide me there."
This was done, but the condemned man refused a handkerchief which
he could drop as a signal to cut the rope. "No, I don't care," he said.
"I don't want you to keep me waiting unnecessarily."

Yet he had to undergo the ordeal of waiting "five minutes or more,"
unable to see, with the halter about his neck, while troops were
wheeled into position. At last everything was ready, the sheriff cut
the rope with a hatchet and Brown fell through the released trap.

"Thus died John Brown, the strange, stern old man, hard and uncouth in character as he was in personal appearance, undemonstrative
and emotionless as an Indian. In the manner of his death there was
nothing dramatic or sympathetic . . . neither the martial dignity of
a chieftain nor the reckless bravado of a highwayman—neither the
exalted enthusiasm of a martyr nor the sublime resignation of a Christian." So wrote David Hunter Strother, later a brigadier general in
the Union Army, in a report not printed until 1955.

Brown's companions, Cook, Coppock, Copeland, and Green, were
hanged December 16, and Stevens and Hazlitt March 16, 1860.

6

John Brown became a symbol both in the North and in the South.

In the North, Emerson proclaimed him a "new saint" who made
"the gallows glorious like a cross." Henry Ward Beecher and other
divines chimed in with similar expressions. Wendell Phillips gave an
eloquent, and inflammatory eulogy when the body was buried at North
Elba, New York.

In the South resentment at the raid was deep, and the deaths of
the conspirators approved. Jefferson Davis, Robert Toombs, Robert
Barnwell Rhett, and William Lowndes Yancey (described by Joseph
Hergesheimer as "the Pillar of Words") united in oratorical denunciation of the "abolitionist attack" on Virginia. There was general fear
that what John Brown attempted—a great slave uprising—might actually take place. Plantation homes were barricaded, patrollers doubled
their vigilance, and in all the Southern states young men began drill-

ing, forming companies to avert a servile rebellion if it occurred, but also to defend their states if secession came.

John Brown left a note in jail when he was taken to the gallows which read in part:

> I John Brown am now quite *certain* that the crimes of this *guilty land:* will never be *purged away:* but with blood . . .

It was a reassertion of his favorite doctrine, but it also was a prophecy. Within less than two years armies, marching to the bloodiest battles ever fought on this continent, would be singing of "John Brown's body."

In the midst of the public excitement, the first Northern voices were raised in moderation. William H. Seward denounced Brown's raid as an "act of sedition and treason." Edward Everett and Caleb Cushing spoke of Brown's "blood guilt." Stephen A. Douglas referred to Brown as "a notorious man who has recently suffered death for his crimes."

And out in Kansas, on a speaking tour, Abraham Lincoln heard of Brown's sentence to the gallows, when he was at the little frontier town of Troy. He said:

"We cannot object, even though he agreed with us in thinking slavery wrong. That cannot excuse violence, bloodshed, and treason."

CHAPTER TWENTY-EIGHT

A New Hand for the Rudder

1

To unhappy James Buchanan, the last months of his administration must have seemed a nightmare. Though he was President of the United States and titular head of the Democratic party, the power was gone from him. He one day exclaimed to General Winfield Scott, "The office of President of the United States is not fit for a gentleman to hold!"

He had lost control of his party. Stephen A. Douglas, whom he had threatened to break and who had defied him, had far greater power among the Democrats than did Buchanan; and the party itself was bitterly divided on the slave question, with animus growing daily between some leaders in the North and South.

Buchanan was no man of action, of bold decisions. He knew that the ship of state was drifting into unthinkable disaster, but it drifted without a hand on the rudder. Without solid party support he could do nothing to avert the rising crisis, even if he had been able to think of anything to do. Nearing seventy, the President was discouraged, forsaken, and frightened. He seemed only to hope that he could defer eventualities so that at least the Union would not be destroyed while he was its Chief Magistrate.

John Brown's fanatic effort at Harper's Ferry only increased Buchanan's distraction. Through force of circumstances, tensions of feeling, and the ever vociferous press, Brown had become a far more menacing figure in death than ever in his life.

Blame for the mounting feelings of hostility by no means lay entirely with the South. Sectional differences of an economic nature had long existed, but the rise of abolitionism was the beginning of the really severe resentment in the South. Calhoun said that abolitionism "originated in that blind, fanatical zeal which made one man believe that he was responsible for the sins of others; and which, two centuries ago, tied the victim that it could not convert to the stake."

There was some little truth to that statement. Oral and written

abuse of slaveholders, and indeed the entire South, became an abolitionist obsession, and went to extremes. Southern men were pictured
as sadistic and greedy upholders of "unbridled licentiousness and despotic control."

Sex, an ever-sensational subject, was brought in with wildest exaggerations, to fan public opinion to heat. For example, Wendell Phillips characterized the South as "one great brothel where a half million
of women are flogged to prostitution."

The Southern people responded with wrath and shock and struck
back by comparing the treatment of slaves with the condition of many
free laborers in the North. Thousands of white children in the North,
said they (with some truth) labored fourteen hours a day in mills and
shops at an age when slave children of the South were free to play.
They cited legislative reports showing that the factory system of the
North made virtual slaves of white workers by binding them econom-
ically to crushing and ceaseless toil.

In the North the net product of the ceaseless drumfire of abolitionist
denunciation created first contempt for, then detestation of the *whole
South*. Slavery was wrong. The stubbornness with which the slaveholders clung to it turned Northern opinion against them.

Advocacy of slave revolts in the South by some irresponsible extremists in the North, touched upon a very real danger. Furthermore
the South faced severe economic problems which the North little considered. It was keyed to slave labor, but this could be changed—in
fact it has been changed. But much of the South's capital was in-
vested in slaves. Coercion and insult were motives for resistance, but
complete financial prostration was an even greater cause.

Finally there was the problem of race. *If* the Negroes were to
remain in the United States, Southerners could see no solution for the
distinctive problems they presented.

These were the irritations and problems which provided, in the
words of Albert J. Beveridge, "the spectacle of fewer than six million
white people defying more than three times their number, their resources even smaller than their man power, the very spirit of the age
against them . . . to take the field and fight, suffer, and sacrifice
with a desperation not often surpassed in the history of the world."

Slavery was an unmitigated evil. It belonged to the dark ages and
backward peoples. It caused extremes of wealth and poverty and
hindered development in the districts where it existed. It was doomed
for its very injustices and for its economic faults. Yet the badgered
Southern people sought to preserve it even as the catastrophe of Civil
War stared them in the face.

2

Two new states, Minnesota and Oregon, had been admitted to the Union, by 1859, and both were free states. But men looked for a bitter fight when Kansas again asked for admission.

In the Senate and House debates grew noisier and angrier. Southerners openly charged that the John Brown raid was instigated by the Republican party; a charge which was indignantly denied by the Republicans. Some lawmakers took to carrying weapons, and it was told how Senator Benjamin F. Wade of Ohio stalked into the Senate chamber before a debate, and laid a pair of horse pistols on his desk with such ostentation that they could not fail to be noticed.

The momentous Presidential question was in all minds, for 1860 would be an election year. It was uppermost in William H. Seward's mind. In spite of his fiery utterances previously, he now sought to heal, rather than create wounds, for he had Presidential aspirations. While Lyman Trumbull of Illinois, Zach Chandler of Michigan, and Ben Wade of Ohio crossed verbal swords with John Slidell of Louisiana, Louis T. Wigfall of Texas, and Robert Toombs of Georgia, Seward was so conciliatory that it was even rumored that he favored secession, something very far indeed from the truth.

Others in the Senate were also interested in the Presidency. Living in fine houses side by side were Senator Stephen A. Douglas and Vice-President John C. Breckinridge who presided over the Senate's deliberations. Both were aspirants for the White House, Douglas the choice of the party in the North, Breckinridge the present hope of the party in the South.

And then Abraham Lincoln made a speech.

He had spoken often in the West; but this time he spoke in the East, at a meeting held especially for him at the Cooper Union in New York, under the sponsorship of the Young Men's Central Republican Union.

Though the organization that invited him said its purpose was only to provide lectures on political subjects "for the general education and enlightenment of the public," it actually was dominated by a group of Republican politicians who wished to prevent the nomination of Seward. Among these was Horace Greeley, once a strong supporter of Seward, but now opposed to him. That night of February 27, 1860, Greeley sat on the platform at the Cooper Union, to which Lincoln was conducted by David Dudley Field and William Cullen Bryant. In spite of a heavy snowstorm more than 1500 persons attended, the largest gathering "of the intellect and culture of our city" since the days of Clay and Webster, Greeley said.

Lincoln had spent much time preparing his address, for he knew it would be important. But when he was introduced he rose, tall and awkward, and appeared sad-faced and embarrassed. He knew his rural colloquialisms and his high-pitched voice might work against him. Though he had bought a new broadcloth suit for the occasion, he somehow still managed to look rumpled.

Once he began to speak, however, he forgot himself and he held the rapt attention of his audience. First he gave a clinching argument against Douglas' favorite theme of popular sovereignty, by proving that the framers of the Constitution "certainly understood that no proper division of local from federal authority . . . forbade the federal government to control slavery in the federal territories."

Then he appealed to the Southern people, in behalf of the Republican party. There was nothing sectional about the party, he said, except that the South made it so by refusing to accept it. The party was not radical or revolutionary; it was in fact conservative. The Republicans did not instigate John Brown's raid, and the party policy was contrary to all such acts of violence. The threat voiced by some Southerners that in event of a Republican victory secession would follow, he compared to a footpad on the road holding a pistol to his victim's head.

From that he turned to the Republicans, enjoining them to do their part in maintaining peace, by placating their Southern brethren and showing that they did not seek to disturb them. But would the South be convinced? Lincoln feared that nothing short of the acceptance of the rightfulness of slavery would satisfy them.

"All they ask, we could readily grant, if we thought slavery right," he said earnestly. "All we ask they could as readily grant, if they thought it wrong. Their thinking it right, and our thinking it wrong, is the precise fact upon which depends the whole controversy. Thinking it right, as they do, they are not to blame for desiring its full recognition as being right; but thinking it wrong, as we do, can we yield to them? Can we cast our votes with their view, and against our own? In view of our moral, social, and political responsibilities can we do this?

"If our sense of duty forbids this, then let us stand by our duty fearlessly and effectively . . . Neither let us be slandered from our duty by false accusations against us, nor frightened from it by menaces of destruction to the government nor of dungeons for ourselves.

"*Let us have faith that right makes might, and in that faith let us, to the end, dare to do our duty as we understand it.*"

That finish brought the crowd to its feet, waving hats and handkerchiefs, in a long-sustained roaring ovation. Every word Lincoln had spoken was evocative of thought. There was not a trace of malice or prejudice in his clear arguments.

He had not so much as hinted that he might have any idea of becoming President. But the Cooper Union speech, which was published in full by four New York papers and others over the land, and was issued in pamphlet form by the *Chicago Tribune,* had much to do with making him President.

Going from New York he made a brief tour of the East, speaking in various New England cities. Everywhere he was greeted by enormous crowds. His progress became a sort of triumphal tour, with torchlight parades, bands, banners, and constant demonstrations of warm admiration by the people.

3

When at last he was back in Springfield, Illinois, he had to face, "yea or nay," the question of whether or not he would be a candidate for President. Previously he had shunned all talk of such an idea. The first proposal of it, which was made to him in Illinois before the Cooper Union speech, almost shocked him. To one man, Thomas J. Pickett, he said, "I must, in candor, say that I do not think I am fitted for the Presidency." What he really wanted to do was run against Douglas again for the Senate, in 1864, and this time beat him.

But upon his return from the Cooper Union speech and the experience of the ovations which followed it, he seemed to feel a stir of power, a gathering confidence. After all, he *might* be of national caliber. When his friend, Senator Trumbull, asked if he would be a candidate, he confessed wryly, "The taste *is* in my mouth a little."

He even furnished a brief autobiography—written in the third person—for publication, with the warning, "I wish it to be modest, do not go beyond the materials furnished." And now he told his friends that even if he were to run only for the Senate, he would appreciate it if his home state delegation was for him in the Republican national convention that was to meet in Chicago the next May.

The state convention, meeting at Decatur, May 9 and 10, only a few days before the national convention, was treated to a novelty. A banner was brought forward, supported by two fence rails, and on it was the legend: "ABRAHAM LINCOLN, The Rail Candidate for President in 1860." It proclaimed that these were two of a lot of three thousand rails split in 1830 by Lincoln and "Thomas" Hanks.[1]

[1] It should have read John Hanks.

Splitting rails had special meaning in the Illinois of that day. It meant hard work, skill, sweat, and the creation of humble but necessary articles for use on the land by the strength of humble men. As if by a common impulse the nickname "Rail-Splitter" was coined for Lincoln, as a great cheer went up. Called upon for remarks, Lincoln rose and said in his inimitably quizzical manner, "I cannot say for certain whether I made those two rails or not, but I have surely mauled out some better ones." He sat down, and the convention enthusiastically and unanimously voted to put the state's twenty-two delegate votes behind him in the national convention.

Almost immediately, on May 16, the national convention opened in Chicago. A rambling frame building of raw lumber, called the Wigwam, had been erected to house it, designed to seat 10,000 people, although more than that crowded into it. More than 2000 came from New York alone to cheer William H. Seward. Another 1500 were from Pennsylvania, where Simon Cameron was the favorite. In addition to these notables, Salmon P. Chase of Ohio, twice governor and once Senator; Edward Bates of Missouri, governor of that state; Justice John McLean, of the Supreme Court; and William L. Dayton of New Jersey, Senator and running mate of John C. Frémont in the previous national election, all were candidates.

Against such an overpowering roster, Lincoln felt his own chances were poor. Not so his managers. While he remained in Springfield, his old friend Judge David Davis, huge and Falstaffian in appearance, but with keen intelligence and full of expedients, organized the Lincoln forces in Chicago. First Davis and his immediate council conned over the weaknesses of their man's rivals.

Seward, while popular and renowned, had made some bitter enemies, including Horace Greeley,[2] and because of his "Higher Law" and "Irrepressible Conflict" speeches he was considered a radical, although in reality he was conservative and inclined to compromise and ingratiate himself. He was the pre-convention favorite to win the nomination.

Salmon P. Chase was actually more radical than Seward, and less popular because of his stubborn nature. Edward Bates had once been associated with the Know-Nothings, and therefore was opposed by the various elements offended by that movement. Simon Cameron was a political boss with a none too savory reputation, and not even all of his own delegation were for him. William L. Dayton had no real strength outside of his own state.

[2] Greeley was prevented by the Seward-Weed forces from having a seat in the New York delegation. He managed however to have himself chosen a delegate from Oregon, and sat with that group.

In contrast, Abraham Lincoln had no public record that he must defend; he had sprung from lowly birth to eminence; and he had sounded the greatest of all Republican keynotes. Though he had wired his convention manager that he authorized no bargains, Judge Davis went ahead like the practical politician he was, promising that Caleb B. Smith should be Secretary of the Interior, in return for the support of Indiana; promising a cabinet post also to Cameron; and making other political bargains in spite of the orders from his candidate. Later Lincoln, though he had nothing to do with these maneuvers, felt impelled to fulfill the promises made, in part at least.

On the day the balloting began Davis, who had had thousands of bogus tickets printed, provided them to all the Illinois and Lincoln men and urged them to go to the Wigwam early and occupy their seats. By this piece of political trickery the Seward thousands, who had paraded before going to the convention, found there was not room for all of them. Those who held legitimate tickets but were barred showed great indignation outside the Wigwam, and there were even a few fisticuffs. But Davis' plan had worked. Lincoln men inside the convention hall outnumbered all others.

The convention proceeded with its business. Seward was nominated with a great roar from his followers, not all of whom had been barred from seats. Next came Lincoln, nominated by Norman Judd, and his name evoked clamor that, according to a witness, "made soft vesper breathings of all that had preceded. No language can describe it. A thousand steam whistles, ten acres of hotel gongs, a tribe of Comanches, headed by a choice vanguard from pandemonium, might have mingled in the scene unnoticed."

Dayton, Cameron, Chase, and others were put in nomination amid scenes of growing excitement. At last came the roll call.

A total of 233 votes was required to nominate. After the first ballot the votes stood: Seward 173½, Lincoln 102, Cameron 50½, Chase 49, Bates 48, the remainder scattered among various "favorite sons."

On the second roll call Seward had 184½, a gain of eleven; but Lincoln had shot up to 181, a gain of 79. Chase had 43½ and Bates 35, while Cameron had dropped out of the running.

Everyone suspected that the third ballot would be decisive. As the roll call proceeded, it was seen that Lincoln was gaining strength. Perhaps he would gain the nomination on this very ballot. When the final count was in, however, he had 231½—1½ votes short of nomination.

Suddenly there was a flurry and increased excitement. Ohio notified the chairman that it had changed four of its votes to Lincoln. The man from Illinois was nominated!

Tumultuous celebrations ensued. A cannon on the roof of the Wigwam blasted a salute. Bells all over Chicago were rung, adding to the noise. Great crowds of people cheered in the streets. The news was flashed over the nation by telegraph. The Republicans had their greatest of all candidates for President of the United States, although at the time few may have realized it.

4

Stephen A. Douglas was "hoist on his own petard." It may be speculated with considerable logic that had it not been for his Kansas-Nebraska bill and his popular sovereignty doctrine, he might have been nominated by a united Democratic party and hence in all probability elected President in 1860. But the die was cast, and in his later actions Douglas must be given credit for sincerity and also for integrity, for he believed his theory was integral to the rights of the American people, and upheld it fearlessly and eloquently, in the Senate and on public platforms. It was a theory, however, that was fatal to his cause.

The Democrats held their first, but indecisive, convention even before the Republicans, gathering at Charleston, South Carolina, in April. Already Jefferson Davis had given notice of the will of the South by introducing in the Senate a resolution calling for a slave code for all the territories.

The convention was a living attestation of the nation-wide scope of the party Andrew Jackson had created. Tall silk hats of city men from the North mingled with wide-brimmed felt hats of planters, wool hats of countrymen, caps of various descriptions, even an occasional coonskin or fox headpiece from the frontiers. Long hair was in evidence, falling over the ears, sometimes to the shoulders. Many men were bearded; it was the new style, which would be almost universal during the Civil War, coming in. Broadcloth suits and white cotton or linen, were side by side with homespun farmers' garbs, for the back country had sent its delegates as well as the population centers.

At the outset the division in the party made itself manifest. The platform committee split 17 to 16—and the 16 were in favor of Douglas, the 17 opposed to him. Two platforms were reported, that by the majority aggressively pro-slavery, including the Jefferson Davis resolutions, and demanding federal support of slavery. The Douglas group reported a conciliatory platform, kindly to Southern sentiments, endorsing the Dred Scott Decision, but favoring popular sovereignty.

William Lowndes Yancey, the Georgia fire-eater, in one of his great oratorical outbursts declared that the abolitionists "who were once pelted with rotten eggs," had grown into three bands, the Black Republicans, the Free Soilers, and the Squatter Sovereignty men. But the convention with its large numbers of Northern Democrats voted down the "Davis platform" in spite of Yancey's denunciations; and adopted instead the one favored by Douglas.

At this point almost all the delegates from South Carolina, Georgia, Florida, Alabama, Mississippi, Louisiana, Texas and Arkansas, rose dramatically from their seats and withdrew from the convention. The Democratic party saw itself riven in two.

The Democratic convention rule was that two-thirds of the qualified delegates must vote for any candidate to nominate him. That two-thirds made necessary 202 votes out of 303 eligible delegates. With the withdrawals Douglas, though the chief remaining candidate, could poll no more than 152½ votes. After eleven days the convention adjourned, to meet again at Baltimore in June. The seceders also voted, to meet at Richmond, Virginia.

Now the scene shifted North, with the party still in complete disorder. When the regular Democrats convened at Baltimore, some of the seceders journeyed thither and sought to regain admission. They were seated. But again at the raising of the prime issue of slavery they withdrew, and in the convention only 192½ votes remained, so that 202 ballots for any candidate was impossible.

In this emergency the Baltimore convention ruled that two-thirds of *those present* could nominate. On the second ballot Douglas was chosen to carry the banner of the Northern Democrats.

The disgruntled Southern seceders, who changed their meeting place from Richmond, convened also in Baltimore, where they gathered not only the dissident South, but also some delegates of doubtful eligibility from the North, chiefly Buchanan supporters. They then proceeded to nominate John C. Breckinridge of Kentucky, an action endorsed by the Richmond convention when it reconvened.

The action in effect made the election of a Republican President certain. To make things even "cosier," the two Democratic parties had no sooner divided and destroyed their strength, than to add to the confusion still another party—making four in all—appeared in the field. It called itself the Constitutional Union party, was composed chiefly of former Whigs and Know-Nothings, and nominated John Bell of Tennessee for President.

With their opposition now divided three ways, the Republicans made all haste to follow up their advantage. Seward, who had suffered terrible disappointment when he failed of the party nomination, nevertheless rallied to the cause, and made effective speeches over the country for Lincoln. Salmon P. Chase and Edward Bates, also disappointed candidates, likewise took the stump for the nominee.

All over the North the campaign was vigorously conducted. A biography of Lincoln was published in the newspapers telling of his early struggles, his background of pioneer poverty, his slow rise upward, his integrity, and his genius. "Honest Abe" took its place alongside "the Rail-Splitter," as a tag to rally the voters. Torchlight parades, rallies, barbecues, and oratory stimulated Republican enthusiasm.

Throughout it all Lincoln remained at his home in Springfield. He received floods of visitors, and with his usual modesty and patience he talked to hordes of office-seekers, advice-givers, politicians, and simple well-wishers. A little girl, eleven-year-old Grace Bedell of Westfield, New York, wrote him one of the thousands of letters that his two secretaries, John G. Nicolay and John M. Hay, read, sorted, and sometimes answered, sometimes referred to Lincoln himself. Grace's letter was one of those referred to him. She asked him to grow whiskers "since all ladies like whiskers." Lincoln grinned at the advice, then grew the famous beard with which his image is usually associated in the American mind today.

On crashed the campaign to its close. Reports came from the South that the fire-eaters insisted that if the Republicans won, secession was sure. Lincoln did not believe it. He cited the overwhelming odds against the South in case of a civil war,[3] and expressed the opinion that the people of the South had too much good humor and common sense to break up the government.

His greatest rival, Douglas, felt no such optimism.

By October, state elections in Vermont, Maine, Ohio, and Pennsylvania showed a Republican trend so unmistakable that Douglas, who had stumped the country in his own behalf, recognized that he was almost sure of defeat.

"Mr. Lincoln is the next President," he told his secretary. "We must try to save the Union. I will go South."

Then Douglas did one of the most courageous things in his life. Into the South he went, and there, in spite of hostility in some areas, made speeches that were fiercely Unionist, even when he knew that his utterances were cutting off much support that he might have won. A Republican victory, he said, would be no justification for secession. Even if that party won a majority of seats in the House, he pointed

[3] The census of 1860 gave a total population in the states and territories, as 31,443,790, of which 27,008,081 were whites, 482,122 free Negroes, and 3,953,587 slaves. The latter were all in the slaveholding states of Alabama, Arkansas, Delaware, Florida, Georgia, Kentucky, Louisiana, Maryland, Mississippi, Missouri, North Carolina, South Carolina, Tennessee, Texas, and Virginia. But of the slave states, Delaware, Maryland, Missouri, and Kentucky did not secede. In the remaining eleven states which did secede the total white population was only 5,450,711 whites, 131,401 free Negroes, and 3,540,902 slaves. In the final contest, therefore, 5,450,711 white people faced the overwhelming odds of 21,557,370 white people.

out, the Senate would remain in the control of the Democrats with Southern sympathies for a good while at least. How, therefore, could Congress do anything inimical to the South?

But Southerners were both fearful and antagonistic. He achieved little, though he traveled and spoke until he was hoarse and ill with the labor and stress.

There is no record of what Lincoln thought of this effort by Douglas. But, knowing Lincoln's utter dedication to the principle of the Union, one must be sure that he applauded the gallant actions of his rival, and in a subtle way, his friend.[4]

Election Day that year came on November 6. Lincoln remained at Springfield, sitting in the governor's office in the state house, while crowds surged outside with much shouting and some band music. He voted in the middle of the afternoon, received a cheer from those who saw him, then returned to the governor's office where he chatted with his friend Senator Trumbull, and others.

Early bulletins indicated the Northwest was overwhelmingly his. About nine o'clock in the evening he went to the telegraph office to hear the returns. Pennsylvania, Illinois, and Indiana, the key states that Frémont failed to carry, were all in the Lincoln column. There was some worry over New York, where the Democrats in the big city might swing that important state. But before ten o'clock word came that New York was assured for the Republicans.

At midnight Lincoln went to a hall where he was given a late supper, together with his chief advisers and backers, by a hundred Springfield women. News of the New York results had swept the streets and there was tumultuous uproar from the crowds outside.

Victory for Lincoln was won. As it turned out he carried all of New England, New York, all the Midwestern states north of the Ohio, Pennsylvania, and the three new states of Oregon, Minnesota, and California, in all seventeen. Breckinridge carried the solid South, together with Delaware and Maryland. Bell captured the border states Tennessee, Kentucky, and Virginia. Douglas carried only Missouri and New Jersey.

Of the popular vote Lincoln received 1,866,452, Douglas 1,376,957, Breckinridge only 849,781, and Bell 588,879. In the Electoral College

[4] It was recorded that two months before the election Douglas believed the election of Lincoln was certain, and exclaimed to a friend Anson Burlingame that four Illinois men, all friends, would be in Washington together. "Won't it be a splendid sight, Burlingame," he said, "to see McDougall returned Senator from California, Baker from Oregon, and Douglas and Old Abe all at Washington together?" E. D. Baker was a close friend of Lincoln's, and James A. McDougall an equally close friend of Douglas', and all four men knew each other, and judging by this statement thought highly of each other.

the votes were even more strangely divided: Lincoln 180, Breckinridge 72, Bell 39, and Douglas 12. Never was the archaic system of
the Electoral College so glaringly inadequate in its failure to reflect
the will of the people as in the 1860 election. Lincoln who polled
nearly 1,000,000 less than his combined opposition, received nearly
half again as many electoral votes as all of his opponents put together,
and Douglas who was by far closest to him in the popular poll, received the fewest electoral votes of all.

Late at night, weary from his long vigil, Lincoln returned to his
home—and underwent an eerie experience. He lay down on a couch
to catch a brief rest. As he lay there he gazed at a mirror on the wall
opposite and there distinctly saw *two* images of himself. One of the
images had "the glow of life and breath, the other showed ghastly
pale and white." Both, unquestionably, were his images.

Doubting his eyesight he rose, then lay down again. The two
images appeared as before. Always a little inclined to the supernatural, he spoke of it to his wife. Mary Lincoln considered it, and her
interpretation was that her husband would have not one, but two
terms as President; and that he would not survive his second term.
Later Lincoln tried again to conjure up the double image in the mirror. It never again appeared.

Perhaps as Dr. Rudolph Marx has speculated, the two images were
due to some trick in the lighting of the room at the time; or perhaps
they may have been the result of a slight and temporary imbalance
of his eyes, due to excessive weariness. Whatever may be the explanation of the phenomenon, that the incident actually took place is
certain for Lincoln later described it himself, with a sense of foreboding, and not long before his tragic assassination.

5

James Buchanan now knew who his successor would be; but not
until Lincoln was inaugurated the next March could he shift from his
own shoulders the responsibility of the nation's dark hour. He knew
America was being drawn into a terrible maelstrom of destruction and
that the country he sincerely loved might never survive that vortex.
How he could hold the Union together for four months he hardly
knew, for in spite of Lincoln's optimistic view, secession was the single greatest issue in the South as soon as the results of the election
were known.

The Republican leaders tried to, or appeared to, ignore the impending crisis. As Allan Nevins wrote:

The cardinal error of the Republicans was their failure to treat the now imminent danger of secession with the candor and emphasis it required. The failure had various roots. It seemed to the Party's interest to minimize a peril which, if nakedly exposed, might drive many to vote for a candidate acceptable to the South; optimism is always easier than pessimism; and many honestly believed that the cry of "wolf, wolf!" would prove as empty now as before.[5]

But in the South slaveholders conceived that the Republican victory meant ruin for them. Right after the election the *Charleston Courier* estimated that the drop in the price of slaves, which took place immediately, would amount to $430,000,000 for the entire South. How the newspaper arrived at this figure is hard to see. There were at the time approximately 4,000,000 slaves, and their value to their owners ranged from as much as $1200 or even $1500 a head for prime field hands, to what amounted to worthlessness or even considerable liability in the cases of slaves incapacitated by age, sickness, or other causes, from doing any work, but yet must be fed, housed, and cared for as part of their masters' responsibility. The *Courier* went on to say:

> Slave property is the foundation of all property in the South. When security in this is shaken, all other property partakes of its instability. Banks, stocks, bonds, must be influenced . . . The ruin of the South, by the emancipation of her slaves, is not like the ruin of other people . . . It is the loss of liberty, property, home, country—everything that makes life worth living.

This sort of thing was said in spite of the fact that Lincoln, the President-elect, was not and never had been an abolitionist. Repeatedly he had declared that he had no intention of interfering with the states which legally held slaves. In his clear estimation the preservation of the Union far outweighed the slave question. As late as August 22, 1862, a month before he issued the Emancipation Proclamation (which was essentially a war measure), he was to write to Horace Greeley:

> My paramount object in this struggle is to save the Union, and it is not either to save or destroy slavery. If I could save the Union without freeing any slave, I would do it; and if I could do it by freeing all the slaves, I would do it; and if I could save it by freeing some and leaving others alone, I would also do that.

[5] See Allan Nevins, *The Emergence of Lincoln.*

Even after emancipation he clung to the hope of reimbursing the South to some degree at least for its lost property. As late as February 1864, he held that the North and South were equally responsible for slavery, and proposed to his cabinet a $400,000,000 appropriation for reimbursement, provided that hostilities ceased by April 1 of that year. The cabinet unanimously voted down the proposal, and Lincoln laid it aside, temporarily as he thought, but in reality permanently, for his assassination prevented its possible revival.

In 1860 the South did not believe Lincoln's protestations, nor, indeed, could he in likelihood have carried them out. In the high councils of the Republican party were men who would yield no mercy to slaveowners, especially since to many of them the entire South, including both holders and non-holders of slaves, had become an object of hatred. These radical Republicans (Jacobins, John Hay called them for they soon attempted to take over the real power of the Republic), included men like Charles Sumner, Ben Wade, Thaddeus Stevens, Zachariah Chandler, Henry Winter Davis, J. A. Logan, James A. Ashley, George S. Boutwell, G. W. Julian, and Ben Butler. They hectored Lincoln throughout the war, set up the notorious "Committee on the Conduct of the War" which ruined many valuable generals and tried to get its political pets into high command, and put through the Confiscation (or Treason) Act of 1862. This group eventually impeached and almost unseated President Andrew Johnson for attempting to put into effect Lincoln's policies for rehabilitating the South after the war, and was primarily responsible for the severities and corruptions of the so-called Reconstruction era.

The South feared these men with reason. It knew it would never be compensated for its losses in slave property; and although the number of slaveowning families was relatively small, the whole section was irretrievably bound together.

In point of fact the North and South had become almost different nations. Buchanan helplessly watched the ominous approach of disaster and longed for his term to end.

CHAPTER TWENTY-NINE

Secession

1

THE four months of waiting before he could assume office were filled with growing anxiety for Abraham Lincoln, and the nation as a whole. With impatience he watched Buchanan's vacillating policies. "He ought to have a little of Andrew Jackson in him," he once exclaimed concerning the outgoing President. "'I take the responsibility, sir'—that was Old Hickory's strength."[1]

Selecting a cabinet from the wildly divergent elements of his party was a task requiring tact and patience. Seward, who still considered himself head of the Republican party, was offered the portfolio of Secretary of State. He accepted, then withdrew, and finally was persuaded to remain in that important post. Salmon P. Chase was given the Treasury office, Edward Bates became Attorney-General, Montgomery Blair was Postmaster-General, Gideon Welles, Secretary of the Navy, Caleb Smith, Secretary of the Interior, and Simon Cameron, Secretary of War.

Some of these appointments were forced upon him by promises made by his lieutenants, against his instructions, during the Chicago convention. Chase, Smith, and Cameron fell into the category of "bargains made." As it turned out Cameron did a bad job in the War Department and was replaced in 1862 by Lincoln's old legal acquaintance, Edwin M. Stanton, who proved to have the drive necessary to prosecute the war as it had to be prosecuted.

Four weeks remained after the election before Congress would meet in session. The situation grew ever more critical.

The very day after the election, Colonel John L. Gardner, in command of United States troops at Charleston, attempted to transfer ammunition from the government arsenal in the city, to Fort Moultrie at the harbor's mouth. He was resisted by a gathering mob of angry

---

[1] The sentiment must have been felt in different words by many persons. In his diary George Templeton Strong, who like Lincoln had never been a follower of Jackson, but admired his strong qualities, wrote December 21, 1860: "O, for an hour of Andrew Jackson, whom I held (when I was a boy and he was 'taking responsibility') to be the embodiment of everything bad, arrogant, and low."

civilians, and was forced to give up the project, his only alternative, from which he shrank, being to order his soldiers to fire at the crowd.

He appealed to John B. Floyd, Secretary of War. And now came a significant development. Floyd was a Virginian and a Southern sympathizer. Instead of aiding Gardner, he relieved the colonel of his command, and sent Major Robert Anderson to replace him. Anderson was a Kentuckian, who had married a Georgia woman. Floyd evidently thought he would not resist the manifest wishes of the Charleston population.

Instead, Anderson treated the situation as the military problem it was. After an inspection of Fort Moultrie, Castle Pinckney, and Fort Sumter, he wired for reinforcements. Buchanan at first instructed Floyd to send the reinforcements, then rescinded his instructions. Instead, Anderson was ordered to avoid offending the populace, but to defend his position if attacked.

The divided Congress (the Senate was Democratic, the House Republican) had lost all faith in Buchanan, and now the more stable and calmer elements sought to bring the two opposing factions of North and South together by some sort of a compromise. Buchanan's message was received December 4. It contained Buchanan's one feeble and futile effort in behalf of the Union. He declared that secession was "unconstitutional." This was all right, as far as it went. But it did not go any farther. These were words, mere words. Almost at once Buchanan qualified his statement by adding that the Union "rests upon public opinion, and can never be cemented by the blood of its citizens shed in civil war. If it cannot live in the affections of the people, it must one day perish."

He assailed the anti-slavery extremists in the North as being chiefly responsible for the bitterness in the South, spoke of the fear of servile revolt in many sections of the slave states, and made the astounding statement that if the peril of such a revolt increased, "then disunion would become inevitable," since self-preservation would make it a necessity.

The message was practically a concession to secession; it offended the South by declaring that secession was unconstitutional; and it irritated the North by blaming it for conditions then existing.

Four days later, December 8, Howell Cobb of Georgia, an outright secessionist, resigned as Secretary of the Treasury. On December 13 the veteran Lewis Cass, after a last effort to persuade Buchanan to send reinforcements to Charleston, resigned as Secretary of State. Cobb, the secessionist, and Cass, the strong Union man, had turned in their portfolios almost simultaneously. It was an ugly omen of things to come.

Now old Senator John Crittenden of Kentucky, seeking anxiously for some way to heal the dreadful breach in the nation, proposed a compromise whereby the territories should be divided between the free and slave states on the basis of the Missouri Compromise line. In the common peril, Douglas receded from his popular sovereignty doctrine, and joined with Crittenden, in the hope the compromise might satisfy both sections. Other brave men, including Tom Corwin of Ohio,[2] John Sherman of the same state (brother of the later famous General William Tecumseh Sherman), and Andrew Johnson of Tennessee, destined to become President on Lincoln's death, added their influence to the proposal.

Rallying to the idea of the Crittenden compromise as being an expedient most likely to smooth out the difficulties of the times, the Senate voted to form a committee, consisting of thirteen members, which should be headed by Crittenden, and which included among its number such men as Stephen A. Douglas and William H. Seward of the North, and Jefferson Davis and Robert Toombs of the South, to seek a solution for the crisis.

The "Committee of Thirteen" had its first sitting December 20.

That was a fateful day; a day on which two events of mighty importance took place.

Abraham Lincoln had remained quietly in his home at Springfield, although he was in constant conference with Republican leaders. Among these was Thurlow Weed, Seward's political partner and campaign manager, who on instructions from the Senator asked the President-elect directly if he would accept the contemplated compromise. On December 20, Lincoln closed the door to such a compromise by issuing what was virtually an ultimatum. "Let there be no compromise on the question of extending slavery," was his forthright statement. He once more underlined his previous agreement to let slavery alone where it existed, and even advocated strenuous enforcement of the Fugitive Slave laws, but on the matter of devoting any of the territories to future slavery he was adamant.

Lincoln was motivated by deep principles and foresight. He was thinking not only of the then existing territories, but of other territories that might be acquired through the activities of filibusters, who would be stimulated by such a concession to warlike actions. (Only about

---

[2] Corwin was rotund, witty, and so dark in complexion that once or twice—as he related with glee—he was taken to be of African descent. "There is really no need of my working," he once said, "for whenever I cannot support myself in Ohio, all I should have to do would be cross the river, give myself up to a Kentucky Negro-trader, be taken South, and sold for a field hand." On another occasion, when a political opponent asked him if Negroes should be permitted to sit at table with white people, he brought a roar of laughter by asking, "Is it proper to ask such a question of a gentleman of my color?"

four months before, on September 12, William Walker had been executed in Honduras, but others were ready to emulate him.) In his mind was the agitation in California to acquire Sonora; the repeated efforts, not only by Walker but by others in Central America; even the possible annexation of the Hawaiian Islands which lay south of the 36°30′ parallel—all of which presumably would become slave territory if the compromise was enacted.

It was one of the most fatefully important decisions of Lincoln's life, for it put an end to the compromise idea and led straight to war.

On that same day, December 20, there was stunning news from the South. South Carolina had called a state convention which met December 17 at Columbia, adjourned next day to Charleston because of an outbreak of smallpox, and on December 20 adopted an ordinance of secession. There were still stanch Union men in South Carolina, and elsewhere in the South. But the Charleston convention was dominated by the radical secessionists and characterized by fiery oratory. Lincoln had expected that good sense and a cool appraisal of the odds against them would prevent the Southern states from taking immediately any irrevocable action. But good sense and cool appraisal were notably absent in Charleston that day.

Caught up in emotional excitement there was hardly a dissenting voice in the city. Those who thought the ordinance of secession a mistake were forced to keep silent. All the others—and vast crowds thronged the streets—went fairly wild with enthusiasm. They roared thunderous acclaim; cannons boomed in salute; the bells of the city's churches were rung as if in joyous celebration of some famous victory; bands played martial music; the palmetto flag appeared everywhere; and telegraph stations flashed the news to every Southern capital, and to Washington, the capital of the nation.

Fire-eating orators, from balconies, did a good deal of posturing, and made scornful utterances about money-grubbing, deceitful, and meddling Yankees who (presumably) would be too busy counting their money bags to do any fighting. Prevailing public opinion seemed to be that the nation as a whole would not attempt to coerce South Carolina back into the Union, and if it did so South Carolina was well able to repel any such "aggression." Young men, carried along on the wave of false confidence fostered by older men who should have known better, enlisted in state regiments and began to drill. Women joined in the emotional hysteria and presented silken banners to these military units, embroidered by their own fair hands. The *Charleston Mercury* headlined clear across its front page: THE UNION IS DISSOLVED!

Other Southern states were affected by the South Carolina act; and yet men remained who strove to check the hysteria. Among those who

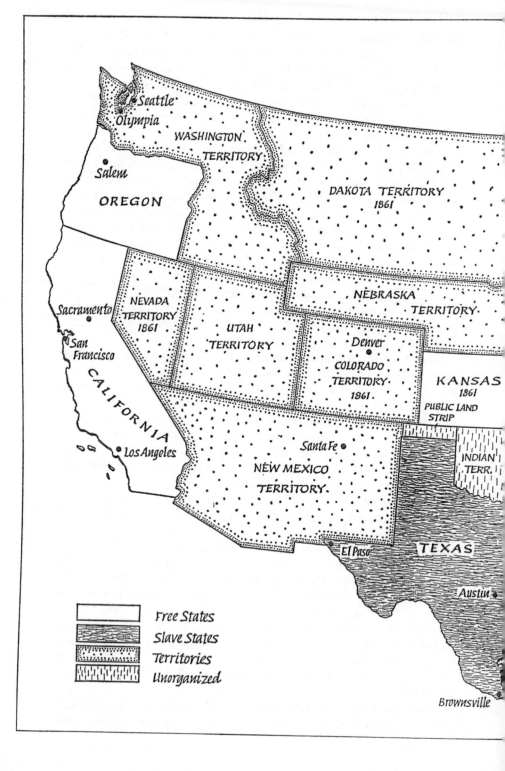

UNITED STATES
A Divided Nation, March 4, 1861

palacios

tried to hold back the avalanche of feeling was old Sam Houston, who
had left the Senate to run for governor of Texas, and had been elected.
Houston, true to the principles of his old chief Andrew Jackson,
sacrificed his political career in his dedicated effort to keep Texas
from seceding, and was at length thrown out of office.

2

Late in December, Buchanan, who by now was beside himself with
anxiety, summoned aging General Winfield Scott from his home at
West Point, New York, to Washington for conference. The old general,
a majestic ruin of a man, seventy-four years old, six feet four inches tall,
dropsical and portly with a weight of about three hundred pounds,
was addicted to the showy uniforms, including gold epaulets and sash,
which no longer looked well on his rotund but sagging figure. But for
all his age and failings, he was still the Commanding General of the
U. S. Army, and he was still able to give the President clear military
advice.

Scott already had written Buchanan that the Southern forts should
be strongly garrisoned, and that measures should be taken like those in
which he himself had participated in the nullification crisis during
Andrew Jackson's time. On his arrival in Washington he repeated
this advice. But like others, the old general was baffled by the President's lack of decision; Floyd, the Secretary of War, turned the cold
shoulder to him; and nothing was done. Scott withdrew to his quarters,
and devoted himself to the pleasures of the board—he was a renowned
eater, and his favorite dishes were canvasback duck, woodcock, snipe,
capon, Virginia ham, and terrapin, all cooked in the French manner,
and complemented with the finest wines and liquors he could obtain.

General Scott knew that the entire military establishment of the
United States contained no more than 16,000 soldiers, and that these
were mostly stationed in posts far out on the Western frontiers. A
Virginian himself, he believed that Southerners, with their martial
spirit and "habit of command," made the best army officers; and he
had given preference to such men as Braxton Bragg, Joseph Eggleston
Johnston, James Longstreet, and a handsome Virginian named Robert
E. Lee, in whom the old general saw some extraordinary military
promise, and of whom he said "he is worth 50,000 men."

As a result some Northern officers became discontented and resigned
their commissions to go into private pursuits; and these included men
like George Brinton McClellan, William Tecumseh Sherman, and
Joseph Hooker, as well as a scrubby short man named Ulysses S.
Grant.

But Virginian though he was, and in spite of his preferences for Southern officers, Winfield Scott was loyal to the core to his flag and the Union for which it stood. He was perhaps not as closely abreast of the political situation as he might be, for though he had run for President in 1852 on the Whig ticket, he had since lost touch with the politicians. Old, swollen, and feeble physically, Scott still could see that the military situation was acute. For the time being, however, after the brusque treatment he received from Secretary Floyd, he offered no more advice; but waited in silence for the time when his voice would be listened to again.

Meantime the tension in Charleston increased. South Carolina now regarded herself as an independent nation, and Governor Francis W. Pickens wrote to Buchanan demanding that the troops of the state be allowed to take possession of Fort Sumter and other federal fortifications in Charleston Harbor immediately, adding that if this were not done he would "not be responsible" for the consequences.

The covert threat seems to have angered Buchanan. He had been almost compliant thus far, but his attitude hardened somewhat after the Pickens letter was received—even though Pickens made haste to "withdraw" the letter. John Floyd, the Secretary of War, however, made haste to pledge that the War Department would take no action to "injure" South Carolina—and this without taking the trouble to consult the President.

But neither Floyd nor Buchanan had fully considered the character of Major Anderson, who had been sent to take command of the United States forces at Charleston.

The people of that city had devoted all their wonderful charm to making Anderson a friend of their cause. He had been wined and dined, the most luxurious homes threw their doors open to him, the loveliest ladies gave him their dazzling smiles, the "highest toned" gentlemen displayed toward him their finest courtesies. Charleston felt that Anderson, a Kentuckian with a wife from Georgia, and sent by that good friend of the South, Secretary Floyd, must be in thorough sympathy with the secession movement.

But Anderson was a soldier, true to his oath of allegiance, and he proved a disappointment to both Charleston and Floyd, though not to his nation as a whole. On Christmas Day, 1860, he attended a gay Yuletide party at the home of Captain J. G. Foster, his subordinate in command at Fort Moultrie. On that day he made his decision. The night of December 26 he quietly transferred his men and such arms as he could transport from Fort Moultrie, which was indefensible, to Fort Sumter, which was not much better. The cannon at Fort Moultrie were spiked, the gun carriages burned, the flagstaff cut down.

When Charleston discovered what he had done next morning, it

loudly proclaimed that he had committed an "overt act." Governor
Pickens called out ten units of the militia, placed guards over the
arsenal and other government buildings, and in place of the flag of
the United States raised the palmetto flag of South Carolina.

Requested to withdraw from Fort Sumter, Anderson refused. The
archaic old stone fort stood right in the throat of Charleston Harbor.
Commerce could not enter or leave without its permission. Talk filled
the streets that the fort would be attacked immediately. And yet, for
various reasons, a sort of quasi-truce existed between the city and the
fort for three and a half months before final action was taken.

3

Anderson's bold move created something akin to panic in Washington. Buchanan was far from ready for an immediate showdown. Floyd
raved and sent a telegram to Anderson demanding an explanation of
his action in the absence of direct orders. To this Anderson replied in
formal military language, that he had abandoned Fort Moultrie because he could not defend it if attacked.

Buchanan actually received first news of Anderson's move from
three Southern spokesmen who called on him December 27. They
were Jefferson Davis, R. M. T. Hunter, and W. H. Trescott.

"My God," cried the old President, "are misfortunes never to come
singly? I call God to witness . . . that this is not only without, but
against my orders. It is against my policy."

But when the spokesmen urged him to command Anderson to "restore the former position," Buchanan delayed, refused to be rushed into
action, and insisted on discussing the matter with his cabinet before
doing anything at all.

The cabinet meeting was furious and exciting. Floyd denounced
Anderson and demanded an immediate order to remove all troops
from Charleston Harbor. He was countered by E. M. Stanton, who
had become, in the cabinet shakeups, Attorney General, and by Jere-
miah Black, who had replaced Cass as Secretary of State. Stanton, with
excitement, said that such an act as Floyd advocated would be equivalent to Benedict Arnold's treason. And the poor bewildered President
tried to assuage the heated atmosphere by crying out, "Oh, no! Not
as bad as that!"

The cabinet adjourned, met again the same day, and in the end
voted, four to three, against sending an order to Anderson such as
Floyd desired. The situation became more tense when three commissioners from South Carolina appeared, called upon the President, and

officially *demanded* the withdrawal of the troops from Charleston Harbor.

At this point a scandal concerning Floyd entered into the stream of events. There had been—to give it the most favorable interpretation—incompetence, imprudence, and negligence in the War Department, whereby some $870,000 was lost from the Treasury, in dealings largely with William H. Russell, of the frontier freighting firm of Russell, Majors & Waddell. This firm had furnished both supplies and transportation to the troops during the so-called Mormon War, and had suffered severe financial losses through the guerrilla tactics of the Mormons. Attempts at restitution for Russell were irregular; and while it has never been proved that Floyd personally received one penny of these lost funds, a kinsman of his, Goddard Bailey, who was a government clerk, had a share in the abstractions. In any case Floyd was guilty of extreme carelessness and inefficiency, if not worse.

Another sudden charge was made against him. As Secretary of War he had, on December 20—the very day South Carolina seceded—ordered 46 cannon shipped from Pittsburgh, Pennsylvania, to Ship Island, Mississippi, and 79 cannon from the same place to Galveston, Texas. Pittsburgh citizens made an aroused protest to the President, and Buchanan countermanded the order.

Previous to that Floyd already had sent 105,000 muskets and 10,000 rifles from Northern to Southern arsenals. This had the appearance of treason. Most historians today agree that the transfer of the muskets and rifles was legal and perhaps proper, to make room in Northern arsenals for newer and better weapons. But what about the order to send 125 pieces of artillery into the deep South at the very onset of secession? It created enormous excitement at the time.

Floyd was asked by Buchanan to resign. After delay the resignation was given and the disgraced former Secretary of War went to Virginia, where he began making secessionist speeches. He was indicted for misfeasance in office, but shortly after the Civil War began, the case against him was dropped.

Now again old General Scott was heard from. He had made an emphatic appeal that he be permitted to send a reinforcement of 250 soldiers, together with supplies, arms, and ammunition, to Fort Sumter.

In agonized indecision Buchanan first drafted a letter making concessions to the South Carolinians, then, faced by threats of resignation by Black, his Secretary of State, and Stanton, his Attorney General, allowed them to rewrite it, converting it into a blank refusal to remove United States troops from Charleston Harbor, and to disavow Anderson's action. Furthermore it notified the rebellious state that Sumter would be defended "against hostile attacks from whatever quarter they may come."

At last attention was paid to General Scott's appeal. The sloop-of-war *Brooklyn* was made ready to sail for Charleston with troops and supplies. But now it was learned that vessels had been sunk in the harbor mouth to block it. Scott therefore decided to send, instead of the *Brooklyn*, an unarmed steamer of lighter draft, the *Star of the West*, with two hundred soldiers and war matériel. On January 5, 1861, the relief ship sailed on an errand she did not complete.

By that time batteries had been placed about the entrances to Charleston Harbor. When, on January 9, the *Star of the West* attempted to pass into the channel, she was greeted by cannon fire. Unarmed, a merchant vessel, the ship could make no reply; and her captain followed the only possible course: retreat.

The flag of the United States had been fired upon.

A boat approached Fort Sumter. It carried Colonel Johnson Pettigrew, of the 1st South Carolina Rifles.

To Anderson he said, "The governor directs me to say to you, courteously but peremptorily, to return to Fort Moultrie."

"Make my compliments to the governor," replied Anderson, "and say to him that I decline to accede to his request; I cannot and will not go back."

The battle lines were drawn in Charleston Harbor. Fort Sumter had become a symbol that would plunge the nation into civil war.

4

January was a month of gathering forces. On January 9 Mississippi passed an ordinance of secession similar to that of South Carolina. Florida followed January 10, and Alabama January 11. Georgia, on January 19, voted secession and invited other seceding states to meet at Atlanta with the object of forming a confederacy. Louisiana joined the movement January 26, and Texas—against the fierce resistance of Houston—February 1.

Seven states now had declared themselves independent of the Federal Union, and everywhere in those states fireworks displays, band music, speeches, and cheering advertised these departures. Virginia, North Carolina, Arkansas, and Tennessee thus far held aloof. In the border slave states—Missouri, Kentucky, Maryland, and Delaware—opinion was so divided that the outcome could not be predicted.

On January 8, Jacob Thompson, Secretary of the Interior and last of the radical Southerners on the cabinet, resigned in anger, perhaps forecasting the future action of his state, North Carolina.

And what was Abraham Lincoln doing during this period of great stress and excitement? He watched the progress of events from his home in Illinois, concentrating his hopes on retaining those border states in the Union. He was beset by "advisers" from both the conservative and the extremist wings of the Republican party. And he remained silent, refusing invitations to speak, even to make public statements on the critical issues.

Though the portents grew more ominous each day, Lincoln seemed calm in Springfield—too calm to suit a nation that was crying aloud for someone to save it in its time of tragic dissolution. It was as if, out of his own wonderful goodwill, he could not believe that there were other men who might be lacking in goodwill.

And this in spite of letters that came daily in his mail, some of them friendly, of course; but others calling him fantastically insulting names like ape, baboon, abortion, idiot, and monster, and saying that he should be tarred and feathered, hanged, even tortured.[3]

So menacing were some of the inimical letters and threats that a friendly Iowan, A. W. Flanders, wrote to John Nicolay, one of Lincoln's secretaries, offering to have a shirt of flexible chain mail made for the President-elect to wear under his clothing, to protect him from assassination attempts. The offer was refused, with thanks.

It should not be supposed that such abuse and such threats left Lincoln unmoved. He had great courage, yet he told Donn Piatt that he "felt like a surveyor in the wild woods of the West, who, while looking for a corner, kept an eye over his shoulder for an Indian."

The New York *Herald,* owned by James Gordon Bennett, now boldly suggested that Lincoln withdraw as President, in favor of some man who would be acceptable to both North and South, adding:

> If he persists in his present position . . . he will totter to a dishonored grave, driven there perhaps by the hands of an assassin, leaving behind him a memory more execrable than that of Arnold—more despised than that of the traitor Catiline.

To this Lincoln was as indifferent as he was to the offer of a mail undershirt.

But down in the South, at an Alabama mass meeting, a banner proclaimed, "Resistance to Lincoln is Obedience to God!"

There was a report, well grounded on plans actually made, that the South would attempt to seize the national capital. If both Virginia

---

[3] A painting on canvas was sent to him, which Mrs. Lincoln unwrapped. It depicted her husband tarred and feathered, chains fastening his feet, and a rope about his neck.

and Maryland seceded, the District of Columbia and Washington would be completely cut off from the non-secessionist part of the country. Nothing would then be required but that the forces of rebellion should march in and take possession of the Capitol, the White House, the Treasury, the Navy Yards, the War Department, and other federal structures, together with all records, documents, stores, supplies, and moneys contained therein.

The plan was frustrated. Virginia did go out of the Union, but not until April 17, 1861. Maryland in the end was prevented from seceding by strong measures instituted by Lincoln himself. In truth, although there was a continual howl that Lincoln was indifferent to, or ignorant concerning, the perilous state of affairs, the tall lonely man was spending all the time he could get alone by himself in solemn, complete, and probably anguished concentration on the problems confronting his beloved nation.

As the day of his inauguration approached, Lincoln was warned again and again of the danger to which he would expose himself, unless he agreed to take his oath of office quietly, in some guarded chamber. His reply to these warnings was that he "would rather be hanged by the neck until he was dead on the steps of the Capitol, than buy or beg a peaceful and safe inauguration."

Abraham Lincoln had something he felt he must say to the people of the United States, and the inauguration was the time and place to say it.

From the old war horse, General Scott, loyal to his fingertips, came a message for Lincoln through Thomas S. Mather, adjutant general of Illinois: "Say to him that, when once here, I shall consider myself responsible for his safety. If necessary, I'll plant cannon at both ends of Pennsylvania Avenue, and if any show their hands or even venture to raise a finger, I'll blow them to hell."

Already at the general's orders troops were trundling by railroad across the country—twenty-two carloads of them—from Fort Leavenworth to the threatened capital. They would be there and on hand Inauguration Day.

One of Lincoln's last acts in that January was a farewell visit to his stepmother, Sarah Bush Lincoln, whom he loved as his real mother for her kindness to him. Part of that ride was in the caboose of a freight train, and he was unaccompanied.[4] At his destination he got out of

---

[4] Perhaps the most unpretentious man in history, it is likely that nobody in the caboose knew he was the President-elect. Recently the New York *Herald* had printed an anecdote that illustrated his unassuming and humorous nature. At a time when a comet appeared in the sky, some passengers with whom he was riding in a coach took him to be an old farmer, wrapped in a gray shawl, lean and long, with ill-fitting garments, uncombed hair and muddy boots. Thinking to have

the caboose, a shawl over his shoulders, and sloshed the length of the train through mud, snow, and ice, to the railroad station. There he found a buggy and friends awaiting him, who took him to Sarah Bush Lincoln's home. The old woman embraced her boy, and he kissed her. They talked far into the night. Lincoln slept in his stepmother's home, next morning had breakfast with her, kissed her goodbye, and went back to the worry and care with which life had surrounded him. That short, peaceful and deeply affectionate interlude in his strife-torn life was the last time he was to see his "angel mother."

So January passed, and Abraham Lincoln prepared for his journey to Washington, where he would assume the staggering burdens of the President of a nation already rent asunder.

5

From the South came more ominous news. On February 4, representatives of six seceding states, South Carolina, Georgia, Florida, Alabama, Mississippi, and Louisiana, met at Montgomery, Alabama. They designated themselves a Congress, and drew up a "Constitution for the Provisional Government of the Confederate States of America."

In that constitution were two provisions that many political students believe were improvements on the Constitution of the United States, upon which it was modeled. The first of these two provisions was that the President, instead of having to veto a bill as a whole, or else accept and sign it, was empowered to veto specific sections of it, thus preventing an enormous amount of useless expenditures and nuisance amendments. The other was that members of the cabinet should be given seats in the Confederate Congress, and take part in debates; which added one of the most valuable features of the British parliamentary system, to the American congressional system. But there was one fatal defect as time would show: extreme deference to state's rights.

On February 9 the Congress unanimously elected Jefferson Davis President of the Confederacy. Davis was not at Montgomery, but he read the telegram notifying him of his election at his plantation, Brierfield, below Vicksburg, Mississippi. When he told his wife, Varina, of

---

some fun with him, they began by asking him about his hogs and crops, and then one of them slyly asked what the old "farmer" would do when the comet hit the earth. With a straight face and not revealing his identity, Lincoln replied, "Wall, that'd be just too bad for that comet. If it hits aroun' our neighborhood us boys 'ud lasso the darn thing. We been a-needin' a light for corn shuckin's an' cider makin's."

the message, he spoke "in a voice of tragic emotion . . . like the voice
with which a man might say he had been sentenced to death."

He was not well, and accepted the office with reluctance. Nevertheless he packed and traveled to Montgomery. It was raining when
he arrived but cannons boomed, and crowds cheered. Later the clouds
cleared away and the rain ceased. Davis seems to have regarded this
as a favorable augury. That night, at shouts from a crowd in the street,
he appeared on a balcony of the Exchange Hotel. William Lowndes
Yancey introduced him with the words, "The hour and the man have
met!" And Davis, in his brief remarks, said, "It may be that our career
[as a nation] will be ushered in, in the midst of storms—it may be that
as this morning opened with clouds, mist, and rain, we shall have to
encounter inconveniences at the beginning; but as the sun rose, lifted
the mist, dispersed the clouds, and left a pure sunlight, heaven so will
prosper the Southern Confederacy, and carry us safe from sea to the
harbor of constitutional liberty."

His inaugural address, delivered February 18, was more foreboding,
for like Lincoln he must have counted up the long odds against the
Confederacy should it come to war. He described the separation from
the Union as a "peaceful achievement," based on the desires of the
voters of the seceding states, and reaffirming the principle that proper
government depended always on the consent of the governed.

Then he went on to outline necessities of the new government, such
as a monetary system, a postal service, and an army and navy. And he
once more expressed the hope that the Confederacy would achieve
friendship and peace with the Union. But he added, warningly, that
if the Union offered violence ". . . a terrific responsibility will rest
upon it, and the sufferings of millions will bear testimony to the folly
and wickedness of our aggressors."

A separate nation had been formed. Texas, though not represented
at Montgomery, had voted to join it; and Virginia, North Carolina,
Tennessee, and Arkansas soon would do so.

One stalwart soldier refused to recognize the secession. On February 22 Major Anderson, isolated with his handful in lonely Fort Sumter, fired a salute of cannon in honor of the birthday of George
Washington, the Father of His Country. The salute was of thirty-four
guns—one for each state, including newly admitted Kansas, and including also all seven of the seceded states.

Charleston denounced this as "insolence," but Anderson grimly
manned his guns.

CHAPTER THIRTY

An Oath Registered in Heaven

1

IT WAS raining in Springfield, Illinois, the morning of February 11, 1861; not a hard rain but a thin gray drizzle, wetting the fields and houses, and dampening the spirits of the hundreds at the railroad station.

In the South, the Congress of the Confederate States of America was engaged in forming the machinery of the new government. In Washington, John J. Crittenden, in brokenhearted despair, was fighting for some last semblance of a meeting ground of minds between the states.

And in Springfield, Abraham Lincoln, standing in the slow rain, said goodbye to his friends before he boarded the waiting train. To them he said with affection:

"My friends—No one, not in my situation, can appreciate my feeling of sadness at this parting. To this place, and the kindness of these people, I owe everything. Here I have lived a quarter of a century, and have passed from a young to an old man. Here my children have been born, and one is buried. I now leave, not knowing when, or whether ever, I may return, with a task before me greater than that which rested upon Washington. Without the assistance of that Divine Being, who ever attended him, I cannot succeed. With that assistance, I cannot fail. Trusting in Him, who can go with me, and remain with you and be everywhere for good, let us confidently hope that all will yet be well. To His care commending you, as I hope in your prayers you will commend me, I bid you an affectionate farewell."

He stepped on the train. The engine puffed as it gathered speed. Lincoln was gone to his rendezvous with an amazing and heroic Fate.

He was to cross several states, meet many people, speak briefly here and there, and his colloquialisms would create criticism, almost scorn in some places. George Templeton Strong, the diarist, who saw him during a procession in New York, thought he had "a keen, clear, honest face, not so ugly as his portraits." Later, when Strong interviewed Lincoln after the Civil War had started, he thus portrayed the President:

He is a barbarian, Scythian, yahoo, or gorilla, in respect of outside polish (for example, he uses "humans" as English for *homines*), but a most sensible, straightforward, honest old codger. The best President we have had since old Jackson's time, at least as I believe . . . His evident integrity and simplicity of purpose would compensate for worse grammar than his, and for even more intense provincialism and rusticity.

In these days, a century after Lincoln's time, it is difficult to reconcile the great phrase-maker, the author of the Gettysburg Address, with the man who in his ordinary conversation was careless, almost crude at times. It was this very contrast that at first caused some people to look askance at him, and it was long before they realized that the great mind of the magnificent speeches was finding relaxation and perhaps comfort in the homely phrases of its youth on the frontier.

Still the nation waited to hear what the President-elect would say concerning the lowering black storm clouds overspreading the nation. For the time being, he chose to forebear such expression. The speeches he did make were almost wistfully humble. At Albany, New York, for example, he said, "It is true that while I hold myself, without mock modesty, the humblest of all individuals that have ever been elevated to the Presidency, I have a more difficult task to perform than any of them. When the time comes I shall speak as well as I am able for the good of both the North and the South . . ."

Almost breathlessly the people waited to see how Lincoln would behave when the time came for action. A good deal of sentiment, based perhaps on his countrified speech and ways, held that though he probably was a good country lawyer and a fair stump-speaker, he lacked the great qualities that made for statesmanship. Some astute political leaders believed that Lincoln, like the four men who had preceded him in office, would be guided, if not controlled, by his associates. They could not have been more mistaken. The man who was heading East to take the helm of the ship of state was to prove as mighty in will as old Andrew Jackson himself.

It was not generally known, but Lincoln's Inaugural Address had been written for weeks, and even placed in print, though held in complete secrecy. Early in the game Seward, to be the new Secretary of State, learned that he was dealing with something different from a country cousin seeking "guidance." He tried to get Lincoln to change this speech. Lincoln accepted some suggestions but on the major points he refused to alter the principles he set forth. And when Seward sent him a somewhat florid peroration for the speech, Lincoln accepted the heart of it—"we are not enemies but friends"—but trimmed it down, and with the sure touch of genius made it one of the most beautiful passages in all the public utterances in the history of America.

2

At Philadelphia the President-elect received a grim warning. A blocky, bearded man, who habitually chewed at a cigar, and had a curiously veiled expression in his eyes beneath their lowering brows, was waiting with Lincoln's friend, Norman B. Judd, at the hotel. His name was Allan Pinkerton, a private detective. He was a strong abolitionist who had furnished $500 in cash and part of the supplies for John Brown when the latter made his raid on Harper's Ferry.

Pinkerton informed Lincoln that there was a plot to assassinate him; that it would take place in Baltimore when the special train carrying the President-elect passed through there; and he even furnished names of some conspirators. One in particular was an Italian barber named Fernandia, who had told Pinkerton, "As Orsini gave his life for Italy, I am ready to die for the rights of the South"—by killing Lincoln.

The detective advised the President-elect to board a train that night for Washington, taking care that his presence on it be kept secret. At first Lincoln listened and asked questions. Never afraid to die, he seemed unable to accept the belief that anyone might make an attempt on his life. He refused to take the night train to Washington, because he had promised to appear at Philadelphia and Harrisburg next day.

But that night Frederick W. Seward, son of William H. Seward, arrived with a letter from his father. It contained substantially the same information Pinkerton had provided.

When he had read this letter Lincoln asked, "Did you hear any names mentioned? Did you, for instance, ever hear anything said about such a name as Pinkerton?"

Young Seward had heard no such name.

"If different persons, not knowing of each other's work, have been pursuing separate clues that led to the same result," said Lincoln, "why then it shows there may be something in it. But if this is only the same story, filtered through two channels, and reaching me in two ways, then that don't make it any stronger."

As a matter of fact the two reports came from two separate investigators, neither of whom knew of the work of the other. Seward's information was from a detective named Bookstaver, who had been assigned to check reports of a plot in Baltimore, by John A. Kennedy, superintendent of the New York police department.

Lincoln's friends convinced him that for the sake of the country, more than for his own, he should take reasonable precautions. Next day he spoke in Philadelphia, and then in Harrisburg. That night, right after dinner, he left Harrisburg in a "special train" consisting of a lone locomotive drawing a lone car, and proceeding without lights. Telegraph wires were cut so that no information by telegraph could go out from Harrisburg.

A change was made at Philadelphia. In the last car of the New York to Washington train a woman detective had reserved two berths, one of which was to be occupied by her "invalid brother." In that berth, with curtains drawn, Lincoln spent the night. He was guarded by armed men, but nobody on the train knew that they had so distinguished a fellow-passenger.

Baltimore, the danger spot, was reached at 3:30 A.M. Since the official special train was not due until 10 A.M., there of course was nobody at the station to make a demonstration. Lincoln's journey continued quietly and he arrived in Washington at 6 A.M. Except for "a joke or two in an undertone," he had hardly spoken throughout the night.

Afterward this clandestine arrival in the capital was ridiculed by some of Lincoln's opponents. There was even a story (completely untrue) that he had disguised himself with a plaid Scotch cap and a long cloak.

He himself hated the thought of taking precautions on the word of "a professional spy." Yet it may have been the wisest of courses for him to do so.

The head of the Baltimore police department, George P. Kane, was an out-and-out secessionist. According to the plan as revealed by Pinkerton, Kane was to send only a handful of policemen to the station. The assassination plotters would be there in numbers. They would create a disturbance which would engage the attention of the officers, and in the confusion murder the President-elect.

As it turned out more than ten thousand persons jammed the railroad station at Baltimore when the announced special train came in. It was a hostile mob, as shown by the fact that, "supposing that Lincoln was aboard, the most terrific cheers ever heard were sent up, three for the Southern Confederacy, three for 'gallant Jeff Davis,' and three groans for 'the Rail-Splitter,'" as a friend wrote to Howell Cobb, then in Georgia.

Lincoln, of course, was not there to hear the angry shouts, and there must have been considerable frustration in certain quarters when this fact was ascertained. But from that time on he was never free from imminent peril of assassination, according to the belief of his friend, Ward H. Lamon. Lincoln himself accepted this fact. Any man who wished to kill the President of the United States, he once calmly stated to his friends, could always do so provided he was willing to pay with his own life for the act.

3

Beset by office-seekers, and by politicians, devoting his best thought and diplomacy to the effort to keep the two wings of his own party—the moderates led by Seward, the radicals by Chase and Sumner—in some sort of harmony, Lincoln spent a disproportionate amount of his time on what appeared to be trivialities as he waited for March 4.

Threats against his life continued to be made; but to these he seemed to be indifferent. About him continually eddied currents of intrigue, as the Republicans, in power for the first time, sought to check and countercheck each other in the scramble for preferments. It was difficult for him to know who were his true friends and who were not. Horace Greeley, after a visit to the capital, wrote:

> Old Abe is honest as the sun, and means to be true and faithful; but he is in the web of very cunning spiders and cannot work out if he would. Mrs. Abe is a Kentuckian and enjoys flattery—I mean deference. And God is above us, and all things will be well in the end. Life is not very long, and we shall rest by and by.

How little Greeley understood Lincoln!

Inauguration Day approached, and old James Buchanan, taking cognizance of the threats, turmoil and danger in the capital, stoutly said, "I will ride with old Abe to his inauguration."

General Scott roused himself to make dispositions like the canny old soldier that he was. On the roofs of houses along Pennsylvania Avenue, down which the inaugural procession would pass, he placed in concealment trusted riflemen. At every hundred yards along the route stood a platoon of infantry, with fixed bayonets. Cavalry patrolled the side streets watching with sharp suspicion for any who appeared to be lurking there. In the windows of the Capitol, sharpshooters bent their gaze on the crowd below, looking for any sign of trouble. A battery of artillery, loaded and shotted, the gun crews ready for action, was posted just north of the Capitol, commanding the eastern side where the spectators would watch the ceremony. A guard of honor, chosen from the army and marine corps, was told off to sur-

round the Presidential carriage, marching on either side, and before
and behind it.

Morning dawned bright and pleasant on Monday, March 4, but
soon clouds overspread the sky and temperatures went down until
the day was raw and chilly. Noon came, and Lincoln was arraying
himself for his inauguration, in a new black suit, well-polished shoes, a
white-bosomed shirt, a resplendent tall black silk hat, and an ebony
cane with a solid gold head to lend him dignity.

At 12:30 o'clock there was a cheer outside the Willard Hotel. President Buchanan had arrived, in an open carriage, accompanied by
Lincoln's old friend, Senator Edward D. Baker of Oregon, and Senator James A. Pearce of Maryland. The President, silk-hatted and
frock-coated, stepped down from the carriage and entered the hotel. A few minutes later the crowd set up another roar, as Buchanan
appeared again, arm in arm with Lincoln. The two proceeded to the
carriage through a path kept open for them by officers.

The bands struck up. A float carrying thirty-four lovely girls—one
for each state—preceded the Presidential carriage. Troops marched,
and people cheered. Down the avenue, gaily decorated with bunting,
Abraham Lincoln was riding into history.

4

At the east portico of the Capitol a wooden platform had been
erected, decorated with the national colors. Upon this sat dignitaries,
among them Lincoln's old rival, Stephen A. Douglas, who in defeat
had turned his distinguished talents to the support of the man who
had won from him, for the welfare of the nation they both loved.[1]

Lincoln and Buchanan appeared on the platform, and ten thousand

---

[1] Douglas died in the service of his country. He threw himself wholeheartedly
in the war effort, conferred with Lincoln, and issued a statement that though he
opposed the administration politically, he would sustain the President in the
exercise of every power to preserve the Union. Though he was ill, he made his way
to Illinois, and especially to the section of the state called "Egypt," to rally support
for the government among those Democrats many of whom had Southern
sympathies. He spoke to the legislature, and his influence was such, not only in
Illinois but throughout the North, that party differences seemed to be submerged
in the major cause of saving the Union. But his physical resistance was low, and
after the Springfield speech he felt increasingly ill. Nevertheless, going to Chicago
where his home was, he summoned strength to tell a large audience in the Wigwam, "Before God it is the duty of every American citizen to rally around the flag
of his country." Then he went to his home, overlooking Lake Michigan, to die. His
ailment had been diagnosed as typhoid fever, and death came June 3, three months
after he saw Lincoln inaugurated. As Carl Sandburg wrote: "Northern Democrats
mourned the lost giant of their party, while Republicans paid tribute to a leader
who in a crisis had hushed mutiny among his followers."

people below applauded. There were many men in Washington wearing blue cockades, signifying sympathy with the secessionists, but very few blue cockades were seen in that crowd on that day.

Senator Baker stepped forward, and introduced "Abraham Lincoln, President-elect of the United States."

So eagerly did the crowd watch that it almost forgot to applaud as a gaunt figure, towering over everyone on the platform, moved forward. There was a movement of awkwardness as one observer later reported. Abraham Lincoln looked around for a place to lay his tall hat. Then a friendly hand reached out, took it from him. The hand belonged to Stephen A. Douglas, who seeing Lincoln's momentary embarrassment, offered the courtesy of relieving him of the hat, which he held upon his lap throughout the rest of the ceremony.

A fumbling. The tall man on the platform brought from a pocket a folded paper—his speech. A return of the gnarled hand to the pocket, and out came a pair of spectacles, steel-rimmed, for which he had paid thirty-four cents years before.

The crowd had been prepared for awkwardness, even *gaucherie*. There may have been smiles on some of those faces below.

Abraham Lincoln began to speak. The smiles faded. Somehow he did not seem awkward as he delivered to them, and to all the nation, his message. He seemed instead charged with intense meaning, extraordinary presence, the genius of history in the making.

His first words were a reassurance to the South. "I have," he said, "no purpose, directly or indirectly, to interfere with the institution of slavery in the states where it exists. I believe I have no lawful right to do so, and I have no inclination to do so."

He affirmed the legality of the Fugitive Slave law, and that it should be enforced.

But then, "A disruption of the Federal Union heretofore only menaced, is now formidably attempted.

"I hold, that in the contemplation of universal law, and of the Constitution, *the Union of these states is perpetual* . . . no state, upon its own mere motion, can lawfully get out of the Union . . . resolves and ordinances to that effect are legally void; and acts of violence . . . against the authority of the United States, are insurrectionary or revolutionary, according to circumstances.

"I therefore . . . shall take care, as the Constitution itself expressly enjoins upon me, that the laws of the Union be faithfully executed in all the states. Doing this I deem it to be only a simple duty on my part; and I shall perform it, so far as practicable, unless my rightful masters, the American people, shall withhold the requisite means, or . . . direct the contrary. I trust this will not be regarded as a menace, but only as the declared purpose of the Union that it *will* constitutionally defend, and maintain itself.

"In doing this there needs to be no bloodshed or violence; and there shall be none, unless it be forced upon the national authority."

There followed a brief, clear enunciation of the fallacy of the very idea of secession. If a minority seceded, what was to prevent another minority again from seceding from the seceders?

"Plainly," the tall man went on, "the central idea of secession is the essence of anarchy . . ."

He pointed out that physically the two sections of the country could not separate. It was impossible to build a wall between them; all of the people were entitled to the benefits and the institutions of the nation as a whole. He pleaded for patient confidence in the ultimate justice of the people.

"My countrymen, one and all," he earnestly said, "think calmly and well, upon this whole subject. Nothing valuable can be lost by taking time . . . Intelligence, patriotism, Christianity, and a firm reliance on Him, who has never yet forsaken this favored land, are still competent to adjust, in the best way, all our present difficulty."

There followed a solemn adjuration:

"In *your* hands, my dissatisfied fellow countrymen, and not in *mine*, is the momentous issue of civil war. The government will not assail *you*. You can have no conflict, without being yourselves the aggressors. *You* have no oath registered in Heaven to destroy the government, while *I* shall have the most solemn one to 'preserve, protect and defend' it."

And at the end, having so laid the case before the nation, he concluded with a movingly beautiful appeal to his countrymen:

"I am loth to close. We are not enemies, but friends. We must not be enemies. Though passion may have strained, it must not break our bonds of affection. The mystic chords of memory, stretching from every battle-field, and patriot grave, to every living heart and hearthstone, all over this broad land, will yet swell the chorus of the Union, when again touched, as surely they will be, by the better angels of our nature."

He had spoken. The crowd, moved and awe-stricken, hardly applauded but paid him the deep tribute of almost breathless silence.

He turned to aged Chief Justice Taney, laid his left hand on the extended open Bible, raised his right hand, and repeated the oath of office prescribed by the Constitution:

"I do solemnly swear that I will faithfully execute the office of President of the United States, and will, to the best of my ability, preserve, protect, and defend the Constitution of the United States."

Cannon boomed. Bands played *Hail to the Chief*. The crowd, released at last from its emotional silence, roared a great cheer of welcome and mighty approval.

Abraham Lincoln, duly elected and now qualified, stood forth before them, the President of the United States.

5

Of Lincoln's role as President many historians have written and many more will write. Fort Sumter marked the opening of the Civil War, Gettysburg its high tide, Appomattox its finish; and then the shot in Ford's Theater dropped the curtain on an epoch—the Jackson-Lincoln epoch.

Every schoolboy can recite Lincoln's tribute to "the brave men, living and dead, who struggled here." In that Gettysburg Address Lincoln never once spoke of *Union* men, or *Northern* men, as distinguished from *Confederate*, or *Southern* men. To him all were Americans, and he prayed that "this nation, under God, shall have a new birth of freedom, and that government of the people, by the people, for the people, shall not perish from the earth."

Every schoolboy remembers also the moving eloquence of his Second Inaugural: "With malice toward none; with charity for all; with firmness in the right, as God gives us to see the right, let us strive to finish the work we are in; to bind up the nation's wounds; to care for him who shall have borne the battle, and for his widow and orphan— to do all which may achieve and cherish a just and lasting peace among ourselves and with all nations."

The course had been set that day in March 1861 when Lincoln, in the tradition he had inherited from Andrew Jackson, spoke the prophetic words that inspired his course and made this nation's history: "The Union of these states is perpetual . . . an oath registered in heaven to Preserve, Protect and Defend it."

Notes on Bibliography

For the general reader who wishes to pursue any or all phases of the history covered by this work, a few books which should be readily available, either in any good library, or currently in book stores, ought to be suggested by an author. With this in mind the following easily available books are suggested, as a sort of preface to a more general bibliography.

The Jacksonian era is well encompassed by Marquis James' *The Life of Andrew Jackson*. Not only is this volume authoritative but it is highly readable, and touches most facets of the period it covers. In this connection, *The Age of Jackson*, by Arthur Schlesinger, Jr., a careful discussion and analysis of the stormy administration of the Seventh President, and *The Era of Good Feelings*, by George Dangerfield, which penetratingly traces events up to Jackson's rise to power, are of great interest and great value.

A broad general knowledge of the furious adventure of the American frontier can be gained from four recent books by Dale Van Every, which in lively and readable fashion cover the westward push of the American people from 1754 to 1845. In order of the periods they discuss, they are, *Forth to the Wilderness, A Company of Heroes, Ark of Empire,* and *The Final Challenge.*

The outstanding works, easily available, on the period of United States history from the close of the War with Mexico to the onset of the Civil War, are those of Allan Nevins, *The Ordeal of the Union* (two volumes), and *The Emergence of Lincoln,* (also two volumes). Nevins, one of the greatest living American historians, writes with zest, immense detail of interest, and strong interpretive powers.

Those readers unable to obtain *Abraham Lincoln* (two volumes) by Albert J. Beveridge, will do well to consult Carl Sandburg's *Abraham Lincoln: The Prairie Years* (two volumes) and *Abraham Lincoln: The War Years* (four volumes), which are written with the fervor of a poet and the careful study of a scholar. For a single volume, easily obtainable, *Abraham Lincoln,* by Benjamin Thomas, is readable, authoritative, and perhaps the best one-volume life of Lincoln.

Beyond these suggestions, the following selective bibliography is offered. These volumes include only a small number of all the sources consulted for the present work, but they are recommended for additional reading in the particular areas covered.

Bancroft, Hubert Howe, *History of California* (7 vols. 1886), *History of North Mexican States and Texas* (2 vols. 1886), *History of Mexico* (6 vols. 1887), *History of Central America* (2 vols. 1887), and *History of Arizona and New Mexico* (1889).

Benton, Thomas Hart, *Thirty Years' View* (2 vols. 1854).

Beveridge, Albert J., *Abraham Lincoln* (2 vols. 1928).

Buell, Augustus C., *A History of Andrew Jackson* (1904).

Carr, Albert Z., *The World and William Walker* (1963).

Casteñeda, C. E. (translator), *The Mexican Side of the Texan Revolution* (1928).

Channing, Edward, *A History of the United States* (6 vols. 1905–25).

Chittenden, Hiram Martin, *The American Fur Trade of the Far West* (2 vols. 1935).

Connelly, W. E. (editor), *The Doniphan Expedition* (1907).

Dangerfield, George, *The Era of Good Feelings* (1953).

DeQuille, Dan (pen-name of William Wright), *The Big Bonanza* (1877).

De Voto, Bernard, *The Year of Decision* (1943).

Dictionary of American History (James Truslow Adams, editor), (5 vols. and index 1940).

Dunbar, Seymour, *A History of Travel in America* (4 vols. 1915).

Gregg, Josiah (Max L. Moorehead, editor), *Commerce of the Prairies* (new edition 1954).

Helper, Hinton Rowan, *The Impending Crisis* (1857).

Irving, Washington, *Astoria* (1836), and *The Adventures of Captain Bonneville* (1837).

James, Marquis, *The Life of Andrew Jackson* (1938) and *The Raven: A Biography of Sam Houston* (1929).

Kansas Historical Society Collections.

Kennedy, William, *Texas: The Rise, Progress and Prospects of the Republic of Texas* (1841).

Lavender, David H., *Land of Giants* (1958).

Leech, Margaret, *Reveille in Washington* (1941).

Malin, James C., *John Brown and the Legend of Fifty-six* (1943).

Martineau, Harriet, *Retrospect of Western Travel* (2 vols. 1838).

Marx, Rudolph, M.D., *The Health of the Presidents* (1960).

Meigs, William C., *Life of John Calhoun* (1917).

Nevins, Allan, *The Ordeal of the Union* (2 vols. 1947) and *The Emergence of Lincoln* (2 vols. 1950).

Olmsted, Frederick A., *A Journey in the Seaboard Slave States* (1856), and *The Cotton Kingdom* (1861).

Parkman, Francis, *History of the Conspiracy of Pontiac* (1851), and *A Half Century of Conflict* (2 vols. 1892).

Poore, Ben: Perley, *Perley's Reminiscences* (2 vols. 1886).

Robinson, Charles, *The Kansas Conflict* (1898).

Ruxton, George Frederick, *Life in the Far West* (1848).

Sandburg, Carl, *Abraham Lincoln: The Prairie Years* (2 vols. 1926), and *Abraham Lincoln: The War Years* (4 vols. 1939).

Schlesinger, Arthur, Jr., *The Age of Jackson* (1945).

Stone, Irving, *They Also Ran* (1944) and *Men to Match My Mountains* (1956).

Thomas, Benjamin P., *Abraham Lincoln* (1952).

Trollope, Mrs. Frances M., *Domestic Manners of Americans* (1832).

Van Buren, Martin (John C. Fitzpatrick, editor), *Autobiography of Martin Van Buren* (1920).

Van Deusen, Glyndon G., *Life of Henry Clay* (1937).

Van Every, Dale, *Forth to the Wilderness* (1961), *A Company of Heroes* (1962), *Ark of Empire* (1963), and *The Final Challenge* (1964).

Villard, Oswald Garrison, *John Brown, 1800–59, a Biography Fifty Years After* (1910).

Wellman, Manly Wade, *They Took Their Stand* (1959), and *Harper's Ferry* (1960).

Wellman, Paul I., *Glory, God and Gold* (1954).

Index

DATE DUE			
			ALESCO